Mastering
Maya® 8.5

Mastering
Maya® 8.5

JOHN KUNDERT-GIBBS | MICK LARKINS

DARIUSH DERAKHSHANI | ERIC KUNZENDORF

WILEY PUBLISHING, INC.

Acquisitions Editor: MARIANN BARSOLO
Development Editor: JIM COMPTON
Technical Editors: KEITH REICHER AND GEORDIE MARTINEZ
Production Editor: SARAH GROFF-PALERMO
Copy Editor: JUDY FLYNN
Production Manager: TIM TATE
Vice President and Executive Group Publisher: RICHARD SWADLEY
Vice President and Executive Publisher: JOSEPH B. WIKERT
Vice President and Publisher: NEIL EDDE
Media Project Supervisor: LAURA ATKINSON
Media Development Specialist: KATE JENKINS
Media Quality Assurance: STEVE KUDIRKA
Book Designer: CARYL GORSKA
Compositor: CHRIS GILLESPIE, HAPPENSTANCE TYPE-O-RAMA
Proofreader: NANCY RIDDIOUGH
Indexer: TED LAUX
Anniversary Logo Design: RICHARD PACIFICO
Cover Designer: RYAN SNEED
Cover Image: JOHN KUNDERT-GIBBS

Dear Reader,

Thank you for choosing *Mastering Maya 8.5*. This book is part of a family of premium quality Sybex graphics books, all written by outstanding authors who combine practical experience with a gift for teaching.

Sybex was founded in 1976. More than thirty years later, we're still committed to producing consistently exceptional books. With each of our graphics titles we're working hard to set a new standard for the industry. From the writers and artists we work with to the paper we print on, our goal is to bring you the best graphics books available.

I hope you see all that reflected in these pages. I'd be very interested to hear your comments and get your feedback on how we're doing. Feel free to let me know what you think about this or any other Sybex book by sending me an email at nedde@wiley.com, or if you think you've found an error in this book, please visit http://wiley.custhelp.com. Customer feedback is critical to our efforts at Sybex.

Best regards,

Neil Edde
Vice President and Publisher
Sybex, an Imprint of Wiley

To our family and friends whose support makes our work possible, especially Kristin, Joshua, Kenlee, and Megan

About the Authors

Mastering Maya 8.5 was written by a diverse group of authors from both professional and academic environments, each with a particular strength in one or more aspects of Maya.

John Kundert-Gibbs is an associate professor of animation in the Theatre and Film Studies Department at the University of Georgia. He has written extensively on Maya and 3D-related topics, including contributing to all the *Mastering Maya* editions and the two *Maya: Secrets of the Pros* books. He's also written on the intersection of media design and theatrical production. John is proud of his graduates, many of whom now work in the best effects houses in the industry.

Mick Larkins is the technical art lead at Hi-Rez studios in Atlanta, Georgia, and is a contributing author of the *Mastering Maya* books and a co-author on *Maya 8 at a Glance.* He holds a master of fine arts degree in digital production arts from Clemson University and a bachelor of science degree in computer science from Furman University. His expertise includes technical animation for games, hair, and cloth. His animated contributions have been exhibited in the Eurographics Animation Theatre, the South Eastern Digital Animation Festival, and the Cineme International Film Festival. Mick wants to dedicate his contributions in this book to his wonderful wife, Megan and furry friend Fozzie. Visit Mick's website at `www.micklarkins.com`.

Eric Kunzendorf teaches as a digital fine arts faculty member at the New Hampshire Institute of Art. Previously, he served as cochairman of Electronic Arts in the areas of computer animation, digital multimedia, and digital art at the Atlanta College of Art and has been teaching computer graphics and animation at the college level for the last 13 years. He has also taught computer art at the School of Visual Arts' Savannah campus. He holds a bachelor of arts degree in art history from Columbia University and a master of fine arts degree in drawing and painting from the University of

Georgia. Eric coauthored *Mastering Maya 7* and *Maya 5 Savvy* and contributed to *Maya: Secrets of the Pros, 1st Edition*. His animations, "Final Project Assignment" and "Mime in a Box," have appeared at the Siggraph Computer Animation Festival.

Dariush Derakhshani is a creative director with visual effects boutique Radium, and a writer and educator in Los Angeles, California. He is an award-winning digital effects  supervisor and author of several bestselling Maya books, including *Introducing Maya 8: 3D for Beginners* and *Maya Secrets of the Pros*, and also co-wrote *Introducing 3ds Max 9: 3D for Beginners*. For almost a decade, he has worked on feature films (*Fantastic Four, The Visitation, The Adventures of Shark Boy and Lava Girl*), national TV commercials (BMW and Lexus), TV series (*South Park*), and music videos (Cake and Linkin Park). Dariush shares the 2003 London Advertising Award for commercial effects, won the Bronze Plaque from the Columbus Film Festival, and received a fellowship from Paramount Pictures. Dariush has a master of fine arts degree from USC Film School and teaches Maya and animation classes.

Eric Keller has been using Autodesk's Maya to create professional animations since version 1 was released and has been an enthusiast ever since. He is currently a high-end  animator for film, television, and scientific visualization. His clients include Disney, ESPN, Hewlett-Packard, CBS, and ABC. Prior to that, he created animations for some of the world's top researchers at the Howard Hughes Medical Institute. He wrote *Maya Visual Effects: The Innovator's Guide*, and is a contributing author to the *Mastering Maya* books.

Boaz Livny has been working for more than 10 years with 3D for film, TV, and multimedia content. He specializes in lighting and rendering but is experienced working in the entire

pipeline. His New York studio Vision Animations Inc. (www.vision animations.com) provides regular services to clients and freelance support for studios. He is a professor of master's level courses at NYU's Center for Advanced Digital Applications (CADA). Boaz regularly writes articles demonstrating advanced techniques with Maya and mental ray in *HDRI 3D* magazine, and he is the author of

mental ray with Maya, XSI and 3D studio max: A 3D Artist's Guide to Rendering (Wiley). Boaz is currently developing an advanced training center for computer arts and science in NYC. Information is available at www.3DArts.org.

Mark E. A. de Sousa is a graphics supervisor in the Cloth and Hair division at Sony Pictures Imageworks. He most recently worked on the full CG feature adaptation of *Beowulf*. Mark's

screen credits also include supervising the cloth dynamics team on *Open Season*. In the past nine years, he has worked on more than 14 feature films, including *Beowulf, Open Season, Spider-Man 2, Polar Express, Stuart Little 2, Harry Potter and the Sorcerer's Stone, The Hollowman,* and *Star Trek: Insurrection*. Mark is also a part-time instructor at the Gnomon School of Visual Effects in Hollywood,

California. He is a graduate of Centennial College's Digital Animation Program in Toronto, Canada.

Ed Siomacco is a technical director for Cloth, Hair, and FX at Sony Pictures Imageworks. His most recent work includes *Spider-Man 3, Open Season* and *The Chronicles of Narnia: The Lion, The Witch, and The Wardrobe*. He is a graduate of North Carolina State University and Clemson University. You can check out his website at www.idgit.com.

CONTENTS AT A GLANCE

Contents

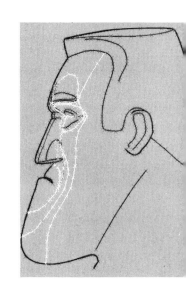

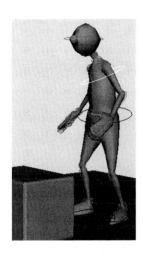

Introduction

Welcome to *Mastering Maya 8.5*, the newest evolution of one of the most popular, well-respected books on Maya! This book aims to cover the needs of artists no matter their level of experience with Maya or CG in general, allowing beginners to gain insight quickly into work flows and allowing more experienced users to get into the nitty-gritty of the program to improve on their own work flows.

In this book, we cover the important theory behind every major component of Maya's software and show you the ins and outs of how to accomplish tasks for vital steps of the production process, from modeling to rendering. Simple exercises throughout each chapter illustrate the points made by the writing team, and more in-depth tutorials take you step-by-step into more advanced methodologies.

We trust you will enjoy the information contained in this book and, more important, will come away from reading *Mastering Maya 8.5* with a deeper knowledge of, and appreciation for, Maya and its place in CG production. Maya is a vast, deep program that allows the user an almost infinite range of possibilities. No one way of working is better than another, so hang with us, grab your mouse, and dive in. The best way—nay, the *only* way—to learn CG is to practice and work diligently. We think you will find that the samples and lessons in this book will give you a great way to start or continue your education.

What You Will Learn from This Book

What will you, gentle reader, get from this book? You will find in these pages an introduction not only to Maya as a software package, but to the way Autodesk's software plays a starring role in the creative and technical process known as the CG production pipeline. You will find a wealth of information in the following pages, with intensive discussions on everything from modeling to rigging to production-quality cloth and hair simulation. For readers both new and old, we cover the creative elements of a production (something that, we think, is unique in how-to software books), and we reveal secrets, tips, and tricks of getting real CG production work done—little work flow speed-ups, settings adjustments, and management techniques that are not important to small tutorials but become critical to getting real-world 3D animations done. In short, we examine how Maya is used, in production houses large and small, to create all the wonderful, spectacular, resonant images seen on television, in still images, and on film.

Mastering Maya 8.5 is a comprehensive guide to the rich and ever-growing software package known as Maya. Rather than only discussing how to click each individual radio button or control, this book presents Maya's tools in a manner revealing *why* you would change settings or adjust certain channels. This method teaches you the underlying reasons and methodology for using a tool, allowing you to feel comfortable enough with each tool to continue learning and experimenting on your own. Additionally, through the various hands-on tutorials, you will learn how to use Maya most efficiently for your project needs so you won't have to figure out work-flow secrets on your own.

You will begin your journey by getting to know Maya's interface and node structure. Next, you will learn how to model using NURBS, polygons, and subdivision surfaces and how to use these modeling tools to create refined, animation-ready models. You will learn how to rig a model (make it move) and animate said model, including lighting, texturing, and rendering (with a look at both Toon Shading and the mental ray renderer). You will also learn how to use MEL (Maya Embedded Language), expressions, particles, and rigid bodies to automate your work and expand the range of animation you can create. We also explore Paint Effects and the high-end tools of Maya Unlimited—Fluid Effects, Hair, Fur, and the new nCloth simulation system—to create unique effects that are normally the realm of proprietary software. (In addition, the CD includes a chapter on Classic Cloth, the implementation used prior to Maya 8.5.)

Who Should Read This Book

This book is intended for a wide range of Maya users, from experienced beginners who need a guided approach to experts who need to brush up on topics or have a need to reference certain techniques to improve their work flow. There is something in *Mastering Maya 8.5* for everyone, but we expect most readers will be in the advanced beginner to intermediate range. We assume that most people who invest in a professional-quality 3D graphics program (and the hardware on which to run it) are serious about 3D animation. We assume you have already done some work with 3D modeling, animation, and rendering and are now ready to hone your skills and take advantage of the breakthroughs that Maya makes available. You may be already working in a production environment, in a training or educational program, or in a related field and preparing to make the jump to 3D modeling and animation. Or you might be a person who has always been interested in 3D animation and, with Maya's free Personal Learning Edition (PLE), have decided to take the plunge and learn the best tool around. In any case, whether you're a neophyte or a guru, you will certainly learn something here, whether it's how to use the Maya interface or some cool new way to perform a complex task.

If you're a relative beginner or feel your background in the fundamentals of Maya and 3D animation has a few holes in it, start at the beginning and work through the book from start to finish. You will learn how the Maya interface works and how each stage of a 3D production is executed.

Users at the intermediate level will find plenty of interest beyond the fundamentals. Various chapters introduce more advanced topics such as organic modeling, character rigging, mental ray rendering, particle and rigid body dynamics, and nCloth, fur, and fluid simulation.

And certainly if you are experienced in another animation package such as 3ds Max or LightWave, you can easily transfer your experience into Maya by using this book as a guided reference to open you to new ways of doing things you've become accustomed to in another package.

No matter what your background or level of experience, you will find valuable information in practically every chapter, including exciting secrets, tips, and techniques that will improve your work and/or work flow.

How to Use This Book

Mastering Maya 8.5 is not just a reference manual. As working animators, 3D artists, and teachers, we knew from the beginning that simply explaining the settings of menus and dialog boxes would not be an effective way for you to learn how to use the software—or for us to share insights and experiences. We knew that "hands-on" would be the best approach for learning this complex software—and for retaining that knowledge. Each chapter goes into lessons that illustrate the appropriate points to give you a chance to get hands on right away with every new method and concept.

To implement this approach, we've created a fully integrated book and CD. The companion CD contains working files—Maya scene files, TIFF and JPEG images, MEL scripts, and corollary resources—that will get you up to speed on each chapter or let you check your progress against a finished version of what you are working on.

Many of the exercises are intended to give you a chance to challenge your understanding of the material. Retaining information is much easier with practice, so plan to use this book side by side with your computer so that you can follow along with the lessons, from the quick introductions to the heavier in-depth exercises.

Even though the book flows in a typical production manner, from modeling through to rendering, you do not need to read the chapters in order: we have provided intermediate scene files that allow you to "step into" the process at any point for any exercise, whether connected with another chapter or not. As with any how-to book, you can focus on the subjects that interest you or the tasks you need to accomplish first, particularly if you are already an experienced animator. However, should you find the book hard to put down once you start reading it, we won't complain!

How This Book Is Organized

Depending on your interests and skill level, you can either study every chapter from beginning to end or start with what you need to know first. Here's a quick guide to what each chapter covers.

Chapter 1, "The Maya Interface," introduces the elements that make up models, windows, menus, and other parts of Maya, with a thorough reference for you to come back to as needed through your progress in the book.

Chapter 2, "Quick Start: Creating an Animation in Maya 8.5," gets you moving in the program straight away and will help you understand Maya's innovative node structure and other crucial Maya components. Chapters 1 and 2 work together to give you a solid foundation in the Maya program.

Chapter 3, "Polygonal Modeling," begins your modeling experience in Maya by going from modeling principles through to creating a full character. This chapter takes care to go through all the parts that will make up the character Machismo while explaining how things are done every step of the way.

Chapter 4, " NURBS Modeling," opens up the world of NURBS modeling, showing what elements make up a NURBS curve or surface, how to edit them, and finally how to apply these concepts with examples to light the way.

Chapter 5, "Subdivision Surfaces," explores the basic ingredients for creating and editing polygons and subdivision surfaces. Various techniques are employed to extend the modeling done in Chapters 3 and 4. This chapter also gets into creating Machismo's head.

Chapter 6, "Blend Shapes: Advanced Modeling," teaches you about blend shapes and how to create models using less traditional methods for creating geometry, particularly for animation.

Chapter 7, "Basic Animation," is where you'll learn all you need to know to get started creating, controlling, and editing animation in Maya. Exercises in this chapter take you through using the Dope Sheet for timing as well as making extensive use of the Graph Editor.

Chapter 8, "Character Setup and Rigging," discusses the use of deformers such as lattices and joints to move portions of a completed model skin. IK (Inverse Kinematics) handles and splines are covered as well. This chapter takes a hands-on approach to setting up a character for animation, complete with painting weights and creating controls to animate him. The chapter also covers using expressions to automate your character's rig.

Chapter 9, "Character Animation," dives into the principles and nuances of character animation by starting right off with the animation for a fully rigged character. The chapter also shows you how to pose, block, and refine your animation for the most efficient and effective work flow in character work.

Chapter 10, "Nonlinear Animation," introduces techniques for creating clips of animation that characters and scenes can use and share. You will create walk cycles and learn how to work with clips to animate a complicated scene.

Chapter 11, "Lighting for Animation," examines the Maya lighting system, the shadow types available, how to add effects to lights, and proper studio lighting of your subjects. You will learn how to balance speed and quality with depth-mapped shadows and when to use raytraced shadows. You will also be exposed to lighting effects, volumetric lighting, and glow.

Chapter 12, "Shading and Texturing for Animation," presents a thorough introduction to creating and editing Maya's materials and textures. The chapter takes you through using the Hypershade window and how to create expansive shader networks to create almost any shading effect. Also, you will see how to create and edit UVs for texturing polygonal models.

Chapter 13, "Rendering Basics," explores the way Maya defines a rendered image and how to use IPR (Interactive Photorealistic Renderering), image planes, and depth of field. Also, cameras and render layers are covered.

Chapter 14, "Advanced Rendering with mental ray," exposes you to the mental ray rendering system in Maya, which has been extensively revised in Maya 8.5. This chapter will show you the ins and outs of rendering with mental ray from Final Gather to Global Illumination and Caustics.

Chapter 15, "Toon Shading," gets you up to speed with Maya's Toon Shading module so you understand how to apply fills, generate lines, use different Paint Effects strokes, and apply toon line modifiers.

Chapter 16, "Maya Embedded Language (MEL)," introduces MEL and shows you how to effectively use scripting to increase your productivity and to automate and simplify work flow. You will also learn how to create expressions to control your animation and create relationships between scene objects.

Chapter 17, "Paint Effects," takes you into the world of Maya's tube-based scene-generating tool. You will learn what's possible with Paint Effects and what the hundreds of attributes mean to help you understand and use Paint Effects to its fullest potential.

Chapter 18, "Rigid Body Animation," shows you how to animate using Maya's dynamics engine instead of traditional keyframing techniques. You'll learn what rigid bodies are and how to control them, and you'll put them to use. You will learn how to use fields and forces for different results and how to "bake" the animation when you are done.

Chapter 19, "Using Particles," brings you up to speed with Maya's powerful particle system. You will work with emitters and fields and learn how to create expressions to control particles. Using ramps to control particle behavior and collisions is also covered and put into practice in this chapter.

Chapter 20, "Fluid Effects," introduces Maya Unlimited's volume fluids simulation engine. We take a quick look at the complex theory behind this tool and then show how to use—and adjust—Maya's built-in preset scenes and make your own to create astoundingly complex effects such as a stormy ocean using Maya's Ocean Shader.

Chapter 21, "Maya Hair," shows you how Maya's dynamic curves work to create fantastic effects and dynamic simulations. You will also see how to use the rendering capabilities of Maya Hair to create lifelike hair for your character.

Chapter 22, "Maya Fur," introduces this module for creating and modifying fur descriptions and fur attributes. We take a character through the furring process to illuminate the lessons in this chapter, and we show you how to control your fur with dynamic movement using fur attractors.

Chapter 23, "Cloth Simulation with nCloth," discusses the use of Maya 8.5's completely reworked Cloth tool, known as nCloth, to simulate cloth-type objects from bed sheets to multipaneled garments such as shirts. You will see how to create cloth for your scenes and how to edit and deal with cloth simulations and caches.

The CD also includes a chapter on Classic Cloth, covering Cloth features used prior to Maya 8.5.

Hardware and Software Considerations

Because computer hardware is a quickly moving target and Maya 8.5 runs on Windows, Linux, and Macintosh operating systems, specifying which particular hardware components will work with Maya is something of a challenge. Fortunately, the Autodesk website provides a list of the latest hardware to be qualified to work with Maya for each operating system:

```
http://usa.autodesk.com/adsk/servlet/index?siteID=123112&id=7639522
```

Although you can find specific hardware recommendations on these web pages, we can make some general statements about what constitutes a good platform for Maya. First, be sure to get a fast processor (or a dual- or quad-processor machine if you can afford it); Maya eats through CPU cycles like crazy, so a fast processor is important. Second, you need lots of RAM (memory) to run Maya; 1GB is a minimum, but 2 to 4GB is ideal, especially if you are working with large scene files. Third, if you expect to interact well with your Maya scenes, a powerful GPU (graphics processing unit, or video card) is a must. Although Maya will putt along with a poor graphics card, screen redraws will be slow with complex scenes, which gets frustrating quickly, and occasional display anomalies will certainly be annoying. A large hard disk is also important, but most computers these days come with huge drives anyway. Some suggested setups might be as follows (current at the time of writing):

Windows or Linux

- AMD Athlon XP; 2GB RAM; NVIDIA Quadro FX5500 or ATI FireGL V7350; 400GB hard disk

- Intel Pentium 4 3.2GHz with HyperThreading; 2GB RAM; NVIDIA Quadro FX5500 or ATI FireGL V7350; 400GB hard disk

Mac OS X

- Mac Pro quad core; 2GB RAM; NVIDIA Quadro FX 4500; 500GB hard disk

Fortunately for us users, computer hardware is so fast these days that even laptop computers can now run Maya well. (Indeed, we used laptop computers running Maya while working on this book.) You will find amazing workstation laptops from Apple, Boxx, Dell, and HP. Additionally, even hardware that is not officially supported by Autodesk can often run Maya—just remember that you will not be able to get technical support if your system does not meet the qualifications chart, and you may have to put up with the occasional display glitch with gaming video cards such as the GeForce or Radeon.

The Book's CD

The CD accompanying this book has been tested on Windows and Macintosh and should work with most configurations of these systems.

The CD provides all the sample images, movies, code, and files that you need to work through the projects in *Mastering Maya 8.5*, as well as a chapter on Classic Cloth for Maya users who need backward compatibility. It also includes a link for you to download Maya Personal Learning Edition.

If you don't already have a version of Maya, you might want to install the Maya Personal Learning Edition, which is a special version of Maya that gives you free access to Maya Complete for noncommercial use. Maya PLE works on Windows 2000 Professional, Windows XP Professional, and Mac OS X (10.3 or better). See www.autodesk.com/maya for more information.

The Next Step

By the time you finish *Mastering Maya 8.5*, you'll be well on your way to mastery of Maya. Several chapters provide suggestions for further reading related to animation and 3D graphics and to some of the most important websites in the field. Be sure to check these websites, as well as the Wiley website (`www.wiley.com`), for updates on Maya and for bonus materials and further information.

As you work through this book and begin exploring Maya on your own, you'll probably think of topics you'd like to see us cover in future editions of this book, as well as other improvements we might make. You can provide feedback at `www.wiley.com`. We welcome your input and look forward to hearing from you!

Now it's up to you to make the most of the tools that Maya offers. Have fun, work hard, and remember that the most important tool you have as an artist is your imagination—so get out there and make yourself proud!

Mastering
Maya® 8.5

CHAPTER 1

The Maya Interface

The Maya interface can be a bit intimidating, and it's not fair to expect yourself to pick it right up and remember where everything is. As you will see throughout this book, the best way to learn Maya is to put it to task, and you can use this chapter as a reference to the interface and the many windows and functions you will find yourself using in your work.

Try not to rush it, and don't be overly concerned with customizing the keys and using shelves or the hotbox for now; just access your commands and functions through the menus. Of course there are a few exceptions to this, as we'll see in Chapter 2, "Quick Start: Creating an Animation in Maya 8.5," but for the most part it is highly recommended that you familiarize yourself with where everything roughly should be through the menu system.

This chapter is a look at how to access functions and a fairly complete rundown of the often-used windows in Maya to get you familiar with their workings. Without further ado, let's get to the interface that makes Maya what it is.

- **The interface**
- **Getting around**
- **Scene windows**
- **Window layouts**
- **The hotbox**
- **Menus and shelves**
- **The Outliner and the Hypergraph**
- **The Channel Box and the Attribute Editor**
- **The Timeline**
- **The Command line, the Feedback line, and the Script Editor**
- **Customizing the interface**

The Interface

You can perform almost every task in Maya in more than one way. The most common way to access functions and tools is through the menu. In addition to menus, you can access functions through icons in the shelf, through hot keys, through marking menus, and through the hotbox. This is one of the charms of Maya and helps make it one of the most powerful CG creation tools on the market. Its adaptability to individual work flows makes it an essential tool for artists. This can be a double-edged sword for beginners though, since they often find themselves overwhelmed as to where to go or how to proceed. You will see all these options throughout the book and a rundown of them in this chapter. We recommend you familiarize yourself with the menus first and then get into the productivity-enhancing shortcuts.

If you are already experienced with other CG software and find it easy to get around in Maya, you can just use this chapter as a reference to come back to when you're already steeped in your scene. Artists who used other packages say that Maya's work flow and interface are important to learn because they can offer a faster, more efficient way of working.

If you're new to Maya and have not had a chance to set any defaults for yourself, reset the interface to the default settings to make sure everything lines up between your work and the exercises in this book. Choose **Window → Settings/Preferences → Preferences**. In the Preferences window, choose **Edit → Restore Default Settings**. This should restore settings to their original state. Be careful not to reset someone else's settings, though, if you are on a multiuser computer.

Let's take a look at what elements make up the default Maya screen, which is shown in Figure 1.1.

The reason we specifically mentioned the *default* Maya screen is that Maya has a highly customizable interface that you can tailor to the way you like to work. As you become experienced with Maya, you will begin customizing the interface for yourself easily. As an inexperienced user, it's best to leave everything at the default to have a level playing field.

In addition, for those systems that have multiple displays, Maya fully supports using a secondary display as long as your video card is capable. Keep in mind that both displays should be set to the same resolution and refresh rate for best OpenGL performance.

Experienced users should focus on the section "Customizing the Interface" later in this chapter.

The Nickel Tour

Let's take a look at the interface and identify the parts of the UI.

Running across the top of the screen (see Figure 1.1) are the *main menu bar*, the *Status line*, and the *shelf*. These provide access to the many functions in Maya. Running vertically to the left of the screen is the *Tool Box*, giving you fast access to common tools to manipulate your objects. Across the screen are the *Channel Box/Layer Editor* and sometimes the *Attribute Editor*. (The Attribute Editor is not displayed in Figure 1.1.) This part of the

Tool Box
Shelves
Status line
Main menu bar   Title bar   Scene menu bar   View Compass

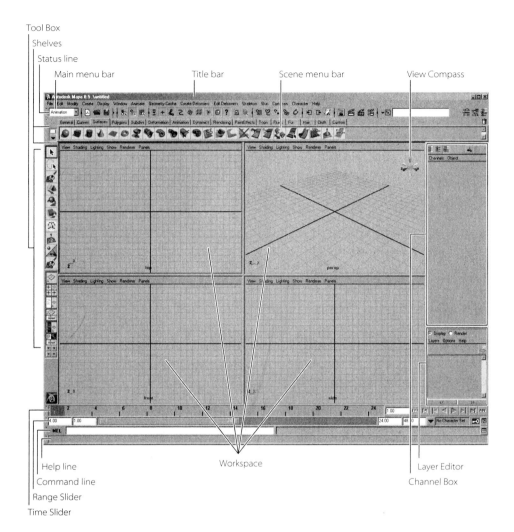

Figure 1.1

**The Maya 8.5
interface**

Help line   Workspace   Layer Editor
Command line   Channel Box
Range Slider
Time Slider

screen gives you access to information on the objects in your scene and allows you to manipulate and organize them as well.

Running horizontally at the bottom of the screen are the *Time Slider* and the *Range Slider*. These give you access to various functions and feedback from Maya itself.

In the middle of all these elements is the *workspace*, which hosts your view *panels* (or scene windows) and their own *scene menus*. These panels are known as views or viewports in some other 3D packages. You can change the options for each panel through its scene menus, from changing its view to changing how objects are displayed. Essentially, these panels are where you create and manipulate your 3D scenes. Figure 1.1 shows the panels with a grid displayed. This grid represents the ground axis of your 3D space and is useful for orienting yourself, especially in the perspective views.

The Workspace

When you first launch Maya, you will be presented with a full-screen perspective view, as shown in Figure 1.2. This view is essentially the view from a camera and shows real-world depth through the simulation of perspective. You use this window to see your scene in three dimensions. You can also move around a perspective view in real time to get a sense of proportion and depth.

Press the spacebar while in the panel to switch from the full-screen perspective to the four-panel layout originally shown in Figure 1.1. The four-panel layout shows the perspective view as well as three orthographic views (top, front, and side), each from a different side. Pressing the spacebar again returns your active view panel to full-screen mode.

Orthographic views are usually used for modeling and scene layout, because they convey exact dimensions and size relationships better than perspective views, as shown in Figure 1.3. Even though the cubes in this scene are all the same size, the perspective view displays the cubes farther away as being smaller than those closer to you. Orthographic views display proper proportions so you can see the four cubes identical in size and shape as well as their position in the scene.

Figure 1.2

The full perspective view

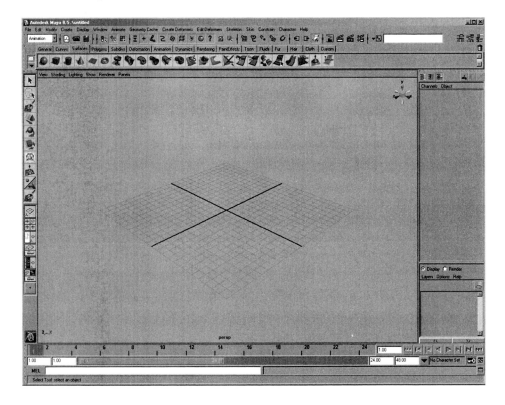

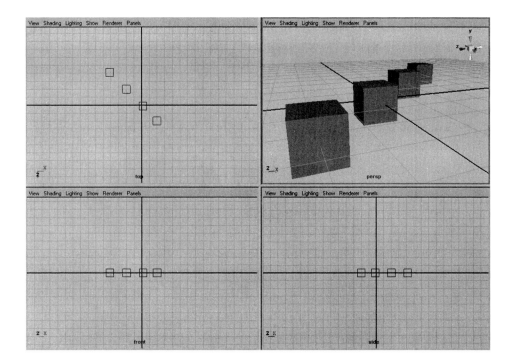

Figure 1.3
The four-panel layout

You can use any of the six presets in the Tool Box on the left side of the screen to adjust the panel layouts of your screen. You can also go through the main menu to make adjustments by choosing **Window → Saved Layouts**. Furthermore, you can change any panel's view by choosing another panel name from the Panels menu (this menu is found just above any panel), shown in Figure 1.4. You can choose any modeling view, orthographic or perspective, or another window to best suit your work flow. Last, you can change the size of any of the panels by clicking and dragging the separating borders between the panels.

The panels display a grid that you can use to align objects and for a general sense of placement and position. You can adjust the size and availability of the grids by choosing **Display → Grid □**. The grid is made of actual units of measure that you can adjust. Choose **Window → Settings/Preferences → Preferences** to open the Preferences dialog box, and in the Settings section make your adjustments.

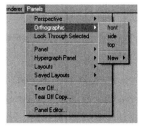

Figure 1.4
You can change your panel view through the scene menus in each of the panel views.

Getting Around

What's the use of all these views and UI elements if you can't get around? Just as with every other program on a computer, you will be using the keyboard and mouse to interact with Maya, although perhaps more in tandem with each other. Maya relies on the Alt key a great deal for the navigation in its work windows. Also, Maya requires the use of a three-button mouse, even with a Macintosh system. On a Macintosh, the Option key doubles as the Alt key. You use one of the mouse buttons in conjunction with the Alt key to move in your scene.

The Mouse Controls

The left mouse button (LM) is the primary selection key in Maya and is the most often used, obviously. But as far as getting around in a scene, when used with the Alt key, the LM button tumbles or orbits around your scene in perspective (camera) panels. The right mouse button (RM) activates shortcut menus, as it does in many software programs, and also Maya's system of marking menus, which are similar to shortcut menus. (For more on marking menus, stayed tuned to this chapter.) The RM button also allows you to dolly into or out of your scene. Dollying moves the camera closer to or farther from your subject in the scene. It is not accurate to call this type of move a zoom, though it often is, because a zoom changes the focal length of the lens of the camera as opposed to physically moving it in relation to the subject. Finally, the middle mouse button (MM) used with the Alt key allows you to pan around the scene, as well as acting as a *virtual slider*. You will see an example of a virtual slider later when we discuss the Channel Box.

Also note that if your mouse has a clickable middle wheel, you can use the wheel itself to dolly into or out of a Maya scene simply by rolling it up or down. This move is the same as an Alt+RM move. You may have to set up your mouse functions (through the mouse driver itself) for the mouse wheel to behave as a mouse's middle button when pressed.

View Compass

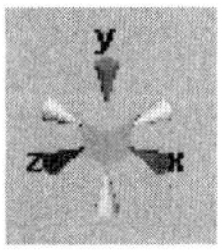

Figure 1.5

The View Compass

The View Compass, shown in Figure 1.5, lets you switch your view in the active panel. A panel, of course, is one of the working views in Maya; the workspace is shown through the panels in Maya's UI. By clicking one of the compass's axes, represented by the cyan, red, green, and blue cones, you can quickly change the active view to an orthographic view. Clicking the cyan cube at the heart of the View Compass returns you to your perspective view.

The Main Menu Bar

Starting with the menu bar, shown in Figure 1.6, you'll find a few of the familiar menu choices you've come to expect in many applications, such as File, Edit, and Help.

Figure 1.6

The main menu bar

File   Edit   Modify   Create   Display   Window   Animate   Geometry Cache   Create Deformers   Edit Deformers   Skeleton   Skin   Constrain   Character   Help

CAMERA MOVEMENT TERMINOLOGY

Every kind of camera move has a different name. The following lists the type of camera moves you have and what each one means:

- Rotate (Tumble) view means to rotate the (perspective) camera; hold down the Alt key and the left mouse button, and then drag in the perspective window to rotate the view. This action physically moves the camera around the subject and can be effective only in a perspective view panel.

- Move view means to move any camera; hold down the Alt key and the middle mouse button, and then drag in any scene window. This will move the camera horizontally or vertically in the scene, effectively panning the view.

- Dolly view means to scale—commonly called a zoom—any camera; hold down the Alt key and the right mouse button (you can also hold down both the LM and MM), and then drag in any scene window to zoom (or scale) the view in or out.

This setup allows a straightforward Alt key plus mouse button mapping of left=rotate, middle=pan, and right=zoom.

In Maya, your exact menu choices depend on your current menu set. By switching *menu sets,* you change your menu choices and the set's corresponding toolset. It may seem strange at first, but it makes the best sense to divide the menu headings into what kind of task you are involved in. The menu sets in Maya Complete are Animation, Polygons, Surfaces, Dynamics, and Rendering; Maya Unlimited adds the Classic Cloth, nCloth, and Maya Live menu sets to those four. The menu sets are available through the Status line, which is discussed in the next section.

The first six items in the main menu are constant, no matter what menu set you are in: File, Edit, Modify, Create, Display, and Window. The last menu, Help, is also constantly displayed. Their functions are as follows:

File Contains file operations, from saving and opening to optimizing scene size and export/import.

Edit Gives you access to the commands you use to edit characteristics of the scene, such as, for example, deleting and duplicating objects or undoing and redoing actions.

Modify Lets you edit the characteristics of objects in the scene, such as moving or scaling them or changing their pivot points.

Create Lets you make new objects, such as primitive geometries, curves, cameras, and so on.

Display Contains commands for adjusting elements of the GUI (graphical user interface) in Maya as well as objects in the scene, allowing you to toggle, or switch on and off, the display of certain elements as well as components of objects, such as vertices, hulls, pivots, and so on.

Window Gives you access to the many windows you will come to rely on, such as the Attribute Editor, Outliner, Graph Editor, and Hypergraph. The Window menu is broken down into submenus according to function, such as rendering editors and animation editors.

Help Gives you access to the extensive Maya help documentation in HTML format.

You'll notice two different icons to the right of some menu items: arrows and boxes (called *option boxes*). Clicking an arrow opens a submenu that contains more specific commands. Clicking an option box (▢) opens a dialog box in which you can set the options for that particular tool.

Tear-Off Menus

At the top of every menu is a double line. Clicking the double line allows you to tear off the menu and place it as a toolbox anywhere on your screen (or screens if you have dual displays enabled). These tear-off menus are also called floating menus. Creating a tear-off menu makes accessing menu commands easier, especially when you need to use the same command repeatedly. Let's say, for example, that you need to create multiple polygonal spheres. You can tear off the **Create → Polygonal Primitives** menu and place it at the edge of your screen. You can then click the Sphere command as many times as you need without opening the dual-layered menu every time.

Click here and drag to tear off menu.

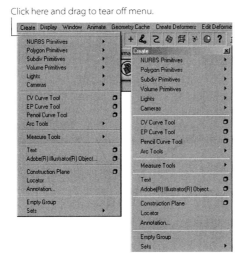

The Status Line

The Status line (see Figure 1.7) contains some important icons.

The first item in the Status line is the menu set drop-down menu. Selecting a particular menu set changes the menu headings in the main menu bar as we discussed earlier. You

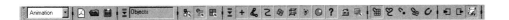

Figure 1.7

The Status line

will notice immediately after the menu set drop-down menu, and intermittently through-out the Status line, black vertical line breaks with either a box or an arrow in the middle. Clicking a break opens or closes sections of the Status line.

Scene File Icons

The first section of tool icons in the Status line deals with file operations:

ICON	NAME	DESCRIPTION
	New Scene	Creates a new, blank scene file
	Open Scene	Displays a window in which you can find and open any scene file you've saved
	Save Scene	Displays a window in which you can specify a filename and location to save a new scene or, if the current scene has already been saved and named, save it to that location

Selection Modes

The second section is the *Selection Mode field*. This drop-down menu lets you use presets for *selection masks*. Selection masks give you the opportunity to choose one kind of object but not another. You can, therefore, select all the particles in the scene and none of the polygon models. This is useful when you have a heavy scene and you need to select some objects and not others. By choosing the *type* of objects you want to be able to select, you can speed up your work flow in large scene files. The menu selections here give you a few presets to optimize the selection modes for your convenience according to your current work flow (for example, select only deformers in a scene, or select from just the dynamic objects such as particles).

Presets are fine and good, but you might prefer to use the individual selection mask icons farther down the Status line to gain more control—you can turn on and off whether you can select individual object types such as particles, NURBS, polygons, and so on. We will cover these in just a moment.

The next group of icons in the Status line lets you click into three distinct *selection modes*. Maya is based on object hierarchy, in which components make up objects that can make up larger objects and so on. You will see this in action in the next chapter in the Quick Start exercise. Selection modes let you choose different levels of an object's hierarchy. For example, using a selection mode, you can choose an entire group of objects, only one of the objects in a group, or just the points on the surface or the poly faces that make up an object. The primary selection modes are *object mode* and *component mode*:

ICON	NAME	DESCRIPTION
	Hierarchy Mode	Lets you select groups of objects or parts of a group
	Object Mode	Lets you select objects such as geometry, cameras, lights, and so on
	Component Mode	Lets you select an object's components, such as vertices, faces, or the control vertices (CVs) of NURBS surfaces

For example, if you have grouped several objects together, being in hierarchy mode and clicking any of the member objects selects the entire group of objects. Being in object mode selects just the object you click. To toggle between object and component modes, press the F8 key, the default hot key.

Individual Selection Masks

The next set of icons between the section breaks deals with individual selection masks, which give you control over which objects or components you want to select. Exactly which icons are displayed here depends on the selection mode you're currently in. If you have many objects in your scene and you are having difficulty selecting a certain type of object with your cursor, you can use these filters to single out the object(s):

ICON	NAME	DESCRIPTION
	Set Object Selection Mask	Turns on or off all selection icons
	Select By Handles	Allows selection of object handles
	Select By Joints	Allows selection of joints
	Select By Curve	Allows selection of curves
	Select By Surfaces	Allows selection of surfaces
	Select By Deformations	Allows selection of lattices and other deformers
	Select By Dynamics	Allows selection of particles and dynamic objects
	Select By Rendering	Allows selection of rendering nodes and objects such as lights and cameras
	Select By Miscellaneous	Allows selection of miscellaneous objects such as locators and dimensions
	Lock Selection	Keeps selected objects locked in as selected
	Highlight Selection Mode	Turns off the automatic display of components when selecting in selection mode

You can get a quick preview of what each icon is called by rolling your mouse pointer over and hovering on each icon to see a pop-up tooltip that gives the icon name and describes its function. As a matter of fact, this is a great way to get to know Maya's UI— in addition to reading every word of this chapter, of course.

Snapping Functions or Snaps

The "magnet icons" are called snaps. Snaps let you snap or lock your cursor or object to specific points in the scene. You can snap to other objects, to CVs or vertices, and to grid intersections and more by toggling these icons. You can also enable some snaps by holding down their respective hot keys. While the respective key is pressed, your manipulator cursor will turn from a square to a circle.

ICON	NAME	HOT KEY	DESCRIPTION
	Snap To Grids	x	Lets you snap objects to inter sections of the view's grid.
	Snap To Curves		Lets you snap objects along a curve.
	Snap To Points	v	Lets you snap objects to object points such as CVs or vertices.
	Snap To View Planes		Lets you snap objects to view planes.
	Make The Selected Object Live		This has nothing to do with snapping. It lets you create objects such as curves directly on a surface.

Input and Output Connections

The two icons to the right of all the filters list the input and output connections of an object, and the third icon toggles on/off construction history. Objects in Maya can connect with each other for any variety of purposes, from animation to rendering. When an object is influenced by any attributes of another object or node in Maya, that object has an *input connection*. When a node's own attribute(s) is influencing another object, that node has an *output connection*. Now these icons aren't used that often in a typical work flow, but it's good to know what they are nonetheless. You will see much more work with input and output connections throughout this book, especially when rigging scenes for animation or creating shaders.

This third icon is for toggling on and off *construction history*. Construction history keeps track of the nodes and attributes that help make up an object, making it easier to edit those objects that have history.

ICON	NAME	DESCRIPTION
	Input Connections	Lets you select and edit all the input connections for the selected object. That is, you can select and edit any object that directly influences the selected object.
	Output Connections	Lets you select and edit the output connections or any objects the selection affects.
	Construction History	Toggles on/off the construction history.

Render Controls

The next three icons give you access to render controls:

ICON	NAME	DESCRIPTION
	Render Current View	Renders the active viewport at the current frame.
	IPR Render Current View	Renders the active view at the current frame into Interactive Photorealistic Rendering (IPR). You can change certain shading and texturing settings and view real-time updates in the IPR window.
	Render Settings	Opens a window that gives you access to all the rendering switches such as resolution, file type, frame range, and so on.

Input Box

New to Maya 8.5, the Input Box allows you to quickly transform, rename, or select objects and components. By clicking the arrow icon to the left of the input fields, you can choose the following operations:

ICON	NAME	DESCRIPTION
	Absolute Transform	Translates an object or component in a specified axis in reference to their original creation position.
	Relative Transform	Translates an object or component in a specified axis in reference to their current position.
	Rename	Edits the name of the currently selected object.
	Select By Name	Selects objects by their name. You can use the asterisk and text to select all objects with specified prefixes or suffixes.

The Channel Box/Layer Editor

The last part of the Status line deals with the area defined as the Channel Box/Layer Editor. These icons toggle through three available views in the area on the right side of the screen. Clicking the first button displays the Attribute Editor on the right part of the screen, with which you can edit Maya's object attributes. Clicking the second turns on a window called Tool Options on the right part of the screen, giving you access to options for the currently active tool. Clicking the last icon restores the Channel Box/Layer Editor, showing you the most commonly animated attributes of an active object as well as the display and render layers in your scene.

ICON	NAME	DESCRIPTION
	Show/Hide Attribute Editor	Displays the Attribute Editor in this area
	Show/Hide Tool Settings	Displays the current tool's settings
	Show/Hide Channel Box/Layer Editor	Displays the Channel Box and Layer Editor

The Shelf

The *shelf*, shown in Figure 1.8, is an area where you keep icons for tools. The icons are separated into tabs that define the functions for the tool icons in the shelf. Select the appropriate tab in the shelf for what you're doing to access an array of common tool icons for that work flow. You can populate a Custom tab with the tools you find most useful for your own work flow.

Figure 1.8

The shelf

To customize the shelf so that your favorite tools are immediately accessible, click the Menu icon (   ) to open a menu to edit the shelf. To simply add a menu item to the shelf, press Ctrl+Alt+Shift while selecting the command from any main menu (for Mac users, press ⌘+Option+Shift). That tool's icon will then appear on the current shelf.

To get rid of a shelf item, MMB drag the icon to the Trash icon to the right of the shelf. You can create multiple shelves, stack them on top of each other, and access them by clicking the Shelf Tab icon (☰) above the Menu icon to the left of the shelf. As with the icons on the Status line, moving your mouse pointer over an icon in the shelf displays a tooltip that gives you the name and a description of that icon.

It's a good rule of thumb to know where the tools in the shelf are found in the menu, so if you are just starting out in Maya, try using the menus first before getting used to the shelf. It may be a bit more work, but it will give you a better understanding of how Maya is laid out.

The Tool Box

The Tool Box, shown in Figure 1.9, displays the most commonly used tools: Select, Lasso Select, Translate (or Move), Rotate, Scale, Universal Manipulator, Soft Modification, and Show Manipulator. These tools are most often accessed with hot keys. By default the layout is simple. The most-used tools—Select, Move, Rotate, and Scale—are mapped to the keys Q, W, E, and R, as shown in the following list. (Keep in mind that Maya's hot keys are case sensitive, which means that all commands in this book should be read as lowercase, even though they may be printed as uppercase. When an uppercase hot key is needed, it is referred to in this book as Shift+key.)

Figure 1.9

The Tool Box

ICON	NAME	HOT KEY	DESCRIPTION
	Select	q	Lets you select objects
	Lasso Select		Allows for a free-form selection using a lasso marquee
	Paint Selection Tool		Allows you to select components by painting over them with a brush (new to Maya 8)
	Translate (Move)	w	Moves selection
	Rotate	e	Rotates selection
	Scale	r	Scales selection
	Universal Manipulator		Allows for translation, rotation, and scale within one tool
	Soft Modification		Allows you to modify an area with a gradual drop-off of its effect
	Show Manipulator		Displays an object's specific manipulators
	Current Tool Display	t	Shows the currently selected tool (shown as blank)

In addition to these common tools, the Tool Box contains icons for several choices of screen layouts to let you change your interface quickly. This is convenient because different scenes and work flows can call for different view modes. Experiment with the layouts by clicking any of the six presets in the Tool Box.

The Channel Box

The area running vertically on the right side of the screen is usually for the *Channel Box* with the *Layer Editor* immediately below it. The Channel Box is a key element in Maya. It lists the commonly animated attributes of a selected object and lets you quickly adjust attributes and add animation and expressions without having to open the Attribute Editor (which is the window that lists *all* the attributes of an object; more on this later in this chapter). In addition, you can easily see input connections on an object's attributes through color coding. This way you can tell if an object is animated, constrained to another object, has an expression controlling it, is dynamic, or so on. Figure 1.10 shows the Channel Box with the Layer Editor just below it. The selected object shown in the Channel Box here is a polygon sphere with several connection types displayed as different colors.

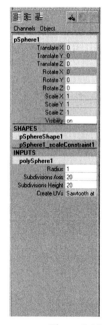

Figure 1.10

The Channel Box and Layer Editor below

Attribute Display in the Channel Box

The following list shows the colors and their connections for the attributes in the Channel Box:

INPUT CONNECTION	COLOR	DESCRIPTION
Keyframed	Orange	A keyframe is set for the attribute at some point in the Timeline.
Connected (to another attribute) or is dynamic	Yellow	This attribute shares the same value as another attribute on another object or has dynamic forces affecting it.
Expression Control	Purple	A written expression controls the value of this attribute.
Constraint	Blue	The attribute's value is constrained to the value of an attribute of another object.
Locked	Gray	You cannot change the value without first unlocking the attribute.
Muted Animation	Brown	There is animation on the attribute, but it is currently muted so it will not play back until it is unmuted.
Blended (with another attribute)	Green	The value of this attribute is blended with the value of another attribute.
Nonkeyable	Light Gray	This attribute cannot be animated.

Editing Attribute Values in the Channel Box

When an object is selected, its name appears at the top of the Channel Box. You can click the name and type a new name to rename the selected object. The channels (keyable attributes) for that object are listed vertically below with the attribute name to the left and the attribute value to the right in text boxes. You can click in the text box to change the value through the keyboard. You can also use a virtual slider in Maya by clicking a channel's name in the Channel Box and using the MM in a view panel to drag left or right to decrease or increase the value of the selected channel.

If you RM click an attribute name in the Channel Box, you will see a context menu that gives you access to several common commands, such as keyframing or locking and unlocking the selected channel or channels. You can animate any channel here by RM clicking the attribute name and choosing **Key Selected** from the shortcut menu. RM clicking the value itself displays a shortcut menu from which you can cut and paste values.

Another useful shortcut menu command is Break Connections, which removes any connections for the selected attributes and returns the value to a normal white color in the Channel Box. For example, if you have keyframes on the Rotate X channel of an object (with the text box shown in orange), clicking Rotate X in the Channel Box and right-clicking and choosing **Break Connections** from the shortcut menu deletes the keyframes and returns the text box to white. You will see more of this usage later in this book and as you learn how to animate in Maya.

Below the channel values in Figure 1.10 (shown in the previous section), you can see the headings SHAPES and INPUTS. These correspond to the connections the selected polygon sphere already has. In this case, under SHAPES we see the selected pSphereShape1 and the pShpere1_scaleConstraint1 nodes. These nodes have inputs to the selected sphere and help define the object in Maya. In short, nodes in Maya are groups of attributes that define an object, its location, shape, and so on. There is animation and an expression on this sphere as well, shown under the INPUTS heading. Clicking the node names here gives you access to their own attributes so that you can quickly make adjustments to the selected object and its connected nodes.

Changing the Channel Box/Layer Editor View

Although it's typical to display the Channel Box and the Layer Editor all the time, you can replace this panel with one of two other windows—the Attribute Editor or the Tool Settings window—by clicking one of the three icons in the upper-right corner, shown in Figure 1.10. This gives you quick access to the three windows you may find most useful to have on screen.

Some find it inconvenient to have the Attribute Editor and Tool Settings windows open in this area. That's why it's wise to set Maya to open these tools in their own separate windows. To do this, choose **Window → Settings/Preferences → Preferences**. The Preferences window (Figure 1.11) is opened. Under the Interface category (on the left side of the window), set the settings Open Attribute Editor and Open Tool Settings both to In Separate Window.

Figure 1.11
The Preferences window

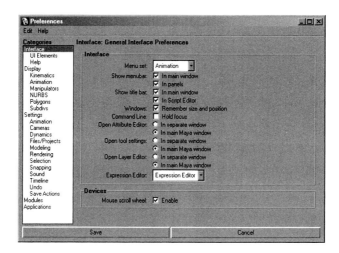

You can switch between the Channel Box and the Layer Editor by toggling one of the icons in the upper-left corner. (See Figure 1.10.) The following list shows the icons that switch the views in this area of the UI:

ICON	NAME
	Show The Channel Box
	Show The Layer Editor
	Show The Channel Box And The Layer Editor

You can resize this area by clicking either of the double arrow buttons at the bottom of the panel below the Layer Editor, which we will look at next.

The Layer Editor

Immediately under the Channel Box is the Layer Editor. This layout with the Channel Box and Layer Editor together is opportune for most scenes since it gives you immediate access to the layering of a scene as well as the channels of a selected object or objects. The Layer Editor has a twofold purpose: displaying layers and rendering layers.

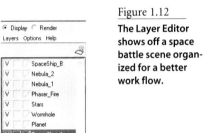

Figure 1.12

The Layer Editor shows off a space battle scene organized for a better work flow.

Display Layers

The first and immediately useful aspect of the Layer Editor is display layers. You can create display layers and assign objects to them to organize your scene. With objects on organized layers, you can quickly turn selections on and off by just toggling the View icon in the Layer Editor next to the appropriate layer name. Figure 1.12 shows just the Layer Editor with several layers already added to the scene.

To create a new layer, click the Create New Layer icon ( ). To add items to a layer, choose **Layers → Membership**. You can also select the objects for your layer and then choose **Options → Add New Objects To Current Layer** to automatically place those objects in the current layer. You can also use the layers to select groups of objects by choosing **Layers → Select Objects In Selected Layers.** To change the name and color of a layer, simply double-click the layer to open the Edit Layer dialog box.

Render Layers

Like display layers, render layers control what objects are on which layers so that you can separate your renders into different layers or passes. Rendering in layers is powerful for later editing in a compositing package such as After Effects or Shake because it gives you ultimate control over the objects in your scene and how best to color correct or even place them. To see the render layers in your scene, click the Render Radio button to toggle away from the display layers. Creating and adjusting render layers is the same as display layers. We will cover rendering in layers in detail in Chapter 14.

The Time Slider/Range Slider

Horizontally across the bottom of the screen are the Time Slider and the Range Slider, shown in Figure 1.13. The Time Slider displays the range of frames currently in your animation. The gray bar on the Time Slider is known as the *Current Time Indicator*, which you can click and drag back and forth in a scrubbing motion to move through time in your sequence. Clicking the Time Slider will also position the slider to whatever frame you clicked, allowing you to jump around in your Timeline.

The text box to the right of the Time Slider displays the current frame. You can also use it to enter the frame you want to access. Immediately next to the current time readout is a set of VCR or DVD playback controls that you can use to play your animation.

Below the Time Slider is the Range Slider, which you can use to adjust the range of animation playback shown in your Time Slider. The text boxes on either side of this slider give you readouts for the start and end frames of the scene and of the range selected to display in the Time Slider. You can adjust this range by either typing in the text boxes or lengthening or shortening the slider with the handles on either end of the Range Slider bar.

When you change the range, you change only the viewable frame range of the scene; you don't adjust any of the animation. This just makes longer animations easier to read and deal with. Adjusting actual animation timing and lengthening or shortening animations are accomplished differently (see Chapters 8 and 10).

Figure 1.13

The Time Slider and the Range Slider

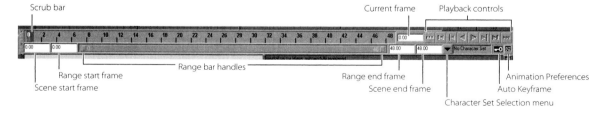

Scrub bar

Current frame   Playback controls

Range start frame   Range bar handles   Range end frame   Animation Preferences

Scene start frame   Scene end frame   Auto Keyframe

Character Set Selection menu

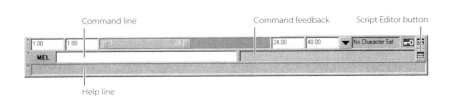

Figure 1.14

The Command line and the Help line

To the right of the Range Slider are the Character Set Selection menu (which deals with the automation of character-animated objects), the Auto Keyframe button (which sets a keyframe automatically when an animated value is changed), and the Animation Preferences button. Clicking this button opens the Preferences window shown earlier in Figure 1.11.

The Command Line/Help Line

Maya is based on Maya Embedded Language (MEL), and all its functions and commands invoke an appropriate MEL command. MEL is a user-accessible programming language and is mostly what allows Maya to be as resourceful and flexible as it is.

You can write your own commands or scripts in MEL, entering them into either the Command line or a window called the Script Editor. Use the Command line (see Figure 1.14) to enter single MEL commands directly from the keyboard in the white text box portion of the bar. The Command line also displays command feedback and messages from the program in the gray portion of the bar. Try entering the following into this box: `sphere`. A new sphere should pop up in your Maya panels. You've created a basic sphere using the MEL command. To delete it, click it to select it and then press Delete.

Clicking the icon at the end of the Command line opens the Script Editor window, in which you can enter more complicated MEL commands and scripts.

Below the Command line is the Help line. When you hover your mouse pointer over an icon, the Help line tells you what it is. This is a terrific way to learn the UI. The Help line also prompts you for the next step in a particular function or the next required input for a task's completion. It's a great way to understand how some tools work when you're not really sure about the next step in a command, such as which object to select or which key to press to execute the command. You'll be surprised at how much you'll learn about tool functions by reading the prompts displayed here.

Working in View Panels

Let's get a quick taste for working in the view panels. Create a NURBS sphere by choosing **Create → NURBS Primitives → Sphere** and then clicking in any viewport. (With Maya 8, primitives are typically created by choosing a primitive from the Create menu and then click-dragging in the interface.) A sphere will appear in your panels and will be selected, as shown in Figure 1.15. Notice its primary attributes in the Channel Box.

Now, press 2 and you will see the wireframe mesh become denser, as in the middle frame of Figure 1.15. Press 3 and the mesh becomes even denser (bottom frame). You can view all NURBS objects in three levels of display, such as this sphere. Pressing 1, 2, or 3 toggles between detail levels for any selected NURBS object. NURBS, as you will see in further detail in Chapter 4, are types of surfaces in Maya that can adjust detail level at any time to become more or less defined as needed. As such, the 1, 2, and 3 toggles only work on NURBS objects.

When working in the 3D views, you can view your 3D objects in *wireframe mode*, where you can see through each polygon (as in Figure 1.15), or in *shaded mode*, where objects are solid-looking (see Figure 1.16). Wireframe gives you the best performance on your computer's graphics system when working in a large scene, as well as the chance to see through the wireframe of one object to another object for position or comparison's sake.

> When you increase the display feedback of your view panels, such as using shaded mode or textured mode, you increase the work your system and your graphics card have to do. This is not a concern until your scenes get larger and heavier, but if you notice that your computer is not responding as fast as you'd like with a scene, try decreasing the visual feedback of your scene to wireframe view or turning display layers on and off as needed.

Within shaded mode, you have a few display options to help you in your work. You can choose to display the wireframe mesh on top of a shade view to help you better model and manipulate the objects. To turn on wireframe shaded view while in shaded view, in the Scene menu, choose **Shading → Wireframe On Shaded**. Figure 1.17 shows a sphere and cube with wireframe on shaded view enabled. Also, you can make your objects shaded but yet semitransparent in the panel so you can see through them but still get a sense of volume. For X-Ray view, choose **Shading → X-Ray**. Figure 1.18 shows X-Ray as well as wireframe on shaded modes enabled. You will see under the Shading menu that you can change your view to flat shaded (which is faster than smooth shaded but still shaded), bounding box (which merely displays the extent of the objects in the view and is the fastest view), or even points (which shows just the points of the objects in the panel).

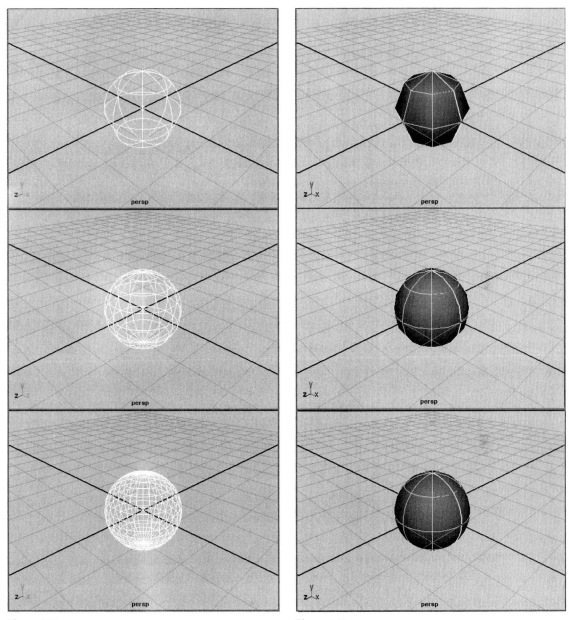

Figure 1.15
NURBS display smoothness.

Figure 1.16
Shaded NURBS display smoothness.

Figure 1.17
Wireframe on shaded view gives you a good view to model on your shaded objects.

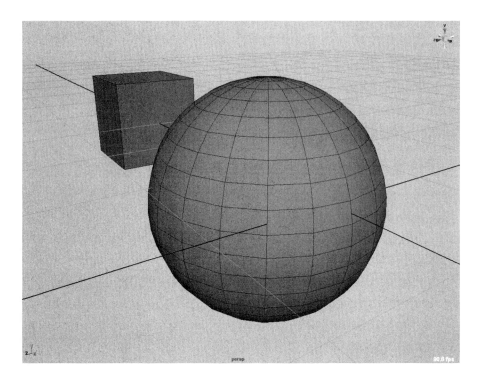

Figure 1.18
X-Ray view allows you to see through an object while still seeing it shaded and in this case with wireframe on shaded as well.

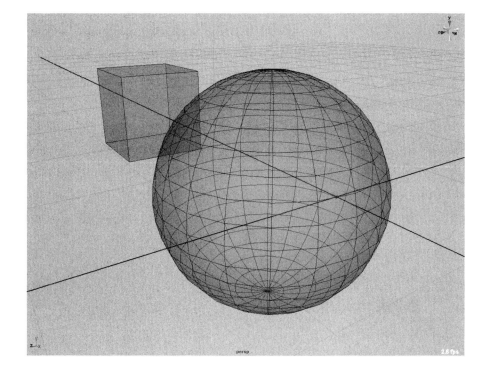

Shaded, Textured, and Lighted Modes

You can select from varying degrees of shading detail, going as far as seeing your objects with textures and lighting detail. You can cycle through the levels of detail by pressing 4, 5, 6, and 7. Wireframe mode is 4, shaded mode is 5, texture shaded mode is 6, and lighted mode is 7. Lighted mode will only work if you are already in mode 5 or 6. While in mode 6, pressing 7 will give you a lighted and textured mode. These modes give you a basic idea of lighting and/or texture detail.

Texture shaded mode (6) displays the actual image textures that have been applied to the object as long as Hardware Texturing is already enabled. (In the view panel, choose **Shading → Hardware Texturing** and make sure it is checked on.) Lighted mode (7) is a hardware preview of the object or objects as they are lit in the scene. Its accuracy depends on your graphics hardware. Here's a summary:

KEY	FUNCTION
4	Toggles into wireframe mode
5	Toggles into shaded mode
6	Toggles into textured mode
7	Toggles into lighted mode

It is handy to toggle between modes 4 and 5 to get a good feel for the weight and shape of your objects. Furthermore, lighted mode (mode 7) is useful for spotting proper lighting direction and object highlights when you first begin lighting a scene. It helps to see the direction of lights within your scene without rendering frames all the time. The number of lights you see in the modeling window depends on your computer's graphics and overall capabilities.

You can display a higher-textured view of your models by enabling High Quality Rendering view. In your view panel, choose **Renderer → High Quality Rendering**. This will give you a good idea of the texturing and lighting in your scene but at the expense of speed.

Display Shortcuts

In the view panel's View menu, you will find two handy UI features, Frame All (hot key A) and Frame Selection (hot key F), and a third slightly homely cousin, Look At Selection. Frame All animates the camera or orthogonal views in or out to see all the objects in a scene. Frame Selection animates the camera view to focus on the selected object or the center of selected objects. Look At Selection snaps the selected object into the middle of your view without moving in close to it.

If you find yourself wondering why pressing a hot key isn't working, Caps Lock may be enabled. Some hot keys have multiple meanings for the lower- and uppercase of the same letter, so check the Caps Lock key.

The Manipulators

Manipulators are on-screen handles that you use to *manipulate* the selected object in true form. Figure 1.19 shows the four distinct and most common manipulators for all objects in Maya: Move, Rotate, Scale, and Universal Manipulator. You use the handles on the manipulators to adjust your objects in real time in any of the axes, as we discuss later in this section. Some tools or objects have *special manipulators* that allow you to interactively adjust certain attributes particular to the tool or object, such as the cone angle of a spotlight.

You can access the manipulators using either the icons from the Tool Box or the following hot keys:

KEY	FUNCTION
W	Activates the Move tool
E	Activates the Rotate tool
R	Activates the Scale tool
Q	Deselects any translation tool to hide its manipulator and reverts to the Select tool

Figure 1.19

Manipulators let you control your object's position, rotation, and scale with ease.

The default hot keys let you easily select your transformation tools (Move, Rotate, Scale) since they rest on the left side of the keyboard. You can, of course, change these key layouts as you see fit. We'll discuss how to customize the interface at the end of this chapter.

Each of the manipulators has a handle for a particular axis, designated by its color. Red is for the X axis, green is for the Y axis, and blue is for the Z axis. A cyan colored axis allows for free movement in both axes of the active panel view. When you select a particular handle, it turns yellow. You can then only transform (move, scale, or rotate) the object in that axis.

As shown in the first panel of Figure 1.19, the Move tool (a.k.a. the translate tool) displays arrows for the axis of movement. You can grab any one of the handles (axis arrow lines) to move the selected object in just the translation axis. The Rotate tool (shown in the second panel) displays circles around the object's pivot point that act as axis handles. You drag on one of the circles to rotate the selected object in just the rotation axis. The Scale tool (shown in the third panel) displays handles with colored cubes, which, when dragged, scale the object in the scale axis.

The Universal Manipulator is shown in the fourth panel of Figure 1.19 and acts in place of all three tools. You can select the arrows to move the object with the Universal Manipulator just like with the Move tool. Select any of the curved arrows in the middle of the box edges of the manipulator to rotate the object in the Universal Manipulator's axis. Finally, selecting and dragging the cyan boxes in the corners of the manipulator box lets you scale the sphere. If you hold down the Ctrl key as you drag, you can scale the sphere in just one axis.

It is much easier to use the default hot keys defined for these transformation tools than to select them from the Tool Box. If the keys aren't working, make sure Caps Lock is off. You must use the lowercase keys.

The Universal Manipulator interactively shows you the movement, rotation, or scale as you manipulate your object. As you move an object, the Universal Manipulator shows you the coordinates. Likewise, rotating with the Universal Manipulator displays the degree of change. Last, scale values in dark gray on the three outside edges of the manipulator box are displayed as you scale the sphere with the Universal Manipulator.

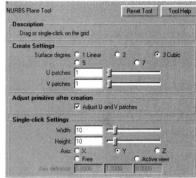

Now these four tools offer you two different ways to move, rotate, or scale your objects. However, the next tool down in the Tool Box is a bit different. The Soft Modification tool allows you to select an area on your surface or model and adjust the surface. The adjustments gradually taper off away from the initial place of selection to "soft modify" an area of the model.

For instance, create a NURBS plane by choosing **Create → NURBS Primitives → Plane** ❐. This opens the options for creating a plane. Set both the U Patches and V Patches sliders to 10 and click/drag your mouse cursor to create a plane on the grid.

Select the Scale tool and scale the plane up to about the size of the grid. Then, select the Soft Modification tool (🖌) from the Tool Box and click the plane, somewhere just off the middle. This will create an *S* and a special manipulator to allow you to move, rotate, or scale this soft selection.

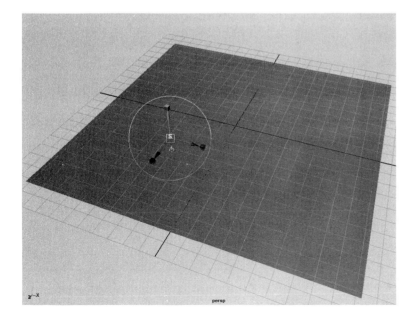

Grab the cone handle and drag it up to move the soft selection up. Notice the plane lifts up in that area only, gradually falling off as if you were picking up a napkin.

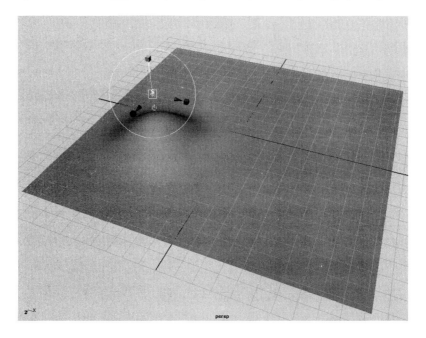

The cube handle on the Soft Modification tool scales the soft selection, and dragging on the circle rotates it. Simply select another transformation tool to exit the Soft Modification tool. You can always go back and select the *S* on the surface to edit the selection or even keyframe it for animation. You can place as many soft selections as you need on a surface.

Tip: To scale the manipulator handles to make them more noticeable or less obtrusive, press the plus key (+) to increase a manipulator's size or press the minus key (−) to decrease it.

The Hotbox

The hotbox (see Figure 1.20) gives you convenient access to all menu commands in Maya. It is a quick way to get to the menu selections without accessing the menu bar itself. This is useful if you want to turn off the menu bar and other UI elements to give you the maximum screen space for your scene. To open the hotbox, simply hold down the spacebar in an active view panel. You can then select menu options with the mouse.

All the menu commands that are available from the main menu bar are available through the hotbox. You can display some or all of the menu headings to give you quick access to whatever commands and features you use most. The hotbox is separated into five distinct zones, delineated by short black diagonal lines: North, East, West, South, and

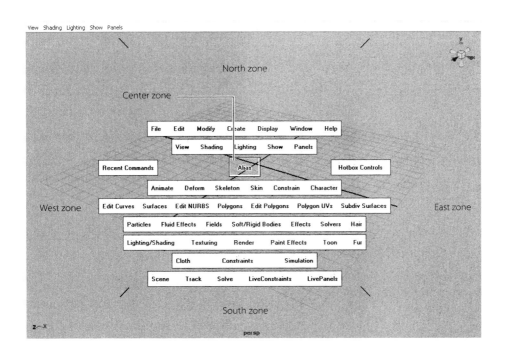

Figure 1.20

The hotbox and its zones

Center. To adjust the hotbox to your liking, press and hold the spacebar and click Hotbox Controls to the right of the Center zone. From here you can select to display some or all of the menu headings.

Activating the hotbox and clicking a zone with the mouse displays a set of shortcut menu commands called *marking menus*, discussed in the next section.

Marking Menus

In addition to menu selections, the hotbox has *marking menus* in each of the five zones. Using marking menus is yet another way to quickly access the commands you use the most. The marking menus are classified as follows:

ZONE	MARKING MENU
North Zone	Selects the display layout, similar to the display layout buttons in the Tool Box.
East Zone	Toggles the visibility of UI elements such as the Help line or Status line. You can quickly toggle the display of several UI elements to maximize your screen space.
South Zone	Changes the current view panel to an information panel window such as the Outliner or Hypershade windows.
West Zone	Activates Selection Masks, as if using the Selection Mask icons in the Status line discussed earlier in the chapter. You can use a marking menu like this to quickly set your selection to vertices without needing to access the Status line, for example.
Center Zone	Sets the view panel to any of the modeling or perspective windows in your scene.

Figure 1.21

The menu sets drop-down menu

As you become more familiar with Maya, your use of the hotbox and the marking menus will greatly increase your productivity. If you are just starting out, it's advisable to begin with accessing the menus and commands such as selection sets through the Status line and main menu bar until you are familiar with where everything is. It is easy when you're a beginner to get lost in all the options you have when selecting some tools and work flows, so it's best to start with the plain and simple and work your way up to the faster work flows such as marking menus.

Menu Sets

As we discussed earlier, menu sets are organized according to function. The menu sets are Animation, Polygons, Surfaces, Dynamics, and Rendering, all of which are available in Maya Complete and Maya Unlimited. However, with Maya Unlimited, you are given access to the Classic Cloth, nCloth, and Maya Live menu sets as well. Each menu set gives you access to the commands associated with its broader function set. The Polygons menu set, for example, displays in the main menu bar all the menu headers that correspond to polygon modeling functions.

The menu sets drop-down (shown in Figure 1.21) is the first thing on the Status line. Changing between menu sets is simpler if you use the default hot keys shown here:

KEY	FUNCTION
F2	Animation menu set
F3	Polygons menu set
F4	Surfaces menu set
F5	Dynamics menu set
F6	Rendering menu set

Customizing Menu Sets

New to Maya 8, you can customize menu sets by opening the Menu Set Editor and choosing the Customize option in the menu sets drop-down. The Menu Set Editor (Figure 1.22) allows you to modify existing menu sets or to create your own. To make your own menu set, select the New Menu Set button and enter a name for your set. To add menus to your set, scroll through the available menus on the right, highlight the ones you wish to add, right-click and select Add to Menu Set.

This wraps up the interactive parts of Maya's UI. You will find all this information a bit much at first, but as soon as you begin using Maya, you will find it becomes second nature quickly. You might want to skip ahead to the next chapter to begin working a simple scene in Maya to apply what you've learned here and then come back for a description of the windows you will be using, or you can stick around and get your feet wet on the most commonly used Maya windows in the next section.

Figure 1.22

You can create your own menu sets or edit existing ones.

The Main Maya Windows

Maya has a few important windows in which you will be working frequently. The following sections introduce the location and function of each window, tell you when you will come across them, and describe how to use them.

The Attribute Editor Window

As you've already seen to some extent, every object is defined by a series of attributes, all placed in nodes. You can edit some of these attributes in the Channel Box as you have seen, but to see all the attributes available for a selected object, you will need the Attribute Editor, which is possibly the most important window in Maya. Through this window you can change an object's attributes, set keyframes, connect to other attributes, attach expressions, or simply view their values.

Create an object in Maya. Choose **Create → NURBS Primitives → Sphere** and then click anywhere in the scene view to put a NURBS sphere in your scene.

With the sphere still selected, open the Attribute Editor by choosing **Window → Attribute Editor** or by pressing the default hot key Ctrl+A.

You will see that the Channel Box displays the commonly used attributes for the sphere but that the Attribute Editor shows an entire collection of attributes. Figure 1.23 shows the sphere and its attributes. The attributes in the Channel Box and Attribute Editor are the same. If you move or otherwise transform the sphere, the values are consistent in both displays.

Connected Nodes

Notice the tabs running across the top of the Attribute Editor. These tabs correspond to the object's node structure. Each tab displays the attributes of another tab that is in some way connected to the sphere that is currently selected. You can easily adjust any of the settings for any node that is linked to the selected object by just selecting its tab in the

Figure 1.23

The Attribute Editor and Channel Box display the values for the selected sphere.

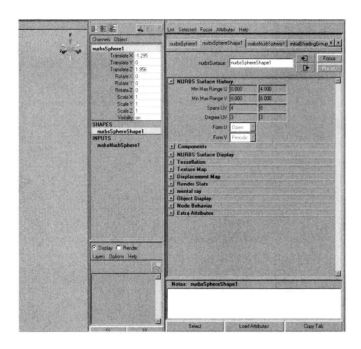

Attribute Editor. For example, if you click the nurbsSphere1 tab, you will see the *DAG node* attributes. A DAG node is the placement, or transforms node, of the object. This node tells the object where it is and what its rotation and scale is. Click the nurbsSphere-Shape1 tab to see the *shape node* of the sphere. The shape node contains the attributes that define the shape of the object. Click the makeNurbsSphere1 tab to access to the *creation node* of the sphere.

The creation node displays attributes for *how* the object was made. For example, try changing the value for the **Start Sweep** attribute. This will change the sweep of the sphere, effectively slicing a chunk out of it, so it looks like a cut-open, hollow orange, as shown here.

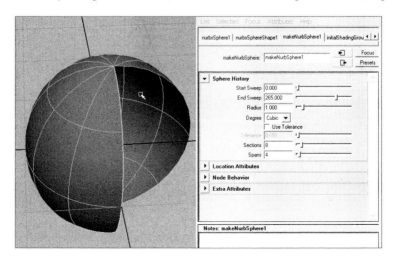

What's more, you can animate almost any of the attributes in any of these nodes (Attribute Editor tabs). All you need to do is RM click the attribute in the Attribute Editor and choose Set Key from the shortcut menu . This sets a keyframe for that attribute at the current frame, just like RM clicking in the Channel Box.

> If your sphere does not have a makeNurbsSphere1 tab in the Attribute Editor, check to make sure the Construction History button in the Status line is toggled on. Without it, the sphere is created without history, so its creation node is deleted right after the sphere is made.

Notes

At the bottom of the Attribute Editor is a Notes area where you can type and record comments that stay with the object's Attribute Editor window. Simply drag the separator bar as shown to create more or less space in the Notes section; this area is handy for remembering how certain things are set up or to pass secret notes about your boss around the studio.

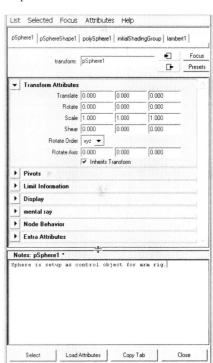

Multiple Selections

The Attribute Editor can display only one object at a time. If you have multiple objects selected, you can toggle through them through the Attribute Editor's menu by choosing Selected and then choosing the object from the menu.

The Outliner

The Outliner and Hypergraph (covered next) use two different approaches to the same end: organization. Maya is based on node structure, meaning every object in Maya is represented by a node. A node is a collection of attributes that define how the object looks, to make a long story short. Some nodes interconnect to form more complex objects or to give you the best control over their shape or behavior.

As you grow your scene, you will create more and more nodes, and you will need a way to organize your objects. Furthermore, you can group objects and place objects into hierarchies. By creating *groups*, you can control objects as a single unit in which all the members of the group move, rotate, and scale as one. Additionally, with *parenting*, you place one object (the child) under the influence of another object (the parent) to control the objects together.

With a parent-child hierarchy, the child can move independently under the parents as well as inherit the movements of the parent. The child node inherits the transforms (movements) of all the parents above it and moves (or rotates or scales) however the parents move, but it can move on its own as well. Imagine, if you will, a ball bouncing on a cart.

Figure 1.24

The Outliner

The cart rolls along while the ball bounces on top. The ball is a child of the cart and moves along with the cart as it rolls along, but the ball has its own movement on the cart as it bounces up and down. Creating good hierarchies is the backbone of animation in Maya and is covered throughout this book.

Both windows display the objects in your scene and allow you to make hierarchy (or grouping) decisions, as well as more intricate connections between attributes. The Outliner displays your scene objects as an outline, and the Hypergraph uses a flowchart layout that gives you more finite control. You access the Outliner by choosing **Window → Outliner**.

The Outliner (see Figure 1.24) displays all the objects in your scene as an outline. You can select any object in a scene by simply clicking its name.

You can reorganize objects listed in the Outliner by MMB dragging an object to a new location in the window. By default, objects are listed in order of creation in the scene. You have easy control over organization in your scene:

- You can select objects in your scene by selecting them in the Outliner.

- To rename a node, double-click its Outliner entry, and type the new name.

- To relocate an object's entry in the Outliner to another location in the Outliner, MM drag the node's entry and place it in-between two other node entries.

- To parent one object under another, MM drag the node onto the new parent.

- To pull an object out of a group, MM drag the node to a different location in the Outliner.

You can separate the Outliner into two independent scrolling displays, which is useful when you have a large scene with a long Outliner list of nodes. The separator bar is located at the bottom of the Outliner window; simply click it and drag it up or down for a second Outliner display area. This is also useful when you need to parent one node at the bottom of the list onto another node toward the top of the list.

The Hypergraph

Using a flowchart or graph view, the Hypergraph (see Figure 1.25) also displays all the objects in your scene. The Hypergraph, however, is a more detailed view of your nodes and how they connect with each other. You can easily parent objects to each other through this window by MM dragging the node to be parented onto the node you wish to be the parent, just as in the Outliner. And since you can have several objects in your scene (indeed hundreds or more), you will need to move around in the Hypergraph. Navigating the Hypergraph is the same as navigating in any modeling panel using the familiar Alt key and mouse combinations for tracking and zooming. You access the Hypergraph by choosing **Window → Hypergraph:Hierarchy Or Hypergraph:Connections.**

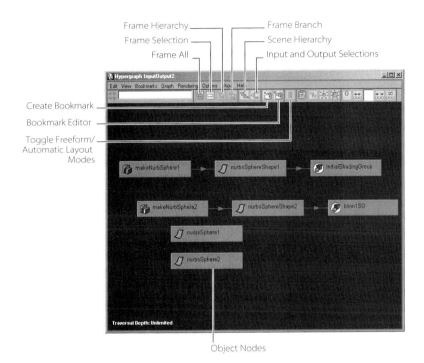

Figure 1.25

The Hypergraph displays your objects in a flowchart format.

Connections and the Hypergraph

You can edit connections of attributes between nodes graphically to set up some rather complex relationships, though this is not immediately evident when you first open the window. Create a NURBS sphere and cone in a scene, place them side by side, and open the Hypergraph window.

In Figure 1.26, you see the simple scene in the Hypergraph's main node view. The Hypergraph shows nodes for the four panel views (persp, top, front, side) as well as the NURBS sphere (nurbsSphere1) and the NURBS cone (nurbsCone1). Select them both in the Hypergraph, and then click the Input And Output Selections icon (see to Figure 1.25 for its location). This connections view shows you all the nodes that interact with the selected node(s). In this case, as shown in Figure 1.27, you see our object's DAG nodes (nurbsSphere1 and nurbsCone1) and their shape nodes (nurbsSphereShape1 and nurbs-ConeShape1) and creation nodes (makeNurbSphere1 and makeNurbCone1) as well as the default gray shader they are assigned to upon creation (initialShadingGroup). For more on hierarchies, see Chapter 2.

The lines connecting the nodes represent connections, with the arrows displaying which node is feeding the other. Here, the creation nodes feed the shape nodes. The DAG nodes are displayed separately on the left. In the example in Figure 1.27, the nurbsCone1 node is connected into the nurbsSphere1 node. The line represents a connection made in this example to lock their rotations together. You will get more practice on this in Chapter 8, but for now, as an exercise in how the Hypergraph works, we'll show you how to make this connection yourself, to match Figure 1.27.

In this connections display, if you MM drag one node on top of another, Maya presents an option to connect attributes between the nodes. The node you drag will connect *into* the node you drag it to. In this case, MM drag nurbsSphere1 onto nurbsCone1. A pop-up menu appears, as shown in Figure 1.28.

Figure 1.26

A scene in the Hypergraph

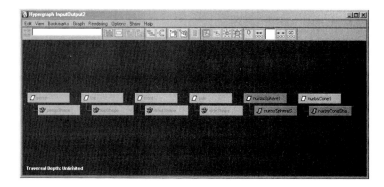

Figure 1.27

Detailed connections are displayed and edited in the Hypergraph display.

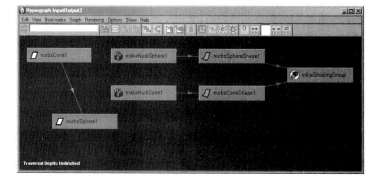

Figure 1.28

Connecting attributes in the Hypergraph

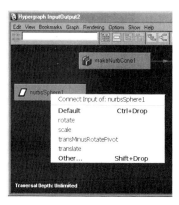

Select Other from the menu to open a new window called the Connection Editor, shown here and explained later in this chapter. In the Connection Editor, scroll down and select Rotate on both sides of the window.

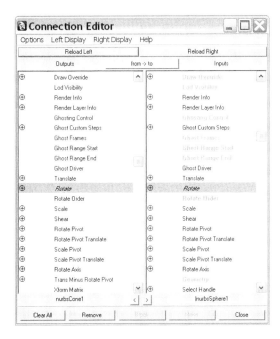

This action connects the rotations of the sphere to the cone. Select the cone and rotate it in the perspective view. You will see the sphere rotating as well. In the Hypergraph, move your mouse over any of the connecting lines to display the attributes that are connected, as shown here.

The connecting lines are also color coded. A green line, as in our example, represents a *vector* connection. A vector connection is a connection of three attributes (or channels),

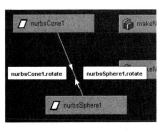

such as **RotateX**, **RotateY**, and **RotateZ.** A single channel connection is made with a blue line.

Notice now that you can no longer rotate the sphere directly if you select the sphere and try to rotate it in your scene. The sphere's rotations are locked to the cone until you sever the connections either through the Channel Box (RM click the attribute in the Channel Box and choose Break Connection) or through the Hypergraph. To disconnect in the Hypergraph, click the green connecting line and press Delete.

To see additional connections between nodes, such as expressions and deformers, choose **Options → Display** and select the type of connection you want to see.

To return to the regular node view at any time when you are editing connections in the Hypergraph, simply click the Scene Hierarchy icon.

Figure 1.29

**The Hypergraph's
vertical layout**

Changing Layout

Using the icons across the top of the window, called out in Figure 1.25 earlier in this chapter, you can change your view quickly. For example, if you select an object in the perspective panel but can't find it in the Hypergraph view, just click the Frame Selection icon. If you prefer a vertical layout similar to the Outliner (shown in Figure 1.29), in the Hypergraph menu choose **Options → Orientation → Vertical**.

The nodes in the Hypergraph are lined up by default. If you would like a free-form display so that you can move your nodes however you wish (instead of horizontally or vertically), click the Toggle Freeform/Automatic Layout Modes icon shown in Figure 1.25. You can also import an image as the Hypergraph background in free-form mode to place nodes on parts of an image. Just toggle **View → Show Background Image** and select your image by selecting **View → Set Background Image**. This is handy for making character rigs when you want to place the appropriate character nodes on the character's parts for making selections and reference faster.

Bookmarks

Another convenience of the Hypergraph is the use of bookmarks. When you frame a certain selection of nodes in the window, you can bookmark the view to return to it later easily. To bookmark a Hypergraph view, choose **Bookmarks → Create Bookmark,** or click the Create Bookmark icon called out in Figure 1.25 earlier in this chapter. You can then just select the view from the Bookmark menu at a later time.

Traversal Depth

To help better organize complex connection hierarchies, you can specify a traversal depth when viewing input and output connections in the Hypergraph. You can set the depth by using the icons and text field in the toolbar, as shown in Figure 30. By default, the depth is set to infinity (−1). The lower the traversal depth, the more pruned the hierarchy will appear.

Containers

New to Maya 8.5, containers let you organize nodes within the dependency graph, allowing you to simplify your layout by grouping nodes together. Container nodes differentiate themselves from other nodes by their thick outline, as seen in Figure 1.31.

To create a container, select the nodes in the Hypergraph that you wish to add, and choose **Edit → Create Container**. To look inside a container, simply double-click on the container node. To add a node to a container, Alt+Shift+drag the node on top of the container node. Likewise, to remove a node from a container, Alt+Shift+drag the node outside of the container. Nodes within a container do not change their hierarchy or connections; they simply act as organizational groupings.

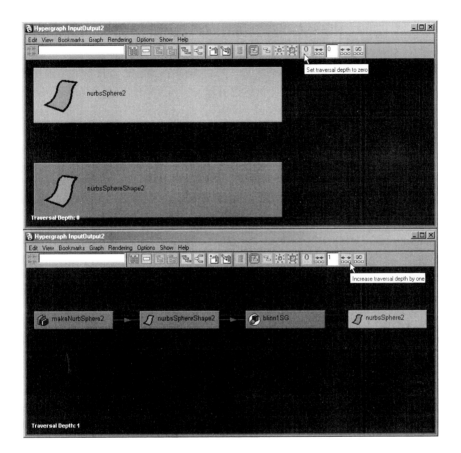

Figure 1.30

Traversal depth prunes a displayed connection hierarchy.

The Connection Editor

You can use the Connection Editor (choose **Window → General Editors → Connection Editor;** see Figure 1.32) to connect attributes between almost any two objects, as you have just seen in the discussion on the Hypergraph. The connection we made there attached the rotations of a sphere to that of a

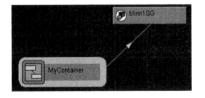

Figure 1.31

Containers allow you to group similar nodes in the Hypergraph without changing their input and output connections.

cone. Simple enough, but we can make connections far more complex. For example, the height of a cube in the Y axis can control the amount of red in a sphere's rendered color. You will see how to make complex animations and relationships later in this book, in Chapter 8, when you begin to rig a scene for animation.

Figure 1.32

**The Connection
Editor**

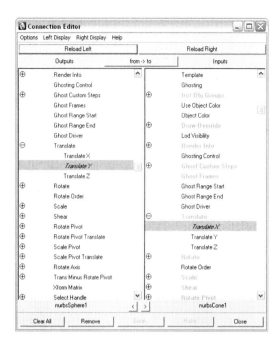

Creating and Editing Connections

The Connection Editor is separated into two vertical panes. Each pane represents one of two objects in the connection. By selecting an object and clicking the Reload Left button, you can load into the Connection Editor's left column all the attributes of the selected objects. By selecting a second object and clicking Reload Right, you can load the attributes of the second object. As you saw earlier, clicking attributes in both columns creates a direct relationship between the two objects' attributes.

When you want to edit connections on attributes or channels already connected, simply click one object's attribute to show you what channel it is connected to on the other object. Maya will highlight the other connected channel when you select the first object's attributes in one of the panes. To disconnect a connection through the Connection Editor, click the channel and simply click the other object's highlighted channel(s).

Connections are the cornerstone of animation and a significant reason for animation being so open ended in Maya. You can create any kind of relationship between almost any attributes of almost any object to create highly complex, interconnected animations.

Filtering the Display of Connections

Since there can be so many attributes and connections even between just two objects, you can filter the view in the Connection Editor to show or hide attribute *types* entirely. You can access view filters through the window's menu bar. Choose **Left Display** or **Right Display** menu headings to toggle the connections you want to display.

CHANNEL FILTERS	DESCRIPTION
Readable	Displays all the attributes of an object, regardless of whether they can be keyframed
Outputs Only	Shows attributes that can only be connected *to* other nodes
Inputs Only	Presents attributes that can only be connected *into*
Non-Keyable	Displays attributes that you cannot create connections with or for
Connected Only	Shows attributes that already have connections
Hidden	Displays hidden attributes for that node

The Multilister

As the Outliner and Hypergraph list the objects in the scene, the Multilister and Hypershade (see the next section) windows list the render nodes of your scene—textures, lights, cameras, and so on. In Maya terminology, adding textures and such to objects is called *shading* (called surfacing in Lightwave-speak, for example). And as with the Outliner and Hypergraph, these windows approach presenting the shaders of your scenes differently to accommodate the best of options in your work flow. You will have a small taste of shading in the next chapter.

The Multilister (accessed through **Window → Rendering Editors → Multilister**; see Figure 1.33) lays out not just the shaders of your scene, but also lights, cameras, and the shaders' textures, in a table format. All the shaders in the scene are displayed under their respective tabs in this window and are represented by named thumbnail icons.

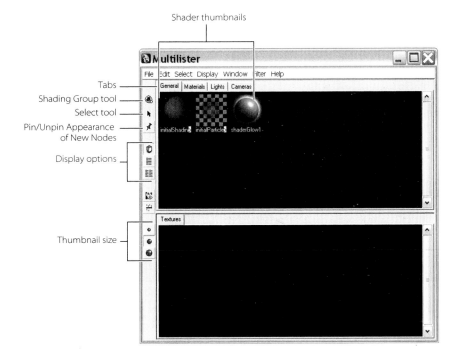

Figure 1.33
The Multilister

Double-clicking any of the names under the thumbnails lets you change the name of the shader or render node. Clicking the thumbnails themselves selects the shader for use, and double-clicking the thumbnail (and not the name) opens its Attribute Editor.

The Multilister is in two panels. Both panels let you select what type of shading/render node is displayed. By default, the top panel displays all the shaders in the scene in the General tab—with materials, lights, and camera nodes under their respective tabs. The bottom panel is typically used to display texture nodes that are in use or are already connected to shaders.

You can add or edit tabs to filter just the nodes you need to work on. For example, if you would like to view only the type(s) of nodes you want, pay a visit to the **Display → Tabs** menu. There you can create new tabs with special filters using the Create Filtered command from that menu.

Many of the commands accessible through the menu system are also available through shortcut menus when you RM click the shaders in the Multilister panes. To assign a shader, for example, select your object in Maya, click your desired shader to select it, and then RM click and choose **Edit → Assign** from the shortcut menu.

You can customize the look of the Multilister by clicking the option display icons of the thumbnail size icons running down the left side of the window, shown in Figure 1.33. Each thumbnail has a small arrow in the lower-right corner. Clicking this arrow expands on that shader's network of connection nodes, if you have textures or images attached.

The Multilister is good for fast shader management and assignment if you are connecting and editing attribute connections, even more so than the Hypergraph. It does, however, lack the brawn of the Hypershade to get into serious shader network management.

The Hypershade

The Hypershade is accessed through **Window → Rendering Editors → Hypershade** (see Figure 1.34) and displays the shaders and textures in your scene in a graphical flowchart layout similar to the Hypergraph window. You connect and disconnect render node attributes through the Hypershade to create shader networks from the simple to the intricately complex. The Hypershade window has three main areas: the *Create/Bins panel*, the *render node display*, and the *work area*. The three icons in the upper right let you switch views.

The Create/Bins Panel

The Create/Bins panel on the left is divided into two tabs: Create and Bins. Selecting the Create tab displays the icons to create several render nodes from materials such as Lambert and Blinn to procedural textures such as ramps and fractal noise. To create a node, simply click its icon in the Create panel and it will appear in the node display and work area for immediate editing. The Create icons are separated into types of render nodes, from surfaces to utility nodes. You will have plenty of exposure to these nodes and how to best edit them in Chapter 12.

The bar at the top of this pane lets you select the kind of node you want to create; you can switch between Maya shading nodes and mental ray nodes. Since mental ray is a fully integrated plug-in, you will need to make sure it is loaded before you see the mental ray option in this panel. We'll discuss plug-ins later in this chapter in the section "Customizing the Interface."

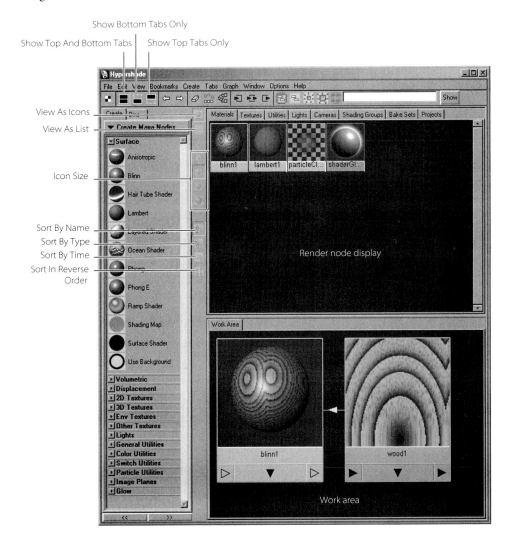

Figure 1.34

The Hypershade

The Bins tab lets you store sets of shaders in bins to manage them better, especially if you have a heavy scene to work in. You use the icons at the top of the Bins tab to organize your shaders. If you hover the mouse pointer over the icons, Maya will show you a pop-up description for each.

The Render Node Display Area

After you create render nodes, they appear in the display area as thumbnail icons. Clicking a render node's icon selects that node for use, and double-clicking it opens the Attribute Editor. If you want to edit a shading network, MM drag the thumbnail icon to the work area below. Navigating in this area of the Hypershade, as well as the work area, is similar to navigating the Hypergraph and work windows in that you use the Alt key and mouse controls. The Hypershade zooms in levels as opposed to the smooth zooms in a work panel, though it still uses the Alt+RM. And although you cannot freely pan around this window, you can use Alt+MM to scroll up and down when you have enough shaders to fill the panel. The bottom panel, the work area, however, reacts much the same as a normal view panel with the panning and zooming moves.

The Work Area

The work area is a free-form workspace where you connect render node attributes to form shading networks for your scene. This is by far the easiest place to create and edit complex shaders, because it gives you a clear flowchart of the network, much like the Hypergraph view of object nodes. To work on a shading node from the node display panel, just MM drag it down into the work area.

The most efficient way to work with shaders is to use marking menus in the Hypershade window panels. RM click a shading icon to display a marking menu. This marking menu lets you assign the shader to the current selection of objects, select objects that have that shader already assigned to them, or to graph the network. Graphing the network of a shader gives you a display similar to the Hypergraph's connection display. Also like the

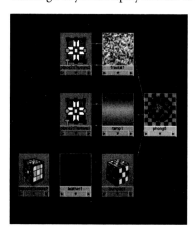

Hypergraph, Maya 8.5 introduces containers to the work area, helping you to group nodes together. See the Hypergraph section on containers for details on how to create and modify container nodes. Figure 1.35 shows how you can edit the connections between shading nodes graphically.

As you saw with the Hypergraph earlier in this chapter, the connections between nodes is handled with color-coded lines and arrows. In this example, a Phong material has connections coming in from a fractal node, a ramp node, and a bump map with a leather node.

Figure 1.35

Seeing a render node's network gives you access to editing its connections.

Using the Hypershade

Open the Hypershade and create a Phong shader by clicking the Phong icon in the Create Maya Nodes panel. Double-click the Phong's thumbnail to open the Attribute Editor (Figure 1.36). In the Attribute Editor, if you click the color swatch next to the **Color** (or other attribute) of the shader, you can change the color of the material. To map a texture (such as a procedural texture—that is, a texture that is created entirely in Maya) or an image file to a color or other attribute, click the map icon (the checkered button) to the right of that attribute. For this example, click the map icon next to the **Color** attribute. The Create Render Node window opens (Figure 1.37). Click the Ramp icon to create a ramp node for the color of this Phong material. If you open your Attribute Editor, you'll notice a green line connecting a new ramp node to the Phong material.

As with the Hypergraph, you can mouse over the connecting lines to see which attributes are connected. You can also select the connection lines and press Delete to disconnect those connections.

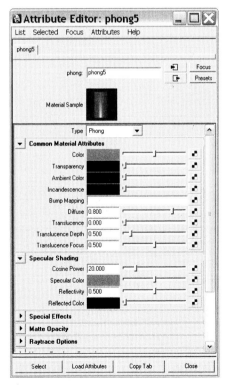

Figure 1.36

A Phong shader

Figure 1.37

The Create Render Node window

The Graph Editor

Maya's Graph Editor (choose **Window → Animation Editors → Graph Editor**) is a truly powerful editing tool for the animator (see Figure 1.38).

Since 3D data is stored digitally as vector information, every movement that is set in Maya generates a graph of value vs. time. The Graph Editor provides direct access to the curves generated by your animation to let you fine-tune and edit, even create, your animation in this window.

The left panel of the Graph Editor is much like the Outliner and displays the selected objects and their hierarchy along with a listing of their animated channels or attributes. By default, all of an object's keyframed channels display as colored curves in the display to the right of the list, with red, green, and blue for the X, Y, and Z axes, respectively. Selecting an object or an object's channel in the list, you isolate only those curves you want to see on the right.

The Graph Editor displays these animation curves as value vs. time, with value running vertically and time horizontally. Keyframes are represented as points on the curves that can be freely moved to adjust timing and/or value. This is where most animators spend their time animating.

Figure 1.38

The Graph Editor

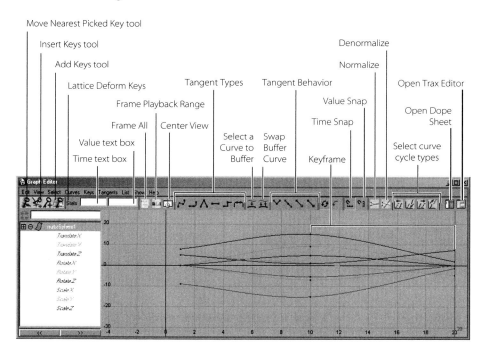

To move a keyframe in the Graph Editor, click to select (or drag a marquee around the keys to select them) and MM drag the keys as needed. You can also select the entire curve or curves and move them with the MM as well. Using the snap icons shown in Figure 1.38, you can snap your keyframes to whole numbers in time or value. This is useful for snapping keys to whole frames.

Navigation in the Graph Editor is the same as the Alt+mouse combinations you are familiar with by now. You can pan and zoom in this window with Alt+MM and Alt+RM respectively.

You can adjust the Graph Editor's curve display with Normalize or Denormalize functions. For example, when you have a translate X curve with vertical values from 1 to 3, and a Rotate Y curve with values from 1 to 360 degrees, seeing the detail of the curves in relation to each other is difficult since you would need to zoom out in the Graph Editor to see values as high as 360. Figure 1.39 shows an animation in which the curves' values stretch up high. In Figure 1.40 we have normalized the curve view so that the full range of values fits between –1 and 1 in the Curve Editor, giving you the opportunity to compare timings between curves with very different value ranges. To normalize the view, click the Normalize icon shown in Figure 1.38. To return to your regular view, click Denormalize.

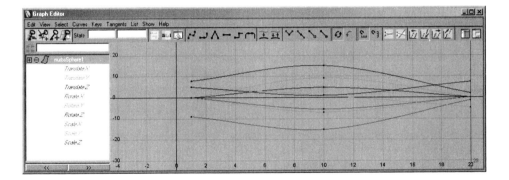

Figure 1.39
Different value ranges can make it difficult to compare timings in animation curves.

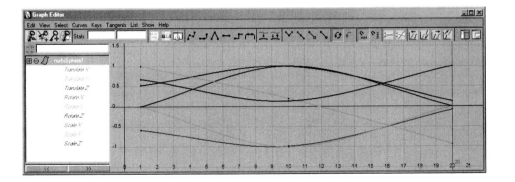

Figure 1.40
Normalizing the view makes it easier to compare timings.

Keep in mind that normalizing does not change the animation in the scene. It only allows you to see all the curves and their relative motions. Normalizing your view is particularly helpful in busy scenes when you want to adjust both the smallest scale of values alongside the largest scale of values without having to constantly zoom in and out of the Graph Editor to see the appropriate curves.

You will get hands-on experience with the Graph Editor in Chapter 7 of this book.

The Script Editor

You access the Script Editor (see Figure 1.41) by clicking the icon in the bottom-right corner of the screen at the end of the Command line or by choosing **Window → General Editors → Script Editor**. Since almost everything in Maya is built on MEL, every command you initiate generates some sort of MEL script or MEL argument. A history of these commands is available in the Script Editor.

You can use this window when you need to reference a command that was issued or an argument or a comment that was displayed in the Help line but was too long to read on one line.

Of course, this window is also useful in scripting or creating macros of MEL commands to execute compound actions. When you want to create a custom procedure, you can copy and paste MEL from this window to form macros. As a matter of fact, the Script Editor is great to use to learn how to script in the first place. By reading the command feedback and the MEL commands issued whenever you execute a button or tool, you will start to pick up on how MEL works. Maya 8.5 introduces support for Python commands. Python support and other new Script Editor features are discussed in Chapter 16.

Figure 1.41
The Script Editor

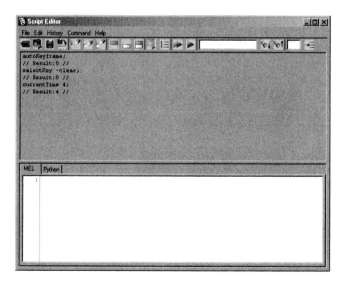

The window is in two halves. The top half is the Script Editor's feedback history, and the bottom half is its Command line, where new MEL commands can be issued. By highlighting text in the upper window, you can copy and paste the command back into the Command line. Once you have some commands that are working for you, you can add them to the shelf by highlighting the text and choosing **File → Save Script To Shelf**.

Using the Script Editor is also a good way to check on error messages that are too long to fully view in the Command line's feedback box. If you see an error message pop up and something goes wrong, open the Script Editor to see what sort of error(s) have scrolled by.

Customizing the Interface

You've probably noticed that we've run into the same tools more than once as we've gone through the aspects of the user interface so far. Simply put, for everything you need to do in Maya, there are not only a few ways to do so, but at least a couple of ways to access the tools to do so.

Most of Maya's commands and tools can be found in at least two places. This may be confusing at first, but you'll discover that in the long run it is most advantageous. It allows for the greatest flexibility in individual work flow and in part accounts for Maya's being easily customized.

Once you are confident with your Maya know-how, you'll develop your own ideas about how to use all the other user interface methods to customize your work flow. You'll want to return to this section when you're ready to do some serious customization.

User Preferences

To customize Maya, you use the Preferences window (choose **Window → Settings/Preferences**), as shown in Figure 1.42.

The Preferences window is separated into categories that define aspects of the program.

- Interface options to change the main user interface:

  - UI Elements lets you change which parts of the UI are displayed. You've seen in this chapter how you can access these preferences through marking menus, but you also have access here.

  - Help lets you specify whether you want tooltip pop-up windows when you mouse over icons or buttons, as well as how you view the HTML documentation that comes with Maya.

- Display options to specify how objects are displayed in the workspace.

Figure 1.42

**The Preferences
window**

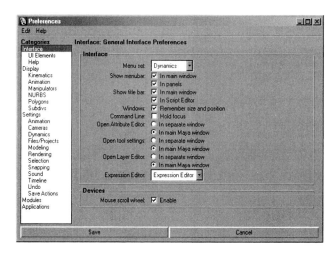

- Settings lets you change the default values of several tools and their general operation. An essential aspect of this category is the Working Units section under the Settings category itself. These options set the working parameters of your scene, including the frame rate. It's important to set the time units and frame rate properly. Some important subsections are as follows:

  - Files/Projects initially specifies where Maya looks for your projects and files. Maya keeps things organized as projects. This setting allows you to specify where Maya always goes first when you try setting a project or loading/saving a scene.

  - Timeline sets your playback rate for the scene. Keep in mind this is *not* the same as setting the scene's frame rate, but merely adjusts how fast Maya will attempt to playback your animation in the view panels.

  - Undo sets the size of the undo queue. It is a good idea to set this to Infinite, which will give you the opportunity to undo almost all your actions in any working session in case something does not work out quite as planned. This will not use up that much more memory, so it's quite worth it.

  - Selection allows you to specify the order of preferred selection. Maya has a selection queue that marks some objects as more selectable than others. If you marquee select a bunch of objects of different types in the scene, Maya will select the more important object types instead of the others. This is where you set your preference of what is selected over another object.

- Modules specifies which modules are loaded by default whenever you start Maya. By default, both Dynamics and Paint Effects are loaded. This is not the same as loading plug-ins such as fur and mental ray, which are accessed through the Plugin Manager (covered later in this chapter).

- Applications lets you set the path of applications that are commonly used in conjunction with Maya. This makes work flow much faster, allowing you to launch an application such as Photoshop to edit a texture map from within Maya itself.

Colors

You can change just about any of the UI and object display colors in Maya by choosing **Window → Settings/Preferences → Color Settings** to open the Colors window, as shown in Figure 1.43. You can click the color swatch to change the colors or use the slider to toggle through common preset colors.

For example, to change the background color of the 3D view panels, click the 3D View heading and select your color. The Active and Inactive tabs give you access to colors of objects that are currently selected (or active) or not selected (inactive).

As you will see throughout exercises in this book, organizing your scene elements using groups with different display colors is different from using the Colors window. These changes affect all scenes and UI elements for the particular user in Maya and are used to customize the display for your convenience, not for scene management or organization. You will be using display layers and the like for organizing.

Shelves

Choose **Window → Settings/Preferences → Shelf Editor** to manage your shelves (see Figure 1.44). You can create or delete shelves or manage the items on the shelf with this function.

Figure 1.43

Adjusting the colors of your UI elements, windows, and scene objects is easy.

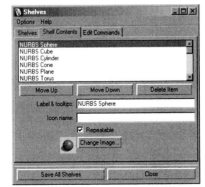

Figure 1.44

The Shelves window

You can easily add any menu item or Toolbox item to your shelf:

- To add an item from the Toolbox, simply MMB drag its icon from the Toolbox into the appropriate shelf.

- To add an item from a menu to the shelf, hold down Ctrl+Shift+Alt while selecting the item from the menu.

- To add an item (a MEL command) from the Script Editor, highlight the text of the MEL command in the Script Editor, and MMB drag it onto the shelf. A MEL icon will be created that will run the command when you click it.

- To remove an item from a Shelf, MMB drag its icon to the Trash icon at the end of the shelf, or choose **Window → Settings/Preferences → Shelf Editor**.

Hot Keys

Hot keys are keyboard shortcuts that can access almost any Maya tool or command. You have already encountered quite a few so far in our exploration of the interface. You can create even more through the Hotkey Editor, shown in Figure 1.45.

Figure 1.45

The Hotkey Editor

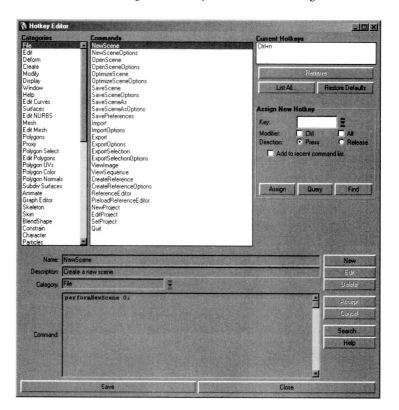

Through this monolith of a window, you can set virtually any key combination to be used as a shortcut to virtually any command in Maya. Since so many tools already have hot keys assigned by default, it is important to get to know them first before you decide to start changing things around to suit how you work. If you are coming to Maya from another 3D package, you can set up your hot keys to resemble your old work flow.

Every menu command is represented by menu categories on the left, and the right side allows you to view the current hot key or to assign a new hot key to the selected command. Ctrl and Alt key combinations can be used with any letter keys on the keyboard. Keep in mind that Maya is *case sensitive*, meaning it differentiates between upper- and lowercase letters. For example, one of our personal hot keys is Ctrl+h to hide a selected object from view, and Ctrl+shift+H is to unhide it.

When you are ready to start setting your own hot keys, query your intended hot key with the Query button to find out if it is assigned to a command that suits that hot key better.

The lower section of this window displays the MEL command that the menu command invokes. It also allows you to type your own MEL commands, name them as new commands, categorize them with the other commands, and assign hot keys to them.

Marking Menus

Customizing your marking menus can give a huge boost to your work flow. You might want more modeling tools at your fingertips than general UI controls such as the defaults. You can customize the marking menus by choosing **Window → Settings/Preferences → Marking Menu Editor**. Figure 1.46 shows the Marking Menu Editor window.

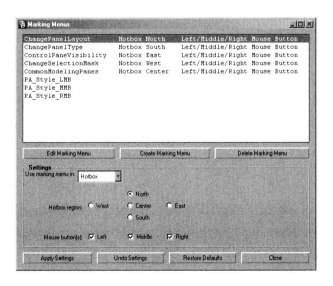

Figure 1.46

The Marking Menu Editor window

The marking menu is divided into zones. Select the zone you want to customize in the top panel and click Edit Marking Menu, as shown in Figure 1.47.

To change a marking menu entry, drag its icon or menu item directly onto the location where you want it to appear in the marking menu for the current zone.

The Plugin Manager

The Plugin Manager, accessed by choosing **Window → Settings/Preferences → Plug-in Manager**, lets you load and unload plug-ins for Maya. For example, mental ray for Maya is a plug-in that must be loaded to have mental ray rendering in your scenes. You load a plug-in by clicking the Loaded button. To unload, simply uncheck the box. If you want the plug-in to always load on Maya startup, check the Auto Load box. You can load third-party plug-ins by clicking the Browse button at the bottom of the window. Most third-party plug-ins provide instructions for installing them properly.

Summary

Once you have wrapped your head around how the challenging Maya interface works at its defaults, you will applaud the ability to change it to make it work best for you.

This chapter gave you an overview of all the major components of Maya's UI and major windows and will be useful as a reference whenever you need a quick brush-up on how something works or is loaded. We explored the interface, navigation, scene windows, and window layouts before looking at the hotbox, menus, and shelves. You should also have a good idea of how to use the Outliner and Hypergraph as well as the Channel Box and Attribute Editor. We also explored the Timeline, Command line, Feedback line, and Script Editor before discussing the interface customization options available.

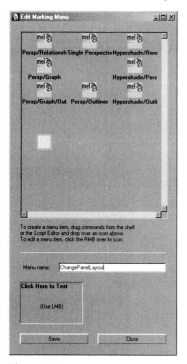

Figure 1.47

Editing the North Zone of our marking menus

CHAPTER 2

Quick Start: Creating an Animation in Maya 8.5

Maya is an intricate, sophisticated software package, yet it is engineered to be easy to use (that is, once you understand its structure!). For the novice, though, the interface and sheer size of the Maya program can be quite daunting. By reading the first few chapters in this book, you will learn the prerequisites to make your artistic vision a reality. The previous chapter showed you the basic Maya interface and controls. This chapter covers the basics for creating a simple animation from start to finish, exposing you to how Maya structures its scenes, animates objects, and renders frames. Most of the information presented here only scratches the surface of Maya's features—this chapter is meant to introduce you to common work flows and organizational structure. If you are an experienced Maya user, you may skip this chapter in favor of more detailed, advanced topics covered later in this book.

- **Maya project structure**

- **Creating and editing objects**

- **Pivots and placement**

- **Maya node structure**

- **Assigning materials**

- **Setting keyframes**

- **Basic lighting**

- **Rendering frames**

Maya Project Structure

Three-dimensional art is composed of many parts that work together to create the final rendered product. These parts include various types of motion data, textured art, rendered images, and scene files. They are collectively known as projects, and Maya allows you to easily organize them. Knowing how to use projects helps tremendously for organizational purposes; before you know it, you will have hundreds of files, so use projects to your advantage!

A project is simply a collection of folders that contain files that relate to your scenes. Scenes are the Maya files (with a suffix of .mb or .ma in their filenames) containing all the Maya data you create. Any modeling, animation, shading, or other resources you create in Maya are saved within these files. Scenes and their external reference files are automatically saved to projects based on a folder structure you create when making a new project.

To start a new project, choose **File → Project → New**. In the New Project window (see Figure 2.1), type the name for your project in the Name field. (This is what the root folder will be called.) Location specifies the folder where your project will be saved; unless you definitely want to specify a new location for your projects; the default \maya\projects is recommended.

Figure 2.1

The New Project window allows you to organize all the files your Maya scenes use.

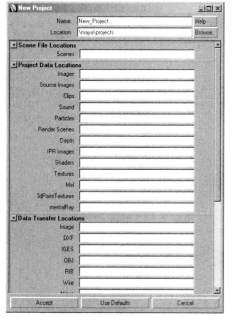

When creating your projects, do not use any spaces in the folder names. Use capitalization or underscores for word breaks to ensure that Maya and its plug-ins can correctly be referenced.

Although you can specify the folder names for each type of asset in your project, it is recommended to use only the default folder names by clicking the Use Defaults button at the bottom of the New Project window. You can indicate a subfolder by using a backslash. Maya will not create folders for attributes corresponding to location fields left blank.

If you are involved with multiple projects at one time, you can easily switch the current project by choosing **File → Project → Set**. Select the desired root project folder and click OK. To edit the paths of a current project, choose **File → Project → Edit Current**. A window just like the New Project window will be available for you to edit.

Incremental Saves

Incremental saves are a highly recommended safety feature for your scene files. As your scenes grow, they become more complex, which means they are more prone to errors! Nothing is worse than accidentally losing a crucial part of your scene or, worse, unintentionally corrupting your scene file. Incremental saves automatically create backups of your previous saves when you save a current scene.

To enable incremental saves, choose **File → Save Scene ❐**. Check the Incremental Save check box. If you do not specify a limit to the increments, backups will never be deleted. This can be a bit excessive though (and can take a lot of hard drive space!), so a limit of 5 to 10 is usually plenty. Be aware that scenes can become enormous, so if storage space is a concern, set lower limits.

Hammer and Nail Part I: Setting the Project

Throughout this chapter, we will create a simple animation of a hammer hitting a nail. The goal of this exercise is to familiarize you with the Maya work flow and environment. Although we won't go into anything too advanced just yet, there is plenty to learn, even for the simplest scenes.

1. Create a project so that your scenes and any associated files you create stay organized. Open Maya and choose **File → Project → New**.

2. In the New Project window, click the Use Defaults button and type **hammer_and_nail** (or some other relevant name of your choice) in the Name field.

3. Click the Accept button to create your project. Maya has now created folders for each of the project attributes. As long as this is your current project, your scenes will be saved in the hammer_and_nail\scenes folder.

Creating and Editing Objects

An object refers to any entity in a scene. It is a general term that can represent a piece of geometry, a light, a locator, or any other spatial object with translation, rotation, and/or scale attributes. The Create menu gives you access to geometric primitives, lights, and tools to create objects in your scene. For more information on these objects, refer to subsequent chapters on modeling (Chapters 3 through 6) and lighting (Chapter 11).

Specifically, the Create menu contains the following:

OBJECT	DESCRIPTION
NURBS Primitives	Basic shapes of 3D and 2D NURBS objects
Polygon Primitives	Basic geometric polygonal objects
Subdiv Primitives	Basic subdivision surfaces primitives
Volume Primitives	Sphere, cube, and cone volume primitives
Lights	Various types of light sources
Cameras	Various methods of creating new cameras
CV Curve Tool	Tool to create a CV curve
EP Curve Tool	Tool to create an EP curve
Pencil Curve Tool	Tool to draw a freehand NURBS curve
Arc Tools	Tools to create arc NURBS curves
Measure Tools	Tools that let you measure distance in various ways
Text	Creates 3D custom text

continued

continues

OBJECT	DESCRIPTION
Adobe Illustrator Object	Allows you to import Adobe Illustrator vector objects into Maya
Construction Plane	An aid when creating objects that aren't aligned to the XYZ orientation
Locator	A null object that does not render but has a position, rotation, and scale in the Maya interface
Annotation	A nonrenderable note or memo that displays in 3D space
Empty Group	A null group with no objects in it
Sets	A collection of objects

Object Organization

Just as it is important to keep your Maya projects clean and organized, so should your scene files be well structured. By using proper object names, groups, and layers, you can make scenes much easier and efficient to work with. Maintaining organized scenes is crucial for projects that require multiple artists.

Naming

It is always a good idea to have a set naming convention for your objects. In Maya, you don't always have a visual representation of a simple object. It is frustrating to search through an Outliner or see nodes that point to poorly named objects. Since many objects in Maya are created out of primitives, it is not uncommon to click the head of a character and see its name pCube1. No one convention is correct for naming your objects; you have to find a method that works for you and your production team. In typical scenarios, geometry objects simply have descriptive names. As you add other types of assets to the scene, adding prefixes and suffixes to names helps organize your scene. If you were to follow the formatting presented in this chapter's examples, a geometrical object would be called MyObject, and its material would be called MyObjectMaterial.

To rename an object, simply select it, view either the Attribute Editor or Channel Box (pressing Ctrl+A switches between these two editors when you have the Open Attribute Editor setting set to In Main Maya Window in the Interface Preferences section), and change the name in the text field toward the top of the panel. Alternatively, if you are working in the Hypergraph view, you can RM click the object's node and select Rename. If you are more technically oriented, you can use the `rename` command. For instance, if you want to rename pCube1 to MyCube, type **rename pCube1 MyCube** in the Command line and press Enter.

Scene Hierarchies

Although it's visually difficult to notice in the 3D view window, objects in Maya are stored and referenced within hierarchical trees. Storing objects in this manner not only makes it easier for the artist to organize scenes, it also defines how objects move in relation to one another. Complex groupings and parent-child relationships between objects are used extensively in modeling, rigging, and animation.

PARENT-CHILD RELATIONSHIPS

A parent object controls the attributes of another object, said to be the child. Although a parent can have multiple children, a child can only have one parent. Children inherit the transform properties of their parent but also can have their own independent transformations. Figure 2.2 shows a Hypergraph view of an object, pSphere1, parented to two children, pSphere2 and pSphere3. If pSphere1 moves 5 units to the left, both children also move 5 units to the left. The children pSphere2 and pSphere3 can still move *in addition* to their parent's movement, as an offset to pSphere1's transforms.

You can parent one object to another in various ways. In any view where you can select objects (3D view, the Outliner, the Hypershade), select two objects by holding down the Shift key as you click. Choose **Edit → Parent** or press the P key. The object you first selected is a child to the object you selected last. In the Outliner and Hypergraph view, MM drag one object onto another. The object dragged is a child to the object you dragged to.

To unparent one object from another, select a child and choose **Edit → Unparent** or press Shift+P. The child object will become unlinked from the parent and move to the root of the scene hierarchy. Alternatively, you can MM drag a child to empty space in the Outliner and Hypergraph windows.

GROUPS

Occasionally you want two objects to move, scale, or rotate together as siblings, yet you do not want to parent them to a piece of geometry or other object. Objects can be grouped to achieve this effect. Although the group node is not an actual object, it is still considered the parent of its members. Groups are also great for keeping your Maya scenes organized. To group objects, select them and choose **Edit → Group** or press Ctrl+G. To destroy a group without deleting its members, select the group and choose **Edit → Ungroup**.

As a scene grows, you might want to add selection sets to access certain objects more easily. A selection set is a group of objects that exists external to the scene hierarchy and is used to cluster objects so that they can be easily selected.

Selection sets can be composed of objects and components. Try creating a few objects using the Create menu. Shift+select some of them, choose **Create → Sets → Quick Select Set**, and click OK in the pop-up window to accept the default name. In the Outliner, notice that a new node called set has been created. Whenever you need to select those objects again, RM click set in the Outliner and choose Select Set Members.

Figure 2.2

pShere1 is the parent of pSphere2 and pSphere3. The two children inherit the transforms of the parent.

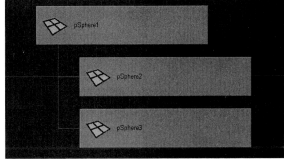

Figure 2.3

Display layers allow you to group objects so that you can alter their real-time render appearance.

Display Layers

Display layers encapsulate user-specified objects and are created in the Layer Editor. They are similar to selection sets but easier to manage. Creating display layers ensures that your scene is organized into modules that control the objects' visibility and whether they can be selected.

Chapter 1 showed how to create new display layers in the Layer Editor and how to add new objects to them. There are three boxes to the left of a layer's name (see Figure 2.3). Clicking the box on the far left toggles on or off the visibility of the layer. Clicking the middle box cycles between three modes: Normal (blank box), Template (T), and Reference (R). If set to Template, the object displays in wireframe, regardless of the current real-time 3D viewing mode. Template objects cannot be selected in the 3D viewing area. If a display layer is set to Reference, its members appear normally in the 3D viewing area yet cannot be selected there.

The last box controls the wireframe color of the objects. Setting this value is especially helpful in scenes that require a lot of wireframe viewing because it helps keep objects from appearing to run together. You can choose the color of the layer by double-clicking on this box or the layer name.

Object and Component Modes

Every geometric object in Maya is made up of smaller pieces of geometric data called components. In object mode, you select and manipulate an entire object. In component mode, you have access to select and manipulate the actual components that are the building blocks of your object. Use object mode to treat the object as a frozen collection of components, and use component mode to modify the shape of the object (based on whichever component type you selected).

Each geometric object type has its own set of components. Polygons contain arrays of vertices, faces, UVs, and edges. NURBS contain arrays of control vertices, surface patches, possible surface points, hulls, and isoparms.

Test these two modes by creating a polygon cube. First, make sure Interactive Creation is on by choosing **Create → Polygon Primitives → Interactive Creation**. Then, choose **Create → Polygon Primitives → Cube** and LM drag your mouse in the perspective viewport for the base and height.

INTERACTIVE CREATION

New to Maya 8, Interactive Creation (found in the **Create → Polygon Primitives** and **Create → NURBS** menus) allows you to drag your mouse cursor to specify basic shape attributes of your primitives. If you choose to disable this option, then primitives will be created using the specified default attributes.

To toggle between object and component modes, press F8 or select the appropriate user-interface icons (see Chapter 1). Once in component mode, you can specify which type of component you want to modify. You can either select the component icon in the Status line or use Maya's unique context menus.

Most artists prefer to use the menus to quickly and easily select components. To do this, RM hold over your polygon cube. You should see a menu pop up that will allow you to choose from the available components. The items in this menu depend on the type of object you click. Select a component by releasing the RM. See Figure 2.4 for an example of this handy menu.

You can also click an icon on the Status line to change a component type to edit. Remember that these icons are visible only if you are in component mode (by pressing F8 or selecting the component mode icon in the Status line).

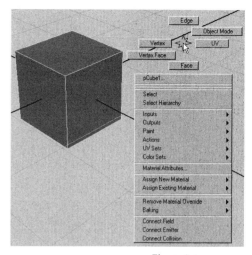

Figure 2.4

To access a context menu, hold down the RM on an object.

ICON	NAME	DESCRIPTION
■	Select Point Components	Lets you select points and vertices of an object
●	Select Parm Points Components	Lets you select parameter points and UVs of an object
⬦	Select Line Components	Lets you select isoparms and polygon edges
◈	Select Face Components	Lets you select faces and patches
⬔	Select Hull Components	Lets you select NURBS hulls
◉	Select Pivot Components	Lets you select rotate, scale, and joint pivots
+	Select Handle Components	Lets you select Handles
?	Select Miscellaneous Components	Lets you select by miscellaneous components such as image planes and local rotation axes

Hammer and Nail Part II: Modeling the Objects

We will continue our project created in the previous section by creating simple hammer and nail models. We will use polygon primitives and parenting to build the various parts of our models.

1. In a new Maya scene file (choose **File → New Scene**), create a new polygon cylinder by choosing **Create → Polygon Primitives → Cylinder**. If Interactive Creation is enabled for your polygon primitives, then click anywhere in the scene to see a new cylinder.

    This cylinder will serve as the head of the hammer. Press 5 to see the cylinder in shaded mode. To change back to wireframe mode at any time, press 4.

2. Using the Channel Box (see Chapter 1), change the **scaleY** attribute to 1.6 to elongate the hammer head, as shown in Figure 2.5. Be sure that the translateX, translateY, and translateZ attributes are 0. Also in the Channel Box, change the name from pCylinder1 to HammerHead.

3. To create the handle, make another polygon cylinder. Translate this cylinder to 0, 0, and 3.7 units in the X, Y, and Z axes respectively, rotate it 90° about the X axis, and scale it 0.5, 3, and 0.5 units in the X, Y, and Z axes respectively. Rename this cylinder HammerHandle. See these results in Figure 2.6.

4. Select HammerHandle and Shift select HammerHead. Choose **Edit → Group** to group these two objects as one. Open the Outliner by choosing **Window → Outliner**. Click the plus sign next to the group1 object to see that the two cylinders are children to the group. Rename the group Hammer.

5. Create a new display layer by clicking the Create A New Layer icon ⬦. To learn more about layers, see Chapter 1. Rename the layer HammerLayer by double-clicking it.

6. Select Hammer from the Outliner, right-click HammerLayer in the Layer Editor, and choose Add Selected Objects. Adding objects to layers like this allows you to keep the scene organized and lets you easily turn off the visibility of objects. Turn off the visibility of HammerLayer by clicking the *V* next to the layer's name.

7. To create a nail, create a polygon cone and rename it NailBottom. Rotate it 180° in X and scale it to 0.2, 0.9, 0.2 in X, Y, and Z respectively. Next, create a polygon cylinder and rename it NailTop. Translate it 0.9 in Y and scale 0.6, 0.05, 0.6 in X, Y, and Z respectively. Figure 2.7 shows the nail parts.

Figure 2.5

The cylinder scaled up along the Y axis represents the hammer's head.

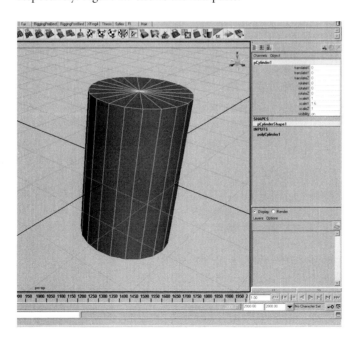

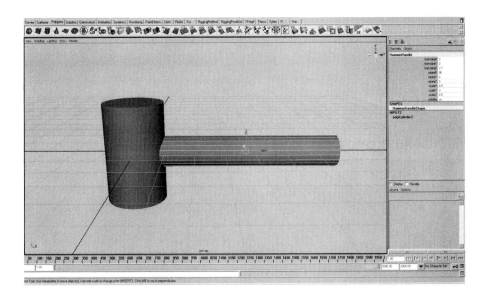

Figure 2.6

Create another cylinder to represent the hammer handle.

8. Select the two nail parts and create a new group called Nail. Create a new layer called NailLayer, and add Nail to it. Your scene should now have two groups and two layers containing the hammer and nail objects.

9. The last object to create is a wooden floor. We want to make sure it is large enough in relation to the size of the hammer and nail. Be sure that each layer's visibility is enabled by clicking in the far-left box next to the layer name. (A *V* should fill the box.) Also for each layer, click the center box until it shows *T*. The hammer and nail objects should now be unselectable in the 3D perspective view and should remain in wireframe mode regardless of the perspective's view mode. We change these properties so that we can see the scale of our floor in relation to the hammer and nail objects and to protect us from inadvertently selecting them.

Figure 2.7

A cone and cylinder make up a nail object.

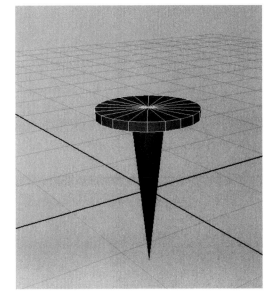

10. Make the floor by creating a polygon cube and renaming it Floor. Set translateY to −1, and set scaleX, scaleY, and scaleZ to 22, 2, and 22 respectively. Since we have a new object, create a new layer called FloorLayer and add Floor to it. Your results should resemble Figure 2.8.

11. Set the hammer and nail display layers back to normal mode by clicking the middle box next to the layers' names. (Normal mode should be enabled after two clicks until the box is blank.) Save your work and continue with the following section to prepare your objects for animation.

Figure 2.8

Templating display
layers allows you to
see how new objects
compare with exist-
ing scene objects.

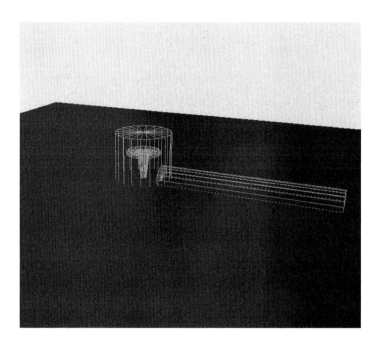

Pivots and Placement

Every object in Maya can rotate in 3D space. The point about which an object rotates is called the pivot point. By default, the pivot point is at the center of a newly created object. As you modify an object, the pivot point will not automatically reposition itself.

Naturally, you will want to specifically reposition the pivot point at times. If you have modified a primitive nonuniformly, you might want to specify the center of gravity about which the object spins. Perhaps you want to rotate an object about a specific surface point, such as a glass tipping over on a table.

To reposition a pivot, select an object, switch to move, rotate, or scale mode (press W, E, and R, respectively), and press the Insert key to enter edit mode. You will notice that the move, rotate, or scale control gizmo will change into straight-colored lines along each axis. Figure 2.9 shows an object in edit mode. LM click any of the axes to move the pivot point where you want it. Press Insert again to exit edit mode. To center a pivot in an object, select the object and choose **Modify → Center Pivot**.

An object can have only one pivot point, and pivots cannot be keyed (meaning they cannot be animated; you'll find more on keys later in this chapter). Suppose you want a glass to fall off the edge of a table and then roll around after it hits the ground. This scenario requires two pivots (one for the bottom edge of the glass so it can tip off the table, the other at the object's center so it can roll), but Maya allows at most only one pivot point on an object. The solution is grouping.

Figure 2.9

To edit an object's pivot location, press Insert and reposition the control gizmo.

Although groups do not have geometry, they can move, rotate, and scale like any other object. A common trick for artists who need multiple pivots is to group the object to itself. This trick allows you to use the group's pivot point independently of the object's pivot point, but since the object is a child of the group, it will inherit any rotation. Grouping objects in this manner is especially common in complex character rigs that require multiple ways to rotate and move.

Hammer and Nail Part III: Pivots

We will continue the hammer and nail project by placing the pivot in the hammer to prep it for animation. Our goal is to hit the nail a total of four times—two small taps and then two large swings. This motion will look best if we rotate the hammer close to the head for the taps and then rotate it close to the handle's tip for the more powerful swings.

1. Continuing from the previous exercise, select the Hammer group from the Outliner and switch to the side camera view. (In the 3D view window, choose **Panels** → **Orthographic** → **Side**.) You can also continue the exercise at this point by opening step2.mb from the included CD.

2. Ensure that you are in wireframe mode by pressing 4, and enter rotate mode by pressing E. You should see the rotate control gizmo at the origin. This is the current pivot point for the hammer.

3. We want to set up the pivot for the large swings, which means we need to move the pivot toward the end of the handle. Press Insert and move the pivot along Z until you get near the tip of the handle, as shown in Figure 2.10. Press Insert to exit edit mode.

4. To ensure that your pivots line up with this example, open the Attribute Editor by pressing Ctrl+A. Twirl down the Pivots section, and then twirl down the Local Space section. Here you will see exact values for the pivot's local space translation. Set the Z value (the last input box) to 5.8622 for Local Rotate Pivot and Local Scale Pivot, as shown in Figure 2.11.

5. Since we also want to the hammer to make a few small taps, we need a new pivot point closer to the hammer's head. With the Hammer group still selected, make a new group by choosing **Edit → Group**. Rename this group HammerSmallTaps. For naming consistency, rename the Hammer group HammerLargeSwings. Keeping appropriate names for objects makes this scene easier to work with later in the pipeline.

6. Select the HammerSmallTaps group and move the pivot point along Z until it is just to the left of the head, as in Figure 2.12. For consistency with this example, open the Attribute Editor to set the pivot (as we did in step 4) and set the local Z attribute to 2.4854. Press Insert to exit edit mode.

7. Since we made a new parent group for the hammer, we need to add it to Hammer-Layer. With the HammerSmallTaps group still selected, RM click HammerLayer in the Layer Editor and choose Add Selected Objects. Save your work and continue with the following section to learn about Maya's node structure.

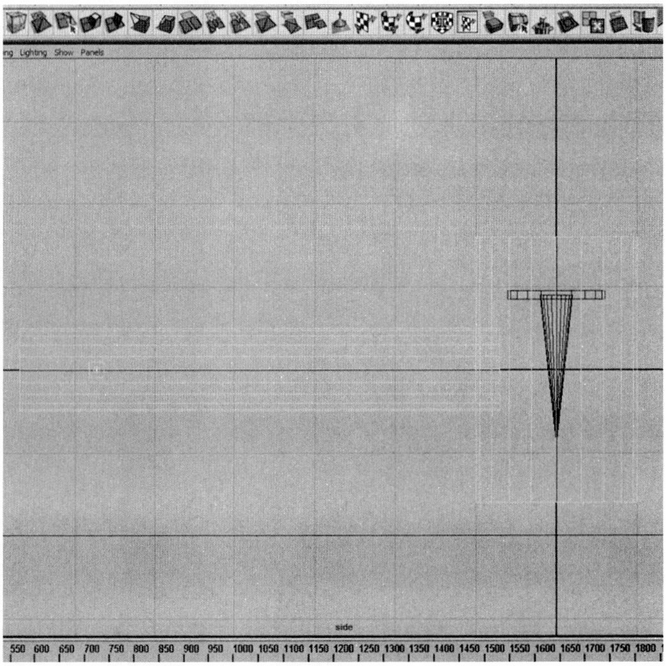

Figure 2.10

To add a second pivot point, group the object to itself and modify the group's pivot point.

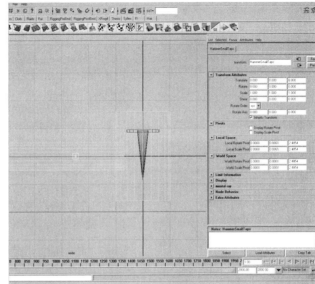

Figure 2.11

By accessing the Attribute Editor, you can specify exact locations for your pivot points.

Figure 2.12

To add a second pivot point, group the object to itself and modify the group's pivot point.

Maya Node Structure

Maya uses a node-based system to interconnect data from one object to another. Nodes are basically encapsulations of data that can be children or parents to other nodes; a parent node will alter the child depending on both nodes' type.

For a newcomer to node-based software, the idea of nodes can seem confusing. Maya tries to keep these nodes out of the artist's way, unless you specifically want to edit the nodes themselves through the Outliner, Hypergraph, Hypershade, or other editors. Imagine you create a sphere in your scene. Although you see a single sphere, Maya creates several nodes that hold attributes (properties) of that sphere. A shape node contains the sphere's geometry, a transform node controls its transform (position, rotation, scale, visibility, and so on) information, and a shading group node tells the sphere geometry which material to use. The shape node is a child of the transform node, which is a child of the shading group node, as shown in Figure 2.13. Together, these nodes represent what you see when you create and place a sphere in your scene. For more on nodes as they relate to the Attribute Editor, Hypershade, Outliner, and Hypergraph, see Chapter 1.

Figure 2.13

Shape, transform, and shading group nodes are basic nodes that define a geometric object.

Transform Node   Shape Node   Shading Group Node

Working with a node-based structure is advantageous because you can easily create, delete, copy, paste, or manipulate attributes of an object independently from other attributes of that object. In an alternative, history-based system that blatantly stacks operations on an object, it is impossible to go back and alter a specific operation without undoing or affecting other operations.

Construction History

As you perform operations on objects, new nodes are created. This network of nodes is referred to as an object's construction history. At any point, you can go back and edit any of the attributes of the nodes in the construction history. Follow these steps to see an example of how to use construction history.

1. In a new Maya scene (choose **File → New Scene**), create a polygon cube by choosing **Create → Polygon Primitives → Cube**.

2. Select the cube. In the Channel Box (see Chapter 1 for more on the Channel Box), LM click polyCube1 in Inputs, and change Subdivisions Width, Subdivisions Height, and Subdivisions Depth to 2. This will subdivide the cube into a finer resolution of faces, as seen in Figure 2.14.

3. Be sure you are in the Polygons menu set. (Chapter 1 explains how to switch between various menu sets.) Bevel the cube by choosing **Edit Mesh → Bevel**. Smooth the cube by choosing **Mesh → Smooth**. Beveling and smoothing are just two of the many operations you can perform on a polygonal mesh; these and the other operations are covered in Chapter 3. Your object should now resemble Figure 2.15a.

4. With the cube selected, notice the inputs listed in the Channel Box (see Figure 2.15b). These inputs are nodes that make up the construction history of your cube.

Figure 2.14

A polygon cube with two subdivisions in width, height, and depth

Because Maya stacks these operations on top of each other, the order of the history matters. Figure 2.16a shows the cube beveled and then smoothed, and Figure 2.16b shows the cube smoothed and then beveled.

At times you need to delete the construction history of an object. As the history grows, Maya spends more time calculating the nodes, which impedes your system performance. Furthermore, certain operations simply do not work well with other operations, especially those that depend on deformation order. (For more on deformers, see Chapter 5.) To delete the history of an object, select the object and choose **Edit → Delete By Type → History**. To delete history on everything in your scene, choose **Edit → Delete All By Type → History**. (Keep in mind that an object's history includes its future as well as its past. Deleting the history will bake and delete all construction nodes related to that object.)

To completely disable construction history, toggle off the Construction History button in the Status line. For most situations, it is not recommended to turn history off.

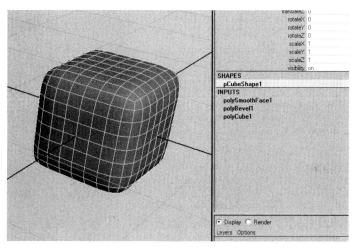

a   b

Figure 2.15

By subdividing, beveling, and smoothing the cube (a), Maya builds a construction history of nodes (b).

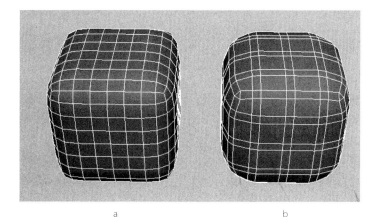

a   b

Figure 2.16

The order of the construction history is important. Cube (a) was beveled and then smoothed, and cube (b) was smoothed and then beveled.

Hammer and Nail Part IV: Exploring the Nodes

In the following example, we will not make any alterations to the hammer and nail scene. Instead, we will explore the Outliner, Hypergraph, and Attribute Editor to see how Maya handles nodes. Although they reference the same nodes, each editor has its own strengths for node handling. For a more complete introduction to each of these editors, see Chapter 1. This exercise will help you better understand when to use each editor depending on your personal goals.

Nodes and the Hypergraph

Artists tend to use the Hypergraph when they want to quickly create, delete, or edit relationships between nodes. To a novice, the Hypergraph may seem a bit daunting since it displays nodes that are normally not seen in the Outliner or in your 3D view. The experienced Maya user depends on the Hypergraph to better organize and set up complicated relationships and scene hierarchies.

1. Continuing from the previous example (or by opening `step3.mb` from the included CD), open the Hypergraph by choosing **Window → Hypergraph: Hierarchy**.

2. In the Hypergraph, click the Scene Hierarchy button 🔣 and choose **View → Frame All** to see all the objects in your scene. Your Hypergraph should look like the one in Figure 2.17.

3. Each box in the Hypergraph is a node that represents the various scene objects. Notice that the icon for the nodes changes depending on the type of object; the group objects have a white parallelogram icon, and the polygonal objects have a blue plane. You can easily see the hierarchical structure of the hammer and nail groups by the connecting lines and placement of the nodes.

4. Remember that geometric objects are made up of many nodes that you can view and edit. Select the HammerHead object by LM clicking its node, and click the Input And Output Connections button 🔁 in the Hypergraph's toolbar. All the dependencies and interconnections of the HammerHead object are shown in Figure 2.18.

Figure 2.17

Hypergraph view of the scene's objects

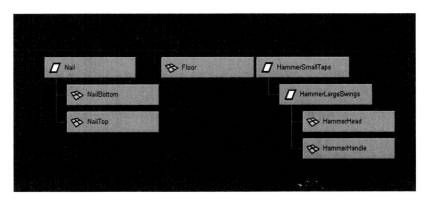

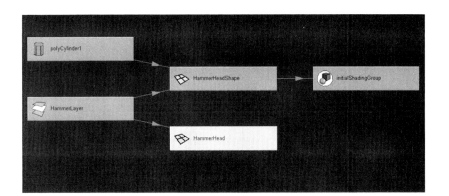

Figure 2.18

The input and output connections of a geometric object

Let's go through each node shown here in the Hypergraph and look at its significance to the scene. The polyCylinder1 node holds the information about the cylinder that HammerHead is based on, including the **radius**, **height**, **subdivisionsAxis**, **subdivisionsHeight**, and **subdivisionsCaps** attributes.

If you select the polyCylinder1 node and view the Channel Box, you will see these attributes exposed for your edit.

polyCylinder1's output connects to the inMesh input of the HammerHeadShape node. This node is the shape node for the HammerHead object. Although it only has one incoming connection, it serves as the "central hub" for how the HammerHead is shaped. Any additional inputs affecting the object's shape (these polygon edits will be covered in Chapter 3) will connect into this shape node.

Since objects must have a shading group in order to be seen by a camera, the HammerHeadShape node is a child of the initialShadingGroup. The initialShadingGroup node represents the default gray Lambert material seen on objects when you create them. If you create a new shader (covered in the following section), you can then assign it to the shape node to change its material.

The HammerHead node represents the transform node for the hammer head object. When you select and name objects in the 3D view, these transform nodes are what you are actually modifying.

The HammerLayer node represents the layer you created when you modeled the objects. When you add an object to a layer using the Layer Editor, Maya automatically links the layer to the children of the object and their shape nodes. To see the contents of the HammerLayer, select the HammerLayer node and click the Input And Output Connections button. Now the HammerLayer node is the central focus in the Hypergraph and has six outputs: the HammerHead, HammerHeadShape, HammerHandle, HammerHandleShape, the HammerSmallTaps, and the HammerLargeSwings groups (as shown in Figure 2.19). The layerManager node is a constant node in Maya that contains all the layers in your scene.

Close the Hypergraph when you are finished exploring the nodes within your Maya scene.

Figure 2.19

A layer-centric layout in the Hypergraph

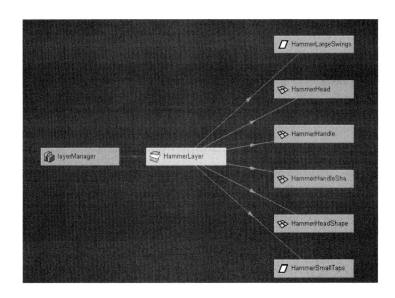

Nodes and the Attribute Editor

The Attribute Editor allows you to change the attributes of the nodes in your scene. Although it does not clearly lay out the hierarchies as well as the Hypergraph, it does present the modifiable attributes in an organized way. Refer to Chapter 1 for more on how to use and navigate the Attribute Editor.

1. Continuing from the previous example (or by opening step3.mb from the included CD), open the Attribute Editor by choosing **Window → Attribute Editor**.

2. In the 3D perspective view, select the cylinder representing the hammer head. Notice that the Attribute Editor loads the HammerHeadShape node as current and creates tabs for any related nodes, as shown in Figure 2.20.

3. Select the polyCylinder1 tab. This node holds the geometric information about the cylindrical hammer head object. Notice how you have access to change the same attributes as when you created the cylinder.

4. Select the HammerHeadShape tab. Twirl down the Render Stats section (see Figure 2.21) and note all the overrides that are possible. Although we won't change any of these attributes for this example project, it is useful to know how to override, on a per-object basis, basic rendering attributes, such as shadowing and visibility. For instance, if you were animating a bright, emissive ball of energy, you would probably not want it to cast a shadow in your rendered frames.

Nodes and the Outliner

The Outliner is an orderly list of the objects, cameras, lights, and other items in a scene. Although similar in function to the Hypergraph, the Outliner always displays the hierarchies of a scene. Although you cannot view a select few objects as you can in the Hypergraph, the Outliner typically hides construction nodes, is a nice supplement to your workspace, and is compact enough to keep on-screen as you work. Many artists keep it open in their workspace as a reminder to group and name objects and to easily access any object within their scene. Refer to Chapter 1 for more information on the Outliner and its uses.

Figure 2.20

The Attribute Editor displays all editable attributes for the currently selected node and creates tabs for its relatives.

1. Continuing from the previous example (or by opening `step3.mb` from the included CD), open the Outliner by choosing **Window → Outliner**.

2. In the Outliner, you should see the default perspective and orthogonal cameras, the nail and hammer groups, and the default light and object set nodes. (Don't worry about defaultObjectSet and defaultLightSet; these are sets that Maya initially creates and are not important for now.)

3. Click the plus sign next to Nail. As in Figure 22.2, you should see the two polygon objects, Nail-Top and NailBottom, displayed as children to the Nail group.

4. Sometimes it is useful to display where in the scene hierarchy an object resides. In the perspective view, select the hammer handle. Notice that in the Outliner, the parent node that contains a child (or any downward relative) highlights green. RM click anywhere in the Outliner and choose Reveal Selected. The parent (and any upward relative) expands to display the selected object's position in the hierarchy.

The Hypershade is another editor that extensively uses nodes. It is responsible for creating and organizing materials used by scene objects. The following section is an overview on how to use the Hypershade.

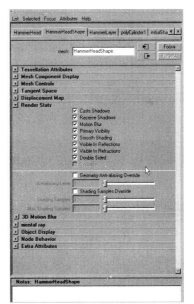

Figure 2.21

The Render Stats section of a shape node allows you to override basic rendering attributes.

Figure 2.22

The Outliner concisely displays the scene hierarchy.

Assigning Materials Using the Hypershade

A material (also known as a shader) is a collection of nodes that determine what an object looks like when it is rendered. You create and edit materials using the Hypershade. For basic information on the Hypershade, refer to Chapter 1.

Surface Materials

Surface material nodes serve as the base for how a material looks when applied to a surface. They control the basic color, highlight, and reflectivity. There are many types of surface materials, but the most commonly used are Blinn, Lambert, and Phong (see Figure 2.23). Lambert surface materials are solid colors that can shade (meaning they get lighter or darker depending on the light affecting them) but have no specular highlight. Specular highlights are shiny reflective highlights on an illuminated object.

Although Phong and Blinn surface materials look fairly similar, Phong surface materials have more pronounced specular highlights and Blinn materials have a softer highlight. Both types have potential disadvantages; Phong materials can flicker during animation renders, but Blinns are a bit more computationally expensive. Both material types are isotropic, meaning they reflect specular light identically in all directions. To create a nonuniform highlight, create an anisotropic surface material type. These surface materials, plus many more, are further described in Chapter 12.

Nodes and the Hypershade

The Hypershade is a node-based editor in which you can build complex materials. At this point in our exploration of Maya, we will only scratch the surface of the many types of nodes at your disposal. The goal here is to see how the Hypershade functions, to explore how to create basic materials, and finally to look at how to apply them to your objects.

Upon opening the Hypershade (choose **Window → Rendering Editors → Hypershade**), you should see the three default materials that Maya automatically generates: lambert1, particleCloud1, and shaderGlow1. Since objects must have materials applied to them in order to render, these serve as the default materials applied to newly created objects.

To create a new shader, start by clicking a surface shader node in the Create panel on the left side of the Hypershade (see Figure 2.24). With your new material selected, open the Attribute Editor by pressing Ctrl+A. Here you can edit all the properties related to your

Figure 2.23

Lambert, Blinn, and Phong surface materials

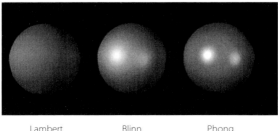

Lambert   Blinn   Phong

new material. To apply a material to an object, either select the object, RM click the material in the Hypershade, and select Assign Material To Selection, or simply MM drag the material from the Hypershade Material Editor onto the object in the 3D perspective view.

There are two types of textures in 3D graphics: image and procedural. Image textures are 2D images that are created in an external photo- or paint-editing software package. Procedural textures are created dynamically inside Maya and require additional computation. Procedural textures usually are a bit more computationally expensive.

The following short exercise shows how to create a material with a premade 2D image texture file. Although you can also add textures to materials through the Attribute Editor, we'll be using the Hypershade most of the time in this example to better expose you to Maya's node-based structure.

Figure 2.24

The Create panel allows you to build new shaders in the Hypershade.

1. Before adding any kind of texture to a surface, you must create a surface material. Save previous work (if any) and create a new scene. In the Hypershade, under the Create Maya Nodes section, select Lambert. A shader called lambert2 will appear in the render node display area. For more information on the render node display area and the work area, see Chapter 1.

2. Be sure you are working in the split pane view by clicking the Show Top And Bottom Tabs button in the upper-right side of the Hypershade window. The top pane holds your scene's shaders. The bottom pane represents your work area and can display material hierarchies.

3. Select lambert2 in the top pane. Choose **Graph → Input And Output Connections**. The work area should show the input and output nodes of lambert2. Since we haven't added any additional nodes to it, you should see only the lambert2 surface material connected to a shading group node, as shown in Figure 2.25.

4. RM hold lambert2 and choose Rename. Type **ImageTextureExample** in the Text field. Renaming this node has set the overall material name to ImageTextureExample.

5. In the Create Maya Nodes section, scroll down, and under 2D Textures, click the File button. A place2dTexture node and a file node should appear in your workspace. You may need to select and move them with the LM to see them properly. The place2d-Texture node is responsible for telling the texture how it maps to a surface. For more on place2dTextures, see Chapter 12.

6. The file node represents the actual 2d texture image. Its thumbnail image is black because we have not told it which image to use yet. Select the file node and open the Attribute Editor (press Ctrl+A). Back in your Maya workspace, the Attribute Editor should now be visible, with the file1 node attributes displayed.

7. In the Attribute Editor, click the folder icon button next to the Image Name text field, as shown in Figure 2.26. In the browser window pop-up, navigate to the Chapter 2 folder on the included CD and select TextureExample.tga (see Figure 2.27).

Figure 2.25

The top Hypershade pane contains all the scene's materials. The bottom pane represents the work area, which allows you to build material hierarchies.

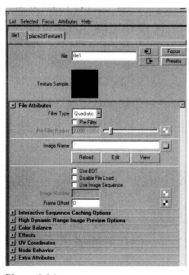

Figure 2.26

A file node's attributes allows you to browse for a texture.

Figure 2.27

A sample image texture originally exported from an external 2D paint package.

8. Back in the Hypershade window, you should now see a thumbnail image of Figure 2.27 in the file node. In the workspace, MM drag from the file1 node to the ImageTexture-Example node. A new menu appears; choose Default. MM dragging one node to another links them, and the dialog box tells how the nodes should connect. Selecting Default tells Maya to link the image to the **Color** attribute of ImageTextureExample. Instead of having its gray color, the material now shows the imported image.

9. Now that we have created a material with an imported image, we want to apply it to an object. Minimize or move the Hyperhsade. Back in the Maya workspace, create a polygon cube (choose **Create → Polygon Primitives → Cube**). Press 6 to enter textured viewing mode. The new cube should be its default gray material.

10. Select the cube and switch back to the Hypershade. In the top pane, RM click Image-TextureExample material node and choose Assign Material To Selection from the context menu. In the perspective view, the texture should now show on each face of the cube, as in Figure 2.28.

Procedural textures are made in a similar way. Instead of creating a file node and importing an image (steps 5 and 7 in the preceding example), you can choose any of the "patterns" found in the 2D and 3D Textures sections in the Create Maya Nodes area of the Hypershade. We will create some of these procedural textures in the following hammer and nail exercise.

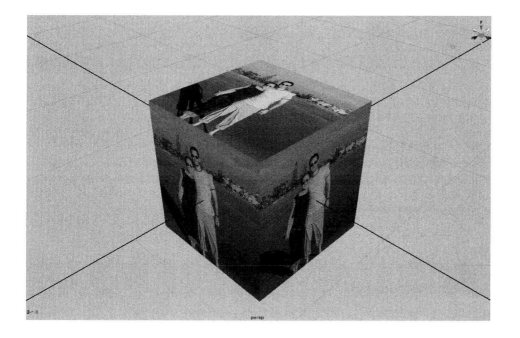

Figure 2.28

A material with an image texture is applied to the cube.

Hammer and Nail Part V: Creating and Assigning Materials

In this exercise, you will create several materials in the Hypershade and apply them to the various parts of your models. We will keep the material networks relatively simple so that you will be exposed to basic material nodes. Since the objects in this scene aren't positioned for animation yet, be sure to use the display layers' visibility toggle to see the various components.

1. Continuing from the previous hammer and nail exercise (or by opening step3.mb from the included CD), from the view panel choose **Panels → Layouts → Three Panes Split Right**. You should see your workspace now divided into three viewing panes. We will customize these panes to give us a good layout that will let us easily access the editors required for this exercise.

2. When you choose a layout as we did in step 1, Maya chooses which editors and views to put in each pane. We will override these panels so that our workspace looks like Figure 2.29. In the left panel, choose **Panels → Panel → Outliner**. By default, this panel is too wide, so LM drag its right divider so that the panel's size is similar to the size of the one in Figure 2.29.

3. Place the Hypershade in the top panel by choosing **Panels → Panel → Hypershade**. As for the bottom panel, choose **Panels → Perspective → Persp** to switch it to the 3D perspective camera. Your layout should now look similar to Figure 2.29.

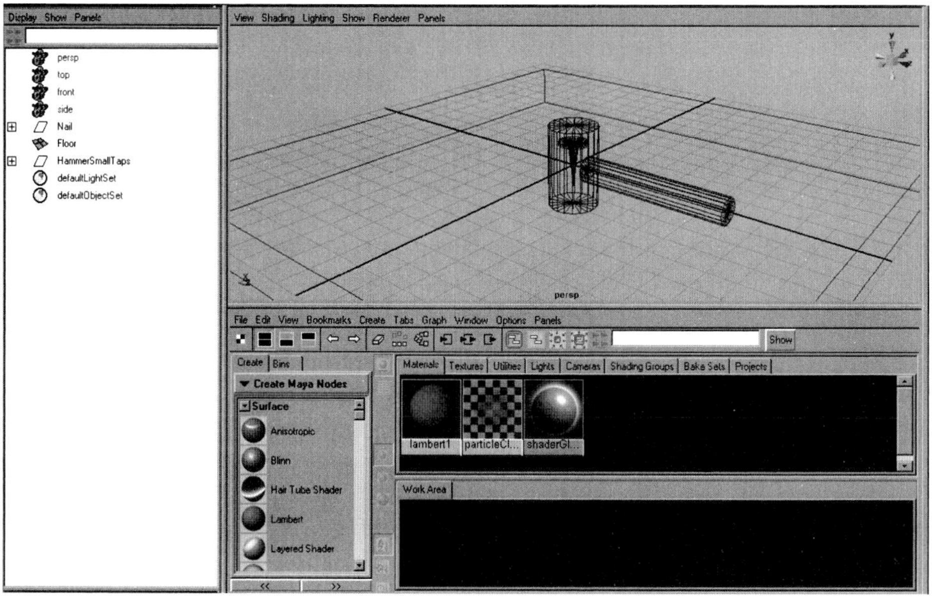

Figure 2.29

You can customize your workspace by choosing a panel layout. You can switch the contents of each pane to any editor or camera view.

Some artists prefer to work in split panels while others prefer floating windows. Split panels allow you to easily access important editors, but floating windows give you more space to work with. As you continue to explore Maya, you will discover your preference.

4. The goal is to create four materials: the hammer's handle, the hammer's head, the nail, and the wood floor. Let's start with the nail. A smooth, shiny, gray, metallic material is a good fit for a nail, so in the Hypershade's Create Maya Nodes section on the left, choose Blinn.

5. In the upper pane of the Hypershade, RM hold blinn1 and choose Rename. In the text field, name this material NailMaterial.

6. In the Outliner, select the Nail group. RM hold NailMaterial and choose Assign Material To Selection. Notice that when you apply the material to a group, all its members receive it.

Although the default gray Blinn material is close to a nail's material, it could use some tweaks. Its color needs to be lighter and its specular highlight needs to be broader to better simulate metal.

7. Select NailMaterial and open the Attribute Editor by pressing Ctrl+A. Under the **Color** attribute, move the slider to about 80%. Under the Specular Shading section, set Eccentricity to 0.8. (For a glossy plastic effect, choose a low eccentricity specular value. For a metallic effect, choose a high eccentricity specular value.)

8. The next step is to create the hammer handle material. In the Hypershade, create a new Blinn material and rename it HammerHandleMaterial.

9. We'll try a new way of applying this material. MM drag HammerHandleMaterial to the handle in the 3D view. The handle should now have the HammerHandleMaterial.

10. Select HammerHandleMaterial in the Hypershade. In the Attribute Editor, click the color swatch next to the **Color** attribute, and in the Color Chooser, select a shade of brown to your liking.

11. Create another Blinn material and rename it HammerHeadMaterial.

12. Change the **Color** attribute of HammerHeadMaterial to a dark gray. If you want, you can play with any of the material's other attributes to see their effect.

13. Apply HammerHeadMaterial to the hammer head object.

14. Create a new Lambert material and rename it FloorMaterial.

15. Change the **Color** attribute of FloorMaterial to a good wood color and apply it to the floor. Save your work and continue with the following section to learn about setting keyframes.

Keyframe Animation

Setting keyframes is the primary way to animate objects in Maya. You set keyframes when you want to record a particular attribute for an object at a frame in the Timeline. If an attribute has keys at different times, the value for that attribute will interpolate as the Timeline passes between the keyframed times.

For example, if you create a ball, keyframe its position at (0, 0, 0) at time 1, and then set another keyframe at position (0, 10, 0) at time 50, the ball moves from (0, 0, 0) to (0, 10, 0) over the course of the 50 frames. So at time 25, the position of the ball is at (0, 25, 0).

To animate, you need to properly set up your scene's animation preferences. To access them, click the rectangle icon to the right of the key in the lower-right corner of Maya's workspace (see Figure 2.30).

You can also specify your scene's Timeline range by setting the Playback End Time and End Time text boxes just to the right of the Timeline (see Figure 2.31). For the exercises in this chapter, set both values to 300. For additional instruction on how to use the Timeline, see Chapter 1.

Figure 2.30

You use the Preferences window to specify the scene's animation configurations such as Timeline range and playback settings.

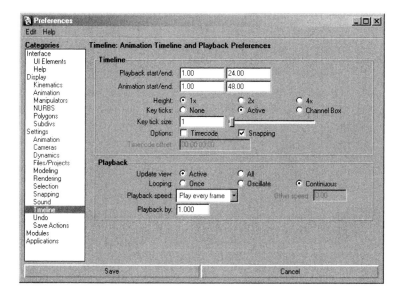

Figure 2.31

The Playback End Time (left text box) sets the end of the playback range, and the End Time (right text box) sets the end of the animation range.

How to Set a Keyframe

You can create keyframes in several ways. The following sections discuss each of them, along with any advantages or disadvantages.

The S Approach

The simplest way to set a keyframe is to press the S key on a selected object. This creates a keyframe for all position, rotation, scale, and visibility channels. Although it might be easier to just press S whenever you want to keyframe an object, it is usually bad practice and can lead to frustration while animating because artists often need to keyframe channels independently from each other. The following exercise shows an example of the S approach and its limitations.

1. In a new Maya scene, create a polygon cube by choosing **Create → Polygon Primitives → Cube**.

2. Be sure your start frame is set to 1 and your end frame is 300. (Set these values on either side of the Timeline.) Your Timeline should look like Figure 2.32.

3. Set the Current Time Indicator (the gray vertical bar on the Timeline) to frame 1. Press S to keyframe all the cube's transform channels. Notice in the Channel Box that all the channels turn from white to a peach color. This means the selected object has a keyframe set.

4. Scrub to frame 300 by moving the Current Time Indicator. Set the TranslateX value to 10 and press S to set another keyframe. If you play back the animation by clicking the Play button in the playback controls, the box moves from (0,0,0) to (10,0,0) over the course of 300 frames.

5. Suppose you wanted to add a curve to the box's trajectory. Scrub to frame 150 and set the TranslateZ value to 5. Press S to set a new key here. Now if you play back the animation, the box moves in an arc from (0,0,0) at frame 1, to (5, 0, 5) at frame 150, and finishing at (10, 0, 0) at frame 300.

6. So far, setting keyframes by pressing S seems to be just fine. Let's suppose you want to make the box spin completely around once from frame 1 to frame 300 (so that RotateY is 0 at frame 1 and 360 at frame 300). Since we already have a keyframe set for the RotateY value at frame 1, we don't need to set it again. Scrub to frame 300 and set RotateY to 360. Press S to set a keyframe here.

7. Play back the animation. Notice that the box doesn't rotate until after frame 150. This is because we initially keyframed all

Figure 2.32

The start frame is set to 1, and the end frame is set to 300. Assuming the playback speed is the default 24 frames per second, the Timeline will take 12.5 seconds to play from start to finish.

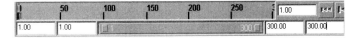

the channels at frame 150, which had 0 for the RotateY value. So the box has no difference in rotation between frames 0 and 150 and has a 360° difference between frames 150 and 300. Figure 2.33 shows the trajectory of the box.

8. Fix the animation by scrubbing to frame 150, set RotateY to 180, and set a keyframe. Now the box spins completely around once during the course of its trajectory. Explicitly setting this rotation value at frame 150 would not have been needed had we used a better keyframing approach.

Animation is often blocked out, meaning the major keyframes are set, and then smaller details are added in between. Adding and editing the smaller details is frustrating when keyframes are blindly set for all the channels at each keyframe. Use the S keyframing method only when you know you want to keyframe every channel. The following section describes an alternative, more common method for setting keyframes.

Keyframing Specific Channels

When animating, you only want to set keyframes on channels that are significant to the motion you are trying to achieve. If you are animating a spinning globe, for instance, you ideally want to keyframe only the rotational values that change as the globe spins. That way, if you decide later you need to move the globe, you can freely do so without messy, unneeded keyframes on the translation getting in the way. The following exercise creates an animation exactly like the previous example, only using this alternative keyframe approach.

1. In a new Maya scene, create a polygon cube by choosing **Create → Polygon Primitives → Cube**.

Figure 2.33

Setting keyframes by pressing S can make it difficult to edit or fine-tune animation.

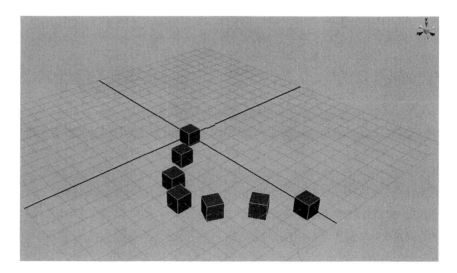

2. Be sure your start frame is set to 1 and your end frame is 300.

3. Set the Current Time Indicator to frame 1. With the cube selected, RM hold the TranslateX channel and choose Key Selected. A keyframe is now set on the TranslateX channel of the cube at frame 1. Do the same for TranslateZ. Notice that only the TranslateX and TranslateZ channels are peach colored.

4. Scrub to frame 300. In the TranslateX channel of the cube, enter the value of **10**. Set a keyframe on this channel only. Since we are going to eventually make our box move in an arc, set a keyframe on TranslateZ as well. (Its value should still be 0.) If you play back the animation by clicking the Play button in the playback controls, the box moves from (0, 0, 0) to (10, 0, 0) over the course of 300 frames.

5. Scrub to frame 150. In the TranslateZ channel of the cube, enter the value of **5**. Set a keyframe on the TranslateZ channel. The other channels have no keyframes set. Now if you play back the animation, the box moves in an arc from (0, 0, 0) at frame 1, to (5, 0, 5) at frame 150, and finishing at (10, 0, 0) at frame 300.

   It is often sufficient and easier to keyframe all three translation, rotation, or scale channels at once. Shift+W sets keys on TranslateX, TranslateY, and TranslateZ; Shift+E sets keys on RotateX, RotateY, and RotateZ; and Shift+R sets keys on ScaleX, ScaleY, and ScaleZ.

6. Since no keyframes are set on the rotational values of the box, we can freely animate rotation without it being dependent on the translation keyframes we just set. Scrub to frame 1 and set a key on the RotateY channel at value 0.

7. Scrub to frame 300, set the value of RotateY to 360, and set a keyframe on that channel. If you play back the animation, the box spins around once as it moves from frame 1 to 300.

Auto Keyframe

Another way to set keyframes is by enabling Auto Keyframe, which you do by clicking the key icon in the lower right of the Maya workspace. When this key is enabled (highlighted red), Maya automatically sets keyframes on channels that change from one frame to another. To see it in action we will re-create the box example using auto keyframes.

1. In a new Maya scene, create a polygon cube by choosing **Create → Polygon Primitives → Cube**.

2. Be sure your start frame is set to 1 and your end frame is 300.

3. Enable Auto Keyframe by clicking the key icon in the lower right of the Maya workspace (see Figure 2.34). It is enabled when it's high-lighted red.

Figure 2.34

Click the Auto Keyframe button to let Maya automatically generate keyframes.

4. Although Auto Keyframe is on, we still have to tell Maya to keyframe initial channels. Set the Current Time Indicator to frame 1. With the cube selected, LM click the TranslateX channel, and then Ctrl+LM click the TranslateZ channel so that both are highlighted. RM hold in the Channel Box and choose Key Selected.

5. Scrub to frame 300. In the TranslateX channel of the cube, enter the value of **10**. If you play back the Timeline, notice that Maya automatically created a keyframe for you in the TranslateX channel at frame 300.

6. Since the TranslateZ value did not change from 0, Maya did not set a keyframe for it. Although we could explicitly set a keyframe of 0 for TranslateZ at frame 300, we'll wait and let Maya automatically create it later.

7. Scrub to frame 150. In the TranslateZ channel of the cube, enter the value of **5**. If you play back the Timeline, the box should move in an arc to frame 150 and then continue in a straight line to frame 300.

8. To make the box move in an arc for the whole Timeline, scrub to frame 300 and set the TranslateZ value to 0. Since TranslateZ was modified in an earlier frame (frame 150), Maya will now automatically set a key for 0 at frame 300.

9. At frame 300, set the RotateY channel for the box to 360. Notice the RotateY channel remains highlighted white since there are no existing keyframes to compare it to. Manually set a keyframe on RotateY and scrub to frame 1. Change RotateY to 0. Maya should automatically create a key here for RotateY. If you play back the animation, the box will spin around once as it moves from frame 1 to 300.

The Graph Editor

The Graph Editor allows you to see and edit animation curves for each keyframed attribute of an object. Chapter 1 exposed you to the basic functionality; refer there for a more complete introduction. Although animation is typically roughed out in the 3D workspace and then fine-tuned and edited in the Graph Editor, we'll try the rotating cube example using the Graph Editor as much as possible.

1. In a new Maya scene, create a polygon cube by choosing **Create → Polygon Primitives → Cube**.

2. Be sure your start frame is set to 1 and your end frame is 300.

3. In the Toolbox on the left side of the Maya workspace is a series of preset panel layouts. Select the fourth icon down. (If you hover your mouse pointer over it, the tooltip should read Persp/Graph.) If you are unable to find this icon, choose **Panels → Saved Layouts → Persp/Graph**. Your workspace should show the perspective camera view in the top pane and the Graph Editor in the bottom pane, as in Figure 2.35.

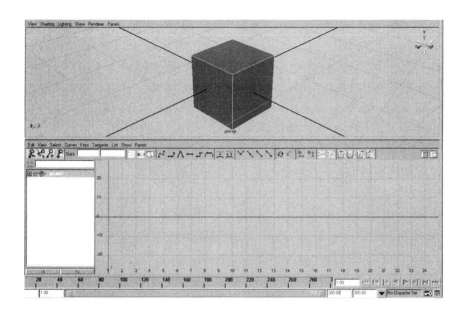

Figure 2.35

The Perspective/ Graph Editor layout allows you to easily see both the 3D scene and the Graph Editor for easy editing.

If you feel that your workspace is too cluttered using this pane setup, you can access the Graph Editor in a floating window by choosing **Window → Animation Editors → Graph Editor**.

4. Be sure Auto Keyframe is disabled. Set the Current Time Indicator to frame 1, and set keyframes at 0 on the TranslateX, TranslateZ, and RotateY channels of the cube by selecting the channels in the Channel Box and choosing Key Selected.

5. Notice that once keyframes are set on the TranslateX, TranslateZ, and RotateY channels, they appear in the Graph Editor's left pane.

6. Scrub to frame 300. Instead of altering values in the Channel Box, let's just create keyframes at the value of 0 for TranslateX, TranslateZ, and RotateY. In the Graph Editor, you should see a straight line and two black dots at 1 and 300 (see Figure 2.36).

7. If you scrub through the Timeline, nothing happens since we have not changed any keyed values. Our first goal is to make the box move 10 units along the X axis for 300 frames. Highlight the TranslateX channel in the left pane of the Graph Editor. In the actual graph, LM click the black keyframe marker to select it. Hold down Shift (so we drag in a straight line) and MM drag upward. (Note that you must be in translation, rotation, or scale mode for MM dragging to work in the Graph Editor.) Notice that as you do this, the box moves down the X axis in the perspective view. Move the keyframe marker up the graph until it is around the value 10. You may need to zoom out (Alt+RM drag left) to do this.

Figure 2.36

Keyframes are set at values of 0 for TranslateX, TranslateY, and TranslateZ at frames 0 and 300.

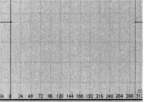

8. Notice how difficult it is to get the value of TranslateX to be exactly 10. You can enable vertical snapping by clicking the magnet icon on the right in the Graph Editor's icon menu. Try dragging the keyframe again and see how it snaps to whole integers. Snap it to 10 so it resembles Figure 2.37.

9. You can also create keys in the Graph Editor. Select the Add Keys tool by clicking the Add Keys Tool icon on the left of the Graph Editor's icon menu ![icon]. Select the TranslateZ channel in the left pane of the Graph Editor, and then LM click anywhere on the blue graph line to select the graph.

10. When selected, the line turns white. Add a key by MM clicking near the center of the line. A new key marker appears (see Figure 2.38).

11. Chances are you did not insert the key exactly at frame 150. LM click anywhere in the graph and press W to return to selection/move mode. LM click the new keyframe and Shift+MM drag it horizontally so that it's at frame 150. (You may have to zoom in your view.)

> In the Graph Editor, press F to frame the graph vertically and horizontally so that you can more easily edit keyframes.

12. Shift+MM drag the key vertically up 5 units. The graph should now resemble Figure 2.39.

Figure 2.37

Move keys in the Graph Editor by MM dragging a key marker.

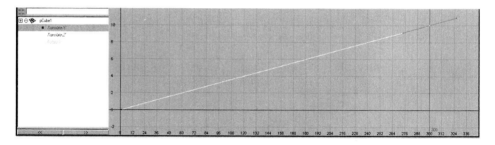

Figure 2.38

Add a keyframe to a graph by using the Add Keys tool and MM clicking where you want the key created.

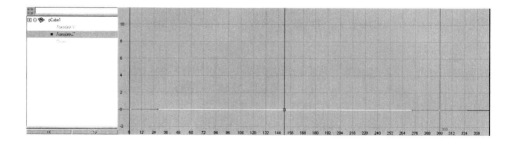

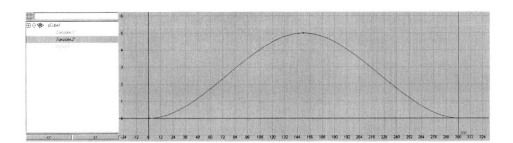

Figure 2.39

The arc in this graph represents the arc animated in the TranslateZ direction.

13. The final task is to add the rotation to the cube. In the Graph Editor, select the RotateY channel and move its key value at frame 300 to a value of 360.

14. If you play back the animation, the box will spin around once as it moves from frame 1 to 300.

Locking Channels

When animating, sometimes you want to lock certain channels that you know you won't use. Locking channels for objects that should only move, rotate, or scale along a certain axis keeps you from inadvertently keyframing channels, especially if you use the Key All or Auto Key features.

To lock a channel, simply select it in the Channel Box, RM hold anywhere in the Channel Box, and choose Lock Selected. The selected channel will highlight gray and you will not be able to edit or key it. To unlock a channel, select it, RM hold in the Channel Box, and choose Unlock Selected.

There are many other options for channel control that we won't get into in this chapter. For more, see Chapter 7.

Hammer and Nail Part VI: Animation

In this next exercise, we will continue the hammer and nail project by animating the hammer hitting the nail into the floor. We will employ many of the techniques described earlier in this section. The motion will have a total of four hits—two small taps and then two large swings. By the fourth swing, the nail will be driven into the floor.

This exercise consists of many steps, most of which are fairly repetitive. Luckily the animation is straightforward, and the repetitiveness forces you to become more used to the animation process in Maya.

1. Continuing from the previous hammer and nail exercise (or by opening step4.mb from the included CD), create a new camera by choosing **Create → Cameras → Camera**. A new camera object appears at the origin.

2. Select the camera and choose **Panels → Look Through Selected**. You now see whatever the camera sees, and when you move your view around the scene, this new camera follows.

3. Looking through the new camera, position your view to −14, 5, −6 in TranslateX, TranslateY, and TranslateZ, respectively. Rotate the view to −17, −115, 0 in RotateX, RotateY, and RotateZ, respectively. Your view should match Figure 2.40. Lock the camera down to this location and rotation by selecting Camera1, selecting all its translation and rotation channels, RM holding in the Channel Box, and choosing Lock Selected.

4. Under the Timeline in the main Maya window, set Start Time and Playback Start Time to frame 1, and set End Time and Playback End Time to frame 200.

5. To easily select objects to animate, open the Outliner by choosing **Window → Outliner** or by choosing the Persp/Outliner pane layout.

6. Select the Nail group and set its TranslateY value to 0.5.

7. Select the HammerSmallTaps group, and set its TranslateY value to 2.5 and its TranslateZ value to 0.35. Since our goal is to only rotate the hammer from now on, lock the translation channels of this group.

Figure 2.40

Use the Look Through Selected command to see what a particular camera sees.

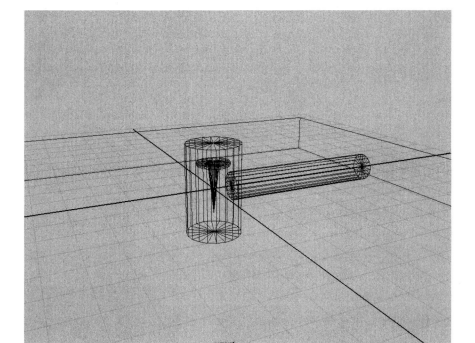

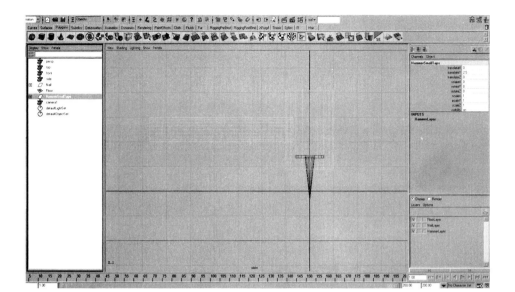

Figure 2.41

A side wireframe view of the objects ready to animate

8. In this example, we will have one object (the hammer) interacting with and driving another object (the nail). To precisely see any intersection when these objects touch, we'll switch our views to the side orthographic view. Do this by choosing **Panels →
Orthographic → Side**. Also, enable wireframe by pressing the 4 key. Your scene should resemble Figure 2.41.

9. Scrub to frame 1. With the HammerSmallTaps still selected, set the RotateX channel to 20. Select the RotateX channel in the Channel Box, RM hold in the Channel Box, and choose Key Selected.

10. Go to frame 20. Set a key on the RotateX channel of HammerSmallTaps at a value of 25. This pose will serve as the anticipation of a small tap on the nail coming up next.

11. Go to frame 25. Set a key on the RotateX channel of HammerSmallTaps at a value of 2.3.

12. We'll leave the hammer in this position for a few frames, so scrub to frame 35, and set another key on the RotateX channel of HammerSmallTaps at the value of 2.3.

13. If you scrub to frame 22, you should see that this frame is where the hammer actually makes contact with the nail. Since the nail should move after this frame, set a key-frame on the TranslateY channel of Nail.

14. Scrub to frame 25. Set a key on the TranslateY channel of Nail at a value of 0.025.

15. Scrub to frame 55. Set a key on the RotateX channel of HammerSmallTaps at the value of 25.

16. Scrub to frame 60. Set a key on the RotateX channel of HammerSmallTaps at the value of –5.

17. Scrub back to frame 59. Select the Nail and set a keyframe on the TranslateY channel. (It should still be 0.025 from the previous keyframe.)

18. Scrub forward one frame to frame 60. Set a key on the TranslateY channel of Nail at a value of –0.36.

19. If you play back the animation, you should see two small taps by the hammer onto the nail. The nail moves slightly into the floor on each hit.

We will now animate the larger hammer hits. In the Outliner, expand the Hammer-SmallTaps group to expose the HammerLargeSwings group. Since the pivot of the Ham-merLargeSwings group is set farther back, the hammer will appear to hit with larger force.

20. Scrub to frame 75. Set a key on the RotateX channel of HammerLargeSwings at a value of 0.

21. Since we are dealing with larger swings, we'll let the hammer take more time to pull back. Scrub to frame 100, and set a key on the RotateX channel of HammerLarge-Swings at a value of 40.

22. Scrub to frame 105. Set a key on the RotateX channel HammerLargeSwings at a value of –3.5.

23. In the Outliner, select the Nail and scrub to frame 104. Set a key on the TranslateY channel of Nail at the value of –0.36.

24. Scrub to frame 105. Set a key on the TranslateY channel of Nail at the value of –0.7.

25. Leave the hammer resting for a few frames by scrubbing to frame 115, selecting Ham-merLargeSwings, and setting a key on the RotateX channel. (It should be at the previous keyframed value, –3.5.)

26. Scrub to frame 135. Set a key on the RotateX channel of HammerLargeSwings at the value of 40.

27. Scrub to frame 140. Set a key on the RotateX channel of HammerLargeSwings at the value of –4.

28. For our final hammer movement, we'll slowly draw it back up in the air. Scrub to frame 180, and set a key on the RotateX channel of HammerLargeSwings at the value of 45.

29. The final element to animate is the motion of the nail on the final swing. Scrub to frame 139 and set a keyframe on the TranslateY channel of Nail at –0.7.

30. Scrub to frame 140. Set a key on the TranslateY channel of Nail at the value of –0.83.

31. Change views back to Camera1 by choosing **Panels → Perspective → camera1** and play back your animation! Save your work and continue with the following section to learn about lighting your scene.

Although we won't do any graph editing here, feel free to select any of the animated groups and view their animation curves in the Graph Editor.

Basic Lighting

Although lighting is covered in Chapter 11, we'll look at the basics here so that you can see your objects when they render. The most common lights include Spot, Point, and Directional. Figure 2.42 shows a sphere rendered with the three types of light.

A Spot light has a specific direction and location. The tip of its light cone is placed anywhere in 3D space, and the direction of the light is determined by its RotateX, RotateY, and RotateZ parameters. Any object passing inside a Spot light's light cone becomes illuminated. To control the size of the Spot light's cone, modify its **Cone Angle** attribute. The Penumbra Angle and Dropoff control the Spot light's edge softness and intensity dropoff.

Point lights spread light rays in all directions and have a specific location. Think of a Point light as a lightbulb. As the light rays travel over a distance, they lose their energy, causing soft dissipation.

Directional lights are used mostly for distant light sources, such as the sun. They do not have a specific location, but they do have a direction.

Figure 2.42

Rendered effect of (a) Spot light, (b) Point light, and (c) Directional light

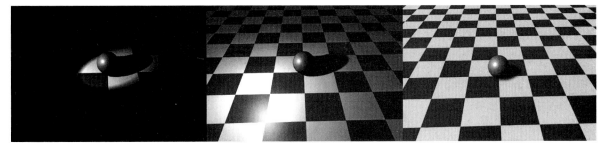

Spot light   Point light   Directional light

Hammer and Nail Part VII: Lighting

In this next exercise, we will add some basic lighting to the hammer and nail scene. We won't get into any complexities such as shadows; the lights you will create here will simply illuminate the scene's objects.

1. Continuing from the previous hammer and nail exercise (or by opening `step5Part2.mb` from the included CD), create a Directional light by choosing **Create → Lights → Directional Light**.

2. With the Directional light selected, set the RotateX, RotateY, and RotateZ channels to –50, –70, and 0, respectively. Since a Directional light has no positional source, we do not have to set translation values.

3. Open the Attribute Editor. Under the directionalLightShape1 tab, set the **Intensity** attribute to 0.5. The intensity controls how bright the light is.

4. Create a Spot light by choosing **Create → Lights → Spot Light**.

5. With the Spot light selected, set TranslateX, TranslateY, and TranslateZ to –10, 15, and 3, respectively. Set RotateX, RotateY, and RotateZ to –57, –82, and 0. Through a zoomed-out perspective view, your scene should resemble Figure 2.43.

6. In the Attribute Editor, set the Spot light's Intensity value to 0.7 and Penumbra Angle to 4. These settings will create a soft white spotlight shining on your scene. Save your work and continue with the following section.

Figure 2.43

A Directional light and a Spot light will emit enough light to render the animation.

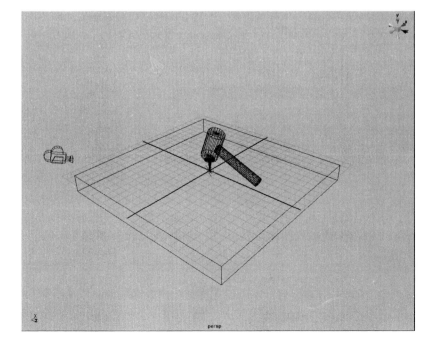

The next section will go through the basics of rendering so that you can see the results of this lighting setup. As you begin to render test frames, feel free to explore other lights and their attributes.

Rendering Frames

The last step of the production pipeline for a Maya animation is rendering frames. Rendering is the process of calculating geometry, lighting, materials, special effects, motion, and so on in order to make an image. Chapters 13 and 14 are devoted to rendering, but we'll cover the basics here.

Render Settings

Before you begin rendering, Maya needs to know a few things. Are you rendering out a single image or a sequence? What size are the images? Would you prefer longer render times to get better-looking results or faster render times to get decent image quality? All these factors, plus many more, are set in the Render Settings window. To access the Render Settings window (see Figure 2.44), choose **Window → Rendering Editors → Render Settings**.

The settings in the first drop-down box determine which renderer Maya will use. Each has its own purpose, but until we get into more advanced topics, we'll keep this on Maya Software.

The first main section, Image File Output, deals with how Maya will name and save the images you render. File Name Prefix determines the name of the image or movie you render. Frame/Animation Ext determines how single and sequence frames are named (more on this in a bit). Image Format determines the format of the saved image once it's rendered. In the Renderable Cameras section, the Renderable Camera drop-down list allows you to specify which cameras you render from.

In the Image Size section, you specify the size and aspect ratio of your images. Note that the larger the image size, the more Maya has to render, which slows render times.

When you choose a renderer, a tab for it appears in the Render Settings window. Click the Maya Software tab to display settings that relate specifically to Maya's software renderer. Figure 2.45 shows this window.

Although we won't cover all the many Maya Software settings, we'll focus on a few that can dramatically affect render times and image quality. Under the first section, Anti-aliasing Quality, notice you can specify the overall settings quality in the Quality drop-down list. Typically, choosing a preset quality level is sufficient. Preview Quality is ideal for rendering test frames (covered in the next section), and Production Quality is usually sufficient for final renders.

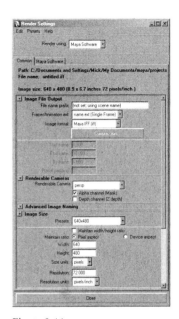

Figure 2.44
The Render Settings window

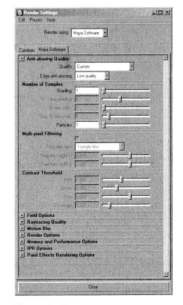

Figure 2.45
The Maya Software settings tab in the Render Settings window allows you to change the software renderer settings.

Once you have chosen the proper render settings for your goals, close the Render Settings window. All subsequent renders will use the settings you chose. The settings are also saved in the project so that you do not have to reset them if you ever close and reopen your scene.

Rendering Test Frames

After specifying render settings, you are ready to render. Typically, test frames are rendered throughout the production pipeline to test materials, models, lighting, effects, and efficiency. Since they are for testing purposes alone, you should generally use lower-quality render settings.

To render a frame, click the Render The Current Frame button on Maya's Status line . Alternatively, open the Render View window (see Figure 2.46) by choosing **Window → Rendering Editors → Render View**.

To render the current frame from the current camera angle, click the Redo Previous Render icon on the left side of the Render View's icon bar or by choosing **Render → Redo Previous Render**.

As your scene grows in complexity, it usually takes longer to render. Sometimes you don't need to render the entire frame, especially if you want to see how only one part of your scene looks for testing purposes. Clicking the Render Region button allows you to draw a box on the image and render just that region. Simply LM click anywhere on the image and draw a box to specify a region; then click the Render Region icon or choose **Render → Render Region**.

Figure 2.46

The Render View window allows you to see renders for the current frame.

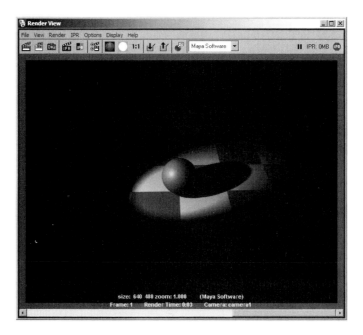

Interactive Photorealistic Rendering (IPS) allows you to quickly render adjustments made to material and lighting attributes. Although we won't get into technical specifics of IPR in this chapter, know that it is useful if you are trying to tweak a material, light, or motion blur without having to recalculate the entire render process.

To use IPR, open the Render View window and render the current frame. Using the LM button, draw a region on the image, and then select the IPR icon or choose **IPR → Redo Previous IPR Render**. As you make changes to the material, light, or motion blur attributes, the IPR region will automatically re-render quickly to show you the rendered result.

Note that although IPR is great for tweaking various attributes, it will not update any moved object or altered view. If you make any of these types of major changes to your render view, you must rerender without IPR to see the changes.

Rendering Animation

An animation is a sequence of rendered images played back at a specified frame rate. Although you use the Render View to render single frames, image sequences are rendered with the Batch Render command found in the Render menu of the Rendering menu set.

In order for Batch Render to work, you need to set some properties in the Render Settings menu. Notice that in the Render Settings window (Figure 2.44), in the Image File Output section, the Start Frame, End Frame, By Frame, and Frame Padding settings are disabled by default. In the Frame/Animation Ext drop-down list, choose name.#.ext. This setting indicates that the name of your outputted images will be of the following format: `MyScene.001.iff`, `MyScene.002.iff`, and so on.

Once you select a valid animation Frame/Animation Ext setting, the Start Frame, End Frame, By Frame, and Frame Padding options become active. Set the first frame you want to render as your start frame and the last frame you want to render as your end frame. By Frame refers to the increment between the frames you want to render. Typically you want to keep this value at 1. Frame Padding refers to the number of digits used in the frame number extensions. For instance, a frame padding value of 4 would yield the following syntax for your filename: `MyScene.0001.iff`. A frame padding value of 2 would yield `MyScene.01.iff`. Always make sure you have enough padding for the number of frames you are rendering or else your frames could be overwritten.

Hammer and Nail Part VIII: Rendering

Now that we've animated and lit our project, we can render out the animation. Follow these steps to perform a batch render on your scene.

1. Continuing from the previous hammer and nail exercise (or by opening `step6.mb` from the included CD), open the Render Settings window by choosing **Window → Rendering Editors → Render Settings**.

2. Make sure you have Maya Software selected as your renderer. In the Common tab, set File Name Prefix to HammerAndNail. In the Frame/Animation Ext drop-down menu, choose name.#.ext. Keep Image Format set to Maya IFF.

3. Set Start Frame to 1 and End Frame to 200. Change Frame Padding to 3. These settings will cause the output filenames to be in the following format: HammerAndNail.001.iff. Your Render Settings window should match Figure 2.47.

4. In the Renderable Camera drop-down list in the Renderable Cameras section, select Add Renderable Camera. Camera1 should now appear as a renderable camera. Click the trashcan icon next to persp to prevent the perspective view from rendering.

5. Switch to the Maya Software tab. Under the Quality setting, choose Production Quality. This will automatically set various render settings to a high-quality level. Close the Render Settings window. If you got lost at any point during this hammer and nail exercise, take a look at step7.mb on the included CD, which represents the scene at this step.

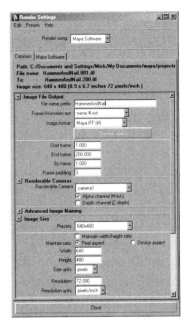

Figure 2.47

These render settings will cause Maya to output a series of frames from frame 1 to 200.

6. Switch to the Rendering menu Set. Choose **Render → Batch Render**. Maya will then render the 200 frames.

7. After rendering is complete (the Command Feedback line in the lower-right side of Maya's workspace will read "Rendering Completed"), you can view the animation by using FCheck, an image-viewing application that comes with your copy of Maya. In FCheck, choose **File → Open Animation** and choose the first frame of the rendered animation in the hammer_and_nail\images folder.

Summary

Although we have just scratched the surface of all areas in the production pipeline, this chapter provided you with a good start for your journey with Maya. We looked at project structure, experimented with how to create and edit objects and their structures, worked with pivots, explored Maya's node structure, and then learned how to assign materials, set keyframes, and light and render your scenes. While reading and following the examples, you probably thought of many questions about how to do more complex tasks. The remainder of this book will help guide you through those tasks and all aspects of Maya as it serves as a cohesive reference for both beginners and advanced users.

CHAPTER 3

Polygonal Modeling

In this chapter, you will "learn by doing" with Maya 8.5's strengthened and enhanced polygon modeling toolset. Our example character is called Machismo, and he is a strongman in the same vein as Bob Parr of *The Incredibles*. Unlike Mr. Incredible, however, Machismo tends to put his body in gear while his brain is still in neutral!

We will create him using many of the polygon tools Maya has available (and possibly some MEL scripts, which extend Maya's capabilities). We will also explore the areas of Maya's interface and display capabilities that are best learned in the process of creating models. After reading this chapter, you should have a good handle on poly modeling tools and techniques.

- ▪ **Understanding polygons**
- ▪ **Polygonal modeling principles**
- ▪ **Preparing to model**
- ▪ **Creating the Machismo model**
- ▪ **Modeling Machismo's body**

Figure 3.1

Two polygons with point order and normals made visible. Note that the point order of the polygons determines which direction the polygon is facing.

What Is a Polygon?

Simply put for our purposes, a polygon is a 3D mathematical construct composed of three or more sets of points having X, Y, Z coordinates in 3D space. These points not only have positional values, they are also connected in a particular order, which determines the way the polygon is said to face. (We'll explore this in the next section.) This facing direction is shown by a polygon's surface normal, as Figure 3.1 shows.

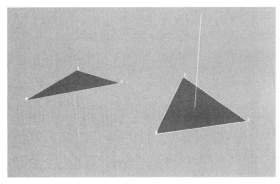

Polygons are the oldest modeling paradigm; their pedigree extends back decades. Nearly supplanted by Non-Uniform Rational B-Spline (NURBS) modeling for organic character work, they have most recently been resurrected by the advent of faster computers, inexpensive RAM, more powerful graphics cards, and to a certain extent, subdivision surfaces. Once Maya's weakest of toolsets, the polygonal modeling tools have evolved into extremely powerful and versatile sculpting commands that allow the artist to create any form imaginable.

Illustrating Surface Direction

Let's illustrate basic polygon concepts in a quick tutorial.

1. Open the `Triangles.mb` file from the CD.

2. Select both triangles either by marquee selecting or by the Shift+selection method.

3. These triangles have been set to display surface normals and vertex numbers using the Custom Polygon Display option box (choose **Display → Polygons → Custom Polygon Display** ❐), shown in Figure 3.2. The vertex numbers indicate the order in which the vertices were created. Note that the vertices on the right were created in counterclockwise order, and the vertices on the left were created in clockwise order.

Figure 3.2

The Custom Polygon Display Options box

The hairlike line extending out from the center of the polygon is called a surface normal, and it indicates the direction the polygon is facing. Creating a polygon in a clockwise direction results in it facing away from the viewport, and creating vertices in a counterclockwise direction points the face toward the viewport.

Why is this important? In the Custom Polygon Display option box, change Backface Culling to On and click Apply. Notice that the triangle whose normal faces away from the camera disappears—the back faces have been culled so that you don't have to see them. Often, modelers working on complex models will turn on Backface Culling to speed the display of their work and make vertex and face selection easier. Also, when joining two polygonal objects, it is important to make sure that the polys from the two objects are facing in the same direction. Turning on Backface Culling or displaying normals make this comparison easy.

Polygonal Modeling Principles

In polygonal modeling, we follow several principles. They form a "best practices" list that you will do well to follow. Following them can take more time but will save you extreme headaches down the line. They are as follows:

- Four-sided polygons, or quads as they will be referred to from here on, are the best type of polygons to use because they deform well, they convert to other types of surfaces well, and you can cleanly use many of Maya's editing tools on them.

- Triangles are okay if you must use them, but if you can figure out a way to make them quads, do so.

- Never use more than four-sided polygons, or *n*-sided polygons. At render time, they almost inevitably cause such problems as texture warping or even complete render failure.

- Keep your model in a clean, quad-based topology while you are working; this will save clean-up time at the end of the process. Figure 3.3 illustrates some ways to convert *n*-sided polygons (N-gons) into quads.

- Always model with construction history turned on. This will allow you to use the inputs to do some powerful editing after the fact, and adjusting the attributes of a node in the Inputs list is often the fastest way to learn about a new feature.

- Delete history often. This prevents modeling slowdown from unnecessary node evaluation.

- Get help if you need it. Maya's Help menu system links directly to the documentation for each command. Also, within each tool's option box is a menu item that can be extremely informative.

- Save often and incrementally. If you model yourself into a corner or make a mistake that you can't undo out of, going back to a previous version can save time. The further back you have to go, the more time you will have wasted.

Figure 3.3

Converting 5-, 6-, 7-, 8-, and 9-sided polys (top row) to quads (bottom row)

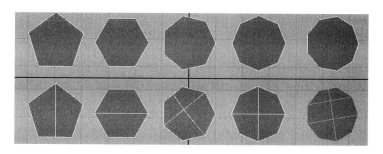

Creating Machismo

Machismo's form offers the right balance of bulk and detail for learning polygonal modeling. We will start with a drawing, which we will convert into a linear NURBS curve template. We will do this to make modeling the body easier. We will then begin box-modeling the body using Maya's various polygon modeling tools.

Machismo gets around—at least he gets around in this book. In Chapter 5, the subdivision surfaces chapter, we will continue modeling using the linear NURBS template and will create the head polygon by polygon. We will then convert the head to subdivision surfaces and create surface details using hierarchical edits. In Chapter 6, which covers advanced modeling, we will concentrate on creating blendshapes for Machismo using some of Maya's deformer tools. We will create a UV map for him in Chapter 12, which covers the texture mapping.

Start with a Plan, and Prepare, Prepare, Prepare

No professional-level modeler starts without a plan, and neither should we. Once a design has been finalized, artists draw the character in a variety of poses to give the animators examples of who the character is and how they should act. More important for our purposes, these drawings help determine how the character should be built, where we need to add detail/polygons, and where can we let the model remain "light."

At the bare minimum, one should strive for a good schematic drawing showing the front and side of a character. What is a good schematic? The first and most important requirement of such a drawing is that the details of one view match or line up with the details in the other drawing. (See Figure 3.4.)

Figure 3.4

Machismo's body and head schematic. Notice how the details depicted in the front and side views all line up.

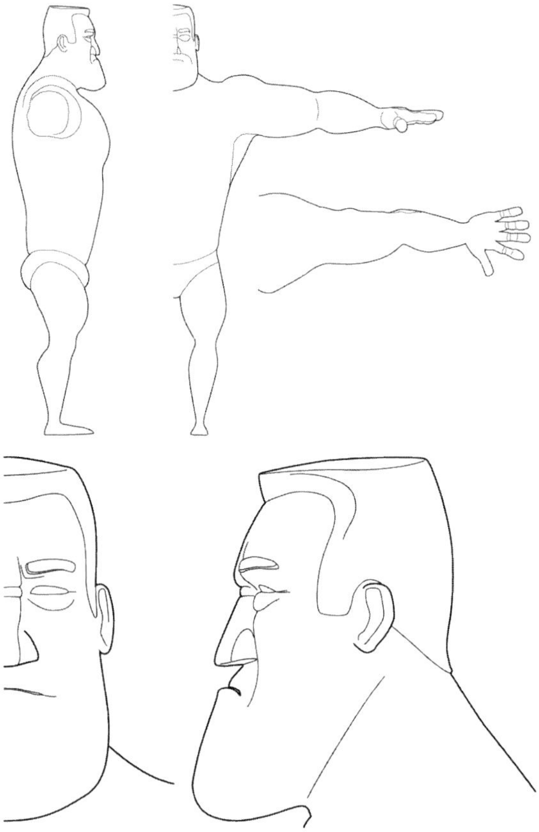

Linear NURBS Curves: The Polygonal Modeler's Best Friend

Before we create the first polygon or primitive (base shapes from which polys are created), we need to translate our conventional drawing into a form that we can use to effectively place faces, vertices, and objects in their proper locations. Traditionally, modelers have used drawings mapped to image planes or polygons as a guide for modeling. A more effective method is to use first-degree or linear NURBS curves.

SETTING UP THE INTERFACE

We will want to first set up Maya's interface to facilitate modeling. Working in Maya involves some degree of interface fluidity, so paying attention to how we do this at the beginning will make it easier to manipulate the interface later during animation and rendering. Here's how to set up the interface for the following modeling exercises.

1. Choose **Window → Settings/Preferences → Preferences**. In the Preferences option box, change the menu set to Polygons in the Menu Set pop-up contained inside the Interface settings box.

2. Set both Open Attribute Editor and Open Tool Settings to Open In Separate. Set Open Layer Editor to In Main Maya Window.

3. In the Categories section at left, click Polygons Settings. This accesses the display settings for all new polygon objects, which is similar to the Custom Polygon Display option box from earlier. Uncheck everything except Edges Standard.

4. Click Selection under Categories at left, and in the Polygon Selection section, click Select Faces With Whole Face. This will allow you to click any part of a polygonal face to select it. Selecting Faces With Center requires that you click the center of a face to select it, which is awkward.

5. We will leave the Camera preference alone for now, but you will need to remember where it is. Under the Cameras category is an Animate Camera Transitions section. The ability to animate the modeling view transitions is a wonderful tool but could result in seasickness. More likely, however, is that an underpowered machine might be slow to handle these animations. This is where you can turn these off. You can now close the Preferences option box.

6. Choose **Display → Heads Up Display → Poly Count** to display useful information concerning polygon components in a scene, an object, and a selection.

We now have a modeling window that will be uncluttered yet still give us the information we need to create this model. Just as important, we now know where to make changes in how Maya displays polygons.

Many modeling applications can create polygonal objects that have length and width but no depth. These are generally called polylines, and they are often used as a base off of which modelers will create polygons by extrusion, appending, lofting, and so on. Maya does not support this topology; instead, it has something better and more flexible: first-degree or linear NURBS curves.

Linear NURBS curves are composed of straight segments drawn between edit points. They have one control vertex (CV) for each edit point (EP), so each segment stays straight

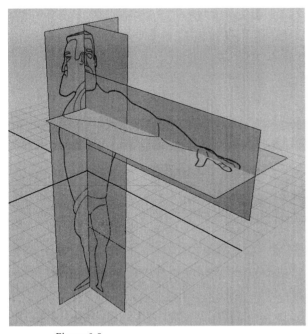

Figure 3.5

The polygon mapped with the schematic drawing, split into three separate views and arranged in XYZ space

no matter how you move the CV or EP. These points can then be moved in X, Y, and Z in predictable ways. This contrasts with second- or third-degree NURBS curves whose movement depends on the component moved. And as a modeler can do with NURBS curves of any degree, they can move from EP to EP or from CV to CV using the arrow keys. This makes selecting individual points easier when in the orthogonal views.

Many modelers begin with three-view polygonal objects as shown in Figure 3.5. The modeling techniques we will use to create Machismo make such a template problematic. We will use Maya's Subdiv Proxy command to establish a version of Machismo to see what the low-resolution model will look like when it is smoothed for rendering. While the flat polygonal template is visible, it is impossible to see the other smoothed side of the model. To see the smoothed side, we must rotate the view to the smooth side and back, which breaks our modeling flow, or set up a camera view on the smooth side, which eats up screen real estate, or hide/show the polygonal template on a layer, which is unacceptably slow. What we need is a modeling template that can remain visible at all times and not obscure our views. Enter the linear template.

To import an image onto a specific viewport or camera, choose **View → Image Plane → Import Image**. You can then manipulate the image properties in the Attribute Editor.

Creating the Linear Template

Let's continue by using the BodyDrawing.mb file from the CD. Open it and set your modeling window to the front view using the hotbox or Panels menu in the viewport. Let's trace the front view.

1. Choose **Create → EP Curve Tool** ❐. Under EP Curve Settings, set Curve Degree to 1 Linear, and set Knot Spacing to Uniform.

2. Zoom in your view so that the head, chest, and arm are centered in your viewport.

3. Click at the very top of the head on the center line to begin creating your tracing.

4. Continue around the drawing, staying on the outline of the drawing as shown in Figure 3.6. Stay to the outside of the line, and if you make a mistake, go back by pressing the Delete, Backspace, or undo (Z) key. If you need to move the viewport, Alt+MM+drag to dolly the camera view.

If you cannot see the line you are creating, first make sure you have the EP Curve tool activated. Then translate the front view polygon back in Z. Keep in mind that the EP Curve tool always operates on the Cartesian plane that is perpendicular to the view window. In this case, it is the YX plane.

5. When you reach the center line around the groin area, press Enter to create your line. If you created the line and are not happy with it, you can edit it by component selecting (RMB) on the line and choosing Edit Point. Then use the Move tool to drag the points where you want them, as shown in Figure 3.7. RMB again on the line and choose Select to select the object. Alternatively, you can toggle between component and object selection modes by pressing F8.

6. Trace all the details inside the outside contour of your line. Because we will be modeling the head separately, tracing the facial features is optional.

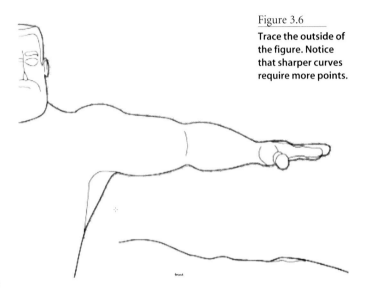

Figure 3.6

Trace the outside of the figure. Notice that sharper curves require more points.

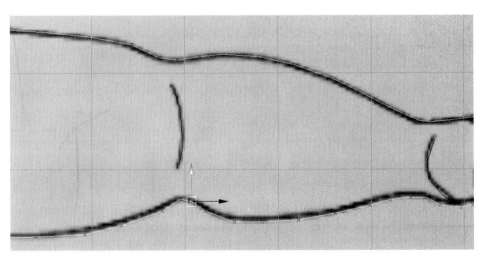

Figure 3.7

Changing the shape of the line by moving the EPs

Figure 3.8

**The front view
traced, selected, and
grouped**

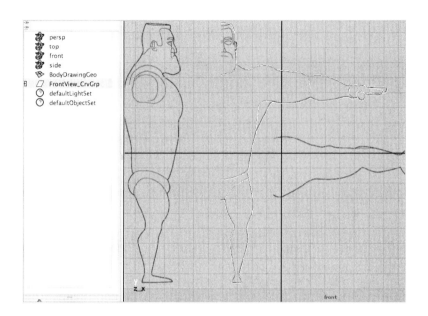

7. When you are finished tracing these details, select all the curves you have drawn in the Outliner, group them, and name the group FrontView_CrvGrp. Your viewport should look like Figure 3.8.

8. Repeat steps 1 through 7 for the top and side views. Name them TopView_CrvGrp and SideView_CrvGrp, respectively.

Now we have to arrange these groups into a useful template by translating and rotating them into position.

1. Select SideView_CrvGrp and press the W key to open the Move tool. Note that the pivot point of this group is at 0,0,0 in XYZ space. We need to center it on this group. Choose **Modify → Center Pivot** to center the pivot point inside this group.

2. Rotate this group –90 degrees in Y to orient it properly.

3. Move this group in X to about 8.786 so that the center line touches the YZ plane exactly.

4. Select FrontView_CrvGrp and move it in X so that the ends of the line at the top of the head and the groin area are lined up with the YZ plane. Because we created the curve in the front view, it should be already set in the YX plane.

A good way to select is to click a curve and press the Up arrow on the keyboard. This will move the selection up the hierarchy, selecting the group node above it. Unfortunately, pressing the Down arrow does not move down the hierarchy. Using the Down arrow selects the shape node for an object.

5. Select the TopView_CrvGrp and choose **Modify → Center Pivot**.

6. Rotate TopView_CrvGrp −90 degrees in X, and set translateX channels to 0.57, translateY to 5.242, and translateZ to −.068 to line up the top view properly, as shown in Figure 3.9.

7. Select these three groups and group them. Call this group BodyCrvTempGrp.

8. Assign this new group to a new layer called BodyCrvTempLyr. You should now have something that looks like Figure 3.10.

9. Save the file as Mach_CrvTemp.mb.

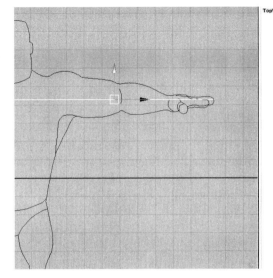

Figure 3.9

The top view rotated and translated into position as seen from the front view. The polygon has been hidden for clarity.

Always give your objects, groups, and layers distinctive names. Maya doesn't recognize the difference between DrawPoly the layer and DrawPoly the object. Use the suffixes *Geo*, *Grp*, *Lyr*, and *Crv* to distinguish geometry, groups, layers, and curves. This avoids renaming and other, nastier little conflicts when two elements have the exact same name. It is a good habit to start and keep!

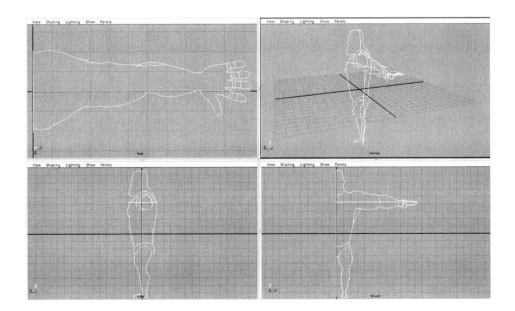

Figure 3.10

The linear template without the polygon base drawing

Finishing the Template

We now have a 3D template made of linear NURBS curves. We can, if need be, begin modeling here, but a little extra work at this stage will reap enormous timesaving benefits down the line. Currently, the lines are flat to the orthogonal planes, and this flatness is a problem in that it does not always accurately reflect the actual points on the figure where the contour will turn away. This problem can best be seen in the wrist area. In the top view, the arm bends a little back from the center line of the figure, but the front view stays flat to the camera. This indicates that the thickest part of the wrist will be at the front of the wrist instead of in the middle. It's worth our time to line up these elements. Do so using the following steps.

1. Deselect all the lines by clicking in the background of the modeling window.

2. RMB click the outside contour line of the front view curves, and choose Edit Point.

3. In component mode, marquee select all the EPs that make up the outside of the hand.

4. Shift+select all the inside contour lines that make up the hand. This should select them as objects.

5. Translate all back along the Z axis only until they extend from the middle of the wrist, as shown at left in Figure 3.11.

6. Select the first EP on the arm, and move it in Z only until it sits where the tip of the arm would be on the character. This requires you to give thought to the anatomy of the forearm and where those muscles will insert into the wrist. If you are in doubt, use the middle of Figure 3.11 as your guide. Remember that we will be lofting these curves later in the chapter. You can move them around later.

Figure 3.11

(a) Move the EPs of the hand to rest along the axis of the arm. (b) Adjust the EPs along the top of the arm. (c) Move the EPs along the bottom of the arm.

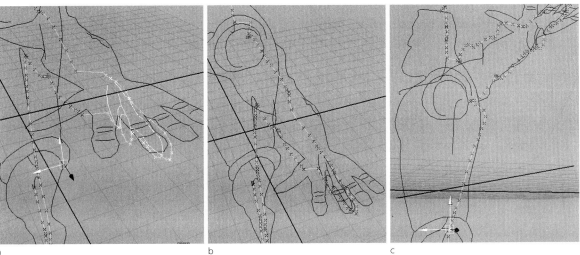

a   b   c

7. Walk your selection up the arm (this is a great place to use the Left and Right arrow keys), and translate the points back or forward in Z as you need to, to match the contour of the character. When you are finished, you should have something roughly resembling the middle image in Figure 3.11.

8. Repeat for the bottom of the arm and continue down the body to the waist. Try for a smooth transition from where the arm meets the body at the latissimus dorsi muscle of the back and the waist where the contour is largely in the middle of the body. When you are finished, you should have something close to the right image in Figure 3.11. Note that the widest part of the upper arm will be the belly of the bicep muscle, so the line should be in the front of the arm.

The top view curve also needs to be edited. The contour along the arm is fine, but where it intersects the side view at the chest should be lower to better reflect the thickness of Machismo's pectoralis muscles. Also, the hand/wrist area needs to move down a little bit as well. So let's change that by doing the following.

1. RMB the top view curve; choose Edit Point.

2. Moving each point along the Y axis, create a smooth transition between the area where the arm intersects the body and where the chest muscle is at its thickest, as shown in Figure 3.12.

Now let's duplicate and mirror the FrontView_CrvGrp and TopView_CrvGrps to create a right side to our template.

1. In the Outliner, open BodyCrvTempGrp by clicking the plus sign to the left of the name.

2. Select FrontView_CrvGrp and press W to open the Move tool.

3. Notice that the pivot point of this group is not at the world origin. We need to change this. Press the Insert key (Home key on the Mac) to enter move pivot mode. Notice how the cursor changes.

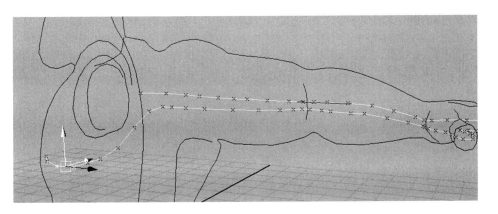

Figure 3.12

The top view curves edited to better reflect the contours in the chest and hand areas

4. Hold down the X key to snap to grid, and move the pivot point of the group to the world origin, as shown in Figure 3.13.

5. Press Insert again to leave move pivot mode.

6. Choose **Edit → Duplicate** ❑.

7. Type **–1** in the Scale X field (that is the one farthest left). Set Geometry Type to Copy, and set Group Under to Parent. This will create a copy of this curve group under the parent BodyCrvTempGrp and mirror it in X by scaling it to –1. Click Duplicate to create the copy.

8. Repeat steps 2 through 7 with TopView_CrvGrp to create a scaled X.

9. Save the file as `Mach_CrvTmpDone.mb`.

Modeling Machismo's Body

We have a good plan, and we have a great base from which to work. We are now ready to create the model. We will be using relatively few tools. First we will generate a cube primitive that we will edit into the shape of Machismo's body using Maya's extensive polygonal editing toolset.

> All directions in the following tutorials assume that all tools start from their default settings. We will adjust them as needed.

Figure 3.13

Moving the pivot point of the front view group. Notice how holding down the X key temporarily invokes Maya's Grid Snapping feature.

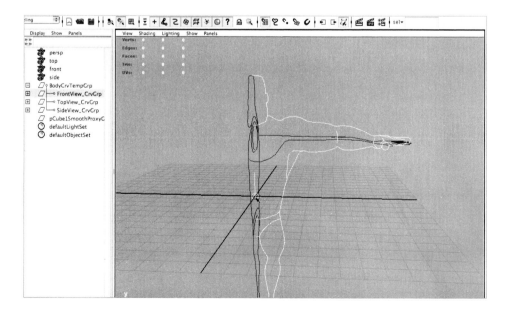

Let's begin by creating the cube for the body.

1. Open `Mach_CrvTmpDone.mb`. Click the Four View Layout Shortcut button, and set windows to the top, front, side, and perspective views if they are not set already.

2. Choose **Create → Polygon Primitives → Cube ❑**. Maya offers Sphere, Cube, Cone, Cone, Cylinder, Torus, Prism, Pyramid, Pipe, Helix, Soccer Ball, and Platonic Solids primitives. For our purposes, the Cube primitive offers the most flexibility for the intended shape.

3. From the Edit menu in the Polygon Cube option box, choose Reset Settings to reset the settings to their "factory defaults." (It's a good idea to reset tools after using them, to keep unexpected behavior to a minimum.)

4. New to Maya 8, you can click-drag to create and position new primitives if Interactive Creation is enabled (this option is found in **Create → Polygon Primitives**). Try it out by clicking in the scene and then dragging to create a cube. You can also single-click to place a default-sized cube at the point you clicked.

5. Using the Universal Manipulator tool, move and resize the cube to match Figure 3.14. To see the cube's relationship to the template better, change to wireframe view by pressing the 4 key. Also, to avoid accidentally selecting and editing the template, make it a referenced layer by clicking twice in the middle box next to the layer name in the Layer Editor (see Figure 3.15). The first click templates the layer, graying it out. When you click the second time, the NURBS lines turn black and an *R* appears in the box, indicating that the curves are in reference mode: you can see them, but you can't select them.

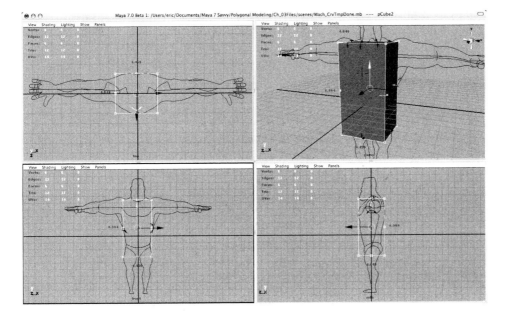

Figure 3.14

The cube scaled and translated to roughly match the template. Note the numeric values; these indicate the scale along the various axes.

Figure 3.15

The Layer Editor with the Template layer set to Reference

Setting Up a Subdiv Proxy Modeling Work Flow

One of the most powerful aspects of modeling with polys in Maya is the program's Subdiv Proxy command. With this tool, Maya duplicates the original low polygon object—called a proxy object from here on—mirrors it along an axis, and then smooths it using a poly-SmoothProxy node. We'll call the duplicate the smooth object from now on. Editing the original proxy shape causes the smoothed shape to update automatically, creating a smoothed preview of what the shape will look like when smoothed at rendering. This allows the modeler to work with as low a polygon count as possible, and that makes rigging, weighting, and animating easier. As we will be working on one half of the body, we will mirror the smoothed shape so that it will always be in view. To create the Subdiv Proxy, do the following.

1. Choose **Edit Mesh → Cut Faces Tool** ❑. Most often, this tool is used to make an interactive cut to basically split polygons using a plane. Alternatively, you can select the plane in which you want to cut by choosing YZ Plane, ZX Plane, or XY Plane. Selecting the plane can yield easier placement of points. For this exercise, try YZ Plane.

    By clicking the Extract Cut Faces check box, however, we can create polygons that are not connected and that can be separated into objects using the **Mesh → Separate** command. You can even offset the extracted polygons by entering Extract Offset values in the provided fields. What we want to do here, however, is to delete the cut faces; so check the Delete Cut Faces check box.

2. Using the View Compass command, go to the top view by clicking the Y cone.

3. Click the Enter Cut Tool button in the Cut Faces Tool Options window, and in the top view hold down the Shift key and drag vertically from top to bottom, as shown in Figure 3.16. The dotted line that appears indicates which set of polys will be deleted. Dragging in the opposite direction deletes the opposite side.

Figure 3.16

Dragging vertically from top to bottom deletes the left side of the cube. The image at right shows the result with the Delete Cut Faces option checked.

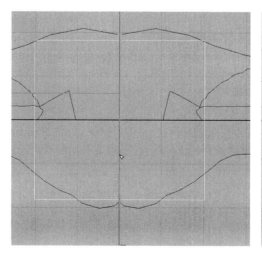
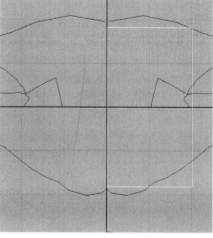

4. Drop the tool by pressing the Q key to open the Select tool.

5. With the half cube selected, choose **Proxy → Subdiv Proxy** ❑. Set the options as shown in Figure 3.17. Specifically, we want to uncheck Keep Geometry Borders and change Mirror Behavior to Half. Also change Mirror Direction to –X. This will automatically mirror the smoothed half shape in the X direction. Also, set Subdiv Proxy Shader to Keep. This will give the smoothed object the same shader as the original shape. We could set Subdiv Proxy In Layer and Smooth Mesh In Layer. This would place both shapes in separate layers, but they would be named pCube1Proxy and pCube1Smooth, respectively. We can create new layers and assign the shapes if and when we need them.

6. Click Smooth to set up the Subdiv Proxy. You should have something that looks like Figure 3.18.

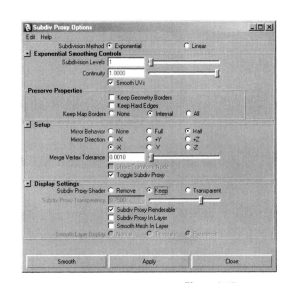

Figure 3.17

The Subdiv Proxy option box

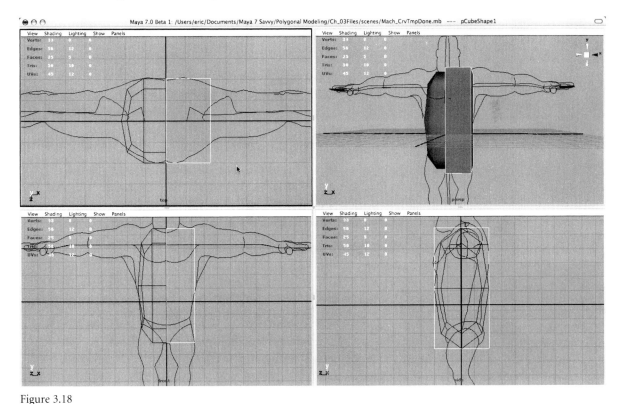

Figure 3.18

The smoothed object at left will update interactively when you perform operations on the proxy object at right.

Several hot keys are associated with this methodology.

KEY	ACTION
Tilde key (~)	Toggles the display of the proxy or smooth mesh
Shift+~	Turns on both proxy and smooth objects
Ctrl+~	Chooses **Polygons → Subdiv Proxy**
Shift+Ctrl+~	Chooses **Polygons → Subdiv Proxy Options**
Page Up	Increases the divisions of the smooth object
Page Down	Decreases the divisions of the smooth object

Editing the Body

Fleshing out the body involves splitting polygons and moving vertices into position. Splitting polys effectively involves judicious use of Maya's splitting and cutting tools and a working knowledge of how those split polys will be smoothed. Our goal is to create a model with as low a polygon count model as possible while still creating the detail necessary so that when smoothed at render time, the model will look good. Maya's smooth function is powerful, but it can be difficult to control.

Figure 3.19 illustrates how Maya's polySmoothProxy node works and provides a guide for how we will be modeling. Figure 3.19a shows that Maya smooths two polygons into eight and demonstrates that the act of subdividing polygons by a factor of 1 actually increases the polygon count by a power of 4. This is why judicious and careful use of the splitting, cutting, and subdividing toolsets is an important skill to master. Splitting the proxy object in the middle of the polygons tightens the bend somewhat in Figure 3.19b, but moving that edge down to the corner in Figure 3.19c tightens the bend in the smoothed object. Figure 3.19d through f illustrate how to tighten an edge to bring back the hard corners by splitting the polys near the edge. The closer the polygon edges on a proxy model, the tighter the corner or other detail on the smoothed model.

> Maya's polySmoothFace node (choose **Mesh → Smooth**) smooths in much the same way as Smooth Visually, but the point order of a polySmoothFace object will be different from that of a polySmoothProxy object. This is crucial if you are using deformers such as BlendShapes that rely on point order to work properly.

Figure 3.19

This Subdiv Proxy example illustrates how to control Maya's smooth function.

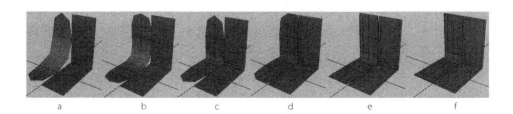

a   b   c   d   e   f

In editing Machismo's body, it is useful to try to do as much with the points you have to match the desired shape, and only when you have done all you can should you cut or split polygons. It is far too common for beginning modelers to subdivide the model too much at the outset and then have to contend with large numbers of points. We will subdivide/smooth the model once and move points into position. This box modeling technique works much like sculpting clay. We will work from large general shapes and model down to specific details. This is the essence of box modeling. Let's edit this model as follows.

1. RMB click the proxy object and choose Vertex. Select and pull the vertices to match the shape shown in Figure 3.20. While you are translating the vertices on the proxy object, you want to watch the smoothed object on the right. If the smoothed object is too rough at this stage, you can press the PageUp button to increase its density.

2. With the model selected in object mode, choose **Mesh → Smooth ❑.** Under the Exponential Controls section, uncheck all the properties under the Preserve label. Map Borders can be set to Smooth Internal.

3. Click Smooth. You should have something like Figure 3.21.

Figure 3.20

Moving the vertices at the start of editing. Notice how the vertices on the proxy object extend far outside the lines of the template while the smoothed object stays largely within the outline.

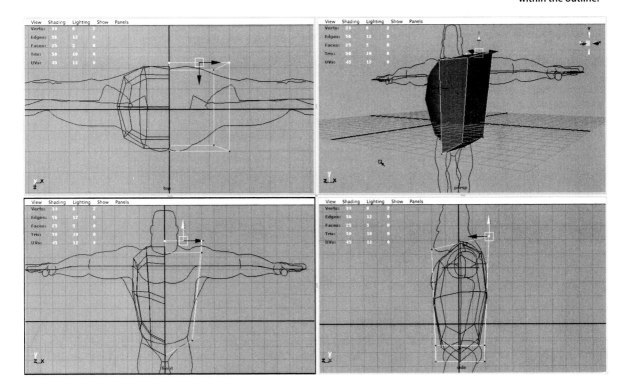

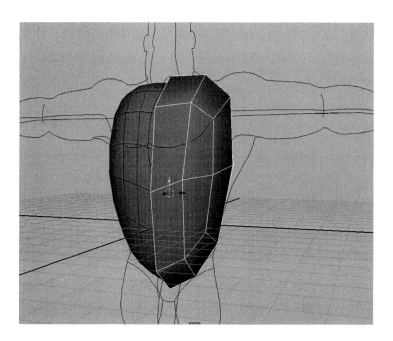

We will now edit the smoothed proxy object using Maya's Move Normal function along with "pick-walking" polygonal vertices using the keyboard's arrow keys. We'll edit this model as follows.

1. RMB click the proxy object and choose Vertex.

2. Hold down the W key and click a vertex to open the Move tool's marking menu. Select Normal. This feature is usually used with NURBS CVs. But when pulling individual vertices, it can be used to quickly move points either along the surface or outward along the vertex normal. This makes it useful for our purposes because many times when editing, it makes more sense to pull points once along the normal as opposed to pulling them in X, then Y, then Z.

3. Select the vertex shown in Figure 3.22. Note that the manipulator is oriented on the U, V, and N axes. This makes it useful for editing individual points as we can move the points more along the surface of the model.

4. With the top view active (MMB click in that window), press the Down arrow key. Note that the U and V axes flip. This shows why the Move tool set to Normal is effective only with single points: if you try to use this tool to move multiple points in U or V directions, they will move in unpredictable ways.

5. Pull the front three vertices outward along the normal until the smoothed object expands to match the template. Notice that when you pull the center line vertex, it does not pull parallel with the center line plane; it overlaps the smoothed object. This is generally undesirable. You may need to pull it back along the U axis until it lines back up.

6. Continue around the figure either using the arrow keys or simply clicking to select each vertex. Move vertices either along the normal or local axes (by using LM with the W key held down to switch between them) to model the figure to match what you see in Figure 3.23. Notice that we moved the points at the bottom of the proxy figure up. We will extrude the waist and legs later.

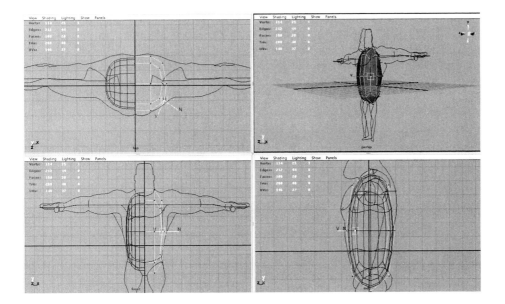

Figure 3.22

Choose the vertex in the front corner of the model. Then use the arrow keys to pick-walk around the model.

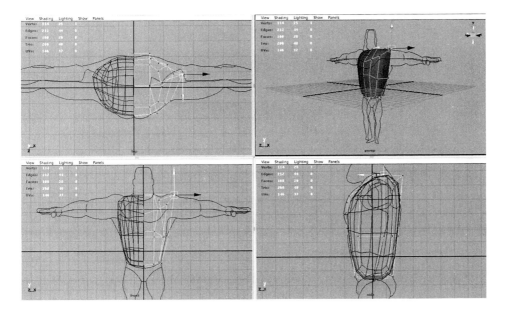

Figure 3.23

The model at this point

Splitting Polygons: It Ain't Splitting Hairs!

The general work flow for effective box modeling is to create a row of edges/vertices and move them into position. We will use several tools to create detail in this way. One tool, Cut Faces, we have already explored. Here we'll look at the Split Polygon tool and the Edge Loop tool. First, we will use the Split Polygon tool to create an edge loop along the chest, shoulder, and back.

1. RMB click the proxy object and choose Select from the pop-up menu. The Split Polygon tool will only work in object mode.

2. Choose **Edit Mesh → Split Polygon Tool** ❐. Set Divisions to 1 and uncheck Split Only From Edges and Use Snapping Points Along Edge. A division factor of more than 1 creates extra vertices along the new edge, which we don't want. Split Only From Edges won't let us split from the middle of a polygon. Later, we will want to change the direction of a line of edges and will want to place a point in the middle of a face and continue in a perpendicular direction. Use Snapping Points Along Edge places a user-specified set of snapping points along the edge where you click. We want to be able to place points wherever we want to along an edge. Snapping points prevent this.

3. In the perspective window, LM click and hold on the front edge of the proxy object as shown at left in Figure 3.24a. With the mouse button held down, you can move the green dot along that edge. Keep in mind that this dot represents where the new vertex will go on the model.

4. Release the mouse button to set the first point. Keep in mind that you can still move that point by MM clicking and dragging it along that edge. If you accidentally click again on the point with the left mouse button, you will be setting another cut point and will need to delete it by pressing the Backspace (Delete) key.

5. Click the next edge to set a point as shown in Figure 3.24b. Keep in mind that what we are doing here is creating a line of edges that will run along the bottom edge of the chest muscle, up around the outside edge of the shoulder muscle, and down toward the middle of the back.

Figure 3.24

The process for using the Split Polygon tool

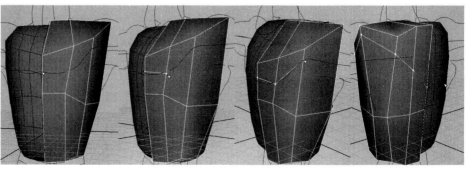

a   b   c   d

6. Continue up to the next point using the template as a guide, as shown in Figure 3.24c.

7. Continue the split as shown in Figure 3.24d.

8. Once a complete loop has been made, press Enter to make the cut.

9. RMB click the proxy object and choose Vertex. Using the Move tool, model the vertices of the upper torso to match what you see in Figure 3.25.

Next, we will want to place a vertical line of edges/vertices down the side of the model. We will want to place it in the center of all the edges that extend around and down the side of the proxy. We could use the Split Polygon tool to perform this operation, but a cool tool, Edge Loop, performs this task much faster. We will use the Edge Loop tool as follows.

1. Choose **Edit Mesh → Insert Edge Loop Tool**.

New to Maya 8.5, you can specify the number of edge loops to insert by choosing the **Multiple Edge Loops** attribute and a desired number of edge loops in the Insert Edge Loop tool's options.

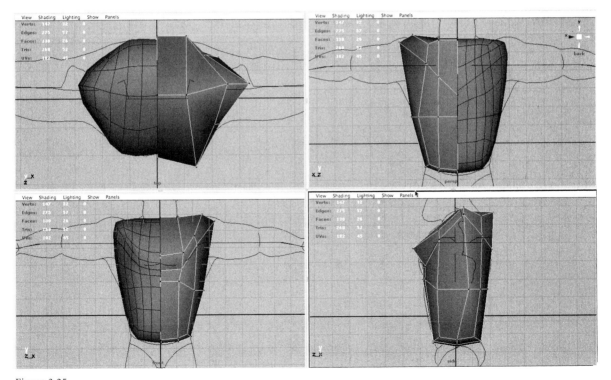

Figure 3.25

The proxy object so far. Note that the perspective window has been set to show the back of the model using the View Compass.

2. Click and hold the LMB along the edge shown at left in Figure 3.26. Don't let go of the mouse button just yet, but do drag the cursor along that edge. Note the dotted line that runs through the faces on either side of the edge as shown in the middle image of Figure 3.26. This is where the edge will be split.

3. Release the LMB to make the loop. If you release the mouse button and then realize that you want the split in a different place along the edge, you can either undo the split or go to the Inputs list in the Channel Box and find the polySplitRing$n$ node. Click the name to display a Weight field. Click the attribute name, and MM drag in the viewport to interactively change the location of the split.

4. After slicing through the model, it is essential that you move the points of the sliced edge as well as the points on either side of the sliced edge. This keeps your model from looking boxy. Fortunately, the Move Normal tool makes this quicker than moving vertices along their local axes. Round out the shoulder muscle as well as the rib cage and neck area. When finished, you should have something that resembles the image at left in Figure 3.27.

Let's do the same thing on the back of the model. Which tool you use is up to you: both the Split Polygon tool and the Edge Loop tool can do the job. The Cut Faces tool is probably not appropriate for this task because it cuts straight through an object, which will leave the vertices far from where they will need to be after editing. So use the Edge Loop or Split Polygon tool to create a line of edges like that depicted on the left in Figure 3.27. Then, move the points to match the final state on the right of the same figure.

Remember to watch the smooth object while you are editing the proxy. This will reveal how the final model will appear once it is smoothed for final rendering. Also remember that you will need to go back and edit previous points again. Adding detail in a local area changes the necessary positions of the vertices around your edits.

Figure 3.26

Using the Edge Loop tool to cut a line of edges down the front of the proxy

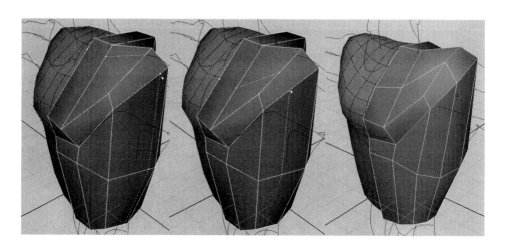

Let's view these new edits two at a time. This will speed up the process. We are working largely from the top of the model down now. We will complete the shoulders and chest area and work down from there. We will create two lines of edges beginning above and below the line defining the bottom of the chest and use them to help define the shoulder muscle and add detail in the back. The left two images in Figure 3.28 show the raw splits; the right two images show the model edited after the split. Because the split needs to begin tight to the line of the chest and then extend to the middle of the faces of the shoulder and back, we should use the Split Polygon tool for this operation.

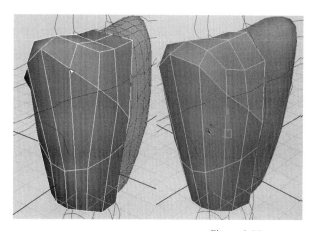

Figure 3.27

The back edges after cutting and editing. Notice how the vertices at the bottom of the torso have been rounded off.

> You can add additional edge loops on either side of an existing loop by using the Offset Edge tool. To use this tool, choose **Edit Mesh → Offset Edge Loop Tool**.

The Shoulder Saddle and Neck Hole

We need to refine the shoulder and collarbone area as well as create a hole for the neck where the head will fit onto the body. Let's use the Split Polygon tool to create two lines of edges around the upper torso. Currently, the front top of the shoulders is a straight, grid-like quad formation. We want a row of polygons that circles the neck like a collar. (In fact, you will use this row to create an actual shirt collar later.) We use the Split Polygon tool to change the flow of these polygons. Figure 3.29a and b show this process.

1. In the top view, begin by clicking the center line edge as shown in Figure 3.29 and then click the next edge down.

2. Click in the middle of the next face down. If we had left the Split Polygon tool set to use snapping points, we would not be able to do this.

Figure 3.28

The next series of edits should start above and below the line at the bottom of the chest.

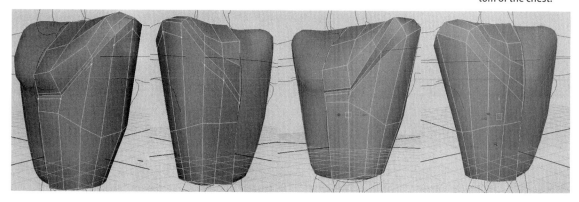

Figure 3.29

Creating the shoulder saddle line of edges. (a) Creating a ring of edges by changing direction in the middle of the faces in the bottom corners. (b) Making those bottom corner faces quads by splitting them from corner to corner.

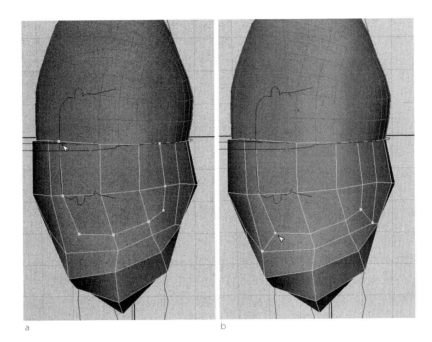

a   b

3. Click the edge perpendicular to the one from which you originally entered the face.

4. Continue across the bottom polygon, clicking each edge as you go. If you are ever unable to click the next edge, you set the previous point in the face instead of on the edge of the polygon.

5. Click in the middle of the next face over and then click the edge above.

6. Continue splitting vertically, and finish by clicking back on the center line edge in the back of the proxy, as shown in Figure 3.29a. Press Enter to make the cut.

7. You now have *n*-sided polygons where you cut across the faces at the bottom corners of your split. Use the Split Polygon tool to connect the corners of the faces you have created, as shown at right in Figure 3.29b.

8. As always, once you have created edges, you must pull the vertices into position to avoid a boxy-looking model.

Now let's create the hole for the neck.

1. Using the Split Polygon tool, create an oval line of edges inside the shape you just cut as shown at left in Figure 3.30a. Try to intersect where the edges or faces cross the template lines.

2. As in the previous set of steps, connect the corners of the faces to the outside corners you just created, as in Figure 3.30b. Notice what we've done: we have changed the direction of the edges from running perpendicular to one another to radiating outward from what will be the neck.

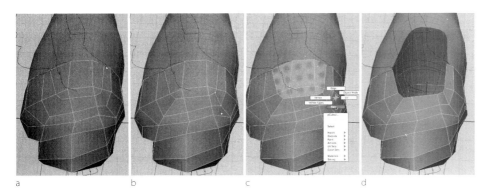

a   b   c   d

Figure 3.30

(a) Cut a line of edges inside the loop created in the previous exercise. (b) Split the bottom polys by splitting the corners. (c) Pick-mask Face and select the faces inside the loop you just cut. (d) Delete those faces.

3. RMB the proxy object and choose Face. Select all the faces inside the edges you just split, as shown in Figure 3.30c.

4. Delete the faces to create the neck hole as shown in Figure 3.30d.

Defining the Shoulder

Machismo is a bulky character, but even so, his shoulders will require a little more definition than he has now. So let's define the deltoid muscle area with an edge loop and introduce a useful command for polygon editing: Merge To Center. Up to now we have been working around the character horizontally, vertically up and down the torso, or radially out from the neck. We will now work independently of those directions. Create the loop as follows.

In the perspective view, select the Split Polygon tool and create a line of polygons around the shoulder area. Continue around the back of the character. The two images in Figure 3.31 illustrate this process.

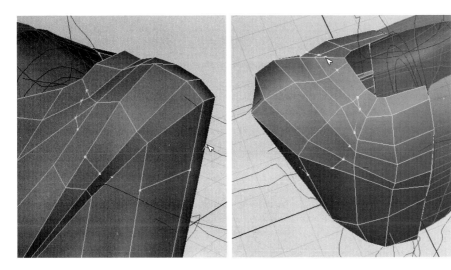

Figure 3.31

Creating the first line of edges for the shoulder

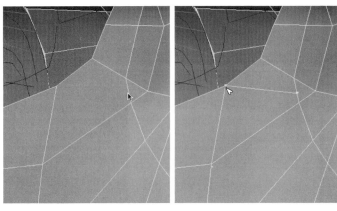

By crossing over the corners of quad polygons, we have created three- and five-sided polygons. We need to correct this for some, but not all, of these polygons. We can do this in two ways. The first is to split the five-sided polygon from the center of one of the triangular face's edges to the far corner of the five-sided poly. Figure 3.32 shows this splitting technique. This creates three quad-sided polygons. This technique is useful if you will need that detail later in the model.

Figure 3.32

Correcting the five-sided polygon by splitting it and the triangle into three quads

A more poly-count conservative way is to get rid of the triangle by collapsing its edge.

1. RMB click the proxy object and pick-mask Edge.

2. Select the edges at the base of the two triangular polygons in the front of the torso and the one triangle in back, as shown in the left column of images in Figure 3.33.

Figure 3.33

Selecting and collapsing the proper edges on the front (left column) and back (right column) of the torso

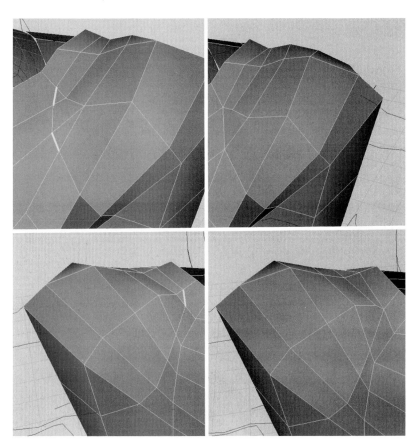

3. Choose **Edit Mesh → Merge To Center** to delete the triangles and change the five-sided polygons into four-sided polys. (See Figure 3.33 at right.) Merge To Center is also useful on faces where it works like a black hole that sucks all the bordering points to a single point in the middle of the collapsed face.

4. As always after creating new edges, edit the vertices to take advantage of the new detail you have added. Move the vertices near the neck area to roughly match the left image in Figure 3.34.

5. Split a line of edges inside those you have just created to match the middle image of Figure 3.34.

6. Edit the vertices to roughly match what you see at right in the small images of Figure 3.34.

7. Delete history on the proxy object, and you have defined the shoulder.

> You might wonder why we haven't corrected the triangles and the five-sided polygons on the side of the torso—we'll do so when we create the arm.

Subdivide the Stomach

Currently there is little detail to Machismo's stomach. If we are to animate him later, we should make sure we create new lines of edges to promote smooth deformation. We'll use the Edge Loop tool to do this,

1. Click one of the edges with the Insert Edge Loop tool. Move the cursor to where you want to insert the edge and press Enter. You should have something resembling the left image of Figure 3.35.

2. Edit the points in front and in back of the torso to begin to create the side bulge of the oblique muscles.

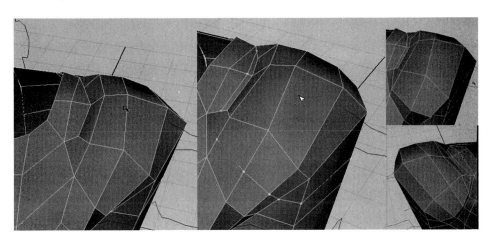

Figure 3.34

Defining the shoulder muscle with a second set of edges

3. Push points in to create the faintest bulge of abdominal muscles in the front and you should have something like the middle image in Figure 3.35.

4. Pull in the points in back to create more of a slope down to the waist, as shown at far left in Figure 3.35.

5. To duplicate edge loops through an offset, use the Offset Edge Loop tool. Choose **Edit Mesh → Offset Edge Loop Tool**.

6. LM click and hold on one of the horizontal edges you just created. You should see two dotted lines appear as shown at left in Figure 3.36. With the mouse button still held down, dragging left and right moves the dotted line closer to and farther from, respectively, the original edge. Place the cuts in the middle of their respective faces, and release the mouse button to make the split. Use this tool carefully because you can rapidly create more points than you can easily edit.

> You can pick-walk several rings or lines of vertices using the arrow keys to move up a model by pressing the direction arrows. This can be a big timesaver.

7. Edit the points as shown in the middle and right images of Figure 3.36.

Figure 3.35

Beginning the belly line using the Insert Edge Loop tool

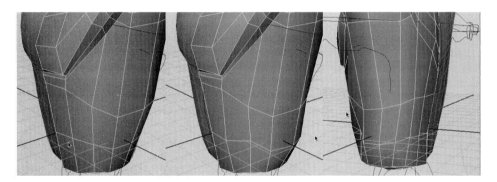

Figure 3.36

Fleshing out (pun intended) the oblique, stomach, and back area using the Offset Edge Loop tool

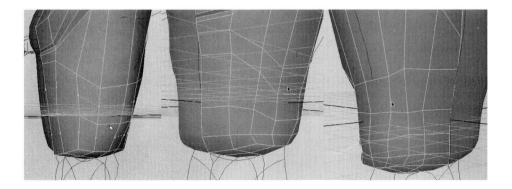

YOUR FRIEND: THE POLYGON COUNT HEADS UP DISPLAY

During this modeling exercise, you should work with Maya's Polygon Count Heads Up Display (HUD) visible because it gives you several important pieces of information. The following illustration shows the HUD active with the five rows of information.

The rows of information are fairly self-explanatory; they relate the number of vertices, polygonal faces, edges, triangles, and UVs. It is the columns of information, however, that are of interest here. The leftmost column shows the entire number of these items in the scene. The middle column shows the numbers for the currently selected object. The rightmost col-

umn will interest you the most while you are modeling. It shows the number of vertices, edges, faces, tris, and UVs in the current selection. So when you are in component mode, you need to keep an eye on this column, and the graphic shows why. It appears that three vertices have been selected by the marquee selection method of vertex selection. But the HUD clearly shows that four vertices are in the current selection. Clearly, a vertex is selected on the back of the model. Translating vertices at this point could be a disaster, so you would need to rotate the model, deselect the stray vertex, and make your edit. Some other uses for the HUD information are as follows:

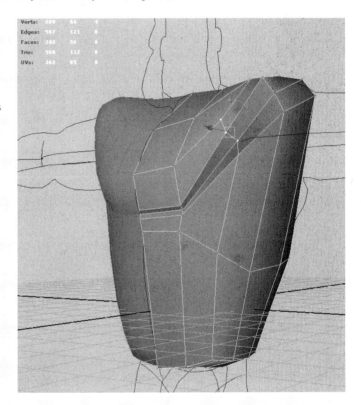

- Checking to make sure only the correct number of faces and edges are selected before extruding

- Ensuring that the correct number of vertices are merged when merging vertices along the edges of two objects

Extruding the Waist and Leg

Let's take a break from slicing and do some extruding on the waist. Extruding is a preferred tool for modelers since it always produces quads and can quickly add clean geometry to a defined area without terminating edge loops. Machismo's legs represent appendages with long areas of relatively smooth patches that will give us the opportunity to explore the Smooth function of the Sculpt Geometry tool. But first, let's extrude the waist.

1. RMB click the proxy object and pick Face.

2. Select the faces on the bottom of the torso as shown in Figure 3.37a.

3. Choose **Edit Mesh** and make sure the **Keep Faces Together** option is checked.

4. Choose **Edit Mesh → Extrude** and you will see something similar to Figure 3.37b. This shows the extrusion is active and is ready to be extended away from the body. The Extrude command defaults to using local space (indicated by the solid blue icon) to move the extrusion. Generally, this is undesirable as it often moves the faces out from the center of the extrusion. Clicking the World/Local Space toggle changes these axes to match the world space (now the icon is hollow) and makes moving, rotating, and scaling much easier.

5. Drag the extruded faces down until they are roughly in line with the crotch as shown in Figure 3.37c.

6. Notice how the smooth object appears distorted. This happens because the Extrude command extrudes all the faces, including the faces along the center line. To keep this area open and the smooth object undistorted, select the faces that are parallel with the center line and delete them. The waist should resemble Figure 3.37d.

7. Translate the points to begin to define the waist and buttocks area as shown in Figures 3.37e and f.

8. Delete history and save your model as Mach_Body01.mb.

Figure 3.37
Extruding and shaping the waist

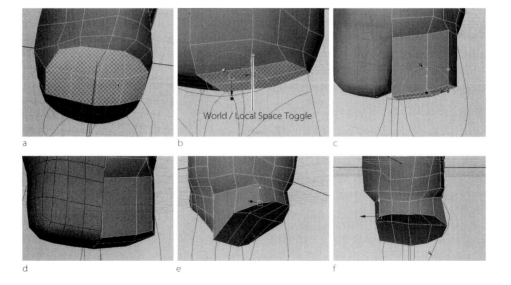

a b World / Local Space Toggle c

d e f

Before we can extrude the leg, we need to form the crotch and rear cleavage.

1. Using the Split Polygon tool, cut two lines of edges as shown in Figure 3.38a and d.

2. Edit the points to create a bulge in the groin area and a crease in the rear of the character, as shown in Figure 3.38b.

3. Slice a line of edges horizontally using the Insert Edge Loop tool and use that detail to round out the front and back of the figure as shown in Figure 3.38e and f. Leave the side of the waist relatively flat. Pull out points to give the "rear cleavage" some volume.

Let's move on to the leg.

1. Pick-mask Face on the proxy object.

2. Select the faces on the bottom of the torso as shown in Figure 3.39a.

3. Choose **Edit Mesh → Extrude** and immediately click the Local/World Space toggle to go to world space.

4. Translate the extrusion down until the manipulator handle is even with the bottom of the groin area as shown in Figure 3.39b.

5. Scale the extrusion down in Y until the extruded faces are flat, that is, parallel to the ZX plane as shown in Figure 3.39c. This will make it easier to contour the leg during further extrusions.

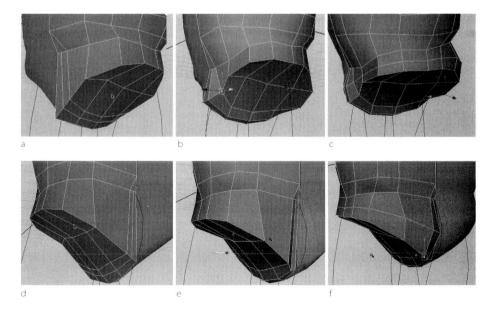

a b c

d e f

Figure 3.38

Creating detail in the groin and rear of Machismo

Figure 3.39

Starting the leg extrusion

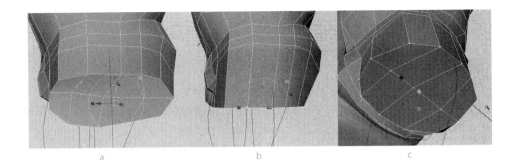

a   b   c

6. Translate, scale, and point edit to get the cross-section shape of the leg shown in Figure 3.39c.

7. Pick-mask Face again, and select the same polys you selected in step 2.

8. Choose **Edit Mesh → Extrude** and once again set the toggle to world space and translate the extrusion straight down until it matches the thickest part of the front of the knee.

9. Translate, scale, and point edit as needed until that section of the leg looks right.

10. Repeat steps 7 through 9, and work your way down the leg until you get something that looks like Figure 3.40.

Begin to make the foot using the Split Polygon tool and extruding as shown in Figure 3.41. This is not difficult: simply extrude in the same way as you did the leg, and scale and translate the vertices into the shape of the foot. Finish the foot as shown in Figure 3.42.

Figure 3.40

Extruding, translating, and scaling to make the leg

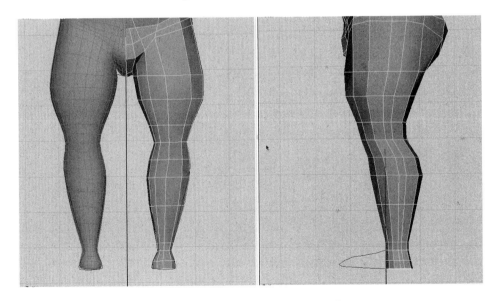

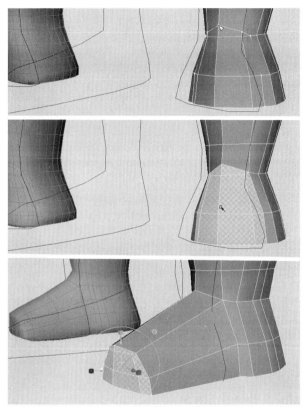

Figure 3.41

Cut faces all the way around the stump of the foot. Delete the 3/5 edges, and select the faces to extrude. Extrude the first half of the foot.

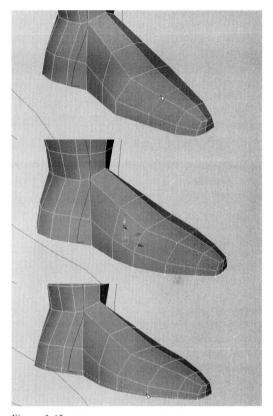

Figure 3.42

Extrude the tip, and pull the inner faces to more of a point. Use the Edge Loop tool to make two cuts around the foot. Scale and translate the cross-sections to their proper widths. Select all the vertices on the bottom of the foot and scale them flat. Use the Edge Loop tool to sharpen the bottom edge of the foot.

Finish the Knee

The knee joint rotates only on the X axis, but as the leg is currently constructed, it will not deform properly. The faces on the front of the knee will stretch unacceptably, and the faces on the back of the knee will crinkle unpleasantly. What we need to do is create room for the knee to bend by shrinking the faces on the front of the knee while expanding the faces on the back of the knee. We could do this by pulling points, but there is a better way. Let's edit the knee as follows.

1. In the side view, use the Cut Faces tool to slice diagonal rows of edges as shown at left in Figure 3.43.

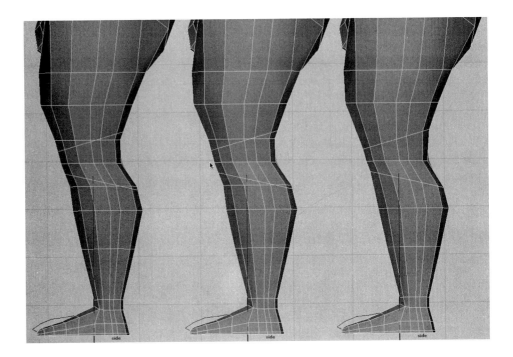

2. Choose one edge on the top and bottom horizontal edges, and then choose **Select →
   Select Contiguous Edges** to select the loop. If this doesn't work, select the edges manually as shown in the middle image of Figure 3.43.

3. Choose **Edit Mesh → Delete Edge/Vertex** to delete the selected edges, leaving no vertices behind. Pressing the Delete key would delete only the edges, leaving the vertices in place.

Create the dimple on the back of the knee and the kneecap using the Offset Edge Loop tool as follows.

1. Pick-mask Edge on the proxy object, and select the two edges on the back of the knee as shown at left in Figure 3.44.

2. Choose **Edit Mesh → Offset Edge Loop Tool** ❐. This tool lets you add localized detail in a model while maintaining an all-quad topology to the model. The Edge Offset is how far from the original selected edges the duplicated edges will be placed. The default, 0.5, places the duplicated edges in the middle of the faces surrounding the edges. We want them closer, so set this to 0.25.

3. Click Offset Edge to see the effect of this command. Figure 3.44 reveals just how useful this tool will be.

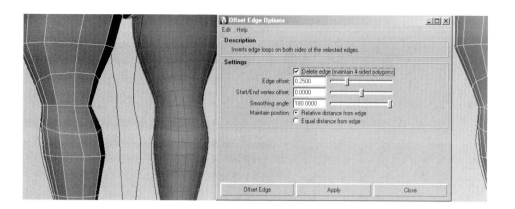

Figure 3.44

Using the Offset
Edge Loop tool to
create the dimple on
the back of the knee

4. As with many tools and commands in Maya, the best way to see how they work is to explore them through the Inputs list in the Channel Box. Click in the Inputs list, find the polyDuplicateEdge1 node, and click it. As you can see, this node's attribute list contains all the settings present in the tool's option box, as shown at right in Figure 3.44. Take a moment and play with the settings to see what they do. Simply click on the attribute name and MM drag left and right in the viewport to interactively change the settings. If you set the Delete Edge attribute to Off, you will see that the diamond shape polygons that the command creates to blend the duplicated edges into the surrounding topology are divided into triangles. One advantage the Inputs list has over the tool options is that you can use it to adjust the startVertexOffset and endVertexOffset attributes separately.

5. Translate the original edges inward to create a small indention in the back of the knee. Also, if you desire, feel free to move the duplicated edges around to better facilitate rigging and animation later.

6. Delete history on the model.

The kneecap serves two functions on this model. Visually, it provides a point of reference that points back to reality. Given that this model is stylized and Machismo has a huge upper body in relation to his legs, his leg structure should convince the viewer that it can support the large torso. A detailed kneecap helps make this argument. Geometrically, the kneecap provides detail that will let the knee expand when the leg is bent. When properly weighted, this will keep the front of the knee from collapsing. Let's create the kneecap as follows.

1. Pick-mask Edge on the proxy object, and select four edges on the front of the leg as shown at far left in Figure 3.45.

2. Choose **Edit Mesh → Offset Edge Loop Tool** to begin adding detail to the knee.

Figure 3.45

Creating the knee using the Offset Edge Loop tool. Note how the Scale tool is used to move points inward along the X axis.

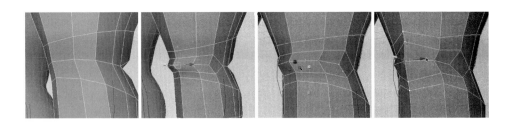

Figure 3.45

Creating the knee using the Offset Edge Loop tool. Note how the Scale tool is used to move points inward along the X axis.

3. Select the middle two edges and pull them out in Z, as shown at left in Figure 3.45.

4. Select the two points on either side of the knee, and move them into the knee along the X axis as shown at right in Figure 3.45.

5. Select two points above the line of edges you selected along the vertical center line and translate them up and out. Select two points along the vertical center line below the line of edges and translate them down and out. (See the far right in Figure 3.45.)

6. Delete history, and save your model as Mach_LegDone02.mb.

Building the Arm

We are going to explore a rather unorthodox use of Maya's surfacing tools to create the arm. We could extrude the arm from the body, but our surfacing method offers us the advantage of tailoring the torso topology to facilitate joining the arm to the body. Furthermore, we devoted a great deal of time to creating the curve template, and we can use this to our advantage here.

Figure 3.46

Select the curve points in the shoulders and wrist areas.

If you cannot find a menu item, be sure you are in the correct menu set. Curves are found in the Surfaces menu set.

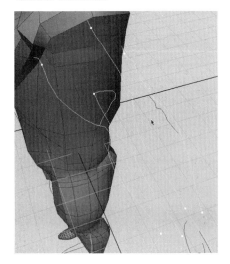

Let's loft the arm as follows.

1. Unreference the template layer by clicking the middle button in the Layer Editor. This allows us to edit the curves directly.

2. RMB click the top and front view curves, and choose Curve Point.

3. Shift+select points on each curve near to, but not right on top of, the torso as shown in Figure 3.46.

4. Shift+select points on each curve near the wrist as shown in Figure 3.46.

5. Choose **Edit Curves → Detach Curves** to separate the curves at the Curve Point locations. This gives us four curves from which to loft.

6. We must rebuild these curves because each has a different number of spans, which will create an ugly loft. Choose **Edit Curves → Rebuild Curve ☐**. Figure 3.47 shows the option box set with the proper values for our purposes. We will explore this command in depth as well as the Rebuild Surfaces feature in Chapter 4.

7. Reselect the curves in order front, top, back, and bottom. This is important in that selection order provides direction for the loft.

8. Choose **Surfaces → Loft ☐**. Figure 3.48 shows the proper options for how we want to make the loft, along with the final result.

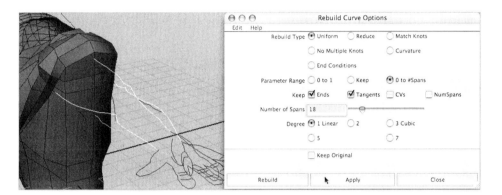

Figure 3.47

The proper settings for the Rebuild Curves option box

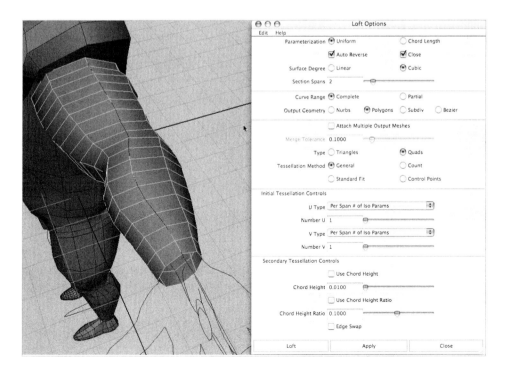

Figure 3.48

The loft settings with the polygonal loft they produce

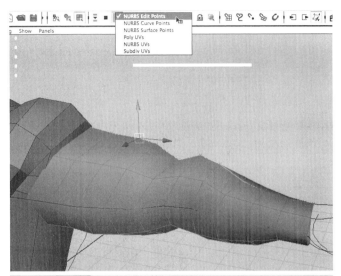

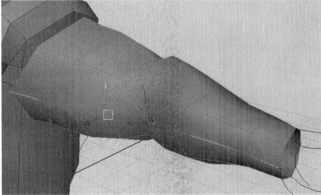

Figure 3.49

Editing the loft by editing the loft curve components. Try to line up the top and sides of the arm to make joining it to the body easier.

What we want to do now is fine-tune our loft. The rebuilding process has produced two undesirable results: it has moved some of the edit points out of position, and it has produced too dense a mesh over the surface of the arm. Let's correct the last problem first.

1. We need to select only the curves that we've lofted, but the polygonal object gets in the way, so uncheck Surfaces Selection Mask in the Status line above the view window.

2. Marquee select all four curves, and choose Edit Curves → Rebuild Curve ❑.

3. Enter 10 in the Number Of Spans field and click Rebuild. This decreases the density of the mesh. Notice that the size of the polygons is similar to the size of the polygons in the body.

4. To correct the edit points problem, click the Select By Component Type button in the Status line.

5. In the Selection Mask section, RMB click the second button from the left, which is the Select Param Points. Choose NURBS Edit Points from the pop-up list, and you are ready to edit points, as shown in the upper image of Figure 3.49.

6. Translate the edit points of each curve until you get something resembling the lower image in Figure 3.49.

7. Press F8 to enter object selection mode, and check Surfaces Selection Mask.

8. Be sure you have completed all editing, select the arm geometry, and then delete history.

Joining the Arm to the Body

We will now join the arm to the body using the Combine command coupled with the Append To Polygon tool. Join the arm to the body as follows.

1. Assign the arm geometry to a separate layer and unshade it by choosing **Layers → Set Selected Layers → Unshaded**.

You can set individual layers to shaded or unshaded (wireframe) view, textured or untextured, and you can also play back each layer from the Set Selected Layers submenu.

2. Use the Split Polygon tool to split an edge in the torso as shown in Figure 3.50a. This corrects two *n*-sided polygons on the side of the torso.

3. Select the faces as shown in the middle two images in Figure 3.50 (b and c). Don't select the last line of polys extending down from the triangle; we can use that triangle to add detail to the back of the shoulder.

4. Delete those faces to create the hole for the arm as shown in Figure 3.50d.

5. Delete history on the torso.

6. We need to make sure the polygons of the torso and the arm are facing in the same direction. If they are different, we won't be able to connect them by using the Append To Polygon tool. Shift+select the arm to add to the selection list.

7. Choose **Display → Polygons → Face Normals**. You will probably see the face normals facing outward on the torso but inward on the arm.

8. Select the arm only, and choose **Normals → Reverse** to flip the face normals for the arm. Figure 3.51 shows the before and after of this operation.

9. Shift+select the torso, and delete history on both objects.

10. Create one object by choosing **Mesh → Combine**. Note that when you do so, the smooth object no longer updates. You can delete the smooth object and choose **Proxy → Subdiv Proxy** to get the smooth reference back.

11. Choose **Edit Mesh → Append To Polygon Tool** ❑, and make sure that Keep New Faces Planar is unchecked.

12. Click an edge of the armhole as shown in Figure 3.52a.

Figure 3.50

(a) Split an edge in the torso. (b) Select the faces to be deleted. (c) Don't select the faces extending down from the triangle on the back. (d) Delete the faces.

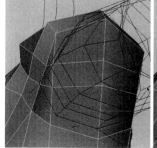
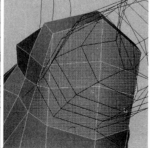
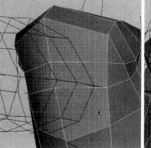

a b c d

Figure 3.51

Reversing the normals on the arm. Note how the torso normals are facing outward.

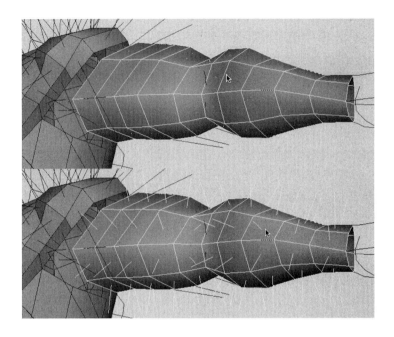

Figure 3.52

Joining the arm to the torso using the Append To Polygon tool. Create the five-sided poly by clicking the edges in order.

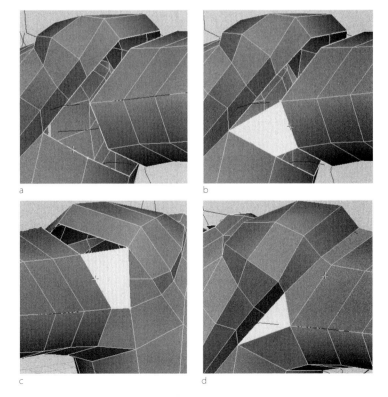

a

b

c

d

13. Click the opposite edge on the arm as shown in Figure 3.52b. A pink polygon appears, indicating that the polygon is ready to be created. If you are not happy with it, press Delete and choose another edge. If you are happy, press Enter and the polygon will connect the torso and arm. Take a look at the smooth object to see the effect.

14. Continue around the object, creating polygons to connect the two parts, as shown in Figure 3.52c. To create the five-sided polygon in the back, click the edges in the indicated order.

15. Finish in the front as shown in Figure 3.52d.

16. Merge To Center the fifth edge of the five-sided polygon in back by selecting the edge and choosing **Edit Mesh → Merge To Center**. Edit the vertices to smooth out the shoulder.

17. Select the torso, delete history, and save as `Mach_ArmDone03.mb`.

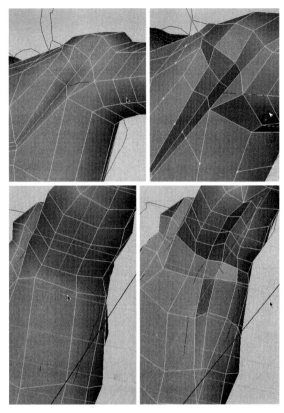

Figure 3.53

Detailing the underarm

Finishing the Body

All the major parts of the body have been defined in our efforts so far. All that is really left is to define details such as the underarm, tricep/elbow, bicep, and chest areas. Figures 3.53 through 3.56 describe this process.

1. Cut a line across the chest and around the rib cage. Then create an indention running vertically down the body from the underside of the bicep to the middle of the back of the rib cage where the latissimus dorsi muscle inserts into the back (Figure 3.53).

2. The tricep/elbow region involves splitting an area for the elbow and then using the Offset Edge Loop Tool to add detail at the elbow (Figure 3.54).

3. The bicep can be as complex or as simple as you want. Figure 3.55 shows diagonal splits connected to define the end of the bicep. Try to eliminate any triangles either by collapsing or connecting to the neck hole or wrist.

4. The chest area (Figure 3.56) is actually quite complex. We want to create definition where the chest muscle connects to the rib cage. To do this, we connect the edges of the groin area to the neck hole. Manipulate vertices to define the lower inside corner of the chest muscle. Split a line of vertices across the chest muscle and around the back to help define the rib cage area. Last, add detail around the trunk, but pull the vertices up to help define the front of the rib cage. This also will provide some room for those faces to contract when Machismo bends at the waist during animation.

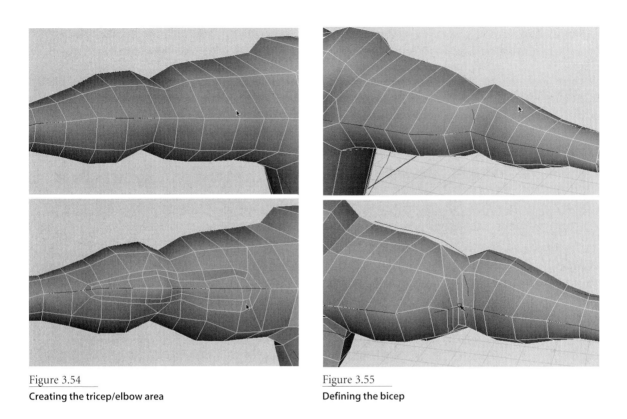

Figure 3.54

Creating the tricep/elbow area

Figure 3.55

Defining the bicep

Figure 3.56

Defining the inside of the chest and the rib cage area

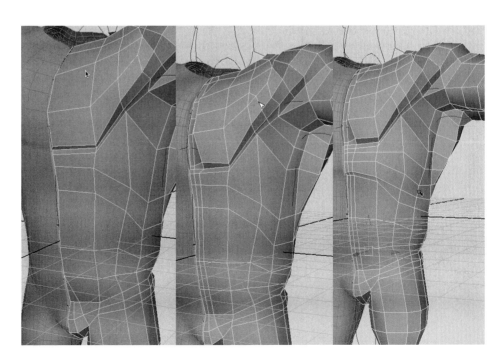

But What about the Hand?

Given that there are so many hands-on tutorials available in books or on the Web, detailing the actual building of a hand would take up unnecessary space in this book. What we will do instead is import the HandGeo.mb file from the CD and explore joining the hand to the arm using the Merge Edge tool. Import the hand and prepare it for joining as follows.

1. Choose **File → Import** ❏. Uncheck Group and Preserve References, and then click Import. Select HandGeo.mb and import it. You should now see a hand appear in the general area of the end of the arm. If it does not, move and scale it into position.

2. Check to see if the polygons of the hand and arm are facing outward by selecting both objects and choosing **Display → Polygons → Face Normals**. If they are not, reverse the normals on the hand by selecting the hand only and choosing **Normals → Reverse**.

3. Choose **Mesh → Combine** to merge the two objects.

4. Choose **Edit Mesh → Merge Edge Tool** ❏. This will cause merged edges to snap together.

5. Click an arm edge as shown at left in Figure 3.57.

6. Click a corresponding wrist edge as shown in the middle of Figure 3.57.

7. Click a third time on either edge to merge edges as shown at right in Figure 3.57.

8. Continue around the wrist until all the edges are merged.

The Sculpt Geometry tool, which has been updated for version 8.5, allows you to mold the shape of a mesh object by using a 3D paintbrush. There are five operations on this tool: Push, Pull, Smooth, Relax, and Erase.

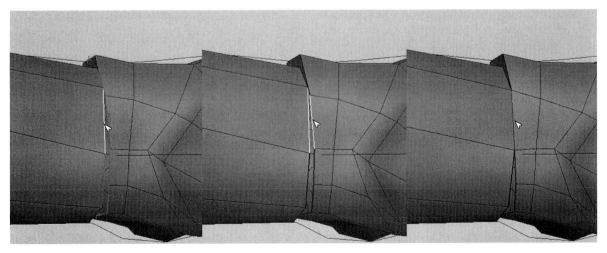

Figure 3.57

Using the Merge Edge tool

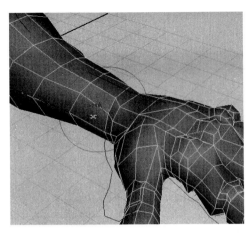

Figure 3.58

Changing the size of the Sculpt Geometry tool brush by holding down the B key and LM dragging in the view port

The Push operation will push vertices inward on a selected mesh, while the Pull operation pulls vertices outward. The Smooth operation will cause vertices to move to new positions influenced by their neighboring vertices. Sharp edges on a model can be smoothed out as long as there are enough vertices to work with.

A new operation for Maya 8.5 is Relax. Relax is similar to Smooth, but it tries to retain the original shape of the object when moving the vertices. The Erase operation erases the effects of the previous four operations.

Now, let's use the Sculpt Geometry tool to smooth out the distortions in the wrist and thicken the forearm.

1. With the body selected, choose **Mesh → Sculpt Geometry Tool ❑**. Under Sculpt Parameters, set Operation to Smooth and set Max. Displacement to about 0.0442. This will help correct the distortion caused by joining the two geometries.

2. The size of the brush will be too large, so hold down the B key and LM drag to the left to make the brush smaller (see Figure 3.58).

3. Lightly touch around the wrist to smooth out the vertices. It is easy to overdo it, so keep it simple.

4. Edit vertices using the Move tool set to Normal to bring back any volume you might lose through smoothing with the Sculpt Geometry tool.

Clean Up!

We have several operations to perform before we can call this model finished. They are what separates a well-built model from a well-built model that others in the pipeline can easily use. Let's finish the model as follows.

1. Select and delete the useless smooth object.

2. Select and name the proxy object. Call it BodyGeo.

3. Choose **Edit → Select All By Type → NURBS Curves**, and delete them.

4. In a last effort to stamp out *n*-sided polygons, pick-mask Face on the model and choose **Select → Select Using Constraints**. This powerful command selects all topologies in any model. Figure 3.59 shows how to set the selection constraints to select *n*-sided polygons; match your dialog window to that in Figure 3.59. Under Constrain, click the All And Next radio button. Immediately look at the HUD. If the right column under Faces reads 0, you have been diligent in your modeling habits and need do no more. If it reads a number greater than 0, you will need to find those *n*-sided polys and get rid of them using the techniques discussed earlier.

5. When polygons are split or new polygons are created, they appear faceted or flat shaded. To smooth the shading across these polygons, select BodyGeo and choose **Normals → Soften Edge**. The edges in the entire model should now be softened.

6. Delete unused layers.

7. In the Outliner, select and delete any unused groups.

8. Choose **Mesh → Cleanup**. This box can help you clean geometry that may have escaped your notice when working on a model. This is a powerful command, but as with all automatic functions in Maya, you must watch it carefully to make sure it does not delete things you might need later. For example, under Fix By Tessellation is an option to tessellate (triangulate) all four-sided faces. Running this command with Select And Cleanup Operation selected will make all the quad geometry in your scene triangular. This is not desirable. As always, if you are unsure about a particular option, check the Help menu for information.

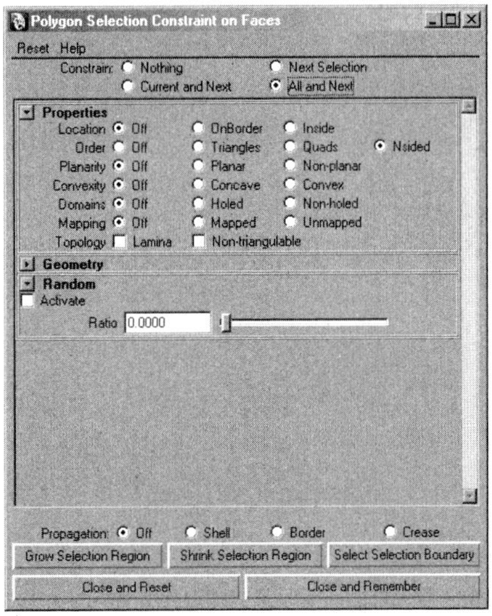

Figure 3.59

The Polygon Selection Constraint On Faces option box set to select all the *n*-**sided polygons in your model. Click All And Next to make the selection.**

9. Since we have been working with the Subdiv Proxy command, it is probably a good idea to choose **File → Optimize Scene Size** ❏. This command will delete any unused nodes in your scene. Sometimes in the course of working in Maya, nodes get disconnected from each other. They stay in the scene but do not affect any geometry, animation, or texture maps. This increases scene size unnecessarily and slows down Maya. Running this command will help lighten the file.

10. Delete history, and freeze transformation on the geometry.

11. Save as Mach04_BodyFin.mb.

Summary

Although it is the oldest of modeling paradigms, polygonal modeling in Maya offers an extremely powerful and flexible toolset. In this chapter, you learned how to manipulate and sculpt using both box and extrusion modeling techniques, taking a simple cube and developing it into a muscularly organic body type using many of Maya's most powerful modeling tools.

In Chapter 5, you will learn to build the head using the polygon-by-polygon technique in preparation for using subdivision surfaces. In the rigging chapters, you will create a rig for the model, and in the texturing chapter, you will create UV and texture maps for this character. But in the next chapter on NURBS modeling, we will create a vehicle for Machismo: the Mighty MaGizmo!

CHAPTER 4

NURBS Modeling

NURBS (Non-Uniform Rational B-Splines) used to be the paradigm of choice
for organic character modeling, but more powerful computers, subdivision surfaces, and
other technological advances have breathed new life into organic polygon-based models.
Buildings, spaceships, and other inorganic surfaces are now mostly built in NURBS. In
this spirit, we will build our own craft in this sophisticated paradigm. Unlike polygons,
however, NURBS require a grasp of some basic concepts before you can effectively work
with them. Maya hides most of the hard math involved with using splines, but some basic
knowledge will enhance your explorations here. After you read this chapter, you'll understand how NURBS work and how you can quickly model with them.

- **Curves**

- **Parameterization**

- **NURBS surfaces**

- **Modeling the MacGizmo**

Understanding NURBS

If polygons represent a sculptural approach to 3D modeling, NURBS modeling is analogous to a manufacturing process. Whereas polys are carved, extruded, merged, and shaped, NURBS are bent, welded, attached, and rebuilt in a process that is more akin to an assembly line. Whereas polygons relate directly to marble or clay sculptural processes, NURBS relate to using welded sheets of steel as the sculptural medium. It is no coincidence that the existence of NURBS and all spline-based technology stems from car manufacturing. Indeed, NURBS, by virtue of their inherent mathematical precision, are the paradigm of choice for most CAD/CAM (computer-assisted design/computer-aided manufacturing) software.

As you know, all 3D computer software provides a visual reference for some heavy-duty mathematics taking place in the software code as it runs. You don't have to type in math formulas to make a curve; Maya does the math for you. You simply manipulate control vertices (CVs), edit points (EPs), and hulls; Maya draws the curves. It is here we'll start.

Curves

Working with curves is the key to working effectively with NURBS surfaces because so many surfacing tools such as Loft, Boundary, Revolve, and Square build surfaces from curves. Figure 4.1 shows the anatomy of Degree 1 Linear, Degree 2, and Degree 3 Cubic curves. We will most often work with first- and third-degree curves, but looking at the second-degree curve as a point of contrast helps this discussion. The middle and left curves were duplicated from the cubic (third-degree) curve at right. They were then rebuilt into second- and first-degree curves respectively using the Keep CVs option checked to minimize distortion in the final product.

> If you have not done so, read the section in Chapter 3 on creating a linear NURBS template ("Linear NURBS Curves: The Polygonal Modeler's Best Friend"). It deals with the basics of drawing using first-degree, or linear, NURBS. We will expand on this information later in the chapter.

NURBS CURVES: A QUICK PRIMER

NURBS curves are a modeling topology consisting of edit points (or knots), spans, control vertices (CVs), and hulls. EPs/knots mark the coordinates in space through which the curve flows. Spans are the lengths of the curves between each EP. CVs control the degree and intensity of the curve between each EP. Hulls are lines that connect the CVs and provide a quick way of selecting the entire curve's shape node. Every curve has a direction marked by a first, hollow CV.

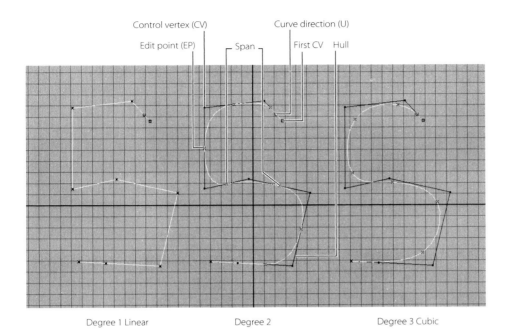

Control vertex (CV)

Edit point (EP)

Span

Curve direction (U)

First CV   Hull

Degree 1 Linear   Degree 2   Degree 3 Cubic

Figure 4.1

The anatomy of first-, second-, and third-degree NURBS curves

The linear curve has nine spans, and the second-degree curve has eight spans, but the original cubic curve has seven spans. This is the trade-off with these three curves: higher-degree curves are smoother with fewer spans. All three curves have the same number of CVs, which means that higher-degree curves have more CVs for fewer spans. Thus, more control is available on higher-degree curves. But to get small details—that is, sharp changes of direction—you'll have to add more spans and therefore more CVs. Let's look at how much control each CV has.

1. Open ThreeCurves.mb from the CD.

2. Choose **Window → Settings/Preferences → Preferences** to open the Preferences option box, and in the Display Category, make sure that Region Of Effect is set to On.

3. In the Status line, make sure Select By Component Type is selected as well as Points, Parm Points, and Hulls, as shown at the top of Figure 4.2.

4. Shift+select each line to open component selections for each.

5. Shift+select each point as illustrated in Figure 4.2.

The white highlighted part of the line shows how much of that line will be affected by the selected CV and is called the region of effect. Each linear curve CV affects only two spans; each CV affects three spans on a second-degree curve. And each CV affects four spans on a cubic curve. This can make third-degree curves somewhat difficult to control because moving one CV warps a larger part of the curve.

Figure 4.2

Illustrating the region of effect for each degree curve. The number of spans affected by moving a CV increases as the degree of the curve increases.

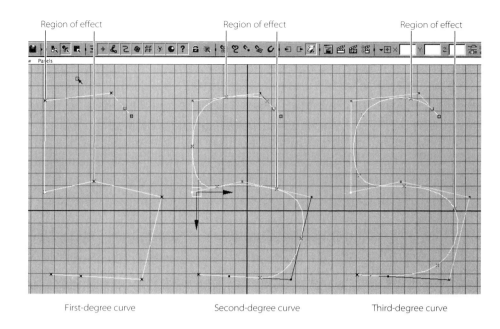

First-degree curve   Second-degree curve   Third-degree curve

So far, so good. From our explorations up to now, you might think second-degree curves offer the best balance between spans and control of the three curves. This is unfortunately not the case, as we will now illustrate.

1. Uncheck the Select By Points button in the Status line to hide the CVs, leaving the edit points and hulls visible.

2. Select and move an EP on the linear curve, making sure your Move Tool option is not set to Normal. You see that the line moves predictably.

3. Now move an EP on the second-degree curve. The whole line distorts horribly. Later, when we create surfaces, we will translate EPs on the curves we use to create the surface. If we use second-degree curves for surface creation, the whole surface will warp as nastily as this line does.

4. Select and translate an EP on the cubic curve and notice that the curve does distort somewhat, but not unacceptably.

Because of the distortion that occurs with second-degree curves, our methodology for working with curves will be to draw them using linear curves first and then rebuild them to cubic curves to create surfaces.

Parameterization

In its simplest form, parameterization refers to where EPs lie on a curve or a surface. Both curves and surfaces require proper parameterization to work effectively, and most problems that artists have working with NURBS can be linked at some point to improper parameterization. Proper parameterization is important when working with curves because it facilitates surface construction when a surface is revolved, lofted, or squared. Beginning with properly parameterized curves will result in well-built surfaces.

Although parameterization itself is difficult to define and understand without lengthy explanations of parametric equations and other forms of math, proper parameterization is fairly easy to explain. Proper parameterization for modeling means making sure each EP on a curve is represented by a whole number (*x*.0) instead of a decimal number (*x.xxx*). In the course of modeling with NURBS curves and surfaces, you will insert knots or isoparms along curves or surfaces. They will be created in between whole-numbered knots or isoparms. These curves and surfaces will need to be rebuilt so that they lie on whole numbers. Let's illustrate this concept using the ThreeCurves.mb file again.

1. If you don't already have the Help line displayed, choose **Display → UI Elements → Help Line**. The Help line will give us feedback on our curves parameterization.

2. Choose Select By Component Type, and make sure that all the NURBS components— edit points, CVs, curve points, and hulls—are displayed.

3. Select the cubic curve at the right to display its components using the Select tool. The following step will not work if you use the Move tool.

4. LM click, and hold and drag anywhere along the right line. You should see a yellow dot appear at the point you clicked. If you drag along the curve with your mouse button pressed, the dot or curve point will be red. Without releasing the mouse, look down at the Help line. It will read Curve Parameter 2.251 or something similar, as seen in Figure 4.3. In this case, this means that we are about one quarter of the way between the third (2.0) and fourth (3.0) EPs. (Remember that the numbering system starts at zero.)

5. Now let's disrupt this evenly parameterized curve by adding a knot (EP) at the current location. Choose **Edit Curves → Insert Knot ❑**. Insert Location determines where the knot will be inserted. At Selection creates the knot at the chosen curve point. Between Selections creates a knot in between two selected components. Multiplicity sets the number of knots to insert. For now, set Multiplicity to Increase By, and set the Multiplicity field to 1. Click Insert.

> You can select anywhere on a line by using the Select tool along with a surface point coordinate in the Command line. To select a particular surface point, type **select <curvename>.u[x.xxx]**. To select a particular EP, type **select <curvename>.ep[x]**. And to select a particular CV, type **select <curvename>.cv[x]**. To select a range of any components, simply place a colon between the values. For example, to select a range of EPs, type **select <curvename>.ep[0:3]**. Edit points 0, 1, 2, and 3 will be selected.

6. We have now created a knot at u[2.251] and therefore have a curve that is out of parameterization. To illustrate this, RMB click the line and choose Select from the marking menu.

7. Open the Attribute Editor (press Ctrl+A) and see that the Min Max Value of the line reads 0.000 and 7.000 and that the number of spans reads 8. To be properly parameterized, the Max value should always equal the number of spans, and the Min value should equal 0. We must rebuild this curve.

8. To see this operation in action, with the curve still selected, choose **Display → NURBS** and show edit points, CVs, and hulls.

Figure 4.3

Surface parameterization illustrated. The parameter reads whole numbers at the EPs, and the numbering begins at the first CV.

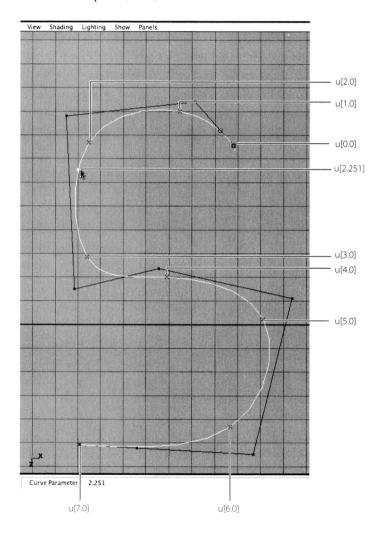

9. Choose **Edit Curves** → **Rebuild Curve** ❐ to open the Rebuild Curve option box (see Figure 4.4). Rebuilding a curve tends to distribute knots (EPs) more evenly along the curve and tends to change its shape; we want to minimize this. To do so, set Rebuild Type to Uniform. Set Parameter Range to 0 To #Spans. This will set the Min Max Value to equal the number of spans. Set Keep to CVs, which will minimize the distortion that comes with rebuilding.

10. Click Rebuild to make the change. Notice that the EPs changed location but the CVs stayed in place. Now pick-mask Curve Point and select along the line near the EPs you created. The EPs are now on whole numbers, which indicates a properly parameterized line.

11. With the line selected, open the Attribute Editor. The maximum value of the Min Max Value should equal the Spans value.

NURBS Surfaces

NURBS curves are visual representations of parametric equations. NURBS surfaces extend those equations into a second dimension and add shading to the mix. Curves are parameterized in the U direction, and surfaces add the V direction. Therefore, NURBS surfaces are said to have a U and a V direction. UVs define points along a specific surface; they are Maya's way of mapping 2D coordinates to a 3D surface.

NURBS surfaces are *tessellated* at render time. This means that when you render a NURBS surface, Maya converts it to polygons. NURBS surfaces were originally conceived as stand-ins for large polygonal datasets. They were much more efficient because you could manipulate a surface using simpler controls and have the patches tessellate to completely smooth shapes at rendering time. In effect, you could manipulate huge numbers of polygons with a few control points.

Figure 4.4

Before and after rebuilding curves. Note how the EPs shift position.

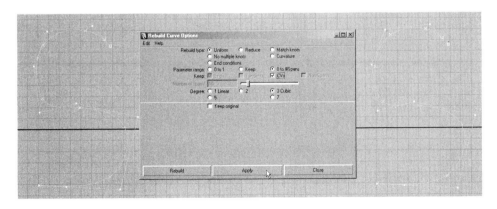

Figure 4.5

A NURBS sphere is really only a rectangular patch that has been automatically formed and closed by choosing Create → NURBS Primitive → Sphere.

All NURBS surfaces and shapes are composed of one or more four-sided *patches*. Figure 4.5 shows how even a NURBS sphere breaks down into a rectangular patch. There is no actual way of changing this; when modeling with NURBS you must create and manipulate four-sided patches. As you will see, there are various quite powerful tricks and techniques for working around this limitation, but it exists nonetheless.

Each NURBS surface is composed of one or more patches. Each patch is formed by the intersection of two *spans* that are demarked by lines called *isoparms*. These isoparms are the 3D equivalent of knots, or EPs, on a curve. Unlike EPs, however, they cannot be moved in 3D space. You can and will insert new isoparms during the course of modeling.

Inserting isoparms increases the number of CVs available to manipulate the surface of the shape. This fact reveals a disadvantage of NURBS surfaces: it is impossible to manipulate the actual surface of a NURBS shape directly. The only way to edit a shape is to manipulate a CV or group of CVs. Maya offers another topology called hulls to make selecting rows or rings of CVs automatic.

The best way to learn to use NURBS surfaces is to build something using this type of surface.

Modeling the MacGizmo

Figure 4.6 shows the schematic drawing of the MacGizmo, a vertical takeoff and landing (VTOL) craft used by Machismo to travel between his various exploits. It contains front, side, and top/bottom views as well as details such as the drive wheel, front wheel, and engine. Many of these details have dotted lines running through them. These are center lines running through the shapes of the drawing. These center lines can be tremendously important timesavers when modeling in that they provide an axis around which we will be revolving/lathing forms to construct these details. So without further exposition, let's begin.

For our purposes, this schematic drawing is a guide. Although we will use this drawing to trace curves for generating surfaces, you will see throughout this chapter that our curves and surfaces don't always match up perfectly. Although a greater degree of precision is needed for CAD/CAM operations, our purposes are geared toward learning Maya's NURBS modeling toolset. We can adapt to any inconsistencies we may create.

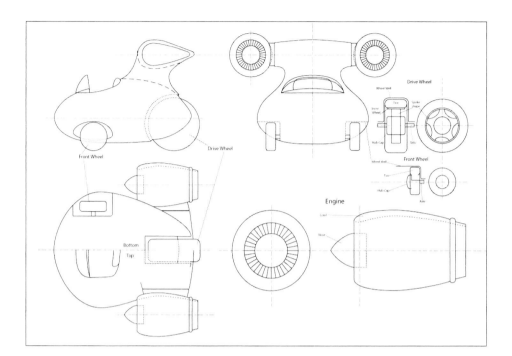

Figure 4.6

The schematic drawing of the MacGizmo

The Front Wheel

We'll begin with the simplest forms in the model and progress to more involved shapes. Let's use the Revolve tool to create the front wheels and the front wheel wells.

1. Open `MacGizmoStart.mb` from the CD. This file contains a single polygon plane mapped with the schematic drawing. We will use it as a template drawing to create the Mac-Gizmo. The drawing is placed so that the world origin is at the center line of the front wheel, with the X axis aligned with the center line or axis of revolution of the wheel. This will help us use the Revolve tool more efficiently.

2. Choose **Create → EP Curve Tool** ❏ to open the Tool's option box and set Curve Degree to draw a linear (first-degree) EP curve.

3. Go to the top view and trace the hubcap/axle curve as shown at the top of Figure 4.7. Be sure to use at least three points to define any sharp transitions in the curve. We have displayed EPs here for clarity.

4. Choose **Edit Curves → Rebuild Curve** ❏ to open the Rebuild Curve option box. Check Keep CVs and set Degree to 3 Cubic as shown in the middle of Figure 4.7. Click Rebuild to rebuild the curve as the cubic curve shown at the bottom of Figure 4.7. Notice that this operation softens the corner edges of the hubcap and axle.

5. Pick-mask Control Vertex on the rebuilt curve.

6. To sharpen the corners, snap the two CVs on either side of the corner CV to the corner CV by clicking the Move tool and holding down the V key. This "snap to point" option works on CVs and EPs as well as vertices (see Figure 4.8). To straighten and sharpen the edge of the front of the hubcap, move only one CV.

Figure 4.7

Changing the degree of a curve tends to soften sharp edges.

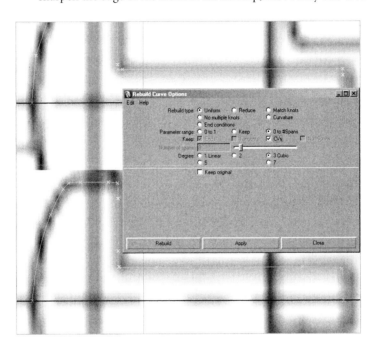

Figure 4.8

Sharpen the corners on the curve by snapping CVs to the corner CV. (The DrawingLyr is hidden for clarity.)

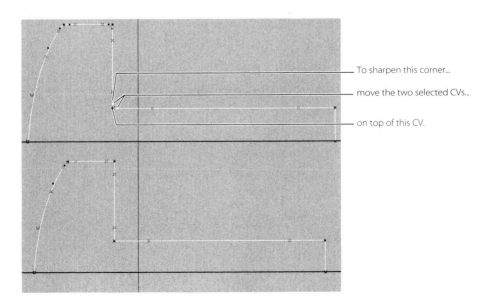

To sharpen this corner...

move the two selected CVs...

on top of this CV.

MAKING CUSTOM SHELF BUTTONS

We will be using the Rebuild Curve option box often, but opening it through the menu or hotbox is time-consuming, so let's make a shelf button to open the option box in one click.

1. Make sure the Curves shelf is in the forefront. This is where our new buttons will be created.

2. Hold down the Shift and Ctrl keys and choose **Edit Curves → Rebuild Curve ❑**. You will not see the option box, but you will see a new button on the shelf. It will look like the Rebuild Curve button farther over to the left. Click this new button to open the option box.

3. If you want to more precisely edit your custom shelves, open the Shelf Editor by clicking the black arrow icon to the left of the shelf and choose Shelf Editor or choose **Window → Settings/Preferences → Shelf Editor**. In the Shelf Editor, you can rearrange your shelf elements, choose new icons for them, edit the MEL command that drives them, and create new shelves.

We will also be using the Rebuild Curve command to make linear curves into cubic curves quite often over the course of this chapter, so it would be wise to automate this process. We will create a shelf button as our automatic solution.

1. Choose **Window → General Editors → Script Editor** to open the Script Editor.

2. In the bottom pane of the Script Editor, type the following code exactly as it appears here:

    ```
    rebuildCurve -ch 1 -rpo 1 -rt 0 -end 1 -kr 2 -kcp 1 -kep 1 -kt 1 -s 8 -d 3
    -tol 0.01;
    ```

    If you scroll up through the History pane of the Script Editor, you will see a line that reads exactly like this, except with curve1 listed after tol 0.01. This tells us that the Rebuild Curve command has been applied to that particular curve. If your typing skills are suspect, you can simply drag select that line of code, MM drag it to the input line (Option drag on the Mac), and delete the name of the curve (but keep the semicolon).

3. LM+drag+select the entire line of code including the semicolon at the end.

4. In the Script Editor menu, choose **File → Save Script To Shelf**. Name your new shelf button D3kCV for degree 3, keep CV. You can name it whatever will remind you of its function.

From now on, whenever you need to convert a linear NURBS curve to a cubic, simply click this button. Use this technique to convert any often-used menu command to a single mouse click.

Repeat steps 2 through 4 to create the tire and wheel well curves. We now have three good curves that are ready to revolve, so let's create the front wheel surfaces.

1. Select the hubcap curve as shown at left in Figure 4.9. Note how its pivot point is centered on the world origin.

2. Choose **Surfaces → Revolve ❑** and set Axis Preset to X. This will revolve the surface around the X axis. Most often, you will want to revolve your curve around one of the orthographic axes. Setting Pivot to Object uses the object's pivot point, which in this case is set to the world origin. Set Surface Degree to Cubic with a Start Sweep Angle of 0 and an End Sweep Angle of 360. This creates a cubic surface that sweeps through 360 degrees. Should you ever need to create a half surface, set the end angle to 180 degrees. Set Segments to 8, the default. It's a good setting unless you believe you need more detail in your revolved surface, in which case you should set it higher. As before, if you are creating a half object, set Segments to 4 instead of 8. Set Output Geometry to NURBS, but recognize that all of Maya's surface tools can be set to output polygons, subdivision surfaces, or, rarely, Bezier surfaces. Also note that Segments, Pivots, Start Sweep, End Sweep, and Degree can all be set in the Inputs list of the Channel Box. Find the revolve$n$ node and adjust accordingly.

3. Rename this object HubcapGeo. You should have an object that looks similar to the middle image of Figure 4.9.

4. Delete history.

5. Repeat steps 1 through 4 with the tire and wheel well curves. Name the resulting objects TireGeo and WheelWellGeo, respectively.

6. Select all three objects and group them by choosing **Edit → Group**. Name the group FrontWheelGrp.

7. Create a new layer called FrontWheelLyr and assign the new group to it.

Figure 4.9

Using the Revolve tool to create the hubcap/axle and moving the Front-WheelGrp's pivot point

8. With FrontWheelGrp selected, move the pivot point even with the narrow end of the WheelWellGeo (as shown at right in Figure 4.9) by pressing the Insert key and moving it into place. Press Insert again to leave move pivot mode.

9. Hide the new layer.

10. Select all the curves and assign them to a layer called CurveLyr. Hide this layer as well. We want to keep these curves in case we need them later.

11. Save the file as `MacGizmo01_FrontWheel.mb`.

We need to model only one wheel because we can create the wheel on the other side of the vehicle by duplicating. We'll do this later when the time comes to put everything together.

Modeling the Drive Wheel with the Circular Fillet and Trim Tools

We will find the next level of complexity in the drive wheel. The drawing calls for a five-spoke hubcap, but the spokes have a modern styling that differs from the standard cylindrical spoke on most wheels. This is the perfect opportunity to use and discuss the Circular Fillet and Trim tools. First, however, we need to set up the drawing so the drive wheel is centered on the grid.

1. In the top view, select DrawPolyGeo.

2. Move the drawing's pivot point to the exact center of the front view of the drive wheel drawing as shown at left in Figure 4.10.

3. Leave the move pivot mode, and holding down the X key to enter grid snap mode, move DrawPolyGeo to the world origin as shown at right in Figure 4.10. Notice that when you hold down X, the Snap-To-Grid button in the Status line depresses, indicating that you are in snap-to-grid mode. When you release the key, the button deselects.

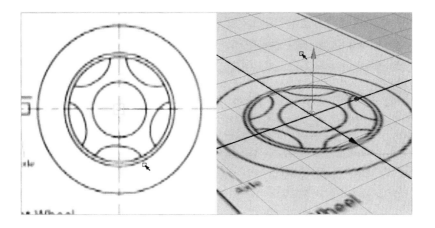

Figure 4.10

Arranging the drawing to facilitate modeling the drive wheel

4. Move the drawing down along the Y axis to a negative number (–.036 is the value shown here) in the Channel Box; otherwise, you won't be able to see your lines as you draw them.

5. Set DrawingLyr to Reference so that you don't select the DrawPolyGeo by mistake. Now that the drawing is arranged properly, let's create the drive wheel.

1. Using the technique from the previous tutorial, draw linear curves for the hubcap, inner wheel, tire, and wheel well as shown at left in Figure 4.11. Name them Hub-capCrv, InnerWheelCrv, TireCrv, and WheelWellCrv, respectively. Notice how the hubcap includes the shape for the spokes, hubcap, and axle.

    The drawing was constructed with versatility in mind. The inner wheel, spoke shape, hubcap, and axle can be constructed as one piece or as separate pieces depending on the needs of the design. In this case, we will combine the spoke shape, hubcap, and axle into one piece.

2. Rebuild each curve as a cubic curve and adjust as needed. Make sure to leave the outside edge of the spoke shape rounded to avoid problems with circular filleting later. You should have something resembling the middle of Figure 4.11. Do not rebuild the inner wheel because we want to keep those bevels when we revolve it.

3. Revolve only the spoke shape as shown at right in Figure 4.11. Immediately delete history. This will be our subject for the bulk of this tutorial.

4. Name this SpokeBaseGeo.

    Although it is possible to add enough spans to the surface to model the five-pronged shape of the spokes, it would be time consuming and inefficient to do so. Maya provides a way to use a line or a surface to hide part of another surface. This process is called *trimming*.

Figure 4.11

Creating curves and revolving SpokeBaseGeo

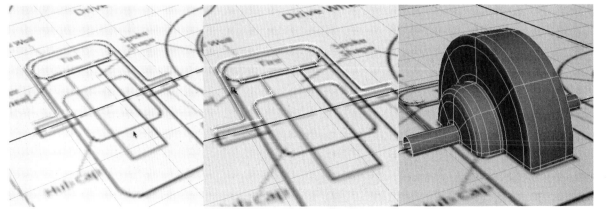

Unfortunately, trimming alone results in a perfectly sharp edge where the trim ends, and this makes surfaces created using trims appear synthetic. Fortunately, Maya provides a way to bevel NURBS surfaces using one of three surface fillet tools: Circular Fillet, Freeform Fillet, and Fillet Blend. To bevel the spokes, we will use the Circular Fillet tool.

> The term *bevel* here should not be confused with the **Edit Mesh → Bevel** command. The Polygon command is a way of softening the edge where two polygons meet. Beveling, or in this case, filleting NURBS surfaces, involves hiding the place where two surfaces meet or intersect by adding a third surface to give the illusion that the original two surfaces are blending into each other.

Let's dive into our exploration of these two powerful tools by first creating the shapes we will use to trim the spokes of the drive wheel.

1. We will use a cylinder to create the trim surfaces, so choose **Create → NURBS Primitives → Cylinder** ❑. Set Axis to Y, Radius to 0.65, and Height to 1.000. Click Create.

   You could go with the default settings and scale the cylinder to the right size as long as you remember to freeze transforms when you are done.

2. Move the cylinder so that it meets the drawing as shown in Figure 4.12a.

3. RM click the cylinder and pick isoparms on the cylinder.

4. Shift+select isoparms on either side of the cylinder as shown in Figure 4.12b.

5. Choose **Edit NURBS → Detach Surfaces**. The default for this command is Keep Original turned off. If the original object is still there, delete it.

6. Immediately, with both objects selected, choose **Edit NURBS → Rebuild Surfaces** ❑. From the default settings, check Keep CVs and click Rebuild.

7. Delete history and freeze transformations on your selected objects.

Figure 4.12

The process of creating the trim objects for the spokes of the drive wheel

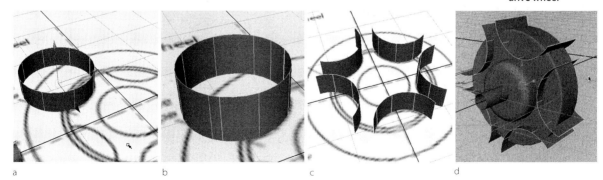

a   b   c   d

8. Delete the outside portion of the cylinder.

9. Move the pivot point of the inside portion to the world origin.

10. Choose **Edit → Duplicate Special** ❏ to open the command's option box. Set Rotate Y to 72, and set Number Of Copies to 4. Set Geometry Type to Copy, and set Group Under to Parent. Click Duplicate Special and you should see something similar to Figure 4.12c.

> When duplicating a number of objects evenly around a circle, simply divide 360 by the number of objects you want. Place that value in the Axis Rotation field, and set Number Of Copies to the number of objects you want minus one (for your original copy).

11. Shift+select your original object and choose **Edit → Group** with the default settings. Name this group TrimObjectsGrp. Note how the pivot point for this group is centered perfectly in the middle of the objects and at the world origin. This is why we arranged the DrawPolyGeo object the way we did earlier.

12. Rotate TrimObjectsGrp 90 degrees in Z, and translate it in X until the cylinder pieces intersect SpokeBaseGeo as shown at in Figure 4.12d.

The Circular Fillet tool uses the surface direction of two intersecting objects to derive a fillet direction in which to create the surface that blends the two objects. The documentation provides a fine example of how this works on two flat planes. However, it is impractical to expect the user to know the surface direction of two objects. In practice, therefore, it is most often easier to create the circular fillet and adjust as needed in the Inputs list in the Channel Box. When you find the right settings, you can adjust the Circular Fillet ❏ to quickly dispose of the other four fillets. Let's create the fillets.

1. Set up the interface to display the Channel Box and Outliner. (Choose **Display → UI Elements → Channel Box / Layer Editor** for the former, and click the Persp/Outliner Layout Shortcut button under the Toolbox for the latter.)

2. Select the SpokeBaseGeo and one of the partial cylinders in that order as shown in Figure 4.13a.

3. Set the view window to wireframe as the fillet surface we want will be inside the object when we get it right.

4. Choose **Edit NURBS → Surface Fillet → Circular Fillet** ❏. Make sure Create Curve On Surface is checked. This will create a curve on both SpokeBaseGeo and the partial cylinder that we will later use for the trim operation. Leave Reverse Primary Surface Normal and Reverse Secondary Surface Normal unchecked. Next, make sure that

Radius is set small, in this case 0.03. Setting the radius value too large can cause problems with the fillet node evaluating. Too large a value could result in an extremely distorted fillet or no displayed fillet. Click Apply. Depending on the speed of your computer, this could take a few seconds or a few minutes. You should see something resembling Figure 4.13a. Notice that the fillet surface is pointing the wrong way.

5. In the Channel Box, under the Inputs list, you should see a node called rbfSrf1. This is Maya's rather cryptic name for the controlling node for the circular fillet. Click it to display a list of attributes if they are not already displayed.

6. Under primaryRadius and secondaryRadius, drag select both input fields, enter –0.03, and press Enter. This will reverse the fillet direction. You should see something resembling Figure 4.13b.

7. That didn't work! Now reset primaryRadius to 0.03 and press Enter to see something resembling Figure 4.13c.

8. It's still not right, but we have only one option left. Set primaryRadius to –0.03, set secondaryRadius 0.03, and press Enter and you should see something that resembles Figure 4.13d. This is what we want.

9. Because the negative value on the primaryRadius attribute gave us the fillet we wanted, we now know how to set the Circular Fillet option box. So open that box now if it is not already open. Check Reverse Primary Surface Normal.

10. Select SpokeBaseGeo and the next partial cylinder in that order, the same as before. The first object selected contains our primary surface normals, and the second surface contains the secondary surface normals.

11. Click Apply to make the fillet.

12. Continue around SpokeBaseGeo, selecting it and the next partial cylinder and clicking Apply. Your wheel should resemble Figure 4.14. The circular fillet operation places curves on surfaces on both the SpokeBaseGeo and the partial cylinders. We will use these curves to create trims later.

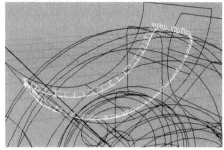

a. primaryRadius 0.03, secondaryRadius 0.03

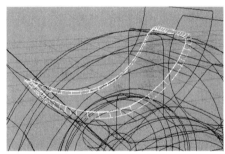

b. primaryRadius –0.03, secondaryRadius –0.03

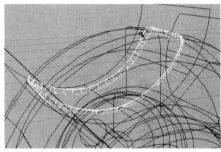

c. primaryRadius 0.03, secondaryRadius –0.03

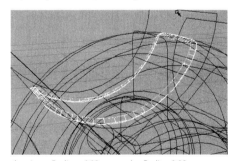

d. primaryRadius –0.03, secondaryRadius 0.03

Figure 4.13

The effect of four surface normal settings on the circular fillet operation

Figure 4.14

The five circular fillets in all their glory!

TROUBLESHOOTING CIRCULAR FILLETS

Fillets involve some of the more complex and memory-intensive modeling operations available to Maya users. They are powerful but finicky. There is a lot that can prevent a fillet from appearing after you invoke the command. Here are some guidelines for creating circular fillets.

- As always when modeling, use clean, properly parameterized geometry. Improperly parameterized geometry and/or geometry that has construction history attached to it can cause horrendous slowdowns, mangled fillets, and even program crashes.

- Avoid trying to fillet sharp edges. These will most often result in tangled or segmented fillets. Remember that a circular fillet is trying to create geometry with a quarter-circle cross-section between two pieces of geometry. Sharp corners are virtually impossible to fillet.

- If a large radius fillet isn't displaying, try either undoing and filleting with a smaller radius or adjusting the radius attribute in the rbfSrf*n* node in the Inputs list.

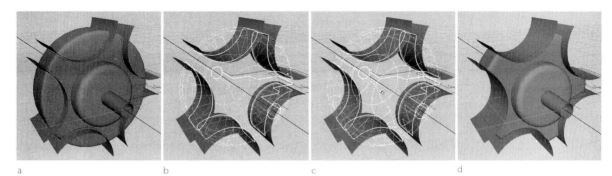

a   b   c   d

Figure 4.15

Trimming the SpokeBaseGeo shape

We now have to trim off the parts of the surfaces that we don't need. A NURBS trim operation usually does not change the surface itself; rather, it hides the part of the surface you specify. Here we will set the Trim tool to keep a specific part of the geometry and hide the rest.

1. This operation can be completed in shaded mode, so press the 6 key on your keyboard to display the perspective view in shaded mode. Your object should look something like Figure 4.15a.

2. Choose **Edit NURBS → Trim Tool** ❏ to open the Trim options panel. Click the Reset Tool button to reset the tool to its default settings. Set Selected State to Keep. Make sure Shrink Surface is unchecked because it will change the surface if checked, and because of this, it is rarely used.

3. Click in the center of SpokeBaseGeo, and you will see something like Figure 4.15b.

4. Click again in the center of SpokeBaseGeo, and a yellow dot will appear as in Figure 4.15c. This specifies which part of the shape you have selected, and because you set the selected state to Keep, it is the part that will remain unhidden.

5. Press Enter to perform the trim and you should see a five-pointed spoke shape as in Figure 4.15d.

6. Now repeat this operation for each of the partial cylinders, and you will have a shape like that shown in Figure 4.16.

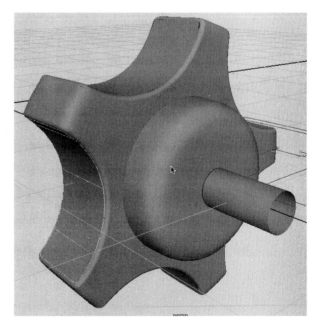

Figure 4.16

The final trimmed SpokeBaseGeo

We have created our spoke object, but we need to clean it up. Each of the fillets is a piece of geometry that has a construction history that we need to delete. As it stands, attempting to move the geometries and fillets as a unit will result in slowly displaying double transforms because the fillets depend on the geometries. Deleting history removes that dependency. Let's clean up and group this assembly.

1. In the Status line, RMB click the Select By Object Type: Curves button and uncheck NURBS Curves. This prevents selecting the revolving curves drawn earlier.

2. In the viewport, marquee select the entire unit you created. Manually select each component in the Outliner if necessary.

3. Delete history and group these pieces of geometry. Name the group DriveWheel-SpokesGrp.

4. Choose **Modify → Center Pivot**.

5. In the Outliner, select and delete the empty TrimGeoGrp and the five circularFillet-Surface*n* nodes.

Let's finish the drive wheel.

1. Select and revolve InnerWheelCrv, TireCrv, and WheelWellCrv around the X axis. After revolving InnerWheelCrv, click the object to select it and open the Attribute Editor. Notice that the degree curve for the U direction is linear and that the degree in the V direction of the object is cubic. This lets you keep a sharp edge on the rim without having to add detail or resort to other tricks.

2. Delete history on both objects.

3. Rename the objects InnerWheelGeo, TireGeo, and DriveWheelWellGeo, respectively.

4. Select DriveWheelSpokesGrp, TireGeo, InnerWheelGeo, and DriveWheelWellGeo and group them. Name the group DriveWheelGrp.

5. Center the pivot of this group.

6. Create a new layer called DriveWheelLyr. Assign DriveWheelGrp to DriveWheelLyr and hide the layer.

7. Select the curves you used and assign them to the Curves layer. They will disappear.

8. Save as `MacGizmo02_DriveWheel.mb`.

Creating the Engine

Our last use of the Revolve tool will be to create the engine. What will be different here will be how we will build the profile curve we use to make the engine. We will use Intersect

Curve, Detach Curve, and Attach Curve as precursors to similar commands we will use with NURBS surfaces. Let's create the profile curve.

1. Move DrawPolyGeo's pivot to center on the engine as you did with the drive wheel in the last tutorial.

2. Draw linear curves around the contours of the nose and cowl as shown in Figure 4.17a. Begin and end the cowl curve in the middle of the inside of the engine. There is no reason to model geometry that won't be seen.

3. Rebuild the linear curves into cubic curves.

4. Choose **Create → NURBS Primitives → Circle** ❑ to open the Circle option box. Set Normal Axis to Y and Radius to 0.2. Number Of Sections defaults to 8; leave it there. Click Create to create a small circle at the world origin.

5. Move the new circle into position as shown in Figure 4.17a.

6. Shift+select the cowl curve to add it to the selection list.

7. Choose **Edit Curves → Intersect Curves** ❑ to open the option box. Reset the settings from the Edit menu and choose Intersect. Using these settings with this command places intersection points on both curves as shown in Figure 4.17b. Because we have been working in the orthogonal planes to create our curves, they overlap exactly. This facilitates the intersect operation.

8. Pick-mask Curve Points on the circle.

9. Hold down the V key and drag a curve point to one of the intersect points.

10. Hold down the Shift and V keys to drag a second curve point to the other intersection point, as shown in Figure 4.17c.

11. Choose **Edit Curves → Detach Curves** to separate the circle into two parts as shown in Figure 4.17d.

12. Repeat steps 8 through 11 to separate the cowl curve into parts.

13. Delete the waste portions of the curve to end up with what is shown in Figure 4.17e.

14. Immediately choose **Edit Curves → Rebuild Curve** ❑ and check the Keep CVs option. Click Apply and then Close on the Rebuild Curve option box.

Figure 4.17

The process of detaching curves. (The drawing layer has been hidden for clarity in the left-most images.)

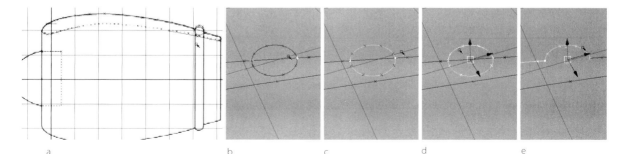

a   b   c   d   e

Now let's attach these curves to make the profile for the engine cowl.

1. Select two of the three curves as shown in Figure 4.18a.

2. Choose **Edit Curves → Attach Curves ❑** to open the Attach Curves option box. Set Attach Method to Connect, and set Multiple Knots to Keep. This will attach the curves with minimal distortion to the shape of the lines.

New to Maya 8.5, you can attach multiple selected curves in a single operation, saving you from repeatedly selecting pairs of curves.

3. Immediately rebuild by checking Keep CVs to get a curve shaped like that in Figure 4.18b.

4. Shift+select the remaining curve and repeat steps 2 and 3 to complete the attachment. You should have a complete line as shown in Figure 4.18c.

5. Delete history on the cowl curve.

6. Rename the nose and cowl curve to NoseCrv and CowlCrv, respectively.

Now we will actually create the engine. We'll use the curves we've just created as well as a linear NURBS plane to create the turbine blades. Let's start with the turbines.

1. Choose **Create → NURBS Primitives → Plane ❑** to open the Plane options box. Set Width to 0.5 and Length to 1. Set Surface Degree to 1 Linear. Click Create.

We are using linear curves to create the turbine blades because one-degree curves are easier to edit and are less processor intensive to render.

2. Name this new shape TurbineGeo.

Figure 4.18

Attaching the curve to create the cowl curve

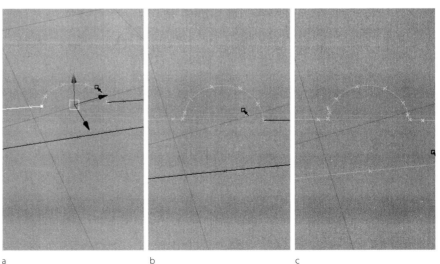

a   b   c

3. Make one side narrower than the other by pick-masking CVs and scaling them down a little bit.

4. Select the object and rotate TurbineGeo 55 degrees in Z.

5. Translate TurbineGeo back in Z until it overlaps both the NoseCrv and CowlCrv as shown at left in Figure 4.19.

6. Move TurbineGeo's pivot back to the world origin.

7. Choose **Edit → Duplicate Special** ❐. We want to create 60 turbine blades, so set Number Of Copies to 59, and set the X rotation to 6. Click Duplicate Special and you should see something like the right image in Figure 4.19.

8. Shift+select the original TurbineGeo, and group the blades under a group called TurbineGrp.

9. Select and revolve the NoseCrv in X. You may see a problem like that depicted at left in Figure 4.20. The revolved surface appears crinkled at the very tip of the nose. This happens when the revolved curve slightly overlaps the axis of revolution. If this is the case, correct it by moving NoseCrv's end CVs back in Z a little until the dark area around the nose disappears as at right in Figure 4.20.

10. Rename the surface created by revolving NoseCrv, and delete history on it.

11. Select and revolve CowlCrv. This will result in a surface that is way too heavy in the U direction because of the intersect, detach, and attach operations we performed on the curve earlier; it will have to be rebuilt. After the revolve operation, notice that the revolve node is selected in the Inputs list in the Channel Box. This allows you to manipulate those attributes, but it can interfere with further operations. You will need to click the surface again before you can edit the revolved surface.

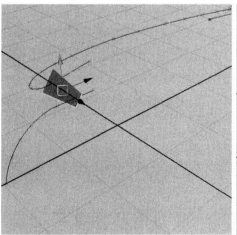 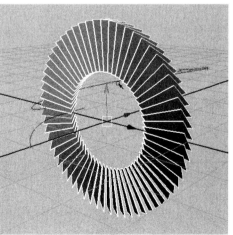

Figure 4.19

Creating the turbines by editing and duplicating a linear first-degree NURBS plane

Figure 4.20

**Revolving and fixing
problems with the
nose surface**

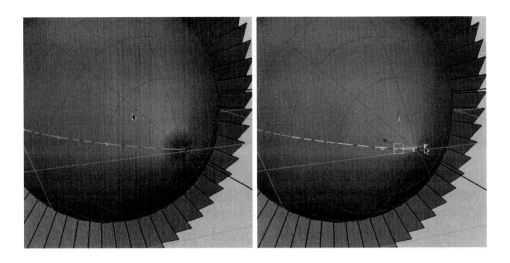

CONSTRUCTION HISTORY

Maya's construction history, coupled with the NURBS surfacing tools such as Revolve, Loft, Extrude, Boundary, and so on, is a powerful force because by making changes to the curve or curves used to make the surface, you change the resulting surface itself. Let's take the NoseSrf, for example. Before deleting history, we can change the shape of the profile curve and that change will propagate to the surface, but we can also change the properties of the line. We can insert EPs, rebuild, change the degree, and so on, and those changes will propagate to the surface created from those curves. As an exercise, edit NoseCrv to create the shape shown in Figure 4.21 by inserting knots, moving CVs, and rebuilding with Keep CVs.

12. With the revolved surface selected, open the Attribute Editor. You will see that while the surface is properly parameterized (that is, the Spans UV values equal the max values for the Min Max Range settings for U and V), the spans in U equal 37. (This value may differ in your model.) This results in long, thin patches on the surface, which is not optimal.

13. Choose **Edit NURBS → Rebuild Surfaces** ❏. The key to properly rebuilding NURBS surfaces is for the surface to have as few isoparms as possible while making sure it retains its shape. To rebuild this surface, we will need to set Rebuild Type to Uniform. This gives us access to the Number Of Spans U and Number Of Spans V boxes below and will distribute spans in those directions evenly across all the surfaces. Set Parameter Range to 0 To #Spans to rebuild the surface with the specified number of spans.

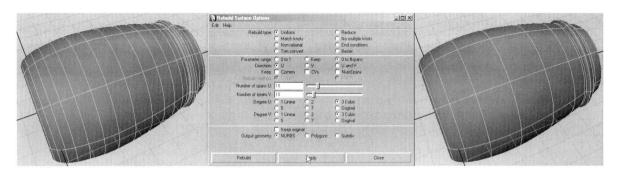

Figure 4.21

Rebuilding the EngineCowl surface using Rebuild Surfaces options. Undo and try larger or smaller values for Number Of Spans U to see the results.

The range 0 To 1 rebuilds the surface with chord length coordinates, which are useful for texturing but not for modeling. The Keep option doesn't change or reparameterize the surface and should be avoided. Since the U direction is heavy and the V direction is fine, set Direction to U. This rebuilds the surface along the U direction only. Set Number Of Spans U to 18. You can try it with a lower value, but that may distort the circular bulge that we worked so hard to add to the cowl curve earlier. Of course, we will be outputting NURBS geometry. Click Apply to display the results shown in Figure 4.21. Notice that the surface patches are squarer and that the ring around the back of the engine doesn't lose detail. This is the key to properly rebuilding a surface.

14. Delete history on this surface and rename it EngineCowlSrf.

15. Select EngineCowlSrf, NoseSrf, and TurbineGrp, and group them under a group named EngineGrp.

16. Create a layer called EngineLyr and assign EngineGrp to it.

17. Assign NoseCrv and CowlCrv to the CurvesLyr.

18. Save the file as `MaGizmo03_Engine.mb`.

Modeling the Body and Wing

We have done extensive work with the Revolve, Trim, and Fillet tools. Now we will use the Fillet Blend tool along with Maya's extensive NURBS editing toolset to create the relatively complex body. But first, we have to create a better template.

1. Unreference the layer called DrawingLyr.

2. Move the DrawPolyGeo so the middle of the top view drawing sits on the world origin.

3. Use the Cut Faces tool from the top view to split faces as shown in Figure 4.22a.

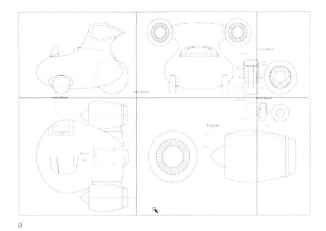

a

b

c

Figure 4.22

Editing the drawing polygon to create a 3D template. Note how each view lines up using the dotted center lines.

4. Pick-mask Faces and extract and separate the side and top view faces as shown in Figure 4.22b. Choose **Mesh → Extract** ❐ to open the Extract option box. Make sure the Separate Extracted Faces box is checked, and extract each face separately.

5. Rotate and translate the polygons into place as shown in Figure 4.22c. Choose **Modify → Center Pivot** to make these operations easier. Also, use the dotted center lines to help line up the views.

6. Delete history on all the pieces and assign them to DrawingLyr.

We will now begin constructing the body using a sphere primitive. Rather than try to draw curves and loft or boundary, we can more efficiently construct the teardrop shape of the body by splitting a sphere into two parts and reconnecting them using the Free Form Fillet tool. Let's create and split the sphere.

1. Choose **Create → NURBS Primitives → Sphere** ❐ and create a sphere with 16 sections and 8 spans along the X axis and a radius of 2.

2. Pick-mask isoparms on the sphere, and choose the isoparm directly in the center of the sphere. If you look in the title bar, the last item should read nurbsSphere1.u[4]. It is crucial that you click directly on the span so that the line is solid yellow and the number of the isoparm is whole with no decimals. Otherwise, the operation will detach in the wrong place and cause problems with rebuilding and modeling down the line.

3. Choose **Edit NURBS → Detach Surfaces**, and split the surface at the location of that isoparm.

4. Immediately, with both new surfaces selected, choose **Edit NURBS → Rebuild Surfaces** ❐ with Keep CVs checked. Delete history.

5. Move the half spheres to either end of the body as indicated in the drawing of the MacGizmo on the polygon. Name the surface in front NoseSrf and the one in back TailSrf.

REBUILDING WITH CVS

Any time you perform an operation that changes the span count of an object, it is wise to immediately rebuild with CVs. This keeps your geometry clean and properly parameterized. As such, it is worth creating a shelf button using the following code:

```
rebuildSurface -ch 1 -rpo 1 -rt 0 -end 1 -kr 2 -kcp 1 -kc 0 -su 18 -du 3 -sv 8
-dv 3 -tol 0.01 -fr 0 -dir 2;.
```

Whenever you need to rebuild with CVs, just click the button.

Because we are going to model with surfaces, we are confronted with the necessity of moving large volumes of points into their proper positions. To do this most efficiently, we need a process for moving CVs en masse into position. Trying to model CV by CV at the outset will be time consuming and inefficient, so adopt these strategies:

- Start with the Translate, Scale, and Rotate tools to move the object into the general position and shape you require.

- Use deformers such as a lattices, joints, or even wrap deformers to reshape the surface without resorting to moving components. A lattice, for example, can move CVs within its volume.

- Begin moving components by moving, scaling, and rotating hulls, which represent rings and rows of CVs.

- Move CVs in as large a group as possible.

- Move points on a CV-by-CV basis.

Following these principles, let's begin massaging the half sphere into shape.

1. Select NoseSrf and scale it into shape as shown in Figure 4.23a.

2. From the Animation menu set, choose **Create Deformers → Lattice**, and use the default settings. Immediately find and select the ffd1LatticeShape node in the Shapes section of the Channel Box. The tDivisions value defaults to 5, which is too high, so change it to 2. Practically speaking, it is difficult to anticipate the direction into which these divisions will divide the lattice, so simply change the values of each attribute until you get the right direction. In this case, change sDivisions to 3.

Scanning the Outliner will show two lattices in the scene, named ffd1Lattice and ffd1Base. Maya compares the location of the points on the lattice with the points on the base object and deforms the CVs or vertices based on that comparison. This makes lattices useful for deforming objects without having to move points around. The base object is currently invisible, but you can select it to see the how the comparison works.

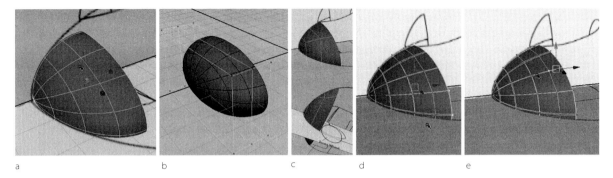

a   b   c   d   e

Figure 4.23

Working from the broad to the specific by scaling/translating the geometry, deforming with a lattice, component editing with hulls, and manipulating points with CVs

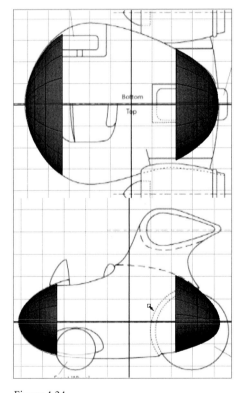

Figure 4.24

NoseSrf and TailSrf of the MacGizmo

3. RMB click the lattice and pick-mask Lattice Point. This will allow you to manipulate the shape of the lattice by moving its points. You should see bright purple dots much as in Figure 4.23b.

4. Translate and scale the points of the lattice until you get something that resembles both images in Figure 4.23c. Remember that we are trying to match the surface of the half sphere with the drawing on both sides and top and bottom, so rotate your view as you model. Also, don't forget that you can scale entire rows of lattice points; you are not confined to moving one point at a time. If your lattice gets too wildly out of shape, you can reset it by choosing **Edit Deformers → Lattice → Reset Lattice**.

5. When you have done all you can with the lattice, select the half circle and delete history to remove the deformer.

6. You might be able to deform the lattice to get the surface to match the drawing. But if not, feel free to pick-mask Hull on the half circle and manipulate the hulls to get the shape as shown in Figure 4.23d.

7. When you are ready, pick-mask Control Vertex and edit the CVs to fine-tune your shape as shown in Figure 4.23e, but realize that this may not be necessary.

8. Repeat steps 1 through 7 for the half sphere in back. Remember, when the shape looks right, you are done. You should have two shapes resembling those in Figure 4.24.

The ship body has a nose and a tail; now we need to fill in the body. We will fill in the bulk of the body using the Fillet Blend tool. NURBS modelers use the Fillet Blend tool to blend between surface and curves that are separate. They do so when the blend between the surfaces must maintain continuity or tangency (see the next section "What Is Surface Continuity?") between the two surfaces. This contrasts with the Circular Fillet tool, which blends between two surfaces that intersect. Let's dive right in and explore this tool while creating the body.

> Although you can fillet blend directly between spans of different objects, the other Fillet tools require you to pick-mask isoparms, so it is the best practice to remain consistent with the other tools and pick-mask isoparms first.

Figure 4.25

Using the Fillet Blend tool to create the body of the MacGizmo

1. Pick-mask isoparms on both objects. The Fillet Blend tool blends between curves, curves on surfaces, and isoparms. When using the last named, the blend inherits properties from both surfaces, so this is what we will use.

2. Choose **Edit NURBS → Surface Fillet → Fillet Blend Tool** ❑. Reset the defaults, and then uncheck Auto Normal Dir and Auto Closed Rail Anchor. Click Fillet Blend Tool. This puts you in the tool and out of the option box.

3. Click the open edge of the front half sphere. It will light up as if you had selected the isoparm, though you will still be in object selection mode.

4. Press Enter to select the next edge. This tool can blend between multiple edges and, as such, needs your input to determine which edges to blend to and from.

5. Click the open edge of the other shape as shown in Figure 4.25a. Again, it will light up like an isoparm selection, which is what we want.

6. Press Enter to generate the fillet and you should have something like that shown in Figure 4.25b.

7. Rename this surface BodySrf.

8. In the View Window menu, choose **Shading → Wireframe On Shaded** to see how this geometry blends with the other two shapes (see Figure 4.25c). Although there are three patches, they show no seam, and as such they are said to have surface continuity.

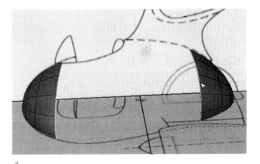

a

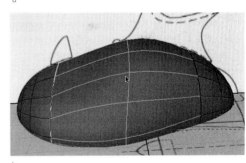

b

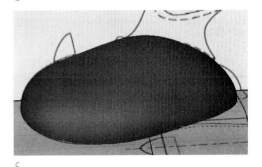

c

What Is Surface Continuity?

This is the perfect time to go off on a tangent (pun intended) and explain the concept of surface continuity. Surface continuity describes how two separate curves or surfaces visually flow across a common edge; this is a fundamentally important concept to NURBS modelers. There are three types of continuity: positional, tangent, and curvature.

- Positional (G0) continuity simply means that the edge CVs of one patch occupy the same spatial coordinates as the edge CVs of the other. The left column of images in Figure 4.26 illustrates positional continuity. This inevitably results in a seam or a break in the surface where the two patches meet. The direction and position of the hulls illustrate how this works.

- Tangent (G1) continuity requires not only that the edge points have positional tangency, but that the next row of CVs on each patch line up at least on the same plane and preferably on the same line so the curve or surface appears to flow seamlessly across the edge. The middle column of images in Figure 4.26 illustrates this flow.

Figure 4.26

Positional, tangent, and curvature continuity illustrated using curves, surfaces with CVs and hulls, and shaded surface only

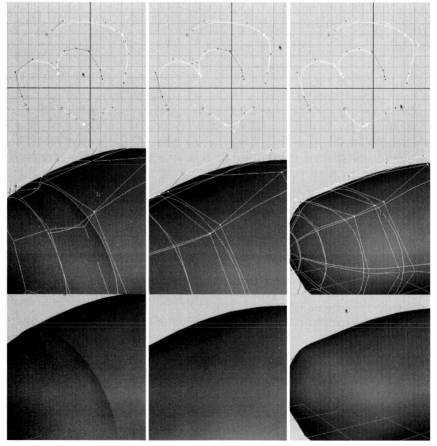

| Positional | Tangent | Curvature |

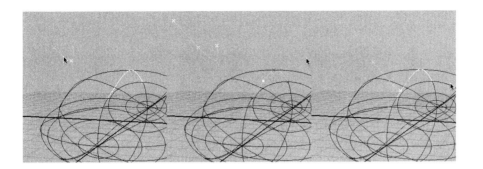

Figure 4.27

Aligning a free-floating curve with a curve derived from a surface isoparm. Note that the floating curve aligns along the derived curve starting from where the curve point was chosen.

- Curvature (G2) continuity incorporates both positional and tangent continuity plus adds the requirement that both curves and surfaces have largely the same slope as they move away from the edge. The problem with this method is illustrated in the right column of images in Figure 4.26. Curvature continuity has distorted the surface of the model unacceptably because it has affected a larger number of points out from the edge. You can see this most clearly in the curves example.

Methods of Achieving Surface and Curve Continuity

Maya offers many methods of achieving surface and curve continuity. Knowing how and when to use each method is largely a matter of experience, but if you understand the types, you will be better able to know when to use the following tools:

- The Align Curves and Align Surfaces commands match one curve or surface to another with positional, tangent, and curvature continuity. However, you are aligning one curve or surface using the curvature of another and therefore the shape being aligned may distort unacceptably. One excellent use of the Align command is to align a free-floating curve with a curve on a surface or a curve derived from an isoparm using the Duplicate Surface Curves command. By selecting a curve point on the derived curve and aligning curves with curvature continuity, you can bring the free-floating curve into near perfect alignment with the derived curve at any point along the derived curve's length, as shown in Figure 4.27.

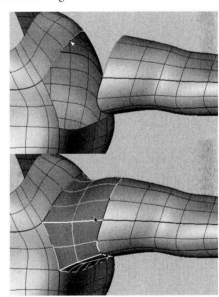

Figure 4.28

Using the Fillet Blend tool to join the patches on the arm to the patches on the body. Note how each fillet maintains tangent continuity with both the arm and body patch.

- Filleting two separate curves or patches generates geometry that automatically has tangent continuity with both original separate pieces. This means that you can use fillets to close gaps between patches. Figure 4.28 illustrates the use of the Fillet Blend tool to create geometry bridging the gap between the patches of the arm and the body. (Open Continuity01_Fillet.mb from the CD if you want to give this a try.)

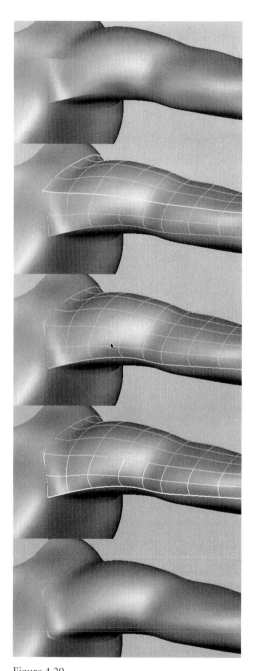

Figure 4.29

The process of using the Attach/Detach Surfaces command to create tangent continuity

- And as you've seen, the Circular Fillet tool places a piece of geometry having tangency with two intersecting surfaces and can be set to blend in any direction.

- Attaching and detaching curves and surfaces are often the simplest and easiest means of attaining tangency between two adjoining patches. Figure 4.29 shows this process. In the top image, the fillets from the previous example have been attached to the arm patches and the surfaces rebuilt with Keep CVs. The arm patches have positional continuity, but there are seams where the surfaces are out of tangency. By pick-masking isoparms and selecting the edge isoparm on each patch (which is the most exact way of beginning the attaching process), you can easily attach and immediately rebuild with CVs. Then detach the new patch (and immediately rebuild) along the isoparm where you just joined them. You now have two patches with tangent continuity between them. Continue around the arm, attaching, rebuilding, and finally closing the surface using the Open/Close Surface command to close the surface in the correct direction.

- The Stitch Edges tool and Global Stitch command can also create tangent continuity between two or more patches. Although they only work on patches, they can close gaps between patches while also achieving tangency. The Stitch Edges tool works on two patches and creates a "master/slave" relationship between them. The first patch selected becomes the master, and the second moves according to how the CVs on the master patch are edited. Use the Global Stitch command to join multiple patches with varying degrees of continuity. Both tools work best when the patches on which they are used are positioned as close together as possible.

- You can also manually achieve tangent continuity by carefully moving CVs or through an automatic process codified in a MEL script. One such script is Matthew Gidney's mAlignCVs script, available at www.highend3d.com. It allows you to select two CVs as anchors followed by the CVs you want to align to the anchors. The script calculates a vector between the two anchors and snaps your CVs along that vector. Figure 4.30 shows how this works.

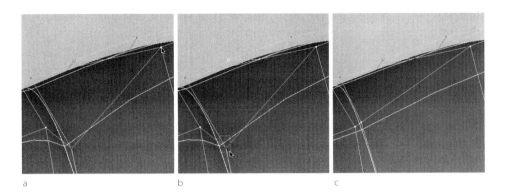

a   b   c

Figure 4.30

How to use mAlignCVs: (a) Select two CVs. (b) Select a CV or a group of CVs to align and run the script. (c) The CVs you pick will align along the vector created by selecting the first two CVs.

Familiarity with the types of surface continuity comes with working with surfaces and curves. Tangent continuity is the most useful to the NURBS modeler because it creates a smooth flow across the edge of two patches without distorting them by changing the curvature too drastically. Which method you use to achieve this smooth flow is, in most cases, a question of personal taste and experience.

Finishing the Body

By properly preparing NoseSrf and TailSrf and applying the Fillet Blend tool, we have generated a piece of geometry that closely matches the drawing. We could have created this shape out of a sphere and added isoparms and pulled hulls and CVs, but the method we used cut our time dramatically.

Interestingly, this new piece of geometry is interactive by virtue of its construction history. This means that the ffBlendSrf node in the Inputs list will move the hulls and CVs on the fillet patch in a "teeter-totter" relationship. Upon examination of the model, you will see that the contour of the tail doesn't quite match with the drawing. Figure 4.31 illustrates both how to correct this and how the CVs move in relation to the edits on the tail cap.

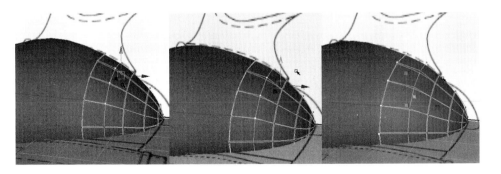

Figure 4.31

Notice how the CVs on the body patch move in relation to the edit on the tail. Moving the CVs forward causes the body to expand, and scaling them outward causes the body to contract.

This approach keeps with our preference for modeling from the general to the specific. With interactive patches such as the fillets, we can edit the shape of the whole surface just by moving a CV or a hull.

All that is left is to flatten the bottom of the body. The fillet operation leaves this too thick. Select the CVs along the bottom, and flatten them by translating or scaling to make them conform more to the drawing. Avoid selecting both the edge CVs and the next row in on either side because this will disrupt the surface tangency.

> If you disrupt tangency a little bit, it will not hurt. When we attach these three surfaces together, any breaks between them will be smoothed out, so don't worry too much here.

1. Let's delete history on BodySrf to make it noninteractive and prepare it for rebuilding and attaching to the nose and tail. If you look at the Attribute Editor with this surface selected, you will notice that it is parameterized with chord length (0–1) parameterization. We will need to change this and add detail to the body at the same time. Notice that settings for the number of spans in U and V are 2 and 16 respectively but the Min Max values are 0 and 1. Rebuild in U and V with Number Of Spans U equaling 6 and Number Of Spans V equaling 16. Click Rebuild.

2. Attach NoseSrf to BodySrf by selecting both surfaces and then choosing **Edit NURBS → Attach Surfaces ❑**. Set Attach Method to Blend, and make sure Insert Knot is not checked. This will attach the surfaces with minimal distortion in this case. Click Apply.

3. Rebuild this new surface with Keep CVs checked.

4. Delete history on the new surface. This is *very* important. Failing to do so can result in the model being distorted irreparably.

5. Select this new piece of geometry, Shift+select TailSrf, and click Attach to attach the surfaces and close the option box.

6. Rebuild with Keep CV and delete history. Rename the surface BodySrf.

7. Freeze transformations on BodySrf.

Lofting the Wing

The wing surface is a fairly simple loft operation. We must be mindful that it does have a slight curve along its length, but a simple two-curve loft will do most of the "heavy lifting" for this piece. In this exercise, we will also explore other ways to create a sharp edge and end caps on shapes. Let's create the wing.

1. Use the EP tool to trace the interior wing cross-section shape in the front view.

2. Rebuild the curve as a 12-span cubic curve.

3. Choose **Edit Curves → Open/Close Curves** ❐. Set Shape to Blend, and uncheck Insert Knot. Click Open/Close. This will convert it from an open to a periodic or closed shape.

4. Manipulate the curve's CVs to conform the shape of the curve to the drawing.

5. Choose **Edit → Duplicate**. This will create a copy in place.

6. Scale the duplicate curve up until it is similar in size to the larger wing shape in the drawing.

7. Manipulate this curve's CVs to match the drawing more exactly, as shown in Figure 4.32a.

8. Select and translate the smaller curve over to line up with the engine, as shown in Figure 4.32b.

9. Shift+select the larger curve and then the smaller curve, and then choose **Surfaces → Loft** ❐. The Loft command extends a surface between multiple curves of varying shapes. This command generally works best with curves that are equally parameterized and with the knots lined up as closely as possible. In this case, set Parameterization to Uniform, check Auto Reverse, set Surface Degree to Cubic, and set Section Spans to 2. Click Loft.

10. Immediately rebuild surfaces with Keep CVs checked.

11. Adjust the CVs to match the drawing as closely as possible, as shown in the two images in Figure 4.32c. It will be necessary to look to the other side of the drawing and try to match it. If you need to change the location of the ends of the surface, move the curves and the entire surface will follow.

12. Delete history on the wing shape and name it WingSrf. Assign the curves used to create it to the Curves layer.

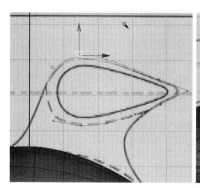
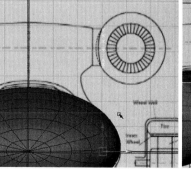

a b c

Figure 4.32
Lofting the right half of the wing

We want to create two surfaces, one for the wing body and a separate and much shorter piece that we will circular-fillet to the engine. Of course, we will detach the wing surface at the point of the break, but it is how we will treat the ends of the wing that will occupy the bulk of the next exercise. Let's create these two surfaces.

1. Pick-mask isoparms on WingSrf and select an isoparm most of the way to the engine. The V value in the feedback line should read close to 1.667 or so.

2. Detach the surface at this point. Immediately rebuild surfaces with Keep CVs checked. Rename the detached surface EngineWngSrf.

3. Pick-mask isoparms on WingSrf. Select an isoparm at about 1.954 in the V direction. (Remember, you can select this exactly by typing **select WingSrf.v[1.95]** in the Command line.) We are going to create a crease right at the end of WingSrf and pull in the end CVs to create a flat surface at the end of the shape.

4. Choose **Edit NURBS → Surface Editing → Break Tangent**. This inserts three spans into the surface and gives the surface enough detail to create a sharp edge. We will use this detail to create a sharp edge.

5. Pick-mask Hull and select the last row of CVs by clicking them directly or clicking any row, and use the arrow keys to pick-walk to the last row.

6. Scale down these end CVs until the hole is close to the size shown at left in Figure 4.33.

7. Because the engine will eventually pivot from the center of the large part of the wing, we need to move the hole over so that when the engine does rotate, the hole won't show. This is also shown at left in Figure 4.33.

Figure 4.33

Creating the flat end surface on the wing surfaces. Centering the pivot point on EngineWngSrf makes moving it much easier.

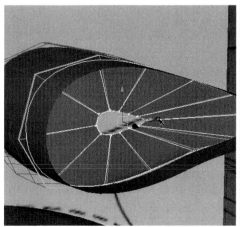
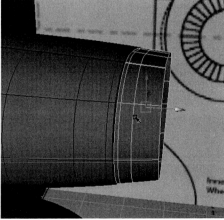

8. Select WingSrf as an object and rebuild surfaces with Keep CVs.

9. Repeat this procedure with the detached wing surface.

10. Move EngingWngSrf so that it is closer to WingSrf. When you are finished, you should have something that appears similar to that shown in the right of Figure 4.33.

Attaching the Engine

Let's attach the engine that we built earlier to EngineWngSrf by circular filleting. First, however, we will need to make some changes to CowlSrf.

1. Make the EngineLyr visible.

2. Translate and scale EngineGrp into position as shown in the drawing from the front and side views. Scaling this group to 0.572 should bring it into alignment.

> Unfortunately, going to the generic side view in the hotbox is useless as the drawing polygon obscures the side view. But using the View Compass in the perspective view lets you view from the other side, which is what we want to do here.

3. Because of the way we built EngineCowlSrf, its seam (the place where the first and last U or V meet in a closed or periodic surface) intersects EngineWngSrf. This placement will interfere with the fillet operation, so we will need to move it. Move the seam by pick-masking isoparms on EngineCowlSrf.

4. Select the isoparm opposite where the seam sits at present.

5. Choose **Edit NURBS → Move Seam**. You will see the surface twist over its length as the seam moves. This can be disconcerting the first time you see it, but rest assured the surface will right itself.

6. Select CowlSrf, Shift+select EngineWngSrf, and choose Edit **NURBS → Surface Fillet → Circular Fillet** ❑. Uncheck Create Curve On Surface, check Reverse Secondary Surface Normal, set Radius to 0.05, and set Tangent Tolerance to 0.001. This creates a much more detailed fillet surface. Click the Fillet button and you should see something that looks like Figure 4.34.

7. Immediately delete history on the fillet surface.

Figure 4.34

**The circular fillet on
the wing**

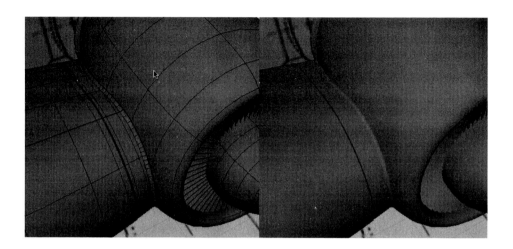

8. In the Outliner, find the object called circularFilletSurface*n*. (Ours was called circularFilletSurface6.) Click the plus sign to the left of the name to open that node.

9. In the Outliner, MM drag the fillet geometry (marked by the blue NURBS symbol) to the left of the name up to EngineGrp.

10. Do the same for EngineWngSrf.

11. Move the pivot point for EngineGrp to the middle of the fat part of the wing surface as shown in Figure 4.35. This allows the technical director in charge of rigging the MacGizmo for animation to rotate the entire engine assembly from the proper place by simply selecting and rotating this group.

12. Select WingSrf, Shift+select EngineGrp, and group them under a new group called WingGrp.

13. Duplicate this group across the Z axis to create a copy.

14. Pick-mask isoparms on the WingSrf from each group. Select the isoparm along the interior edge of each shape as shown in Figure 4.36.

15. Attach these surfaces using the Blend option without inserting knots.

16. Rebuild with Keep CVs, and delete history.

17. In the Outliner, open WingGrp1, which is the name given to the duplicated group created earlier.

18. Rename the EngineGrp inside WingGrp1 to REngineGrp.

19. MM drag REngineGrp to the original WingGrp, and delete WingGrp1.

20. Save the file as MacGizmo04_BodyWing.mb.

You now have a completed wing assembly!

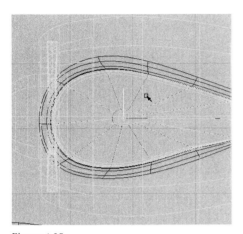

Figure 4.35

Moving EngineGrp's pivot point. Note that doing this from the front view in wireframe view makes this much easier.

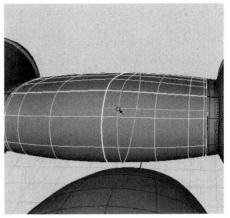

Figure 4.36

Selecting the middle two isoparms of two surfaces before attaching can best be accomplished by selecting the next isoparm out from the middle and sliding the selection inward as shown here.

Connecting the Wing to the Body

We will connect the wing and body by bringing their surfaces together using the Sculpt Surfaces tool and blending the surfaces using the Circular Fillet tool to cover where they intersect.

1. We need to add detail to the center of WingSrf by pick-masking isoparms and selecting the two isoparms out from the center line as shown at left in Figure 4.37.

2. Choose **Edit NURBS → Insert Isoparms** ❏, and set Insert Location to Between Selections. Set # Isoparms To Insert to 4. Click Insert.

3. Immediately rebuild with Keep CVs.

4. Choose **Edit NURBS → Sculpt Geometry Tool** ❏. Here we want to set the Radius (U) value to 0.5. Under the Sculpt Parameters rollout, set Operation to Pull. This will pull the surface out along the reference vector, and Reference Vector should be set to Normal in the option box. Set Max Displacement to 0.25; this value determines how far the surface will move with each mouse click. Under the Stroke rollout, check Reflection and set Reflection Axis to Z. This will help maintain symmetry with our sculpting.

5. In the perspective viewport, move the mouse until the two reflected brush shapes overlap, and then begin painting. As you paint, rotate your view to the opposing side and paint there. Continue until you have something that looks like Figure 4.38a and b. Show and hide the DrawingLyr as needed to check your work.

6. RMB click BodySrf below, and repeat the painting operation until the surfaces intersect as shown in the two smaller images in Figure 4.38c.

Figure 4.37

Inserting four isoparms between the selected isoparms

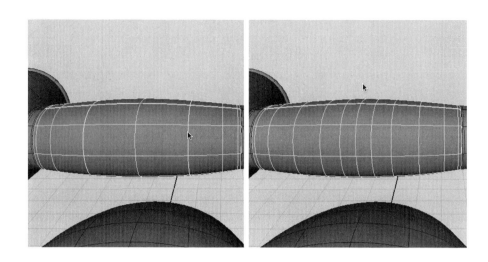

7. Select both surfaces and create a circular fillet, leaving Create Curve On Surface, Reverse Primary Surface Normal, and Reverse Secondary Surface Normal unchecked. Set Radius to 0.7 and leave Tangent Tolerance at 0.01. Click Fillet, and you should see something like Figure 4.38d.

8. Delete history on this new surface and rename it ConnectSrf.

9. Group ConnectSrf, WingSrf, and BodySrf under a new group called BodySrfGrp.

10. Assign this group to a new layer called BodyLyr.

11. Assign WingGrp to EngineLyr.

12. Save the file.

These surfaces will appear to form one continuous surface by virtue of the circular fillet's tangent continuity at the time of its creation.

Figure 4.38

Sculpting WingSrf and BodySrf until they intersect and then circular filleting to join them

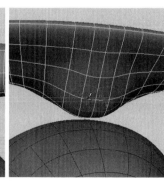

a   b   c   d

Trimming and Styling the Wheel Wells

Now we'll create the wheel wells using the Trim command. We will also create a rim around the wheel wells using the Extrude Surface command. Using an extrusion lets us hide the trim edge completely. Given that trim edges sometimes don't render smoothly, you want to learn ways to work around this shortcoming. Let's insert the drive wheel.

1. Make DriveWheelLyr visible. Move and rotate DriveWheelGrp until it intersects the body shape as shown in Figure 4.39a.

2. In the Outliner, make DriveWheelGrp a child of BodyGrp by MM dragging it into BodyGrp.

3. Select BodySrf and DriveWheelWellGeo, and choose **Edit NURBS → Intersect Surfaces** ❑. Set Create Curves For to Both Surfaces, and set Curve Type to Curve On Surface. This will place a curve on the surface of both objects, and we will use the curves to trim both surfaces. Click Intersect and you should see a curve like that shown in Figure 4.39b.

4. Use the Trim tool to trim the well by keeping both the outer surface of BodySrf and the inner surface of DriveWheelWellGeo as shown in Figure 4.39c.

5. RMB click BodySrf and pick-mask Trim Edge. Click the trim edge to select it as shown in Figure 4.40a.

6. Choose **Edit Curves → Duplicate Surface Curves**. Immediately choose **Edit Curves → Rebuild Curve** with Keep CVs checked. You should see something like Figure 4.40b. This creates a curve around the trim edge and rebuilds it to properly parameterize it for extruding a profile curve.

7. Create a NURBS circle in the Z axis. This will be our profile curve. Snap drag it to the middle top EP on our duplicated curve. Scale it until it looks something like Figure 4.40c.

Figure 4.39

Trimming the wheel well

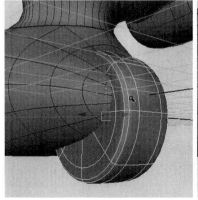
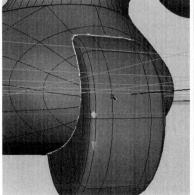

a   b   c

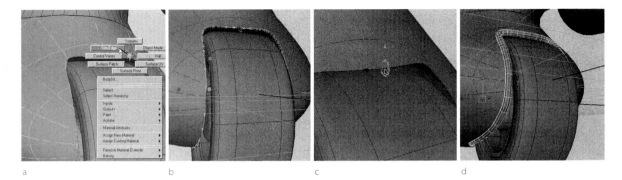

a   b   c   d

Figure 4.40

Extruding a profile circle around the rim of the wheel well using a curve duplicated from the trim edge

8. Shift+select the curve duplicated from the trim edge earlier. This will be the path along which we extrude the circle.

9. Choose **Surfaces → Extrude ❑**. Set Style to Tube, set Result Position to At Path, set Pivot to Component, and set Orientation to Profile Normal. These settings will extrude the profile along the path curve. Click Extrude, and you should see a surface like that shown in Figure 4.40d.

10. Due to the construction history associated with the Extrude command, this new extrusion is interactive. Changing either the profile curve or the path curve will result in a change to the final rim. So at this stage, scale or translate the profile circle and observe the effect that has on the extrusion.

11. When you are finished, delete history on the extruded surface and rename it DriveWheelRimSrf.

12. In the Outliner, add the extruded surface and DriveWheelWellGeo to the BodyGrp by MM dragging them on top of BodyGrp as shown in Figure 4.41.

13. Delete both the profile and path curve.

Figure 4.41

The before and after view of the Outliner after adding Drive-WheelRimSrf and DriveWheelWellGeo to BodyGrp

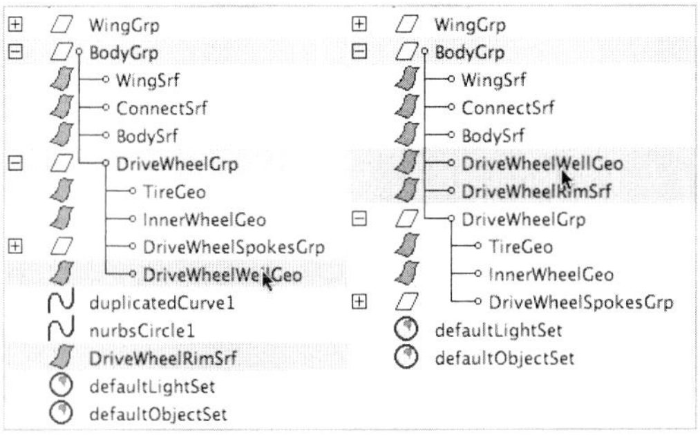

Using this technique, you can create any type of rim on these wheel wells that you like. Now let's duplicate this procedure for the front wheels.

1. Make FrontWheelLyr visible, and move and rotate FrontWheelGrp into position as shown in Figure 4.42a. Notice that part of the narrow, open side of the wheel well sticks out from the bottom of the body in the top image. Unless we correct this, we won't be able to trim either surface.

2. Pick-mask CVs on WheelWellGeo. Select and move the CVs of the left side of the wheel well over until it is completely enclosed by BodySrf as shown in Figure 4.42b. This will ensure that the curve generated by intersecting BodySrf with FrontWheel-WellGeo will be periodic.

3. Hide BodyLyr and show DrawingLyr if it is not visible already.

4. Select FrontWheelLyr, RMB in the Layer Editor, and choose **Set Selected Layers →
Unshaded**.

5. In the front view, manipulate the CVs of WheelWellGeo to better match the shape of the wheel well as shown in the drawing in Figure 4.42c. The wireframe layer view makes this operation a little easier.

6. RMB again in the Layer Editor and choose **Set Selected Layers → Shaded**.

7. Duplicate FrontWheelGrp across the Z axis by scaling –1 in X in the Duplicate Special option box. (Move the group's pivot point to the world origin first.) We are duplicating in X because we have rotated the group 90 degrees in Y.

8. Rename the children of this new group RHubcapGeo, RTireGeo, and RWheelWell-Geo, respectively.

Figure 4.42

Positioning Front-WheelGrp and editing WheelWellGeo to set up the trim operation

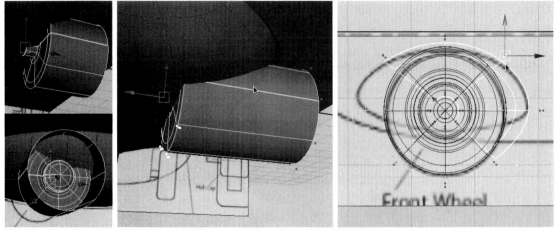

a   b   c

Figure 4.43

Adjusting the wheels and extruding the rim geometry

9. Intersect and trim each wheel well surface with BodySrf.

10. Extend the axles by pulling the CVs of Hubcap-Geo and RHubcapGeo into the body, and move both wheels into the body so they are closer to the inside of the wheel wells as shown in the top of Figure 4.43.

11. As you did with the drive wheel, extrude a profile along the edge of the wheel well by duplicating the trim edge and extruding a circle along it as shown at bottom in Figure 4.43. This time, however, create the circle in X.

12. Delete history, and rename the extruded geometry LWheelWellRimSrf and RWheelWellRimSrf, respectively.

13. Make all WheelWellGeos and WheelWellRim-Srfs part of BodyGrp. Notice that when you add the second WheelWellGeo to the BodyGrp, Maya appends a number at the end of the geometry's name.

14. Rename all surfaces and groups with appropriate L or R prefixes.

15. Delete the path and profile curves associated with this process.

Installing the Cockpit

The final element to add is the cockpit. We will import the cockpit fully constructed. You can easily build the cockpit with the information you have learned in this chapter, and you may choose to do so. The walls of the cockpit were extruded from simple curves. The windshield is lofted from three curves and then edited by pulling points. The dashboard and seat pieces are simple NURBS cylinders modeled into position and closed with a simple planar surface. (Simply select the end isoparm and choose **Surfaces → Planar**.) But a completed cockpit has been provided on the CD, and we will use that. We will add details such as a rim around the cockpit and windshield. Let's add the cockpit.

1. Import CockPit.mb from the CD.

2. Select CockPitInteriorSrf and BodySrf.

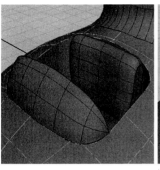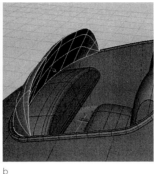

a   b   c

Figure 4.44

Trimming the cockpit and styling the windshield

3. Choose **Edit NURBS → Intersect Surfaces** ❒. As previously, we need to create a curve on each surface to use to trim both surfaces, so select Create Curves For Both Surfaces and set Curve Type to Curve On Surface.

4. Trim both surfaces and you should have something like Figure 4.44a.

5. Pick-mask Trim Edge and select the edge you just trimmed.

6. Duplicate that curve and rebuild the curve with Keep CVs.

7. Create a NURBS circle and point snap (hold down the V key) it to the curve you just created.

8. Shift+select the curve and extrude along the path.

9. Translate the profile so that there are no unsightly intersections.

10. Delete history on the extrusion and rename it CockPitRimSrf.

11. Pick-mask isoparms on WindShieldSrf, and select the edge isoparm as shown in Figure 4.44b.

12. Duplicate Surface Curves, and snap a circle to an edit point on the duplicated curve.

13. Extrude the circle along that curve and you should have a surface like that shown in Figure 4.44c.

14. Save your file as `MacGizmo06_CockPit.mb`.

And now the MacGizmo is complete!

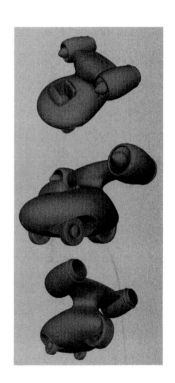

Cleanup

We need to get this model ready to pass off to the rigging and texture mapping technical directors. We need to make sure that all surfaces have no construction history and are grouped properly and that no unused groups or transforms are lying around the scene.

Can you proceed without doing this? Yes, but this is the type of cleanup that professional modelers do to make their files production ready.

1. Place WindShieldRimSrf and CockPitRimSrf into CockPitGrp by MM dragging them in the Outliner.

2. Place CockPitGrp into BodyGrp using the same method.

3. Select RFrontWheelGrp, LFrontWheelGrp, WingGrp, and BodyGrp and group them under a group named BodySrfGrp.

4. Choose **Edit → Select All By Type → NURBS Surfaces** and delete history on them. This is important to clean any construction history out of the surfaces.

5. Choose **Edit → Select All By Type → NURBS Curves** and delete them. If you lose any of your trims, undo and repeat step 4. Deleting curves before deleting trim history causes you to lose your trims.

6. In the Outliner, delete DrawPolyGeo and any empty transformations you can find.

7. In the Layer Editor, delete all layers except BodyLyr. Rename that layer BodyGeoLyr and assign BodySrfGrp to it.

8. This step may be optional. We have modeled the MacGizmo oriented along the X axis as we were following our drawing. The needs of the project may dictate that the model be oriented along the Z axis. If so, rotate BodySrfGrp 90 degrees in Y to orient it properly. If not, proceed to the next step.

9. Freeze transformations (Translate, Rotate, and Scale) on BodySrfGrp. This will zero out transformations for BodySrfGrp and all child nodes.

10. Choose **File → Optimize Scene Size**.

11. Save your file as `MacGizmo07_FinalGeo.mb`.

Summary

In this chapter, you learned how important parameterization is for turning curves into surfaces and then experimented with many techniques for working with NURBS surfaces in the context of building the MacGizmo. We dealt with several ways of hiding trim edges using extruded surfaces or circular fillets. We explored tangency and different ways of generating surfaces using fillets, and we used Maya's construction history to adjust surfacing operations after the fact. Last, you learned proper surface and group organization for passing the model down the pipeline.

In the next chapter, we will explore a variation on the theme of Machismo's head using subdivision surfaces. You will use a 3D template to create a low-resolution cage of Machismo's head and refine the surface using Maya's hierarchical editing capabilities. You will then apply blendshapes to the lowest level of the head and see how these changes propagate up to higher levels of detail.

CHAPTER 5

Subdivision Surfaces

Polygons offer a sculptural modeling technique, but they require a significant addition of detail to create smooth, organic models. NURBS offer smooth surfaces, but they require the adoption of an alien modeling paradigm that involves concepts such as stitching, parameterizing, and trimming. Subdivision surfaces offer a compromise between the smoothness of NURBS and the sculptural quality of polygons by providing a paradigm that combines some of the best features of both modeling types. Subdivision surfaces are typically used toward the end of the modeling production process in order to add smoothness and detail to models that would otherwise be too computationally expensive to deal with earlier in the production pipeline. This chapter will follow that workflow, modeling Machismo's head in polygons before converting it to subdivision surfaces for smoothing and detail work.

- Understanding subdivision surfaces

- Start with a template

- Modeling the head

- Details, details, and subdivision surfaces

Understanding Subdivision Surfaces

A subdivision surfaces (subD) is a hybrid surface combining many of the advantages of both NURBS and polygons. Like NURBS, subDs represent a large number of polygons that can be increased or decreased depending on the needs of the artist. A relatively small number of knots (control points) control a surface, which is tessellated into levels of smoothness that are appropriate for anything from interactive display on the computer monitor to high-resolution models for rendering to High Definition Video (HD) or film. Unlike NURBS, which are limited to manipulating four-sided patches into models, subDs also support polygonal topologies and modeling methods. Indeed, as you will see, it is most advantageous to begin modeling in polygons and switch to subDs for detailing. In fact, at the most basic editing level of a subD object (level 0), polygon vertices share the placement of the subD surface.

The greatest advantage of subDs is their hierarchical nature. Subdivision surfaces can create increasing levels of detail and you can switch between the display of higher and lower levels of detail while modeling. Also, changes made to the model at a lower level of detail propagate up to the higher detail levels. Furthermore, this varying level of detail can be localized so that surface detail and complexity can be added only where needed. With NURBS, modeling detail requires that the number of U and V spans be increased across the entire patch or object. This approach increases the computational weight of the model and is largely undesirable. Even polygons require a high degree of modeling to add localized detail without increasing the entire object's resolution. Figure 5.1 shows the relative surface resolution needed for each modeling paradigm. Notice how the subD surface in the middle has detail added only where needed.

Artists typically approach a model first by creating a low-resolution polygon version and then converting it over to subDs. After the conversion, the mesh becomes quite smooth; creasing is often used to retain intended harder edges.

Subdivision surfaces can be deceptive, however, in that they can promote bad modeling practices. You know that a primarily quad-based modeling effort is the best practice when modeling with polys. Triangles work, but *n*-sided polys should be avoided because they smooth strangely. Subdivision surfaces smooth *n*-sided polys fine, but the *n*-sided polygons

Figure 5.1

A NURBS, subdivision, and polygon surface manipulated with the Sculpt tool. Notice the different resolution for each with specific attention to the additional detail up through the center of the subD model.

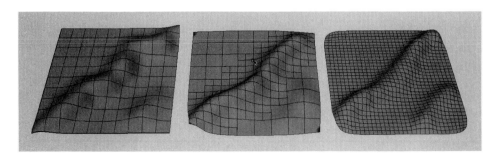

are not supported by mental ray for Maya; those objects containing polygons other than four sides will not render and may crash the renderer.

Subdivision surfaces can be edited in two modes: standard mode and polygon proxy mode. Standard mode allows you to edit the subdivision components of the model and view it as a true subdivision surface. In this mode, you can use the standard subdivision modeling tools and refine components into levels. At any point, you can switch the model into polygon proxy mode, which allows you to edit the general hull of the object as if it were a low-resolution polygon model. Also in this proxy mode, you can use any of the polygon modeling tools.

Start with a Template

We will be modeling Machismo's head using primarily polygonal modeling techniques. We will convert the head into subDs at the end of the process to add details such as veins and wrinkles using the Sculpt Geometry tool. But first, we need to start with a template.

We will be modeling the face poly by poly. This is sometimes called *point modeling*, because it involves creating each poly by placing points in 3D space. Unfortunately, Maya makes this difficult in that the program wants to place points on the nearest orthogonal plane; it is difficult to place points exactly where you need them. The way we can get around this problem is to provide curves on which to snap the points we will place. Figure 5.2 shows the completed template in 3D.

In *Maya: Secrets of the Pros 2nd Edition* by John Kundert-Gibbs, Dariush Derakhshani, et al. (Wiley, 2005), Tom Capizzi and Krishnamurti Costa wrote an excellent chapter outlining the process of planning and executing a cage for a head during the head-modeling process. They emphasize the need for planning the head through extensive drawing and edge-loop articulation.

Figure 5.2

The 3D template complete

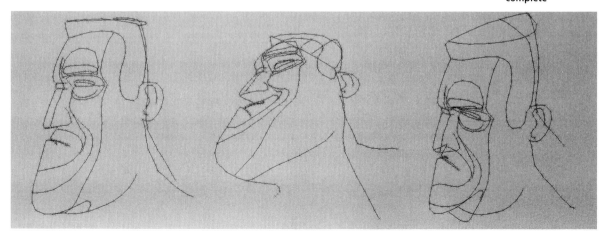

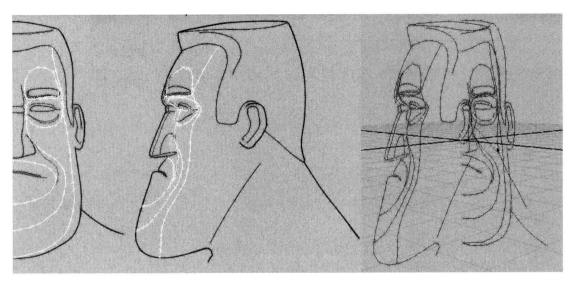

Figure 5.3

The template traced and arranged in perpendicular orientation. Notice the edge loops and contour lines selected at left

Creating this template is not terribly difficult; you can use the techniques you learned in Chapter 3 while working on Machismo's body. Create the 3D template like this.

1. Trace the head drawing with linear curves. Make sure, as always, to trace all the details. But also try to estimate in both views where edge loops and plane changes will occur. The left two images in Figure 5.3 show these tracings with edge loops and plane change lines selected. Note that, with the exception of the line on the side of the nose, these are not contour lines per se. They are simply indicators of where the surface will change direction. We will use them to snap polygons in areas with no obvious detail.

2. As you did with the body template, group and rotate the side view so as to line up parallel with the YZ plane and translate the front view to be perpendicular with the side view as shown at right in Figure 5.3.

3. Switch your layout to Two Panes Side By Side, and make one front and the other side orthogonal views.

4. Place the side view and front view lines on separate layers. Template the side view lines.

5. Select each line in the front view and pick-mask Edit Points.

6. Move each EP on each front view line. Select and translate each EP in the Z axis only to match the side view line. Figure 5.4 shows this process for the edge loop around the eye. Do this for each line in the front view group. Don't forget that you can use the arrow keys to pick-walk down the line and save yourself some mouse clicks.

7. Some lines that run around the volume of the head, most notably the line of Machismo's flat-top haircut and his neckline, will have to be pulled out of the side view to line up with the front view template.

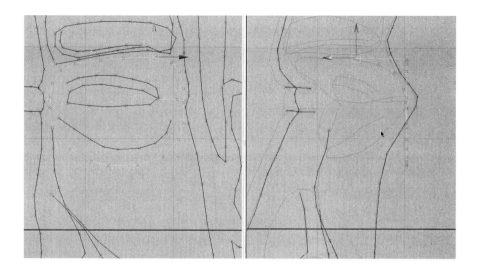

Figure 5.4

Pick-mask Edit Points on the lines in the front view, but pull them in Z from the side view.

8. When you have pulled all the lines you need, go back and delete the interior lines of the side view template. These lines have served their purpose and will get in our way when modeling.

9. Save your file as Head3dTemplate.mb. It should resemble the template shown in Figure 5.2, earlier in this chapter.

Modeling the Head

We will be modeling the head using primarily the Create Polygon and Append To Polygon tools. Remember, we are going to rough out the general shape using polygonal modeling practices and then convert the head into a subdivision surface toward the end. We will start with the eye cavity, which has certain constraints placed on its shape. No matter what 2D shape the eye itself takes, it must conform to the 3D shape of a spherical eyeball. Failure to allow for this will cause enormous headaches later when the eyeballs and eyelids are rigged. So let's begin modeling the head at the eye.

1. Open Head3dTemplate.mb.

2. Create, translate, and scale a NURBS sphere into the position shown in front and side views at the top of Figure 5.5.

3. Make the sphere live by clicking the Magnet button in the Status line. This will turn it into a green wireframe. Now the EPs of the line of the eye can be snapped to it.

4. Pick-mask Edit Points on the eye template line as shown in the middle of Figure 5.5. Notice that when you select the Move tool, there is a circle at the center of the manipulator instead of the usual square. This shows that Maya is going to constrain the movement to some element, in this case, the live object.

5. Snap the points to the live surface by moving them slightly back and forth in the front view. You will notice them snapping to the surface in the side view.

6. Continue until all the EPs are snapped as shown at the bottom of Figure 5.5.

7. Edit the wrinkle line to match the edge of the eye. Don't worry about the eyelid line at this point.

8. Deselect everything and click the Make Live button to make the sphere not live.

9. Delete the sphere.

10. Save the file as `MachismoHead01_EyeCavity.mb`.

> You may have noticed that the descriptions in this chapter are more general than they were in earlier chapters. They are becoming broader because as you work you will become more proficient and should need less specific direction, and you may even make variations that will make this character yours.

Figure 5.5

The process of conforming the eye line template to the live sphere

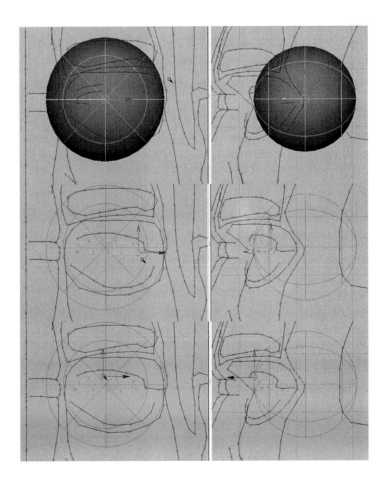

Now we are ready to begin the eye cavity. But remember that this template is there to make your modeling task easier. It is not the end in itself; the model is. Therefore, if you need to deviate from the template, feel free to make the change. With that in mind, let's begin to model the eye cavity area.

1. We will begin this model with a single polygon, so choose **Mesh → Create Polygon Tool**. For some reason, Autodesk does not include this tool on the default polygon shelf, so let's add it by MM dragging the icon from the Tool Box to the shelf.

> You can also add menu items to the current shelf by holding down Ctrl+Shift and selecting an item from a menu.

2. Holding down the C key to temporarily enter Snap To Curve mode, click the eye template line created earlier. This sets the first point on the line.

3. With the C key held down, immediately click to the right of the first point. The image in Figure 5.6a shows this step.

4. Still snapping with the C key, click the edge of the brow loop, as opposed to the eye cavity edge loop below it, to set the next point, as shown in Figure 5.6b. Notice the pink triangle that forms; this is how the shape will materialize.

5. Hold down the C key, and click the fourth point to the left on the brow loop as shown in Figure 5.6c.

6. To change the location to a different line, MM click with the C key held down and drag on the new line. You should see the point snap to the eye cavity curve as shown in Figure 5.6d.

7. Press Enter to create the polygon. If you need to step back during the course of creation, press the Backspace key.

Figure 5.6

The process of creating the first polygon on the eye cavity

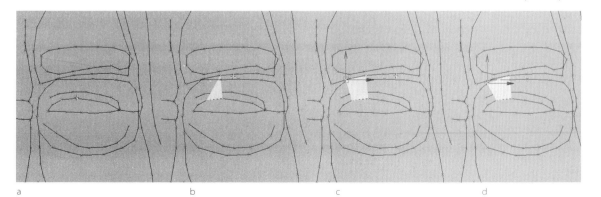

a   b   c   d

We could have entered Snap To Curve mode by clicking the button in the Status line. You may find, however, that holding down the C key to temporarily enter Snap To Curve mode gives you more flexibility by allowing you to leave it by letting go of the key. Although requiring a little more manual dexterity, it is a quicker and more versatile way of working.

We now have our first polygon. Remember that at the beginning of Chapter 3, you saw that point order—the order in which the points of a polygon were created—determined surface direction. By clicking in the counterclockwise order in this example, we created a polygon that faces out from the model, which is what we want. Note, however, that we are constrained from here on to appending polygons to this polygon in a counterclockwise clicking order. Let's append some polygons and complete this stage of the eye cavity.

1. Choose **Edit Mesh → Append To Polygon Tool** and immediately MM drag the tool's icon from the Tool Box to the shelf.

2. If it is not already selected, click the first polygon. Notice that when you do, all the edges light up thicker than normal.

3. Click the right edge to start appending polygons. You will see arrows pointing along each edge that you can append to, and a point will appear at the bottom corner of the polygon, as shown in Figure 5.7a. The append process will begin from this edge.

4. With the C key held down, click to the right along the eye template curve. This sets the next point as shown in Figure 5.7b. Notice the pink shape beginning to form just as with the Create Polygon tool.

5. With Snap To Curve enabled, click the bottom of the brow edge loop line as shown in Figure 5.7c.

6. Instead of pressing Enter, press the Y key to append the polygon and reengage the tool. You are now ready to append again. Click the edge of the new polygon as shown in Figure 5.7d.

7. Continue around the eye, creating about 13 polygons as shown in Figure 5.7e. For the last polygon you append, you will not need to click the curve but rather from edge to edge.

Figure 5.7

Using the Append To Polygon tool to create the eye cavity

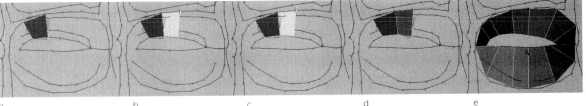

a   b   c   d   e

You have now completed this stage of the eye cavity. Let's begin the nose and combine it with the eye cavity we just created. We will then set up a smooth preview on the right side by creating a subdiv proxy. Doing this allows us to preview what the head would look like if it were already a subdivision surface. Begin the nose.

1. At the top middle of the forehead, create and append polygons as shown in Figure 5.8a. Remember to click in a counterclockwise order. Also, note that although the polygons were appended by snapping to the curve at the tip of the nose, their edges were moved inward along the X axis because we want the nose to be a little sharper than the drawing indicates.

2. Select both the nose and eye objects and choose **Mesh → Combine**. This creates one object out of both surfaces.

3. Use the Append To Polygon tool to create another line of polygons as shown in Figure 5.8b. Append from edge to edge to connect the two shapes. And as always, don't be afraid to pull vertices to change the shape of the model to get what you want.

4. If the polygon folds over in the course of appending, as shown in Figure 5.8c, immediately undo, select all the faces of either object, and choose **Normals → Reverse**.

5. To help match edges, choose **Edit Mesh → Split Polygon Tool** to split an edge out from the eye, as shown in Figure 5.8d.

6. Append another row of polygons up the center of the forehead as shown in Figure 5.8e.

To see how the model will increase in resolution either by smoothing at render time or by converting into subDs, we will create a subdiv proxy. Creating a subdiv proxy is beneficial because we can preview an

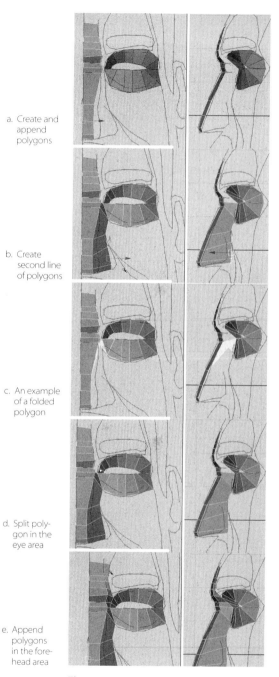

a. Create and append polygons

b. Create second line of polygons

c. An example of a folded polygon

d. Split polygon in the eye area

e. Append polygons in the forehead area

Figure 5.8

Combining the nose and eye shapes, and using the Append To Polygon tool to connect them accurate smoothed head without committing the polygonal model to a subdivision surface. Create a subdiv proxy and be sure to mirror across the X axis to create a higher-resolution duplicate. (If you are not sure how to do this, review the process in Chapter 3.)

After setting up the subdiv proxy, we will extend a line of polygonal skin down the sides of the cheek. We will use this as a base to append polys into the mouth area. Figure 5.9 shows this process.

1. Append polys to the nose and eyes to create the cheek as shown in Figure 5.9a.

2. Create a five-sided polygon as shown in Figure 5.9b. To do this, click the inside edge, place a point on the inner curve and then the outer curve, and then click the outside edge. This will allow you to append quads around the face and then use the Insert Edge Loop tool and Split Polygon tool to split these quads and convert the five-sided polygon to quads.

3. Append quad polygons around the mouth area all the way to the center line. At the bottom near th e chin, you will have to place the points freely by clicking to set the point and MM dragging in both front and side view to place them correctly. Notice how the edges all appear to radiate outward from the mouth. This will allow the mouth to deform properly.

4. Use the Insert Edge Loop tool to split this row of polygons automatically. Then use the Split Polygon tool to correct the five-sided polygon. Figure 5.9c shows how to finish this row.

5. As always, move the vertices created by this new edge outward to avoid allowing this area to look flat. Remember, any time you split a flat polygon, you need to manipulate the new edge or vertices to give some definition and break that initial flatness.

6. Finish by deleting history on this geometry.

Figure 5.9

Creating the rows of polygons around the cheek area

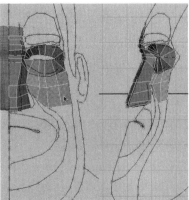 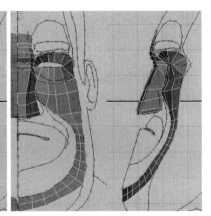

a. Append polygons in the cheek area.   b. Create five sided polygon.   c. Finish the row of polygons.

Defining the Mouth

We will use the same basic procedure to define the mouth area. You may have noticed by now that while appending on a polygon-by-polygon basis is powerful, it can be slow, so whenever possible we will create a single polygon and create edge detail later. Let's define the mouth.

> When defining the edges and inside of the lips, keep two things in mind. First, don't model the lips together or too far apart. Try to leave them slightly open and slack. This will make either weighting or selecting vertices when modeling blend shapes easier. Second, when modeling the inside of the lips, don't go too far. Just model the inside of the lips area. Otherwise you run the risk of the inside of the mouth protruding outside the face when animating.

1. Append a polygon from the bottom of the nose to the mouth line as shown in Figure 5.10a.

2. Split a line of edges down from the tip of the nose to the mouth line using the Split Polygon tool.

3. Append a six-sided polygon as shown in Figure 5.10b. This will allow you to append quad polys around and into the mouth.

4. Append quads all around the mouth using the curves as shown in Figure 5.10c.

5. Split the six-sided poly you created in step 3.

6. Split a thinner line of polys just outside the inside edge with the Insert Edge Loop tool, and then finish with the Split Polygon tool. You can see this completed in the top corner of Figure 5.10d.

7. Use the Insert Edge Loop tool to split a line of edges that will serve as the front of the top and bottom lip as shown in Figure 5.10e.

Figure 5.10

Building the cheek and mouth area using the Append To Polygon tool and the Insert Edge Loop tool

   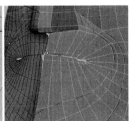 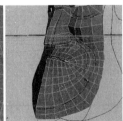

a. Append a polygon from the nose to the mouth.

b. Append a six sided polygon.

c. Append polygons around the mouth.

d. Split the edges of the lip.

e. Split further edge loops around the mouth.

Figure 5.11

Extruding and defining the inside of the lips

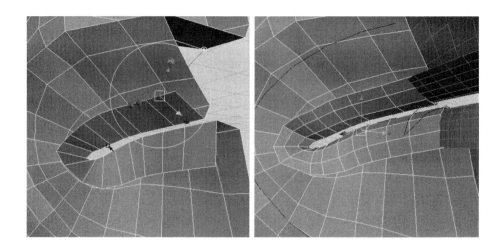

8. Pull out the vertices at the top and bottom of the lip to match the contours of the template drawing.

9. Add two rows of edges radiating outward from the lip area.

10. Pull vertices outward as needed to round out the surface of the mouth.

11. As always, delete history when finished.

Define the inside of the lips with three lines of polygons as shown in Figure 5.11. Select and extrude the inside edge of the lips back and up into the mouth; then add edges and pull the resulting edges to define the lips.

Modeling the Forehead and Eyebrows

Here is where our 3D template will truly help create the forehead. We will work around the eyebrow and finish by extruding the eyebrow slightly in anticipation of adding creases when we convert to subDs. Let's create the forehead/eyebrow area.

1. Append two polygons at the corners of the eyebrow as shown in Figure 5.12a.

2. Append polygons all around the eyebrow as shown in Figure 5.12b. Split a line of polygons down the center of the brow to the eye. Pull them into position as shown in Figure 5.12b. It is crucial that there be an equal number of edges at the top and bottom of the brow.

3. Append polygons to fill the brow shape, and then split as shown in Figure 5.12c.

4. Extrude the brow faces as shown in Figure 5.12d. Round out the brow vertices as shown in Figure 5.12d.

5. Continue appending polygons to fill out the brow to the hairline as shown in Figure 5.12e.

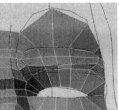

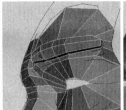

a. Add polygons at the inside and outside corners of the brow.

b. Build up the forehead using the Append To Polygon Tool.

c. Fill in the eyebrow by appending polygons.

d. Extrude the eyebrow faces.

e. Complete the brow by appending polygons.

Figure 5.12

Filling out the forehead and eyebrows

Finishing the Nose and Eyes

We now need to extrude the nostrils on the nose and create more of an eyelid than we have now. Let's finish the nose.

1. We will actually begin finishing the nose by adding a line of edges from the top center of the brow down around the bottom of the nose as shown in Figure 5.13a.

2. Select and extrude the six faces at the bottom side of the nose. The first extrusion should contract inward toward the center rather than project outward from the nose. The top image in Figure 5.13b shows how this works.

3. Translate some of the vertices of the nose to round out the top of the nostril. The result can be seen in the bottom of Figure 5.13b.

4. Select the same six faces and extrude them as you did in step 2. Pull these out and round out the side of the nostril as shown in Figure 5.13c.

5. On the bottom of the nose, create the nostril hole by splitting polygons as shown in Figure 5.13c; then delete all the edges on the interior of the shape you created. This will create one polygon, which will allow you to extrude the nostril hole more easily.

Figure 5.13

Finishing the nose and nostril hole

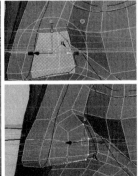

a. Split a line of polygons down the side and bottom of the nose.

b. Extrude and round out the polygons.

c. Select and delete the edges.

d. Extrude and delete the *n*-sided polygon.

6. Extrude the nostril at least three times up into the nose. After each extrusion, scale and translate the extrusion to go back into the nose.

7. Delete this single polygon and you should have something similar to Figure 5.13d. Delete history on the face and you are finished.

We will approach the eye cavity differently. Machismo has somewhat recessed eyes with pronounced bags under them. We will finish his eye by adding rings of detail around the eyehole and edit the model accordingly.

1. Pull all the vertices of the eyehole out from their current location just enough so that you can extrude or append a line of polygons, giving the eyelid some thickness.

2. Either by extruding these edges or appending, create this row of polys extending back into the head.

3. Immediately extrude the back edge of polygons and pull them out to create the smallest hint of an inside edge of the eyelid. This operation is similar to what we did with the lips.

4. Using the Insert Edge Loop tool, split a line of edges around the outside of the eye cavity. Push the vertices along this edge back into the head at the inside and outside of the eye and out from the head at the top and bottom of the eye.

5. Create another line of edges and repeat the previous step. When you are finished, you should have something similar to Figure 5.14.

Finishing the Polygonal Version of the Head

The next series of images detail the completion of the head. There are no modeling techniques used in the next series of images that you haven't seen before. Figure 5.15 outlines the procedure used to finish the head. Append and split polygons to add a couple of lines

Figure 5.14

The finished eye. Note at left how the back of the eyelids projects away from the edge of the eyelid.

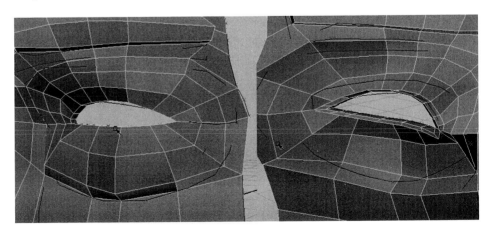

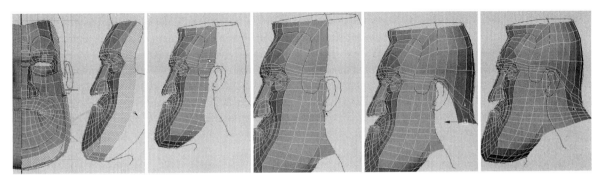

Figure 5.15

Finishing the head by appending, splitting, and extruding polygons

of polygons extending back from the side of the head. Add a construction like that shown in the middle of the head of the middle image. This will form the ear later. Extend the hairline around the back of the head. Then extrude the back of the hairline down to form the back of the neck. Close up the side of the neck and then extrude the neck down.

The top of Machismo's flattop is fairly simple. Figure 5.16 shows how to append polygons to the center curve and then split a line of edges one polygon in from the center line. Then connect the triangles that result.

The process for creating the ear is shown in Figure 5.17. With a stylized character such as Machismo, it is acceptable to leave the ears as tabs as in the top middle image here, but some creative splitting, collapsing, and deleting of edges will allow you to create the detailed ear shown at the lower right.

Figure 5.16

Finishing Machismo's flattop

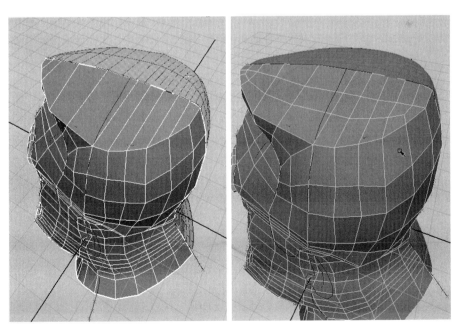

Last, add a line of edges around the front of the bottom edge of the flattop and down around the sideburns, and connect it to the back edge of the hairline above the ear as shown in the middle of Figure 5.18. Pull the sideburns out to provide an edge to the hairline as shown on the right in Figure 5.18.

Figure 5.17

Creating Machismo's ear. If realistic detail is not important to your project, you can leave the ear as shown in the top middle image.

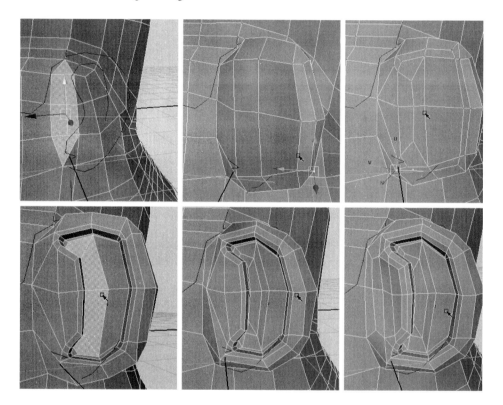

Figure 5.18

Finishing the hairline

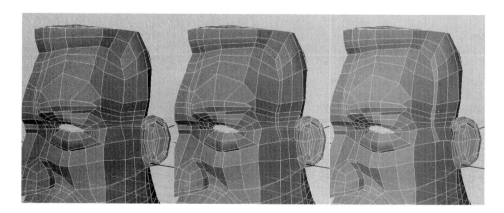

Details, Details, and Subdivision Surfaces

We have created all the broad features of Machismo's head and are ready to dive into creating the finer details that will give Machismo his individual character. But because we are going to convert this model to subDs with that paradigm's hierarchical level editing capability, we need to plan ahead to determine which details we need to model into the head's base-level surface and which we will want to leave for higher-level edits. A fundamental rule of thumb for creating detail in a subD model should be this: If the detail will be moved, either through a deformer or a blend shape, model it into the base mesh. On the other hand, if the detail can be carried along the surface of the model, model it into a more refined level. We do this because we will want to apply deformers and blend shapes to the base zero level mesh.

The polygon-by-polygon modeling technique we used to create the head mesh has the benefit of making an organized mesh. However, at this stage, the model is also smooth. Details that should be sharp—the hairline, the creases in the bag under the eye, and the folds on the nose—are soft and undefined.

Open `MachismoHead04_PolyDetail.mb` and examine it. All these details have been added and sharpened by adding polygons at key places on the face. If you create a quick subdiv proxy, you will see that the model sharpens quite nicely in those areas. However, this has come at the cost of a higher polygon count. Also, any additional details such as secondary wrinkles along the bottom of the eye or on the forehead would also have to be modeled into the base polygonal mesh or created using a bump map.

With Maya's subdivision surfaces, however, we layer these sharper details on a finer mesh and use the coarser, base 0 mesh to drive the deformation. Open `MachismoHead05_SubDHeadStart.mb`. This is the original modeled but undetailed head, mirrored and welded using the Merge Edge tool. So let's convert the head and begin modeling details.

> Our normal work flow would be to create UVs on the half head before mirroring and welding the halves together, but as that is beyond the purview of this chapter, we will save it for Chapter 12.

1. Select the head (SubDHeadGeo) and choose **Modify → Convert → Polygons To Subdiv □**. What you need to remember about this box is that the Maximum Base Mesh Faces field number shown here *must* be equal to or higher than the number of faces in the polygonal mesh you are about to convert. The number of faces in this head equals 1590; setting this number higher than that will result in a successful conversion. Setting it lower will cause the operation to fail. If you have been modeling efficiently, you shouldn't have to set this value much higher than 3000. The Maximum Edges Per

Vertex value defaults to 32, which is way more than you should need if you model with any degree of efficiency. Click Create.

2. We now have our subD mesh, but we want to set up our preferences to see what level we are working in a little better. Choose **Window → Settings/Preferences → Preferences** and choose Subdivs from the Categories window pane.

3. Under Subdivs Display, switch from Points to Numbers as your Component Display option. Click Save to make the change.

4. Pick-mask Vertex to display the 0 level vertices. You will see that these vertices conform to the original polygonal vertices on the model.

5. RMB pick-mask Display Finer. Notice that 1s appear above the more refined areas of the model. This is the level 1 mesh that Maya creates on top of the level 0 base mesh.

6. Pick-mask Display Finer again to display the level 2 vertices on the mesh. Only a small number of these vertices exist on the model, but their existence will serve our purposes nicely later. Also note that you can pick-mask the level of display by choosing the display level directly in the marking menu.

7. Pick-mask Object Mode, select the model, and then press the 1, 2, and 3 keys on your keyboard to see how Maya smooths the display of the subD head interactively.

Edges are extremely important to subD modeling because it is possible to create creases along the surface of the model automatically using the Full Crease Edge/Vertex command of the Subdiv Surfaces menu. As we are working on the full head model, we can add some asymmetry to our modeling efforts if we so choose. Let's add creases to this model.

1. Pick-mask Edges on the head. Also, if you are not displaying level 0 edges, pick-mask Display Level 0.

2. Select the edges that run along the brow furrows as shown in Figure 5.19a.

3. If you haven't already, switch to the Surfaces menu set. Choose **Subdiv Surfaces → Full Crease Edge/Vertex** to create a crease and add level 1 topology to the furrow. The edges you selected should now be dotted lines as shown in Figure 5.19b.

4. Translate these creases back in Z to see how they work as shown in Figure 5.19c. Immediately undo as we will be animating these creases later.

Create full creases at different places on the model. Figure 5.20 shows all the edges that have been made into full creases depicted in white; all partial creases are indicated in black. All parts should be fairly clear except the eyes. The front of the eyelids should be partially creased, and the back part of the eyelid that rubs against the eyeball should be fully creased.

Figure 5.19

Select edges and create creases. The effect of moving the creases back temporarily is shown at the bottom. (Edge selections thickened at top for clarity.)

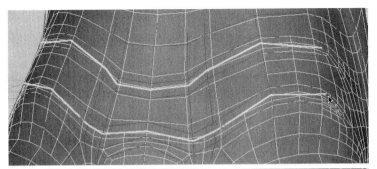

a. Select edges.

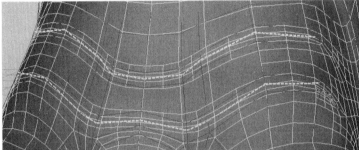

b. Create full crease.

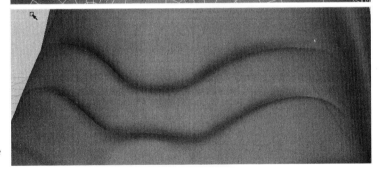

c. Pull edges back into the head to form the creases.

Figure 5.20

The base level 0 model at left is smooth before creasing. Full creases are drawn in white on the middle image, and partial creases are drawn in black. The final model is shown at right.

As stated before, any details modeled at a more refined level will be carried along by deformations applied at a coarser level. So let's edit our base head at a more refined level by using the Sculpt Geometry tool. Let's place a scar on Machismo's lip.

1. Open `MachismoHead06_SubDHeadfin.mb` or continue working on the file from the previous tutorial.

2. Zoom in to the lip area, RMB pick-mask edges, and Display Level 1 as shown in Figure 5.21a.

3. Select a set of edges on either side of where you want your scar, and RMB select Refine Selected. This will add selective detail to that area of your lip as shown in Figure 5.21b. If you make a mistake, immediately choose **Subdiv Surfaces → Clean Topology** to go back to a simpler surface.

4. Choose **Subdiv Surfaces → Sculpt Geometry Tool** ❑. As with all other times you've used this tool, set the brush size appropriately, probably to about 0.1 or so. Use the solid blue brush as we will want as sharp a drop-off as possible. Set your max displacement to something small, probably to about 0.2 or so.

Figure 5.21

Machismo likes to brag that he got this scar in a bar fight in Mombassa, but he really got it when he tried to open a glass bottle with his teeth!

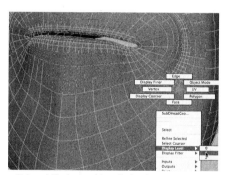

a. Pickmask Display Level 1 on the head

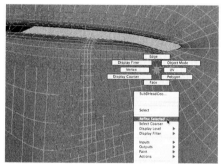

b. Refining the area of the scar

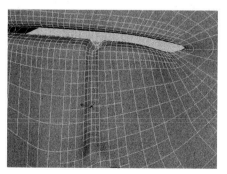

c. Create the scar with the Sculpt Geometry tool.

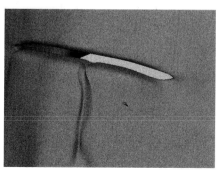

d. Create a wavy edge to the scar.

THE SCULPT GEOMETRY TOOL HOT KEYS

The hot keys for using all the sculpt tools are as follows:

- Hold down the U key to choose Push, Pull, Smooth, and Erase functions and set reflection axes.

- Hold down the B key and LM drag to set the diameter of the brush interactively.

- Hold down the M key and LM drag to set the Max Displacement value. This is indicated numerically and by the length of the arrow that changes as you drag.

- Hold down the N key to set the brush opacity, which is not useful here but is great for weight painting.

5. Sculpt a depression in the lip running down to the middle of the chin as shown in Figure 5.21c.

6. And for that real, broken-bottle scar look, select some of the edges along the sides of the scar and crease them. Select individual edges and translate them so that the scar has a wavy irregular shape as shown in Figure 5.21d.

7. Choose **Subdiv Surfaces → Clean Topology** to remove unnecessary detail in the more refined levels. Delete history to complete the model.

8. Save your file.

Now let's see how this detail rides on a blend shape deformer applied on the level 0 base mesh.

1. Import `SneerBlendShape.mb` from the CD. Note that it is not only coarser than the subD head we've been working on, but it is also still in polygonal form! It is often easier to model in polygonal form and convert than it is to model broad shapes in subD surfaces, especially on underpowered computers.

2. Select the new object and convert it to a subD surface.

3. Pick-mask Vertices on both SubDHeadGeo and polyToSubd1. Set both to display Level 0. Marquee select the new mesh, and then Shift marquee select the detailed mesh as shown in Figure 5.22a. Unless all the vertices on both objects are selected, the blend shape operation won't work.

4. From the Animation menu set, choose **Create Deformers → Blend Shape ❒**. Name the node L0BlendShape, and make sure that Check Topology is checked. Click Create to create the blend shape node on the base head.

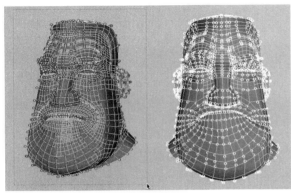

a. Select the Level 0 vertices on the blendshape geo.

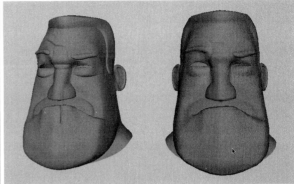

b. The blendshape drives the subdivision surface head and the scar moves too.

Figure 5.22

Selecting both meshes at Level 0 and the two meshes after the blend shape is applied and activated

5. Choose **Window → Animation Editors → Blend Shape** to open the Blend Shape Editor, or find the node in the Inputs list in the Channel Box and change the blend shape's single target value to 1. You should see something like Figure 5.22b. Notice how the scar travels with the lower lip. It does this because the topologies at Level 0 on both models match perfectly.

Setting the blend shape at the object level would force the topologies of both levels to match, meaning that Maya would place level 1, 2, 3, and 4 topology on the blend shape target to match the base head. This would not only slow down the whole operation, it would cause the scar and all creasing to vanish as the blend shape would apply to *all* hierarchical levels in the model.

Summary

Maya's subdivision surfaces are improving with each new release of the software. In this chapter, you have seen how they offer the ability to apply deformations at lower, coarser levels of a model to carry more detailed levels with no deleterious effects. With single-level topologies, such as NURBS or polygons, point order prevents blending objects with different levels of detail. This is the great advantage of using subdivision surfaces.

In the next chapter, which covers advanced modeling techniques, we will explore a way to create blend shapes quickly.

CHAPTER 6

Blend Shapes: Advanced Modeling

In this chapter, you will learn a unique technique for accelerating one of the more tedious tasks associated with character modeling: creating blend shapes. Blend shapes are parts of a series of models that can morph into each other and are used primarily for facial animation. Creating these models can often be quite complex; we will discuss using joints to help model a large number of blends quickly.

- **About blend shapes**

- **Assembling Machismo**

- **The incredible (edible) blend shape machine**

- **The Paint Blend Shape Weights tool**

About Blend Shapes

Blend shapes modeling involves the tedium of creating many variants of the main head of your character. In creating these variants, you are usually limited to changing or deforming one particular part of the head or face—the mouth, eyes, brow, cheek, and so on—to create a series of different facial expressions. Some may require a great deal of modeling; others might just need a few vertices pushed in or pulled out.

Often, the modeler has to roll up their sleeves and begin massaging points to get what they want. Some modelers use clusters, lattices, or wire deformers as a sophisticated means to create individual blends. Nothing discussed here prevents you from using any of those techniques.

Maya's blend shapes are a special type of deformer that deforms the vertices of one object, called the base object, to conform to the vertices of one or more target objects. In other software packages, this process is called morphing or shape matching. Maya's blend shape node compares the position of every vertex in the base object with the matching vertex in the target object and moves the base object's vertices to match. The blend shape node makes allowances for offsets of the target object's position in space, and for this reason you must *never* freeze transformations on a target object.

The blend shape node identifies each vertex by *point order*. In Chapter 3, you saw that each vertex in an object is numbered; Maya uses these numbers to determine which vertex on the base object will be controlled by the same-numbered vertex on the target object or objects. Therefore, once blend shape targets have been modeled, no points can be added to or deleted from the base object.

Blend shape deformations are additive, meaning that they compound on top of one another. This can be counterintuitive. For example, a vertex on two blend targets is moved 0.5 units in Y. When these two targets are applied to the base object, the corresponding vertex on the base object will move 1 unit in Y.

Each blend shape node has an envelope that globally controls the effect of each blend target's weight in deforming the base object. The envelope works like a multiplier for the node. If the envelope value is 2, each weight factor doubles; if it is 0.5, each weight value has half its strength. Changing the envelope value is inefficient compared to achieving the same effect on an individual target level by changing the weight of each target. You can double the effect of a target by changing its weight to 2. This is much more flexible and efficient than using the envelope value.

Rather than trying to model both sides of the head, we will model only half and use Maya's wrap deformer to help us create both halves of the face. This will allow us to create many more blend shapes than if we had to work on both sides at the same time. We will discuss a two-stage process using nonhierarchical joints constrained to geometry to create half-head shapes. We'll then use those as blend shapes on a wrap deformer to mold each half of the symmetrical, full-head, final blend shape. And, as an addition, we will discuss applying a partial body blend shape to a single skin character. In fact, we must do this first.

Assembling Machismo

Open `Machismo01_HeadBodyStart.mb` from the CD to see the polygon detailed head and body sized to match the schematic drawing. If you are combining your own files, see the sidebar "Completing Machismo's Head in Polygons" before importing the head into the body file. The actual size is unimportant; the head should be sized to match the body. Most likely, the number of vertices in the neck area of the head will not match the number around the neck hole of the body. In this case, the head has 13 faces and the neck hole has 11. This is common; it is difficult enough to model the head and body without having to worry about how the actual number of vertices is going to match in the future, and we can correct the problem. So with this in mind, let's join the head.

1. If a part of the neck is too close to the body to effectively append polygons between the two objects, delete the bottom row of faces to make room. In this case, that leaves a lot of room in the back, but that is okay because that will provide room for the polygons to contract when Machismo raises his head.

2. Check Normals on both objects to make sure they all face in the same direction by choosing **Display → Polygons → Face Normals**. If the normals do not match, reverse them on the object where they face inward by selecting that object and choosing **Normals → Reverse**. Both objects' normals should face outward.

3. Freeze transformations and delete history on both objects.

4. With both selected, choose **Mesh → Combine** to fuse them into one object.

5. Use the Append To Polygon tool to join the two objects as shown in Figure 6.1. Note the method used to combine two head edges to one body vertex by creating a diagonally oriented quad polygon as indicated by the pointer. This is a common way to join an area of higher detail to an area of lower detail.

COMPLETING MACHISMO'S HEAD IN POLYGONS

You may have noticed that the head we have joined to the body is different from the way we left it in Chapter 5. The base head we converted to subdivision surfaces and then detailed had no sharp detail. We added detail using creases and hierarchical edits later in the chapter. We do not have that luxury here. Open `HeadSidebarComparison.mb` from the CD and compare the two heads. The edits that have been made to DetailedHead are simple furrow cuts hooked onto existing edges. Figure 6.3, later in this chapter, shows the creation of the brow furrows in the forehead. These furrows will actually be used to animate the wrinkling of the brow when we create blend shapes, but they are a broad example of how to create details that sharpen edges by hanging edge rows onto existing vertices. Details you will want to sharpen using this technique are the bags under the eyes, the crinkle at the edge of the eyes, and the wrinkle along the bridge of the nose.

The other details consist of mainly adding rows of edges near an edge that needs to be sharpened when the model is smoothed. These consist of primarily the hairline, eyebrows, eyelids, and the front edges of the upper and lower lips. These additional lines will sharpen those details when the model is smoothed.

Figure 6.1

Using the Append To Polygon tool to join the head and body

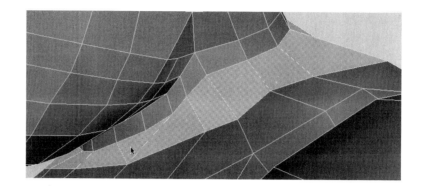

6. Split this new line of polygons down the middle. To deal with the five-sided polygon/triangle combination created, split the diagonal quad by either collapsing the triangle or splitting the five-sided polygon.

7. Soften the transition between the head and body by either pulling points or using the Sculpt Geometry tool set to smooth. You can also choose **Mesh → Average Vertices** ❑ and set the Smoothing Amount option to 5. Figure 6.2 shows how to smooth the transition between the head and neck. Using the pick-walk command to move the selection row is useful here (pick-walking is the action of pressing the arrow keys to select neighboring components of a currently selected component). The Average Vertices command averages the locations of the selected vertices with those around them to get the new location. How close it gets to the final averaged location with each command is controlled by the iteration factor. Generally, it is wise to start with a low number of iterations. Pick-walk around the head using the arrow keys and choose Average Vertices as needed. Finish by manually smoothing the chest area edge vertices.

Figure 6.2

Smoothing out the transition between neck and head

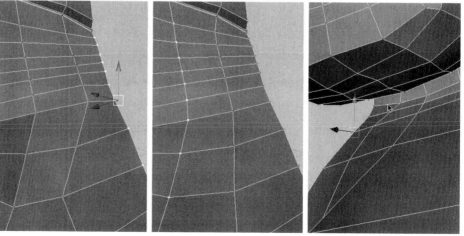

a. Manually smooth the edge vertices.   b. Pick-walk around the head.   c. Manually smooth the chest area edge vertices.

8. Soften the normals to remove the faceted look at the joint (and on the head) by choosing **Normals → Soften Edge**. (See Figure 6.3). Under the Normals menu, the Soften Edge and Harden Edge options are actually presets of the Set Normal Angle menu item. Soften Edge sets the normal angle on edges to 180 and blends the shading across all the faces to give a soft look. Harden Edge sets the normal angle to 0 and yields a faceted look.

9. Delete history.

Having joined the head to the body, we are now ready to mirror and sew up the body to make a complete piece of geometry. At this stage, however, it is wise to create your UV map for this single-skin character. We will create the map in Chapter 12, but for now, we will simply cut some more details into Machismo's costume. We should create a neckline for the shirt, glove edges for the hands, boot edges for the feet, and shorts lines for his tights. This will make our UV mapping operation much easier, as we will be able to build seams into our maps. When you are finished, save your file as Machismo03_HalfBodyNoUVs.mb.

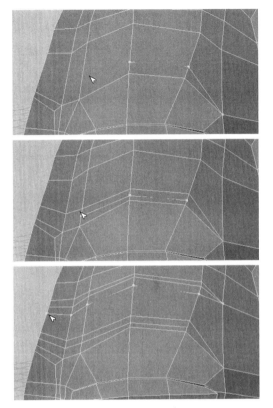

Figure 6.3

Creating furrow lines in the brow

Off with His Head!

Machismo is at present a single-skin mesh with 4624 faces and 4653 vertices. To create blend shapes conventionally, we would need to create duplicates of the entire mesh to deform one part of the face. Clearly, the additional 4624 faces added to the file for each facial shape multiplied by the 30 or 40 shapes needed for even a basic set will cause file size and memory requirements for Maya to explode. We need to be able to separate the head from the body to make the blend shapes.

Splitting the head from the rest of the body destroys the single skin, makes weighting difficult, and makes texture matching, if the split occurs in the middle of a UV patch, much more complex. So what we will need to do is combine the head back to the body and merge the vertices back into the body.

Wait a second! Didn't we just join the head to the body? Why are we splitting it again? We joined the head to the body to blend two completely separate objects into one mesh. And remember that we joined the half head to the half body; now we are working on the completed body mesh. But won't that disrupt the point order on the head? After all, aren't we adding the points in the body to the head of the base object? The answer is that if the points of the head of the base object match the points of the head of the target object, the blend shape will work. You can blend between objects of different vertex totals if the vertices of the area on the base object match the numbers of the vertices on the blend target. So first, let's separate the head.

> This technique is somewhat complicated. Be sure to read each step *very* carefully. Mistakes early on may not be apparent until later when the entire technique fails, so be patient and careful as you work through this tutorial.

1. Open `Machismo05_BlendShapeStart.mb` from the CD. This file contains the full body mesh with UVs (which will be created later in Chapter 12). We will use these UVs to help select the faces we want.

2. Choose **Window → UV Texture Editor** and then select BodyGeo. You will see the UVs appear in the UV Texture Editor window.

3. RMB pick-mask UV in the UV Texture Editor window. Select one UV on the face, one UV on the top of the head, and one UV on the bottom of the nose, as shown in Figure 6.4a. If you want, confirm your selections by looking in the perspective window.

4. RMB click in the UV Texture Editor window and choose **Select → Select Shell** from the marking menu, as shown in Figure 6.4b. This selects all UVs on each UV patch where you made the original selections.

5. RMB click and from the marking menu choose **Select → Convert Selection To Faces**, as shown in Figure 6.4c. You can now close the UV Texture Editor window.

6. In the perspective viewport, pick-mask Face on the object as shown in Figure 6.4d.

7. Choose **Mesh → Extract** (with Separate Extracted Faces checked in the Options menu). Make absolutely sure that **Edit Mesh → Keep Faces Together** is checked. This will create two objects grouped under the original object name.

Figure 6.4

The UV Texture Editor can be a useful tool for selecting groups of vertices, faces, and UVs.

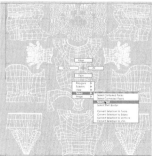

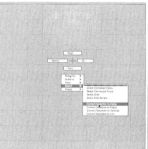

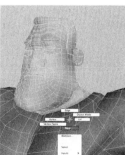

a. The UV layout with one UV selected on all the head pieces.

b. Choose Select Shell from the marking menu.

c. Convert to faces.

d. Pick-mask Face.

8. Select the new head object and duplicate it with the duplicate grouped under the world.

9. Translate the new duplicate head back to –4 in Z so it is arranged behind the head. Center its pivot.

10. Rename this object HeadBlendBaseGeo. We will hook all our further blend shapes to this head because it lets us separate this operation from the main head.

Now we need to reattach the head to the body while keeping the point order arranged properly.

1. Select the head object and then Shift+select the body object. The selection order is *important* because when we combine the two objects, Maya will start ordering the points from the first object selected.

2. Choose **Mesh → Combine** to merge the two objects. Name the new object BodyFinalGeo.

3. Pick-mask Vertex on BodyFinalGeo.

4. Choose **Select → Select Using Constraints** to open the Polygon Selection Constraint On Vertices option box.

5. Under the Properties rollout, set Location to OnBorder and click the All and Next radio button under the Constrain section. This should select all the vertices on the borders of this object. This will include vertices on the inside of the mouth, on the eyes, and on the nostrils as shown in Figure 6.5.

6. Click Close And Reset. This will close the box and undo all the constraint settings, which is important; otherwise the next step will not work.

Figure 6.5

The model with all the border vertices selected as specified in the Polygon Selection Constraint On Vertices options box. HeadBlendBaseGeo has been hidden for clarity.

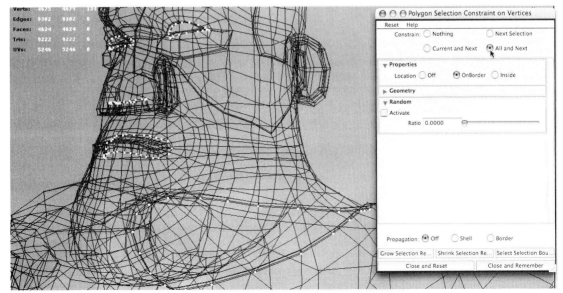

7. Deselect the vertices around the eyes, nose, and mouth by LM Ctrl+clicking and marquee selecting around them. Do not deselect any of the vertices around the collar. Notice how many vertices are left selected in the Heads Up Display (HUD).

   (If you do not see a Heads Up Display in your perspective viewport, enable it by choosing **Display → Heads Up Display → Poly Count**.)

8. Choose **Edit Mesh → Merge** ❏. Reset the settings and click Apply. Immediately note the HUD reading for vertices. The number of vertices selected should now be exactly half of what it was before this operation. If there are more than half, some vertices were too far away to merge with the default value. Undo and raise the Distance value a little; then reapply. If the value is less than half, some pairs of vertices merged. Undo, reduce the distance, and reapply, although it is difficult to see how the default value of 0.0001 could be too large.

9. Select the object and soften normals to remove the faceted edge, although given that this edge met the body at the neckline of the shirt, this step is optional.

10. Delete history on BodyFinalGeo.

Having reattached the head, we now need to apply the HeadBlendBaseGeo as a blend shape. This will confirm that our efforts to preserve proper point order have been successful. Create the blend shape like this.

1. Select HeadBlendBase and then Shift+select BodyFinalGeo. Remember that the blend shape will apply to the last object selected.

2. Choose **Create Deformers → Blend Shape** ❏. Name the blend shape node HeadBaseBlend and uncheck Check Topology. This latter step causes Maya to ignore overall details in object topology. Failure to uncheck Check Topology will prevent Maya from creating the blend shape node. Click Create to create the blend shape node called HeadBaseBlend.

3. Select BodyFinalGeo and you will see the HeadBaseBlend node and a tweak node in the Inputs section of the Channel Box. Click HeadBaseBlend to open it.

4. For the weight, set the field next to HeadBlendBaseGeo to 1. If nothing changes on the model, congratulations! You have a working blend shape and can proceed. If, on the other hand, you end up with something like Figure 6.6, you probably selected the body object before combining. You will need to start over from the beginning. Also, accidentally changing point order by deleting vertices anywhere on either head or body object will cause the model to tear apart because the point order will have changed.

5. If you want to see how your blend shape will deform BodyFinalGeo, select some vertices on the target object and deform them. The matching vertices on BodyFinalGeo should deform to match.

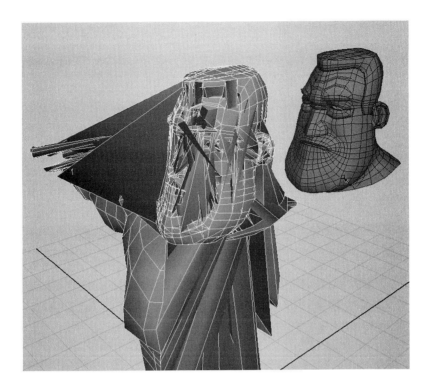

Figure 6.6

When blend shapes go bad! This is what happens when you select the body object before combining.

This technique works because vertices 1 through 1908 on BodyFinalGeo match up exactly with 1 through 1908 on the blend target HeadBlendBaseGeo. Therefore, you must realize that you can only use this for one body part on the single-skin mesh. It would be impossible to extract/separate and recombine the arms or legs for corrective blend shapes, as that would disrupt point order. Now let's set up our Blend Shape Creation Machine.

The Incredible (Edible) Blend Shape Machine

Okay, you can't eat it, but if you model blend shapes for a living, this work flow may make your life and livelihood a little easier. The traditional work flow for modeling blend shapes is to duplicate the base object and then model the duplicate into a target shape. As it is common, best practice to separate shapes into left and right versions—left and right smile, for example—this can get tedious in a hurry.

Some common modeling techniques are vertex modeling; lattice, wire, or cluster deforming; and soft modification of selected components. These are all fine, time-tested techniques with their own unique advantages and disadvantages; nothing disqualifies or makes impossible their use in the blend shape modeling pipeline. Our purpose here is to discuss a new way of modeling using Maya's joints arranged nonhierarchically to deform a half-head object. With minimal setup, we will have a mechanism by which we can quickly model a host of targets that we will then use on a full-head model. Let's begin to create this blend shape by producing a rig.

1. Open `Machismo06_BlendMachineStart.mb` from the CD. This file picks up where we left off after attaching the head to the body in the previous tutorial.

2. Create three layers: BodyLyr, SkullLyr, and SkinLyr. Assign BodyFinalGeo to BodyLyr and hide that layer.

3. Duplicate HeadBlendBaseGeo, name the duplicate SkullGeo, and assign it to SkullLyr. Holding the X key down, snap-move it to the world origin.

4. Assign HeadBlendBaseGeo to BodyLyr. It should disappear.

5. Duplicate SkullGeo, rename it SkinGeo, and assign it to SkinLyr.

6. Hide SkullLyr.

7. Pick-mask Faces on SkinGeo and delete the left half of the face. You can see the result at the left in Figure 6.7.

8. Choose **Skeleton → Joint Tool** and with the X key held down, grid-snap a single joint at the world origin. This will serve to hold the majority of the head vertices in place. Press the Y key to create this one joint and stay in the tool.

9. With the V key held down, click a vertex along the center line on the tip of the nose to place one joint on the end of the nose as shown at the left in Figure 6.7. Press Enter to create the joint and leave the Joint tool.

Figure 6.7

Placing individual joints at the world origin first and proceeding to place them on the surface of SkinGeo

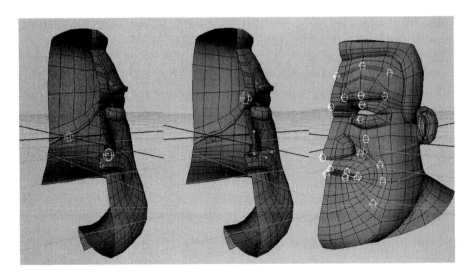

10. Select the second joint you created, duplicate it, and vertex-snap it to the middle of the brow as shown in the middle image of Figure 6.7.

11. Continue duplicating and vertex snapping until you have something like what appears at right in Figure 6.7.

> If the joints are too small to be seen or selected properly, change their default size by choosing **Window → Settings/Preferences → Preferences** and changing the Joint size setting in the Kinematics category. The joints shown in Figure 6.7 are set at about .24.

Virtually every book and tutorial on facial blend shape modeling contains some drawing depicting the muscles of the face and pontificates about how the modeler should conform to the moving points to simulate movement along these muscles. It then leaves the modeler with no actual way of simulating these muscle movements. What we want to do here is make these joints able to slide along the surface of the SkullGeo to better simulate this muscular action. To do that, we will use the Geometry constraint. Let's constrain these joints to SkullGeo.

1. Hide SkinLyr and display SkullLyr.

2. Select SkullGeo and Shift+select the nose joint.

3. Choose **Constrain → Geometry**. This constraint keeps whatever is constrained pinned to the surface of the model. In this case, the joint will slide along the surface of SkullGeo, thus facilitating the simulation of muscle movement.

4. Shift+click the nose joint to deselect it.

5. Repeat steps 2 through 4 for each joint on the surface of the model. Leave the joint at the world origin alone. A fast way of doing this is to Shift+deselect the joint just constrained, Shift+select the next joint, and press the G key to invoke the last menu command. The deselected joint should be purple, which indicates that it is connected in some way to the still-selected surface geometry.

Let's name our joints for the purposes of discussion. Which joint gets which name should be self-explanatory. If you do not do this before binding, you will not have these names to draw on when painting weights.

HeadBaseJNT	NoseJNT	BrowJNT
BrowInsideJNT	BrowMidJNT	BrowOutJNT
EyeBrowInJNT	EyeBrowMidJNT	EyeBrowOutJNT
EyeLidTopJNT	EyeLidBtmJNT	FaceJNT
SneerJNT	CheekTpJNT	CheekMidJNT
CheekBtmJNT	LipTpInsJNT	LipTpMidJNT
LipTpCrnrJNT	LipBtmCrnrJNT	LipBtmMidJNT
LipBtmInsJNT		

Now we need to bind these joints to the SkinGeo. We will use Maya's Smooth Bind command to create a skin cluster for the entire half head. Skinning this head offers several advantages:

- Within the skin cluster, each joint acts like a cluster unto itself, offering the advantages of cluster deformers without the disadvantages of that deformer type.

- Smooth-bound joints can spread the influence of one or more joints as far within the cluster as needed. This allows the joints that control the edge of the mouth to deform the forehead slightly as happens with actual flesh and blood.

- As you have seen, individual joints can be constrained to move along a skull object, thereby simulating muscular deformation of skin.

- Joints and the resulting skin mesh can be reset using the **Skin → Go To Bind Pose** command.

- For modeling purposes, the weights of individual joints can be painted/changed to fit the needs of the target object.

There is one potential disadvantage to using skin clusters to model blend shapes, and that ties in to blend shapes' additive nature. For example, when a person smiles, their entire face moves. The skin on the neck, cheeks, ears, forehead, and eyebrows shifts minutely. If you build that shift into the smile blend target, it could potentially cause problems when you combine the brow lift with the smile targets. You must therefore use care when creating these blend targets.

The other side of the argument is to limit influence to each part of the face, but this can create the problem inherent to using blend shapes. Often, facial animation created solely with blend shapes looks like each separate part of the face is moving independently. The mouth moves, but the eyes don't. This separateness often causes facial animations to look extremely plastic and unconvincing.

So with these advantages and disadvantage in mind, let's bind the joints to the head like this.

1. Hide SkullLyr and display SkinLayer.

2. Marquee select all the joints you created in the last tutorial.

3. Shift+select SkinGeo.

4. Choose **Skin → Bind Skin → Smooth Bind** ❑. Set Bind to Selected Joints, and set Bind Method to Closest Distance. Normally, joints are parented in a chain called a hierarchy, but we are using a nonhierarchical arrangement. Set Max Influences to 4. This will assign no more than four initial influences at binding time. Each vertex will then have no more than four influences, which is enough for modeling. Check Maintain Max Influences After Bind. This will limit each vertex to no more than four influences at any time. The good news is that this should keep joints that are far from a particular

point from influencing that point. The bad news is that if, for some reason, you paint a vertex with influence from a fifth joint, one of the original four influences, usually the one with the lowest amount of influence, will be removed and the other values will be adjusted so that they equal 1. This could lead to unexpected results. Set Dropoff Rate to 10. This creates a sharp drop-off of influence around the joints. Uncheck Remove Unused Influences because we are sure all these joints will be used, and uncheck Colorize Skeleton because the colors it assigns appear somewhat confusing. Click Bind Skin to create the bind.

You should remember that, unlike using weights for binding a character to a skeleton, we will be using these joints to massage this mesh into different shapes. Therefore, the weights are completely malleable throughout the modeling process. This will also provide some good practice for painting weights later during the character setup process. Now save your file; you can save it with a name you devise or as `Machismo07_WeightPaintStart.mb`, as that's what it will be referred to in the next section.

Blend Shapes: Sneers, Blinks, and Smiles

Before we actually begin weighting and modeling, we need to bring in some teeth and eyes to use as reference for our efforts. Few things are as frustrating as spending hours modeling blend shapes only to find that some or all of them cause the base object to intersect internal geometry. So open `Machismo07_WeightPaintStart.mb` from the CD and import `EyesandTeeth.mb`. Immediately assign FaceGeoGrp to a layer called EyeTeethLyr. Reference that layer to prevent accidental selection.

Of course, painting weights at this point would be premature because we don't know what specific shapes we will be making. We need to decide this first. Describing the modeling of a complete set of blend shapes for each facial feature would be long and largely redundant. Our key here will be to model particular shapes and weight-specific joints that are similar to the shapes we'll be creating later each facial feature. For example, weighting and modeling a smile will make creating the frown shape that much easier. To create these shapes, we will weight, translate, and even scale some of the joints on the face. Our list will be as follows:

Nose_Sneer

Lower_Lip_Up

Upper_Lip_Up

Eye_Closed

Eye_Wide_Open

Eyebrow_Up

Smile/MouthWide

Jason Osipa has written an excellent book called *Stop Staring: Facial Modeling and Animation Done Right* (Sybex, second edition 2007) that covers in depth which shapes to create and why. Although our methods and rationalizations for creating shapes differ at times, Jason's book features plenty of material that is useful on the subject of blend target creation.

Nose_Sneer

This shape can emphasize either a smile to create a look of high humor or a frown to create a look of deep disgust. Figures 6.8a and 6.8b show the default weighting for the NoseJNT and SneerJNT. After the basic shape has been roughed in by rotating joints, the weights can be adjusted to refine that shape. For example, weighting the SneerJNT consists mainly of flood painting with the Paint Skin Weights tool set to Smooth. We accomplish this as follows.

1. With SkinGeo selected, choose **Skin → Edit Smooth Skin → Paint Skin Weights Tool ☐**. There really is little difference between this box as applied here and any other sculpt tool.

2. RMB click the SneerJNT and choose Paint Weights from the marking menu. You will see something basically similar to Figure 6.8a. Notice how sharp the transition is between the vertices where the edges intersect. We need to soften this.

3. Set Paint Operation to Smooth and click the Flood button until you see the smoothness extend over several vertices. The transition in the deformation at the bottom of the nose smooths out, and that map resembles Figure 6.8b.

4. Clean up the NoseJNT map (which should initially resemble Figure 6.8c) by selecting Smooth as the Paint Operation and hitting the Flood button. Also change the Paint Operation to Add and paint until the map resembles that shown at far left in Figure 6.8d.

Figure 6.8

The process of moving joints and adjusting weight maps to create the sneer blend

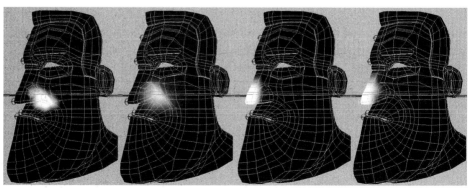

a   b   c   d

Painting weights will also be covered in Chapter 8, so reading that chapter can only help your efforts here.

Now let's create the half blend shape like this.

1. Select SkinGeo and duplicate it as a copy parented to the world.

2. Drag select from top to bottom the attribute list in the Channel Box at right.

3. RMB click the list and choose Unlock Selected. Now you can move the mesh.

4. Rename it Nose_Sneer.

5. In the Channel Box, set Translate X to 2, Translate Y to –7, and Translate Z to –4.

Get into the habit of translating your blend shapes off to the side in whole increments. It makes organizing the locations of blend shapes much easier because it is easier to type whole numbers than numbers with decimal points.

Finish this process by marquee selecting all the joints and choosing **Skin ▸ Go To Bind Pose** to reset the mesh and get ready to create the next blend target.

Lower_Lip_Up

This target will require you to move the joints up off SkullGeo as well as do extensive weight smoothing to achieve the desired shape. Display EyeTeethLyr in the Layer Editor first. Create this target as follows.

1. Shift+select LipBtmCrnrJNT, LipBtmMidJNT, and LipBtmInsJNT.

2. In the Inputs list in the Channel Box, find the geometryConstraint node. It should be labeled something like LpBtmCrnrJNT_geometryConstraint1.

3. Change the nodeState from Normal to HasNoEffect. This basically turns the node off, temporarily allowing us to pull the joints off the surface of the hidden SkullGeo.

4. Move the joints up to above the bottom of the upper lip as shown in Figure 6.9a. You will see that the inside of the lower lip doesn't move much because it is being incorrectly influenced by the upper lip joints.

When modeling blend shapes, it is generally wise to push past what looks natural on a facial pose. You can always dial a target weight back to bring it into line with what looks correct, but it is difficult to push the weight farther than what you have modeled.

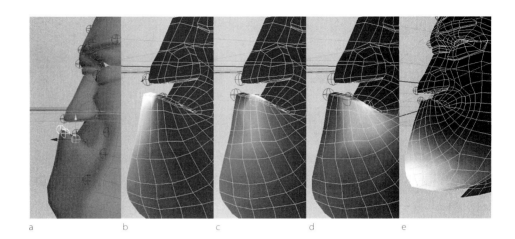

a　　　　b　　　　c　　　　d　　　　e

5. Correct this by add and smooth painting with the Paint Skin Weights tool. You can weight the points on the inside of the lips fully to the nearest bottom lip joint. Figure 6.9b, c, and d show how the outside of the lips should be weighted.

6. Take this opportunity to weight the skin for the top lip as well because these points will be improperly influenced by the bottom vertices.

7. To keep volume in the lower lip, rotate each joint –7 to –10 degrees in X along the local axis. This will cause the lower lip to puff out, but unfortunately it will probably cause the chin to move incorrectly. We will correct this by increasing the weighting of HeadBaseJNT in this area.

8. RMB select Paint Weights on HeadBaseJNT to select its map. HeadBaseJNT is the joint you want to use if you want to move points back to their default state. We don't use this joint to model, so any point influenced by this joint will be dragged back to its default position. Weight the chin area until you get something similar to Figure 6.9e.

9. Duplicate SkinGeo, unlock the attributes, and then move and rename the mesh Lower_Lp_Up.

Don't select Go To Bind Pose just yet. We will create the Upper_Lip_Up blend first.

Upper_Lip_Up

Because we need the lower lip in place to judge the correct position of the upper lip, we will move the upper lip into position and then reset the bottom lip joints. We do this as follows.

1. Shift+select LipTpInsJNT, LipTpMidJNT, and LipTpCrnrJNT and pull them up in Y. This will cause them to slide along the upper lip away from the lower lip.

2. Turn off their geoConstraints and move them forward to match the lower lip, as shown in at left in Figure 6.10.

3. Increase the influence of NoseJNT along the bottom of the nose to correct the distortion that resulted from step 2. (See the image on the right in Figure 6.10.)

Now we need to reset the joints on the bottom lip to their default positions. But Maya's Go To Bind Pose causes all the joints in the skin cluster to return to their positions at the time of binding, so we will need to fool Maya by keying the position of the top lip joints. Do so like this.

1. Move the Current Time Indicator in the Time Slider to frame 5.

2. Select the three upper lip joints. Choose **Animate → Set Key** to record the position, rotation, and scale of those three joints at frame 5.

3. Move the Current Time Indicator to frame 1.

4. Choose **Skin → Go To Bind Pose**. All the joints will snap back to their defaults. Note that a key has been set at frame 1 as well.

5. Return to frame 5 and you should see the upper lip joints move back into position while the lower lip joints stay in the bind pose.

6. Duplicate, move, and rename SkinGeo to Upper_Lip_Up.

7. Select the three upper lip joints. Drag select the attribute names in the Channel Box. RMB click the names, and choose Delete Selected from the pop-up menu to delete the keyframes you set in step 2 and step 4.

On your own, go on to create the Lips_Down blend shapes using this method.

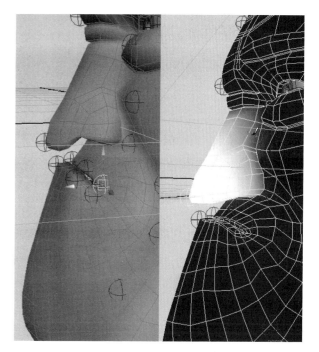

Figure 6.10

Moving the upper lip to match the lower lip and correcting the distortion in the nose by extending the influence of NoseJNT

Eye_Closed

Let's move to a different body part: the eyes. Machismo has a thick, rounded upper eye area. He has no actual eyelid but instead has a rounded area of flesh. That, coupled with his narrow, squinty eyes, makes this blend shape fairly easy to create. If a character had pronounced eyelids, we would want to find another way of closing the eyes because blend

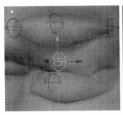

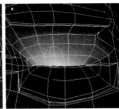
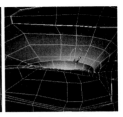

a. Select the joint.

b. Select PaintWeights on that joint.

c. Flood Replace with 0 influence.

d. Paint influence back into the map.

e. Paint the inside of the eyelid.

Figure 6.11

Creating the Blink blend shape by removing influence and painting it back in

shapes move linearly. This can cause the eyelid to move through the eyes when going from open to closed. Let's create this shape.

1. Select EyelidTopJNT and translate it down until it is just a little past where the eye closes completely, as shown in Figure 6.11a.

2. Select SkinGeo and open the Paint Skin Weights Tool options box. RMB select Paint Weights on EyelidTopJNT to select that map. See Figure 6.11b. As you can see, the influence extends too far up the forehead and down to the bottom of the eye.

3. Set Paint Operation to Replace, set Value to 0, and click the Flood button to flood the map so that EyelidTopJNT has no influence, as shown in Figure 6.11c.

4. With a small brush, add paint with a value of 0.1 or lower on the top of the eyelid until you get a shape that looks like Figure 6.11d. Smooth paint as necessary, but be wary of flooding the map with smoothing because that will cause the edges of the upper and lower eye to distort as the influence spreads into those areas.

5. If necessary to keep the area above the eye full, rotate the joint to fill out the area. Add and smooth paint as needed.

6. Hide the EyeTeethLyr and rotate the view to get a look at the inside of the head. Paint the inside of the eyelid until it looks like Figure 6.11e. Given that the influence on the front of the eye never reaches full strength, the weighting of the back of the eyelid shouldn't either.

7. Duplicate the mesh, and then move and rename this shape Eye_Closed.

8. Choose Go To Bind Pose to reset the joints and mesh.

Eye_Wide_Open

Moving EyelidTopJNT will indeed open the eyelid, but as things are now, it will also tuck the eye surface under the eyebrow, which we don't want. Instead of moving EyelidTopJNT, scale it down in Y beforehand. Also, move and scale EyeLidBtmJNT to open the eye wider. As always, paint weights to improve the deformation. Also, you will probably

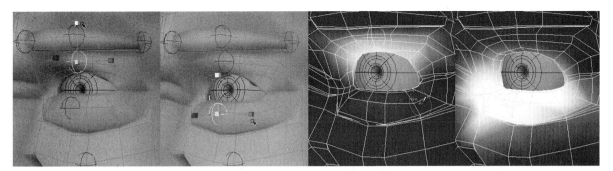

want to disconnect EyeLidBtmJNT's geoConstraint for more freedom of movement. Figure 6.12 details this process.

And don't forget to reset the joints after duplicating, moving, and renaming the mesh Eye_Wide_Open.

Eyebrow_Up

Set nodeStates of the three eyebrow joints to HasNoEffect, and translate them up and back on the head in Y and Z. This will cause the geometry to crinkle where the influence conflicts with the brow joints. Raise the three brow joints along the vertical line of edges on the brow. The hairline as well as the top of the head will move with them. Select the Add Paint Operation and paint the influence of HeadBaseJNT to counteract this effect. It is good for the hairline to move, but the top of the head should remain stable. Figure 6.13 shows what you should try to achieve in the forehead area. At far left, the brow and eyebrow joints have been raised, which affects the top of the head. Add back in HeadBaseJNT influence as shown in the left image. Smooth and add paint as needed as shown in the middle image. If a fold like the hairline fold depicted in the middle and right images develops, it is easiest to duplicate, move, and rename the mesh and then pull points on the duplicate until the fold is corrected. Remember, using joints to model is a fast way to move volumes of points accurately. Nothing stops you from moving individual points once the target is complete.

Figure 6.12

Creating the Eye-Wide target involves scaling and moving both the upper and lower eye joints and then weighting both those joints. You also must increase the influence of the joints around the eye joints and adjust each joint's influence.

Figure 6.13

Creating the Eye-brow_Up shapes by manipulating the eyebrow and brow joints, and then painting influence and correcting folds manually

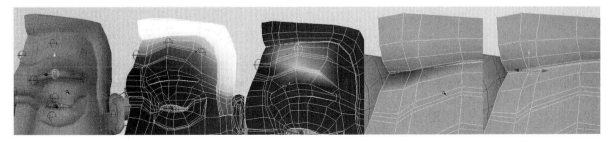

Smile Mouth/Wide

The left image in Figure 6.14 shows which joints should be moved to make the wide mouth target. The best way to approach this is to reconnect the geoConstraints for these joints and move them back along the head. This will cause the jaw and the rest of the head to move. Nail this part of the head in place by painting influence for HeadBaseJNT extensively through the neck and the back of the head, as shown at right in Figure 6.14.

You can now continue modeling blend shapes and painting weights as needed or proceed directly to the rest of the tutorial. Machismo08_WeightPaintFinish.mb on the CD contains an example of our work up to this point.

The Rest of the Shapes

You can use the techniques we've discussed in the preceding tutorials to create a host of expressions and phonemes. The list of shapes you can build will largely depend on the needs of your animation. It is certainly better to build too many than to build too few. The file we will use for the next phase of this tutorial, Machismo09_HalfHeadsDone.mb, contains both what we have already done as well as the following blend targets:

Lips_Pursed	Lips_Closed	Lips_Narrow
Lower_Lip_Dn	Upper_Lip_Dn	Frown
Lips_Curl_Up	Brow_Furrow	Squint
Eyebrow_In	Eyebrow_Dn	Eyebrow_Mid_Up
Eyebrow_Mid_Dn	Eyebrow_Out	Ear_Up

We can now move on to creating our full-head blend targets.

Figure 6.14

Move the indicated joints back along the skull and then lessen their influence by add and smooth painting influence for HeadBaseJNT.

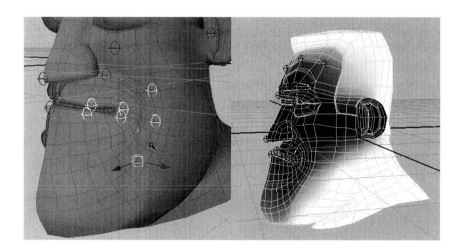

Molding the Full-Head Blend Shapes

No, "molding" is not a misspelling! Our modeling will resemble vacuum molding more than actual modeling. We will set up a procedure that will allow us to rapidly convert our half heads into full-head left and right side shapes. We will use a copy of SkinGeo as a wrap deformer to which we will apply all our half-head targets as blend shapes. We will apply the wrap deformer to a copy of SkullGeo, which will be our base object. Let's begin this process.

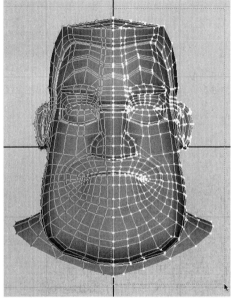

1. Create two layers called BaseHeadLyr and MoldLyr.

2. Duplicate SkullGeo and call the duplicate BlendBaseGeo.

3. Duplicate SkinGeo and call it MoldGeo.

4. Assign each piece of geometry to its respective layer.

5. Select all the half-head blend targets and assign them to MoldLyr.

6. Select all the joints and assign them to SkinLyr.

7. Hide all layers except BaseHeadLyr and MoldLyr.

In the file `Machismo09_HalfHeadsDone.mb`, notice how all the blend shapes are arranged so that blend targets for each facial part are close to one another. This will allow you to select each facial part in a logical order, making our next operation easier. Now we will want to create a blend shape deformer on MoldGeo.

Figure 6.15
Select only half the vertices on the BlendBaseGeo, and then select MoldGeo.

1. Shift+select every one of the half-head blend shapes. The order in which you select them will be the order in which they appear in the target list of the blend shape deformer.

2. Shift+select MoldGeo. Given that it is right on top of BlendBaseGeo, you may need to add-select MoldGeo in the Outliner.

> You can also type **select-add MoldGeo;** in the Command line.

3. Choose Create **Deformers → Blend Shape** ❑. Name the BlendShape Node FaceBlends and check the Check Topology check box. Click Create to create the blend shape node.

4. RMB pick-mask Vertex on BlendBaseGeo, and marquee select the half of the head shown in Figure 6.15.

5. Shift+select MoldGeo. The vertices on BlendBaseGeo should remain selected when you click MoldGeo.

6. Choose **Create Deformers → Wrap** ⬚. A wrap deformer acts like a lattice with a custom shape. Instead of having internal points like a cubic lattice, a wrap acts like a shell whose components deform the object to which the wrap is applied. In the option box, Weight Threshold specifies the amount of influence the wrap object will have, so set it to .01. This setting will work because we are going to check Use Max Distance and set the Max Distance field to .01 also. Max Distance is the maximum distance the components of the wrap object can be from the components of the deformed object. Given that each point of MoldGeo occupies the same point as that on BlendBaseGeo, this value can be small. Click Create to create the wrap object.

Now we have MoldGeo deforming half the vertices on BlendBaseGeo. We will use the blend shape node to create full-head blend shapes.

1. Hide MoldLyr. BaseHeadLyr should be the only layer visible.

2. RMB click on the Layout shortcut button and create a two-pane layout with one pane set to show the Blend Shape Editor and the other pane set to show the perspective view centered on BaseHeadGeo, as shown in Figure 6.16.

Normally, we would use the blend shape node in the Inputs list or custom attributes attached to an animation control to edit our blend shape because the editor takes up too much screen space. However, in this case, the Blend Shape Editor allows us to change target weighting without selecting any particular object. Other blend-editing methods require you to have a particular object selected, which is counterproductive here.

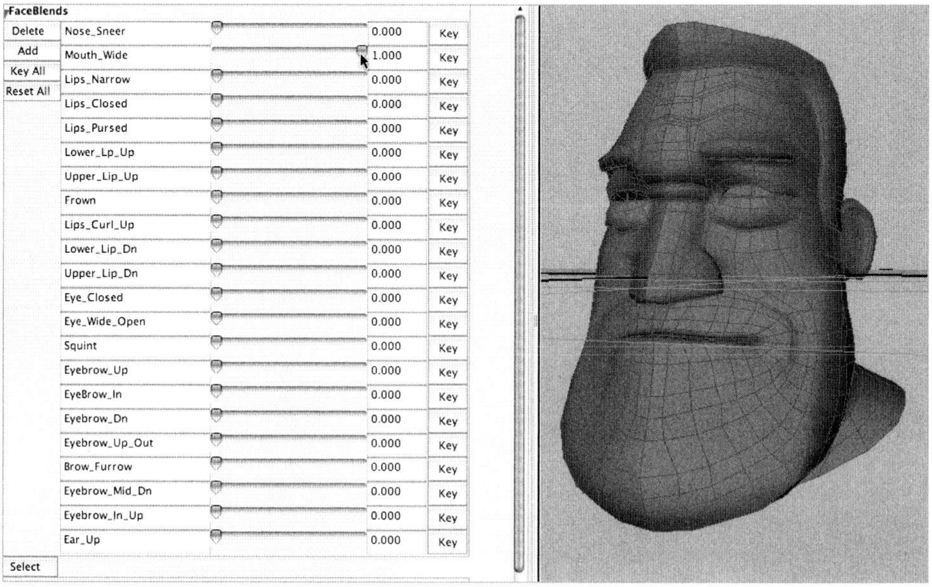

Figure 6.16

The pane layout most ideal for creating blend shapes. Notice how the Blend Shape Editor is set to the horizontal orientation. The Mouth_Wide target is weighted to 1.

Figure 6.17

Machismo and the 22 uglies! Here Base-HeadGeo is shown selected and all blend targets are visible.

3. Move the Mouth_Wide slider all the way to the right. The blend shape node on Mold-Geo draws the vertices of BlendBaseGeo into the same shape. Figure 6.16 shows how this works.

4. Duplicate BlendBaseGeo and rename it Mouth_Wide_L. Move it up and over to the side, but in the opposite direction from the half-head shapes. Remember to be as organized as possible because there will be a lot of shapes.

> You can move from renaming in the Channel Box down the attribute list by pressing the Tab key. This makes direct numerical placement easier than clicking with the mouse in each box.

5. In the Blend Shape Editor, return the Mouth_Wide target weight to 0.

6. Repeat steps 3 through 5 for each target in the list. At the end, you should have 22 targets, as shown in Figure 6.17. Append an _L to the end of the names of each of these heads as they will represent the left side shapes.

> You can make these blend targets less perfectly symmetrical by typing **1.1** or **.95** in the Weight field in the Blend Shape Editor. This either pushes the shape farther or dials it back from the full shape.

And Now, the Right Side

Now we need to create the right side blend shapes after cleaning up our work to this point.

1. Create a new layer called HeadBlendsLyr and assign all 22 targets to it. Optionally, while the targets are selected, you can change the wireframe color by choosing **Display → Wireframe Color**, choosing a separate color for the left side heads, and clicking Apply.

2. Set HeadBlendsLyr to Reference to prevent accidental selection of the targets.

3. Show MoldLyr as we will need to select MoldGeo.

4. Select BlendBaseGeo, Shift+select MoldGeo, and choose **Edit Deformers → Wrap → Remove Influence**.

5. With BlendBaseGeo still selected (MoldGeo deselects as the result of the Remove Influence operation), delete history. Deleting the wrap deformer this way cleans up any base geometry used by the wrap deformer, and then deleting history removes the wrap node completely.

6. Scale BlendBaseGeo −1 in X by typing **-1** in the scaleX field in the Channel Box.

7. RMB pick-mask Vertex on BlendBaseGeo. We are going to select half the head again, but unlike before, we want to leave the vertices along the midline unselected, as shown in Figure 6.18.

8. Shift+select MoldGeo.

9. Choose **Create Deformers → Wrap** using the same settings as earlier.

We are applying the wrap to these particular vertices because otherwise we would have double transformation problems anywhere the center line vertices moved on both left and right blend. By leaving them out of this blend shape set, we avoid this problem. Now let's create the right side targets as follows.

1. Set up the two-pane layout from earlier with the Blend Shape Editor on one side and the perspective view on the other.

2. As before, move the weight slider for Mouth_Wide all the way to the right to set it at 1.

3. Duplicate BlendBaseGeo.

4. Rename it Mouth_Wide_R.

5. Set scaleX to 1. Note how the shape reverses to be on the right side.

6. Move this target model directly above the Mouth_Wide_L target model. This is the procedure for placing our created targets: place them above or below their matching left side target. This will allow us to easily select both left and right side targets in order when applying them to the main head.

7. Repeat steps 2 through 6 for all targets in the list.

8. When finished, select all the new heads and assign them to HeadBlendsLyr.

9. Save the file as `Machismo10_BlendsDone.mb`.

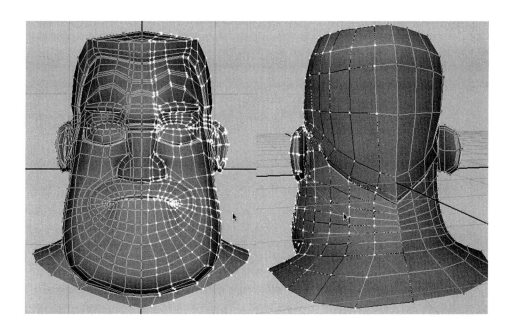

Figure 6.18
Notice how Blend-BaseGeo has all but the centerline vertices selected.

Now all that is left is to apply all 44 of these targets to our main head. Remember, at the beginning of this process, we separated a head to use as our base object. We will apply a blend shape deformer to this head.

1. Hide all layers except HeadBlendsLyr, which should be set to Normal display mode.

2. Select your pairs of left and right targets by holding down Shift and then selecting first the left and then the right shapes. Select each left pair first and each right pair second until they are all selected. Begin with the pair of targets you want to see at the top of the list and select from there.

3. Display BodyGeoLyr, and Shift+select HeadBlendBaseGeo. This is the base object to which we will apply the blend shape node.

4. Choose **Create Deformers → Blend Shape** ❐. Name the node MainHeadBlendShape and check Check Topology. Click Create.

5. Selecting MainHeadBlendShape in the Inputs list in the Channel Box gives instant access to the target weights. Manipulate them to create a variety of facial expressions as shown in Figure 6.19.

6. Group all the geometry we've created as you or the needs of your production require.

Open the file `Machismo11_BlendFinal.mb` to see the final version of our efforts here.

Figure 6.19

**Manipulating the
MainHeadBlend-
Shape on Head-
BlendBaseGeo
to create facial
expressions**

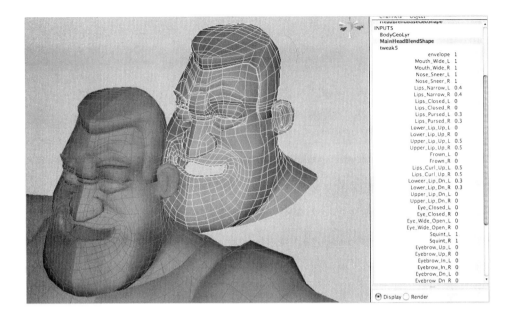

Figure 6.20

**Averaging the ver-
tices at the corner
of the eyelids to
correct the tangled
vertices**

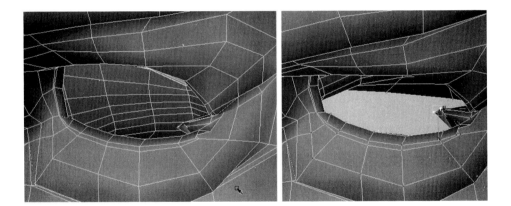

Correcting Problems

Problems don't always present themselves until the end of the process. The Eye_Wide_
Open_L and _R shapes are perfect examples of this. The left side of Figure 6.20 shows how
the corners of the eyes have become tangled. Untangling them is simply a matter of selecting the offending vertices and applying 12 iterations of the **Mesh → Average Vertices** command, as shown in the middle and right images of Figure 6.20. Then tweak the position
of the vertices as needed. Delete history to get rid of the average vertices nodes. Repeat for
the right side shape.

The Paint Blend Shape Weights Tool

You can weight blend shapes like joints, clusters, or other deformers. The mechanism by which they are weighted, however, is somewhat different. Instead of being weighted in a localized area, each target has a weight of 1 over the whole object.

This allows the user to literally paint with shapes! This opens possibilities for animation heretofore unexplored, but for blend shape creation it opens endless possibilities.

In the preceding tutorial, we created half shapes and used a technique to create two symmetrical full-head blend targets. But some people might prefer to model an entire head symmetrically or base their blend targets on entire heads representing single emotions. Painting blend shape weights allows you to recombine full heads to either create entirely new shapes or separate shapes for each facial feature as needed. Let's explore the extraction of half shapes first. Open `BlendWeightToolExample.mb` from the CD and let's begin.

1. Select BaseObjectGeo. This head has a blend shape with the three heads at right serving as targets.

2. Choose **Edit Deformers → Paint Blend Shape Weights Tool** ❒. The base object will immediately turn white as the selected target has an influence of 1 over the entire object. You must remember to separate the concept of target weight and target influence here. A target may have no influence, which will negate any weight it has.

3. From the target list in the option box, select Smug.

4. In the Inputs list in the Channel Box, set Smug Target Weight to 1. You will see the base object change.

5. Go back to the Paint Blend Shape Weights Tool option box. Set Paint Operation to Replace and set Value to 0. Click the Flood button. This will remove all the influence of the Smug target.

6. With a fairly large brush, add paint with a value of about 0.12 to bring back influence in the mouth area. Then select Smooth as the Paint Operation and hit the Flood button to soften the effect, as shown in Figure 6.20 in the previous section. If you need to reduce influence, replace paint with Value set at 0 and Opacity set at a value less than 0.1. In this way, you can get a fine degree of control over the deformation effect.

7. Duplicate BaseObjectGeo to create a new blend target.

Now let's explore creating a new whole-head blend shape with parts of each of these three targets.

1. Select Replace as the Paint Operation and hit the Flood button to replace the influence of the Smug target with a value of 0. You will have to increase Opacity to 1 before you flood to remove all influence.

2. Replace the influence of the remaining two targets by selecting them in the Targets list and flooding with a Replace Value of 0 and an Opacity of 1.

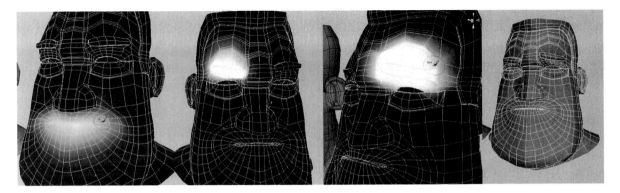

Figure 6.21

Creating an entirely new blend shape using localized influence from three separate blend shapes using the Paint Blend Shape Weights tool

3. In the Inputs list in the Channel Box, set the target weights for all three targets to 1.

4. Now, paint the mouth area with influence from Simpering as shown at far left in Figure 6.21.

5. Paint the right brow with influence from Smug as shown in the second image from the left in Figure 6.21.

6. Paint the left brow area with influence from Scared as shown in the second image from the right in Figure 6.21.

7. When finished, you now have an entirely new blend target as shown at far right in Figure 6.21.

Summary

By using Maya's joint and wrap deformers in nontraditional ways in this chapter, we have opened up a host of possibilities for blend shape modeling. They offer the highly desirable feature of being able to move large numbers of points quickly. Here we have used them with the necessary degree of control to create exactly what we want quickly. Combining blend shapes with Maya's ability to paint weights for blend targets opens up an almost limitless set of shape and emotional permutations.

In the next chapter, we will shift gears and explore some of Maya 8.5's basic animation features. We will discuss different types of animation available in Maya as well as basic keyframing using the Timeline. We will also use the Dope Sheet and Graph Editor to cycle and animate a bouncing ball.

CHAPTER 7

Basic Animation

This chapter introduces you to animating in Maya. We will define what keyframing means in Maya as well as discuss the program's tools for creating and manipulating keyframes. Learning to animate in Maya involves progressing from basic, simple keyframing of simple attributes to bringing characters to life through animating their performances and creating special effects through animating particles, fur, and so on. It also involves writing expressions and MEL scripts, which give the animator exquisite control over every aspect of the animation environment, and supervising and editing motion capture sessions to create extremely naturalistic animations for games, broadcast, or film. This chapter will get you started by introducing the following fundamental concepts and activities:

- **Animation types**
- **Keyframe animation**
- **Understanding animation work flow**
- **Bouncing a ball**
- **Converting cycled animation to curves**

Animation Types

Maya offers a broad range of animation types:

Keyframe Animation   Records the changes in an object's attributes as a curve over time. These recorded values—points along an animation curve—are called *keys.* Flying logos and characters are a simple and well known form of this type of animation.

Dynamic or Effects Animation   Involves the simulation of objects or phenomena using rules of physics as made possible by Maya's internal simulation engines. Fluids, particle effects (such as smoke), hair, fur, and cloth are all examples.

Path Animation   Allows you to specify NURBS curves as paths for an object or character to follow. Using this type of animation, you can have a car travel over land or a spaceship follow a specific path through space.

Motion Capture   A type of animation in which a live-action performance is recorded as a dataset that can drive a skeleton that in turn drives a character. For example, game developers often use motion capture of athletes for sports or fighting games.

Nonlinear Animation   Allows the animator to manipulate and edit groups of keyframes, known as clips in Maya's Trax Editor, much as one would edit video clips in a nonlinear video application. Looping and blending clips allows the animator to leverage a small amount of animation into longer animation performances. See Chapter 10 for more on nonlinear animation using the Trax Editor.

Technical Animation   Involves the use of driven keys, node connections, and expressions to create animation controls that allow the animator to drive characters and effects with a fine degree of control. The best technical directors/animators have an advanced knowledge of Maya Embedded Language (MEL), Maya's internal scripting language, which is introduced in Chapter 16.

This chapter will concentrate on keyframe and path animation. Later chapters will cover other animation topics.

Keyframe Animation

The technical definition of keyframing is the recording of changes in attributes over time, but this is a stale interpretation. Animation, which is a collection of keyframes played back over a set period of time, is properly defined as the act of breathing life into inanimate objects. Keyframes record the little slices of action that make such "life breathing" possible; playing them back over time makes the animation complete. Keyframe animation is simple in concept, but mastering the art of placing keyframes with the proper spacing between them is a lifetime's endeavor.

Creating Keys

Maya offers many ways to set keys. Each method has its own purpose, but some are much quicker and more effective than others.

- The S hotkey, with the **Animate → Set Key** ❏ set to default, is the workhorse of key creation. It sets keys on all keyable attributes on a particular object. Because it is so easy to use—just press the S key—it will serve as the primary means of creating keyframes for most of your animation efforts.

- You can key individual attributes in the Channel Box directly by RM clicking a selected attribute and choosing Key Selected from the resulting pop-up menu. That allows you fine control by placing a key directly on a selected attribute or group of attributes. Figure 7.1 shows the Key Selected command.

- Turning on automatic keyframing allows Maya to record changes to attributes automatically, which is helpful if you tend to forget to set keys yourself, though many animators reject this tool, preferring not to record attribute changes until they are satisfied with them. To enable automatic keyframing, press the black "key" button in the lower-right corner of the main window (the background turns red when auto keyframing is enabled).

- Adding keys on a function curve in the Graph Editor is an effective method for refining animation. Because this action is specifically intended to make small changes in the animation curve, it is not suitable for general keying.

- The Attribute Editor (AE) allows keying of some attributes that are relatively deep in Maya's node structure, but because you are limited to keying attributes one at a time, it is more efficient to key animation by other means when available

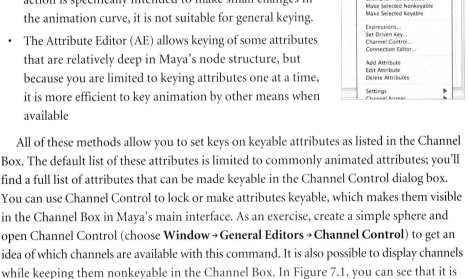

Figure 7.1

The Key Selected command

All of these methods allow you to set keys on keyable attributes as listed in the Channel Box. The default list of these attributes is limited to commonly animated attributes; you'll find a full list of attributes that can be made keyable in the Channel Control dialog box. You can use Channel Control to lock or make attributes keyable, which makes them visible in the Channel Box in Maya's main interface. As an exercise, create a simple sphere and open Channel Control (choose **Window → General Editors → Channel Control**) to get an idea of which channels are available with this command. It is also possible to display channels while keeping them nonkeyable in the Channel Box. In Figure 7.1, you can see that it is possible to hide, lock, unlock, make keyable, make nonkeyable, mute, and unmute selected attributes directly from this pop-up menu.

Setting Breakdown Keys

The **Animate → Set Breakdown** command works much like the Set Key command except that it sets *breakdowns* instead of keys. Breakdowns retain their relationship in time to the keys on either side of them. For example, if you insert a breakdown at frame 5 in between keys at 1 and 10 and then change the last key from frame 10 to frame 8, the breakdown automatically moves itself to frame 4, maintaining its spacing between the two keys. However, often breakdowns land on noninteger frames, which are frames with numbers that end in decimals. They need to be snapped (by RM clicking the Time Slider and choosing the Snap command) to the nearest frame to ensure that the pose will be rendered correctly. Otherwise, breakdowns work exactly like keyframes.

The Time Slider and Range Slider

Maya offers three main controls for editing keyframes: the Time Slider, the Graph Editor, and the Dope Sheet. Figure 7.2 shows the Time Slider and various animation controls, many of which can be set through the Animation Preferences window. Figure 7.3 shows the Animation Playback controls in detail. You can control many of these functions via keyboard hot keys as follows.

Alt (Mac Option)+V	Toggles between play and stop
Esc	Stops the playback
. (period)	Moves to the next keyframe
, (comma)	Moves to the previous keyframe
Alt (Mac Option)+. (period)	Moves to the next frame
Alt (Mac Option)+,(comma)	Moves to the previous frame

Figure 7.2

The Time Slider, playback controls, and the Command, Help, and Feedback lines

The Time Slider and its related controls provide the most immediate, if not the most detailed, animation controls, and it doesn't cost screen real estate like the other two editors.

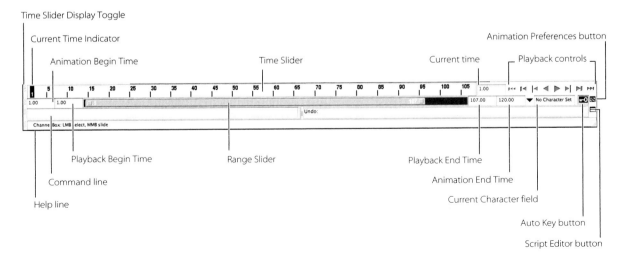

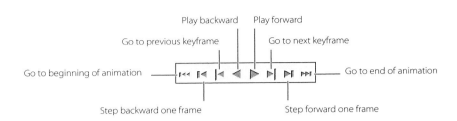

Figure 7.3

Animation playback controls

It allows you to set the beginning and ending of the animation and playback range as well as the current time both numerically and interactively in conjunction with the Range Slider.

Clicking the Time Slider on a given frame moves the Current Time Indicator to that particular frame and sets it as the current frame. LM clicking and dragging in the Time Slider allows you to *jog* or *scrub* through your animation interactively. The quality of playback depends on the complexity of your scene and the power of your computing setup. High polygon or deformer counts, high-resolution textures, or many lights in the scene will cut down on the smoothness of playback, but for the most part jogging through your scene is a great way to focus on the motion of your subject.

MM clicking or dragging in the Time Slider allows you to move the Current Time Indicator without updating the scene in the viewport or the values of attributes in the Channel Box. This is a powerful way to copy keys from one time to another in a scene. Remember that setting a key equals recording the changes in attributes over time, but if the attributes don't change, the previous key is effectively copied when the next key is set. We will use this feature extensively when animating later in the chapter.

RM clicking in the Time Slider displays the Edit Key pop-up menu, which offers the standard key-editing features we will discuss later in the chapter. It also provides access to the following submenus:

- Display Key Ticks lets you display keys from either the active object or the selected attributes in the Channel Box or turn off the tick mark display altogether.

- Under Playback Looping, you can set Maya to play the animation once, repeat continuously, or oscillate forward and backward from the start to end points.

- With the Set Range To submenu, you can control the playback range in various ways. One useful option here is the Sound Length setting, which you can also use to find the length of an audio file that has been imported into a scene.

- With the Sound submenu, you can show, hide, or rename any of the audio files that have been imported.

- With the Playblast function, you can preview your animation as real-time movie clips. We will use playblasting extensively in Chapter 9.

Directly under the Time Slider is the Range Slider, which also contains fields for changing the animation and playback start and end times. The Range Slider allows you to interactively change the range of frames displayed in the Time Slider. By clicking and dragging in the box next to the numbers on either end of the Range Slider, you can shorten or lengthen the size of the slider. By clicking and dragging in the slider itself, you can move the entire range of frames displayed in the Time Slider. The innermost set of fields on either side of the Range Slider sets the playback start and end frames, and the outermost set of fields sets the animation start and end frames.

Understanding Animation Work Flow

When approaching any animation task, it is wise to have a plan for how you craft the performance of your subject. A huge mistake that beginners make when approaching animation is to begin by setting keys indiscriminately. We recommend the following methodology because it works on almost all animations, from the simple to the complex:

- Begin by setting preferences to facilitate animation for a particular output. Animations for the Web, broadcast video, and film all have different parameters, and within each output type, different necessities require changes in the workspace and time settings. Changing those settings in the Animation Preferences at the beginning of the process makes creating animation for a particular output easier. If you'll need to create multiple output types, set your preferences for the highest-quality output to start with (e.g., television output is higher quality than Web, so you should base your preferences on television if animating for both media).

- Create keys in the viewport and do some rough timing in the Time Slider. In the following tutorial, we will be keying one particular attribute on a simple ball rig. In most cases, you will key all attributes on the animation controls of a character at the extremes of motion.

- Last, refine motions and add enhancements using the Graph Editor. In the following exercise, we will adjust how Maya interpolates the frames between keys by changing tangent types and manipulating tangent handles.

Now let's get experience with Maya's animation controls and employ the work flow discussed earlier with a classic "bouncing ball" tutorial.

Hands On: Bouncing a Ball

Let's begin by opening a file and setting up the workspace for animation.

1. Open BallSetup.mb from the CD. This is a simple ball animation rig that we will use to explore some basic keyframing concepts.

2. Choose **Window → Settings/Preferences → Preferences**. Preferences allow us to set up the workspace and, more important, Maya's timeline for animation. We will cover the settings that need to be changed here.

3. In the Interface category, set the Attribute Editor and Tool Settings to open in separate windows, but set the Layer Editor to open in the main Maya window.

4. Under UI Elements, show all the visible UI elements and show the Channel Box/Layer Editor in the main window.

5. Under the Settings category, set Time Working Units to NTSC [30 fps]. This is the proper frames per second setting for broadcast television. If you were working on film resolution files, you would choose Film [24 fps] as your time setting.

6. In Settings/Animation, check the Auto Key check box. Under Tangents, set Default In and Default Out Tangents to Clamped. We will discuss tangents and their relationship to Maya animation later in this chapter when we discuss the Graph Editor.

7. Under Settings/Timeline, set Playback Start/End to 0 and 90, respectively, and set Animation Start/End to 0 and 120. Set Height to 1x and Key Ticks to Active. Set the key tick width to 2 pixels. Under Playback, set the Update View setting to Active. This will update only the active view, making animation playback faster. Under Looping, click Continuous. Set Playback Speed to Real-time [30 fps]. This will give us the most accurate playback setting for this file. For truly accurate playback, you will need to playblast the animation, but for our simple scene, 30 fps will work fine. Also remember that if you were to import and play sound, Real-time is the setting to use.

These will be the basic settings you will want when starting an animation that will be broadcast on TV. If you find yourself constantly changing settings when opening a file, you will want to set up preferences differently so that the file opens with the settings you like.

Bouncing the Ball

Creating a ball bounce seems simple, but all of the basic elements of animation are contained in this simple action, and creating the animation involves more than just moving the ball up and down while scaling it. BallSetup.mb is a relatively simple file that will allow us to separate movement along various axes as well as use Maya's squash deformer to create more convincing deformation in the ball as it bounces. Let's create the bounce.

1. Set the Current Time Indicator in the Time Slider to 1.

2. Select ControlBoxCrv and click the **Bounce_Down_Up** attribute to select it. This attribute is connected to the translateY channel of UpDnGrp, which controls the vertical motion of the ball. You will learn much more about connecting attributes in Chapter 8.

3. MM drag the mouse to the right to move the ball up along the Y axis. Move it until **Bounce_Down_Up** reads 7.

4. RM click **Bounce_Down_Up** and choose Key Selected to key only this custom attribute. The number 7 should now have an orangish background, indicating that the attribute is animated.

Figure 7.4

Selecting a range of frames in the Time Slider by Shift+dragging. Note how the feedback numbers on the selection tell you exactly which frames you have selected.

5. Click frame 15 in the Time Slider to go to that frame.

6. Use Key Selected to set a key on **Bounce_Down_Up**.

7. Go to frame 7.

8. Set **Bounce_Down_Up** to 0. Because the Auto Key button (the red key button at the right of the Range Slider) has been activated, changing the value of the attribute automatically sets the key.

9. Scrub through the animation by dragging in the Time Slider.

10. Shift+drag from frame 1 to frame 14 to select this range of frames, as shown in Figure 7.4.

11. RM click in the Time Slider and choose **Set Range To → Selected** to limit the Time Slider to the length of the ball bounce.

12. Click the Play Forward button on the playback controls to play the animation. Stop play either by clicking the same button (which has toggled to the Stop Play button) or by pressing the Esc key.

This animation is mechanical and unconvincing because the ball reaches the top of the bounce and travels down the same way it rises. Let's change this up with some breakdowns.

1. Go to frame 2 in the Time Slider.

2. Select the **Bounce_Down_Up** attribute on ControlBoxGrp, RM click it, and choose Breakdown Selected to put a breakdown key on that frame. It will show up in green on the Time Slider.

3. Shift+click frame 2 to select that breakdown. Let go of the mouse and click, hold, and drag the selected frame/breakdown to move it to frame 5, as shown in Figure 7.5.

4. Go to frame 14 in the Time Slider and repeat step 2 to place a breakdown there.

5. Move the breakdown from frame 14 to frame 11 on the Time Slider.

6. Play the animation through to see the changes.

By recording the value of **Bounce_Down_Up** at the frame just after and before the top of the bounce and moving those values later and earlier in the bounce, respectively, we made the ball appear to hesitate a little before it drops to hit the ground. The ball eases in and out of the top of the bounce. This little change produces a much livelier bounce, making the animation come alive more than it did with the mechanical bounce we started with.

Figure 7.5

Moving the breakdown key from frame 2 to 5

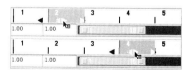

Adjusting Timing with the Dope Sheet

Now let's adjust the overall timing of the bounce using the Dope Sheet (choose **Window →
Settings/Preferences → Dope Sheet**). This will be a simplistic use of the Dope Sheet: normally, you use it to adjust timing on a large number of objects or attributes at once, as it
has the unique ability to adjust timing on the object as a whole and then refine these timings on individual attributes. It is possible to adjust the timing for an entire character
using just the Dope Sheet, and you will explore this further in Chapter 9.

Figure 7.6 shows the Dope Sheet with many of its features labeled. When you see the
Dope Sheet on your screen, you will notice that the green color of the breakdown key is hard
to distinguish against the blue hue of the Dope Sheet summary and virtually impossible to
make out against the green of the object backgrounds. To change this to a contrasting color,
choose **Window → Settings/Preferences → Colors**, click the Animation Editors rollout,
and adjust the Summary Object and Object colors to clarify the Dope Sheet.

Let's adjust timing.

1. Scroll over in the Dope Sheet by Alt+MM dragging horizontally to the left until frame 30
   is visible in the lower right of the Dope Sheet view area.

2. LM click the last key at frame 15 to select it.

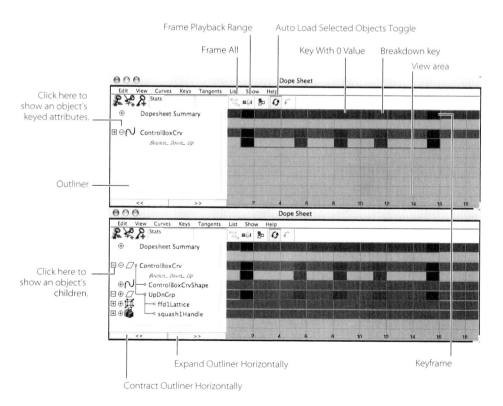

Figure 7.6

**The Dope Sheet
showing Control-
BoxCrv's attributes
and child objects**

3. Select the Move tool by pressing the W key.

4. MM drag the selected key to frame 21. Notice that the breakdown key shifts over to maintain its timing relationship with the end and middle keys.

5. Select and MM drag the middle key from frame 8 to frame 11.

Moving keys in the Dope Sheet adjusts the timing of the bounce, slowing it down to a more leisurely pace than previously. Be sure to adjust the Timeline to play back all 21 frames of your new, slower animation.

Noninteger Keys

We have adjusted the overall timing of the bounce; we now have to manually adjust a problem that arises when moving the keys surrounding breakdowns. The breakdown keys automatically adjust their position, but more often than not, they fail to land on integer keys and come to rest on partial keys—keys with a decimal rather than a whole number. This can cause problems with several of Maya's processes down the animation pipeline. For example, motion blur, which calculates on a multiframe basis, can look distorted if it tries to calculate for keys that are not located on whole numbers. Let's correct the problem.

1. Select the breakdown between the middle and end keys.

2. Move the Current Time Indicator to frame 15 by pressing the K key and LM dragging in the Dope Sheet. Notice that the Stats field reads that the keyframe sits at about 15.29 and that the value of **Bounce_Down_Up** sits at 5.89 for that frame. A look at the Channel Box, however, reveals that the value of **Bounce_Down_Up** reads 5.636. It doesn't take much to realize that such differences will result in problems with any process, renderer, or expression that is based on reading specific values on specific keyframes.

3. RM click the breakdown and choose **Edit → Snap** ❐. Select All for the Time Range and, most important, set Snap to Times. Rarely, if ever, will you want to snap values because this can potentially change the animation in unanticipated ways. Click Snap Keys to snap the selected key to the nearest whole number.

4. Now the Stats field reads 15, which is what we want.

Scaling keys in the Time Slider, Dope Sheet, and Graph Editor can land all keys in a selection on noninteger time values. Although they can be snapped to whole values en masse, you risk throwing the timing of your animation off drastically. It is best to never scale keys; move them individually.

5. Snap the first breakdown by selecting it and repeating step 3. This key snaps up from 6.715 to frame 7 where the first snap operation rounded the key down from 15.29 to 15.

Creating and Editing Keys Using the Graph Editor

One of Maya's most popular and powerful tools for editing and creating keys is the Graph Editor. It works by allowing you access to keys and the interpolation between them. As discussed, a keyframe is a recording of an object's attributes at a certain moment in time. In cel animation, a keyframe is a drawing that records an extreme pose of a character or an object. The lead animator then hands the key drawings off to an assistant who draws the in-between frames, called *inbetweens* (or 'tweens), to finish the animation. The assistant interprets what those inbetweens should look like from instructions given by the lead. Maya serves as the assistant animator in that it interpolates what the motion of an object should look like based on the instructions you give it. How to properly instruct Maya will occupy our efforts here.

In mathematics, to interpolate means to derive from and insert values between two known values. This is exactly what Maya does between keyframes, and the Graph Editor allows you to control how this interpolation is calculated.

Figure 7.7 shows the Graph Editor (choose **Window → Animation Editors → Graph Editor**) with the function curve for **Bounce_Down_Up** shown in its view area. Each dot on the curve represents keys and the curves drawn between them represent how Maya interpolates the motion of the ball between keys. The brown dots and lines extending from each key are *key tangent handles*. They control how the curve travels through the key, and they are your means of instructing Maya how to "draw the inbetweens" between keys. Users of Adobe Illustrator, Macromedia Freehand, or Photoshop's Pen tool will recognize the spline curves seen in the Graph Editor. Let's examine the types of key tangents Maya offers.

Spline   A spline tangent maintains a smooth curve as it passes through the keyframe. It has control handles that, depending on their weighted tangent setting, can be adjusted

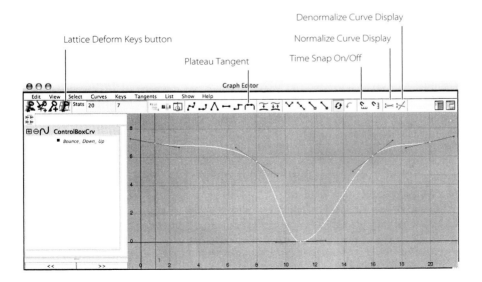

Figure 7.7

The Graph Editor

somewhat like Bezier curves. These tangents provide smooth interpolation between keys, butthey have the disadvantage of being directly affected by the location and values of keys before and after the individual keys. This can result in *spline drift*, in which the curve drifts past the intended key value before curving back through the next key.

Linear Linear tangents represent a constant rate of change between two keys of different values. For mechanical actions or for animations of texture that require a constant velocity or rate of change, use linear tangents. When creating animations of living things, you should use curved tangents instead.

Clamped Some think clamped tangents are the most versatile of all the tangent types because they combine some of the best features of both spline and flat tangent types. Clamped tangents interpolate smoothly between keys of differing values, but remain flat between keys of the same value. Consider using clamped tangents where you would normally use splines. In many cases, they require less repair work than splines.

Flat Flat tangents are simply tangents that extend horizontally from either side of the key. They ensure no motion between keys of the same value, especially when the Out tangents of the earlier key and the In tangent of the later key are set to flat and their values are the same.

Stepped On the surface, there seems to be little use for stepped tangents. These tangents maintain a constant value until the animation reaches the next key. The value of the keyed attributes then jumps or pops to the next value. But as you will see in Chapter 9, these tangents let you separate motion from timing to concentrate on appearance or pose.

Fixed Fixed tangents cement the direction and length of the In and Out tangents of the particular key specified as Fixed. This means that no matter how you change the keys or breakdowns on either side of the Fixed tangent, it will not change.

Plateau Plateau tangents force curves to respect and not go over or under the highest and lowest valued keyframes along a curve. They also maintain flatness between two similar valued keyframes. In practice, there is little difference between keys that have been flattened at the high and low points and plateau keys, but plateaus can reduce the necessity of cleaning up curve drift, which is convenient.

new

New to Maya 8 are several usability enhancements that make the Graph Editor even more useful. First, you can now attach a custom color to any animation curve you wish, which can be very helpful if you want to highlight a particular curve when working on an animation. Select any curve (or curves), then choose **Edit → Change Curve Color** ❑. In the option box, choose any color you wish for your curve and accept the changes to see the curve(s) colored in the Graph Editor window. Figure 7.8 shows the Bounce_Down_Up curve colored a custom green rather than its default black.

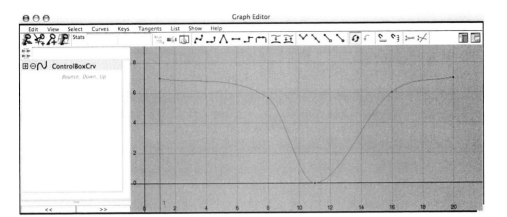

Figure 7.8

Coloring the Bounce_Down_Up curve a custom color

You can now bookmark a particular curve as well, which is very useful when dealing with numerous animation curves while creating a complex animation. With bookmarks, you can quickly frame a particular curve or object rather than having to hunt for it in a sometimes overcrowded Graph Editor. To create a bookmark, select one or more curves (or select one or more objects), then choose **List → Bookmarks → Bookmark Selected Curves** ▢ (or **Bookmark Current Objects** ▢). In the options box, you can name the bookmark to anything you wish. To return to a saved bookmark, choose **List → Bookmarks → <name of bookmark>**.

Finally, you can now load only objects associated with selected curves into the Graph Editor's outliner pane (on the left). As with the other enhancements, this feature reduces clutter in the Graph Editor, making it easier to find objects associated with any given curve. To enable this, choose **Edit → Select Curves**, at which point only objects associated with selected curves will show up in the outliner pane of the Graph Editor.

> In this section we are discussing animation curves at their purest. We are not discussing what makes good and bad animation. You can judge that only by looking at animation as it is played back in the viewport, not by the appearance of the function curve.

Keys can have tangents that are broken or unified and have weights that are either locked or free. Let's examine these and some other useful features of the Graph Editor while we discuss the effects of different tangents and their uses.

1. In the Graph Editor, choose **Curves → Post Infinity → Cycle**. This will repeat our curve forever and give us a good view of the ball as its bounce repeats.

2. Choose **View → Infinity** to display the curve as a dotted line extending forever. To see this, zoom out in the Graph Editor.

Figure 7.9

The Bounce_
Down_Up attribute
curve with the end
keys selected. Note
the dotted-line cycle
curve repeated to
infinity.

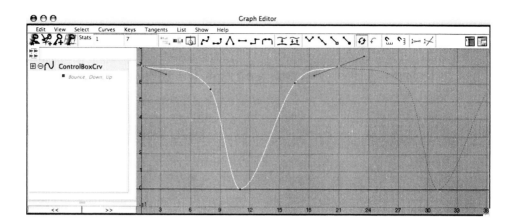

3. Set the Playback Stop value on the Range Slider to 63. At 21 frames for one bounce, this will allow us to see three bounces before the playback repeats.

4. Click Play to see the ball bounce. Notice that there is a hitch in the motion of the ball as it reaches the top of the bounce. This is caused by the little upward tick in the curve at the beginning and end as shown in Figure 7.9.

5. Choose **Curves → Buffer Curve Snapshot** and then immediately choose **View → Show Buffer Curves** from the Graph Editor menu. This will show how the changes we will make will affect the curve and allow you to see and compare the results. It also offers a quick way to go back to what we had originally if we need to

6. Select the end keys as shown in Figure 7.9. RM click in the Graph Editor, choose **Tangents → Plateau**, and play the animation.

The good news is that the hitch is gone; the bad news is that there is now an unhealthy pause at the top of the bounce. This is shown in the Graph Editor as a flattening of the top of the curve. We want a nice, rounded curve at the top. There is no quick fix for this, but it is fixable. Let's do so as follows.

1. We'll begin fixing the top of the bounce by creating a little more "pop" at the bottom of the bounce. Select the key at frame 11, and choose **Keys → Break Tangents**. This allows us to move those tangent handles independently. As a general rule, you will want to break tangents only where you want a sharp change of direction.

2. With the key still selected, Shift+select the two end keys and choose **Keys → Free Tangent Weight**. This will allow us to lengthen or shorten the tangent handles, which will increase or decrease the slope of the curve on either side of the key.

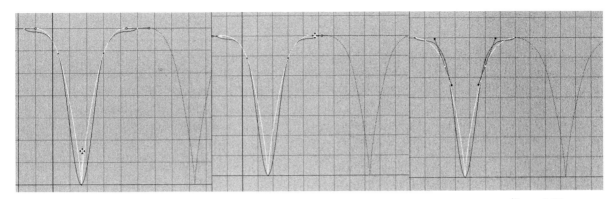

Figure 7.10

Changing the curve
to give the ball
bounce more "pop"

3. Lengthen the handles of the key at frame 11 as shown at left in Figure 7.10. Remember that moving keys, curves, and handles in the Graph Editor is a multistage operation. First, you must select the particular element by LM clicking it. To select a tangent handle, you must LM click the key and then LM click the tangent handle to select it separately. Last, enter move mode by selecting the Move tool or pressing the **w** key, then move the tangent handle by MM dragging it where you want it.

4. Shorten the handles of the end keys to slightly sharpen the curve at the top as shown in the middle of Figure 7.10.

5. Click the Time Snap On/Off button to turn on time snapping. This ensures that all keyframes will snap to an integer frame value, which is useful here.

6. Last, select and move the breakdown keys down until the end of the tangent handle is even with the top of the curve, as shown at right in Figure 7.10.

7. Play the animation and see what the final result looks like.

As an exercise, try freeing the tangent weight on those breakdown keys and moving them up in the graph; then move the tangent handles down to where they were before. Take another buffer curve snapshot before you start. That way you can use the **Curves →
Swap Buffer Curve** command to switch instantly back and forth between the two to see the effect of your changes.

Add "Whiz Bang" Squash and Stretch

Though we now have a serviceable bouncing ball, it lacks some of the "life" that makes for more fun, visually interesting animation. To remedy this, we will add some squash and stretch to the ball, giving the animation more life and the ball more "pop." The **BallSquashStretch** attribute on the ControlBoxCrv is a custom attribute that has a set driven key relationship with a nonlinear squash deformer that deforms the ball. We will use this attribute to deform the ball to add some extra exaggeration or punch to the bounce. Let's create squash and stretch as follows. Open `BallBounce01SquashStart.mb` from the CD and let's begin.

1. Make sure the Graph Editor is open so that you can see how the curve develops as we change the values of **BallSquashStretch**.

2. Go to frame 1.

3. Select **BallSquashStretch** and set a key on only that attribute.

4. Squash the ball a little by MM dragging in the viewport until **BallSquashStretch** reads –0.6.

5. With the K key held down, MM click frame 21 in the Graph Editor.

6. Set a key on **BallSquashStretch**. MM dragging with the K key held down changes the Current Time Indicator without updating either the viewport or the values in the Channel Box. So setting a key at frame 21 essentially copies the frame from frame 1.

7. Go to frame 7, where the breakdown key sits, and set **BallSquashStretch** to 0. This will make the ball perfectly round.

8. With the K key held down, MM click frame 15 and set a key on **BallSquashStretch**.

9. Go to frame 10, which is the frame before the ball hits the ground, and stretch the ball by setting **BallSquashStretch** to about 1.6.

10. Hold down the K key and MM click frame 13. Set a key on **BallSquashStretch** to duplicate the value of frame 11 on that frame.

11. Click frame 11 with the K key to move the Current Time Indicator to the contact frame.

12. Squash the ball by setting **BallSquashStretch** to –1.6.

13. Choose **Curves → Post Infinity → Cycle** to repeat the curve forever throughout the animation.

14. Select the start and end keys on **BallSquashStretch**, and set Tangents to Flat to smooth out the curve.

15. Play the animation to see the ball bounce with the deformation added.

16. Save your file.

Put Some Lean into It!

What we are going to do next is go beyond the bounds of reality by making the ball lean into the bounce using the **LeanBck_Fwd** attribute on ControlBoxCrv. This will make the ball look like it is gathering itself in the air. First, however, we need to move the ball forward to be able to place the lean properly. Let's continue with the file you created earlier, or open BallBounce01LeanStart.mb.

1. On frame 1, set a key on ControlBoxCrv.translateZ in the Channel Box.

> The dot notation (.) is a quick way to specify a specific channel of a particular object. So "set a key on ControlBoxCrv.translateZ" is the same as "Select ControlBoxCrv, then click the translateZ channel in the Channel Box, RM click it, and choose Key Selected."

2. Move the Current Time Indicator to frame 63.

3. Move ControlBoxCrv forward in Z until that channel reads about 8. With the AutoKey button engaged, this should set a key automatically. If it doesn't, key translateZ to set a key. (And then click the AutoKey button.)

4. Go back to frame 1. Notice that you can see the keys in the Time Slider all laid out in front of you. We will use this to our advantage here.

5. Set a key on ControlBoxCrv.Lean_Bck_Fwd. It should be at 0 now.

6. Go to frame 6 or 7. As the ball drops into the fall, lean the ball back some by setting **Lean_Bck_Fwd** to read about –8.5.

7. Go to frame 10 right before the bounce and right where the stretch is at its greatest and emphasize the lean a little by setting **Lean_Bck_Fwd** to about –9.

8. On the impact frame at frame 11, set **Lean_Bck_Fwd** to 0.

9. On frame 12, set **Lean_Bck_Fwd** forward to 9.

10. On frame 15, set **Lean_Bck_Fwd** to about 16.

11. On frame 21, set **Lean_Bck_Fwd** to 0 to complete the motion.

12. In the Graph Editor, select **Lean_Bck_Fwd** curve by LM clicking the curve in the view area and choosing **Curves → Post Infinity → Cycle**.

13. Choose **View → Infinity** for that curve.

14. Play your animation to see what you've created.

It…is….ALIVE! The changes outlined here take the ball bounce animation from mechanical and boring to springy and full of personality, breathing life into this virtual object. By pushing the lean attribute higher on the up side of the jump, you can make the ball lean forward as it goes up, emphasizing the "gathering" at the top of the jump. Manipulate these values to change the amount of lean to see if you can do better.

Converting Cycled Animation to Curves

This animation is fine if all you need is your ball bouncing the same way forever. Most animations will require more. In the next exercise, we will convert the cycled animation to animation curves in an operation called baking. We will then edit those curves to break up the sameness that cycles produce. Let's bake the animation as follows. Open BallBounce02BakeStart.mb from the CD or use the file you saved earlier, and let's begin.

1. Select ControlBoxCrv. In the Graph Editor, select Bounce_Down_Up, BallSquash-Stretch, and Lean_Bck_Fwd in the Outliner portion. Don't select the curves, just the channel names.

2. In the Graph Editor, choose **Curves → Bake Channel** ❒. Set Time Range to Start/End, and change Start and End to 0 and 171, respectively. This will give us exactly eight bounces over a period of just over 5.5 seconds. Set Sample By to 1, and check Sparse Curve Bake; otherwise Maya will put a key on every frame on the curve. Click Bake to bake the cycles into curves.

3. Increase Animation Stop Time to 171, and set the Range Slider to match it.

4. Turn off cycling by choosing **Curves → Post Infinity → Constant**. You can also turn off the dotted lines by unchecking Infinity in the View menu.

Our animation is now 171 frames in length, but it is all the same intensity. Let's use a useful Graph Editor feature, the Lattice Deform Keys tool, to give the animation some decay. But first, let's explore normalizing our keys to better see what is going on in the animation.

In the Graph Editor, you may notice that if you zoom in to edit the ball bounce and squash curves, the lean curve extends out of the frame, but if you zoom out to see the lean curve, the former two curves are too small to edit effectively. There is also a Normalize Curve command that is located in the Curves menu. Its function is to display the curves as if their values were between 1 and 0, no matter what their actual values are. Normalize your curves like this.

1. Select the attribute names in the Outliner of the curves you want to normalize. Click the Normalize Curves button toward the upper right of the Graph Editor. Figure 7.11 shows the before and after (top and middle image) of this operation, and the bottom image shows the display of the normalized curves scaled vertically by Shift+LM and +MM dragging vertically in the Graph Editor. Now all the curves are displayed between 1 and 0. Nothing has changed concerning the values, just the display. You can go back to the previous display by clicking the Denormalize Curves button next to the Normalize Curves button. For some people, it will now be easier to see the

relationships between the curves. For others, it will be confusing. Choose whichever method of viewing the curves works best for you. Fortunately, the rest of this exercise works no matter how the curves are displayed. In this example, we will work with the normalized curves.

2. Move the last key on the translateZ curve out until it rests on frame 171.

3. Edit this curve until it looks like the top image of Figure 7.12.

4. Select all curves except the translateZ curve.

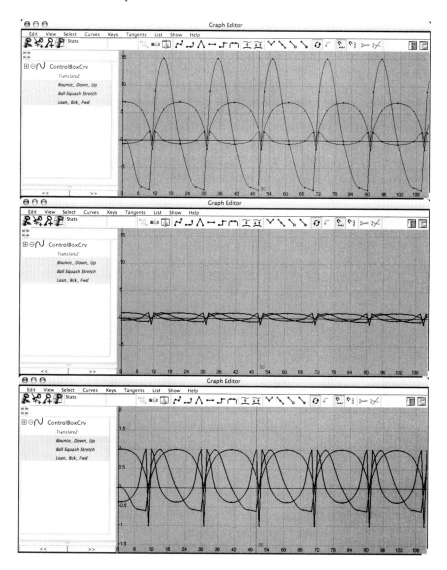

Figure 7.11

The animation curves before and after normalizing

5. Double-click the Lattice Deform Keys button (toward the top left of the button bar) to open the options box for this tool. Because we are going to use this tool to decrease the intensity of the animation, we only want two rows and columns. Also, make sure the Middle Button Scales check box is checked. Your Graph Editor should look like the middle image of Figure 7.12, and you can close the option box.

6. Shift+click the top and bottom right circles on the lattice to select those lattice points.

7. LM drag along the zero line to scale the lattice points down toward 0. They don't need to go all the way down to 0, but the curves should shrink considerably as shown at the bottom of Figure 7.12.

8. With the keys still selected, snap them to their nearest whole frame.

9. The lattice operation introduced some distortion on the curves where it radically shrank their height. Go back in and shorten the tangent handles to smooth out the curve and the animation as shown in Figure 7.13.

BallBounceFinal.mb shows the end product of these exercises.

Figure 7.12

Using the Lattice Deform Keys tool to reshape the animation curves and lower the intensity of the bounces

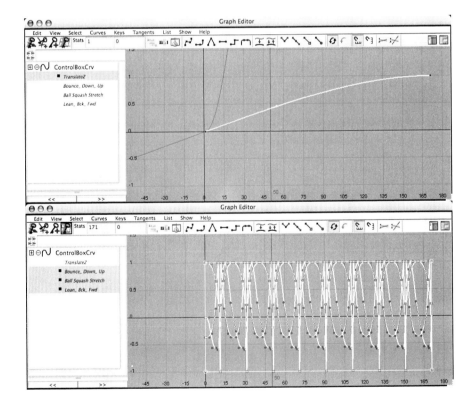

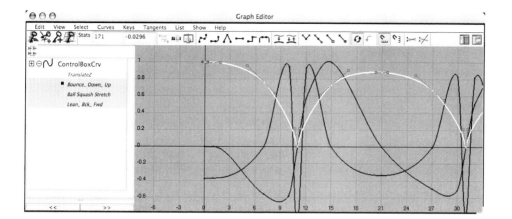

Figure 7.13

Smoothing the curve by manipulating the tangent handles. The buffer curve shows how the curve was before manipulating the handles.

Summary

Even animating a basic shape such as a bouncing ball can be quite sophisticated with the right rig and the right application of animation principles. In this chapter, you learned about animation types, basic keyframe animation techniques, and the tools Maya offers in these areas. In Chapter 8, we will discuss how to rig a complex (humanoid) character. In Chapter 9, you will learn further animation techniques using more sophisticated characters as well as proper methods for previewing animation once the scene gets too complex for playing back in the viewport.

Character Setup and Rigging

This chapter will take you through the steps to create a fully functional rig for a complex character. You build a skeleton rig to move portions of your model—such as arms and legs—around, bind the skeleton to a geometric skin, and use Maya's Full Body IK system to create automatically a control structure for the character.

Whether you intend to rig characters for a living or just use other people's rigs for your animation, understanding how character rigs are set up is essential. You will learn about the limits of animating using any given rig and why things go wrong when they do. You will also learn the language of rigging and how to communicate your needs to a rigger. This chapter covers the following topics.

- **Deformer types: skeletons, clusters, and lattices**
- **Forward and inverse kinematics**
- **Creating a proper bipedal skeleton**
- **Using the Full Body IK skeleton**
- **Skinning a character**

Deformer Types

Deformers are powerful tools used by the rigging artist to alter portions of a continuous geometric shape or to give structure and continuity to a set of geometric shapes that would otherwise have no connection. Without deformers such as skeletons and lattices, you would have to move entire objects or painstakingly move each and every control point on a skin mesh. Obviously, then, deformers—a large group of tools that include skeletons, blend shapes, and jiggle, cluster, and lattice deformers—constitute crucial elements of the animator's toolbox. Although there are a number of deformer types, the four types of deformers most used by Maya riggers when constructing a primary character rig are the skeleton, cluster, lattice and blend shapes. Other deformers, such as the jiggle deformer, are most often used to drive secondary animation (such as a jiggling belly) and are usually added at the end of the rigging process for characters that require them. Since most rigs use the skeleton, cluster, and lattice deformers, we will discuss those three types in detail.

Keep in mind that you can also use joints and other deformers as effective modeling tools. See the previous chapters on modeling, as well as Chapter 10, for more on how to use deformers to alter a model's surface in a static way. Here, we will concentrate on using deformers as animation tools.

Skeletons

Just as with real skeletons, bones and joints are used to build a skeleton in Maya. In real life, a skeleton is an architectural structure that houses and protects the vital organs of people and animals, maintains their shape, and enables them to move around through the use of muscles attached to the bones. In Maya, a skeleton joint/bone combination functions in a way that combines the functions of real bones, muscles, and ligaments: maintaining the overall shape of a character while allowing portions of a continuous geometric skin to move about.

To build a skeleton in Maya, you use the Joint tool (choose **Skeleton → Joint Tool** in the Animation menu set) and "draw" the skeleton into your scene by clicking to place joints where you deem them needed. (Most often this is inside the geometry of a finished character model.) As you click joints into place, Maya will connect them with a visual reference called a bone: joints are the only element in a joint/bone pair that you can select and manipulate. Figure 8.1 shows a set of joints connected by bones.

It is often best to create a hierarchy of joints/bones in an orthographic view (such as the side view). Doing so not only ensures that the joints are all coplanar, it also helps to set the joints' preferred rotation axes, which is important for later animation of the bone. We will discuss the issue of joint orientation in detail in the Hands On section of this chapter.

Some people find it useful to limit the joints they create according to their functions, such as a universal joint or a hinge joint, because it means more efficiency in animation and fewer calculations for Maya to perform. For example, you might use universal joints for wrists and ankles and hinge joints for knees. Through careful skeleton construction and controls, however, you can avoid having to place limits on joints. This can be handy when animating because you can "break" the physical limitations of a knee joint, for example, and bend it forward if a particular pose ever calls for it.

To allow a skeleton hierarchy to affect geometry, you must "skin" a character by binding elements of the geometry to the joints in the skeleton. To do the initial skinning, Maya uses an algorithm to calculate a cylindrical volume around each bone; geometric elements (CVs, vertices, and so on) that fall within that volume around a bone are affected by that bone/joint combination. Elements that fall outside the volume are not affected by that joint. Maya supports two types of binding: rigid and smooth. Rigid binding is a Boolean operation: a CV (or vertex) is influenced 100 percent by one single joint. Smooth binding, on the other hand, allows individual CVs to share influence by multiple joints. For example, if two joints are near a particular CV on a NURBS surface, that CV might be influenced 60 percent by the first joint and 40 percent by the second. (The influences always add up to 100 percent.) If another bone is added near the first two and the skin rebound, the three bones all share influence over that one CV. To get a similar look using rigid binding requires additional deformer tools, such as the Sculpt deformer.

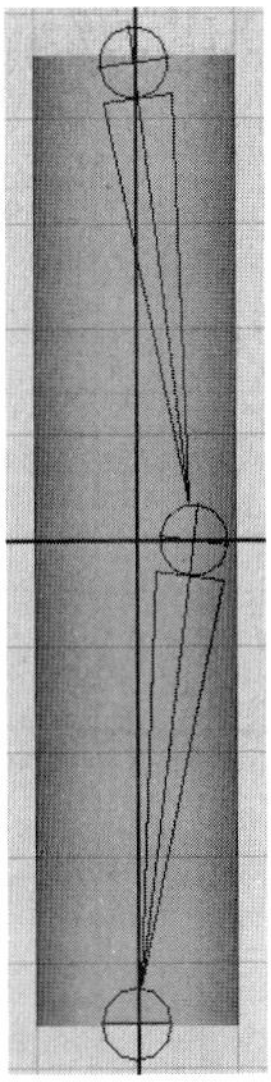

Riggers (and in fact entire studios) have preferred methods of rigging using rigid and smooth binding, but in general, skinning a complex character using smooth binding is more intuitive. The caveat is that you must then adjust, or "paint," the skin influences on a smoothly bound character, a topic we will cover later in this chapter.

To see how rigid and smooth binding differ in their default implementations, let's bind a simple NURBS cylinder using each type of binding. First, create the cylinder and three joints (two bones), as shown in Figure 8.2. (Be sure to add 20 or more spans to the NURBS cylinder so that it bends properly.)

Now rigid bind the cylinder to the joints: select the skeleton root (the first joint created), Shift+select the geometry, and choose **Skin → Bind Skin → Rigid Bind** (with default options) from the Animation menu set. When you rotate the middle joint, you will see something like Figure 8.3,

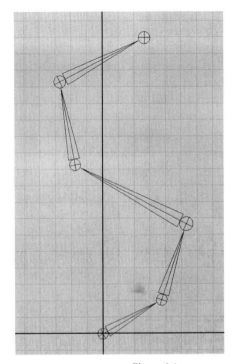

Figure 8.1

Joints and bones connected to form an S shape

Figure 8.2

A three-joint skeleton inside a simple NURBS cylinder

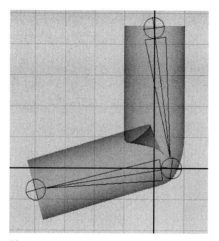

Figure 8.3

Rigid binding a skeleton to a cylinder

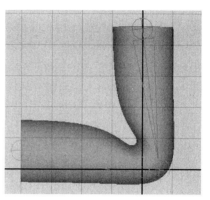

Figure 8.4

Smooth binding a skeleton to a cylinder

which has an unfortunate crease in the "elbow" area. We can eliminate this problem by using a Sculpt deformer, should we want to do so.

Now, to see how smooth binding works, undo the rotation of the joint, detach the skin from the joint chain by selecting the geometry, and choose **Skin → Detach Skin**. Select the skeleton root, Shift+select the cylinder, and choose **Skin → Bind Skin → Smooth Bind** (with default settings). When you now rotate the middle joint, you will see that the elbow area bends more naturally, as shown in Figure 8.4. Unfortunately, even with such simple geometry, the volume of the "elbow" area decreases as the joint is bent, which is unnatural looking. Even with smooth binding there is still work to be done reweighting the elbow area of the cylinder to get the creasing and bending just right. Later in the chapter we'll work with the Paint Skin Weights tool, which can be useful in cases like this.

Clusters

A Cluster deformer is really just a collection of points (CVs, vertices, and so on) that can be manipulated at once. To create a cluster, select one or more points, and then choose **Create Deformers → Create Cluster** from the Animation menu set. To see how a cluster works, create a NURBS plane and increase the patches in U and V to about 20 each. Go into component mode (press F8) and select several CVs near the middle of the plane. Now create a cluster from these CVs. You should see a small *C* appear above the plane; when you select and move this letter, the CVs that are members of the cluster will move along, as in Figure 8.5.

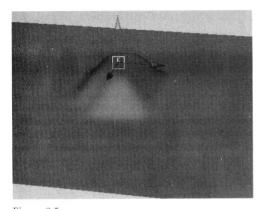

Figure 8.5

The center of a plane deformed using the Cluster deformer

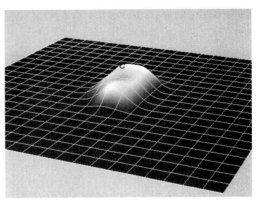

Figure 8.6

The center of the plane after adjusting cluster weights

You can adjust the weighting of each member CV (how much each CV will move in relation to the cluster handle) by selecting the plane, choosing **Edit Deformers → Paint Cluster Weights Tool**, and painting new weights into the scene. Using this tool, you can set the Opacity and Value settings to various levels. Value is how much a cluster CV is influenced by the cluster. (A setting of 1 is fully influenced, which shows white in the scene window, and 0 is no influence, or black.) Opacity is how much strength the brush has. (A setting of 1 is fully opaque, so the brush effect is applied completely, and 0 is fully transparent, so the brush has no effect). You can set the paintbrush width by holding B and dragging the mouse over the NURBS plane until the brush size is what you want. Figure 8.6 shows the same cluster after some weight painting.

Lattices

Although a joint/bone pair is a useful deformer for model elements that should maintain a constant length (as if a bone were inside the skin), a lattice deformer is often more useful when creating a more malleable character or part of a character because it allows distortion of the entire object in any amount. The joint/bone pair creates an endoskeleton (bones inside a skin), but the lattice deformer creates what is effectively an exoskeleton ("bones" outside the skin) of a lattice of points surrounding a geometric skin. To create a lattice, select a piece of geometry (a primitive sphere will do as an example), and choose **Create Deformers → Create Lattice** from the Animation menu set. You will see a subdivided box surrounding the sphere, as shown in Figure 8.7. To alter the number of divisions of the lattice, change the s, t, or u division for the latticeShape in the Channel Box.

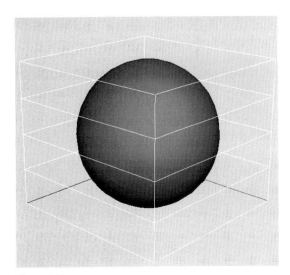

Figure 8.7

A lattice deformer surrounding a sphere

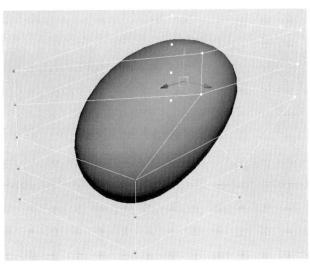

Figure 8.8

The lattice deformer and sphere distorted

To distort the lattice, select it, go into component mode (press F8, or RM click on the lattice, bringing up a contextual menu, and select Lattice Point), select some of the lattice's control points, and move or rotate them. The underlying object will deform as the lattice is moved, as shown in Figure 8.8. Note that the lattice deformer is automatically connected to the object(s) you selected, so no additional skinning process is necessary. In addition, objects deformed by a lattice are much more malleable, or "squishy," than those of a joint hierarchy, allowing for deformations of "boneless" objects such as octopi, sponges, tongues, and balls.

Forward and Inverse Kinematics

Forward and Inverse Kinematics are two different ways to rotate joints in a chain of joints. Forward Kinematics (FK) is the simpler, less processor intensive of the two methods, but it lacks much of the intuitive control that Inverse Kinematics (IK) brings to joint chain rotations.

Forward Kinematics is simply rotating each joint by hand, as we did in the skeleton example in the previous section. When a joint higher in the chain (a hip, for example) is rotated, the rotational motion is propagated *forward* down the joint chain and all child joints are moved by this rotation. Figure 8.9 shows how the entire "arm" structure built in the previous section moves when the "shoulder" joint is rotated. Although this motion is simple to create, and simple for Maya to calculate, it lacks precision placement for joints lower in the chain. If, for example, you want to touch the "wrist" joint to another object, you must first rotate the shoulder, then rotate the elbow, and then probably tweak the rotation of both joints to get the exact lineup you want. Not only is it more time consuming to place an extremity this way, since the entire hierarchy moves when a higher joint up the chain is rotated, the wrist joint in this example will move around if any other joints farther up the chain move, causing it to slide around during animation, which is definitely not a desirable effect and takes a great deal of time and effort to control. On the other hand, FK is ideal for creating arcing motions like arm swings or the motion of legs when doing a cartwheel, so it has its place in the rigging arsenal.

Inverse Kinematics, on the other hand, is much more complex mathematically but allows for fine control of extremity joints and helps control slippage of these joints as the rest of the hierarchy is positioned. In IK, moving the extremity joint (actually a handle controlling placement of this joint) causes joint rotation up the chain, so motion in the chain is propagated *backward*, or in an inverse fashion.

Inverse Kinematics uses *IK handles* and *IK solvers*. An IK chain runs through the joints being affected, a visible handle wire passing from the first to last affected joint. A *handle vector* begins at the start joint and finishes at the end joint, where the IK handle's *end effector* is located. By adding an IK solver, we can animate our example joint chain simply by moving the wrist joint. The shoulder and elbow rotate appropriately so that the entire arm is properly positioned, as shown in Figure 8.10.

An IK solver looks at the position of the end effector of an IK chain and performs the necessary calculations to make the joints rotate properly, from the start joint to the end joint of the IK chain, in such a way that the end joint will be where the end effector is. When the end effector moves, the IK solver converts the translation values of the end effector to the rotational values for the joints and the joints update accordingly. Usually, a simple IK chain will span only three joints, but it can handle more, especially if the IK Spline handle—which controls underlying joints via a curve—is used. Maya has four kinds of IK solvers: the ikRP (Rotate Plane), the ikSC (Single Chain), the IK Spline, and the ikSpring. Each type of IK solver has its own type of IK handle.

Using the ikRP Solver

Since the ikRP solver is likely to be the solver you use most frequently, let's see how it works first. As you go though the following steps, refer to Figure 8.11, which shows the components of an ikRP solver.

1. In the side view, draw a simple three-joint chain by choosing **Skeleton → Joint Tool**, or just use the joint chain from our previous examples. (Switch back to perspective view after creating the skeleton joints.)

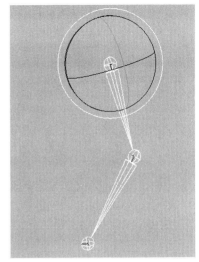

Figure 8.9

Moving an entire joint chain by rotating the top joint in the hierarchy—Forward Kinematics

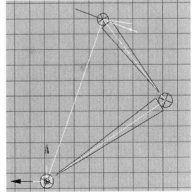

Figure 8.10

Moving a joint chain by moving the end effector of an Inverse Kinematics handle

Figure 8.11

**The ikRP solver
components**

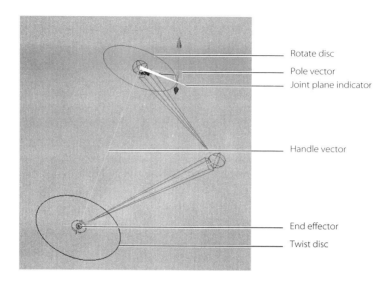

Rotate disc
Pole vector
Joint plane indicator

Handle vector

End effector
Twist disc

2. Choose **Skeleton → IK Handle Tool** ❐, reset the tool to its default settings, and choose ikRPSolver from the Current Solver pop-up menu.

3. Click the first joint you created, and then click the last joint. You should see that an IK handle has been created. The circle at the top looks complicated (as shown in Figure 8.11), but it's actually a fairly simple setup once you've learned what its components are.

The ikRP solver calculates only the positional value of the end effector, which means it ignores the rotational values of the end effector. By default, the joints are rotated by the ikRP solver in such a way that their Y axes are planar, their X axes are pointing to the center of the bones, and their Z axes are perpendicular to the bending direction. If you do not see the rotate disc, select the end effector and press the T key to display the Show Manipulator tool.

The plane along which the joints are bending is represented by the plane indicator. The plane itself is called the *joint chain plane*. You can rotate this plane about the handle vector using the twist disc, which rotates the IK chain. The Twist degree is measured relative to a reference plane created by the handle vector and the pole vector, which can be translated and keyframed. (At times, the way you want the arm to bend will cause the IK chain to flip with the default reference plane setting. To avoid this flipping, adjust or animate the pole vector.)

The advantage of using the ikRP solver over the ikSC solver is that it offers more precise control over the rotation of the IK chain. The disadvantage is that it necessarily has more components to deal with and can be slower to update, though that is a small problem given today's fast CPUs. In addition, the ikRP solver will "flip" when the end effector passes the top joint of the plane (this is due to a mathematical singularity in the calculations Maya's RP solver uses). Though the ikRP flipping can be partially controlled via a pole vector constraint, it is still a difficulty to be aware of when using the ikRP solver. Because the rotation plane is locked with an SC solver, this is not a problem. However, since the SC solver does not allow the joint chain plane to be rotated, it is not very useful for chains that need to represent universal joints like the shoulder or hip joints in a person.

Using the ikSC Solver

The ikSC solver is simpler than the ikRP solver. Let's experiment with it.

1. Go to the side view and draw another simple joint chain, or just select the ikRP handle and delete it.

2. Choose **Skeleton → IK Handle Tool** ❒ as before, but this time select the ikSC Solver setting. Close the option box.

3. Click the first joint, and then click the last joint. You will see the ikSC handle.

4. Select Rotate and try rotating the IK handle. You will notice that only the local X and Y rotate handles seem to have any effect and that they snap back to certain angles after you release the handles.

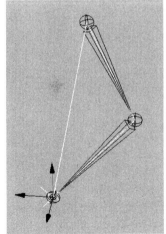

Figure 8.12
An ikSC solver

If you press T to display the Show Manipulator tool, you will see nothing because there are no extra manipulators for the ikSC solver—everything is controlled by the IK handle itself. The ikSC solver calculates the rotational values of the end effector and rotates the IK chain in such a way that all the joints in the chain will have the default local orientation for joints. The joint chain plane exists in the ikSC solver, although you do not see any representation of it in the handle and you have no control over it: the joints are locked into to rotation plane in which the IK handle was created. As with the ikRP solver, the plane cuts across the chain so that the X and Y axes lie on the plane, as shown in Figure 8.12.

In the Attribute Editor for the ikSC solver, under IK Handle Attributes, you will see Priority settings. The ikSC chain can have a priority assignment when two or more chains are overlapping. The chain with the Priority 1 setting will rotate its joints, then the chain with the Priority 2 setting will rotate its joints, and so on. The PO Weight setting determines the handle's position/orientation weight. If the weight is 1, the end effector will try to reach only the handle's position; if the weight is 0, the end effector will try to reach only the handle's orientation. You should leave this setting at the default value of 1.

The advantage of using the ikSC solver is that you need to use only the IK handle to control the IK chain. If you don't need a large number of IK chain rotations—for example, in the rotation of toes or fingers, which don't rotate much around the longitudinal axis—this is the more economical way to animate.

Using the IK Spline Handle Solver

Figure 8.13

Joint chains and the
Spline handle

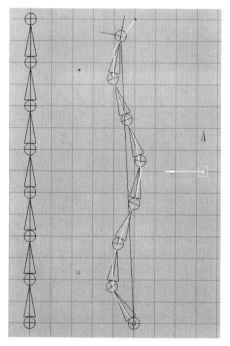

The ikRP and ikSC handles are similar in their attributes, but the IK Spline handle is quite different in the way it functions. The IK Spline solver takes a NURBS curve as part of its handle and rotates the IK chain to follow the shape of the curve. The CVs of the NURBS curve, rather than the end effector of the handle, are animated. The IK Spline handle is ideal for animating curvy or twisty shapes, such as tails, spines, snakes, or tentacles. Let's try out this type of IK handle.

1. In the side view, build a joint chain, as shown on the left in Figure 8.13. For IK Spline handles, the joints need not be built at an angle, but the bones should be short to ensure that the chain will move smoothly.

2. Choose **Skeleton → IK Spline Handle Tool ▯**, and select **Number Of Spans 4**. Leave the other options set to their defaults and close the option box.

3. Click the top joint in the hierarchy, and then click the last joint. You will see the IK Spline handle.

4. In the Outliner, select the joint chain or the IK handle and try moving the joints. The joints have become attached to the curve, and the IK handle doesn't show a manipulator.

5. Select the curve, display its CVs, and move them around, as shown on the right in Figure 8.13.

You can also create your own NURBS curve and have the IK Spline handle use that curve. Turn off the Auto Create Curve setting in the IK Spline Handle option box. Click the root joint, the end joint, and then the curve to create the IK Spline handle.

6. Open the Attribute Editor for the IK handle. You will see the regular attributes and some specifically for the IK Spline handle. Try entering numbers for the **Offset**, **Roll**, and **Twist** settings in the IK Solver Attributes section.

Offset translates the joint chain along the curve, with 0.0 as the start of the curve and 1.0 as its end. **Roll** rotates the whole joint chain. **Twist** gradually twists the chain from the second joint on. If the Root Twist Mode setting is turned on, the twist begins from the root joint. The Root On Curve setting constrains the root joint to the start of the curve. Turn it off and you can move the root joint off the curve as shown in Figure 8.14, but notice that it is still constrained to the curve.

Figure 8.14

The joint chain
dragged to the side
of the curve

Using the ikSpring Solver

The ikSpring Solver tool helps to make multijoint chains work more predictably. In the case of an arachnid leg or a multijointed machine arm, the standard IK handle tool may not prove effective (it might allow joints to bend in strange directions, or it might not bend each joint proportionally), and the spline IK tool tends to make joint chains look like ultraflexible octopus arms more than stiff, multijointed arms. In such a situation, the ikSpring solver comes to the rescue, allowing great control over moving multijointed chains in a proportional manner. Before the ikSpring solver can be used, you must load it using a MEL command. In the Command line (or Script Editor), type `ikSpringSolver`. This enables the solver and places it in the IK Handle Tool Settings options window it will default to the last choice in the Current Solver pop-up menu). Once you have typed in this command once, Maya will remember your preference in the future and automatically load the solver each time you restart Maya.

To use the solver, first create a multijointed skeleton. You can choose to create something like a spider leg, as in Figure 8.15, or something else of your choosing.

Now choose **Skeleton → IK Handle Tool** ❑, and, in the option box, choose the ikSpring-Solver from the Current Solver pop-up menu. Click the first joint, and then click the last to create your new spring IK handle. You should see something similar to Figure 8.16.

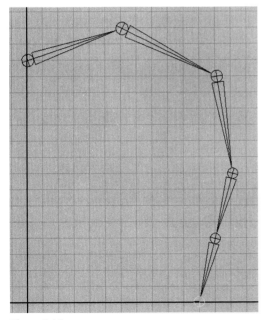

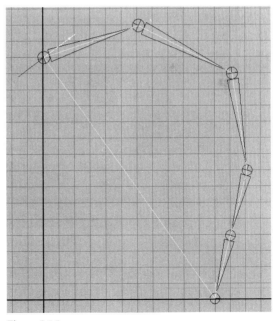

Figure 8.15

A "spider leg" jointed skeleton

Figure 8.16

Adding the IKSpringSolver to the spider leg

On moving the IK handle, you will see that the joints move in a predictable, proportional manner, as shown in Figure 8.17. If you want to see the difference between this tool and the "normal" ikRP solver, try duplicating the joint chain and binding it using the ikRPSolver. On moving this version of the chain, you will see that compression movements cause more kinking when the ikRP solver is used.

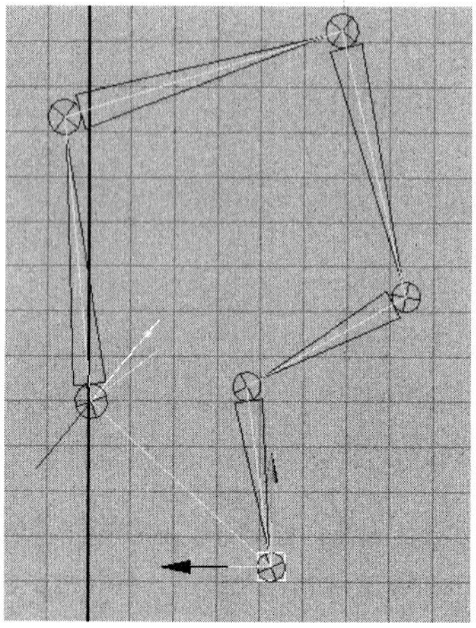

Figure 8.17

Moving the joint chain using the ikSpringSolver

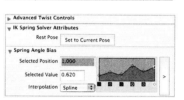

Figure 8.18

Adjusting the Spring Angle Bias graph for the ikSpring Solver tool

For more control over how the spring solver bends each joint in response to handle movement, Maya provides a graphical interface to adjust the response of each joint in the chain. With the ikSpringSolver handle selected, open the Attribute Editor (press Ctrl+A), be sure the ikHandle1 tab is selected, twirl down the IK Solver Attributes pane, the IK Spring Solver Attributes, and then the Spring Angle Bias pane. There, you will see a graph that you can use to alter the responsiveness of each joint, either numerically (using the number fields at left) or graphically by grabbing each point (which represents each joint, in order from top to bottom of the hierarchy as you move from left to right) and moving it up or down. The higher the joint's position is placed in the graph, the more responsive that joint will be to handle movement—thus a value of 0 for any joint will result in that joint's not moving at all in response to handle movement. After some adjustments, your graph might look similar to Figure 8.18.

The Human IK (hik) Solver

The human IK solver is a different IK solver altogether, and is designed to be used with the Full Body IK setup, which we will look at in detail in Hands On section later in this chapter. Briefly, the hik solver allows multiple effectors to be attached to a single IK node; you don't have to use the one-to-one relationship that the other solvers necessitate. Since you can't create a human IK solver without using Maya's FBIK system, we will reserve discussion of this solver for later in the chapter.

Switching between Forward and Inverse Kinematics

Maya lets you switch back and forth between using ikRP and ikSC handles and rotating joints via Forward and Inverse Kinematics, and you can even blend these motions. To switch or blend from IK to FK on a joint chain, you simply need to adjust the **ikBlend** attribute on the IK handle. Let's go through the steps for switching between Forward and Inverse Kinematics using a simple three-joint "arm" setup.

1. Create a three-joint "arm" skeleton, and attach an ikRP solver to it.

2. Keyframe the IK handle, move to frame 10, translate the IK handle, and set a new key.

To set a key, highlight the text of the channels you want to keyframe (the Translate X, Y and Z channels in this case), and RM choose Key Selected from the pop-up menu.

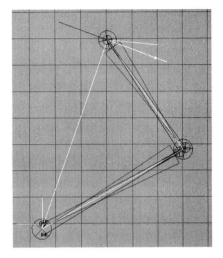

Figure 8.19

Different positions for the FK and IK skeletons, resulting in the final position of the blended joint chain

3. In the Channel Box, set a key (frame 10) of 1 on the **ikBlend** attribute.

4. Go to frame 15 and set a key on the **ikBlend** attribute of the IK handle, setting it to 0 now. Over the six frames from frame 10 to frame 15, the motion of the arm will blend from IK (controlled by the IK handle) to FK (controlled by rotation of the individual joints).

5. Go back to frame 10. Select the two upper joints in the IK chain and keyframe them. Go to frame 20, rotate the joints individually, and then keyframe them.

When finished, play back your animation. (You may need to play it forward one frame at a time so you can see the motion more clearly.) You should see the joint chain rotate to follow the IK handle for the first 10 frames; then it should smoothly blend into the motion of the individual joint rotations over the next 5 frames, finally completely following the motion of the joint rotations, leaving the IK handle behind (at least if you had stickiness turned on), as shown in Figure 8.19. You can keyframe the **ikBlend** attribute back on (value of 1) over more frames and the joints will rotate back to the IK handle position over those frames.

When using IK/FK blending, you will see two colored lines and a joint chain: the FK chain and IK chain are denoted by the lines, while the resulting blended chain rests somewhere between the two "lined" chains. This triple-vision feature enables you to see how the FK and IK chains are being blended to create the position of the resulting chain. You can change the display size of these joints by choosing **Display → Animation → IK/FK Joint Size**.

One more thing to be aware of in switching back and forth between IK and FK is that the movements generated by the rotation of the joints and the corresponding keyframes of the end effector will not always match. They will be roughly the same, but you might need to tweak the end effector's animation.

If you build a chain in a straight line, the ikSC solver or the ikRP solver will not be able to calculate and bend the chain. To fix this problem, first rotate the child joint(s) to angle the chain—even a fraction of a degree should do. Then choose **Skeleton → Set Preferred Angle** or RM choose Set Preferred Angle from the contextual pop-up menu. Delete the existing IK chain and create a new one. Now the ikSC and ikRP solvers should be able to bend the chain. It is best, however, to create all joint chains with slight bends in them in the first place.

Hands On: Creating a Skeleton

The best way to understand how to rig a character is simply to create a rig. The rest of this chapter will be devoted to creating a skeleton with controls and properly binding the geometry to the skeleton.

The first step in creating a rig is to plan your work. The sample rig we will build will be for the character Machismo, created earlier in the modeling chapters. For a complete model, ready to be rigged, you can either use your model or open the MachismoGeo.ma file on the accompanying CD. Since Machismo is a bulky, muscle-bound character, he will require special attention around the torso and arm areas when you skin the geometry to the skeleton. He will also require control over individual fingers, but since he's wearing shoes, he only needs a basic, single-joint chain for each foot.

Creating a Curve Proto-Structure for the Skeleton

Once we determine the general sense of Machismo's skeletal layout, we could just wade in and start building a skeleton. However, this method of building a skeleton is fraught with potential problems, the largest of which is that, when building a complex skeleton, it is nearly impossible to position each joint correctly with the first click. When you inevitably have to move the joints around to fit them correctly into the geometry, rotation axis problems can arise, which will cause all sorts of troubles later when binding and animating the character. In addition, it is easy to forget to include a joint when building a skeleton, which can also cause problems later. You can pre-build a skeleton in Maya in a number of ways; we will create a series of curves for each important section of the skeleton (legs, arms, spine, and so on) that we will use as reference when building the actual skeleton. Because the points on a curve can be moved around freely and the layout of the curves is obvious in the scene window, and since the skeleton can be snapped to the curve, this method allows for quick and accurate creation of the skeleton once the curves have been properly placed within the geometry.

If a joint's rotation axis is not lined up with the bone, the joint will not rotate about the bone when it is later rotated, leading to problems controlling motion during animation. The job of the rigger is to make animation easier, not harder, so it is imperative to create clean rigs without rotation problems, and thus the extra time spent creating the proto-skeleton curves is well worth the effort.

Building the reference set of curves takes just a couple of adjustments. The first is to open the EP Curve Tool option box (choose **Create → EP Curve Tool** ❑) and set Curve Degree to 1 (linear). By doing this, you will only get points on the curve where you click your mouse; since you will be placing joints on each curve point, this is a necessary first step. Second, for ease of selecting and moving the curves, turn off selectability of all scene elements except curves. (In the main taskbar, set the object mask—the black downward facing triangle—to All Objects Off, and then select the Curves icon to enable just curve selection.) You might also want to enable X-Ray mode so you can more easily see the curves inside Machismo's body (choose **Shading → X-Ray** in the Panels menu set).

Building the set of reference curves is as easy as choosing the EP Curve tool and clicking along arms, back, legs, fingers, and so forth to create a curve for each important area of the skeleton. Once you have a basic "layout" for each curve, go into component mode (press F8) and drag each curve point around until it is exactly where you want it. For our skeleton, we added "roll" joints midway down each upper and lower arm and leg; these joints can be used to help create the twisting motion of skin along forearms and calves and are included for completeness of the skeleton. You do not need to include these extra joints if you don't want to. As reference, you can open the MachismoSkelCurves.ma file on the accompanying CD. When you are finished, you should have a set of curves similar to those in Figure 8.20.

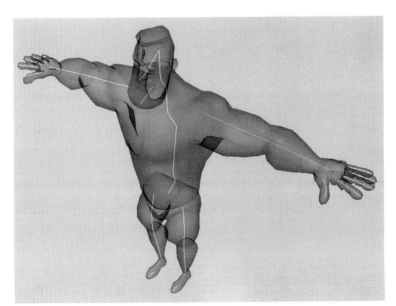

Figure 8.20

The set of reference curves for Machismo's skeleton

Now we need to name the curves appropriately so that we can speed up the work flow later. Because the new Full Body IK can be built using joint names, naming curves (and therefore joints) with exact names is crucial. (Alternatively, you can label joints before creating a Full Body IK skeleton.) For now, name your curves as follows: SpineCurve, LeftLegCurve, RightLegCurve, LeftFootCurve, RightFootCurve, LeftArmCurve, RightArm-Curve, LeftHandThumbCurve, LeftHandIndexCurve, LeftHandMiddleCurve, Left-HandRingCurve, LeftHandPinkyCurve, RightHandThumbCurve, RightHandIndexCurve, RightHandMiddleCurve, RightHandRingCurve, RightHandPinkyCurve, and JawCurve. Be sure the names are exactly as typed here (including upper- and lowercases): these names will be used in a script that will do most of the skeleton building in the next section.

THE IMPORTANCE OF NAMING ALL ELEMENTS

Name *everything* in a rig, especially seemingly unimportant elements such as curves used to create a skeleton. Far from wasting time, this little extra effort will be one of your best timesavers. If you do not, you will find yourself spending a great deal of time trying to figure out what joint143 is and why you placed it where you did. If, however, you name this joint leftUpArm, you will know just what the function of this joint is, as well as why you placed it where you did. Additionally, naming all your rig elements becomes a way to make the rig self-documenting: selecting a rig node—any node—will tell you what that node does just by looking at its name. This self-documentation is invaluable both as the rigger finishes work on the rig and as the character is animated.

Building the Skeleton

You can build the skeleton now in a couple of ways. You can choose the Joint tool, turn on curve snapping (click the Snap To Curves button in the toolbar), drag your joints into place on the curves, and then name them using Table 8.1. But why spend all the time and effort to do this when a MEL script can do it for you? Find the drawBase.mel script on the accompanying CD and source it (choose **File → Source Script** in the Script Editor window). Then just select all your curves, type **drawBase** into the Command line, and press the Enter key. Voilà. A mostly built, properly named skeleton is ready for your use, as shown in Figure 8.21! If you run into any errors with the script, the most likely cause is incorrect naming of the curves; see the previous section and recheck your curve names to be sure you have everything named properly (and remember that MEL is case sensitive). If you want to create the skeleton manually or add or change any skeleton joints, see Table 8.1 for a complete list of joint names that Full Body IK setup supports.

Table 8.1

Proper names for each possible joint in the Full Body IK setup

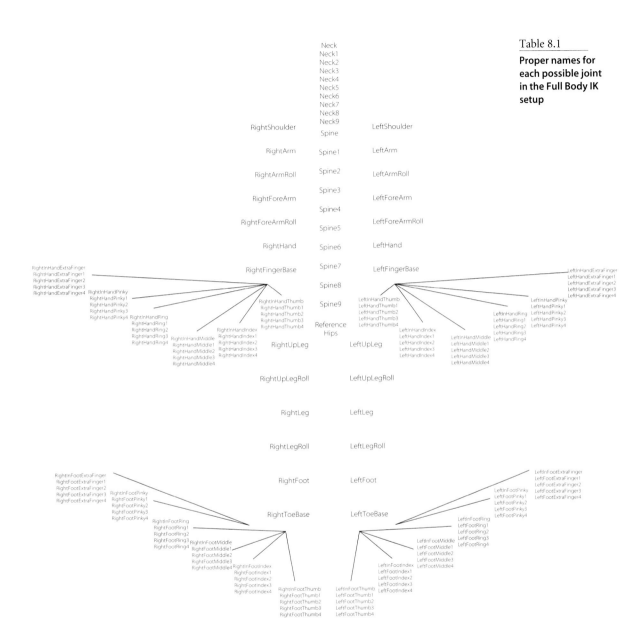

Figure 8.21

Instant skeleton! Using the draw-Base.mel **script**

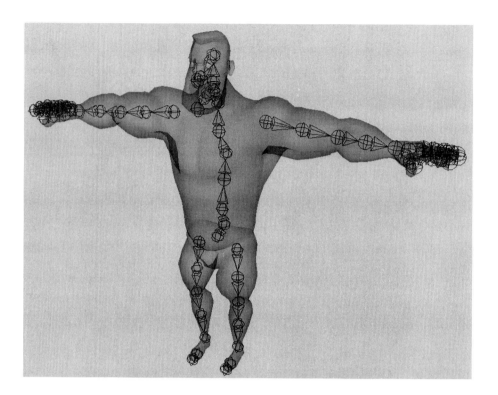

Even though most of the skeleton is built, there's still a bit more work to do. First, the spine/head curve probably has incorrect names: since there's no way to know beforehand how many spine and neck joints a person will create, most of the joints in the neck/head area will likely be named incorrectly. Go to the first neck joint and rename it Neck. The second neck joint (if you have one) should be Neck1, the third should be Neck2, and so forth. The first head joint should be named Head, the second Head1, and so on. (The Full Body IK setup recognizes only the first Head joint, but you can place as many as you want in the head area.) Second, you need to parent together all the skeleton pieces into a complete, hierarchical skeleton. For example, select the LeftUpLeg joint, Shift+select the Hips joint, and press p to parent the two together. Proceed through the skeleton, linking any sections that were not parented before. When you finish, selecting the Hips joint should highlight all the bones in the skeleton. (If not, parent the orphan section into the main skeleton.) Your finished skeleton should look like Figure 8.22. If you need a reference, see the MachismoSkeleton.ma file on the CD.

As Table 8.1 shows, Maya's Full Body IK solution system can use joint names to understand which section of the body it is creating a solution for. Full Body IK creation also supports joint labeling, rather than naming, as a means of telling the system which section

Figure 8.22

The complete hierar-chical skeleton

of the body it is creating as the Full Body IK program is called. Advantages and disadvantages are associated with each method of naming. Naming joints allows for a much larger range of joints to be specified (leftArmRoll, for example) than does joint labeling; however, if your studio has an already-defined joint-naming scheme, using joint labels rather than names allows you to continue using your current naming conventions.

Here, because we have no current naming convention, we will use the joint-naming scheme. If you prefer to use joint labels, select a given joint (the leftArm joint, for example), choose **Skeleton → Joint Labelling → Add FBIK Labels → Label Left** (this step needs to be done only once per side of the character), then choose **Label Shoulder** from the same menu set. Alternatively, you can select the joint, open the Attribute Editor, open the Joint section and then the Joint Labelling section, and choose Left from the Side drop-down menu and Arm from the Type drop-down menu.

Either method will provide the same results; choose whichever method is most efficient for you. The `drawBase.mel` script labels each joint appropriately, in addition to naming each joint, so you can use either method to create the Full Body IK solution in the next section. If you want to use joint labels, be sure to relabel the head and neck regions of the skeleton since they had to be renamed manually as well.

Although it might not be obvious, many of the joints just created have inverted or off-axis joint orientation: the Y axis of individual joints will likely be pointing in unpredictable directions, out of alignment with one another. This may not seem like a big problem, but lack of uniform joint orientation will lead to difficulties in rigging and animating, so we need to solve the problem now. Fortunately, we have created a MEL script that shows joint orientation (local rotation axes) and has some easy ways to fix any orientation troubles. Source the `jointFlip.mel` script that comes on the accompanying CD (choose **File → Source Script** from the Script Editor window). Then type **jointFlip** in the Command line to invoke the script, whose interface is shown in Figure 8.23. If you prefer to use Maya's built-in tools, you can use the Orient Joint tool (choose **Skeleton → Orient Joint ❑** from the Animation menu set), which operates similarly to the jointFlip script. In fact, as each tool has elements the other is missing, you can use both in complementary fashion to resolve even the most difficult join orientation challenges.

You can see the problem with inconsistent joint orientations by looking at the way an S curve of joints rotates. If you create a series of joints like those shown on the left in Figure 8.24, select *all* the joints in the chain (not just the top joint), and rotate them, you will get a compressed S curve, as shown in the center image in Figure 8.24. Although this effect is compelling in a way, it demonstrates that some joints are bending to the left (counterclockwise) and that others are bending to the right (clockwise). This leads the animator and rigger to have to compensate by inversely rotating some joints (that is, by rotating counterclockwise to get a clockwise rotation), which complicates rigging and animation. Additionally, some joints might get out of phase by a strange angle, such as 30 degrees off-axis. This can lead to even stranger behavior and is a real bane of rigging a character. By adjusting the local rotation axes so that the Y and Z axes all point in the same direction, you can achieve consistent rotation. On the right side of Figure 8.24, all joints rotate in a clockwise direction, which is the desired result.

Figure 8.23

The `jointFlip.mel` script user interface window

Figure 8.24

Rotating a joint chain (A) with different orientations (B) and aligned orientations (C)

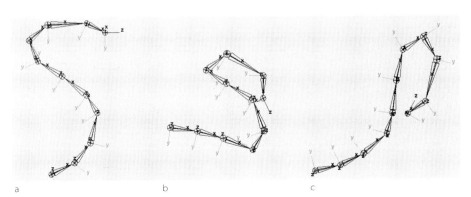

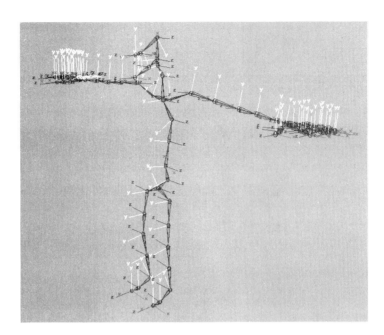

Figure 8.25

Adjusting the local rotation axes of Machismo so that all sections are oriented consistently

With the Machismo skeleton highlighted, run the jointFlip script. In the scene window, you can select the whole skeleton or any subelement of the skeleton (an arm, for example), show rotation axes, move up and down the hierarchy, and change the joint orientation of any joint. For each chain of joints (the back, the arm, the leg, and so on), the goal is for all the Y and Z axes to point in the same direction, as in Figure 8.25. Notice that the orientation of the last joint in each chain (the last finger joint, for example) is unimportant, because rotating that joint does nothing. When all the rotation axes of the various parts of the skeleton face the same direction, the skeleton is ready to be rigged and skinned.

Creating a Full Body IK Skeleton

Creating a skeleton that moves more or less as a bipedal human character has become much easier with the advent of the Full Body IK system. The Full Body IK system is a direct outgrowth of the MotionBuilder system now being integrated into Maya as a first-class plug-in rather than being a stand-alone program as it was previously (one can, of course, still purchase MotionBuilder as a separate application from Autodesk). Full Body IK is a paradigm shift for those who have rigged characters in Maya before: the FBIK system depends on a new, multi-node effector called the human IK Effector, or hikEffector. Whereas all other effectors/IK handles only allow one input to them, the hikEffector places all control elements (feet, hands, and so on) within one node. What this new data scheme allows is automated reaction of body elements as a character is manipulated in the scene window. For example, as a character's hips are moved up and down, the Full Body IK system will cause the spine, arms, and legs to react appropriately, which not only creates realistic secondary animation, it also eases the job of animators.

Full Body IK can also create quadruped rigs, as well as "nonstandard" human rigs (with extra fingers or toes, for example). Although we will concentrate on creating a standard bipedal rig, Maya's documentation explains how to create these other types of rigs, and you can create a sample quadruped (or biped) rig by selecting **Skeleton → Full Body IK → Get FBIK Example**. Included are a camel and a man.

Creating Full Body IK is simple once joints have been named or labeled properly, though you will usually have to take several steps after creating the Full Body IK system to get the desired behavior from the system. To create the Full Body IK system, select the root joint of the skeleton, and then, under the Animation menu set, choose **Skeleton → Full Body IK → Add Full Body IK ☐**. In the option box, set Identify Joints to By Name and leave Posture set to Biped. Click Add, and in a few seconds you should see a rigged skeleton, as shown in Figure 8.26.

Once your Fully Body IK system has been created, try playing around with the effectors: grab any of the boxes or large circles on the skeleton (at the hands, feet, neck, head, and so forth) and move them around. The character's body should react more or less in a natural motion. Note that whenever a Full Body IK effector is selected, all joints that are affected by it turn magenta. (Thus, when the HipsEff is selected, the entire skeleton turns magenta.) For reference, you can open the `MachismoFBIKStart.ma` file on the CD.

Figure 8.26

Adding Full Body IK to Machismo's skeleton

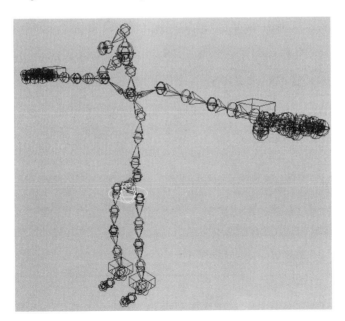

Adjustments to Full Body IK

Although the lion's share of work in creating the rig is done simply by creating the Full Body IK system, you will still want to make some adjustments to get just the right behavior out of your rig. The most important adjustment is to add a secondary effector at each of the character's heels, which will allow for proper foot-roll animation. To create a secondary effector for the left foot, select the LeftFootEff node (the box around the left ankle) and choose **Skeleton → Full Body IK → Add Secondary Effector** (from the Animation menu set). A sphere will appear aligned around the ankle, called LeftFootEffPivot; you might want to rename this node something like LeftFootEffHeel. Translate this new effector to the heel of the left foot, as shown in Figure 8.27.

You can also scale the effector to a smaller size to match the other effectors on the character. With the LeftFootEffHeel still selected, choose **Skeleton → Full Body IK → Activate Secondary Effector** to enable the effector. Repeat this process for the right foot, ensuring as much as possible that the effectors line up in the side view. If you now rotate each secondary effector, you will see that each foot rotates around the heel, providing the correct behavior for a walking motion with the heel striking the ground.

To create a proper heel-ball-toe walking motion, we need to create another secondary effector at the ball of each foot. Following the previous steps, add a secondary effector to each foot (rename them LeftFootEffBall and RightFootEffBall), move the effector into position at the ball of each foot, and activate them. When you're finished, your feet should look like Figure 8.28. After adding these two effectors, the foot will roll properly as each effector/pivot is rotated in turn.

By default, all Full Body IK characters have contact with a "floor" set at the level of the scene grid (0 on the Y axis). Because this is where our character's feet currently rest, we do not need to adjust this setting; however, it is instructive to look at the settings should you

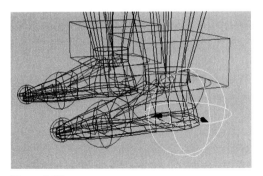

Figure 8.27
The secondary heel effector placed properly

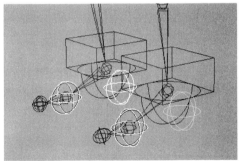

Figure 8.28
Adding heel and ball secondary effectors to Machismo's feet

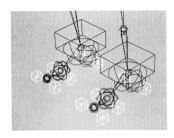

Figure 8.29

Displaying the Floor Contact markers

need to change the floor level for your character. To see the floor contact markers, select the HipsEff node (set at the character root), and then, in the Channel Box under the hikFloorContactMarker1 node, set feetContact On. (Be sure drawFeetContact is also set to On.) You should see a series of boxes around each foot, as shown in Figure 8.29. (You can also turn on floor contact for the hands by turning on the handsContact setting.) Each set of six boxes should just surround each foot, defining the area in which the feet contact the floor.

To adjust the contact markers, you don't directly manipulate the boxes; rather, you adjust settings for the hikFloorContactMarker1 node in the Channel Box. The footHeight control lets you set the height of the floor contact; raising this value will make the skeleton look like it's standing on higher and higher ground. The other settings adjust where the contact markers are located around the feet. FootBack, Middle, and Front set where the back, middle, and front pairs of contact markers are located, and footInside and Outside adjust the location of the three inside and outside markers for each foot.

If your skeleton is well made and the geometry of the character is not too unusual, the initial settings for the contact markers should be close to correct. Feel free to adjust the settings if they are not perfect, remembering that your goal is to surround the geometry of the feet with the markers and that the Back, Middle, and Front marker sets should be even with the heel, ball, and toe effectors, respectively. If you open the Attribute Editor with the contact markers selected, you'll see a few other settings under the Feet To Floor Contact Attributes not available in the Channel Box. Feet Floor Pivot lets you set the foot's pivot point to Auto, Ankle, or Toes. Feet Contact Type can be set to Normal (bipedal feet), Ankle, Toe Base, and Hoof. Feet Contact Stiffness is initially set to 0, but you can set it higher for more stiffness in the joints of the feet. After adjusting the settings for the Floor Contact marker, you can turn off display of the contact markers by setting the Draw Feet Contact to Off; although this turns off display of the floor contacts, they will remain active in the scene. For reference, see the MachismoFBIKComplete.ma file on the CD.

You can also add contact planes at different heights from the base floor level. This can be useful if, say, the character needs to place her hand on a chair as she bends over to pick up something from the floor. To create a floor contact plane, select the effector to which you want to add the plane, and then choose **Skeleton → Full Body IK → Add Floor Contact Plane**. You should see a plane appear just below the effector. Before the contact plane will work, however, the **Hands** or **Feet Contact** attribute must be set to On. If you have not yet turned on **Hand Contact**, for example, select the HipsEff node and set **Hands Contact** to On. Now when you move the hand (or foot), you should see it stop when it reaches the contact plane. You can move the contact plane up or down and translate it across the X-Z plane, and, new with Maya 8, you can also angle these contact planes by rotating them. When it contacts an angled plane, the hand (or foot) will rotate to rest upon the surface. You can add as many floor contact planes for each hand/foot as you want, so creating a staircase or other multitiered contact object is straightforward.

You can also adjust the pinning of each effector. The foot effectors, for example, are pinned in translation and rotation, the hips effector is unpinned, and the hand effectors are pinned in translation only. Pinning states affect how a specific effector will react to body motion. An unpinned effector will move and rotate freely as the body is manipulated. Effectors pinned in translation will remain locked in space, but are free to rotate unless directly manipulated. Effectors pinned in rotation will move freely in space, but will not rotate unless directly manipulated. Effectors pinned in translation and rotation will not move or rotate unless directly manipulated. The exception to this rule is a joint chain that is stretched beyond its maximum (if, for example, you pull the hips up to such an extent that the legs are completely straight). In such a case, the pinned effectors will move so that the bones do not have to stretch. Try pinning and unpinning various effectors on your skeleton and see how this changes the way the body reacts as you move it around in space.

> The shape of the effector changes to reflect different pinning states: unpinned effectors are spherical, effectors pinned in translation are boxes, effectors pinned in rotation are half spheres, and effectors pinned in rotation and translation are boxes with a half sphere. This visual feedback is helpful for quickly noting which effectors will have which behavior. We will discuss the technique, using pinning and unpinning of effectors and subcharacters, to animate the Full Body IK rig in Chapter 10.

Finally, you can adjust a number of attributes in the Attribute Editor to tweak the behavior of your Full Body IK rig as it is manipulated in the scene window and animated. Select the HipsEff node, and then open the Attribute Editor. The HipsEff tab gives you access to basic controls such as whether the effector is pinned, the Pivot Offset (which determines around which point the effector rotates), and the Radius, or size of the effector.

Under the hikHandle node, in the HIK Handle Attributes section, reside a number of controls that let you fine-tune your Full Body IK setup. The basic control is the Activate check box, which determines whether the Full Body IK system will function. Posture Type can be set to either biped or quadruped. Hip Translation Mode can be set to World or Body Rigid; adjust this setting only if you have created separate translation and rotation nodes for the HipEff node. (This is done in the options for creating your Full Body IK rig.) Realistic Shoulder Solving determines whether the clavicle bone will rotate if the arms are raised above shoulder level. A setting of 1 for this will make for fully realistic shoulder motion (full clavicle involvement), and a setting of 0 locks the clavicle joint in place. Depending on the character (cartoon versus photo-realistic, for example), you want to go to either extreme or find a setting in the middle somewhere. Solve Fingers controls whether the Full Body IK system solves motion for each of the fingers. Because solving for fingers involves as many joints as the rest of a normal skeleton, turning Solve Fingers off while blocking out animation can make for faster interaction with the scene.

The Pull sections (Pull, Left Arm Pull, Right Arm Pull, Left Leg Pull, and Right Leg Pull) are all enabled by checking the Expert Mode check box. When this check box is enabled, you can adjust how strongly each body part (head, chest, left leg, and so on) is attracted to the motion of the body as a whole. The greater each pull value, the less effect moving other body parts has on that particular body part. (The Reach Translation, and Rotation values on the individual effector are multiplied by the Pull value, so if the Reach value is 0, even a Pull value of 1 will have no effect). Each Pull twirl-down menu offers even further control over how the Pull function works. One can, for example, adjust how the left elbow pulls or how the hand affects the hips.

The Roll Attributes section allows you to distribute some arm or leg "roll" rotation (rotation around the long axis of the bone) to roll bones, if your character has them. Since we have constructed Machismo with roll joints, you can enable each or some of these joints in the Roll Attributes section. If, for example, you want to share forearm rotation fifty-fifty between the elbow and forearm roll joints, enable the Left/Right Forearm Roll Mode and set the value to 0.5 (or 50 percent). The greater the value, the more of the total rotation the roll joint takes on. It is a little difficult to see the effect of this setting until after the character is bound to the skeleton (see the next section for how to bind the geometry to the skeleton), but the effect is important for more realistic characters.

The Stiffness section (which includes Arm, Leg, and Hips stiffness settings) controls the acceleration speed of each body part *during playback*. (The settings have no effect during scene interaction.) To make a body part—say a leg—begin to move more slowly than the default, set the stiffness to higher than the default 0.5 setting. This makes the particular leg appear heavier when the body is animated. To make the leg appear very light, set the stiffness to close to 0.

The **Kill Pitch** attribute controls, for either the elbows or the knees, the ability of the joint to rotate in the pitch direction (around the Z axis by default). This control can be used to remove unwanted pitch rotation in the knee or elbow joints.

The **Finger** and **Toe Tips Size** attributes are an alternative to creating a floor contact for the hands or feet. Here, instead of the markers associated with the floor contact constraint, the hikSolver creates a sphere around each appendage, whose size can be controlled by the **<node>Tip** attribute. The larger the **Tip** attribute, the bigger the fingers and toes are to the solver, and the feet and hand contacts with any floor planes are adjusted accordingly. Do not use the **Tip Size** attributes in conjunction with a floor contact plane because the contact plane will cancel out the **Tip Size** attribute.

Binding and Weighting the Character

Now that we have an operational character rig, it is time to let it control the geometry of the character. Basic skinning is fairly easy, since Maya does most of the work for you. However, as you will see, adjusting skin weights to make the character deform just right takes time and effort. To bind the skeleton to the skin, follow these steps:

1. Select the root (Hips) joint of the skeleton. Be sure not to select the hips effector but rather the root joint itself. Then Shift+select the body geometry.

2. Choose **Skin → Bind Skin → Smooth Bind** ❐. In the option box, reset all settings (choose **Edit → Reset Settings**). Max Influences determines how many joints might affect a given element of geometry, and Dropoff determines how quickly the influence of a joint disappears as you move farther from the joint. (Higher numbers drop off more quickly.) For this character, Max Influences of 5 and Dropoff of 4 are appropriate values. Also be sure the Colorize Skeleton feature is turned on. This feature colorizes each bone in the skeleton and will be useful shortly as we adjust the skin weights.

3. Click the Bind Skin button, and, within a few seconds, your geometry should be bound to the skeleton.

When you now move your control rig around, Machismo himself should follow, deforming more or less correctly with the motion of the joints, as shown in Figure 8.30. If the default settings do not produce satisfactory results (note especially whether the fingers, toes, and armpits are generally workable), try undoing the skinning process and adjusting the Max Influences and Dropoff settings. For reference you can open the MachismoSkinStart.ma file on the CD.

Figure 8.30

Surfing! Machismo's geometry being moved around by the skeleton.

Unfortunately, while creating a smooth bind is a straightforward process, it does not do a perfect job of deforming our character's geometry. To create a usable character, we must reweight the skin—one of the most tedious and potentially frustrating parts of creating a character rig. Although Maya makes it fairly easy to reweight skin, doing so for a character with dozens of joints is still a long and difficult task because of the sheer number of cross-influences between various joints.

You can adjust the weighting of your skin in several ways, but the most intuitive method is to use the Paint Skin Weights tool, which allows you to use a virtual paint brush to paint on adjustments to the default skin weighting and see these adjustments take effect in real time. Maya 8 includes a color feedback feature that colors the skin, showing the influence of every joint on the skin at the same time and allowing for easier fine-tuning of joint influences on the skin. Figure 8.31 shows Machismo's skin with the multicolor feedback turned on. Joints can also be rotated while still in paint mode, which can speed up weight painting substantially because it removes the need to go back and forth from rotate to paint tools.

To enter weight painting mode, select Machismo's skin geometry and choose **Skin → Edit Smooth Skin → Paint Skin Weights Tool** ❐ from the Animation menu set. The Paint Skin Weights Tool options window will open, as shown in Figure 8.32. This window contains

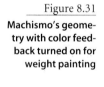

Figure 8.31

Machismo's geometry with color feedback turned on for weight painting

many settings, as well as a pane wherein you can choose the joint for which you will paint influences. Toward the bottom of the window, twirl down the Display tab and check the Multi-Color Feedback option to see Machismo's skin color reflect the weight of each joint.

The basic procedure to paint skin weights is to select a particular joint (a finger joint, for example) and then paint to add, replace, or smooth weights, depending on which radio button is checked. (You can also scale weights, but this is not frequently useful.) Adding weights adds a certain amount of influence—defined by the amount in the Value slider multiplied by the Opacity setting—to the skin from the selected joint. If both Opacity and Value are set to 1, painting adds full influence (value of 1) to the painted vertices. If both are set to 0, painting has no effect since adding 0 doesn't affect the weightings. Replace discards the old weightings and replaces them with the current value (multiplied by the Opacity setting). Smooth adjusts weights so that they approach each other: if a particular CV has 0.8 influence from joint1 and 0.2 influence from joint2, Smooth adjusts these weights so that, eventually, they will both be close to 0.5. Replace is a little dangerous to use with weighting, because it can lead to skin points with less than a 1.0 overall weighting, which causes that piece of skin to "hang back" as the character is animated, since it is not being pulled along at 100 percent. Thus, we will stick to using the Add and Smooth settings to paint weights where possible.

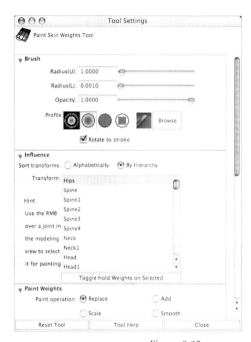

Figure 8.32

The Paint Skin Weights Tool options window

To start, select the LeftForearm joint in the Tool Settings window, and then MM click the joint to go into rotation mode. With the middle mouse button (not the left one), drag one of the rotation axes to bend the elbow joint enough to see creasing in the elbow area, but not enough to overlap any skin, which would make weight painting difficult, as shown in Figure 8.33. (Be sure to write down the original rotation angle of the joint if it's not 0 so you can get back to that angle again.) Select the Paint Skin Weights tool (press the Y key on the keyboard to reselect it again), set the mode to Add, and set the Value slider to something like 0.4 and the Opacity slider to about 0.3. These settings will allow fairly subtle adjustments of the skin weights, which is desirable so as not to create any discontinuities where influence from one joint meets influence from another. If your brush radius (the red circle that appears over the geometry) is too small or too large, hold down the B key and drag the mouse over the geometry to be skinned; the radius of the brush will alter size to better fit your painting needs.

Figure 8.33

Bending the elbow for weight painting

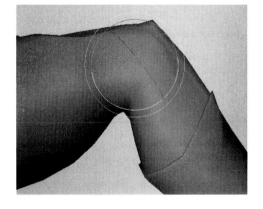

Figure 8.34

The bent elbow with adjusted skin weights applied

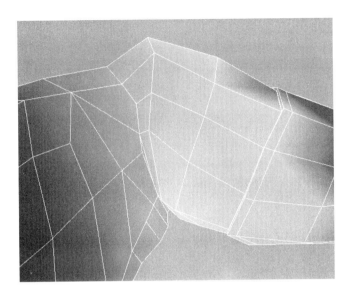

Switch back to paint mode by LM clicking anywhere on the geometry, and then begin painting over the lower inside elbow area to increase the elbow joint's influence over the forearm, thus increasing the inside elbow crease. Switch back and forth between the Left-ArmRoll and LeftForearm joints, adding influence to each to create the crease. You will also want to create a more defined outer elbow on the back of the arm using the same method. As you add influences in this area, you may find that the back of the elbow, especially, is getting very sharp. To smooth out that area, change to Smooth mode and paint over the area until you are satisfied with the look. (You may find that increasing the opacity while using the Smooth tool makes this tool work more efficiently.) When you're finished, your newly creased elbow should look something like Figure 8.34. Once you are satisfied with the elbow area, be sure to select the LeftForeArm joint and reset all the rotation values to 0. (Alternatively, you can select the skeleton and choose **Skeleton → Full Body IK → Go To Stance Pose** to return all joints to their initial bound positions.)

You can select a joint on which to adjust weights by holding the right mouse button down over the joint and choosing Paint Weights from the pop-up menu. This can really speed up weight painting over selecting the joints in the option box.

Now comes the fun part: repeat the process of painting weights for *every* element of Machismo's body! This will take a long time, and getting skin weights set just right is something of an art, so be sure to save different versions of your scene file in case you need to go back to an earlier version. Here are some pointers to help you in the weighting process.

- The multicolor feedback setting will be useful, once you get used to how the colors are generated by various joints, when painting areas with multiple influences, such as the fingers, armpits, and upper legs/hips.

- For particularly nasty areas (such as the armpits), bend the primary joint a little, adjust weights until the area looks good, and then bend the area more and readjust weights.

- Be sure to rotate joints in every direction they can be rotated to check on weighting. Your character may look fine when a joint is rotated in the X axis but terrible when that same joint is rotated in Z.

- For areas that can bend tightly (fingers, knees, and elbows), be sure to adjust weighting throughout the range of motion of the joint. Try bending the joint partially, adjusting weighting, bending it further, readjusting weighting, bending it fully, and then doing final adjustments.

- Continually test your rig in "temp" versions of your scene, and give these temp versions to others to test as well. You will find that all sorts of little problems crop up in the skin weighting as the character is put through complete motions, and it's better to solve these now than in the middle of animating a scene.

- For areas such as the head that don't need to distort at all, you can flood the geometry with a value of 1 for a joint such as head4. This will remove any influences of other joints, such as the neck joints, without your having to paint weights for each joint individually. To flood the geometry, choose the Replace setting (this is one time it's good to use Replace), set the Value and Opacity to 1, and click the Flood button.

- Be sure to write down translation and rotation settings for every joint or effector handle you move. You will want to return them to *exactly* where they were after you finish weighting the skin, and writing these values down is a lot safer than trying to remember them. Although Go To Bind Pose or Go To Stance Pose normally works, it sometimes doesn't return joints to exactly the value they were in initially.

When you finally finish reweighting your model, you should have a definite sense of achievement knowing that you now have a properly bound character that moves just right when various joints are rotated. The MachismoWeighted.ma file on the CD contains a fully weighted rig for your perusal.

Summary

In this chapter, we covered all the basics of building a character rig, from creation of a standard bipedal skeleton, complete with properly aligned rotation axes, to construction of a Full Body IK control rig and skinning the character itself. After completing this chapter, you should be well on your way to creating useful character rigs of your own. Just remember the character setup artist's mantra: Pay attention to every detail, and name every element of your rig!

CHAPTER 9

Character Animation

To animate means "to breathe life into" something. Character animation can be described as the highest form of this act of "life breathing." It is more than just modeling, texturing, rigging, and keyframing; these elements combined with performance and timing elevate the craft of computer graphics to the level of art—the level at which the audience reacts to and empathizes with the actions of the character rather than the technological marvel of computer animation.

The ability to create such a performance takes years to develop, and it does not begin with the animator's computer knowledge or even the animator's knowledge of Maya. An animator can rather quickly grasp Maya's animation tools and editors, but learning the art of character animation takes a lifetime. Each performance brings new challenges and new problems. Character animation techniques can be specific to each performance; what works in one particular animation task may not apply to another. This chapter will introduce you to the time-tested pose-to-pose method of creating character animation as well as discuss some of Maya's key character animation tools.

- **Preparing to animate**
- **The animation process**
- **Pose-to-pose blocking**
- **Establishing timings**
- **Refining animation**

Step Away from the Computer!

A common mistake for novice and advanced animators alike is to sit down at the computer and begin animating. Few, if any, professional animators choose to simply start animating at the computer; almost everyone takes time to prepare in some way. Failing to prepare results in the fundamental mistake of believing that animation can be created without putting thought into the actual motions to be crafted.

With animating, beginning at the computer is much like drawing from memory; novices draw objects and people based on how they think the subject looks, not on how it actually appears. Experienced artists look more often at their subject than they look at their paper to draw their subject more accurately. Novice animators will often try to create motion based on how they *think* their subject moves as opposed to how it *actually* moves. Whenever possible, experienced animators try to view some sort of reference to see how their subject moves in real life. This type of study is called *motion* or *action analysis,* and it is as old as animation itself. All that is required is reference material.

Reference Sources

Early cel animators were largely limited to film, stopwatches, paper and pencil, and mirrors to study motion. We are fortunate to have many more and higher-quality material. Here is a short list of them.

- Video cameras
- DVDs and videotape
- Illustrated books
- Sound recordings

These items can provide an accurate point of comparison for your animation.

The Internet can be used to find reference material for motion study. In particular, sites like www.youtube.com and www.video.google.com are a ready source of video clips.

Video Cameras

The widespread availability of the digital video camera (see Figure 9.1) and inexpensive data cards that are compliant with IEEE 1394 (FireWire) is perhaps the greatest boon to the animator in the last several years. After the computer itself, no tool is more valuable. This may appear to be a bold statement, but consider that the DV camera can serve not only as an instrument with which to shoot reference footage, but also, in conjunction with the data card, as a video I/O device with which you can preview animations on the target video monitor quickly and easily. Furthermore, with the proper video-editing software, this camera can take the final rendered frames out of the computer as near-beta-quality video. Such video is of sufficiently high quality to serve as a demo reel.

Figure 9.1

DV cameras such as this Sony DCRTRV-20 offer a host of features to help in planning animation.

The clear advantage of the DV camera is that you can use it to acquire any type of motion you want. The DV camera is small, and you can take it anywhere. You can then copy this footage into the computer easily and quickly and use it as an exact reference. The disadvantage is that this type of reference is only as good as the actor or the subject being videotaped. A poor performance or poorly timed action will not serve as a good base for animation. Another disadvantage is shared by almost all live-action reference: it is too slow. Almost all footage acquired by the video camera will need to be sped up between 5 percent and 25 percent.

The one caveat with video footage —and all live footage—is that it should be used as a reference upon which you can build a performance, not as the performance itself. You will almost always want to push far beyond what appears on your reference to create a compelling performance. Nevertheless, video reference serves as a good first step.

DVDs and Videotape

Using commercial DVDs and videotapes, you can view motions repeatedly to gain an understanding of how people, animals, and things move on the "big screen." Whether you are a novice or an experienced animator, build a library of DVDs and videotapes. DVDs are more effective because you can access motions and acting performances on a frame-by-frame level. Even inexpensive DVD players have a pause and advance-by-frame function, and you should use these controls extensively. Furthermore, on many DVDs of commercial films, added material provides valuable insight into the animation or acting production processes that went into the film. DVDs also let you jump right to the action you want; by contrast, videotapes are linear, so you have to fast forward and rewind to get to the same point.

Illustrated Books

Books with clear, step-by-step illustrations of actions are excellent references, especially for the pose-to-pose animation we will explore in this chapter. By stringing the poses together, you can create the motions shown. Clearly, however, this technique contains no timing information and is therefore limited to simple pose information. Also, this kind of reference is only as good as the illustrations of which it is composed. If the author of the book did not put thought into how the illustrations fit together, their value to you as an animator is limited.

Paper and Pencil

Conventional drawing media can be of enormous benefit to the animator. If you can thumbnail sketch a motion, you need never worry about not having just the right reference footage or illustrations handy. By planning out a particular motion on paper, you start ahead of the game. Which position you move the character into requires forethought, and this is where drawing can be enormously beneficial. Also, some characters cannot be filmed or have not been animated, so looking at reference footage may not be possible. Sometimes paper and pencil is the only way to go.

Sound Recordings

If the animation is to have a sound track, the wise animator will obtain a copy of the sound track for a shot *before* animating. It is possible to animate to particular beats in music in 10- to 15-frame intervals. Playing the music during animation and including it in the playblasts often eases the task of animating. A performance that might seem slow on its own can be much more lively set to the appropriate music.

Of course, if the animation involves lip-synching, you must have that in place before animating. In many ways, having a voice track to work from makes animating easier. The voice performance will have rhythm and points of emphasis that you can use when animating both the face and the body, and if there is a video recording of the actor performing the lines, it can be studied as well. Animators generally listen to the sound track multiple times before beginning to animate to get an effective internal sense of what is happening within the shot.

Mirrors

Go to almost any animation studio, visit an animator's desk, and somewhere you will find a mirror. Using a mirror, the animator, who in many cases will also be a frustrated actor, can act out a sequence and view it in real time. Good animators have excellent *kinesthetic awareness*—that is, they are supremely aware of the position of their body and its parts in space. They translate this into an understanding of how the character moves onscreen; if they know how *their* bodies move, they can more effectively move the character onscreen. The mirror allows the novice animator to confirm their developing kinesthetic awareness and allows experienced animators to make more effective use of their own abilities in this area. Also, using a mirror, a facial animator can decide which poses to strike at which time for lip-synching.

> Working from mirror views or photos of your own face is a technique strongly recommended by Jason Osipa in *Stop Staring: Facial Modeling and Animation Done Right* (Sybex, second edition 2007). Don't assume this only works for photorealistic faces; Osipa demonstrates that even stylized and toon characters can benefit from this kind of real-world understanding.

Stopwatch

Properly used, a stopwatch can be nearly as effective as a video camera, especially if you are an experienced animator. With it, you can acquire the basic timings of an action quickly. The procedure for using a stopwatch is to perform the action while timing how long it takes. Of course, this also points out the stopwatch's primary limitation: it is great for general timings, but you must time specific actions within the broader motion separately. And unless you are careful, specific timings can lose their relationship to the broader action.

The Animation Process

Three steps to the animation process are described in this chapter. This is a structured keyframing process that is sequential in nature and fairly easy to implement. The steps are as follows:

Posing This step involves moving the character into sequential poses that carry the action. Set stepped keys on sequentially numbered frames (1, 2, 3, and so on). The emphasis is on creating enough keys to carry the action but not so many that the actual flow of animation creation slows to a crawl. Here is where you can use good reference as a base to create strong poses that carry the action you are trying to convey.

Timing This is usually the fastest phase because it involves selecting and translating (*not* scaling) keys in Maya's Dope Sheet or Timeline, changing key tangent types to clamped, and adding keys on individual controllers as needed to create smooth motion. Playblast often during this stage to determine proper timing between keys. Your video reference will help to start the process of timing, but you will most probably need to speed up the action by 10 to 20 percent since animated action almost always appears too slow if it matches live-action timing. At the end of this phase, the animation will appear 90 percent complete, but truly creating great animation involves a great deal of the next step.

Because computer CPUs and graphics cards vary widely, playblasting is the only true way to get an accurate view of how fast or slow your character moves.

Refining   This is the longest phase because it involves adding details that create great animation. This phase will be different from animation to animation. It involves adding keys to extremities, offsetting motions, fighting symmetry, crafting follow-throughs and overlaps, and so on. This last 10 percent of the animation can take 50 percent of the time.

One huge benefit in separating the animation process into these three phases is the amount of experimentation it allows. As you will see later, at many points during the posing process a slightly different approach might be worth pursuing. The posing process is extremely flexible. In fact, you can make changes in posing and timing all the way up to and during the refining process.

Let's apply these ideas by creating a simple jump animation. First, we'll examine a reference movie with an eye toward picking out poses at extreme positions, and then we'll animate the character using our three-step process.

Hands-On: Animating Joe Generic

Before we start animating, let's look at a video for direct reference of a jump. We can learn from it to animate our hero, Joe Generic. Open `JumpReference.mov` in the Chapter 9 folder on the CD. This movie shows one of the authors jumping up onto a short ledge. In the QuickTime Player application, you can press the Left and Right arrow keys to step forward and backward frame by frame. You can use this feature to select key poses or extremes for your animation.

Ideally, you should play `JumpReference.mov` in a player that not only allows you to advance frame by frame, but also allows you to display the frames or timecode down to the frame level. Adobe Premiere and After Effects and Apple's Final Cut are excellent examples of this type of software. Counting frames, while possible and a good exercise to begin your exploration of timing, can be tedious and overly complicated.

If you open `JumpReferenceLable.mov` on the CD, you can see these poses labeled as they occur, as in Figure 9.2. Properly created, these poses will carry the force of the jumper as he springs off of the floor and lands on the box. You will see that what we will be striving for will be the essence of the pose. The person depicted in the reference video has a completely different body style than Joe Generic; therefore, a direct translation is impossible. Not to worry though; this is the case more often than not when using reference material.

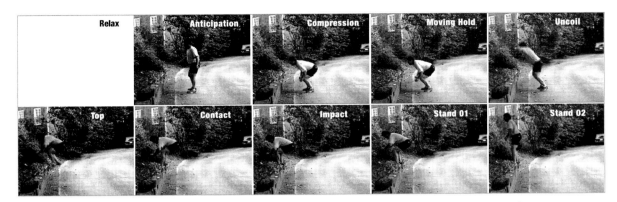

Figure 9.2

The key poses we will be using in the pose-blocking phase. Note that there is no relaxed pose; we will build that on our own.

The Setup: Getting Joe Ready to Go

It does not take a complex character to learn how to animate; in fact, overly detailed characters with many controls are actually counterproductive. You spend so much time trying to control the character that you can't learn animation. Joe Generic is a character with minimal controls designed for the sole purpose of learning body animation. Before we can begin, however, we will need to do some setup. Open `JoeGJumpStart.ma` from the CD and let's begin.

JoeG stands in the common arms-out/palms-down default pose as depicted in Figure 9.3. This is his bind pose, and a copy of this pose should always be stored somewhere in the file. In our case, we will store it on frame 0. But first, we need to create a selection button to select all the controls at once.

1. Create a new shelf called JoeGCtrls by clicking the shelf menu and choosing New Shelf. Name the shelf JoeGCtrls and click OK.

2. In the selection bar, make geometry and joints unselectable.

3. In the perspective view, select the left foot curve.

4. Hold down the Shift key and select the right foot curve, the left hand curve, the right hand curve, the head curve, the chest curve, and the hip curve.

5. Open the Script Editor. In the history pane, you should see the following code:

```
select -r JoeG_LfootCtrl ;
select -tgl JoeG_RfootCtrl ;
select -tgl JoeG_LhandCtrl ;
select -tgl JoeG_RhandCtrl ;
select -tgl JoeG_neckCtrl ;
select -tgl UpperBodyGrp ;
select -tgl COG ;
```

Figure 9.3

The default pose

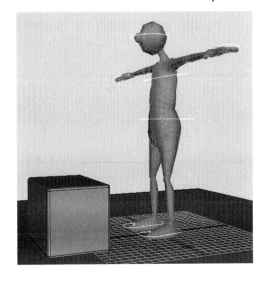

6. Select these lines of code and choose **File → Save Script To Shelf** in the Script Editor's menu set.

7. Type **SAll** to name the button, and click OK.

You should see a button called SAll appear on the shelf. Now when you click it, all the controls should be selected. This will be useful for keying purposes. Later, you might want to use this process to create selection controls for other parts of the body.

You can skip the previous steps 2 through 5 by typing the lines of code directly into the input pane of the Script Editor and proceeding with steps 6 and 7.

Let's set a key on the default pose on frame 0. (You can also set the default pose on a negative frame if the shot needs to include frame 0 for some reason—for example, if you're using cloth simulation run-up.)

1. In the Animation Preferences dialog box (**Window → Settings/Preferences → Preferences**) under the Animation category, set Default In Tangent and Default Out Tangent to Flat and Stepped, respectively.

2. Make sure the Current Time Indicator is set at 0. If it isn't, move it there.

3. Click the SAll button to select all the controls.

4. Choose **Animate → Set Key** □. Choose **Edit → Reset Settings** to reset the default settings, and click Set Key to set the key at frame 0.

From now on, set keys by pressing the S key. When you see "set a key," press the S key.

5. Set Animation Start Time to 1. This will change Playback Start to 1 as well.

6. Move the Current Time Indicator to frame 1.

Animating Joe Generic is a matter of moving and rotating individual controls and manipulating the custom attributes of those controls. For example, the UpperBodyGrp contains rotational controls for the arms, elbows, and wrists, and the hand controls (JoeG_L and _RhandCtrl) contain the controls for opening and closing the hand. Take some time to figure out what each control does. As you experiment with the controls, you will set keys on each control you move at frame 1 because the Autokey button is probably activated (and if not, it should be). But you can delete this Timeline key by pressing the SAll shelf button, RM clicking the key at frame 1 in the Timeline, and choosing Delete from the pop-up menu. Once you are done with this important experimentation and have deleted the resulting key, you are ready to begin the posing process.

The Relax Pose

Although this pose does not exist on the video reference, it is a crucial part of this jump animation. It establishes a starting point for the animation and it informs the audience of Joe Generic's general demeanor. For our purposes, it will also provide a way to establish a work flow for creating these poses. Let's begin to create this pose. Figure 9.4 shows the initial pose, for reference.

1. Click the SAll button and set a key on frame 1. You will always set the key first and then create the pose.

2. In the Layer Editor window, you will see a list of layers. Each contains a piece of geometry that you can use as a guide to create your poses. You don't have to match them perfectly; they are meant to provide a point of reference in Maya that will assure you that you are on the right track. For this first pose, display RelaxLyr in the Layer Editor. This layer has been set to Unshaded, so it will be visible in the form of a wireframe.

3. Begin by moving the control labeled COG. Translate and rotate the COG into position. JoeG is set up so that the entire upper body, arms, and head follow. Change the **Lower Back** and **Upper Back** attributes by clicking the attribute name and MM dragging in the perspective viewport. Try to match the guide geo by sight, but the exact settings are as follows:

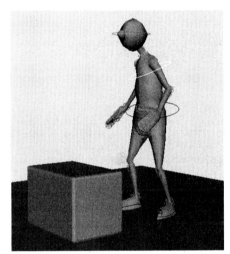

Figure 9.4

Joe Generic in a relaxed pose

translateX	–0.382
translateY	–0.597
translateZ	0
rotateX	11.94
rotateY	1.825
rotateZ	–8.565
LowerBkBend	0
LowerBkTwist	0
LowerBkBank	2.7
UpperBkBend	0
UpperBkTwist	0
UpperBkBank	2.7

4. Move the feet into position as shown in the guides. Sometimes it is advantageous to get the shoulders correct first, but because this is the first frame of the entire movement, it is wise to set the feet first. Again, moving the feet into exact position is not

necessary, but to move the feet to the position indicated in the template, set the foot controls as follows:

JoeG_LfootCtrl

translateX	.76
translateZ	−1.427
rotateY	18.225

JoeG_RfootCtrl

translateX	−0.95
rotateY	−7.701
KneeTwistRL	−3.8

All other controls should be left alone.

Note that KneeTwistRL rotates the knee independently of the foot and hip.

5. Move to the UpperBodyGrp, which has the NURBS circle as a control handle. On it, you will find controls for the arm, elbow, and wrist rotations. Although it is possible to rotate this controller, do so sparingly as a fine-tuning of the shoulder position. Overrotating will bend the torso in an unnaturalistic way. The torso mainly exists as a controller on which to hang the arm, elbow, and wrist controls. These controls have a specific naming convention that you may have already noticed: UpDwn, BckFwd, and SupPr refer to the particular direction you drag to rotate the body part. For example, clicking LshldrUpDwn and MM dragging to the left in the perspective view rotates the shoulder up, and dragging to the right rotates it down. Keep in mind that you can select both attribute names and MM drag to move both parts at the same time. Try to match these settings visually by dragging in the window:

UpperBodyGrp

rotateZ	3.683
LShldrUpDwn	30.2
RShldrUpDwn	20.1
RShldrBckFw	−12.1
LShldrBckFw	5
RElbwBnd	36.8
LElbwBnd	46.9
LWristUpDwn	−5.5
RWristUpDwn	−11.2
LWristBckFw	11.1
RWristBckFw	11.1
LWristSupPr	−17.3
RwristSupPr	13.4

6. Select both hand controllers, and set MiddleCurl and MiddleRot to 21.3.

7. Select JoeG_neckCtrl and set rotateX to 18.46.

You now have a relaxed pose. You should have tried to match the guide geometry visually. You probably didn't match it exactly, but you'll be close, and you will have your own individual pose.

You will repeat this procedure for each of the following poses. Now we'll discuss the particular features of each pose.

The Anticipation Pose

An anticipation is the setting up of a motion in a particular direction by moving opposite to the main motion to begin the motion. In this case, we want to move Joe backward and to the right to set up the jump, which will propel Joe forward.

1. Move the Current Time Indicator to frame 2.

2. Hide RelaxLyr and show AnticipationLyr.

3. Click the SAll button.

4. Set a key at frame 2.

5. Starting with the COG controller, move each controller to match the Anticipation-Geo wireframe as shown in Figure 9.5.

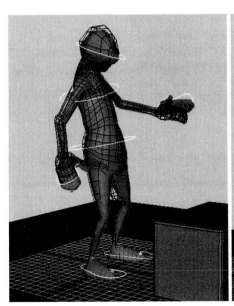
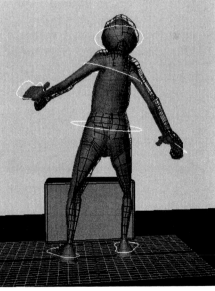

Figure 9.5

The anticipation key. Note how Joe Generic does not match the guide exactly.

Compression

If you look at the compression pose in the reference video, you will see that this pose is the lowest point in the jump—at least the lowest point of this jumping motion where the subject is in *balance*. Properly balancing your character during an animation is key in giving your character the appearance of *weight*. The weight of the character is poised over the base formed by the feet. Given that there is no actual gravity in the computer or on the screen, this weight is visual in nature. This means that the visual bulk of the character, which the viewer expects to be affected by gravity, should be relatively equal on either side of the center line for the subject to be in balance. The center of gravity of the subject is leaning forward, poised over the center line of the feet as shown in Figure 9.6. This balance is crucial because if the subject is not properly balanced at the proper time, any force used to move the character will not be convincing. This animation pathology is a common problem for animators.

Compression is not an exact science, and determining the proper pose here is a matter of experience and purpose in the animation. If the character is slow, lumbering, and/or clumsy, the center of gravity can lag behind the center line. If the character is quick, nimble, and/or light on their feet, the center of gravity can be slightly in front of the center line. If you intend for the character to miss the jump, skewing the position of the center of gravity in relation to the center line is a good first step.

After setting a key on frame 3, adjust JoeG's controls to conform to the guide geo, and move on to the next pose.

The Moving Hold Pose

A moving hold occurs when a character reaches an extreme and needs to hold it for a moment or two. Often, moving holds are installed in the timing or refining phase of an animation, but because this particular pose is so important in terms of the weight shift of the character, we will create it in the posing phase. In snappy, cartoon action, the character

Figure 9.6

In the compression pose, the visual bulk or weight of the subject is balanced over the center line.

Centerline   Center of Gravity

Balance Line

moves quickly from pose to pose while holding each particular pose for a few beats or frames, allowing it to be seen and "read" by the audience. However, the character cannot come to a complete stop without losing the illusion of life; therefore, the character needs to move a little bit throughout the hold. Rather than this being random motion, the moving hold should relate to and complement the next motion in some way.

In this case, the character is to drop down a little lower than the compression pose, which will emphasize the spring that is about to occur. You can see this pose compared with the CompressionGeo in Figure 9.7. In this pose, Joe G's weight shifts forward as he leans into the jump. This pose reflects the idea of dynamic balance as it introduces the aspect of time into the equation. Viewed on its own, this hold appears to be out of balance, but taken in context of the entire animation over time, this out-of-balance frame will actually enhance motion of the jump.

The distance the center of gravity moves forward of the center line will be largely determined by how far forward the character must jump. If the character is going for distance, the center should move farther forward of the center line. If the character is going for height, the center should not move as far forward but should be lower than it would be for a distance jump. Remember that right after this, the actual jump begins. Although this and every pose created in this phase is static, they constitute a sequence that will be put into motion in the timing phase.

On frame 4, set a key and move the character into position.

The Uncoil Pose

The purpose of this pose is self-explanatory: the character is springing into the jump. From the reference, we see the legs are pushing the bulk of the character up and forward. Although this and every pose is important, it is the timing between this frame and the moving hold pose that will carry the force of the action of the jump. Notice also how the arms appear to assist in the force of the jump as they raise at the shoulders

As you can see from the reference, the subject's legs are not perfectly straight in the frame before his feet leave the ground. The reference geometry's pose reflects this, but this is a great time to experiment. It is well worth your time and effort to see what effect a more straight-legged pose will have on the final animation. Figure 9.8 shows what this might look like. Set this pose on frame 5 of the animation.

You will need to turn off the **StretchSwitch** attribute on the foot controllers to straighten the legs by raising COG. Do this by setting its value to 0.

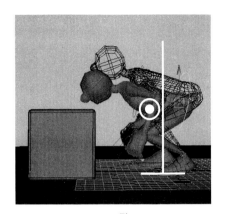

Figure 9.7

The moving hold pose compared with the compression guide geo reveals the movement of the center of gravity relative to the center line.

Figure 9.8

A straighter legged pose than the guide geometry indicates will give the jump a little more "oomph!"

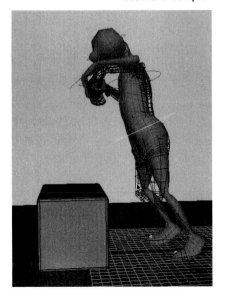

The Top Pose

In the top pose, both JoeG and the reference subject are trying to get their feet under them to make contact with the box/ledge. Surprisingly, the hips do not raise up that much more, if at all, from the uncoil pose. This is where the value of reference becomes apparent. You would think that the force of the uncoil would carry the hips much higher at the top of the jump, but the video reference shows this is not so. The top pose reveals that the hips need to rise only enough to allow the character to pull his feet under him to make contact with the block.

This pose will be the point at which we use lags and overshoots in midair to give this motion a little more liveliness. Set this key pose on frame 6 of the animation.

The Contact Pose

The subject of this pose is the feet first touching the block. It is analogous to the keying of the stretched ball just when it touches the ground on the frame before it squashes that we covered in Chapter 7. The point at which the feet make contact with the box is the point where the character transitions from being totally in the air to being in contact with the box. It therefore requires a key. Place this pose on frame 7 of the animation.

The Impact Pose

Figure 9.9

For the impact pose, the center of gravity should be on the action side of the center line. If it is too far forward, the character will look like it will do a face plant.

This pose is analogous to the squash frame of the bouncing ball in Chapter 7. This pose demonstrates the weight of the character as it translates from transiting through the air to landing with force on the box. The weight must land in balance, but in this case, the momentum of the character requires that the center of gravity stay back of the center line. If the center of gravity is too far forward relative to this motion path, the character should probably overshoot the box and land on his face. If it is too far back, the character will probably look as though he should fall back off the box. In certain circumstances, both these situations could be useful, but we want the center of gravity to be balanced properly as Joe lands. Create this pose on frame 8 of the animation. Figure 9.9 shows the impact pose as it relates to the contact pose.

The best way to determine if this pose is correct is to scrub back and forth from frame 6 to this frame. Look carefully to see if the character catches himself properly, and remember that he can and should extend his arms to help balance himself out as his legs and feet accept the force of his weight as he lands.

The Stand01 and Stand02 Poses

These two poses are really the ease-out keys for our motion. They represent JoeG pulling himself back in from the full extension of the impact pose as he is standing back up. The center of gravity should sit somewhere close to the center line of the figure in these two poses. Place these two poses on frames 9 and 10, respectively.

Save your file as `JoeGJumpPosed.ma`. Also delete all the guide geometry and layers associated with this animation as they create an unnecessarily large file.

Staging and Posing

When you are animating, you are actually using two actors on your stage. The first is your subject: Joe Generic. The second is less apparent, but it represents your entire audience. It is the camera through which you will render the action. Properly placed, it can enhance your audience's experience and complement your character's performance. A thoughtlessly placed camera, however, can make a well-animated performance look haphazard and unclear.

Place the camera so that the action is presented clearly. Many factors influence the audience's ability to read the action, but one of the most prominent is the character's silhouette. The audience reads the outline of the character as an integral part of the meaning of the pose. If the outline of the character's pose does not clearly convey the action, the pose loses its effectiveness. Figure 9.10 illustrates this principle fairly well. The top two images show the contact pose seen from the front. The top-right image shows the outline, but the pose is muddled. No sense of weight shows in the outline; JoeG is simply huddled in on himself. The bottom two images show the same pose from a three-quarter view. The silhouette clearly depicts the essence of the pose.

Figure 9.10

Reading the silhouette as a vital component of the pose

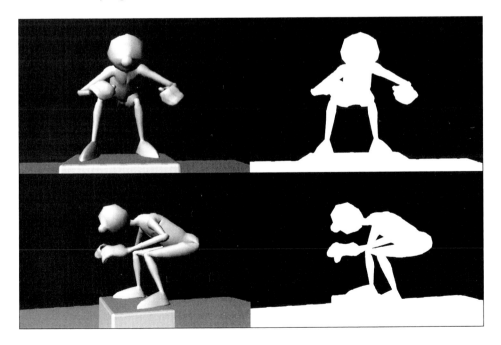

This example clearly points to the need for a rendering camera that is separate from the perspective camera. We will need the freedom to manipulate the perspective camera in the timing and refining phase, so we will need to create a new camera to be our final rendering camera. The good news is that we can use the perspective camera to frame our action and then duplicate it and lock that camera down to use to render the animation later. Let's frame the action and set up the camera.

1. In the perspective view menu set, choose **View → Camera Settings → Resolution Gate** and then choose **Safe Action**. This will create a frame that represents the output resolution of the camera as set in the Render Settings option box. You should certainly have this set to your desired output settings. We would normally lay this animation off to DV tape, so we set this file at 720 × 480. But feel free to set it any way you want.

2. Dolly, pan, and track your camera as needed to frame the action of the animation within the Action Safe line. We use the Action Safe line because if we lay the animation off to tape and play it through a standard TV monitor, the uneven cropping that these devices inflict on video requires us to leave a border around the edge of the screen. Keeping the poses within this frame ensures that no part of the poses will be cropped out if and when the animation is played back on a television.

3. Once you've framed the animation properly, choose **View → Select Camera**.

4. Choose **Edit → Duplicate** to create a copy with its parent as the world.

5. Rename this persp*n* camera RenderCam.

6. In the Channel Box, select all the translate, rotate, scale, and visibility attributes.

7. RM click them and choose Lock Selected.

You now have a rendering camera ready to go when you need it! Let's move on to the timing phase.

Establishing Timings

We need to separate our collection of poses in the Timeline to create motion. During this phase, we want to explore how seemingly insignificant changes of a frame or two at the right time can dramatically change the character of a particular action and thereby change the meaning of the entire animation. We will not worry about changing poses at this phase; we will work on our timing first.

It is possible to create poses at the same time you determine timings; many animators do so as a matter of routine. But the advantage to separating the two phases, especially for learning animation, is that the animator can concentrate on the complexities of each phase without the complexities of the other phase getting in the way.

Where Do We Start?

Arguably the most difficult part of creating timing is beginning the process. For example, how long do you think it should take to go from the relaxed pose to the anticipation pose? Do you simply decide arbitrarily, or can you determine this ahead of time? Fortunately, we have a source from which we can draw ideas: our reference video.

The easiest way to use this source is to simply count frames between each key and then translate that into timings for the animation. We will use these as a start and work from there.

	Actual	**−20%**	**Final**
Relax to Anticipation	12 frames	9 frames	9
Anticipation to Compression	17 frames	14 frames	14
Compression to Moving Hold	2 frames	1–2 frames	7
Moving Hold to Uncoil	8 frames	6 frames	3
Uncoil to Top	8 frames	6 frames	4
Top to Contact	3 frames	2 frames	2
Contact to Impact	3 frames	2 frames	2
Impact to Stand01	5 frames	4 frames	4
Stand01 to Stand02	19 frames	15 frames	14

We'll use the actual timings for our initial animation mostly to show just how slow video reference can be. Let's space out the keys.

1. Open `JoeGJumpPosed.ma` from the CD.

2. Click the SAll button to select all the controls. Each red tick mark in the Timeline represents keys set on all the controls.

3. Select the keys on frames 2 through 10 in the Timeline by Shift LM dragging from frame 2 past frame 10 as shown in Figure 9.11a and b. A red bar will appear indicating your selection (see Figure 9.11b). Go past frame 10 because there is no problem with too large a selection, but too small a selection will wreck your keys, requiring you to start over. This is how you will move keys. Move the selection until the left side of the selection reads the proper number.

4. Drag the middle arrows until the left side of the selection reads 12 as shown in Figure 9.11c. This will leave 12 frames between the relax pose and the anticipation pose. This sets the anticipation frame at frame 12.

5. Click anywhere in the Timeline to drop the selection.

6. Shift+drag+select the keys beginning on frame 13 (see Figure 9.11e), and drag the middle arrows until the left side of the selection reads 30, as shown in Figure 9.11f. This sets the compression frame at frame 30.

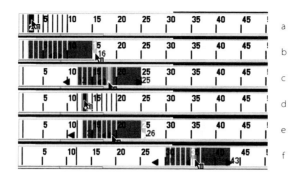

Figure 9.11

The process of selecting and spacing out frames in the Timeline. (a) Frame 2 is the frame we are concentrating on. (b) Shift LM dragging to select the frame range. (c) Dragging the middle arrows to move the range until frame 2 becomes frame 12. (d) Frame 13 is next. (e) Select the remaining keys. (f) Drag the remaining frames until frame 13 rests on frame 30.

7. Drop the selection.

8. Drag the rest of the keys beginning on frame 31 until the left side of the selection reads 32. This moves the Moving Hold key to frame 32.

9. Drag the rest of the keys beginning on frame 33 over to the right until the left side of the selection reads 40. This moves the Uncoil key to frame 40.

10. Drag the rest of the keys beginning on frame 41 over to the right until the left side of the selection reads 48. The top pose is now at frame 48.

11. Drag the rest of the keys beginning on frame 49 over to the right until the left side of the selection reads 51. The contact pose now rests on frame 51.

12. Drag the rest of the keys beginning on frame 52 over to the right until the left side of the selection reads 54. The impact pose is now at frame 54.

13. Drag the rest of the keys beginning on frame 55 over to the right until the left side of the selection reads 59. Stand01 is now at frame 59.

14. Drag the last key to frame 78. This is the Stand02 pose.

15. Change the Playblast End Time to 85.

16. Save your file. You can see the result of our efforts in the file `JoeGJumpActual.ma` on the CD.

Our keys have been created as stepped keys. For some animations, especially those with lip-synch, this situation is ideal because the poses snap or pop from pose to pose while the sound track helps provide flow. For this animation, however, it would be best to have more of a transition between keys, so we will change them from stepped to Plateau-style keys. In the process, you will see what effect Maya's Spline, Clamped, and Plateau key types have on the function curves in the Graph Editor.

1. Click the SAll button to select all the controls, and open the Graph Editor by choosing **Window → Animation Editors → Graph Editor.**

2. Figure 9.12 shows the animation in the Graph Editor with all the keyed channels on the seven character controls shown. The top image (a) shows stepped keys. If you LM drag through the Timeline, you will see the effect of the four types of keys. The poses snap or pop from one to the next with no transition.

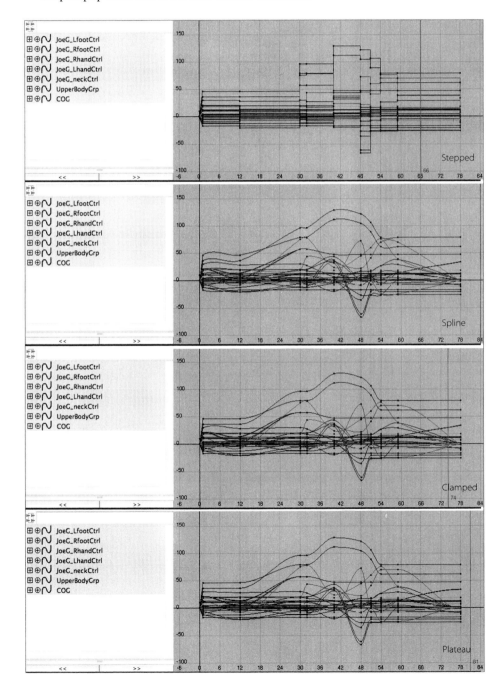

Figure 9.12

Animation Key tangent types as they appear in the Graph Editor.

THE BUFFER CURVE SNAPSHOT

Maya provides a useful tool to view changes to your animation curves as you adjust them: the buffer curve snapshot. The buffer curve snapshot takes a "picture" of the current state of any selected curves, allowing you to refer to that state as you make adjustments to the animation. To create a snapshot, select your animation curves and then choose **Curves → Buffer Curve Snapshot** in the Graph Editor menu. To view the snapshot, choose **View → Show Buffer Curves**. When you now make changes to a curve (by changing the tangent attributes, for example), you will see the original curve in gray, providing a reference point from which to work. You can switch back and forth between the current curves and the buffer curves by choosing **Curves → Swap Buffer Curve**.

3. Double-click the Timeline to select all the keys.

4. RM click the Timeline and set the Tangent type to Spline. You can see considerable spline drift in the early frames in Figure 9.12b. Remember from Chapter 7 that spline drift occurs when the spline curve extends past the value of the key you set, causing unwanted motion in the character.

5. Select all the keys in the Timeline again and change the key tangents to Clamped. In Figure 9.12c, you can see that this operation decreases, but does not eliminate, the curves extending past their extremes, especially at the beginning of the animation.

6. Select all the keys in the Timeline and change the tangents to Plateau. As shown in Figure 9.12d, this curve type eliminates all the spline drift that is present with Spline and Clamped keys. Therefore, we will use it from here on.

7. Set the Default In and Out tangent type to Plateau in the Animation Category of the Preferences window.

Now, let's playblast the animation.

1. RM click the Timeline and choose Playblast □. Click the View option to open the animation when it is done rendering. Turn off Show Ornaments to hide the camera name and XYZ marker in the lower-left corner of the window. Set Viewer to Movie-Player if you are using Windows or Linux or QuickTime if you are using Mac. Leave the Compression settings at their default in Windows. For the Mac, go ahead and set the Compression settings either to Animation or to Sorenson. Since we have the Render Settings set to 720 × 480, use Render Settings for the display size. Set Scale to whatever your computer can handle. If you can view a full-size movie without the computer dropping frames, by all means set the scale to 1. A setting of 0.75 works well for most animation checks. Check Remove Temporary Files and Save To File. Maya will overwrite the previously rendered movie unless you specify a new name. The movie will save to the images folder in your project folder by default. Unless you have

good reason to change this, leave it there. If you do, specify a new folder by clicking the Browse button.

2. Click Playblast to render the animation.

The subject in the reference video weighs about 265 pounds. Joe Generic doesn't look anywhere close to that weight, so directly translating the timings of the video coupled with video's natural tendency to be too slow to begin with makes the animation laughably slow. You can look at `JoeGJumpActualPlateau.mov` on the CD to see the results. We will scale these keys and immediately snap them. Ideally, we would move each key individually, but this technique is so much quicker, we'll save a lot of time by scaling. Let's speed this animation up by 20 percent.

1. Make sure all the animation controls are selected by clicking the SAll button.

2. Shift+select from frame 1 to frame 80 in the Timeline, as shown in Figure 9.13a.

3. Drag the scaling arrow on the selection until it reads 64, as shown in Figure 9.13b. Note that 16 is 20 percent of 80.

4. Immediately RM click the selection, and choose Snap from the pop-up menu, as shown in Figure 9.13. This will snap the keys to the nearest integer keyframe.

5. Set the Playblast End Value field to frame 65.

6. Playblast the animation. You can see the result in `JoeGJumpminus20percent.mov`. The scene file containing this result is `JoeGJumpminus20percent.ma`. Both of these files are on the CD.

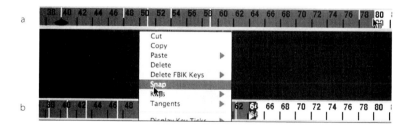

Figure 9.13

(a) Using the Time-line to select frames 1 through 80. (b) Scaling the keys down to frame 64 and snapping them to the nearest inte-ger keyframe.

SCALING KEYS REVISITED

Chapter 7 states that scaling is dangerous and should rarely, if ever, be used. However, this chapter illustrates the rule that rules are made to be broken. Most often, scaling results in the scaled keys falling on noninteger frame numbers. This can cause problems with rendering. Also, scaling adjacent keys can result in keys landing on top of one another, which can cause playback problems. In this instance, however, the keys are well spaced out and each controller is keyed on each keyframe. Scaling followed immediately by snapping the scaled keys should not cause any problems.

The timing is a little snappier, but it still plods, and there is a disturbing little hitch in the movement between the compression and the moving hold poses. This is because there is not enough time between them. Also, JoeG seems to struggle into the air in moving between the Moving Hold and Uncoil keys. We can speed this action up by moving the Moving Hold over closer to the Uncoil frame. This quickness will emphasize the speed and force with which JoeG thrusts himself upward to drag his feet up to the block. So, with all the controls selected, move the moving hold frame from 26 to 29 and playblast to see the result.

This has the desired effect of speeding up the jump, but now the middle of the jump from the uncoil to the top pose looks too slow. With all the controls selected, Shift+select from frame 38 to 42 and move the selection to frame 35. Playblast to see the result. Much better! Now it looks as though the feet are struggling a little bit to catch up to the upper body and hips. This is what we want.

Experimentation is the key here. Try different timings on different parts of the animation. Here are a few examples to try:

- Move the anticipation pose from frame 10 to frame 5.

- Speed up the stand-up motion by moving Stand01 to frame 44 and Stand02 from frame 62 to frame 55.

- Slow down the motion from the compression to the moving hold pose by moving the compression from frame 24 to frame 16.

See how far you can speed up or slow down various parts of the motion without their looking unnaturally fast or slow. Save as many versions as you want, but the final frame locations that we will be working from in the refining phase are as follows and can be found in the file JoeGJumpTimedFinal.ma. on the CD:

Relax	1
Anticipation	6
Compression	20
Moving Hold	29
Uncoil	32
Top	35
Contact	38
Impact	40
Stand01	50
Stand02	62

Refining Your Animation

The refining phase represents the last 10 percent of the animation, which can take an enormous amount of time to complete. In this phase, you install details that can make a decent animation great. Here, art takes over and we depart from the reference video. It is situational in that the moves we create here will be unique to this particular animation.

Up to now, we have been creating a generic archetype for a jump; in this stage, we create the extra motions that make this animation special.

In this phase, we will try to do the following:

- Correct any egregious geometry intersections. For example, right now, the feet pass through the box. This is the time to correct that error.

- Fight "twinning," or symmetry of pose, motion, and timing. Actually, we should fight symmetry of pose during the posing phase. In symmetrical poses, body parts are the same on both sides of the character. In symmetrical motions, body parts move in the same fashion and arrive in a pose at the exact same time. This is a problem with the style of pose-to-pose animation described in this chapter. In symmetrical timings, parts of the animation last the same amount of time. For example, if the time from the relax pose to the anticipation pose were the same as from the anticipation pose to the compression pose, the timing would be symmetrical and would result in the animation looking mechanical and lifeless.

- Add lags and overshoots to the motion of the character. In this case, Joe Generic has oversized hands and feet and an oversized head set on a skinny neck. Subjected to the forces of acceleration, these body parts will tend to lag slightly behind the motion of the larger body and overshoot the extremes of motion.

We will offset, add, and delete keys as necessary to give this motion a bit more life. Furthermore, we will start with the body and work outward. It will be impossible to describe all the additions. Even a simple animation such as this will suggest many more refinements than we have space to cover, so we will discuss some changes to key areas and let you take what you learn and continue as needed. We will do the following:

- Correct the feet passing through the box.

- Edit the foot controllers' keys to make the feet leave the ground and land on different frames.

- Add some lag and overshoot to the head as the body takes off and lands in the jump.

Correcting the Feet

Let's correct the feet and offset their motion.

1. In the Animation Preferences window, change the Default In and Default Out tangent types to Plateau. Failure to do this will result in distorted animation paths.

2. Create a three-pane split-top window layout in the work area. Place the perspective view at the left top, the RenderCam on the right top, and the Dope Sheet below. This will allow you to view the animation from all angles in the persp window and render playblasts using the RenderCam camera. We will use the Dope Sheet for this refinement because it allows us to see the keys for each object independent of any curves or connection. We can move them easily to get the effects we want.

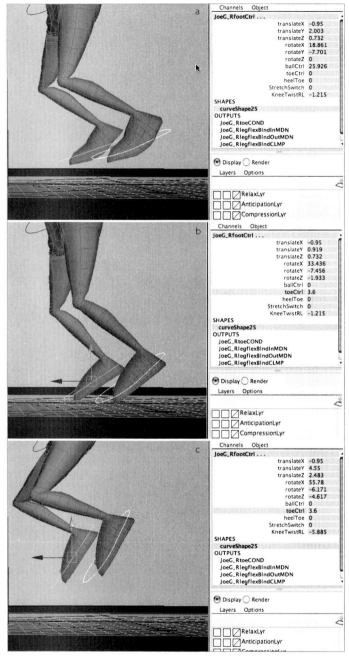

Figure 9.14

(a) Improper feet. (b) The feet after translating, rotating the foot controls, and adjusting ballCtrl, toeCtrl, and heelToe on each controller. (c) Making sure the feet move up rather than forward.

3. Click the SAll button to select the seven animation controls.

4. In the Dope Sheet's List menu, turn off Auto Load Selected Objects. This will let us select and choose which controls we work on while viewing the rest of the controllers' keys for comparison purposes.

5. While holding down the K key, LM drag in the Dope Sheet to advance the Current Time Indicator to frame 32. This is the top pose. Go to frame 33. You will see that the feet are still bent up as they leave the ground, as shown in Figure 9.14a. We not only want to fix this, we want to adjust the rotations so that JoeG's toes appear to help with the jump.

6. Translate and rotate the controllers together or individually to get something like what you see in Figure 9.14b. This corrects the inappropriately bent toes as well as builds in some lag behind for the feet as they try to leave the ground.

7. Adjust ballCtrl and toeCtrl to point the toes down more toward the ground, as shown in Figure 9.14b. You can exaggerate the effect by increasing toeCtrl until the bend in the foot is more noticeable.

8. Advance the Current Time Indicator to frame 34 and you will see that your correction has spawned another problem; namely, the feet move forward rather than up. Correct this by translating and rotating, as shown in Figure 9.14c. Put in motion, the feet will now lag behind the motion of the rest of the body, and they will appear to snap up to the top key more quickly.

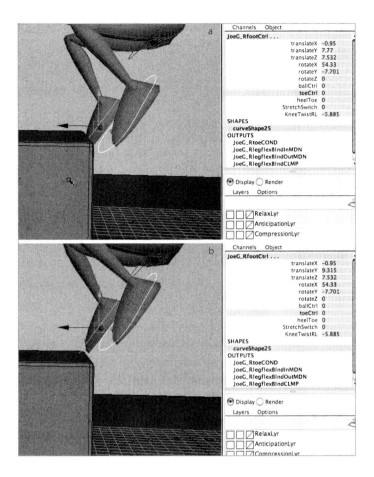

Figure 9.15

(a) The feet about to intersect the box. (b) The feet corrected.

9. Go to frame 36, the frame after the top pose where the feet are clearly about to intersect the box, as shown in Figure 9.15a.

10. Move the controllers up in Y so that the feet avoid the box in the next frame, as shown in Figure 9.15b. Don't go too far or the feet will appear to jerk upward right before they land.

Offsetting the Feet

Currently, both feet land on the box at *exactly* the same frame, which looks a bit unnatural. We can change this by offsetting the keys for the foot controllers in the Dope Sheet.

1. In the Dope Sheet, LM marquee select the keys on frames 29 to 33 for JoeG_LfootCtrl.

2. Press W to choose the Move tool, and in the Dope Sheet, MM drag the keys one frame earlier. This will cause the left foot to take off one frame earlier. It doesn't take much to break the twin on such a fast motion.

3. On JoeG_RfootCtrl, select the keys on frames 29 through 40, and MM drag them one frame *later*. This will cause the right foot to leave the ground two frames after the left foot and land one frame after the left foot.

4. Playblast to see the results. `JoeGFinalFeet.mov` on the CD shows what this should look like.

Experiment, experiment, experiment! How far can you push this and still have the animation look naturalistic? Eventually, you will make the animation look too awkward, but you can always undo your last action. The important thing is to gain the experience of seeing just what offsetting a key or keys one or two frames can do to make or break your animation.

Adding Lag and Overshoot to the Head

Now let's look at editing the head and arms to bring a little flexibility to the upper body. Keep in mind that visually the head and hands are large masses that connect to the body by thin connections at the neck and arms. As the body thrusts upward, it would seem visually logical for the head to lag a bit as the body moves through the jump. The head will also tend to overshoot what are now the extreme poses in the animation. We will do as much as possible with the keys we have and add any new keys sparingly, if at all. It would be nice to be able to distinguish the neck controller keys from the rest of the body during this phase, and fortunately Maya allows us to do this by changing key colors.

1. Choose **Window → Settings/Preferences → Color Settings** to open the Color Chooser window, shown in Figure 9.16.

Figure 9.16

The Color Chooser window

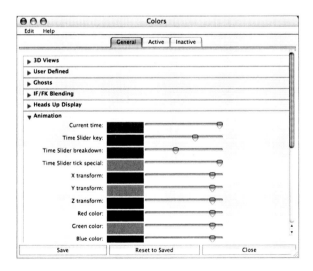

2. In the General tab, click the Animation twirl down. Set a new color for the Time Slider Tick Special color. We will use this to color the JoeG_neckCtrl key ticks. Click Save.

3. Select JoeG_neckCtrl in the perspective view.

4. In the Command line, type **keyframe -tds on;** and press Enter on the numeric keypad. All the JoeG_neckCtrl key ticks in the Timeline should now be the color you specified as the Time Slider Tick Special color. To turn this off, simply type **keyframe -tds off;** with the neck controller selected.

The sudden motion of the jump will cause the head to fall down to the chest until it swings up at the top of the curve and then snaps down when the feet impact the box. Let's edit the motion of the head.

1. With JoeG_neckCtrl selected, move the Current Time Indicator to frame 29.

2. LM drag in the Timeline to scrub the animation to frame 32. Notice that the head drops a little, but it should actually drop more.

3. At the key on frame 32, rotate the head until the **rotateX** attribute reads 64. This shows how the head will be thrust down against the chest by the force of the jump.

4. At the key on frame 35, rotate the head in X to –7. Here the head will flop up at the top of the jump, but we will have to offset this for maximum effect.

5. At the key on frame 38, rotate the head in X back to 0. Once it gets there, the head stays rotated up until the next key.

6. At the key on frame 40, rotate the head in X to 116. This rotation has the head snapping forward on the impact key. Again, we will have to offset this pose to make it work here. Too much rotation will make JoeG look like he has broken his neck!

7. At the key on frame 50, rotate the head in X to 105. The head stays down as he begins to stand up.

8. Playblast to see what you have.

Now let's offset these keys to give this motion maximum effect.

1. Drag the keys from frames 29 to 40 one frame later on the Timeline. You should now have keys on frames 30, 33, 36, 39, and 41.

2. Deselect the key now on frame 30, and drag the remaining keys one more frame later on the Timeline. You should now have keys on frames 34, 37, 40, and 42.

3. To lessen the whip-cracking speed of the last head snap down, move the key at 42 over to frame 45.

4. Playblast to see how it looks. JoeGJumpHead.mov shows the result. If you think the head looks too loose, dial back the **rotateX** value of the keys on frames 37 and 40.

Through proper use of offsets, you can create many looks for this animation. Open `JoeGJumpFinalOffsets.ma` from the CD. Open the Dope Sheet with all the controllers selected. Take a look at the attributes of COG and UpperBodyGrp. You can see them by clicking the rightmost plus sign next to the curve name in the outline view in the Dope Sheet if they are not displayed already. Many of the keys of these custom attributes have been offset to make them occur later (and in some cases earlier) in the animation. Take a look at `JoeGJumpFinalOffsets.mov` in the movies folder in the Chapter 9 folder on the CD to see the results.

Have fun playing with the keys in the Dope Sheet to create different effects. Save incrementally and often to be able to go back to some that you liked.

Summary

In this chapter you explored a particular method of pose-to-pose animation. Starting with video reference, you created the poses that carried the action of a simple jump. While you had guide geometry to use, we hope you went past the constraints of the guides to create a performance that was wholly yours. You then adjusted the time between poses and gained an understanding of the difference just a few frames can make in the clarity and naturalism of an action. Last, you refined the motion of a few body parts to get a feel for what it takes to create a truly compelling animation.

In the next chapter, we will deal with nonlinear animation using Maya's Trax Editor. Nonlinear animation is a method for combining animation "clips" in a nondestructive manner similar to non-linear video editing.

CHAPTER 10

Nonlinear Animation

This chapter covers nonlinear animation, a method of animation that allows you to construct motion out of smaller animation clips in a nondestructive manner, similar to the way modern nonlinear video editing software (such as Apple's Final Cut) works. This type of animation is extremely useful for repetitive motions and is also used extensively by game developers to allow their onscreen characters to react in different ways to changing environments and user input. With Maya's Full Body IK (FBIK) system (see Chapter 8), nonlinear animation using Maya's characters and the Trax Editor can be even more useful because the FBIK setup automatically creates characters to be used in nonlinear animation.

At its heart, nonlinear animation helps solve two of the most time-consuming problems with keyframed animation: the tedium of re-creating identical or similar motion and the difficulty of overlapping two previously keyframed motions atop each other. Because of its nondestructive editing capabilities, nonlinear animation lets you "edit" together motion clips by placing them end to end, or overlapping their motions. In fact, nonlinear animation using the Trax Editor is similar in many ways to video editing, in that you stack clips side by side or on top of each other to create a final motion. Although reuse of animation clips was spurred by the needs of game developers, who needed to be able to reuse and blend short clips, Maya's implementation has advantages that you will find useful in just about any animation project. This chapter covers the following topics.

- **Creating poses**
- **Creating clips**
- **Modifying, blending, and sharing clips**
- **Hands On: Animating with Maya's new Full Body IK setup**

What Is a Character?

Before you can animate using the Trax Editor, you must first create one or more characters. A character in Maya is a collection of disparate attributes that are to be animated. In other words, a character is simply a list or grouping of possibly unrelated attributes on various nodes.

Because it is easier to understand a character by example than by theory, let's create a very simple character to demonstrate what one is. In a new Maya scene, create two primitives, like a sphere and a cylinder. Select the sphere, and then select the X, Y, and Z translate channels in the Channel Box. With these selected, choose **Character → Create Character Set** ❒ from the Animation menu set. Reset the Character Set Options tool, and select **From Channel Box** under Attributes. Give your character a name (like simpleGuy), and click the Create Character Set button to create your character.

If you now look in the Outliner window, you will see a character named simpleGuy at the bottom of the list. If you twirl down the list of attributes associated with this character, you will see the sphere's X, Y and Z translate channels listed, as shown in Figure 10.1. We can add attributes to this character as we wish. First, select the cylinder, and then select the rotate X, Y, and Z channels in the Channel Box. Next, select the character, simpleGuy, in the character selection pop-up menu in the lower-right portion of your Maya window (or choose **Character → Set Current Character Set → simpleGuy**). Finally, choose **Character → Add To Character Set**. As shown in Figure 10.2, this places the cylinder's rotation channels into the character, simpleGuy, allowing you to animate those channels as well when the character is selected.

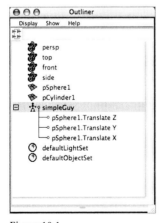

Figure 10.1

The Outliner shows the attributes belonging to the character simpleGuy.

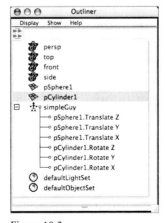

Figure 10.2

Adding the cylinder's rotation channels to the character simpleGuy

To animate using this character, be sure the character is selected in the Characters pop-up menu; then animate any of the character's channels, and press the S key to set keys on all character attributes. You can now animate the translate channels of the sphere and the rotate channels of the cylinder at the same time. While this ability is not particularly interesting for our simple character, being able to collect specific attributes into a character is very valuable for more complex characters, as you will see later in the chapter.

Working with Poses

Creating distinctive poses for a character that can be reloaded on cue can be a useful technique both for pre-animation and during the animation process. Using poses, you can quickly go to any number of predefined character configurations, which can save time during the rigging process and also during animation if your character commonly returns to certain positions during animation.

Let's begin with simple "characters" made from a couple of geometric primitives, which, for the purposes of our initial work, will function well as substitutes for more complex characters.

1. Create a sphere named thing1 and a cube named thing2. (Any model will do for these characters, so feel free to substitute something else if you prefer.)

2. Select thing1 and make it a Maya character by choosing **Character → Create Character Set ❐**. In the option box, choose **Edit → Reset Settings** and click the Create Character Set button. This will create a character, named character1, with keyable translation and rotation channels. Select thing2 and create a second character, character2.

3. Set character1 as the working character set by choosing it from the Character pop-up menu at the bottom right of the Timeline.

4. The easiest way to create a pose is to use the Trax Editor. Open the Trax Editor by choosing **Window → Animation Editors → Trax Editor**. To load the characters, select the geometry for each character (or select the character in the Character pop-up menu), and choose **List → Load Selected Characters** from the Trax Editor window. As Figure 10.3 shows, character1 and character2 are listed in the Timeline, where poses and animation clips will appear once you have created them. The twirl-down menu left of each character name is currently empty because no clips or poses are associated with either character. You navigate the Trax Editor in the same way that you navigate most Maya windows: to zoom in or out, press Alt+RM. To scroll through the Timeline, press Alt+MM.

5. Set character1 as the current character using the Character pop-up menu. If you want to see the character in the Channel Box (to see which channels are keyable, for example), you can select the character in the Outliner.

6. In the Trax Editor window, choose **Create → Pose** ❐. Name the pose Beginning and click the Create Pose button. You will not see any difference in the scene or Trax Editor window, but Maya has saved the current state (translation and rotation) of the sphere—character1—as a clip to be used.

7. To load the pose into the Trax Editor, choose **Library → Insert Pose → Beginning** from the Trax Editor menu set. As Figure 10.4 shows, the pose will be loaded into the Trax Editor under character1. (Twirl down the triangle next to the character1 name to see the clip if you don't already.) Additionally, on the left side of the Trax Editor window, three buttons will appear. The leftmost lets you lock and unlock the clip (making it unselectable if locked). The middle button is the solo button, which, when selected, makes the current clip or pose the only active one. The rightmost button is the mute button, which turns off animation for a given pose or clip.

8. Now create a second pose for character1. Move the sphere to another position in the scene window (there is no need to change to a different time in the Timeline), and in the Trax Editor window, choose **Create → Pose** ❐. In the option box, name the pose Ending and click the Create Pose button.

Figure 10.3

The Trax Editor window

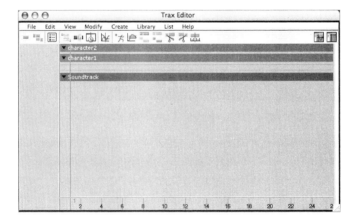

Figure 10.4

The Trax Editor showing a new clip

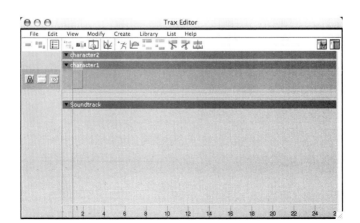

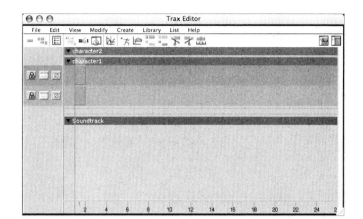

Figure 10.5

Inserting a second pose in the Trax Editor

9. Load the new clip by choosing **Library → Insert Pose → Ending**. The new pose will appear in the Timeline below the beginning pose, as in Figure 10.5.

10. You will notice no changes to the position of the sphere, since the top pose is still controlling its position. Click the mute button next to the beginning clip (the rightmost button in the left pane) and the sphere will "pop" to the position defined by the ending clip. You can also drag the poses around in the Timeline to make the sphere hop from place to place as the Timeline is updated. We will discuss the Timeline more thoroughly in the next section.

CLIP INSTANCES IN THE TRAX EDITOR

When you place a pose or a clip into a track in the Trax Editor, you are creating an instance of the source clip stored in the Visor (choose **Window → General Editors → Visor**). When you drag the Beginning clip, for example, into a track, it is called Beginning1 (or 2 or so on), not just Beginning. Because of this instance relationship, you can make any changes you want to an individual pose or clip in a track without affecting the source clip's values. On the other hand, if you adjust the source clip's settings (via the Attribute Editor), all instances of the clip in the tracks are updated to reflect those changes.

Working with Clips

Although poses can be useful on a limited basis (when you need to return quickly to a specified pose, for example), clips are generally more useful tools for an animator. Clips are short (in general) bits of animation that can be added and/or blended to create longer animations that can be varied and cycled as needed for a given shot. The general flow of work for clips is to create pieces of animation (often different for each body part), store them in a kind of "bin" (similar to bins used in nonlinear video-editing programs), and then stack them together and adjust their parameters in the Trax Editor, creating the desired animation. Since the animation is stored in these clips, multiple clips can be added together in a nondestructive manner, allowing the animator to control large- and small-scale animation of a character without the need to find and adjust specific keyframes. Clips are especially useful when animating repetitive motions that still need potential variety from cycle to cycle, such as blinking, walking, running, or talking. Clips can be scaled up or down to increase or decrease the speed or exaggeration of the action, and they can be cycled to repeat a given motion.

Creating Clips

You create clips the same way that you create poses, except that all of a character's animation keyframes are recorded rather than a single character state. Once created, clips can be used over and over and shared across scenes. A clip actually can be composed of just one keyframe; however, a single-keyframe clip can be difficult to use later because it has no length to adjust or blend with other clips. If you create a one-keyframe clip, you can alleviate its limitations by selecting the source clip in the Visor or Outliner, opening the Attribute Editor, and increasing the Duration setting of the source clip. However, it's easier (and more useful) to create a multi-keyframed clip in the first place.

> To view clips directly in the Outliner, turn off the Show DAG Objects Only option in the Outliner pane's menu set.

Once you have some sort of animation in your Timeline, you can create a clip in the Trax Editor by choosing **Create → Animation Clip** ❒ from the Trax Editor menu set. In the Create Clip options box, shown in Figure 10.6, you can choose how you want to create

Figure 10.6

The Create Clip Options window

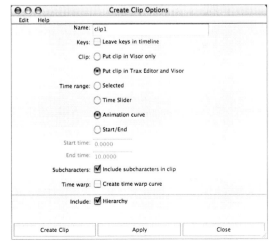

and use your clip. In the Name field, enter a name for your clip. (The default name is clip1.) You will find it helpful to rename the clips to describe what they do. For example, if you are creating clips of words for lip-synching, name each clip for the word you are animating. The Leave Keys In Timeline check box lets you maintain the keyframes you use to create a clip in your Timeline. This can be useful if you want to create several similar clips and don't want to reproduce all the keyframes for each clip. In general, however, it is best to remove Timeline keyframes as you create a clip so that you don't get unexpected animation later. (The Timeline and clip keyframes will work additively, creating unsightly results.)

The Clip radio buttons let you place the clip in the Visor only (if you don't plan to use it right away) or place the clip in the Visor and in a character track in the Trax Editor. The Time Range section provides four choices, plus two selections related to sub characters and time warping:

- Use a selected time range (Shift+drag in the Timeline).

- Use the start and end values of the Range Slider.

- Use the range of animation curves (from the first keyframe to the last for your character, which is the default method).

- Use a manually specified start and end frame.

- Include a Time Warp animation curve, which allows you to remap the timing of a clip; though useful if needed, this feature slows performance in a scene, so enable this function only if you plan to use it.

- Include subcharacter keyframes when you create a clip.

To see how clips work in more detail, let's create a clip.

1. Reuse your scene from the earlier section on poses, or create a new scene with two geometric primitives. Create two characters for the primitives, character1 and character2, with default options.

2. With character1 selected, set a keyframe on the character by pressing the S key. (Be sure character1 is selected in the Character pop-up menu or you will not be able to set keys on this character.) Change the time, move and rotate the primitive associated with character1, and set another keyframe. Continue creating as many keyframes on this character as you desire.

3. In the Trax Editor window, or under the Animate menu in the Animation menu set, choose **Create → Animation Clip** ❏. In the Create Clip Options window, name the clip anything you want, set the clip to go in the Trax Editor and Visor, choose Use Animation Curve Range to set the length of the clip, and click Create Clip. As shown in Figure 10.7, a new clip is inserted in the Trax Editor, ready for your use. In addition, in the Visor (in the Clips tab now, not the Poses tab) is a new source clip.

4. Click Play in the scene window and you will see the time marker move across the Trax Editor Timeline as well. As it crosses the clip, your animation will play back, as it did when the keyframes were stored in the scene Timeline.

Once a clip is in a track, you can interactively change its position, length (or scale), and cycling options, as explained in the next section.

Figure 10.7

Creating a new clip in the Trax Editor

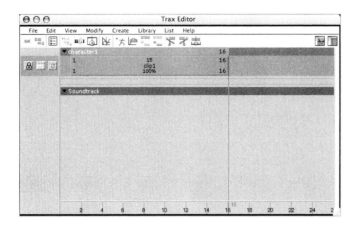

Modifying Clips

Although creating and reusing clips can be useful, modifying the clips to produce varying animation is even more valuable. Figure 10.8 shows a clip in the Trax Editor. The numbers on the blue line above the clip show the in and out points of the clip in the main (scene) Timeline. The middle of the clip itself shows the length of the clip, the name of the clip, and the percentage of the original clip length this current incarnation fills. The two numbers on the left side show the clip in point (top left) and the Timeline in point (bottom left) of the clip. The right side shows the clip out point and Timeline out point of the clip (top and bottom, respectively). All clip information will update automatically as you make changes to this instance of the clip.

Modifying a clip is fairly straightforward once you know how to manipulate a clip in the Trax Editor.

- To change the position (beginning and ending points) of the clip, just drag the clip (by its middle) to a new point in the Timeline.

- To change the length (or scale) of the clip, drag the bottom-right corner of the clip. Your cursor should turn into a double arrow with a dot in between to show that you can now scale the clip. Dragging left reduces the scale of the clip (the animation happens faster), and dragging right makes the animation slower. Alternatively, you can change the Scale value for the clip by double-clicking the lower-right number and typing a new end frame or by loading the character into the Channel Box and changing the Scale value. You can also drag the lower-left number in the clip to scale the clip at the beginning instead of the ending point.

Figure 10.8

A clip loaded in the Trax Editor

Figure 10.9

A cycled clip

- To change the number of times a clip repeats (its cycle settings), Shift+drag the bottom-right corner of the clip. Alternatively, you can set the Post (or Pre) Cycle number in the Attribute Editor or Channel Box. When your track contains multiple cycles of the original clip, Maya places a black tickmark in the clip at each point where the original clip repeats and slightly lightens the color of the bar for all cycles past the first one. In addition, the cycle area of the clip will show the new Timeline out point as well as the number of extra cycles you have created. In Figure 10.9, you can see that we created 1.2 extra cycles, and the C1.2 label in the clip provides this feedback. You can choose to offset the animation cycle for a clip in two ways. If you choose Absolute, the attribute values are reset to the original value on each repetition of the cycle. If you select Relative, the attribute value is added to the original value. For example, a Relative offset is useful when moving a character's feet in a walk cycle so they don't snap back to the origin on each step. To adjust the relative/absolute settings for a clip, select the clip and then open the Attribute Editor, shown in Figure 10.10. Under the Channel Offsets section, you can choose All Absolute, All Relative, or Restore Defaults. (Translations are relative, and rotations are absolute by default). Or you can use the channel radio buttons to specify for each attribute whether its offset is absolute or relative.

Figure 10.10

Changing offsets in the Attribute Editor

- To trim a clip, so that you use only a portion of the animation rather than the entire clip, drag the top-right or -left corner of the clip. (Alternatively, double-click the number fields at the top right or left and type a new start or end frame for the clip.) A trimmed clip will contain animation only for the section of the clip that is still available, so there could be problems with the animation "cutting in" or out as the animation starts or stops in mid-clip.

- You can also create a hold on a clip: a series of frames that freeze the last pose of the character. Although frozen poses are often distracting, a hold can be useful from time to time, especially for background characters. To create a hold, Shift+drag the top-right corner of the clip. (You can't create a hold before the first frame of the clip by dragging on the left.)

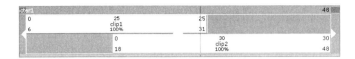

- Two or more clips can be scaled or moved together. Shift+select the clips and then move them (drag the center move manipulator) or scale them (drag the scale manipulators at either end) to alter their settings as a group. Figure 10.11 shows two clips being modified together.

- To set the weight of a track, select the clip and click the clip name in the Inputs section of the Channel Box. Weighting simply multiplies the animation curves by the number in the Weight channel. Setting the Weight equal to 1 (the default) means the animation is just as it was created. Setting the weight higher makes the animation "bigger," and setting the weight lower than 1 produces a smaller effect.

- You can disable a clip's effects to get a better view of how other animation is influencing a certain point. To disable a track, move the pointer over the clip and RM choose Enable Clip (removing its check mark). To re-enable the clip, follow the same procedure.

- Making a clip active allows you to go back and rework the animation in the Timeline, as with "normal" animation, and then load those revisions back into the clip. With the pointer over the clip, RM choose Activate Keys. You will see the keys loaded back into the Timeline, where you can add and remove keyframes and adjust the animation curves to suit your needs. When you have finished working on the animation, choose Activate Keys again to remove the keys from the scene and place the clip back into the Visor and Trax Editor Timeline.

- Finally, you can create a time warp, which allows you to modify an animation clip as a whole without disturbing the individual clip animation itself. Although Scale can only alter the length of a clip, Time Warp can be used to invert the clip (make it play backward) or ease the clip in or out, which can be especially useful if the clip is trimmed to start in mid-animation. To create a time warp, place the pointer over the clip and RM choose Create Time Warp. A green bar will appear at the top of the clip (when it is not selected), reminding you that a time warp is placed on this clip. To alter the time warp curve, select the clip and then click the Graph Animation Curves button in the Trax Editor to load the clip curves into the Graph Editor. Select the time warp curve and adjust to suit your needs. Figure 10.12 shows the time warp curve after creating an ease-in ease-out flatness to the tangent handles.

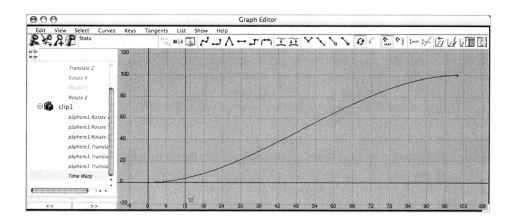

Figure 10.12

A time warp curve in the Graph Editor

By controlling the placement, length, cycling, weight, and animation of a clip, you can fine-tune your animation to an exacting degree using the Trax Editor. If you want even more control over the shape of the underlying curves that make up a clip, you can graph the curves and adjust them as you would any animation curves in the Graph Editor. In the Trax Editor, choose **View → Graph Anim Curves** (or click the Graph Anim Curves button in the toolbar). The Graph Editor will appear with all the curves of your clip loaded in the window. (You might need to press the A key to center the curves.) You can then adjust the curves as you would any other animation curves, tweaking the motion until you are satisfied.

The animation curves of a clip loaded into the Graph Editor can be shown either with weighting and timing changes applied or without, depending on which would be more effective for your editing purposes. To view the original curves, choose **View → Clip Time** to unselect the Clip Time feature. You will see the curves snap back to their original timing and weighting. To re-enable the clip time view, simply reselect the Clip Time option, toggling it back on.

Blending Clips

Although adjusting one animation clip's characteristics is quite useful, the ability to blend animation between clips allows you to marry multiple short animation segments into one longer animation. For example, you might blend between a standing and a walking clip or between a walking and a running clip, reducing the need to keyframe complex transitional states in an animation.

To see how blending works, either use your simple character from the previous sections or create a character out of two primitives (such as a sphere and a cone), and then create two clips: one clip with the sphere and cone moving up and down in the Y axis in opposite directions and the other with them moving in the X or Z axis in opposite directions. You might find it easier to create the second clip if you disable the first one. To disable a clip, select the clip in the Trax Editor, and then RM choose Enable Clip. A disabled clip's track is slightly darker, indicating that it no longer affects the character's motion. Enabling and disabling clips can be a useful way to test individual motion on a character with multiple tracks of animation.

When you finish creating the clips and load them into the Trax Editor, the window should have two tracks for each character (as in Figure 10.13), with the clips stacked on top of each other. Notice that Maya created a new track for each character below the original ones to accommodate the new clips.

If you now play back the animation, the motions from both clips combine, so the sphere and cone travel diagonally opposite each other. To allow each clip to operate on its own, simply move one clip down the Timeline until it is no longer overlapping the other. When you do this, however, you will see that the animation "pops" between the two clips (the animation stops between each clip), a situation for which blending can compensate.

> You can manually create new tracks in the Trax Editor by selecting a track and RM choosing Insert Track Above or Insert Track Below. To remove an unused track, RM choose Remove Track.

Clips are blended based on which clip is first in the Timeline. In other words, if clip1 starts on frame 20 and clip2 starts on frame 30, clip1 will hold the initial values (at 100%) for the blend, and clip2 will hold the final values (100%). This system breaks down if both clips start at the same time on the Timeline, so avoid blending two clips that start at the same time.

Figure 10.13

Two tracks for each character, stacked on top of each other

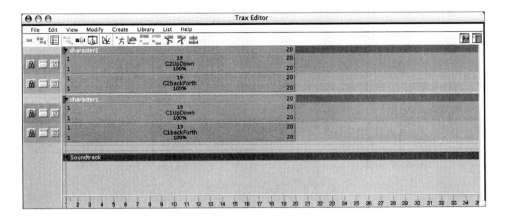

Adding a Blend to Overlapping Clips

Partially overlapping clips create additive animation during the frames when the two clips overlap. The trouble with the overlapped section is that the animation can pop when the new clip is introduced because the values of the animated channels suddenly change.

To resolve the popping problem, you can add a blend to the clips, creating a smoother alteration from the values of one clip to values of the other. To create a blend, Shift+select the two clips and, with the cursor over one of the clips, RM choose Blend. The overlapping area of the clips will turn green, and an arrow showing blend direction will appear between the clips, as in Figure 10.14.

Blending works using the common attributes of the two clips. Blending will not be effective if the clips you are trying to blend do not share common attributes. Also, blending will create a smoother transition if a similar motion is maintained between the two clips.

In the Trax Editor, choose **Create → Blend** ❐. Look at the options in the Initial Weight Curve and Rotation Blend sections. In the Initial Weight Curve section are four choices that give you control over the tangents used to create the blend.

Linear Creates an evenly weighted transition between the clips.

Ease In Assigns less weight at the beginning of the transition and increases the weight given to the next clip as frames in the blend progress. This makes the beginning of the transition less noticeable.

Ease Out The opposite of Ease In; places more weight on the beginning keys. The effect of the first clip is more prominent than the effect of the second clip for a longer amount of time.

Ease In and Ease Out Combines the Ease In and Ease Out options.

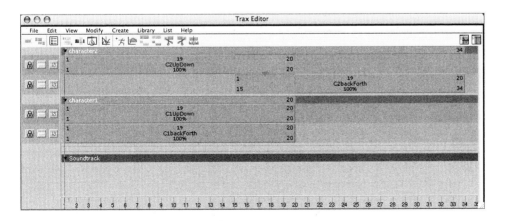

Figure 10.14

Two animation tracks blended

You will discover that you achieve different results with each option. To remove a blend so you can experiment with other settings, select the blend arrow and press the Delete key.

The items in the Rotation Blend section control how the rotation attributes from the first clip are combined with the rotation values of the second clip (assuming, of course, you have rotation keyframes animated). **Quaternion Shortest** uses the least amount of distance between the rotations, and **Quaternion Longest** uses the greatest distance between the rotations. Basically, if you don't want the object to spin in the opposite direction as one clip blends into another, choose **Quaternion Shortest**. The **Linear** option merges the rotation values at a constant rate during the blend. Experiment with these options to see just how big a difference each choice will make. Once you are familiar with the way the blend works, you will more easily achieve a successful transition between the clips.

Modifying Clip Blends

To change the length of the blend (the number of frames over which the blend takes place), slide one track relative to the other, changing the overlap. You can also blend tracks that are not on top of each other—the blend will occur between the last values of the first clip and the initial values of the second clip. Figure 10.15 shows the two clips blended across empty frames.

You can even adjust the curve manually if you want: select the blend arrow and load the animation curve into the Graph Editor. (Click the Graph Anim Curves button, or choose **View → Graph Anim Curves**.) The Graph Editor will open, showing the blend weight curve. As you can see in Figure 10.16, the default blend curve is just a straight line on a scale of 0 to 1 in both the horizontal and vertical axes. When the curve is at 0,0, the blend is completely weighted toward the first clip in the blend. (That is, character channel values are 100 percent those of the first clip.) When the curve is at 1,1, at the end of the blend, the blend is completely weighted to the second clip in the blend.

To create a different shaped curve (for instance, to ease the blend in and out), simply adjust the tangent handles of the two blend keyframes or add other keyframes into the blend shape. Editing the shape of the blend is simple enough, yet if you want ease in, ease out, or ease in and out effects, you might save time by deleting the blend and creating a new blend by selecting the appropriate options from the Create Blend menu.

Because the shape of the blend curve is independent of the length of the blend, you can adjust the shape of the blend and then increase or decrease the length of the blend in the Trax Editor (or vice versa), thus lengthening or shortening a blend without changing its shape. This separation of curve shape from length is one of the work flow benefits of using Trax as opposed to traditional keyframe techniques.

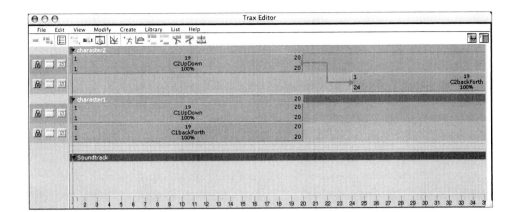

Figure 10.15

Blending across empty frames

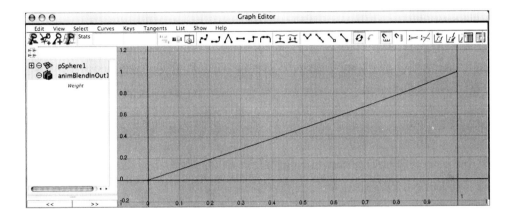

Figure 10.16

Graphing the blend weight curve

Blending clips allows for quick and easy transitions between different character animation states. Although these transitions aren't always perfect, they are generally good, and you can adjust them using the Graph Editor or by changing the blend lengths. Another advantage of using Trax is that it provides the ability to share clips and poses among characters in a single animation or even in multiple, separate scenes. If you invest time planning your characters, you can save time when you are animating.

Sharing Clips

Maya's ability to share animation clips and poses among characters makes possible huge time savings in a complex, multicharacter project or in several projects that can use each other's motion data. To see how sharing clips works, we'll first share clips within a single scene, then use a referenced scene to share clips, and finally use the import/export feature to share clips between scenes.

Sharing Clips in a Scene

You can share clips between characters within a single scene by copying and pasting clips from one character to another. If you have the simple project from the previous sections, you can continue to use it. If not, create a simple character consisting of a geometric primitive, and create two or three animation clips for one of the characters. When one character is animated with clips, create a second, similar character and move it away from the first character in your scene.

> You can share clips between characters that are quite different from each other, but much of the animation of each clip might be lost in the transfer. Thus, it is generally better to share clips between similar characters.

You can copy a clip from one character to another in two ways. The simplest method (if the clip is already being used by the other character) is to copy and paste it from the first character's track into the second character's track. To do so, RM choose Copy Clip with the cursor over the clip you want to copy. Then, load character2 in the Trax Editor Timeline, and with the cursor over the character2 name, RM choose Paste Clip. The new clip will appear in the track for the second character.

The second way to copy and paste is to use the Visor. With character1 (*not* character2) set in the character pop-up menu, open the Visor, and with the cursor over the clip you wish to copy, RM choose Copy. Then, in the Trax Editor, place the cursor in a track for the second character and RM choose Paste, placing the clip into the track. (Answer Yes in the dialog box that asks how you want to paste the clip.) The result is shown in Figure 10.17.

Copying and pasting from the Trax Editor and from the Visor are not identical operations. When you copy a clip from the Trax Editor itself, any clip changes (to scaling, weighting, or cycling) are transferred to the clip for the new character. When you copy and paste from the Visor, the original source clip is copied, with no modifications. Depending on your animation goals, one or the other method may prove more useful.

If you open the option box when pasting a clip (choose **Edit → Paste** ❐ from the Trax Editor menu set), you can paste by attribute name by attribute order, by node name, or by character map, as shown in Figure 10.18.

Figure 10.17

A clip copied from character1 to character2

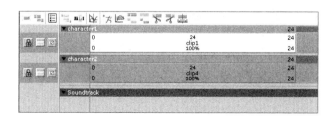

Generally, you want to use attribute name or attribute order to paste because this places the animation curves on attributes in the new character that are either of the same name or in the same order as in the originating character. The By Node Name option will not work properly when the two characters are in the same scene (because two nodes cannot be named the same in a single scene). However, you can use this option when importing or copying clips into a new scene in which all the nodes have names identical to those in the original scene. The By Character Map option creates a

Figure 10.18
The Paste Clip option box

user-modifiable MEL script that maps the curves from one character to another. This method can be powerful for pasting a clip from one character onto a different character, but it is a fairly complex and specialized process and not generally useful for the average Trax user. For information about how to create and use a character map, choose **Character Setup → Character Set → Mapping Animation Between Characters** in the online documentation that comes with Maya.

Upon pasting the clip onto character2, you will likely find that your new character will move to *exactly* the same place as the first character (so the two overlap). If this behavior is acceptable, you are finished with the pasting. If not, you can correct the problem in two ways:

• Activate the clip (highlight the clip to bring its keys into the Timeline for editing, and then RM choose Activate Keys), and move the character to the proper position at each keyframe.

• Graph the animation curves (choose **View → Graph Anim Curves**), and adjust the curves to move your character into position.

Graphing the animation curves tends to work more intuitively because you can move the curve as a whole. Working with the individual keyframes in activate mode can lead to forgotten or misplaced keyframes and thus to unwanted behavior.

Using a Reference Scene to Share Clips

To copy clips from one scene file to another, you can reference a source scene into a new one. Save your current scene (with clips intact), and then open a new scene and create another simple character. Now choose **File → Create Reference** and select the source scene you just saved. You should see the geometry from your old scene appear in the new one, and if you look in the Character pop-up menu, you will see characters 1 and 2 (preceded by the scene filename) in the menu, in addition to the new character you just created.

In the Trax Editor, the two characters from your source scene will appear below your current scene character. You can then copy and paste clips as you want, using the techniques described in the previous section.

When you are finished copying clips, remove the reference from your new scene. To do this, choose **File → Reference Editor**. In the Reference Editor window, select the scene file you referenced, and choose **Reference → Remove Reference**. With the reference removed, all the geometry and extra clips from the source scene are removed and you are left with just the copied clips you want to use in your new scene.

Exporting and Importing Clips

The third way to share clips is to export the clips themselves and then import them into a new scene. The exported scene will contain *only* animation clips (and poses), not geometry.

Reopen your old scene file (with the two characters) and open the Trax Editor or Visor. Select all the clips that you want to export (only selected clips will be exported), and choose **File → Export Animation Clip**. A dialog box will appear, allowing you to save the exported clips into a new scene file (stored, by default, in the Clips folder of your project). Choose a name and export the file.

In a new scene file, create yet another simple character. In the Trax Editor, choose **File → Import Animation Clip** and import the clips you previously exported. When the file is imported, the clips from the other file are stored in the Visor of the new scene, in the Unused Clips tab. You can then use the Visor method to copy and paste clips onto your new character, thus sharing the clips between files in this manner.

By exporting clips from scene files, you can create libraries of clips to use later. For example, if you create walk, run, jump, sit, and stand clips for a character, you can save just the clip data to a scene file (or multiple files if you prefer) and then import this animation data into any other character file you create in the future, saving you the time of rekeying all this motion data.

Using Trax to "create once, use many times" can drastically reduce the need to redo work, either in a single scene file or across dozens of scenes in ongoing projects. This, combined with the nonlinear, additive nature of Trax, makes Trax extremely useful for real-life animation work in which characters—especially background characters—need to perform similar tasks many times or in which a number of characters need to share similar behaviors.

Now that you have a good understanding of clips and the Trax Editor, we'll create some animation using our Machismo rig from Chapter 8. The following examples show how much time you can save using nonlinear animation techniques in Maya.

Using the Geometry Cache

New to Maya 8 is the ability to cache geometry motion and use this animation as a clip in the Trax Editor. Geometry caching saves out the state of each vertex on a skin for each frame, which means Maya does not have to calculate complex skin deformation on each frame, speeding up playback and scene interactivity greatly. This feature is especially useful if you have complex geometry that is slow to play back because the cached geometry will play back in real time. It can also be useful for game animation because the rig for a model can be deleted once the animated geometry is cached. In either case, the goal is to do the complex, slow skin deformation calculations once only, caching them after the first time so that subsequent playback is quick and doesn't use CPU resources. Once cached, animation is stored in the Trax Editor and behaves much like any other animation clip there. Thus, geometry cache clips can be stacked, joined, and adjusted. Additional controls for geometry caches include cache weight painting, merging portions of caches, deleting and replacing individual cache frames, and importing caches from other scenes.

With Maya 8.5, the geometry caching feature is even more useful because caches can be muted or soloed (allowing individual tracks to play back or be removed from playback), new clips can inherit transformation data from old clips (so that they don't pop when a new clip starts), and the tangency of point animation can be adjusted to further help blend geometry cache clips together. All in all, the tools available via geometry caching allow enough control over vertex animation that numerous cached clips can be combined, adjusted, and weighted after being created, which removes the need to go back and re-animate character motion via skeleton animation as long as the original animation was reasonably close to the intended final animation.

To create a geometry cache clip, animate geometry as you wish and then choose **Geometry Cache → Create New Cache ❑** from the Animation menu set. In the Create New Cache option box, seen in Figure 10.19, you can choose the name of the cache, the directory it is stored in (the project's data directory by default), whether one file is created per frame or one large file is created for all animation frames, whether to split the cache up by piece of geometry or not (this only matters if your selected geometry has separate geometric pieces), how to store the point data, and how much of the Timeline to include in the cache.

Figure 10.19

The Create Geometry Cache option box

Once created, the cached clip appears in the Trax Editor as any other clip would. You will notice that the animation continues in the Timeline, however, since there are still keys on the skeleton driving the animation. But you can delete the skeleton animation, enable the geometry cache clip, and watch the animation play back based on vertex position. Figure 10.20 shows a character "walking out of" his skeleton, as the skin animation is controlled via a geometry cache clip.

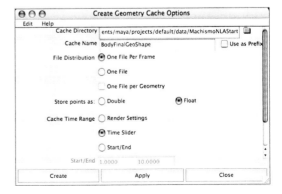

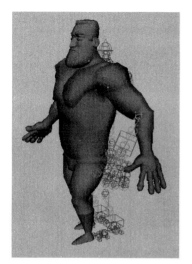

Figure 10.20

Machismo walks out of his stationary skeleton.

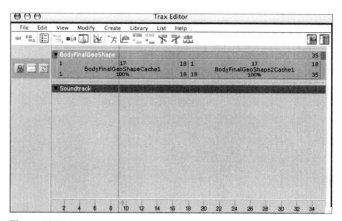

Figure 10.21

Two geometry cache clips in the Trax Editor

If you create two or more clips, they can be stacked atop one another or placed back-to-back to create various animation effects, as shown in Figure 10.21. If your scene is very heavy and you wish to view animation close to real time, or if you are working on creating animation for a game engine, this new feature will come in very handy.

Hands On: Working with a Full Body IK Animation Rig

Figure 10.22

The FBIK character and subcharacters in the Outliner

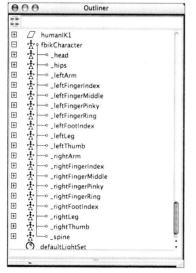

In Chapter 8, we created a rig for the Machismo model created earlier in the book using Maya's new Full Body IK (FBIK) animation system. Here we will make use of that rig, which creates characters automatically, to animate the character using nonlinear techniques.

Since the FBIK system creates a character for the main body and subcharacters for various body elements, little setup is required to begin animating using clips and the Trax Editor. Before animating the character, let's take a look at the character hierarchy FBIK gives us. As Figure 10.22 shows, there is a single main character, named fbikCharacter, for each FBIK setup. Under the character are subcharacters for elements of the body, including the hips, spine, legs, arms, and fingers. Having so many subcharacters reduces the number of extraneous keyframes an animator must set, but it might seem a bit daunting to have to select the proper subcharacter each time a body part is moved. Fortunately, the FBIK system automatically enables the correct subcharacter whenever an FBIK effector is selected, making the process of nonlinear animation that much easier.

Now let's create a few clips for Machismo to see how nonlinear animation works in conjunction with the FBIK system. We will start with a simple "moving hold" clip of Machismo standing and shifting his weight slightly and progress to a more complex walk cycle.

1. Open the MachismoNLAStart.ma file on the accompanying CD (or open your own version of the rig).

2. Place Machismo into a good standing position. You will want to move his arms down to his sides and shift his weight around so he isn't standing completely balanced between his two sides. (Having too much symmetry between sides is called "twinning" and looks unnatural in animation.) The left side of Figure 10.23 shows a good standing position.

3. Select the fbikCharacter character from the pop-up menu, and press the S key to set keys on the entire character. (If you want to reduce the number of keyframes, you can key just the subcharacters that have position data on them.)

Figure 10.23

Machismo in two standing positions

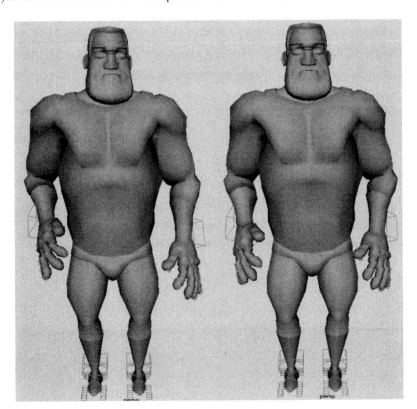

4. Now we need to create a second standing position for our character, slightly offset from the first one. We will use this second position as a transition stance so that as Machismo stands, he will move slightly. First, move to a different place in the Timeline—it doesn't much matter how far the time is moved, since the clip can be scaled to suit your needs later. We chose 10 frames, since it's an easy round number.

5. Now shift Machismo's weight around a bit. You can shift his hips over a bit, move his arms, and maybe tilt his head slightly. Anything you can do to make it look like the character has shifted his weight slightly will work fine. The right side of Figure 10.23 shows the new position. Set a key for the whole character again.

6. On playback, if the motion is too large (or small), adjust it so it is fairly subtle. You will also want to create "ease in" and "ease out" adjustments to the motion. The easiest way to do this is to select the main character and open the Graph Editor to flatten the tangent handles out for all the animation curves. Figure 10.24 shows the adjusted curves in the Graph Editor.

7. Now that you have some animation on the character, create a clip by selecting the fbikCharacter from the character pop-up and choose **Animate → Create Clip** ❐ from the Animation menu set. Call this clip something like shift, leave the other elements in their default states, and create the clip.

8. When you open the Trax Editor and click the Load Selected Characters button (the runner with the + beside him), you will see all the subcharacters listed, with animation clips loaded for most of them (depending on how many subcharacters you set keyframes for). You can now move clips for some body parts around by a few frames, creating overlapping animation. You can select all the clips and retime the animation, making it longer or shorter. And you can reweight any subcharacter's animation to make the motion more or less subtle. Figure 10.25 shows how the clips might look after offsetting them a bit and scaling the animation up to 200 percent, or 20 frames.

Figure 10.24

Flattening the tangents for the character's animation curves

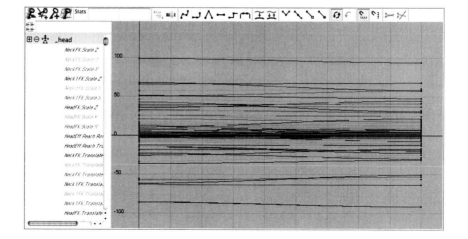

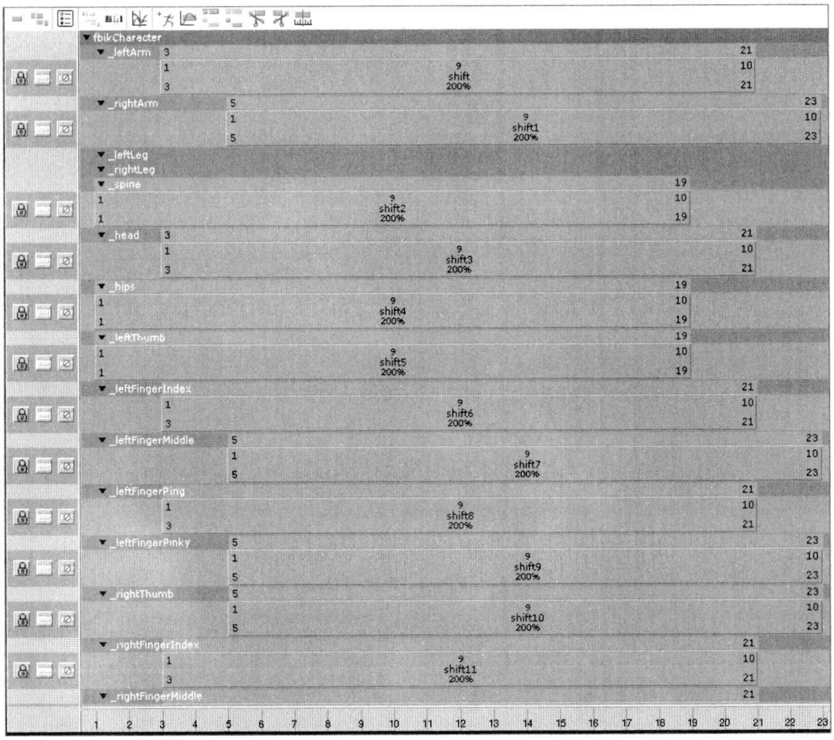

Figure 10.25

Adjusting clips in the Trax Editor

Now that we have created a moving hold, let's create a walk cycle for our character. This movement will be more substantial than the last one, but the principle is the same: keyframe the character into position over time, create animation clips, and adjust the scale, weighting, and cycling of the clips in the Trax Editor.

1. Disable the clips from the last animation so you don't have to worry about them overlapping with your new work. Select all the moving hold clips in the Trax Editor, move the pointer over any clip, and RM choose Enable Clip to uncheck it. Test to be sure you no longer have any movement on the character before proceeding.

2. A basic walk cycle has four positions: left foot passing, left foot forward, right foot passing, and right foot forward. Once we get one cycle finished, we can use the Trax Editor to create several steps. First let's create the left foot passing position. In the side view (or from the side in the Perspective view), move Machismo's left leg up just a bit, move his pelvis forward, and lean his back into the walk just a bit. The rightmost image in Figure 10.26 shows this position. Keyframe all the pertinent subcharacters.

3. Move to about frame 6 on the Timeline. Now place the character's left foot forward and striking the ground with his heel. Adjust the hips down a bit, and swing the arms in the opposite direction, as in the second image from the right in Figure 10.26. Again, set keyframes.

Figure 10.26

The four key poses for Machismo's walk cycle

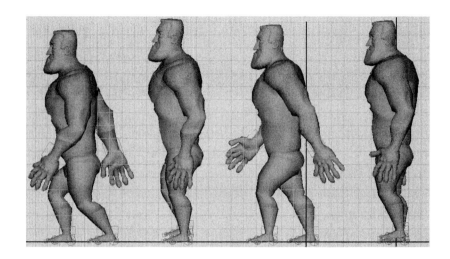

4. Move to about frame 12 on the Timeline and create the right passing position similar to the left passing position, but with the right foot raised now. (See the third image from the right in Figure 10.26.) Set keys.

5. Move to about frame 18 on the Timeline, and create the right foot forward position similar to the left foot forward position. (See the leftmost image in Figure 10.26.) Set keys.

6. Move to frame 24 and create another passing position with the left foot raised, as similar as possible to frame 1. Key this as well. Play back the animation and adjust the walk cycle until you are happy with it. (You might want to key the feet so that the walk pushes off the toes when Machismo moves.)

Now let's create a clip for the walk cycle. Select the fbikCharacter and choose **Animate →
Create Clip** ❑. In the option box, name the clip walk, and create the clip with default settings. When you open the Trax Editor, you should see the new clip layered under the standing clip (which is darkened to indicate it is not active), as shown in Figure 10.27.

Now we can adjust various body parts to create a bit of overlap to Machismo's character so he doesn't look quite so robotic while walking.

1. Move the hips and spine tracks back by about one frame, the arms back by about three frames, and the neck and head back by about two frames. (Adjust these numbers to suit your vision of his walk.) This overlapping motion will create a much more natural-looking walk cycle. You can also load any character clip in the Graph Editor and adjust the curves to make finer adjustments to the walk cycle.

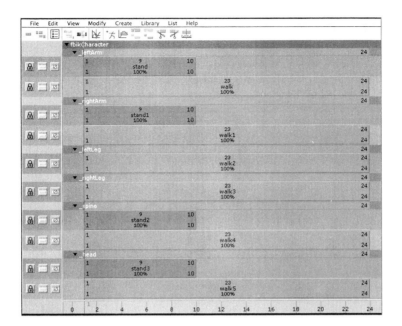

Figure 10.27

The Trax Editor showing the new walking clip

2. Finally, you can retime or cycle the animation by adjusting the weight or cycling of the clip. To cycle through Machismo's new walk several times, select each clip and Shift+drag the bottom right of the clip to pull out several cycles of the animation. To change the weighting of any of the clips, select the clip in the Trax Editor, and then, in the Channel Box, adjust the Weight channel to either increase (more than 1) or decrease (less than 1) the effect of any of the clips.

Now that we have two usable clips—the moving stand and the walk clip—we can blend between them to create animation of Machismo going from a standing position to walking.

1. Select all the walking clips and move them five frames forward in time (so the hips of the subcharacter's walk cycle starts on frame 5).

2. Reenable the standing clip by selecting all the standing clips and RM choosing Enable Clip. If you play back the animation now, you will likely see problems with the way the animation plays back because the clips are not yet blended.

3. To blend the clips, select the standing clip for one subcharacter, Shift+select the walking clip, and RM choose Blend ❏. In the options window, set Initial Weight Curve to Ease In Out, and create the blend. The clips will turn green in the overlapped, blended area, and an arrow will indicate which direction the blend flows (from the standing to the walking clip). Repeat for all subcharacters so your Trax Editor window looks like Figure 10.28.

Figure 10.28

Blending between standing and walking clips

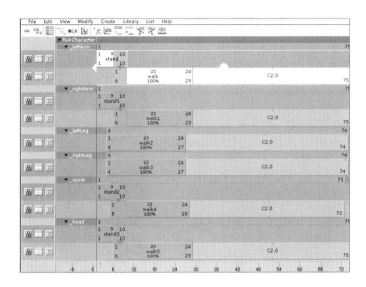

Now when you play back the animation, Machismo should start in a standing position and then move into a walking one. You can adjust the blend settings by selecting the blend itself in the Trax Editor and graphing the animation curve. From there you can change the curve that represents the flow of animation from the first to the second clip. Now that you can create and blend clips, try creating more animation clips for Machismo, cycle them, and blend between them to create a larger animation segment.

Summary

Nonlinear animation has become increasingly popular with animation studios over the past years, spurred on by game developers and large-scale crowd scenes that need similar animation, blended together, for large sets of characters. Maya's Trax Editor is one of the best, most robust nonlinear animators (NLAs) on the market. As you have seen in this chapter, using the Trax Editor can quickly produce animating from simple characters moving in simple ways to complex characters performing complicated actions. If you find yourself spending a great deal of time doing a repetitive animation task, try asking yourself how you can use the Trax Editor get this done. You might be surprised at how the Trax Editor can save you hours of time!

By creating and reusing poses and clips, you can save a great deal of time in animating repetitive tasks. By blending clips, you can fuse different animation states into one another, reducing the need for complex transition keyframes. With time warping, entire animation clips can be readjusted nondestructively to create individual motion for part of a character's animation. Finally, by sharing clips and poses between characters and scenes, you can leverage all the work done for one character or one scene for use in other scenes and projects. Maya's nonlinear animation is so powerful that once you begin using it, the Trax Editor can become your best friend!

CHAPTER 11

Lighting for Animation

Creating successful digital lighting is both a science and an art. Although there are many artistic similarities between stage lighting and digital lighting, Maya presents many technicalities that are quite different from real-world lighting.

As with all current computer-lighting models, Maya's lights simply cannot computationally reproduce a real-world lighting model. But Maya does provide you with tools to produce visually stunning light and shadow that can either mimic real-world lighting or adapt to your own artistic style.

Maya's lights also provide many benefits impossible in the real-world model, including lights with no shadows, negative lights, ambient light that has no direction or source, and the ability to look through a light as a camera. You can place lights anywhere in a scene, at any intensity, in any color. In other words, you have much more artistic freedom with Maya's lighting tools than you do with real-world lighting. There is no one correct way to light any given scene, and the information here will give you what you need to know in order to realize your lighting goals.

This chapter will discuss how to properly use all types of light in Maya and how to generate advanced effects using Maya's powerful tools and attributes.

- **Understanding lighting**
- **Basic work flow**
- **Types of lights**
- **Light manipulator**
- **Using shadows**
- **Light effects**

Understanding Lighting

Understanding the basic qualities and functions of light is crucial for properly lighting your Maya scenes. Although this chapter focuses primarily on the technicalities of how to create and use lights and their effects, knowing how to go about lighting your scenes is an art form in itself. Creating good lighting requires more than just randomly setting up lights in a scene and hoping for the best results. You will find, as you pay more attention to the qualities and functions of light, that your renders will appropriately illuminate your ideas.

Qualities of Light

Light can be divided into four qualities that you as an artist can work with. These qualities may seem basic, but you should consider them for each light you place in your scene; doing so makes each light important to your composition.

Intensity The brightness of your light. Controlling the intensity of your lights allows you to accentuate important areas of your scene.

Distribution The direction and angle of your light. Light direction is computed by vectors and specifies the angle at which your light hits 3D objects. Distribution also refers to the quality of your light source; in some cases, you want soft and subdued edges around your spotlights, and in other cases you want a harsh, stark edge.

Color Lets you convey theme and mood with your lights. Careful consideration must be used when determining your light color. How does the light color look with the material of the object? Is the color well balanced with the other lights in the scene?

Movement Refers to how your lights dynamically change. This can be a change of intensity, distribution, color, position, or rotation. Just as it is important for your models to be dynamic during an animation, so too should your lights change.

Functions of Light

Incorporating light in your scene is more than just a means to make your models visible. There are five specific functions of light in a scene:

Selective Visibility Allows you, through light, to control what the viewer can and cannot see. You can accentuate an action or area of your scene by isolating a pool of light onto it. In compositing, using fade-ins and fade-outs can suggest the passage of time.

Composition Refers to how the lights interact as a whole in relation to the scene. Strong composition allows your audience to fully focus on important elements within your scene.

Revelation of Form Allows you to use different lighting techniques with texture and shape on your scene elements. For example, a face lit by a single light below the chin conveys a much different tone than shining multiple lights from above would convey.

Establishing the Mood Important when presenting the viewer with a scene. Different intensities, distribution, color, and movement of light convey strong, sometimes subliminal, moods to help unify your scene with your story.

Reinforcement of the Theme Important in your lighting setup. The lighting should support, not contradict, the theme of your production.

Properly applying these functions in each of your Maya scenes will ensure that the lighting not only complements, but also strengthens, your artistic vision.

Basic Lighting Work Flow

Lighting is typically implemented toward the end of the production pipeline since textures, modeling, and animation can drastically determine lighting schemes. This, in conjunction with the sheer number of lights common in productions, can lead to long render times. Although every lighting artist will find their own work flow, several basic guidelines can help speed up the lighting process.

Interactive Photorealistic Rendering (IPR)

Interactive Photorealistic Rendering (IPR) allows you to update part of a rendered image in order to quickly see your changes. When using IPR, you can quickly see the results of adjusting color, intensity, and other basic light attributes. Limitations of IPR include the inability to dynamically update depth-map shadow information if a light is moved. Furthermore, IPR does not support raytracing, 3D motion blur, or particle effects.

To enable IPR, from the Rendering menu set, choose **Render → IPR Render Current Frame**. After the render view appears and renders your scene, use your mouse to draw a region on the frame. The area within this frame will then quickly update as you alter your scene. When setting up your initial renders for a scene, try using a series of directional lights with IPR; you can easily transform these lights and they will update efficiently.

Key and Fill Lights

This leads us to the next guideline: start by creating your general key lights and then worry about your kicker and fill lights. Since many lights are required to get a well-lit scene just right, establish your general mood and composition first with the key (main) lights. These lights include any explicit sources of light (such as the sun, lamps, fire, and so on). You can use low-intensity lights representing a bounce to help create a softer, realistic look. See Figure 11.1 for an example of using key and fill lights. Note that all these lights are standard spotlights in Maya; key and fill lights are merely stage lighting terms.

Figure 11.1

When setting up your lighting, place the key lights first and then add fill lights for softness.

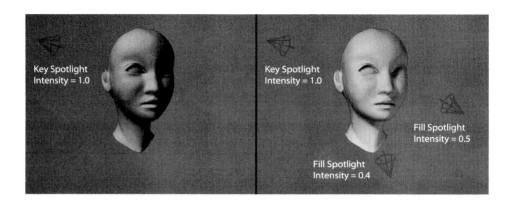

Figure 11.1

When setting up your lighting, place the key lights first and then add fill lights for softness.

Interactive Light Placement

Lights (and any other object) in Maya can be "looked through," meaning Maya creates a camera that positions and orients itself based on the selected object's position and rotation. This functionality really helps when you want a light to target a specific part of your scene. To look through a light, select it and choose **Panels → Look Through Selected**.

New in Maya 8, when creating a Directional, Spot, or Area light, you can turn on interactive light placement so that you will be automatically looking through the new light. To enable this option, choose **Create → Lights → Spot Light□** (or **Directional Light** or **Area Light**) and check the Interactive Placement check box. Figure 11.2 illustrates interactive light placement.

Figure 11.2

Interactive light placement allows you to look through a light to better control where your light points.

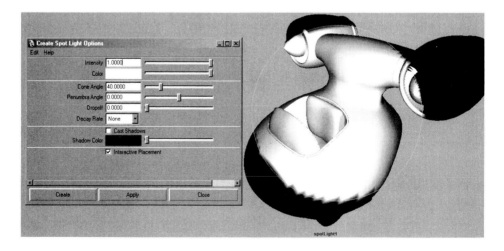

Types of Lights

Maya presents six types of lights: Ambient, Directional, Point, Spot, Area, and Volume (see Figure 11.3). You will often use combinations of these lights to achieve desired effects. Although lights in the real world are additive, and all have directions and positions, Maya gives you access to certain lights that just aren't possible outside the digital realm. Using a proper combination of these realistic and not-so-realistic lights, you can create compelling digital scenes. All of Maya's lights are created by choosing **Create → Lights** from either the main menu or Hypershade menu.

You can easily change from one light type to another for an existing light in the Attribute Editor.

Ambient Light

Ambient light appears to have no source of direction or position. It is most commonly used to control the overall brightness of a scene. Uniformly lit scenarios, such as haze, are best lit with Ambientlights. If used sparingly and carefully, they can be used to help uniformly soften your scene and reduce the number of directional or positional lights. Overuse of ambient light leads to very flat composition, so use it sparingly.

Maya gives you control over how much your Ambient light is omnidirectional (light from all directions) and how much is positional (light from one direction based on its position) through the **Ambient Shade** attribute. Figure 11.4 shows the various Ambient Shade values.

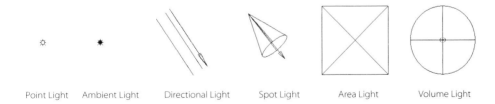

Point Light　Ambient Light　Directional Light　Spot Light　Area Light　Volume Light

Figure 11.3

The various types of lights in Maya, with their control symbols

Ambient Shade = 0.0　　Ambient Shade = 0.5　　Ambient Shade = 1.0

Figure 11.4

Ambient Shade controls how omnidirectional your Ambient light appears.

Directional, Point, and Spot Lights

Directional, Point, and Spot lights are the three most commonly used lights in Maya. Directional lights shine along a vector uniformly throughout your scene. Although their UI gizmos are placed in XYZ positional space, they actually do not have a position. Directional lights are most commonly used as distant light sources, such as the sun. Shadows cast from Directional lights tend to be smaller than shadows cast from other light sources since the light rays are parallel and do not spread. Figure 11.5 shows rendered images using each of the three lights.

Point lights spread light rays in all directions and have a definite world-space position. Think of a Point light as a lightbulb or candle. Point lights can have decay rates (loss and dissipation of energy over distance) and cast larger shadows than Directional lights because of their omnidirectional light rays.

Spot lights are cones of light defined by a position and direction. In addition to a decay rate, a Spot light has **Cone Angle**, **Penumbra Angle**, and **Dropoff** attributes. (These attributes are discussed in more detail later in this chapter in the section "Light Properties.") The control you have over both position and direction of the light makes Spot lights versatile.

Area Light

Area lights tend to be more computationally expensive yet yield softer lighting. Rather than shining a single light ray along a vector, Area lights shine according to a two-dimensional area. The number of rays emitted from the light are controlled by the size of the Area light's rectangular area. Therefore, if you scale the light larger, the light will become brighter.

Use Area lights when you want light to emanate from a large area, such as a white wall, rather than a single bulb. Figure 11.6a is rendered with a Spot light, and Figure 11.6b is rendered with an Area light. Notice how the Spot light creates a strong but smaller specular highlight, while the Area light creates a softer but longer highlight.

Figure 11.5

This chair is illuminated by a single Directional light, Point light, and Spot light. Notice the differences in how the light hits the surfaces.

Specular highlight refers to a shiny, reflective highlight on an illuminated object. Specularity exists on objects with Blinn, Phong, or anisotropic shading.

Directional Light   Point Light   Spot Light

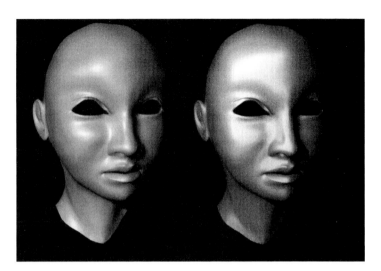

(a) Spot light   (b) Area light

Volume Light

Volume lights allow you to specify a boundary volume in which light shines. A major advantage to these lights is that you can see, in your interactive scene window, the 3D area in which your light exists, enabling you to easily control your light's range. As with Area lights, there is no Decay Rate option for Volume lights; a **Color Ramp** attribute is used for falloff effects. Figure 11.7 shows a spherical Volume light applied in a scene.

Light Properties

All types of light in Maya have attributes that you can modify. Some of these attributes are common to all lights, and others are specialized from light to light. You control all these properties in the Attribute Editor.

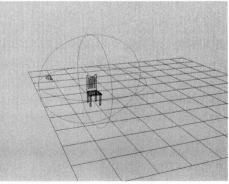

Figure 11.7

A spherical Volume light illuminates the chair. Notice that the brightest point occurs in the center of the volume and then the intensity falls off as the light reaches the edges of the volume.

Color, Intensity, and Gobos

The basic properties of light are color and intensity. Color simply refers to the color that your light emits, and intensity determines the brightness. You typically set these properties first on newly created lights. You can use the Color Chooser to tint your light a specific color. Alternatively, you can specify a texture to act as a mask (or gobo) for your light. *Gobo* is a theater term that refers to cutouts placed over the light to simulate the shadow of a scene element. When used effectively, gobos can save a lot of time by eliminating the need to model unseen scene props. To create a gobo, simply apply a texture to the **Color** attribute of a light. Black sections of the texture will block light, and white sections will allow light to pass through. To change the color of the light shining through this mask, change the Color Gain swatch in the mask's file node. Refer to the tutorial at the conclusion of this chapter for creating animated gobos. Figure 11.8 shows a gobo applied to a Spot light.

Unlike in the real world, you can actually create your lights with negative intensity, which eats up other light! Negative intensities work great for lighting areas that are typically always shadowed, such as a crevice. Since software-rendered digital light is restrained from bouncing realistically, negative lights can help add softness and realism to your scene.

You can create shadow masks by choosing black as the light color and white as the shadow color. The rendered result is a black scene with white shadows; you can then composite this result with other layers of the scene, giving you control of the shadows in postproduction. Note that you will also need to turn off Primary Visibility for the object casting the shadow and change the ground to a plain white color in order to get the best results of shadow masks.

For spotlights, you can create intensity and color curves to control values over time. To do this, twirl the Spot light's Light Effects panel down and click the Create button. You can then open the Graph Editor and edit the newly created lightInfo node's curve values.

Figure 11.8

The texture on the left is applied to the Color attribute of the Spot light to create a cutout gobo.

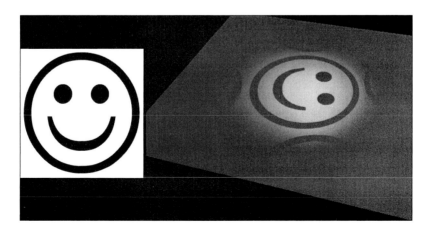

Decay Rate

Spot, Point, and Area lights all have a **Decay Rate** attribute that decays the light's intensity over a distance. You can choose from three decay rates:

Linear Decreases intensity proportionally to the distance.

Quadratic Decreases intensity proportionally to the square of the distance (distance × distance), which is how intensity decays in the real world.

Cubic Decreases intensity proportionally to the cube of the distance (distance × distance × distance). The light's color stays the same no matter how far it is from the light source.

Decay rate begins to affect light intensity at a distance greater than 1 unit from the source.

Decay on Volume lights is created quite differently. Decay is controlled by a gradient specified in the Color Range section of the light's Attribute Editor. The left side of the range represents the color of the farthest end of the light, and the right side controls the color of the light source. Figure 11.9 shows an example of applying dark colors to the color range.

Light Linking

Specific objects that are illuminated by specific lights in Maya are referred to as being *linked*. Each light has an Illuminates By Default option that simply links the light to all objects in your scene. This option is enabled by default when the light is created. If you are working on a simple scene, you usually will keep the default settings and let all your lights shine on all objects. As your scene gets more complex, you will want to control your light linking both for aesthetic reasons and to drastically reduce render times.

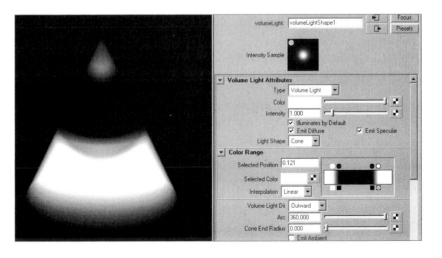

Figure 11.9

Control the decay rate for a Volume light by adding dark colors to the color range.

One way to control light linking is through Maya's Relationship Editor (choose **Window → Relationship Editors → Light Linking → Light-Centric** or **Object-Centric** or choose **Lighting/Shading → Light Linking Editor → Light-Centric** or **Object-Centric**). Light linking simply presents the current linking configuration for the scene. The object-centric viewing mode organizes a one-to-many relationship between a specific object and the scene's lights. Here, you can select which lights shine on the specific object. Light-centric mode organizes a one-to-many relationship between a specific light and the scene's objects. Figure 11.10 shows a light-centric view of the relationship editor and its rendered results.

You can also change the linking relationships through your 3D workspace using several options found in the Lighting/Shading menu. Select the objects and lights whose linking information you want to change. Choose **Lighting/Shading → Make Light Links** to link them or **Lighting/Shading → Break Light Links** to sever them.

Note that breaking a link between an object and all lights will not make the object invisible; light linking affects only how objects are illuminated. If an object in your scene is not linked to any lights, it renders out pure black, occluding other lit objects. This occlusion can come in handy for creating masked render passes for compositing scenes together.

Figure 11.10

This image shows a light-centric view of the Relationship Editor. (a) Since the sphere is unlinked from the Spot light, it does not receive any of its illumination. In picture (b) All objects are linked and therefore illuminated by the Spot light.

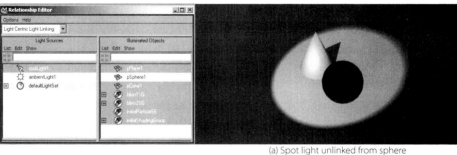

(a) Spot light unlinked from sphere

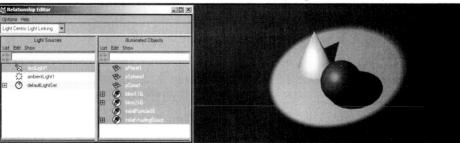

(b) Spot light linked to sphere

You can select objects and lights based on light-linking information. Select a light and choose **Lights/Shading → Select Objects Illuminated By Light** to select all the objects linked to that light. Select an object and choose **Lights/Shading → Select Lights Illuminating Object** to select all the lights linked to that object.

Spot Light Properties

Spot lights have some unique attributes that control Cone Angle, Penumbra Angle, and Dropoff. The Cone Angle attribute controls the spread of the light beam. The default value of 40° typically is sufficient for most Spot lights. A wider angle (up to 180°) can often be used for fill lights.

Penumbra Angle softens the light by blurring the outside edge of the light cone. A positive Penumbra Angle value blurs the outside edge, and a negative value blurs the inside edge. Figure 11.11 shows the effect of altering the penumbra angle.

Dropoff is similar to Linear Decay Rate, but instead of decaying over a distance from the light source, it controls the rate at which light intensity decreases from the center to the edge of the light beam. Typically, appropriate values range from 0 to 50.

Spot Light Effects

Two attributes unique to Spot lights are found in the Light Effects section of the Attribute Editor: Barn Doors and Decay Regions. Both attributes are turned off by default. Barn doors are basically shutters that cover the edges of the light cone and can be applied from the top, bottom, left, and right. The Barn Doors values represent the angle between the Spot light's center and the doors. The Barn Doors attribute is often used to block light from emitting past a certain point in your scene; traditional stage lighters rely on these shutters to control light spillage. See the effects of barn doors in Figure 11.12.

Decay Regions lets you create regions that determine where in the Spot light's beam illumination occurs, as seen in 11.13. You can manipulate these truncated coned regions through the Attribute Editor or by setting decay region manipulators. These manipulators are discussed in the following section.

Figure 11.11

Notice how a negative penumbra blurs the edges inward, while a positive penumbra blurs the edges outward.

Penumbra = –10   Penumbra = 0   Penumbra = 10

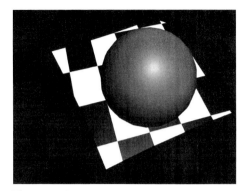

Figure 11.12
You can control hard-edged boundaries of your Spot light by using Barn Doors.

Figure 11.13
Specify regions of illumination on your Spot light by using Decay Regions. (Fog, discussed later in this chapter, was added to the light to better illustrate the regions.)

Light Manipulator

The Light Manipulator is a visual display on the Maya Heads Up Display (HUD) that allows you to control light attributes interactively; it is useful for precisely positioning targets, decay regions, and other light effects. To enable a Light Manipulator control, select a light and choose **Display → Show → Light Manipulators** or select the Show Manipulator tool from the Tool Box. You will then see a series of extra controls surrounding your light.

Below the light's handle, you should see a control (called the Index Manipulator) made up from a circle with a tick mark. Clicking the Index Manipulator cycles through the seven Light Manipulator modes: None, Center Of Interest/Origin, Pivot, Cone Radius, Penumbra Radius, Decay Region, and Origin/Radius Decay. You will notice that the tick mark on the Index Manipulator changes its direction with each mode. To display a specific light manipulator, select a light, choose **Display → Rendering → Camera/Light Manipulator**, and then choose a manipulator. Figure 11.14 maps the seven display modes of the Index Manipulator.

Figure 11.14
HUD icons for the seven display modes of the Index Manipulator

None   Center Of   Pivot   Cone Radius   Penumbra   Decay Region   Origin/Radius
              Interest/Origin   Radius   Decay

Move the Center of Interest/Origin

This manipulator allows you to change the location (Origin) and direction (Center Of Interest) of a light source. Having the ability to visually place the Center Of Interest of a light ensures that you know exactly the direction in which your light is pointing. All lights include this manipulator.

Move the Pivot Point

This manipulator lets you move the pivot point for the vector between the light Origin and Center Of Interest. Click the pivot point (the bull's-eye near the light Origin), and drag it along the vector. Then, move either the light Origin or the Center Of Interest to see the vector between the two rotate about the pivot point.

Move the Cone Radius

Move the yellow Cone Radius manipulator to change the angle of the Spot light's beam. Only the Spot light contains this manipulator.

Move the Penumbra Radius

Like the Cone Radius, the Penumbra Radius modifier controls the value of the Penumbra Angle attribute. As you move the manipulator, you will see an outline of the penumbra on your light. Only the Spot light contains this manipulator.

Move the Decay Regions

This manipulator allows you to visually set the Decay Regions attribute by moving the rings along the light beam. For best results, use IPR renders to preview the results. Only the Spot light contains this manipulator.

Figure 11.15

Looking through the selected light, you can see the Barn Doors attribute represented by vertical and horizontal lines.

Move the Barn Doors

This manipulator allows you to control the Barn Doors attribute on a Spot light, as seen in Figure 11.15. You must be looking through the light (choose **Panels → Look Through Selected**) in order to see the on-screen controls; MM drag the horizontal and vertical lines to adjust Barn Doors values.

Using Shadows

Knowing when and how to use shadows in Maya is important for both render times and aesthetic results. By default, Maya's lights do not cast shadows. Typically you do not want every light casting them since they are computationally expensive. Instead, only key lights should cast shadows. The two types of shadows in Maya's default renderer are depth-map and raytraced.

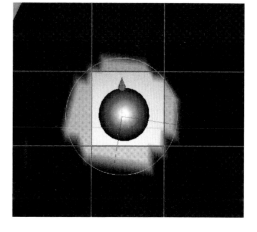

Depth-Map Shadows

Depth maps are data structures within Maya that contain information defining the depth between the light source and the scene's surfaces. This information, referred to as Z-depth, is a grayscale image map that colors surfaces based on their distance from the light. To obtain this information, Maya calculates Z-Depth by looking through the light's point of view and determining which parts of objects are occluded (and therefore in shadow) and which are seen (and therefore shined upon). Logically, the only type of light that cannot produce depth-map shadows is Ambient light, since its source does not have a discrete position and rotation.

To render a light using depth-map shadows, enable Use Depth Map Shadows found in the Shadows section of the light's Attribute Editor. In this section, you can then specify other attributes to tell Maya how your depth-map shadow should look and be calculated.

Color

The default color of shadows is black. Although black shadows may look fairly typical, adjusting the shadow color can create good contrast between light and shadow in your scene. For instance, if you have a warm light color (such as a light yellow-orange), a cool colored shadow (such as a purple-blue) can really give good contrast.

Depth-map shadows do not take into account light rays passing through transparent objects. By making the shadow color lighter, you can simulate transparent shadows, as seen in Figure 11.16.

Dmap Resolution, Filter Size, and Bias

Remember that depth maps are image maps with a finite amount of information. Dmap Resolution controls the size of the depth map; by default, the Dmap Resolution value is 512. The higher the Dmap Resolution value (such 1024 or 2048), the sharper the shadows appear since their increased resolution allows for more shadow data stored. Lower dmap resolutions (such as values of 64 or 128) yield softer shadows.

Figure 11.16

Notice how the shadow of an opaque object (a) is identical to the shadow of a transparent object (b). Solve this discrepancy by choosing a lighter shadow color (c).

(a)   (b)   (c)

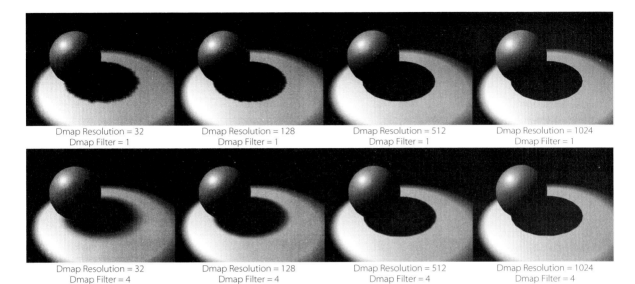

| Dmap Resolution = 32 | Dmap Resolution = 128 | Dmap Resolution = 512 | Dmap Resolution = 1024 |
| Dmap Filter = 1 | Dmap Filter = 1 | Dmap Filter = 1 | Dmap Filter = 1 |

| Dmap Resolution = 32 | Dmap Resolution = 128 | Dmap Resolution = 512 | Dmap Resolution = 1024 |
| Dmap Filter = 4 | Dmap Filter = 4 | Dmap Filter = 4 | Dmap Filter = 4 |

The quality of the depth map is controlled by the filter size. The filter blurs the shadow edges so that aliasing from the dmap resolution disappear. Be warned, though: increasing this filter too much can impact render times dramatically. Experiment with different values based on your dmap resolution (the smaller your resolution, the larger your filter should be); usually a value of 3 or 4 should suffice for most shadow scenarios.

Dmap Bias offsets the depth map either toward or away from the light source. Usually you will keep the default value of 0.001. If your shadows appear to be detached from the casting surface, gradually increase the bias. If you see artifacts such as spots or streaks in your shadows, gradually decrease the bias until they disappear. Figure 11.17 shows the effects of various Dmap Resolution and Dmap Filter settings.

Figure 11.17

Lower dmap resolutions yield softer shadows, but become more sensitive to the filter size.

Disk-Based Dmaps

Depth maps are recalculated and re-created for each light for every frame in the animation. If you are using depth-map shadows in your scene, then for each render, Maya has to calculate depth maps for each depth-map-enabled light source for each frame of animation. You can see how shadows have a significant impact on render time! In many cases, the actual depth-map information of the lights does not change from render to render or even from frame to frame in an animation. Luckily we can use disk-based dmaps to permanently write out the depth information to a file so that Maya does not need to recalculate this information for every render.

So when should you use disk-based dmaps? Depth map information does not change unless the light or objects are moved. Furthermore, even if your camera moves through your scene (as in a flythrough), as long as the objects and light don't move, you can use single-frame disk-based dmaps. You can modify the attributes of the light or objects and still reuse the saved depth maps.

To use disk-based depth maps on a single-frame render or flythrough, choose Reuse Existing Dmap(s) from the Disk Based Dmaps drop-down list in the Depth Map Shadow Attributes section of the light's Attribute Editor. Maya will calculate the depth map for the first time you render and save it to disk. The map will be read from disk during subsequent renders. By default, depth maps are saved in the renderData/depth folder of the current project. You can choose to append the scene name and light name to the dmap file by enabling the corresponding check boxes.

You can also use disk-based dmaps on animated scenes that have moving lights and/or objects. If, for each render, you want to make changes to attributes of the light or objects but do not want change the way they move, you can save a sequence of dmaps to be read for subsequent renders. Do this by enabling the Add Frame Ext check box. Maya will calculate the depth map for each frame the first time you render the animation and save the frames to disk in a sequence. Subsequent renders of the animation will read from this sequence.

If you have previously saved disk-based dmaps and have moved the light and/or objects, the depth maps need to be updated. To overwrite previously saved disk-based dmaps, choose Overwrite Existing Dmap(s) and render your scene or animation. If you are happy with the new placement of the light and/or objects, be sure to choose Reuse Existing Dmaps to read your newly created maps.

If you want to no longer read from saved dmaps, set Disk Based Dmaps to Off in the drop-down menu. Maya will then calculate a new depth map for each render of each frame. By default, Disk Based Dmaps is set to Off.

Raytraced Shadows

Though more computationally expensive than depth map shadows, raytracing produces crisper, and sometimes more realistic, shadows. Raytracing shoots rays from the light source into the scene. Each of these rays then bounces off objects and hits other objects where it reflects again and so on. You can specify the number of reflections and reflectivity of the objects. Although raytracing can do soft shadows, the visual benefits when used for that purpose are minimal over dmap shadows. Raytracing really is beneficial for rendering crisp shadows and lighting transparent objects; unlike rendering with dmap shadows, raytracing accurately creates shadows when the light shines on an object with transparency.

IPR does not support raytraced shadows; you must completely re-render your scene to see them.

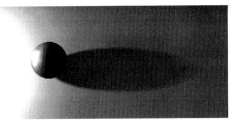

Depth Map Shadow: Dmap Resolution = 512,
Filter Size = 3

Raytraced Shadow: Shadow Rays = 3

Figure 11.18

Notice how the ray-traced shadow actually dissipates the farther it gets from the sphere. The depth-map shadow does not dissipate; its soft edge (based on its Dmap Resolution and Filter Size values) is only elongated.

To render with raytraced shadows, enable the Use Ray Trace Shadows check box in the Shadows section of your light's Attribute Editor. You also need to turn on Raytracing in the Raytracing Quality section of the Render Settings window (choose **Window → Rendering Editors → Render Settings**).

Raytraced shadows produce shadows a bit differently for each type of light. If you want to create a blurred shadow that softly becomes lighter as it goes farther from an object, use raytraced shadows on an Area light. Refer to Figure 11.18 for a comparison between raytraced and depth-map shadows.

Shadow Radius for Ambient lights, Light Angle for Directional lights, and Light Radius for Point, Spot, and Volume lights determine the softness of the shadow edges. A value of zero produces hard, sharp edges; as the value increases, the shadow edge appears softer. You may notice that as these three values increase (each light has its own limits), the edges become quite grainy. Increasing the Shadow Rays value blurs these grains but also can add significantly to render times. Figure 11.19 shows this difference in shadow quality. If you are trying to simply render soft shadows and have no transparent or highly reflective objects in your scene, depth-map shadows tend to be much more efficient with little differences.

Ray Depth Limit determines the maximum number of times a light ray can bounce around your scene. If the Reflections value in the Render Settings window is lower than Ray Depth Limit, Ray Depth Limit will adapt to the lower value. Increasing this limit will allow your scene to more accurately produce shadows, especially those appearing through transparent objects. For more information on using raytracing for rendering scene elements, refer to Chapter 14.

Figure 11.19

The number of shadow rays determines the graininess of the shadow. There is a noticeable difference between the values of 1 and 10 but minimal visual difference between 10 and 20. A higher number causes substantial render-time slowdowns.

Shadow Rays = 1

Shadow Rays = 10

Shadow Rays = 20

Light Effects

Maya gives you the power to create interesting lighting effects such as fog, lens flares, glow, halos, and gobos. Compositionally speaking, it is important to not go overboard with these effects. During the 1990s, a trend was to add lens flares to everything; the industry quickly was oversaturated with this effect and almost ended their use in even proper circumstances. Lighting effects can also dramatically increase your render times, so use them appropriately. Light effects are accessed under the Light Effects section of a light's Attribute Editor.

Fog

Light Fog lets you simulate volumetric lighting by creating a fog effect within the light's beam. You can add a fog effect to Point, Spot, and Volume lights. There are three types of fog in Maya: Light, Environment, and Volume. Under the Light Effects section of the light's Attribute Editor, click the Light Fog checkerboard button. By default, Maya creates and loads a Light Fog node. To change Light Fog to Environment Fog or Volume Fog, open the Hypershade (choose **Window → Rendering Editors → Hypershade**). Scroll down the Create Maya Nodes list and twirl down the Volumetric section. You can create a new node by clicking Env Fog or Volume Fog and then apply it to your light's Light Fog attribute. (MM drag the fog node from the Hypershade to the Light Fog attribute.)

All lights allow you to alter the intensity of the fog in the Attribute Editor. Fog Intensity controls how bright and dense your fog appears. Spot lights allow you to change Fog Spread and Fog Intensity. Fog Spread controls how the fog decreases its intensity as the distance increases from the light source. See Figures 11.20 and 11.21 for examples of Fog Spread and Fog Intensity.

Point lights handle fog attributes a bit differently than they handle Spot lights. Point lights give you control of Fog Type, Fog Radius, and Fog Intensity. The three fog types—Normal, Linear, and Exponential—control the intensity falloff for the fog. Figure 11.22 illustrates these fog types. Normal allows the fog intensity to remain constant regardless of the distance. The Linear option decreases the fog intensity as the distance from the light source increases, and the Exponential setting decreases the fog intensity as the distance increases exponentially. The Fog Radius attribute controls the size of the fog spherical volume.

Figure 11.20

Examples of various Fog Spread values

Fog Spread = 0.5   Fog Spread = 1   Fog Spread = 2

Fog Intensity = 0.5   Fog Intensity = 1   Fog Intensity = 2

Figure 11.21
Examples of various Fog Intensity values

Figure 11.22
Examples of the three types of fog available for Point lights

Light Fog

Light Fog is the most common type of fog you will use on your lights. The primary distinction with Light Fog is that it can cast depth-map shadows; other fog types cannot. Through the lightFog node attached to your light, you can change the fog density and color. By default, Color Based Transparency is enabled. This attribute controls how objects in fog are obscured based on the Color and Density values. If it's enabled, objects are fully shaded, not just flat-shaded silhouettes. Also, Color Based Transparency depends on the brightness of the fog color, so if you have a dark fog, disable this attribute to properly render your fog.

Fast Drop Off controls to what degree objects are obscured by fog effects. If disabled, each object will be obscured by the same amount, based on the Density value. If Fast Drop Off is enabled, objects will obscure to varying degrees based on the Density value and the amount of fog between the camera and the object. Enable this option for more realistic results; be careful to not make your fog Density values too large or you may lose sight of certain objects in your scene.

The shadowing options for light fog are found in the Attribute Editor, under **Shadows → Depth Map Shadow Attributes** section of the particular light (rather than in the fog node's properties). The two fog shadow attributes are Fog Shadow Intensity and Fog Shadow Samples. Fog Shadow Intensity affects the darkness of the fog's shadow, and the Fog Shadow Samples controls the graininess. See Figure 11.23 for visual examples of these two attributes.

Environment Fog

Environment Fog is not directly controlled by particular lights; it represents general fog that exists within your scene. This fog affects how clear or obscure objects appear. Unlike Light Fog, Environment Fog does not cast shadows. To create Fog, open the scene's Render Settings window (choose **Window → Rendering Editors → Render Settings**), and look under Render Options in the Maya Software tab. Here, you can apply a fog shader by clicking the checkered button. The two types of Environment Fog are Simple and Physical, each with unique attributes.

Figure 11.23

Notice the differences in the shadow darkness and graininess with various Fog Shadow Intensity and Samples values.

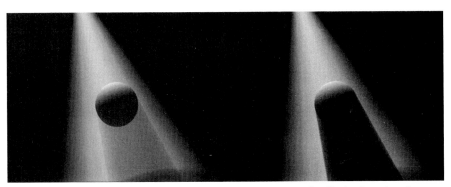

Fog Shadow Intensity = 1   Fog Shadow Intensity = 5

Fog Shadow Samples = 5   Fog Shadow Samples = 30

SIMPLE FOG

By default, an Environmental Fog node is "simple," meaning you have control over only a few controls to make a simple representation of fog. As with Light Fog, the Color Based Transparency attribute controls whether your objects are fully shaded or flat shaded. Saturation Distance is the distance at which the fog becomes completely saturated (the fog's color reaches the Color value), and objects beyond this distance are unseen.

You can use layers to attach textures (typically 3D textures) to control the fog density. Enable layers and apply textures to simulate cloud patchiness within your fog. You can also control where the fog exists by enabling Use Height. Fog renders only within the range between the Min and Max Height values. Control the falloff between the fog height edges by specifying a blend range distance. Figure 11.24 shows an example of simple Environment Fog.

Figure 11.24

Simple Environment Fog with a Height range specified

PHYSICAL FOG

Physical Fog uses a more accurate, physically based system to simulate air, water vapor, and, optionally, a volume of water. These volumes each have their own attributes to create realistic fog. You enable Physical Fog in the Environmental Fog material's Attribute Editor. The following list shows the available Physical Fog types:

Type	Description
Uniform Fog	Fog with uniform density in all directions.
Atmospheric	Fog gets thinner as it moves upward.
Sky	Best for scenes with large skies and long-distance visibility, the Sky fog type blends the fog properly with the horizon.
Water	This fog scatters light from above for underwater scenarios. You can use it for shots that are under water or for objects that are seen under water from above.
Water/Fog	Uniform fog that appears above water.
Water/Atmos	Atmospheric fog that appears above water.
Water/Sky	Full sky fog that appears above water.

The Fog Axis attribute lets you specify which axis serves as "up" for the fog. (This is disabled with Uniform Fog.) Planet Radius controls the number of units in your scene's atmosphere; a larger value simulates a larger atmosphere.

You can change various attributes such as Color, Density, and Volume in the Fog, Air and Water sections. (These are enabled based on the fog type you select.) The Sun section controls the illumination of sunlight in your fog. Clipping planes control minimum and maximum distances in which your fog can exist.

VOLUME FOG

Volume Fog allows you to control a spherical, conical, or cubic volume of air particles. Volume Fog is useful when you want to create encapsulated 3D fogs, such as a cloud. To create, select Sphere, Cube or Cone from the **Create → Volume Primitives** menu. You can either specify a solid color for your fog or use the Color Ramp Input setting for a ramped series of colors.

In the Dropoff section of the Attribute Editor, you can specify the dropoff shape as Off, Sphere, Cube, Cone, or Light Cone (see Figure 11.25). A Light Cone dropoff shape causes the fade to occur toward the point of the cone shape, and a Cone dropoff shape will seem more uniform within a conical shape. Edge Dropoff controls how harsh the density falls off toward the volume edge, and Axial Dropoff (available only with cones) controls the density drop-off down the center axis of a cone.

You can specify two drop-off methods. The default Scale Opacity multiplies the density by the fade value, causing uniform drop-off transparency. Subtract Density is useful to use if you have a texture controlling the transparency of your fog. The low-density regions will be transparent while high-density regions are barely affected. Use this if you want to preserve the texture or puffiness of your fog volume.

Figure 11.25

You can choose from five drop-off types for volume lights. Notice how the Cone type falls off from the center while the Light Cone type falls off from the cone point.

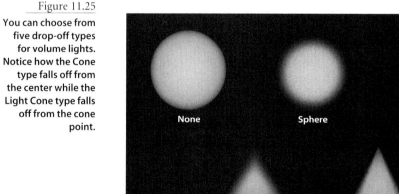

OptiF/X

At times, you might want to add visual effects, such as glows, halos, and lens flares, to your light sources. These light effects are applied in postprocessing (created after the frame is rendered) and are visible only if the light source is visible from your camera view. To create an Optical FX shader on your Point, Area, Spot, or Volume light, click the checkered texture button next to the Light Glow field in the Light Effects section of the Attribute Editor. By default, a four-star glow will be set active on your light.

Glow and Halo

By default, Glow Linear is enabled on an Optical FX shader, and halos are disabled by being set to None. Glow and Halo share other types, including Exponential, Ball, Lens Flare, and Rim Halo. Figures 11.26 and 11.27 show the various Glow and Halo types. Notice that Glow affects the inner portion of the effect and that Halo controls the density of the outer surrounding portions of the light effect.

Glow and Halo sizes are controlled by the Spread attribute. Additional Glow attributes include noise, level and opacity controls. Glow noise is useful if you want to fake something such as smoke or fog distorting the uniformity of the glow. When using noise, be sure to tweak the offset and scale settings in the Noise section in the Attribute Editor.

| Glow Linear | Glow Exponential | Glow Ball | Glow Lens Flare | Glow Rim Halo |

Figure 11.26

The five types of glows

| Halo Linear | Halo Exponential | Halo Ball | Halo Lens Flare | Halo Rim Halo |

Figure 11.27

The five types of halos

You can animate the Uoffset and Voffset noise values to simulate smoke animating over your light.

Glow Star Level controls how sharp the star points appear. A lower value blurs the star effect, and a higher value sharpens. Modifying the Glow Opacity attribute changes how opaque or transparent the glow appears.

Lens Flares

Lens Flares are used to re-create the lens imperfections when strong lights are seen by the camera. To enable, check the Lens Flare check box in the Optical FX attributes. Since Lens Flares represent a portion of the color spectrum, the color depends on the Flare Color and Flare Col Spread attributes. Flare Col Spread represents a range of colors based on Flare Color; a higher Flare Col Spread value produces a wider range of colors. Flare Num Circles controls the number of circles seen by the camera, Flare Min/Max Size determines the size of the circles, and Flare Length modifies the length of the flare beam. Flare Focus blurs and sharpens the flare circles, and Flare Vertical And Horizontal determines the flare's position. Refer to Figure 11.28 for examples of these attributes.

Hands On: Creating Animated Gobos Using Paint Effects

Figure 11.28

Various attributes for changing the way lens flares are rendered.

Common uses of gobos include window silhouettes and tree shadows. The following tutorial shows how to use Paint Effects and spotlights to quickly create great-looking tree

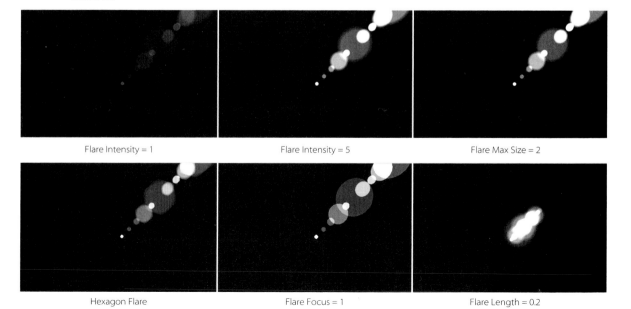

Flare Intensity = 1   Flare Intensity = 5   Flare Max Size = 2

Hexagon Flare   Flare Focus = 1   Flare Length = 0.2

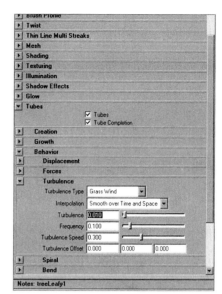

Figure 11.29

Paint Effects is used to create a tree branch in the camera's view.

Figure 11.30

You can adjust animation for the tree branch by accessing the Turbulence portion of the Attribute Editor.

gobos. The basic idea is to create a silhouette of a Paint Effects brush, add animation to it, render it, and then use those rendered frames as an image sequence for a spotlight's texture.

1. Open GoboTutorial01.mb from the included CD or create your own Paint Effects brush stroke. (See Chapter 17 for more on Paint Effects.) Your scene should have a stroke of a simple Paint Effects branch (taken from the TreeLeafy.mel preset in the Visor) that takes up the majority of the camera's frame, as seen in Figure 11.29.

2. There is some default wind animation already on the stroke, but you can adjust the animation by referring to the Attribute Editor for treeLeafy1 and choosing **Tubes →
Behavior → Turbulence** (see Figure 11.30). Set the Turbulence attribute to 0.01. If you play the Timeline, you should see the tree slightly bend and rustle.

Since our goal is to create a mask for the tree and use it as a gobo, we need a way to render the tree all white (which will eventually block light) and the empty space all black (which will eventually allow light to pass). You can do this in several ways. Here we will set the incandescence level for each tube material to 1.0.

3. Select the Paint Effects object and untwirl the Shading section of the treeLeafy1 node. Adjust the Incandescence sliders in the Shading and Tube Shading sections all the way to white.

Figure 11.31

The silhouette of the Paint Effects tree can be used as a mask for the gobo.

Figure 11.32

Applying the frames from the Paint Effects batch render to the color input of the light creates dynamic gobos.

4. Render the current frame to be sure that the Paint Effects object is completely white and looks similar to Figure 11.31.

5. After setting any desired render globals (although the default for the provided scene should be fine), batch-render the scene for 200 frames by choosing **Render → Batch Render**. (For more on render settings and batch rendering, see Chapter 15.) You now have a sequence of images that can be used as an animated gobo.

6. To try out your animated gobo, make a new scene, create a plane, and make a new Spot light. Position the light so that it points to the plane. With the light still selected, open the Attribute Editor and click the checkered Texture button in the Color attribute. Choose File from the Create Render Node window. Under Image Name, navigate to the first frame of the batch-rendered file. Finally, check the Use Image Sequence check box so that Maya knows to cycle through the images for each frame.

If you render this new scene with the applied gobo, you should see the outline of the tree on the plane. You now have a great-looking, moving tree shadow that can be used for outdoor scenes or perhaps casting through a bedroom window. Figure 11.32 shows a render of the tree's projection onto the plane.

Summary

This chapter has explored and explained all the basics you will need to successfully light your Maya scenes. By understanding the artistic qualities and functions of lighting, in conjunction with the power available to you in Maya, you should be able to efficiently illuminate your objects. Because lighting is computationally intensive, it's important to know the many types of lights and the various shadowing methods, fog, and light effects so that you can use them effectively to realize your artistic visions within the inevitable time constraints.

CHAPTER 12

Shading and Texturing for Animation

Creating sophisticated shaders in Maya involves creating complex connections between material and render nodes. Therefore, this operation can be frustratingly confusing for the beginner. In this chapter, you will learn how to texture the inorganic form of the MacGizmo and the highly organic body of Machismo himself. You will learn how to create procedural, computer-generated effects to render highly naturalistic metal surfaces and how to set up UV maps for painting file-based textures for Machismo. We will build shading connections in the Hypershade and learn about the connections between lighting, shading, and rendering your subjects.

- Understanding Maya textures
- The Hypershade window
- Building simple shading networks
- Shading the MacGizmo
- Shading Machismo: The UV foundation
- Creating Machismo's texture

Understanding Maya Textures

No aspect of Maya animation is more intimidating to the new and intermediate user than creating shaders or materials for use in animation. Interestingly, and perhaps ironically, in no aspect of Maya is it more important for the user to understand how Maya's nodal structure works. Creating the exact look you want requires a fairly fine degree of control. It also requires that you know and understand how Maya's nodes connect as well as which of Maya's formidable array of surfaces, textures, and render node utilities to use for a particular application.

Maya offers the user a wide array of procedural shading techniques and powerful methods of introducing file textures into shading networks. Procedural textures are defined mathematically in the computer according to user-defined attributes, while file textures are bitmapped images that can be applied to models using various mapping methods. Either type of shader can be used effectively; sometimes, combining them can result in extraordinarily lifelike shaders. But regardless of which type of shader you use, your efforts in creating convincing shaders inevitably lead to the Hypershade.

The Hypershade

The Hypershade is Maya's primary shading editor, letting you create shading networks of extraordinary complexity and depth. It also lets you see first hand how different nodes connect to form those shaders. It is much like the Hypergraph in that you can see the dependency graph with all a node's upstream and downstream connections, but it has the advantage of showing each node as a swatch icon, which provides visual feedback for the various connections you have made. Figure 12.1 shows the Hypershade with key buttons and areas labeled.

The first thing you might notice is that the Hypershade is a fairly large window, and this is its greatest disadvantage: it takes up quite a bit of screen real estate. Toggle Create Bar On/Off lets you hide the Create portion of the window so you can make the window smaller but still see the same amount of information. The Show Work Area Only and Show Storage Area Only buttons let you further isolate what you are working on. The Clear Graph button lets you hide the shading network shown in the work area. The Graph Materials On Selected Objects button lets you instantly expand the shading network of the object you have selected in the viewport, saving the time you might spend hunting for the proper shader in the storage area. The Show Upstream And Downstream Connections button instantly expands the shading network of the material chosen in the storage area or one that has been placed and selected in the work area. The new Container buttons (four of them) allow for simplification of the Hypershade when excessive nodes exist in the work area.

Toggle Create Bar On/Off

Show Work Area Only

Show Storage Area Only

Clear Graph (work area)

Graph Materials On Selected Objects

Show Up And Downstream Connections

Create/Delete Container

Contract/Expand Container Display

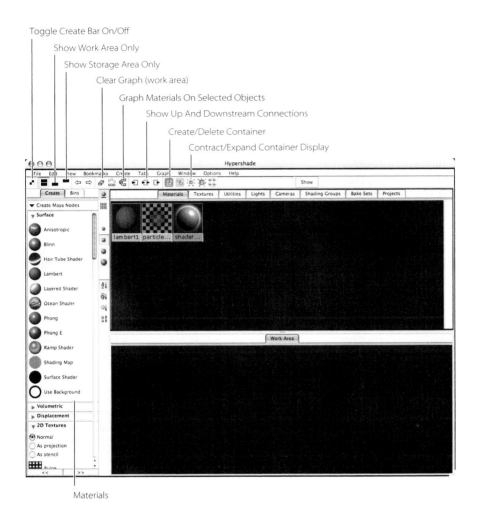

Figure 12.1

The Hypershade in all its glory!

Materials

RMB clicking in either the storage area or the work area displays the entire range of Hypershade menu items. As such, it makes the menu bar above somewhat redundant. You can even access the material creation commands normally found in the Create Bar. For speed, it is often best to work with the Hypershade marking menu accessed by RMB clicking in the window.

In the rest of the chapter, rather than saying, "choose **Create → Node**," we will say, "Create a node" or "Add a node." You will know to access these nodes using either the Create Bar or the Create menu.

The Hypershade is much more than a material-creation or texture-mapping tool. It is also a tool for organizing materials and the textures, utilities, lights, cameras, shading groups, and bake sets associated with them. For large projects with enormous numbers of shaders, this organizational capability is invaluable, but as we will be creating individual shading networks, it will not concern us here.

One new organizational feature of the Hypershade is the ability to create containers, special nodes that (as the name implies) contain other nodes. Container nodes have no function on their own beyond organizational purposes, but they can hide a great deal of detail in the work area, simplifying the structure of complex nodes when that detail is not needed. To create a container node, select one or more nodes in the storage or work tabs, then click the Create Container button on the toolbar (or choose **Edit → Create Container** from the Hypershade menu). In the work area, you will see that the selected items have

Figure 12.2

The new container node

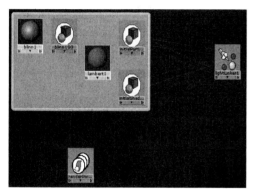

been "absorbed" into a new container node (denoted by its rounded corners). Double-clicking on the container node (or clicking the Expand Container Display button) reveals the contents of the container, as shown in Figure 12.2, while clicking the Contract Container Display button hides the contents. To move items into or out of the container, Alt+Shift+LM drag the nodes into or out of the container. To remove a container, press the Delete Container button with the container selected. Containers can be very useful for complex scenes or render nodes, but as we are mostly working with simple shaders in this chapter, we will forgo use of containers here.

Building Simple Shading Networks

As stated earlier, building shading networks involves making connections between different attributes on different nodes. You can do this in several ways, and we will use the Hypershade. Let's begin by creating a simple texture of the world using two NURBS spheres.

1. Open GlobeTexture.mb from the CD. In it, you will see what appears to be a NURBS sphere located at the world origin. Actually, there are two NURBS spheres, one right on top of and slightly larger than the other.

2. Open the Outliner either as a separate window or by pressing the Outliner/Persp layout shortcut on the toolbar. You can see the two pieces of geometry: GlobeGeo and AtmosphereGeo. It is common to start creating shader networks by RM clicking a piece of geometry and choosing **Materials → Assign New Material** from the marking menu, but when one piece of geometry obscures another, this method is very difficult. Instead, we will create the network, select the object, and assign the network directly.

Proper file management is extremely important to shading operations, especially when working with external files. When you copy these project files off the CD, it is crucial that you set the project to the proper project folder. If you don't, you will still be able to place, see, and render files. However, when you save and reopen the files, you run the risk of losing the link between the Maya file and the external file and all your objects could display without your textures.

3. Choose **Window → Rendering Editors → Hypershade** to open the Hypershade.

4. In the Create Bar, click the Lambert button to create a new Lambert material and place it in the work area. Zoom out by RM dragging to the left with the Alt (Option on the Mac) key held down in the work area.

Do not modify any of the three default materials in the scene, especially the Lambert1 material, unless you want every object in the scene to be created with that surface. This can be particularly irritating if you map an image onto the color channel of the Lambert1 material in the Hypershade. Every object you create from that point on will have that image mapped to it.

5. Ctrl+double-click the title of the Lambert*n* node in the Hypershade and rename it Earth_mat.

6. Scroll down in the Create Bar until you reach 2D Textures. Check Normal as the projection method. As we will be placing this texture onto NURBS spheres, they already have UV coordinates, so Normal works fine.

7. Click the File button to place a file node and a 2D texture placement node in the work area.

8. Double-click the File*n* node to display it in the Attribute Editor. The File node places a single, flattened image in a shader network. The place2dTexture node is the node that tells Maya how the image should be placed and rendered on the surface.

9. Click the File button (the one with the folder icon) next to the Image Name text field to open the Open File dialog box. Select GlobeTexture.tga and click Open. You might have to set the Enable pop-up in the Open dialog to Image (all formats) rather than the default IFF in order for Maya to allow you to open the TGA image file. Notice that if you set the project properly, Maya will default to the sourceimages folder in your project folder. This is the default location for images used in textures.

Now we need to link the file node to the color channel of the Lambert material. It is possible to simply MM drag the File1 node on top of Earth_mat and choose Default to connect the OutColor attribute of the file node to the color channel of Earth_mat, but let's explore the fine degree of control over these connections Maya allows.

1. RM click the Output connection arrow on the File1 node in the Hypershade, as shown at the top of Figure 12.3.

Figure 12.3

The steps for connecting attributes directly in the Hypershade

2. From the marking menu, scroll down and choose **OutColor → OutColor**, as shown in the middle of Figure 12.3. Notice, however, that you can choose to connect the R, G, and B color channels separately, if you want.

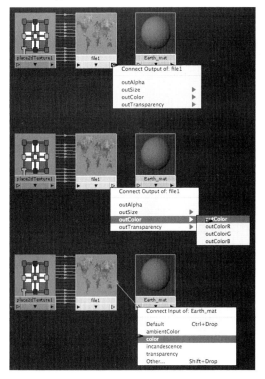

3. When you release the mouse button, a line appears that is attached to the cursor of your mouse. RM click the Connect Input triangle on Earth_mat, as shown at the bottom of Figure 12.3.

4. From the marking menu, choose **Color**. When you release the mouse button, the swatch changes color to reflect the new color map.

5. To apply the map, select GlobeGeo in the Outliner, RM click Earth_mat in the Hypershade, and choose **Assign Material To Selection** from the marking menu.

6. Move AtmosphereGeo away from GlobeGeo (or hide the other globe) and you will notice that the image is mapped improperly on the geometry. To fix this, double-click the place2dTexture*n* node in the work area. If you see nothing but two gray spheres, press 6 on your keyboard to enter shaded/textured view in the viewport.

7. Type **90** in the Rotate Frame field to rotate the image 90 degrees clockwise on the globe. Figure 12.4 shows a before and after example of what this looks like.

THE TRANSLATE FRAME U AND V FIELDS

Right above Rotate Frame are the Translate Frame U and V fields. Each attribute is a floating-point variable. Setting either value to 1 translates the frame an entire frame width and basically places the map back where you started. With the place2dTexture*n* node selected in the Channel Box, select the **translateFrameU** attribute and MM drag in the viewport. The map translates around the globe. Hold down the Ctrl key for a finer degree of change in the attribute value. Keep in mind that this attribute can be keyed.

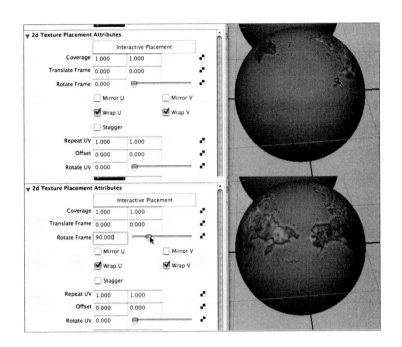

Figure 12.4

Changing the Rotate Frame attribute to fix an improperly oriented image

The color map of the globe represents a simple shader network. Next we'll create some clouds using a slightly more complex network and explore Maya's IPR (Interactive Photorealistic Rendering) in the process.

1. Move AtmosphereGeo back over GlobeGeo by setting its translate attributes to 0 in the Channel Box.

2. In the Hypershade, create a Lambert material and name it Atmos_mat.

3. Create a Cloud 3D texture. A 3D texture is mapped in and through 3D space as opposed to a 2D space, which is generally mapped onto an object using surface coordinates. This characteristic makes for some interesting possibilities in terms of animation.

4. RM connect the **OutColor** attribute of the Cloud$n$ node to the color channel of Atmos_mat.

5. In the Outliner, select AtmosphereGeo, RM click Atmos_mat, and assign the shader to the selected object.

Let's take a moment and set up an IPR process to help us gauge the visual effect of our shading machinations.

1. Choose **Window → Rendering Editors → Render Settings**, and set the Render Using pop-up to Maya Software. In the Common tab, set Image Size Preset to 640 × 480. In the Maya Software tab, make sure that under Raytracing Quality, Raytracing is unchecked because the Maya IPR will not work with raytracing rendering. Close the Render Settings window.

2. Choose **Render → Render Current Frame** to create a render in the Render View window.

3. Click the IPR button in the Render View window to set up a render process and add a directional light to the scene. You will see something like Figure 12.5a.

4. As shown in Figure 12.5a, draw a box around the ball. This will represent the area to update.

Now that we have our preview method set up, let's finish the atmosphere.

1. Double-click the Cloud*n* node to open the Cloud settings in the Attribute Editor. Set Contrast to 0.6. This setting specifies how much Color1 and Color2 will mix. A setting of 0 averages the two colors across the entire texture; 1 separates the colors completely. Set Amplitude to 1.8. Amplitude scales the effect of the noise value in the texture. Higher values increase the separation between the two colors. Check Soft Edges to soften the edges of the cloud texture, and adjust Center Thresh to 0.1 and Edge Thresh to 1.5. These two values combine to adjust how soft or hard the edge roll-off will be. Set Transparent Range to 0.5. This setting controls the range over which the cloud texture goes from solid to clear. The higher the value, the more diffuse the range. Set Ratio to 0.9. The Ratio setting controls how detailed the cloud texture becomes. The higher the value, the more detailed the grain in the noise. As you change the settings, notice how the texture changes in the IPR window. When you finish changing the settings, you will see something like Figure 12.5b.

2. In the Hypershade, connect the OutColor of the Cloud node to the Transparency channel of Atmos_mat. You should see something like Figure 12.5c. The Transparency attribute accepts the color generated by the cloud node as a transparency map, but it reads the white areas as transparent.

3. Under the General Utilities rollout of the Create Bar, create a reverse node in the work area. This type of node takes values or colors fed into it and inverts them.

4. Connect the OutColor of the Cloud node to the Input attribute of the reverse node. OutColor is a 3 component (RGB) attribute composed of floating-point numbers. These types of attributes are called vectors and can represent RGB colors or XYZ coordinates. Because the reverse node's Input connection is also a vector variable, you can connect it directly. If you were working with a single variable, you would need to connect it to one of the attributes that make up the vector (e.g., the G value in an RGB color triplet).

Figure 12.5

Creating and updating the IPR process to see changes in the shader network

a   b   c   d   e

5. Connect the Output of the reverse node to the Transparency attribute of Atmos_mat. You should see the clear areas of Atmos_mat turn white because the reverse node inverts the color generated by the cloud node and feeds it into the Transparency attribute of Atmos_mat. Figure 12.5d shows this.

6. Undo this operation and connect the Output of the reverse node to the Color attribute of Atmos_mat. You should see the areas that were black turn white, as in Figure 12.5e. If you prefer the previous version, undo this operation and repeat step 5.

As an exercise, try animating these textures by rotating the translateFrameU attribute of the place2dTexture node placed on Earth_mat. Then also animate the translate channel of the place3dTexture node of Atmos_mat back in Z. Figure 12.6 shows the place3dTexture node selected in the viewport. The clouds will swirl around the globe as it appears to rotate, as shown in EarthAnim.mov on the CD. Open GlobeTextureAnim.mb to see the Maya example of this.

Shading the MacGizmo

The craft that Machismo uses for his travels will need some form of shading, and that is our next challenge. During this process, we will discuss material types as well as mapping methods. We will discuss more advanced shader network creation coupled with shading work-flow techniques to give those shaders the maximum-quality appearance with minimum rendering times.

The MacGizmo is a one-seated vertical take off and landing (VTOL) aircraft that was designed and built by a scientist saved by Machismo early in his career as a superhero. It is his prize possession, and as such, he keeps it in tip-top condition. Our plan for shading the body will go something like this:

- The engines will be the most complex to shade. The good news is that we will only have to shade them once and then apply the shader to the other engine. The cowl of the engine will have three distinct areas that will have different appearances. The area covered with paint is described in the section "Shading the Engine Cowl with the Ramp Node." The part of the cowl in the turbine area will appear to be polished aluminum or steel, and the back of the engine will be textured with grooves or veins that disperse the heat of the engine exhaust. The nose cones of the engines are chrome, and the turbine blades are a ceramic steel that will need some definition to avoid blending together.

- The skin is a highly advanced alloy that has been coated with metallic paint and polished to a high shine like a brand-new automobile. We will shade the engines first and then extract the paint shader to use on the body.

Figure 12.6
The place3dTexture node selected in the viewport

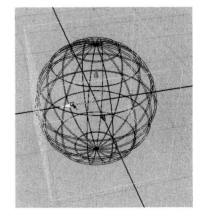

- The rims of the cockpit and wheel wells are steel polished to a high shine.

- The inside of the cockpit can be a matte finish gray or black. We will shade it last so that we give ourselves leeway to use whatever looks good with the rest of the surfaces we create.

- The chair will be leather or vinyl, also depending on what works with the rest of the craft.

LEARNING TO BUILD YOUR OWN SHADERS

The first thing to do when creating shaders for your models is what we have done here: make a plan for what you are trying to achieve. Once you plan what you want to do, it will be easier to find out how to do it. When writing or drawing your plan, describe it in terms that are identifiable. Notice that when we are describing this shader, we use terms such as *metallic paint*, *polished*, and *brand-new automobile*. This gives you something to go out and observe if you don't know how it appears. Those visual properties are the best way to start figuring out what you want to do in Maya.

The next step is to determine which nodes to connect in what manner to get the desired effect. The only sure answer is experience, but you can gain that experience in a number of ways.

The first and best learning method is simply to build shaders, and that is the first method we will use here, but we will, in effect, be following recipes. Just as when following any tutorial, your task is to remember how we used these nodes and think about ways to use them in other shaders. Notes along the way will aid you in this task. It is also helpful to experiment further with the settings for each node we use. Then, when you go on to build your own shaders, you will have a knowledge base that will help with the inevitable problem solving that you will need when building shaders.

Another valuable method in building shaders is to load and read the way the shader nodes are connected in each network. The Shader Library that comes with Maya is an excellent source of shader networks of beginning to intermediate difficulty. The Shader Library tab in the Hypershade gives you access to these shaders. Simply MM drag them to the storage area and click the Show Upstream And Downstream Connections button to display the network. Of course, this assumes you have the Shader Library installed. If you don't, it would be well worth your time to install the library according to the *Installation and Licensing* guide in your Maya documentation. When you have a handle on reading these networks, Highend3d.com is an excellent source of advanced and complex shader networks for you to read.

It is impossible to learn every single aspect of shader building in one book, much less one chapter. Many of the nodes can be used for animation as well as shader building, so there is plenty of room for self-study. The documentation is quite good when describing the basic operation of each node, but is light on applications of those nodes beyond basic suggestions.

Shading the Engine Cowl with the Ramp Node

Since we have a "plan of attack" for creating our shader for the engines, we can begin by planning our areas of separation. Remember that our surfaces are NURBS surfaces and therefore have a U and a V direction. The texture space of a NURBS surface has *implicit UVs*, meaning that these UVs cannot be edited and always exist in a 0 to 1 numeric environment. Remembering this is important because it will allow you to anticipate exactly where a texture will fall on a surface. To illustrate this, and to introduce the extremely powerful and useful ramp node, let's separate the texture into areas in which the colors to fall.

1. Create a new file, and import `MacGizmoEngine.mb` from the CD.

2. Select EngineCowlSrf and choose **Edit NURBS → Rebuild Surfaces** ❐. When modeling, we always want to rebuild using 0 to #Spans, but now we want to rebuild this surface with 0 to 1 parameterization. This is called *Chord length parameterization*, and rebuilding with this type here will facilitate shading by bringing the surface into the same parameterization as the texture UVs. After setting Parameter Range to 0 To 1 and checking Keep CVs, click Apply. Notice that the spans do not move at all.

3. RMB pick-mask Isoparm on EngineCowlSrf and select the isoparm shown at left in Figure 12.7. Note the number in the title bar (.166666666666667), and write it down; you will need it later. Keep in mind that if you are using something that you built, this number may be different.

4. Select the isoparm shown at the right in Figure 12.7 and record the number shown. In this case, it is .722222222222222.

5. Rebuild EngineCowl surface with 0-#Spans set as the parameter range and Keep CVs checked. We only need the 0 to 1 parameters to get the two values listed earlier.

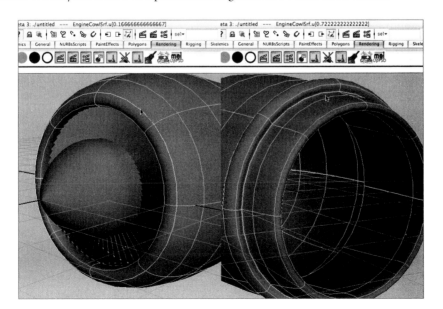

Figure 12.7

Selecting isoparms at the front and the back of EngineCowl-Srf and noting their chord length numbers in the title bar

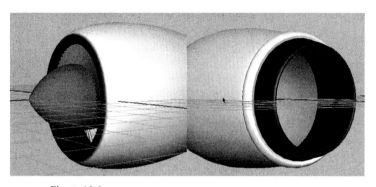

Figure 12.8
EngineCowlSrf with the designated texture areas

6. In the Hypershade, create a Blinn surface named Cowl_mat.

7. MM drag it from the work area of the Hypershade and drop it onto EngineCowlSrf.

8. In the Create Bar, scroll down to the 2D Textures area and click the Ramp button to create a ramp node in the work area.

9. Connect the OutColor attribute of the ramp to the color channel of Cowl_mat. The first thing you will note is that the ramp is going across rather than down the cowl surface.

10. Double-click the ramp node in the Hypershade work area. This will open the Attribute Editor focused on the ramp. Change Type to U Ramp, and change Interpolation to None. This will create sharp bands of color instead of the smooth gradients of the default. The circles at the left of the ramp are called handles and represent the selected position of a color on the ramp. Clicking them selects that handle and changes the Selected Color swatch below the ramp. You can drag these handles vertically to change the position of the color on the ramp.

11. Delete the blue band by clicking the box to the right of the blue color at the top of the ramp.

12. Change the color of the red band by selecting the red handle and dragging the slider next to the Selected Color swatch all the way to the left. This will make it black.

13. Click the green handle and notice that Selected Position now reads somewhere about 0.5. In the Selected Position field, type **.166**. This represents the value of the isoparm in step 3, moving the edge of the black band to the isoparm we selected earlier.

14. Double-click the green color swatch to open the Color Chooser, and change the color to white.

15. LM click in the black area of the ramp to create a new circle, which represents a Color Index Position (see sidebar "The Mighty Ramp Node" for more information on color index positions). Type **.722** in the Selected Position field to move it up to match the position of the isoparm in the back of EngineCowlSrf selected earlier. Your surface should look exactly like that shown in Figure 12.8.

16. Rename the ramp node ColorSep_rmp.

THE MIGHTY RAMP NODE

There are probably a thousand or more uses for the ramp; this chapter discusses only a few of them. Essentially, a ramp creates gradations of color. This gradation can then be connected to various attributes in the Hypershade or the Connection Editor. The output attributes of the ramps we will use have two important types: outAlpha and outColor.

OutAlpha is a grayscale version of the ramp seen in the Attribute Editor. It doesn't matter how colorful the ramp is, the outAlpha will always be grayscale having a numeric value from 0 to 1. This means that any input connection on any node that has a 0 to 1 range can be driven by a ramp.

OutColor is just what it says: it is the RGB color image created by the ramp. It can connect directly to any input that is a triple or vector value. The color output is expressed as outputR, outputG, outputB, where each output is a value of 0 to 1.

Every ramp has a Color Entry List, each member of which shows up as one of the movable handles to the left of the ramp area. Each of those circles has an index number beginning with [0] and increasing vertically as shown here. Each member of the list has a position and color attribute. The color attribute is expressed as an RGB value, and the position attribute is its location on the ramp, expressed as a number from 0 to 1. For more on using ramps, see Eric Keller's new book, *Maya Visual Effects: The Innovator's Guide* (Sybex, 2007).

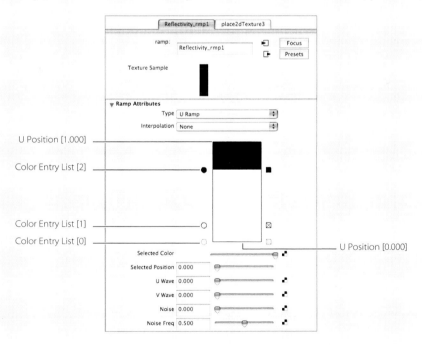

How the colors blend within the ramp is controlled by the Interpolation method set in the pop-up menu at the top of the Ramp Attributes rollout. We will use Smooth, which blends smoothly between each color entry, or None, which creates a sharp division between each color entry.

Over the course of this chapter, we will be using ramps for almost every aspect of creating this shader.

Figure 12.9

**The final shading
network for
Cowl_mat**

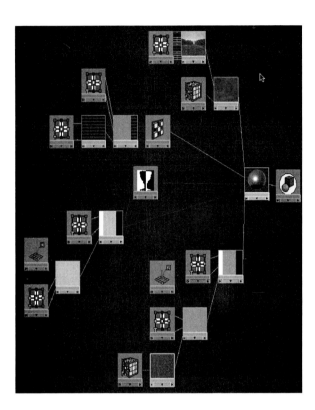

Figure 12.9

The final shading network for Cowl_mat

We have now used the ramp to designate where textures will go on our surface. Ramps of different configurations will figure heavily in our texturing process, and this ramp will be the base from which we will build many of them. Figure 12.9 shows the network we are going to build. Do not be intimidated! We will build this by separating the material components into separate areas in the Hypershade. This "divide and conquer" strategy will allow us to build complex shaders while understanding exactly what we did and how to do it on other shaders in the future.

Mapping the Environmental Reflection

Given that we will be working with reflective surfaces, we will need to give them something to reflect. We will do this by creating an environment sphere using an image from the CD. Let's create the environment map.

1. In the Hypershade's Create Bar, scroll down to Env Textures, click the Env Sphere button to create Environment Sphere, and place3dTexture nodes in the work area.

2. Scroll up to the 2D Textures and add a file texture and its accompanying placement node into the scene.

3. Double-click the File*n* node to open the Attribute Editor and click the File button.

4. Open the `WhiteHouse.tga` file to include the image.

> `WhiteHouse.tga` is a photograph of the White House that we took last summer and
> made into a spherical image map using the technique described on the website www
> `.lizardlounge.com/html/tutorials/c4d/sphericalMap/`.

5. RM click the Output Connections button on the file node, and connect the OutColor
    connection to the image input on the envSphere node.

6. RM click the Output Connections button on the envSphere node, and connect its
    OutColor to the reflectedColor channel on the Cowl_mat.

`MacGizmoEngReflStart.mb` shows the result of all these steps.

Mapping Areas of Reflectivity Using the Ramp Node

One characteristic of Maya that trips up beginners when creating procedural shaders is
that it often separates attributes that we intuitively accept as connected. In this case, the
Reflectivity attribute governs the amount of reflectivity a material has, and reflectedColor
governs exactly *what* that material reflects. Thus it does not matter what is connected to
the reflectedColor attribute if the material's reflectivity channel is set to 0. We want the
back heat sink area of the cowl to have almost no reflectivity while leaving the front two
areas fully reflective, and we will use a copy of the ramp we created to accomplish that.
Open `MacGizmoEngReflStart.mb` from the CD, and set the overall reflectivity as follows.

1. In the Hypershade, disconnect ColorSep_rmp from the color channel of Cowl_mat
    by LM clicking the green line connecting them and pressing the Delete key. Figure 12.10
    shows which line to select and delete.

2. Select ColorSep_rmp, and then choose **Edit → Duplicate → Shading Network**. This
    duplicates the ramp node and its placement node with connections already in place.
    Name the new ramp Reflectivity_rmp.

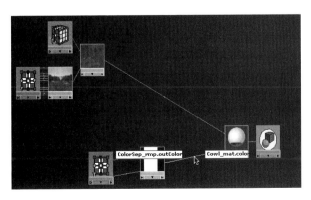

Figure 12.10
**Select and delete
the line connecting
outColor of
ColorSep_rmp
and the color
channel of
Cowl_mat.**

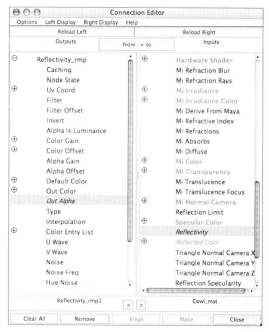

Figure 12.11

Using the Connection Editor to connect the outAlpha output of the ramp to the Reflectivity input on the material

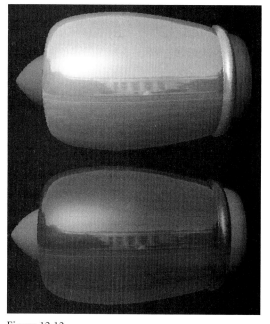

Figure 12.12

The Cowl_mat reflections before (top) and after (bottom) connecting the diffuse channel

3. Double-click the ramp node to open it in the Attribute Editor, and change the color of the bottom color entry to white.

4. Connect the outAlpha of Reflectivity_rmp to the reflectivity input of Cowl_mat. Oddly, you cannot directly connect these two attributes in the Hypershade. You have to use the Connection Editor. So MM drag the ramp node on top of Cowl_mat, and choose Other from the pop-up. This opens the Connection Editor. As shown in Figure 12.11, click outAlpha on the Outputs side. Scroll down the Inputs list in the right window until you see Reflectivity. Click it to connect the attributes. If you click the wrong attribute by mistake, just click it again to deselect it.

5. Open the Render View window and set up an IPR process by clicking the IPR button at the top of the window. The top image in Figure 12.12 shows the result. We have a surface that reflects the environment, but the reflection as well as the entire surface seems washed out. In this case, the diffuse channel of the material is set too high. As a general rule, the reflectivity and diffuse values of a material should equal or come close to 1. But if we are driving the reflectivity value with the ramp, how can we have the two values equal 1? By piping the ramp through a reverse node, that's how!

6. Add a reverse node to the work area by clicking its button in the Create Bar.

7. Connect the outAlpha output of the ramp to the InputX input of the reverse node. You do this by RM clicking the Input button on the reverse node and choosing **Input → InputX**.

8. Now connect OutputX on the reverse node to the diffuse attribute on Cowl_mat. The IPR should update to look something like the bottom image in Figure 12.12. The reflection is richer and much more natural.

Reflectivity Tweaks

For most highly polished, metallic painted cars, reflectivity actually decreases as the surface turns and faces the viewer. This reduction in reflectivity is what allows all the sparkly, shiny bits, which are buried beneath the paint's surface, to show to the viewer. We will add those bits when we add the color component later in the chapter. For right now, however, we want to make the surface facing us less reflective. We will do this by using the Facing Ratio attribute of the sampler info node.

The sampler info node samples points on a surface as they are rendered. This sampling information is expressed in a whole host of attributes contained in this node; we will use Facing Ratio. Figure 12.13 illustrates the concept of the Facing Ratio attribute. All polygon and NURBS surfaces have normals that extend out from the model. The sampler node derives Facing Ratio by comparing the angle of view from the camera to the normal as it extends from the object. If the normal is perpendicular to the angle of view, the surface is at right angles to the camera and Facing Ratio reads 0.0. If the angle of view is inversely parallel to the surface normal, the surface is facing directly toward the camera and Facing Ratio reads 1.0. Let's explore this on the model.

1. In the Hypershade, create a ramp with black at the top and white at the bottom. Note that Maya defaults to creating a V ramp. Leave Interpolation set to Linear. Name it RefTweak_rmp.

2. Scroll down to the General Utilities section of the Create Bar and click the Sampler Info button to create a node in the Hypershade.

3. Hold down the Shift key and MM drag the sampler info node over the ramp you just created to open the Connection Editor.

4. Connect the Facing Ratio attribute of the sampler info node to the V Coord attribute under the grayed-out UV Coord input of RefTweak_rmp, as shown in Figure 12.14a.

Figure 12.13

A normal that is perpendicular to the camera (top arrow) has a 0.0 Facing Ratio, and one pointing toward the camera (arrow pointing right) has a 1.0 Facing Ratio.

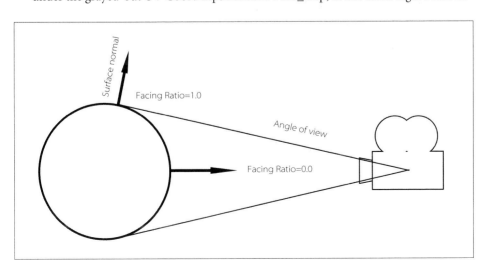

Figure 12.14

**(a) Using the Con-
nection Editor to
connect the Facing
Ratio attribute to the
ramp (b) Connecting
the outColor of the
ramp to the Color
Entry List[1].Color
attribute of the
Reflectivity_rmp**

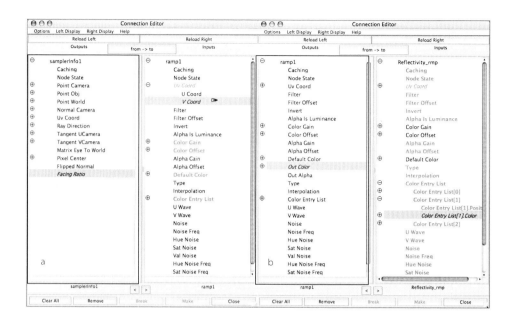

5. Select RefTweak_rmp in the Hypershade and click the Reload Left button at the top
   of the Connection Editor to load the ramp into the Output side of the window.

6. Select Reflectivity_rmp and click the Reload Right button to load this ramp node into
   the Input side of the Connection Editor.

7. Connect the outColor attribute to the Color Entry List[1].Color attribute, as shown at
   right in Figure 12.14b.

8. Manipulate the two handles of the ramp to get the effect you want. Figure 12.15
   shows some rendered examples created from manipulating the ramp handles. If you
   want to make the edges less reflective, change the white of the ramp to a shade of gray.

This technique is extremely powerful. With it, you can control much more than just
reflectivity. Imagine making glass that is less transparent, reflective, and refractive depending on how it faces the camera. You can use this technique to control color or any attribute that might depend on which way it is facing in relation to the camera.

From this point onward, we will call this process the Facing Ratio Ramp technique. So to create a facing ratio ramp, follow steps 1 through 4 of the preceding exercise using names
unique to your situation.

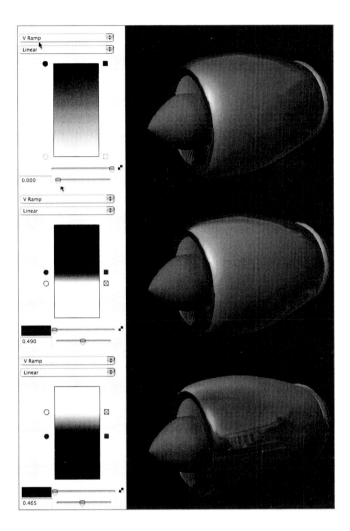

Figure 12.15

Different effects achieved by manipulating the smooth ramp. Notice the effect of flipping the white and black values in the image at bottom.

Creating Metallic Color

As with all the other channels we have explored, color offers several opportunities for manipulation to enhance the overall effect of the shader. The first ramp we created separated the surface into different color areas, so we will use a copy of that ramp to place our colors.

1. Duplicate ColorSep_rmp With Shading Network. Name the duplicate ramp Color_rmp.

2. Connect the outColor attribute of the duplicate to the colorInput of Cowl_mat.

3. Double-click the ramp to open it. Select the bottom handle and change the color from black to white.

4. Change the color on the middle handle to a dark green with HSV values of 120, 0.9, and 0.35.

5. Leave the top color area black. This will be the black of the exhaust area.

6. Create a Granite 3D texture and connect its outColor attribute to the Color_rmp's Color Entry List [2].Color channel by Shift+dragging it over Cowl_mat and connecting the two in the Connection Editor.

7. Open the Granite texture in the Attribute Editor. This texture creates the appearance of granite or other rocklike material suspended in a filler material. We will use it as a metallic undercoat in the color layer. Change the settings of the Granite texture as follows:

Color 1 HSV 354	.3	.6	
Color 2	273	.45	.6
Color 3	180	.25	.76
Filler Color	120	.9	.35
Cell Size	.045		
Density	1		
Mix Ratio	.7		
Spottiness	.63		

Leave all other settings at their defaults. Render the engine cowl. The image at the top of Figure 12.16 shows the result of our efforts so far. This direct connection of the Granite texture to the middle swatch of Color_rmp ties that granite color directly into the color of the cowl. Making the top swatch while in Color_rmp makes for highly reflective metal in the turbine area, which is what we want. Now we are going to use the Facing Ratio Ramp technique to suppress the color of the middle swatch as the surface turns away from the viewer.

Figure 12.16

The results of connecting the granite texture to the color ramp

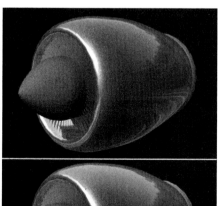
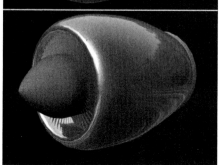

1. Create a facing ratio ramp in the Hypershade work area. Call the ramp ColorRatio_rmp.

2. Connect the **outColor** attribute of the granite texture to the ColorRatio_rmp's **Color Entry List[1].Color** attribute.

3. Open ColorRatio_rmp in the Attribute Editor and make the black swatch at the bottom a mid to light gray.

4. Connect ColorRatio_rmp's **outColor** attribute to Color_rmp's **Color Entry List[1].Color** attribute.

5. Test render to see the result. Notice how the reflection takes over sooner from the color as the surface moves away from the viewer. If this doesn't look right to you, simply reconnect the outColor of the granite texture directly to Color_rmp's **Color Entry List[1].Color** attribute to set it to how it was before.

TEXTURE REFERENCE OBJECTS

An alternative to creating file textures out of 3D procedural textures for an object is to create a texture reference object (TRO) for the geometry you are animating. A TRO is a separate copy of the geometry, placed wherever you create the reference object and hidden from view. It remains static throughout your animation (unless you choose to animate it yourself— but that would defeat the purpose of the reference object!), and the 3D procedural texture is applied to this object first rather than to your animating object, and then the texture is trans- ferred from the TRO to your animated object. The result of this process is that the texture no longer "swims" as your object is animated, instead staying put no matter how wildly the geometry is deformed or transformed in space.

While rendering an object that uses a TRO is somewhat slower and can be more memory intensive than rendering using a file texture, a TRO remains resolution independent, so zooming in and out on the object will not caused aliasing or pixelization of the texture as would happen with a file texture. Additionally, a TRO can sometimes provide a cleaner look for a texture on a complex surface.

To create a texture reference object, add a 3D procedural shader to some geometry, select your geometry, and then from the Rendering menu set, choose **Texturing Create Texture Reference Object**. That's it! Your TRO is now ready to be used in your scene. In the example here, image A is a sphere at the origin with a 3D marble texture applied; B shows the nor- mally textured sphere translated forward in Z, showing how the texture is moving across the surface of the sphere; and C shows the same translated sphere but using a texture reference object—note how the texture is the same as in the left image even though the sphere has been translated.

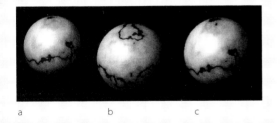

a   b   c

Unfortunately, procedural 3D textures like granite can be slow to render. Also, unless you take care to parent them properly to nodes that are animated, the textures they create can swim through the model. Finally, deforming objects mapped with procedurals will cause the textures to remain stationary as the model moves. Although this can be used advantageously in some circumstances (remember the animated clouds?), it is generally better to convert them to file textures. File textures render faster as well as animate and deform with the model.

1. Select the granite texture in the Hypershade.

2. Shift+select EngineCowlSrf in the viewport.

3. In the Hypershade Edit menu, choose **Convert To File Texture (Maya Software)** ❑. Figure 12.17 shows the settings you should use. We will be using this command extensively later in the chapter and will discuss more of these options at that time. For now, just match settings and click Convert And Close. The computer will render out a file version of the texture and save it in your project's sourceimages folder. This will take a few seconds or a few minutes depending on the size of your rendered texture and the speed of your computer.

Figure 12.17

The Convert To File Texture option box

4. Rename the file texture node that results GreenMetal_file.

Maya automatically duplicates the nodes upstream of the converted texture. Therefore, in this case, the ramps and the Blinn material Cowl_mat have been duplicated and automatically applied to EngineCowlSrf. Feel free to leave this surface on the model, but we will delete everything but the file texture node and pipe it into Cowl_mat in place of the granite texture.

1. RM click GreenMetal_file in the Hypershade, and choose Select Output Nodes from the pop-up menu.

2. Shift+select GreenMetal_file to deselect it.

3. Delete the nodes that remain selected.

4. Connect the outColor attribute of GreenMetal_file to either the Color Entry List[1].Color attribute of ColorRatio_rmp or the Color Entry List[1].Color attribute of Color_rmp.

5. MM drag the Cowl_mat swatch over EngineCowlSrf in the viewport to assign the shader to the surface directly.

6. Test-render to check the new file texture. There should be no discernable difference between your new renders and the image of Figure 12.16.

Creating Grooves with a Bump Map

The exhaust area of the back of the engine cowl should be a dark grooved area with minimal specularity. We will create it by using a ramp as a color entry on a second ramp applied as a bump map to Cowl_mat. Open `MacGizmoEngineBmpStart.mb`, or use your file from the previous section, and apply the bump map as follows.

1. Duplicate ColorSep_rmp With Shading Network, and name it Bump_rmp.

2. Open it in the Attribute Editor and make the bottom two handles a gray value of 0.5 in the Color Chooser. This will distribute a neutral bump value over the entire surface.

3. Create a new ramp. Change the red and blue handles to black. Change the green handle to a 0.25 percent dark gray.

4. Open the place2dTexture node connected to this ramp and change the V field of the RepeatUV field to 200.

5. Connect the outColor attribute of this new ramp to the Color Entry List[2].Color attribute using the Connection Editor as outlined earlier.

6. Connect the outAlpha attribute of Bump_rmp to the bump map input of Cowl_mat. You will need to MM drag Bump_rmp over Cowl_mat and choose bump map from the pop-up menu. This will connect a bump2d node between the ramp and the material. This is common. If you double-click this node, you will see that two values influence the bump map. The ramp (and any other image map used as a bump map) is plugged into the Bump Value channel. The Bump Depth setting controls the height or depth of the bumps. For most applications a value of 1 is too high, so set it to about 0.25.

7. Do a test render to see the results.

   `MacGizmoCowlFinished.mb` shows the final material.

Shading the Turbines and Nose Cone

Shading the turbine blades will be relatively simple. We will create a nose cone material using a layered texture and in the process discuss the merits of the anisotropic material. Open `MacGizmoNoseConeStart.mb` from the CD, or use your file from the previous section, and shade the turbines as follows.

1. If you are working through from the previous exercise, clear the Hypershade work area by choosing **Graph → Clear Graph** from the menu.

2. Create a Blinn shader and name it Turbine_mat.

3. Create a U direction ramp. Make the colors white at the bottom and black at the top.

4. Connect the outColor of the ramp to the colorInput of Turbine_mat.

5. In the Outliner, open EngineGrp and select TurbineGrp.

6. In the Hypershade, RM click Turbine_mat and choose Assign Material To Selection from the pop-up menu.

7. Test-render to see the result. Some options for experimentation are changing the diffuse value to 0.5 to match the reflectivity value, changing the U ramp to a V direction ramp, moving the black handle farther down on the ramp, and turning on Raytracing in the Raytracing Quality rollout in the Maya Software tab of the Render Settings window.

For the nose cone, we want a shader that has a specular highlight that runs the length of the nose cone. For that we will need to use an anisotropic material, but we want the other attributes of the Blinn material, so we need to use a layered shader to combine the two types of materials. Let's shade the nose cone as follows.

1. Clear the work area of the Hypershade.

2. Create a layered shader and call it Cone_mat. Exactly as its name implies, a layered shader layers two or more materials on top of each other. We use it in this case because we want to blend the unique specular highlight of the anisotropic material with the attributes of a Blinn material. For some reason, the layered shader comes with a bright green and partially transparent default material. Drag the Color Slider all the way to the left to black, and drag the Transparency Slider all the way to the right to make it white. The green color swatch should disappear at this point. We will delete it later.

3. Create a Blinn material in the Hypershade and call it Trans_mat.

4. In the storage area at the top of the Hypershade, click the Textures tab.

5. Find the envSphere1 node in the storage area and MM drag it to the work area.

6. Connect the outColor of the envSphere node to the reflectedColor input on Trans_mat.

7. Create two facing ratio ramps as described earlier. Name one Ref_rmp and the other Trans_rmp.

8. Connect the outAlpha attribute of Ref_rmp to the reflectivity input on Trans_mat.

9. Connect the outColor attribute of Trans_rmp to the transparency input on Trans_mat. Remember that transparency is an RGB triple data structure, so we use the outColor attribute instead of the outAlpha attribute.

10. Open Trans_rmp and make the top handle white and the bottom handle black. Set the white handle's Selected Position option to 0.755 and the black handle's to 0.385.

11. Open Ref_rmp. Make the top handle white and set its Selected Position option to 0.790. Make the bottom handle black and set its Selected Position option to .24.

12. Create an anisotropic material and name it Spec_mat. Double-click it to open it in the Attribute Editor. The anisotropic material can have 1 degree of specularity in the X direction and a completely different degree of specularity in Y, which is why it is useful for us here. Reverse the current direction of the specular highlight by setting Spread X to 3 and Spread Y to 24. This will stretch the highlight vertically across the surface. Change the Roughness value to 0.76 to diffuse it a little.

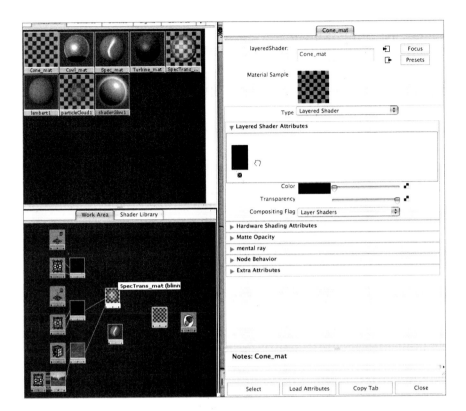

Figure 12.18

MM drag the Trans_mat Blinn material to the Layered Shader window. Delete the default layer.

13. To connect the two materials to the layered shader, open the layered shader in the Attribute Editor. Figure 12.18 shows the Attribute Editor with the Layered Shader window displayed.

14. MM drag Trans_mat to the Layered Shader Attributes section of the Layered Shader window, as shown in Figure 12.18. Delete the black swatch after you do this. This connects Trans_mat to leftmost layer in the shader, left representing the top layer. Given that this shader is partially transparent, it will need to be on the topmost layer to give the effect we want.

15. MM drag Spec_mat to the right of Trans_mat in the Layered Shader window.

16. MM drag Cone_mat to NoseSrf in the viewport to apply the material to the NURBS surface.

17. Test-render to see the result. Figure 12.19 shows the engine cowl from several angles. We are now ready to surface the rest of the craft.

Figure 12.19

The final rendered engine with raytracing enabled

Figure 12.19

The final rendered engine with raytracing enabled

Surfacing the Rest of the MacGizmo

We attacked the engine shaders first for the simple reason that they are the most difficult surface to create. Doing so allowed us to explore ramps and their uses in dividing the surface. Furthermore, the complexity of the color and reflectivity of the engine will transfer to the rest of the craft fairly easily. First, however, we must export our shaders from the file we've been editing and place them into the file with the MacGizmo's geometry. Let's export the shading networks.

1. Open `MacGizmoEngineFinal.mb` from the CD, or use the file you have been editing so far.

2. In the Hypershade, select Cowl_mat, Cone_mat, and Turbine_mat in the storage area.

3. Choose **Graph → Input And Output Connections** to display the entire network in the work area.

4. Select all the nodes in the work area.

5. Choose **File → Export Selected Network** and call the exported file `Engine_mats.mb`. Click Export.

> Maya will store this file in a bit of a strange place. It buries it in a file called shaders in the renderData folder.

6. Open `MacGizmoFinalGeo.mb` from the CD.

7. Save it as `MacGizmoShadeFinal.mb`. Always save before you edit so that you won't accidentally save over your original data.

8. In the Hypershade, choose **File → Import** and select `Engine_mats.mb` from this chapter's shaders folder. You will see all the materials appear in the Hypershade storage area.

9. Apply Cowl_mat, Turbine_mat, and Cone_mat to the appropriate surfaces and groups by selecting them in the Outliner, RM clicking the material, and choosing **Assign Material To Selection** from the marking menu.

10. Test-render to see the results.

These shaders contain much of the work we will need to surface the body and rim geometries. To create the shader for the body and wings, we'll duplicate some of the nodes and connections to Cowl_mat and connect them to a new material called BodyWing_mat. Let's create the new body shader.

1. Graph the Input and Output connections of Cowl_mat in the Hypershade work area.

2. Duplicate Cowl_mat Without Network, and rename it BodyWing_mat. This creates a copy of the Blinn surface with all the nonconnected attributes set the same as they are set for the cowl material.

3. Connect the outColor of envSphere1 to the reflectedColor attribute of BodyWing_mat.

4. RM click ColorRatio_rmp, which is connected to Color_rmp in the Cowl_mat network, and choose Select Input Nodes from the pop-up menu. Figure 12.20 shows which nodes to duplicate. In the Hypershade, choose **Edit → Duplicate → Without Network**.

5. Connect the duplicated nodes by MM dragging the duplicated place2DTexture node over the ramp and choosing Default.

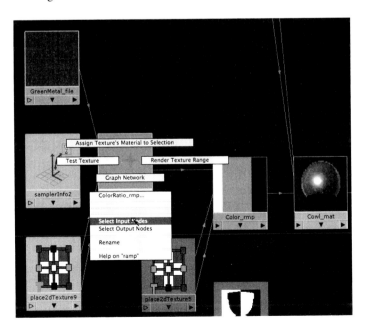

Figure 12.20

Selecting the input nodes connected to FacingRatio_rmp

6. Connect the Facing Ratio attribute of the duplicated sampler info node to the V Coord attribute of the UV Coord Input on the ramp by MM dragging the sampler info node over the ramp and choosing Other from the pop-up menu to open the Connection Editor.

7. Connect the outColor of the duplicated GreenMetal_file node to the duplicated ramp's Color Entry List[2].Color input using the Connection Editor.

8. Connect the outColor of the duplicated ramp to the color input of BodyWing_mat.

9. To create the reflectivity ramp in the new material, select and duplicate the ramp, the sampler info node, the place2dTexture nodes, and the reverse node, all of which are connected to Reflectivity_rmp in the Cowl_mat's shading network.

10. Connect the place2dTexture and sampler info nodes to the duplicated ramp as you did in steps 5 and 6 earlier.

11. Connect the outAlpha of the duplicated ramp to the reflectivity input of Body-Wing_mat. Remember that you will have to use the Connection Editor to do this.

12. Connect the outAlpha of the same ramp to the InputX input of the reverse node. Then connect ouputX of the reverse node to the diffuse input of BodyWing_mat.

13. In the Outliner, select the following surfaces:

      WingSrf

      ConnectSrf

      BodySrf

      EngineGrp|circularFilletSurface6_1

      EngineGrp|EngineWngSrf

      REngineGrp|circularFilletSurface6_1

      REngineGrp|EngineWngSrf

    Assign BodyWing_mat to them.

14. Test-render to see the result.

> Sometimes the surface direction of a NURBS patch or surface can conflict with shader creation. If a surface looks as if it is reflecting incorrectly, first check the direction of the surface by clicking the patch and displaying normals. If the normals are facing in the opposite direction, choose **Edit NURBS → Reverse Surface Direction** with the Swap option checked and rerender. That should fix the problem.

The primary advantage to creating the body and wing shaders in this manner involves the additional control you get from duplicating the two ramps. By adjusting the Color Index handles of these two ramps, you can adjust the way the surface reflects the environment separately from Cowl_mat.

Last in this exercise, we will create the metal shader for all the hubcaps and rim surfaces from Cone_mat using Maya's triple shading switch node. The shading switch nodes are powerful but misunderstood nodes that let you switch attributes of a shader depending on the surface to be shaded. The Single, Double, Triple, and Quad designations refers to the data type used for the switch operation. A single switch node works on a single floating-point variable, like the reflectivity or diffuse channel. A double switch takes a double data type such as the repeatUV, wrapUV, or UVCoord attribute as its input. A triple switch takes a triple data type such as an RGB, XYZ, or vector type variable as the type that will switch between surfaces. Last, the quad switch takes a four-value attribute such as the RGB and alpha value of an image and switches that between separate objects. Let's create the triple shading switch (TSS).

1. Assign Cone_mat to the following objects:

    DriveWheelRimSrf

    RWheelWellRimSrf

    LWheelWellRimSrf

    InnerWheelGeo

    DriveWheelSpokesGrp

    WindShieldRimSrf

    CockpitInteriorSrf

    RHubcapGeo

    HubcapGeo

2. Disconnect Spec_mat from Cone_mat by selecting the green lines connecting them and pressing Delete.

3. Scroll down in the Create Bar and open the Switch Utilities rollout. Click Triple Shading Switch to create a triple shading switch node in the work area.

4. Create a Phong shader and name it RimPhong_mat. This will provide a different color for now. It will also provide a slightly more focused specular highlight than either a Blinn or an anisotropic material.

5. Double-click the shader to open it in the Attribute Editor. Make the color a light dull yellow. Change Cosine Power to 60, and kick up the specular color to a light gray.

6. The triple shading switch node connects a little differently than other nodes. You connect it to the layered shader conventionally by MM dragging the switch node to the Cone_mats.input[3].color input. Remember that the index number (3) must be a higher index number than Trans_mat for the specular and reflective color to show. Figure 12.21 shows how this is done.

7. RM click Cone_mat and choose Select Objects With Material. This selects all the geometry from earlier.

8. Hold down the Shift key and double-click the tripleShadingSwitch node to open it in the Attribute Editor while keeping all the geometry selected.

9. Click the Add Surfaces button to load all the geometry into the inShape side of the Shading Switch window. Notice that groups do not load but all the children of those groups load individually.

10. Scroll down the list and MM drag either Spec_mat or RimPhong_mat to the inTriple side. This assigns that outColor attribute to that shape while keeping all other attributes the same. Figure 12.22 shows how this works.

Test-rendering reveals an omission and a happy accident. The inside of the cockpit was assigned RimPhong_mat instead of CockpitRimSrf. But it looks fine, so we will leave it. Let's add CockpitRimSrf and assign the RimPhong_mat manually.

1. In the Outliner, MM drag CockpitRimSrf to the inShape side of the Triple Shading Switch window.

2. MM drag RimPhong_mat to the inTriple side of the window.

3. Assign Cone_mat to CockpitRimSrf. This step is important. Up to now, CockpitRimSrf has been shaded with the default Lambert surface. For the triple shading switch node to work, its surface must be assigned to the object; simply including it in the inShape list is not enough.

4. Test-render to see the results.

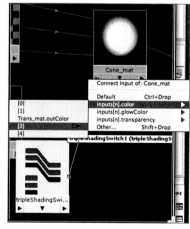

Figure 12.21

Connecting the output of the triple switch to the input of the Cone_mat layered shader

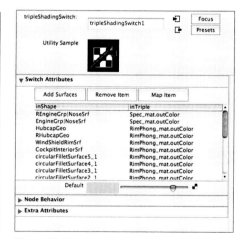

Figure 12.22

The triple shading switch node with inShape and inTriple colors loaded

You now see that every surface assigned to RimPhong_mat is rendered yellow and that the nose cones remain chrome colored. This is true despite all these objects being assigned to the Cone_mat shader. You can, by creating other shaders, create an almost limitless array of looks for each piece of rim and hubcap geometry. To learn about creating shaders using the shading switches, create several materials to feed into it.

Over the course of your renderings, you may find some inconsistencies and imperfections in the color map used to map BodySrf, ConnectSrf, and WingSrf. These flaws come from how we created that map from the 3D texture that we converted into a file texture. Remember that we converted that texture while we had it assigned to the engine cowl surface. As such, Maya rendered it into a file while it was assigned to the EngineCowlSrf UV texture space. The cowl's UV texture space is different from BodySrf, ConnectSrf, WingSrf, the engine wing, and fillet surfaces connecting the wing to the engine. You can see these flaws clearly by opening MacGizmoShadeFinal.mb and doing a non-raytraced test render of the area behind the cockpit. If these flaws are too much to bear, you can take care of them in a number of ways.

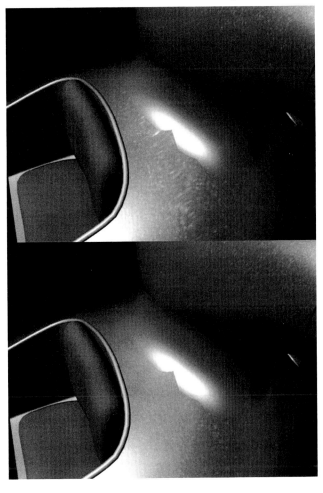

You may also see imperfections caused by geometry intersecting improperly. You can correct those imperfections easily by editing CVs.

The ultimate solution would be to apply the granite 3D texture using the settings described earlier to every one of these surfaces and converting the 3D texture to create a file texture for each surface using the procedure outlined earlier. This would create a separate file texture and material for each surface and would also give you the highest degree of control over the appearance of each surface. It would also consume more disk space and would probably be more hassle than it is worth.

A compromise solution is to open the file texture in Photoshop and use the Rubber Stamp tool to remove all the imperfections (which are starkly visible when you open the file). Save the file as granite1-EngineCowlSrf.tga, and switch it with the file texture that is currently connected to the color channel of BodyWing_mat. Figure 12.23 shows before (top) and after (bottom) renders of the material.

Reading Textures Using the Hypershade

To finish the MacGizmo, you will import a file containing materials for the cockpit glass, the wheel wells, and the pilot's chair. With `MacGizmoShadeFinal.mb` still open, import `MacGizmo_matFinishPack.mb` from the sourceimagesshaders directory on the CD. Go ahead and assign Chair_mat to SeatGrp, Glass_mat to WindShieldSrf, and Tire_mat to TireGeo, LFrontWheelGrp|TireGeo, and RTireGeo. Also, assign the appropriate WheelWell_mat to the correct L-, R-, and Drive-WheelWellGeo. Test-render to your heart's content, but after doing so, open the Hypershade and examine these materials; each has something unique about it.

Glass_mat   This glass shader uses the Facing Ratio Ramp technique, but the ramps are applied to the transparency and reflectivity channels. This creates a convincing glass material without resorting to raytracing. You can certainly up the refractivity of the material if you decide you need reflectivity.

Tire_mat   Tire_mat uses a V ramp with a V wave of 1 to create a simple tread texture. You can create the tread texture simply by piping it into the middle index position of a ramp and then running that ramp through the bump channel of the material.

Chair_mat   This material is derived from Leather_mat, which is included when you import `MacGizmo_matFinishPack.mb` from the CD. Leather_mat has the outColor attribute of a leather 3D texture piped into the color channel and the outAlpha controlling the bump map of Leather_mat. When the chair back is selected and the leather 3D texture is converted into a file texture, Maya creates a color file and a grayscale file and pipes them into the appropriate channels of the new material, which is renamed Chair_mat.

WheelWell_mats   The wheel well materials were all generated from MasterWheelWell_mat, which is unique in how it is built. A 2D noise texture node controls the Blender attribute of a blendColors node. This allows you to control which two colors will be used in the Noise field, a control that the noise node alone does not allow. The Blender attribute controls how the two colors specified by you in the node will be blended. In this case, Color 1 is a dark gray and Color 2 is a light gray. The output of the blender node was connected to the color channel of the material. Because the output of the blender node is always RGB, however, we had to use a luminance node to convert the RGB to black and white. The output of this node could then be connected to the bump map channel of the material. This material was then assigned to the three wheel well objects and converted to file textures, with each piece of geometry selected to create a separate material for each.

From the first part of this chapter, you can see that Maya's selection of 2D and 3D procedural textures can produce sophisticated and convincing results. For shading characters, however, we will need to create layered bitmap textures using Photoshop or other painting tools. But before we paint the first pixel, we need to create the UV map, which is key to optimal texture production.

Shading Machismo: The UV Foundation

File textures involve wrapping an image or a set of images onto a 3D surface. In the previous section, we created procedural textures on NURBS surfaces and then created file textures that Maya automatically placed in the NURBS surfaces' UV texture space.

NURBS surfaces have an implicit UV texture space that dovetails quite well with their UV modeling space. The UV direction of the surface is tied to the UV coordinates of the texture space. The inherent "square-ness" of a NURBS patch accommodates the inherent "square-ness" of the UV space. As an exercise, select one of the NURBS objects on the MacGizmo from `MacGizmoShadeFinal.mb` and open the UV Texture Editor. (Choose **Window → UV Texture Editor**.) From the Image menu, choose **Display Image And UV Texture Editor Baking** to see the image map as it is wrapped onto the UV surface. Figure 12.24 shows the connection between the model and the texture space.

But what about polygons? Polygons have no such inherent connection to UV texture space. Open `Machismo00_BuildUVsStart.mb` from the CD. Select polySurface5 and open the UV Texture Editor. There is a big difference here from our experience with NURBS. Each polygon is created in UV space; but for the most part, they are all on top of one another! Clearly, we will have to change this.

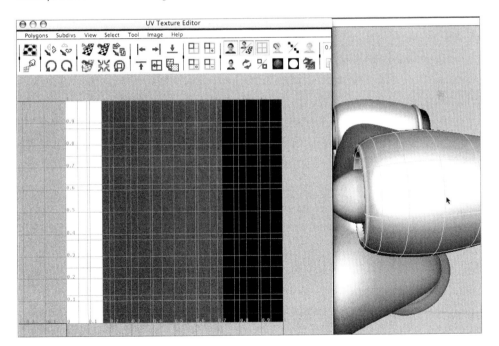

Figure 12.24

EngineCowlSrf is selected, and then the baked ramp color texture is displayed in the UV Texture Editor.

The Successful UV Map

A successful UV map usually has minimal seams and UV distortion. Unlike with cloth sewing, which has certain analogies to UV mapping, seams are not where two pieces of UVs are sewed together; rather, seams are where the borders of mapped UVs are separate in UV space but are connected in 3D space. A seam can be exacerbated if those edges, which are separate in UV space, are of unequal length. These border edges should be equal in length for the texture map to flow across them.

Figure 12.25

The concept painting of Machismo

In the course of creating a UV map for Machismo, we will explore various mapping methods and Maya's UV manipulation tools. Creating a successful UV map is not technically difficult, but it does require a certain forethought that should begin at the character design stage. Because we have included tights, gloves, and boots in the model, we can divide the UV map into smaller areas that will be easier to map. We will then have to tackle the head, which is easily the most difficult part of the body to map.

In every other phase of 3D production, it is essential that you start with some plan of attack; creating a texture is no different. In fact, it is even more necessary when you're planning to paint textures. Figure 12.25 shows a concept painting. You can see that the surfaces of the shirt and leggings are different than the surfaces of the pants, gloves, and boots. This will let us build the map in separate pieces. We will also need to paint bump, color, specular and diffuse maps. Once our plan has been established, we can create the UV map to help facilitate our efforts.

The concept painting was created in Photoshop from a screen capture of a pose created from a preliminary animation rig. Layers of paint and texture were overlaid above the grayscale screen shot to get the image in Figure 12.25.

Dismembering the Body

On opening the initial file for Machismo, you will notice that we are working on half the model. This is to speed up the mapping process. We only have to do half the work this way—mirror the geometry and the UV map and sew the whole thing together. Our first task is to put the head, chest, arm, glove, shorts, leg, and boot into separate areas to make selecting and further mapping easier. You will map the same area several times using different methods. The goal is to map accurately and quickly as many polygons at a time as you can. Let's create a preliminary map.

1. Open `Machismo00_BuildUVsStart.mb` from the CD.

2. Set up the model view with two panes side by side with the right image the persp view and the left the UV Texture Editor. We will be using the latter to help us separate and select components by area.

3. Select the half body and choose **Create UVs → Planar Mapping □**. Check Keep Image Width/Height Ratio (which prevents distortion). Select the Fit To Bounding Box radio button. Select the Z axis radio button to project from that axis onto the model. Click Project and you should see something like Figure 12.26.

> (New with Maya 8.5, the former Polygon UV menu has been split into two menus: one for creating UVs and the other for editing them.)

4. In the Inputs list in the Channel Box, record the projectionHeight value of 17.36. This is the height of the projection in 3D space. We will use it later in figuring the size of the various projections on the body parts. You can see this value depicted in the lower corner of Figure 12.26.

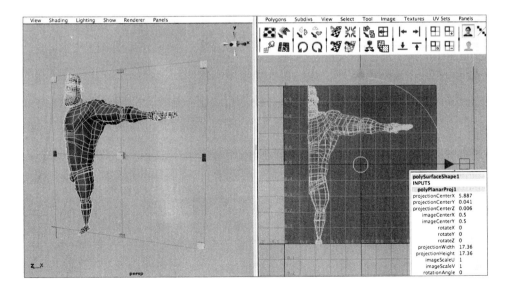

Figure 12.26

The half body planar mapped along the Z axis in the UV Texture Editor and the model view

In the UV Texture Editor, the UV projection is surrounded by the projection manipulator that has controls analogous to the translate, rotate, and scale manipulators in the 3D view. The arrows allow you to move the projection, and the light blue arc allows you to rotate the projection in the UV Texture view. In the perspective view, only the scale manipulators are apparent, but thin colored lines let you translate the map indicator in X and Y. Clicking the red cross in the lower left of the mapping indicator opens the familiar gnomon, which you can use to rotate the map. It is worth a few minutes to try this out and see what effect it has on the map, but make sure you return to the default setting when you finish.

Planar mapping creates a map that represents the flattening of the model in the specified axis. Of course, polygons that are parallel with that axis, such as the sides of the head and thigh, will have no area in the UV map. This makes planar mapping unacceptable as an overall technique, but we will use this preliminary map as a selection tool. Let's separate the head as follows.

1. Zoom in on the collar area of the upper body.

2. Pick-mask Edge on the model, and select an edge at the front and at the back of the collar as shown at the top of Figure 12.27.

Figure 12.27

Selecting the edge loop around the head

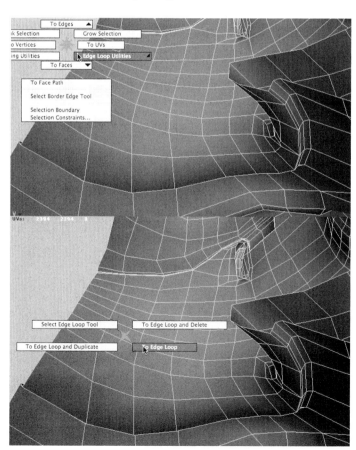

3. Hold down the Ctrl button, RM click in the modeling view, and choose **Edge Loop Utilities → To Edge Loop**, also as shown at the bottom of Figure 12.27. This will select a loop of edges around the entire neck. Simply selecting an edge at the front will not select the entire loop because it intersects with the corner of a polygon, so we had to select an edge in back to complete the loop.

4. In the UV Texture Editor pane you will see that the edges selected in the Perspective view are also selected in the UV Texture Editor pane. This parallel selection is useful when laying out UVs. In the UV Texture Editor menu, choose **Polygons → Cut UV Edges**. This will separate the head area by splitting along the selected edges. We will now move the head away from the body.

5. RM pick-mask UV in the UV Texture Editor. Select one UV anywhere on the head. It will display as a green dot.

6. RM click the head and choose **Select → Select Shell** from the marking menu. Only the head area should be selected. If the entire body becomes selected, undo until the head edges are selected, make sure that the selection goes all the way around the head with no gaps, and then repeat steps 3 through 6.

7. Press W to enable the Move tool, and within the UV Texture Editor, move the head away from the body.

Figure 12.28 shows how to separate the legs from the torso. We will eventually separate the boot as well. Select an edge loop, using the shortcut described earlier, from the middle edge of the border between the shorts and leg. Then follow the preceding steps 1 through 7.

Use the same technique to separate the glove and boot. To separate the arm, select the edge loop shown in Figure 12.29.

Mapping each separate area gives us a chance to explore cylindrical and automatic mapping techniques. We will proceed from the simple to the complex. Our order of mapping will be the leg, arm, boot, shorts and body, glove, and head.

Figure 12.28

Separating the pants from the body and legs

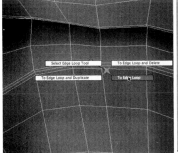
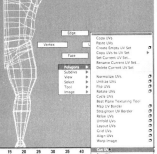
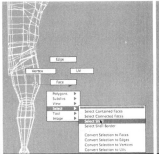
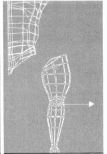

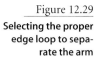

Figure 12.29

Selecting the proper edge loop to separate the arm

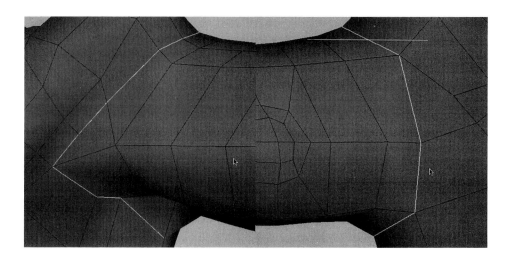

Getting the Dimensions Right

One huge problem with mapping separate parts of the body like this is that Maya, while powerful, is unpleasantly consistent as far as the relative sizes of the maps it creates. It always makes the maps as large as possible within the UV texture space regardless of how large the area being mapped in the view space is, leaving you to try to scale the map down by eye with varying results. By taking the original height of the full body projection and dividing it into the height of the projection of the individual body part, we can arrive at the correct size of the projection as expressed in the imageScaleU and imageScaleV values. This will size the projection within the UV texture space correctly in relation to the other body parts. The formula for this is simple:

Body Part Length/Height of Body = The Size of Projection

We can illustrate this by cylindrically mapping the leg. Open Machismo01_MappingStart.mb from the CD and let's map the leg.

1. In the UV Layout pane, pick-mask Face on the body and select the leg, as shown in Figure 12.30a. Be sure to exclude the boot because we will be mapping that later.

   Using the UV Texture Editor is a fantastic way to select components that may be difficult to get to in the viewport.

2. Choose **Create UVs → Cylindrical Mapping □**. Using the default settings shown in Figure 12.30b, click Project.

3. You will see a half-cylinder projection manipulator and the polyCylProj*n* node in the Channel Box, as shown in Figure 12.30c.

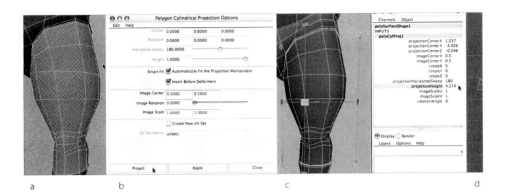

a   b   c   d

Figure 12.30

(a) Selecting the faces of the leg. Note that the boot has been excluded. (b) The Polygon Cylindrical Projection options box with the default settings. (c) The projection node with the projectionHeight attribute highlighted. (d) The projection shrinks in the UV Texture Editor.

4. In the Channel Box, note the projection height channel, which should read 4.274. Divide the original full-body projection height of 17.36 by 4.274 to get a value of about 0.25.

5. Input this value into the imageScaleU and imageScaleV attribute fields of the projection node. You will see the size of the projection within the UV Texture Editor shrink dramatically as shown in Figure 12.30d.

This part of the UV projection is now the correct size in relation to the rest of the body. By dividing the body part height value into the height of all the body part projections, we can make sure that these pieces are sized in proper proportion to one another, which will make sewing pieces and painting the map much easier. We now need to further manipulate the projection itself to narrow it in the UV texture space and to align the edges of the map line more smoothly.

1. Figure 12.31a shows the scaled projection with all the other mapping attributes set to their defaults.

2. The cylindrical map defaults to a 180° projection. We want it to unwrap through 360°, so in the Channel Box, change the projectionHorizontalSweep attribute to 360. This will wrap the projection cylinder all the way around the leg, as shown in Figure 12.31b. Notice how the projection within UV space gets narrower.

3. We want the seam of where the projection meets to be on the inside of the leg (just as it would on a pair of pants). So click the red cross on the manipulator (the cursor is over it in the middle of Figure 12.31b), and rotate the manipulator 90° in Y to properly place the seam, as shown in Figure 12.31c. Now we can move on to mapping the arm.

In the final map, the parts will not adhere to these proportions; we will enlarge the head because it is the most important part and will be seen in close-ups. But for the original creation phase, unifying scaling will help ensure that separate pieces of the same part of the garment, namely the body and arm, will match up properly when the texture is painted.

Figure 12.31

(a) The default mapping. (b) Changing the Sweep attribute from 180 to 360. (c) Rotating the manipulator 90 degrees in Y to correctly line up the seam.

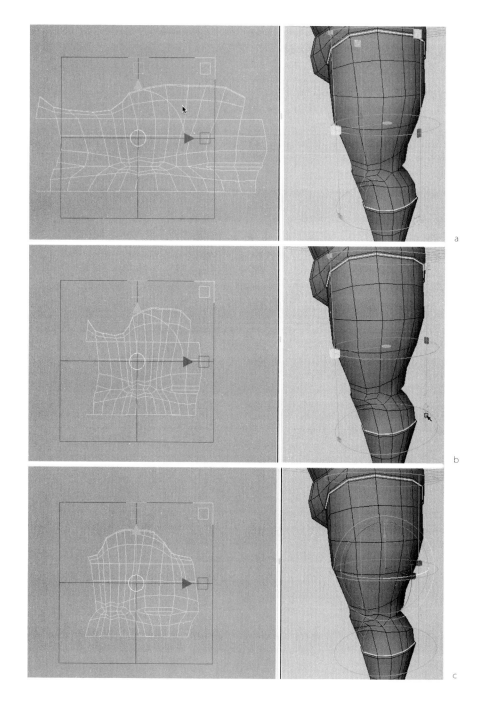

Cylindrical Mapping of the Arm

Mapping the arm involves a different procedure because Maya's cylindrical mapping maps best in the Y direction. You cannot set it to map on any other axis by default. Therefore, the projectionHeight doesn't help us much. We will need to derive that value by planar projecting first.

1. In the perspective view, pick-mask Face on the body geometry, and select the faces in the arm. Exclude the gloved hand as you did the boot. Remember that the glove extends about halfway up the forearm. (Because of the way the glove overlaps the forearm, it is easier to select these faces in the perspective view than in the UV Layout pane)

2. Choose **Create UVs → Planar Mapping** ❑. You can project this throwaway map in Y or Z. Click Project.

3. Record the projectionWidth value of this map. It should read 4.998.

4. Undo this map.

5. Choose **Create UVs → Cylindrical Mapping**. The projection manipulator will be oriented in the wrong direction.

6. Input **4.998** into the projectionHeight attribute of the polyCylProj*n* node in the Channel Box. This will make the projection the correct height in the viewport.

7. Divide 4.998 by 17.36 (the original height) to get 0.29. Set the imageScaleU and V attributes to this value to correctly scale the projection in the UV Texture Editor.

8. Rotate the projection manipulator 90° in Z to align it with the axis of the arm.

9. Change the projectionHorizontalSweep attribute to 360° to wrap the manipulator all the way around the arm and narrow the projection in the UV Texture Editor, as shown in Figure 12.32a.

10. In the UV Texture Editor, rotate the projection 90° to match it visually with what you see in the viewport, as shown in Figure 12.32b. You can also input **90** in the rotationAngle attribute in the Channel Box.

11. In the viewport, grab the red rotational handle on the side of the manipulator and rotate it in Y until the seam (marked by the red cross) runs along the bottom of the arm and there is an even edge of faces at the top and the bottom of the projection in the UV Texture Editor, as shown in Figure 12.32c. Rotate Y in the Channel Box until it reads about 60°.

Save your file. The easy part is over.

Figure 12.32

(a) Setting the sweep value for the cylindrical projection. (b) Rotate the projection in the UV Editor window. (c) Rotate the manipulator (this has been thickened for clarity) until the seam is facing the bottom of the arm and an even edge is at the top and bottom of the projection.

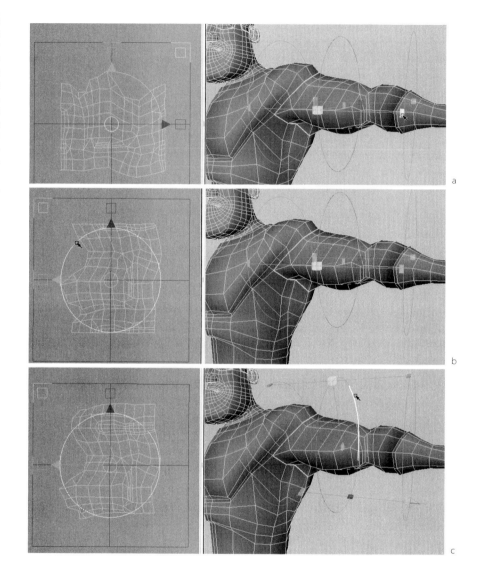

Mapping the Boot

The boot is the first part of the character for which it is just about impossible to create a single, seamless, distortionless section. We will have to combine automatic and cylindrical mapping to create the proper section for the boot. Let's create the map as follows.

1. Select the faces making up the top part of the boot and cylindrically map them as you did the leg earlier. Divide the projectionHeight by 17.36 to correctly scale the projection in UV space. Rotate the projection –205° in Y to point the seam to the front of

the boot. Finally, flip the UVs horizontally to match them with the map for the foot part of the boot.

> It is common to try different settings to determine which are correct for the situation. The Rotate value of –205 and the need to flip UVs was determined after several trials (and errors). Don't think you have to get it right the first time, every time.

2. Select the foot part of the boot as shown in Figure 12.33a.

3. Choose **Create UVs → Automatic Mapping** ☐. Set the number of planes to 6, and check Less Distortion. Leave all other settings at their default, and click Project. You will see something like Figure 12.33b. Maya lets you manipulate the axes of projection for the automatic mapping node. The blue planes represent the axes of projection. Rotating these axes changes the projection angles for these planes together; they cannot be rotated independently.

4. Unfortunately, there is no scale attribute for this automatic projection, so we will have to scale it manually. In the UV Texture Editor, RM click and choose **Select → Convert Selection To UVs** to make the UVs visible.

5. Press the R key to choose the Scale tool, and click and drag the middle, yellow box in the UV Texture Editor until the top UVs of the top of the foot piece match the bottom of the shin part of the boot, as shown in Figure 12.33c. Translate the UVs into position, and zoom into the UV Texture Editor to get this as close as possible.

6. RM click and choose **Select → Convert Selection To Faces**. We need to flip these UVs vertically, but we can't perform this operation on UVs; faces must be selected.

7. From the UV Texture Editor menu, choose **Edit UVs → Flip UVs** ☐, and select the Vertical and Local radio buttons. Click Apply and Close. You should see something like Figure 12.33d.

8. Convert the selection back to UVs, and move the selection off the shin part of the boot.

Figure 12.33

(a) Select the faces of the foot part of the boot. (b) The Automatic Mapping manipulator. (c) Scale the foot pieces to match the ankle UVs. (d) Convert Selection To Faces and flip the UVs.

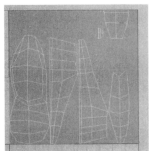
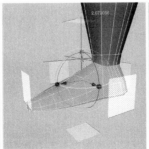
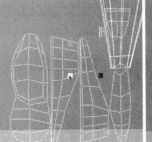
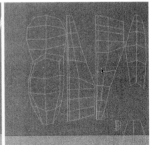

a   b   c   d

Having mapped the foot part of the boot, we now want to sew it so that the seam goes down the top of the foot. We can create a map that will have almost no distortion. But which side of the foot goes on which side of the heel? The connection between the layout and perspective panes helps here. By pick-masking Edge in the UV Texture Editor and selecting an edge along the side of the heel, as shown in Figure 12.34, we see the corresponding edge become selected on the side foot piece. Let's sew the foot together.

1. Select one UV on the side piece, and move it into position, as shown in Figure 12.35a. Because we want as little distortion as possible at the top of the foot, make the side of the foot overlap the heel as much as possible.

2. Select the three edges of the heel as shown in Figure 12.35b.

3. Choose **Polygons → Sew UV Edges** from the UV Texture Editor menu and you should see something like Figure 12.35c.

4. Finish the other side of the foot using this same technique.

5. Connect the tip of the foot to one of the sides.

6. Pick-mask Edge in the UV Texture Editor, and select the edges along the top of the foot.

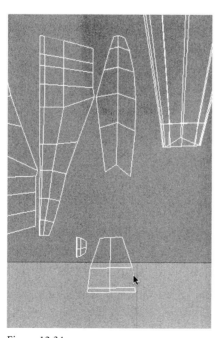

Figure 12.34

Determining which foot piece goes on which side of the heel

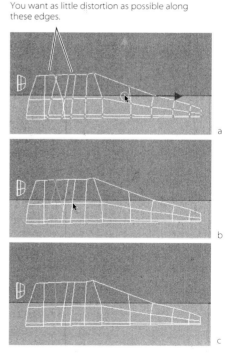

You want as little distortion as possible along these edges.

Figure 12.35

(a) Move the pieces of the foot close to the heel. (b) Select the edges to sew. (c) Sew UVs to close the gap.

7. Choose **Polygons → Cut UV Edges**.

8. Move each half to the appropriate side of the foot, and sew the UVs together.

The bottom of the foot can remain separate because the edge of the foot provides a natural break and will incorporate the seam nicely. Our next task will be to map the shin area of the boot and sew it to the shoe.

Because we rotated the cylindrical projection on the boot earlier, the edges at the bottom of the shin area will line up with the shoe. Right now, however, they are too wide. We could scale them down and move them into position row by row, but now is a great time to introduce the UV Lattice tool.

1. With the UVs selected, choose **Tool → UV Lattice Tool** to select the UV Lattice tool. The defaults of three rows and three columns will work fine for this purpose. Keep in mind that the lattice is active until you select another tool. You will LM click and drag the circles at the intersections of the lattice lines to manipulate the lattice.

2. Figure 12.36a and b show the before and after. Move the circles in the bottom corners inward to scale the bottom UVs downward. The idea is to distort the top lines of the boots as little as possible.

3. Move the middle circles inward to scale the middle of the shin area inward.

4. Pick-mask Edge, and select the bottom edges of the shin area as shown in Figure 12.36c. Note that the top edges of the shoe area are also selected.

5. Sew these edges together to complete the shoe, as shown in Figure 12.36d.

The cylindrical mapping operation has mapped the UVs at the rim of the boot on top of one another in UV texture space. This will cause any texture that is mapped in that area to stretch, probably unacceptably. To correct that, we need to pull the UVs up and space them out.

1. Pick-mask UV in the UV Texture Editor, and select one UV anywhere on the boot.

Figure 12.36

(a) **Apply the lattice to the selection. (b) Move the lattice points to warp the UVs. (c) Select the edges. (d) Sew UVs.**

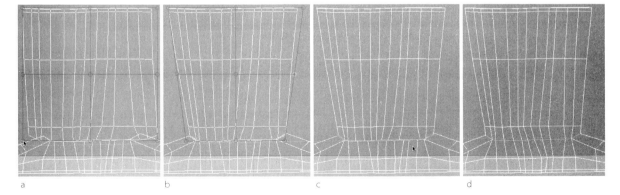

a   b   c   d

Figure 12.37

**(a) Move the top
rows of UVs up. (b)
Move the end UVs
back down.**

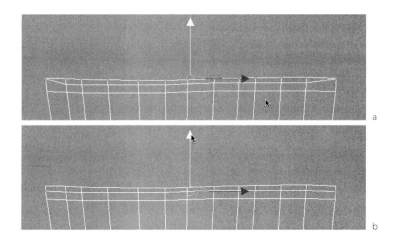

2. Ctrl+RM click in the window and choose **To Shell Border** from the marking menu. Note that this is the same thing as RM clicking and choosing **Select → Select Shell Border**. Select Shell and the Convert Selection To commands are also available using this shortcut, so we will use the Ctrl+RM shortcut from now on.

3. Shift+deselect all the UVs except the top row.

4. Move the top row of UVs upward, as shown in Figure 12.37a.

5. Move the second row edge UVs down, as shown in Figure 12.37b. Sometimes you will need to juggle UVs, selecting them in the perspective view, if more than two are mapped on top of one another.

Mapping the Glove

Machismo's glove is next, and it will require us to cylindrically map the wrist and forearm area while planar mapping the hand as we did with the boot. But the hand is a more complex shape that does not lend itself to any mapping technique. As a result, we will have to move UVs in groups and individually to produce a usable map. Let's map the glove as follows.

1. Planar map the hand part of the glove in Y. Size the projection in UV space by dividing projectionWidth by 17.36, and enter that value (0.17) into the imageScaleU and V fields, as shown in Figure 12.38.

Figure 12.38

**Planar projecting
the hand**

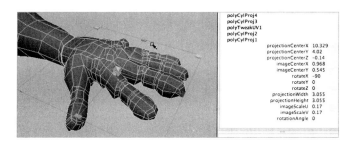

2. In the UV Texture Editor, pick-mask Face and select the faces of the forearm/wrist area.

3. Planar map these faces in Y to get the proper projection size as we did with the arm earlier. Then undo the mapping operation.

4. Cylindrically map this selection with the proportion derived by dividing the projection numbers. Enter this value in the imageScale U and V fields.

5. Change horizontalProjectionSweep to 360. RotateZ to –90, rotationAngle to –90, and projectionHeight to 1.928 in the Inputs list. This will position the manipulator pointing down the axis of the arm and orient the projection properly in the UV Texture Editor.

Figure 12.39a shows the projection in the UV Texture Editor as it is now. The problem is that we will have to cut and sew more UVs than we want to; we are trying to keep this operation to a minimum. We want the edge in front to be the border edge, but which one is it? We can select an edge and use it to line up the projection exactly as follows.

1. Pick-mask Edge in the viewport and select the edge, as shown in Figure 12.39b. Note where it shows up in the perspective pane.

2. Click the Show Manipulator tool in the Toolbox.

3. In the Inputs list in the Channel Box, select the topmost polyCylProj$n$ node. This will be the most recent. The manipulator will appear.

4. Rotate the manipulator around the wrist until the selected edge lines up with the edge of the projection, as shown in Figure 12.39c.

Let's continue mapping the hand.

1. Pick-mask Face in the UV Texture Editor, and select the hand part of the glove.

2. Planar map the hand in Y with a scale of 0.17.

3. Select a line of edges all the way around the hand. Use the Ctrl+RM Edge Loop shortcut discussed earlier.

4. Deselect any stray edges selected on the arm or glove by Ctrl marquee selecting them in the UV Texture Editor. You should have a selection like that in Figure 12.40. Note that in the bottom image the selection zigzags up and down around the base of the wrist.

5. Cut UVs to separate the top and bottom of the hand.

6. Select Shell on the bottom palm of the hand to select all of it. Remember that if the whole hand is selected, you did not select edges all the way around the hand in step 3.

7. Move your selection up above the top of the hand in the UV Texture Editor.

8. Convert your UV selection to Faces, and flip UVs with both Local and Vertical settings.

9. Move and rotate the palm to line it up so that the pinky fingers are side by side, as shown in Figure 12.41a.

Figure 12.39

(a) The starting projection. (b) Selecting the edge in the viewport. (c) Rotating the manipulator after using the Show Manipulator tool. The projection rotates to match the manipulator and line up the edge.

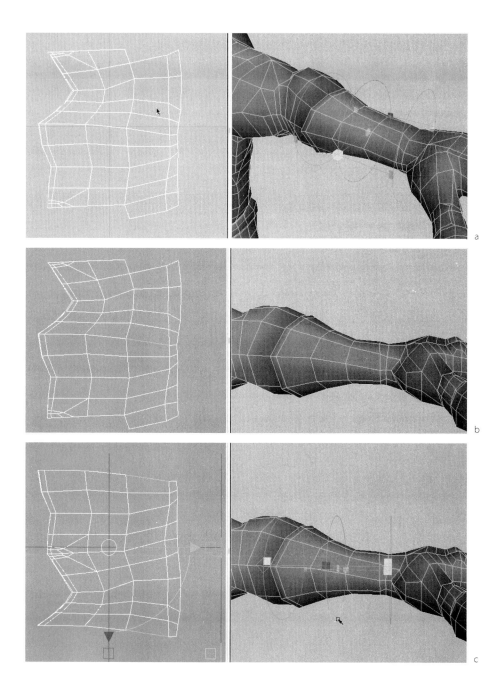

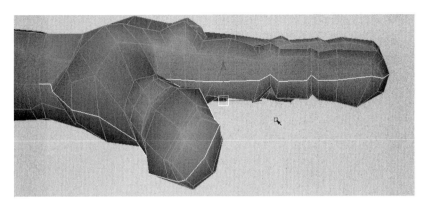

Figure 12.40

The proper selection
path for cutting UVs

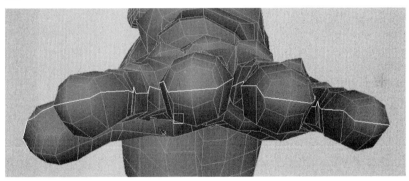

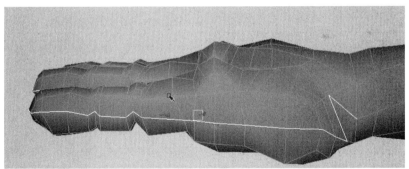

Figure 12.41

(a) The palm
aligned. (b) The shell
border selected. (c)
UVs deselected. (d)
Convert Selection To
Edges. (e) Sew UVs.
(f) Relax UVs.

a　　　　　b　　　　　c　　　　　d　　　　　e　　　　　f

10. Select the shell border as shown in Figure 12.41b.

11. Deselect all UVs not on the common border with the top of the hand. Also deselect any UVs along the border with the wrist area, as shown in Figure 12.41c.

12. Choose Convert Selection To Edges as shown in Figure 12.41d. If any stray edges are selected, pick-mask Edge and deselect them.

13. Sew UVs to sew the two hand projections together, as shown in Figure 12.41e.

14. RM click in the UV Texture Editor, and choose **Select → Select Connected Faces**.

15. Convert your selection to UVs.

16. Choose **Polygons → Relax UVs** with Pin UV Border and Pin Unselected UVs checked. Set Max Iterations to 1 and click Relax. You should have something like that shown in Figure 12.41f.

17. There are some overlapping UVs in the thumbs and fingers area. To help see where these overlaps occur, you can use Maya's new Display Overlapping UVs feature: select the hand and choose **Image → Shade UVs** to show a color representation of the UVs in texture space. The shell will become colored and semitransparent; any overlapping UVs will be visible due to their difference in color and their greater opacity.

18. Pull the overlapping UVs outward individually until you have something that looks like Figure 12.42. Take special care to untangle the UVs between the fingers.

19. Move the hand UVs over to the wrist/forearm. Line them up as carefully as you can for sewing.

20. Select the border edge along the hand/wrist.

21. Sew UVs.

22. Select Connected Faces and immediately convert the selection to UVs.

23. Relax UVs to smooth out the border.

24. Select the whole body mesh and delete history. We won't need any of the projection data.

25. Save the file as Machismo02_ArmLegDone.mb.

WINDING ORDER

In addition to seeing any overlapping UVs when Shade UVs is selected, you will also see the winding order—the direction in which UVs are wrapped—for each polygon face. Elements that appear blue have a clockwise winding order, while those that are red have a counter-clockwise winding order. Being able to see the winding order is important because the order for each shell of UVs should be the same. If one face is reversed, it will distort the eventual texture on the figure, creating undesirable results. If you discover faces that have an inconsistent winding order, you can select these faces and choose **Polygons → Flip** in the UV Texture Editor menu set to flip them into the correct winding order.

Relax UVs is useful for untangling UVs in certain circumstances. But if it is used too much, it can create a mushy and undefined UV map. We will use this map as a basis for painting, so it needs to carry some of the definition of the mesh.

Mapping the Torso

The torso is comparatively easy, now that we have done the glove. Given that in many garments, the seam goes from the neck to the armhole and down the side of the body to the leg hole and then bisects the crotch, we can use that seam as our border edge. We will use planar mapping almost exclusively here. Let's map the torso as follows.

1. Select the faces on the side of the torso, as shown in Figure 12.43a.

2. Planar map this selection in X. Scale the UVs by dividing projection-Height by 17.36.

3. Move them out of the center of the UV Texture Editor for now.

4. Select the faces in the shoulder area, as shown in Figure 12.43b.

5. Planar map this selection in Y, and scale the projection as described earlier.

6. In the UV Texture Editor, select one of the border edges of the leg map.

7. In the perspective viewport (this is important—the selection is different and undesirable if you do this in the UV Editor), Ctrl+RM and choose **Edge Loop Utilities → To Edge Loop**. This will select up the leg and down to the knee, but it is the crotch edge that we want.

8. Deselect the selected edges on the leg map.

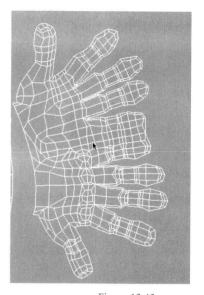

Figure 12.42

The hand map with edge UVs pulled

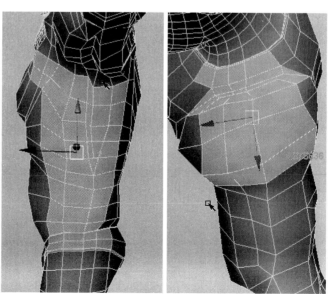

a　　　　　　b

Figure 12.43

Select faces at the side and shoulder area in the torso.

Figure 12.44

Select these edges.

9. Cut UVs.

10. Select a UV on the front of the torso and choose Select Shell. Only the front of the torso should select.

11. Move the front of the torso away from overlapping the back.

We have just created front, back, side, and shoulder panels for the torso. What we want to do now is cut the shoulder and side panels and join the pieces to their appropriate panel.

1. Select the edges on the shoulder and side panels as shown in Figure 12.44.

2. Cut UVs.

3. Move the bottom half of the shoulder map to the front of the torso, and sew UVs to join them.

4. Select the faces of the top half of the shoulder map, and flip UVs in the vertical direction.

5. Move this piece to the top of the back section, and sew it onto the back.

6. Select the faces of the right part of the side panel, flip them in the horizontal direction, move them to line up with the back panel, and sew them together.

7. Move, line up, and sew the left half of the side panel to the front panel. This particular panel poses an interesting problem. The part of the chest that was mapped in X is quite different from the front panel projection of the chest. It is desirable to pull out the UVs in the front panel that are almost on top of one another to make that area more even.

8. Pull down the UVs in the crotch area to give them some area in the final map.

9. Pull out the overlapping UVs in the border between the shorts and legs and in the collar of the shirt.

10. Select an edge loop along the border of the shorts and the trunk of the torso, and cut UVs. Move the shorts out from the trunk, as they will be textured separately.

Open Machismo03_TorsoUVdone.mb from the CD to see the final torso map.

Mapping the Head

Fortunately for us, Machismo is a bit of a blockhead. His melon fits rather nicely into a cube, which will help us immensely. His face is flat, so planar mapping it will be easy. In fact, we've done quite a bit of the work already by making a planar map. Let's separate the sections we already have.

1. Select edges along the natural planes of the head, as shown in Figure 12.45.

2. In the UV Texture Editor, cut UVs to separate the map into its constituent parts.

3. Select UV Shell on the front and back pieces. Move them out of the way.

4. Move the bottom front of the neck piece out of the way as well.

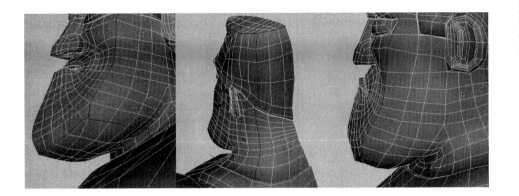

Figure 12.45

Select these edges along the natural planes of the head.

5. Select Shell on the bottom of the neck. This will be the first piece we will add to the puzzle of the face.

6. Convert the selection to Faces.

7. Planar map this piece in Y. Set Image Center to 0.0, 0.8. This will put it right near where our pieces already lie. Make the Image Scale 0.1. This is a guess. You could figure imageScale in U and V, but we will be scaling, flipping, and latticing this piece of geometry so much that just getting the size and location somewhat close at this stage will be helpful. Click Project.

8. Immediately convert your selection to UVs, and move it between the front of the face and front of neck pieces.

9. A check of the edges reveals that this new under-chin piece is upside down, so flip it vertically so that it matches the surrounding face and neck pieces.

10. Unfortunately the shape of this piece is all wrong, but here is where the UV Lattice tool really shines. Click the Lattice tool to choose it.

11. Figure 12.46 shows the process of deforming these UVs.

12. Sew the edges together.

13. Select the back of the head as faces and flip them horizontally.

14. Select the faces of the side of the head and planar map them in X. Set the scale to 0.18, and use the same Image Center settings.

15. Move and rotate the side projection so that it begins to line up with a four-row, four-column UV lattice to deform the side projection, as shown in Figure 12.47a.

16. Use the same 4 × 4 UV lattice and deform the back of the head projection as shown in Figure 12.47b.

Figure 12.46

Deforming the under part of the chin using the UV Lattice tool

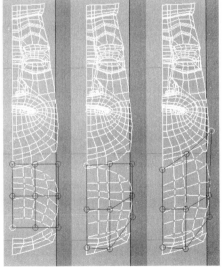

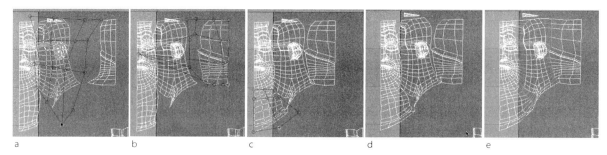

a   b   c   d   e

Figure 12.47

Use the UV Lattice Tool to assist in joining the UV pieces of the head.

17. Use a 3 × 3 lattice to shrink the chin area vertically and stretch it horizontally, as shown in Figure 12.47c.

18. Select the UV Shell Border, and then deselect UVs, as shown in Figure 12.47d.

19. Convert Selection to Edges, and sew UVs, as shown in Figure 12.47e.

20. Smooth out the UV map by pulling individual UVs. Feel free to turn on UV shading (**Image → Shade UVs**) to check for overlapping UVs and winding order problems on the head.

Problem Areas: The Ear and the Nose

The human head is one of the most difficult areas to UV map. The reason is that major details such as the nose and the ear have serious undercuts. The nose, for example, has the entire bottom nostril area, which does not map well in Z. Also, the back of the nostrils where the nose connects to the face actually curves around to face away from any mapping plane we could use. Fortunately Maya provides tools to make this job easier. Let's map the nose as follows.

1. In the perspective view, pick-mask Edge and select around the bottom of the nose, as shown in Figure 12.48a.

2. In the UV Texture Editor, cut UVs.

3. Pick-mask UV, select the shell you just made, and move it out of the way.

4. In the viewport, pickmask Edges, and select those that compose the back of the nostril area, as shown in Figure 12.48b. Let your selection radiate outward from the back of the nostril area and extend down below the hole. If you look at the UV Texture Editor while you do this, you will see where the edges extend into the tangled area at the back of the nostril.

5. RM click in the UV Texture Editor, and convert your selection to UVs.

6. Choose **Tool → UV Smudge Tool** ❑ to select the UV Smudge tool and open its option box. Set Effect Type to Fixed, which will move UVs like the Soft Modification tool moves geometry. Setting Falloff Type to Exponential will decrease the effect, depending on

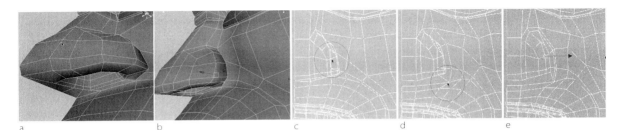

a   b   c   d   e

how far away a selected UV is from the center of the brush. Set Smudge Size small, to about 0.008 or so to get the brush the right size. Note that you can interactively change the brush size by MM dragging with the B key held down.

Figure 12.48

(a) Select the edges around the bottom of the nose. (b) Select the edges around the back of the nostril. (c) Before using the UV Smudge tool. (d) After using the UV Smudge tool. (e) Moving the points manually.

7. Smear the UVs away from the back of the nose. Figure 12.48c and d show the before and after.

8. One last row is folded under the nostril, and you can use the UV Smudge tool or move it manually to get something that looks like Figure 12.48e.

9. Select the UV section you cut earlier as faces and planar map these faces in Y. Make the scale very small, about 0.025 or so. After mapping, rotate the projection manipulator in X to about −107. This will center the mapping projection so that the nostril UVs are not overlapping the bottom of the nose.

10. Flip UVs vertically.

11. Convert the selection to UVs, and move them alongside the face so far.

12. Select the UVs of the nose and use a 4 × 4 UV lattice to begin to move them and create a hole shaped like the nose piece shown in Figure 12.49a.

13. Use a UV lattice to edit the nose piece and bring it into the same rough shape as the hole, as shown in Figure 12.49b.

14. Move the piece into position, select the appropriate edges, and sew UVs as shown in Figure 12.49c.

Figure 12.49

(a) Latticing the nose UVs. (b) Shaping the bottom of the nose. (c) The final nose.

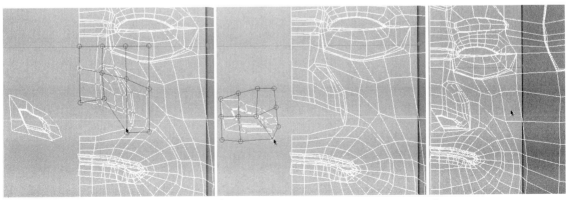

a   b   c

The ear presents a problem seen in the eyebrow and lips area: one area overlapping another. The eyebrow and lips problem can be solved by simply pulling points out from behind the obscuring part, but the ear has a mass of UVs that are difficult to distinguish from one another. Let's map the ear.

1. Select a line of edges around the bottom of the hairline down the front of the ear and around the back as shown in Figure 12.50.

2. In the UV Texture Editor, cut UVs to make a separate piece out of the ear.

3. Select a UV shell of the ear piece.

4. We now need to hide everything except this piece so that manipulating the UVs is easier. Choose **View → Isolate Select → View Set**. Then choose **View → Isolate Select → Add Selected**. This isolates this UV patch.

5. Relax UVs by checking 2 Iterations and Pin UV Border. This will shrink the ear part of the map.

6. Now we need to select everything except the shell border UVs, so select Shell Border and then immediately Shift marquee select the entire patch. This effectively inverts the selection by selecting everything except the shell border.

7. Move and scale the UVs until the interior part of the ear is contained completely within the border of the map.

8. Choose **View → Isolate Select** and uncheck View Set to show the rest of the head map.

9. Select Shell on the ear, convert Selected to Edges, and immediately sew UVs.

Figure 12.50

Selecting the proper series of edges is the key to mapping the ear.

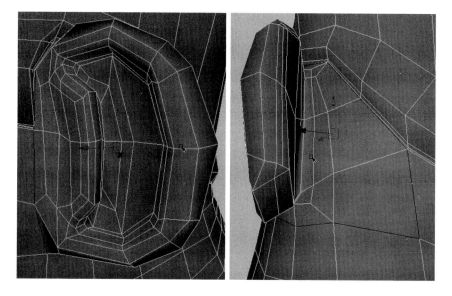

If there were a need to paint a detailed map in the ear area, you would need to go through some more manipulations at the back of the ear to spread out the UVs for painting, but because this area will be a flat color on Machismo, we can stop here.

The last step is to select and map the top of the flattop in Y and move and sew it into position. After our previous machinations, this should be easy. As part of this step, examine all the various parts of the map over the entire body. Wherever you see overlapping UVs, untangle them either by manually pulling them apart or by using the Relax UVs command. Save your file at this point. Our map is in sections, and now we must finish laying out the UV map.

Mirroring Geometry and Laying Out the Map

Up to now, we have not been overly concerned with the organization of our map other than the proportions of our projections, but how we lay out our map is extremely important. Basically, we want the various pieces of the map to fill the square UV space as efficiently as possible. We will be painting a square map, so we want to make sure that our pieces fill up the space well. Unfortunately, at this point, we have only half the geometry and therefore only half the map, so let's mirror the geometry as follows. Open the scene file from earlier or open `Machismo04_UVLayout.mb` from the CD.

1. Select the body geometry in object mode. The pivot point of the geometry should be at the world origin. If for some reason it is not, move it there.

2. Delete history on the geometry.

3. Choose **Polygons → Mirror Geometry** ❑. Set Mirror Options to –X, and make sure Merge With Original is unchecked. Click Mirror.

4. You may notice that the geometry mirrors farther off the center line than expected. To correct this, pick-mask Vertex, and in the UV Texture Editor, select Shell. Only the left half of the geometry should be selected.

5. Move the left half over until the two halves meet at the center line, as shown in Figure 12.51. They can overlap somewhat; the object is to get them as close as possible.

6. In the UV Texture Editor, convert the selection to Faces and flip UVs in the horizontal direction using Global Coordinate. This will spread the various map pieces all over the UV Texture Editor.

7. Use the Merge Vertices tool to weld the body together up the center line. You click each edge to merge and then click a third time to merge your selection. Follow the center line around the model. Use the wireframe view to see the inside edges in the mouth.

8. Rename the geometry BodyGeo.

Figure 12.51

Move the left half over until the two halves meet in the middle.

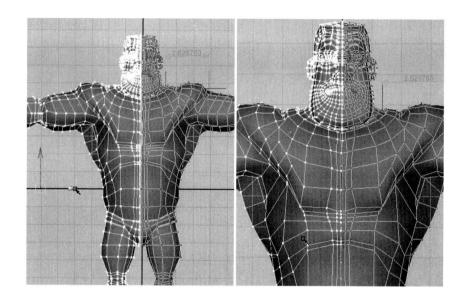

Now we need to weld the head, front of torso, back of torso, front of shorts, and back of shorts in UV space. Our procedure is simple; weld them together as follows.

Figure 12.52

(a) Moving the pieces into position. (b) Selecting the center line of the body pieces. (c) Manually selecting and then deselecting the stray selected edges.

1. In the UV Texture Editor pane, move each left piece in close proximity to the right piece by selecting a UV shell for each and moving it into position, as shown in Figure 12.52a. Make sure the edges of each left piece align with those of the right side.

2. In the UV Texture Editor, select an edge along the center line anywhere on the body.

3. Ctrl+RM click and choose Select Continuous Edge. This will select the center line edges on both pieces of all the body maps as shown in Figure 12.52b.

4. Deselect the loose edges selected on the head.

5. Sew UVs to join the body pieces.

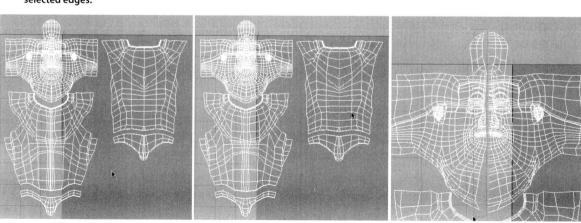

a   b   c

6. Manually select the center line edge of the head by marquee selecting around it.

7. Deselect the loose edges by Ctrl marquee selecting them as shown in Figure 12.52c.

We now need to lay out the UV map. In its final form, it needs to fit into the upper-right square of the UV Texture Editor. But we don't want to cram the pieces into that small square. Instead, at this point, we will lay out the UV map into a larger square as shown in Figure 12.53a. You can scale pieces of the map, but you should scale the right and left hands together to ensure that the maps for each half will match. As you can see, the front and back of the torso have been joined at the shoulder and the head piece has been scaled up.

Once the map is laid out the way you want it, you can fit it into the upper-right corner by selecting the entire map as faces, choosing **Polygons → Normalize** ⬚, and checking Collectively and Preserve Aspect Ratio. Delete history, and congratulate yourself on a well-mapped figure. Save your file as `Machismo06_UVMap.mb`. We are now ready to begin mapping texture maps onto a material's color, diffuse, specular, and bump channels.

No matter how precise your measurements with the Measure tool, the UV map will always be somewhat distorted. This is a natural consequence of using planar mapping for polygons that are not flat toward the mapping plane. To check and help correct the UV map, we will map a checkered file texture onto the surface of the model. This will give us a good sense of the relative size of the pieces of the map in relation to one another. We will be working from `Machismo06_UVMap.mb`. Let's apply the file texture and check the map.

1. Select BodyGeo in the viewport.

2. In the Hypershade, choose **Graph → Graph Materials On Selected Objects**. A Lambert material should appear.

3. Add a file node to the work area, and connect it to the color channel of the Lambert node.

4. Double-click the file node to open it in the Attribute Editor.

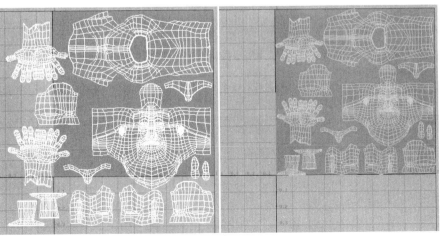

a   b

Figure 12.53

(a) Fit the map pieces within as large a square as you need. (b) Choose Polygons → Normalize r to bring all the pieces of the UV map into the 1.0 UV texture space.

5. Click the folder icon next to Image Name to open up the File Open dialog box. Select UVCheckChecker.tga from the sourceimages folder. Click Open.

6. In the viewport, press the 6 key to enter shaded/textured display mode and you should see the checkered texture mapped to BodyGeo.

Figure 12.54 shows three areas we will want to correct. We will do this in the UV Texture Editor. We use the file checker texture because it shows up nicely in the viewport and will update in real time as we edit the UV map. We'll correct the stretching on the underarm and gloves and let you do the boots on your own. Let's correct these stretched texture.

1. Create a two-pane side-by-side layout with the perspective on the right and the UV Texture Editor on the left.

2. Select BodyGeo. The UV map will display in the UV Texture Editor. The checker texture will probably display as well. If it does not, choose **Image → Display Image** to put a check by it. It should display in the UV Editor. If the image is too bright, choose **Image → Dim Image** to dim the image.

3. In the viewport, pick-mask UV and select a UV on the torso near the stretched texture, as shown at right in Figure 12.55a.

4. In the UV Texture Editor window, press the F key to frame the selected UV. This will zoom that window in close. You can zoom out a little so that the entire area is shown, as at left in Figure 12.55b.

5. The narrow faces need to be stretched to correct the texture distortion. So select UVs as shown at left in Figure 12.55b.

6. Move them up in the editor, and you will see the texture shrink on the model, as shown at right in Figure 12.55b.

Figure 12.54

Three examples of UV stretching

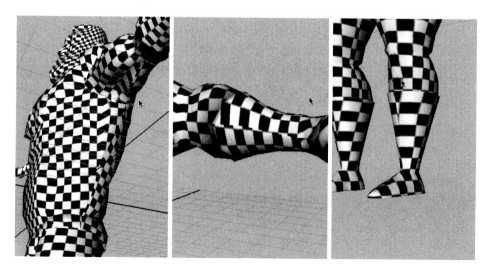

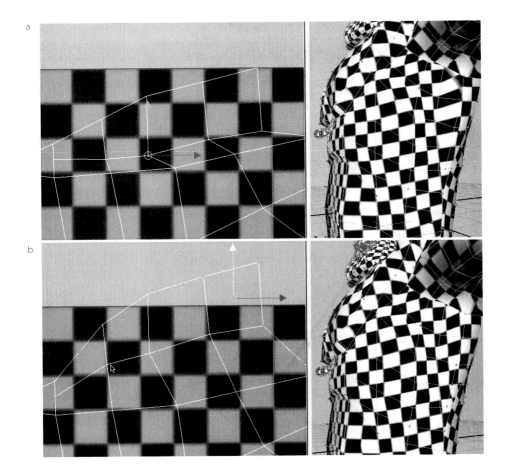

Figure 12.55

(a) Selecting the right UV. (b) Moving the UVs vertically in the UV Texture Editor corrects the stretch on the model.

7. Select Shell on the UV map to select the entire piece and move it down until it is inside the UV border, as shown in Figure 12.56. You may have to move the hand piece to allow room.

8. Repeat steps 3 through 6 on the other side of the torso.

We do not need the squares of the checkers to align perfectly. We need them to be the same size relative to one another on each. Our proportional measurements from earlier have aided a great deal in that. To correct the gloves, throw a UV lattice on it and expand the UVs so that the checkers are not stretched. Figure 12.57a and b show the before and after for that operation. Do the same for the other glove.

Overall, our map is in good proportion and we can use a UV snapshot of it to paint the texture. You should now disconnect the checkered file node from the Lambert shader; it will revert to the material's default gray. Save your file as `Machismo07_UVMapDone.mb`. Let's move on to creating Machismo's detailed texture maps.

Figure 12.56

Move the torso UV map down into the UV border.

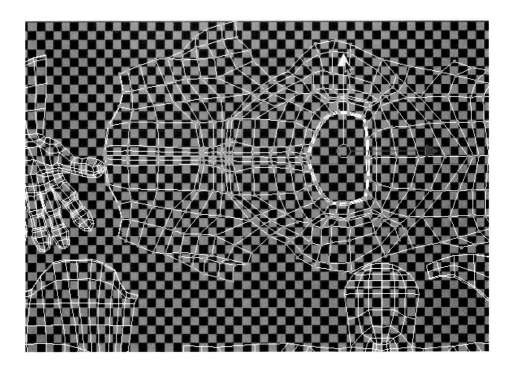

Figure 12.57

Using a UV lattice to correct texture stretching on the gloves

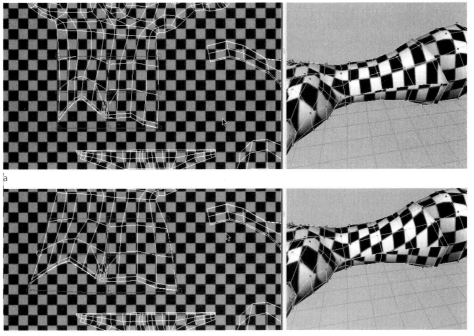

a

b

Creating Machismo's Texture

With our finished UV map, we are ready to begin creating Machismo's material. We will be creating maps for the color, diffuse, bump, and specularColor channels of Machismo's material. In the process, we will explore Maya's powerful interaction with Photoshop in the form of the PSD network node.

> To proceed any further with this section, you will need a copy of Photoshop. Although you can create painted texture maps in any program that can create a TGA, IFF, or TIFF, this section makes heavy use of the PSD file node, which creates and links to an external Photoshop file.

First we need to do some setup. At present, we have a low polygon model, that will have its resolution increased at render time to add polygonal detail and smooth out Machismo's bulky body. Select BodyGeo and choose **Mesh → Smooth** with the default settings to smooth out the mesh. You can manipulate the level of detail using the Divisions attribute of the polySmoothFace node in the Inputs list of the Channel Box. You can go back and forth between the low and high rez version of the mesh to check how textures look on the final model. You must be aware of a few key points, however, when you use this technique:

- Always set the divisions level to 0 before deleting history.
- Delete history and choose **Mesh → Smooth** before you rerender after manipulating the UVs. Otherwise the UV map gets distorted from your earlier manipulations.
- Make changes to the UV map on the low-resolution, 0 division level. Do not change the UV map at a higher division level as this is interpolated from the low-resolution version.

Lighting

The wise texture mapper should always take into account the lighting conditions of the animation for which a character is destined. It is frustrating to paint textures under one set of lighting conditions only to have them look bad under the actual lighting of the final piece. Because we don't know what the final lighting conditions will be at this time, we can only try to create a general soft overall lighting environment for our character.

If you have access to a photograph or render of the final environment, obtain a copy of GI_Joe.mel from Highend3d.com. This MEL script, written by Emmanuel Campin, can take a photograph and create simulated image-based global illumination that looks good and renders extremely fast.

If you don't want to go to the trouble, import `LightDome.mb` into your file. This is a simple globe of 16 directional lights with their intensities and Dmap Resolution attributes connected to custom attributes on a central locator called LightMaster_loc. You can increase and decrease the intensity of the dome lights as well as the softness of the shadows using the custom attributes on this locator. Included in this file is a directional light to simulate the sun. You can rotate it to see how your texture changes with different lighting angles.

One other nice feature of the dome light is that it allows us to use the shadows on the surface as a map in and of itself. We do this by baking the shading group into a file texture as we did with the granite texture earlier in this chapter. We will use this to both demonstrate Maya's ability to bake textures and to create a map that we will use as the basis for a diffuse map later. Let's create this baked lighting map.

1. If you haven't done so, import `LightDome.mb` from the CD.

2. Select LightMasterLoc. This locator contains all the settings to control the lights. Set Globe Intensity to 0.2 and Floor Intensity to 0.1.

3. Do a quick test render to see what you have. Save the image in the Render View by clicking Keep Image.

4. Select BodyGeo. Make the Divisions level on the polySmoothFace node 2.

5. Open the Hypershade. RM click in the work area and choose **Graph → Graph Materials On Selected Objects**.

6. Shift_select the Lambert node that appears in the work area, and in the Hypershade, choose **Edit → Convert To File Texture (Maya Software)** ❑. Click Anti-Alias, Bake Shading Group Lighting, and Bake Shadows. Set X and Y Resolution to 1024, and set File Format to TGA. Bake Shading Group Lighting bakes the lighting information into the file texture; Bake Shadows renders the depth map shadows into the texture as well. Click Convert And Close to bake the map.

This operation will take a minute or two depending on the speed of your processor and how much RAM you have. When it finishes, you will have a file texture linked to a surface shader that is applied automatically to BodyGeo. Now select LightMasterLoc and change GlobeIntensity and FloorIntensity to 0, effectively turning off the lights. Now rerender and compare the two images. Except where the UV map overlaps in the lips, ears, and eyes, the two images are almost identical. The technique of light and shadow baking is often used in video games to bake environment lighting into the texture maps used in corridors and buildings. The right side of Figure 12.58 shows the first render with the lights, and the left shows the render with no lights and the baked surface shader applied to BodyGeo. There is actually little difference except for render times. You can delete the surface shader and all the file texture nodes. The file texture is in the Sourceimages folder of your current project, so you can access it later.

Figure 12.58

The right image shows the Lambert texture rendered under the globe of lights. The left image is with the lighting information baked into the shader.

Let's begin the process of creating Machismo's shader. Our first step will be to create a PSD network to feed into a Blinn shader called Machismo_mat. From that point on, you are limited only by your ability to paint in Photoshop. Create the PSD network as follows.

1. Create a Blinn material and name it Machismo_mat.

2. Assign it to BodyGeo.

3. Select BodyGeo and smooth it by choosing **Mesh → Smooth**. This will give you a smoothed model that Maya will use to create the UV snapshot. This will ensure that your map will work at a high resolution.

4. In the Hypershade menu, choose **Edit → Create PSD Network**. Figure 12.59 shows this option box with the settings you should include. You can specify the image name, and you should do so. Otherwise, Maya calls it some confusing long name that includes the geometry name as well as the material name. You don't need that, so call it Machismo_mat.psd. For the Size X and Y, you can input **2048 × 2048**. If you aren't going to have any close-ups in your animation, go ahead and work at 1024 × 1024. The higher resolution of 2048 × 2048 (2K) will give great detail for close-ups, but working with that resolution causes Maya to render and update slowly. For UV Settings, you want to include your UV snapshot, usually at the top of the file. Maya will not render this layer; it is there for reference only. The Attributes Selection section is where this option box really makes itself useful. From the

Figure 12.59

The Create PSD Network Options box. You can set the Size X and Size Y to 2048 if you are going to view your character close up.

attributes list on the left, choose Color, Bump, Diffuse, and specularColor. Click the right-arrow button to move them over to the right side. These tell Maya to create a separate layer set for each attribute. If you have a procedural already linked to a particular channel, Maya will convert it to a layer based on settings you specify when you click the Convert To File Texture Options button below the Selected Attributes section. When you have finished with your settings, click Create.

5. You will see that the Machismo_mat network looks like Figure 12.60. Each channel is connected to a separate file texture, but each of those texture maps is contained in one PSD file and they all update when you invoke the Update PSD Network command.

The quality of texture map that you will paint depends largely on your skill with Photoshop, which is beyond the scope of this book. Machismo_mat.psd on the CD is the large, 2K map that the authors created for this character. It is linked to MachismoFinalTexture.mb in the shaders folder inside the renderData folder. To create your own, you can modify Machismo_mat.psd or create your own from scratch. If you choose to do the latter, here are some general work-flow suggestions that will be helpful:

- Because you are creating the map, you can delete history on BodyGeo at a higher divisions setting. This will give you a higher-res mesh, but because the UV map is done, you can apply the texture map to an earlier low-res version of the mesh.

- Start by making a separate selection mask for each UV section in Photoshop and saving the sections as alpha channels.

- Create the bump map first, and then save color, diffuse, and specularColor if needed.

- If you need to cut back on the bumpiness of the bump map, you can do so by either decreasing the bump value of the bump2d node in the Hypershade or by cutting down on the contrast of the bump layer in the Photoshop file.

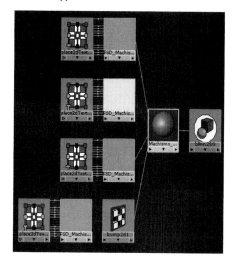

Figure 12.60

The PSD network as shown in the Hypershade

- When creating the bump map, use soft-edged brushes and then use the blur filter to soften your strokes some more. They will be crisper than they seem in the final render.

- If you want to see your map without the inclusion of one or more of the Photoshop layer sets, then hide the layer set, save the file, update the PSD network, and render.

- It is well worth your time to type **psdUpdateTextures;** in the Command line and make a shelf button out of it. This will save you the time of having to use menus to update the PSD file in Maya.

- Be aware of the default color of each layer set. Maya determines it from the default values found in each shader. The default gray of the color channel comes from the default color of the Blinn. To erase any changes in your map, use the Eyedropper tool in Photoshop to grab the default layer color and paint it out.

- Make changes to your map on separate layers. Merge down in Photoshop only when you are finished making changes.

- Too many layers slows down updating and rendering, so be judicious in your use of layers in Photoshop.

- You can give your character a warm lighting scheme by changing the specularColor map to a yellow tone. Similarly, you can make it cooler by shading it toward blue.

- Let your areas of color extend outside the areas shown in the UV snapshot. If you don't, seams can sometimes result.

- Use the light map created earlier for your diffuse map. This will give you more depth to the shading in your character.

- Be careful about editing your PSD network in Maya. You can corrupt your Photoshop file if you are not careful. You can also edit manually. This takes longer, but is safer. Add a new layer as follows.

  1. Create a new layer group in Photoshop. Click the Background layer and choose New Group in the Layer Palette menu.

  2. Name this layer group with the dot notation the same as the other layers (for example, Machismo_mat.reflectivity).

  3. Create a layer under this new group. Fill it with a 50 percent gray.

  4. Save the Photoshop file.

  5. In the Maya Hypershade, select Machismo_mat from the storage area, and graph the network in the work area.

  6. Add a PSD file node from the Create Bar.

  7. Double-click the PSD file node to open it in the Attribute Editor. Rename this node PSD_Machismo_mat_reflectivity.

  8. Click the Load File button, and load `Machismo_mat.psd` from the CD.

  9. Under the Link to Layer Set pop-up, choose Machismo_mat.reflectivity.

  10. Use the Connection Editor to connect the outAlpha of PSD_Machismo_mat_reflectivity to the Reflectivity attribute of Machismo_mat.

- Upon completion of your texture map, you can reduce Maya render time and memory usage by saving out each of the render elements (color, bump, diffuse, etc.) as a separate "flattened" file—like a TGA or IFF file—and then pipe those files into the correct material attributes, deleting the PSD node once you finish. Taking the time to make this switch can save a great deal of time and memory overhead if your scene is complex and/or the animation is long.

The low-res version of the model shaded with Machismo_mat can be found in `Machismo09_Final.mb`.

Summary

This lengthy chapter covers most aspects of creating custom shaders in Maya. You started by creating some simple shader networks in shading the globe and progressed to examining Maya's procedural shading capabilities when surfacing the MacGizmo from Chapter 4. You then learned techniques for creating properly sized and proportioned UV maps, which are the foundation of any good texture map. You finished by learning how to set up and manipulate a PSD network, allowing you to shade many different channels using one Photoshop file. In the next chapter, we will begin our exploration of rendering files, which flows directly out of texturing and lighting.

CHAPTER 13

Rendering Basics

When Maya's software (and your computer's hardware) renders a scene, it creates an image, or sequence of images, based on the lights, models, dynamics, and animation you've spent so much time creating. The machine takes over when you start a render. This might sound like a pleasant notion, but machines do exactly what we tell them to do—no less, no more. So this means that the instructions we have given the machine must be precise; otherwise we're in for a big headache.

This chapter covers how to set up cameras, render an image, create an image sequence, control the size and quality of the images, and render for compositing. We'll also discuss how to render both bitmap and vector images, how to render layers, and rendering using multiple cameras and other new features of Maya 8.5, as well as how to render directly to a layered Photoshop file. Most importantly, you will learn how to develop good rendering habits and avoid common pitfalls that can cause major headaches.

- **Rendering an object**
- **Creating and animating a camera**
- **Setting the camera and resolution**
- **Adding depth of field**
- **Adding motion blur**
- **Using the render settings**
- **Rendering with Maya Software**
- **Rendering with hardware render and the hardware render buffer**
- **Vector rendering**
- **Working in the render view**
- **Using Interactive Photorealistic Rendering (IPR)**
- **Layer rendering, compositing, and editing**
- **Ultimate rendering checklist**

Rendering an Object

Three-dimensional graphics programs render two-dimensional images that are either bitmap or vector images. Bitmap (also referred to as raster) graphics display image information in terms of pixels. A bitmap image can be thought of as being a large mosaic. When you zoom in or enlarge a bitmap image, you can see the individual pixels that make it up. Vectors, on the other hand, can be thought of as shapes made up of lines and filled with colors. They tend to look more like illustrations than the more photo-realistic bitmap graphics. Adobe Illustrator is an example of a vector graphics program.

To render a scene you need three items: a shaded object, a light, and a camera. Create a sphere in an empty scene, and click the clapboard icon at the upper right of the Status line (or choose **Render → Render Current Frame** in the Rendering menu set). The render view window opens and Maya renders a dull gray sphere. Maya has already done some of the work for you. The software has textured your sphere with a default Lambert shader, included a default light in your scene, and used the currently selected view for the camera. So you have your three ingredients for a basic render. Most likely you'll want to change these ingredients, unless a dull gray sphere is your idea of an exciting animation. But at least we have a place from which to begin.

Creating and Animating Cameras

In Maya you can create three types of cameras with which you can render your scene. The cameras themselves are essentially the same, but they come with different types of controls:

- A single-node camera is identical to your perspective camera. In the Create menu it is just called Camera.

- A two-node camera is a camera with a second external control that aims the camera. In the Create menu this is called Camera And Aim.

- A three-node camera is a camera with separate, external controls for aiming the camera and an "up" manipulator that allows you to control the camera's roll. In the Create menu this is called Camera, Aim , And Up.

Let's try these cameras out so the differences become more obvious.

1. Open the `streetScene1.mb` file from the CD. The scene shows a simple street with some simple buildings. Some curves are floating in space above the street—ignore these for the time being.

2. Choose **Create → Cameras → Camera**. An object resembling a camera will appear at the origin; it will be labeled Camera1 automatically.

3. Select the camera and choose **Panels → Look Through Selected** from the perspective camera's viewport. Your view will switch to Camera1's view. You should be able to track, dolly, and tumble using the same controls you use with the perspective camera.

4. In the Outliner, select Camera1 and make sure the Channel Box for the camera is visible. Move the camera using your view controls until you have a pleasing view of the street and the illegally parked convertible.

5. With Camera1 still selected, select all its attributes in the Channel Box, right-click, and choose Lock Selected from the list of options.

6. The camera is now locked down. You should no longer be able to change the view using the tumble, dolly, and track hot keys.

7. Select the attributes in the Channel Box again, right-click, and choose Unlock Selected.

8. With Camera1 still selected, press the S key at frame 1 of the Timeline to set a keyframe on all the channels.

9. Move the Time Slider to frame 120.

10. Use the dolly, tumble, and track hot key combinations to move to a different part of the scene, and try getting a different view from behind the car.

11. Press the S key again to set another keyframe.

12. Play back the animation and make sure you are still looking through Camera1.

UNDOING CAMERA MOVES

By default, you cannot undo a camera move that was made by using the tumble, track, and dolly hot keys. Thus, if you move the camera you're looking through by accident and you want to move back to the previous position, you may be in for some frustration. You can make a camera's movement undoable by checking the Undoable Movements setting in the camera's movement options in the Attribute Editor. However this will add camera moves to your undo queue, which can also add a bit of frustration. One can "back up" with a camera, however, by choosing **View → Previous View** from the current camera's pane, or by pressing the [key on the keyboard. If you want to be sure you don't lose a camera position, put a single keyframe on a camera at a frame you won't use in the animation (frame –1 for example). You can then move the camera and change the time on the Timeline and the camera will snap back into position.

Locking a camera is a great idea when setting up a scene. Doing so can help prevent you from moving the camera by accident once you've set up that perfect shot.

Chances are the camera move isn't quite what you would expect. For basic camera moves, such as pushing in, tracking, or pans, animating the camera this way should work fine. However, you may find it frustrating to animate the camera this way if you want to create more sophisticated moves such as a crane shot. Hence, the other types of cameras.

Let's try a second type of camera.

1. From the Create menu, choose **Cameras → Camera And Aim**. A new camera will be created named Camera2. In the Outliner, you will see that it is a child of a group called Camera2_group.

2. Expand the group in the Outliner and you'll see another node, called Camera2_Aim.

3. Switch to the perspective view and tumble until you can see Camera2 sitting peacefully at the origin.

4. If you select Camera2 and translate it in the perspective view, you'll notice that as it moves, it continues to point at the aim node much like an object with an aim constraint attached.

This camera arrangement makes creating dynamic camera moves easier because you can now set keyframes on the camera and the aim nodes separately. You might find it easier to position the camera and aim node from the perspective view while having one panel set to the camera's view. You can also move the group node, which will move both the camera and the aim. However, this is not always a good idea. If you start setting keyframes on the group, the camera, and the aim node, the animation of the camera can get confusing rather quickly. Select the Camera2 group node and look at its attributes in the Channel Box. At the bottom of the list you'll see an extra attribute labeled twist. If you change the values in this channel, you'll see that it controls the roll of the camera. You can keyframe this attribute on Camera2's group node if you need to correct the roll of the camera.

Let's try the third camera type.

1. From the Create menu, choose **Cameras → Camera, Aim, And Up**. You'll notice that a camera group called Camera3 has been created. It is similar to the Camera and Aim group except that it now has a third node that allows you to control the camera's Up direction.

2. Open the Outliner and select Camera3 from the Camera3 group.

3. Ctrl+click the Camera3_path curve.

4. Switch to the Animation menu set, and choose **Animate → Motion Paths → Attach To Motion Path ❑**.

5. In the option box, make sure that Follow is deselected and set Time Range to Time Slider.

6. Do the same for Camera3's aim node; create a motion path connection between it and the curve called Camera3_aim_path with the same options.

7   Create a motion path connection between Camera 3's up node and the path labeled Camera3_up_path.

8. Arrange the interface so that you have four panels visible. Set the panels to Outliner, perspective, Camera3, and the Graph Editor.

9. Play back the animation and observe how the camera moves in the Camera3 window. Observe how it moves in the perspective window.

10. In the Outliner, Shift+select the nodes for Camera3, Camera3's aim node, and Camera3's up node. Look at the motion path curves in the Graph Editor.

11. Experiment with moving the motion path keys in the Graph Editor.

12. Experiment with selecting and moving the CVs of the motion path curves in the perspective window.

It's not necessary to animate a camera using motion paths, but it can add a new level of control. To see a completed version of this scene, open the file streetScene2.mb from the CD.

Using motion paths is a great way to get some interesting movements out of your camera. It also gives you plenty of control to fine-tune the movement. Experiment with applying different constraints between the camera and moving objects in your scene. You can also try parenting your camera to other objects or even bones.

Using the Show Manipulators Tool

If you like the simplicity of the single node camera, you can use the Show Manipulators tool on a simple camera to achieve much of the same control that you would with the other two types of cameras. Create a new scene and choose **Create → Cameras → Camera**. A basic camera should appear at the origin. Choose the Show Manipulators tool from the toolbar. Figure 13.1 shows a single node camera with the Show Manipulators tool activated.

The camera now has an additional control for its center of interest, much like the aim node on the camera and aim. With the camera selected, from the Channel Box right-click Center Of Interest and choose Key Selected.

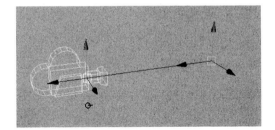

Figure 13.1

A single node camera with the Show Manipulators tool activated. You can set keyframes on either transformation tool to animate the camera's movement and center of interest.

As long as you have the Show Manipulators tool active, you can cycle through the various controls by clicking the circular switch close to the camera in the perspective view. You can then interactively adjust some of the same controls that you control numerically in the camera's Attribute Editor. These include the camera's pivot point and the clipping planes.

Viewing Clipping Planes

A camera in Maya is different from a real camera in that Maya's cameras are mathematical constructs that simulate how a real-world camera functions. The most important difference between Maya's cameras and real ones is that Maya's cameras can only "see" a certain chunk of space (called the frustum) due to the math involved in calculating what the camera sees. Clipping planes are slices of space beyond which a camera will no longer display or render objects in a scene. There is a near clipping plane near the camera and a far clipping plane at a distance. Objects between these two planes will be rendered. One might be tempted to make the near clipping plane very small and the far plane very far away, but since Maya uses clipping plane information to help determine the distance between the camera and the objects in a scene, there can be only so much distance between the near and far clipping planes before the math used to determine depth (the resolution) breaks down and render artifacts appear.

Let's explore clipping planes.

1. Open `clippingPlanes.mb` from the CD.

2. Make sure you are looking through Camera1.

3. Open the Attribute Editor for Camera1.

4. Set the far clipping plane to 12. Notice how the objects in the distance disappear.

5. Set the far clipping plane back to 1000, and set the near clipping plane to 11.

6. Notice how the objects in the foreground disappear. Furthermore, one of the hydrants is intersected by the near clipping plane (see Figure 13.2).

7. If you render this scene, you will still see all the fire hydrants. This is because Auto Render Clip Plane is on by default. Turn this option off and then render the scene again to see the results of your changes.

> Sometimes when you are working in Maya, you find that a camera is not displaying objects correctly or that nothing at all can be seen. This is often because the clipping planes have been accidentally set incorrectly.

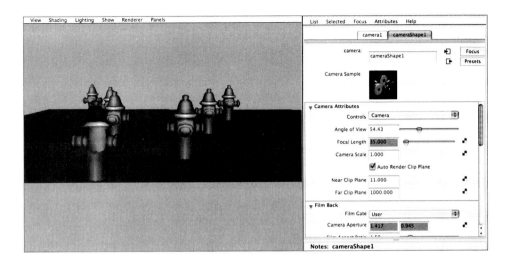

Figure 13.2
With the near clipping plane set to 11, the fire hydrant in the foreground is being sliced in half.

Another important camera control is the focal length. The Focal Length and the Angle Of View settings in the Attribute Editor are inversely related: increasing one decreases the other. The shorter the focal length, the wider the view and the more exaggerated the perspective. This is similar to switching out the lens of the camera and, if used in an animated scene, can act as a type of zoom. By default, the focal length is set to 35, which is a common length for real-world cameras. A popular technique in horror movies, called the dolly-zoom, is to animate the shortening of the focal length while pushing the camera in toward a subject, keeping the main subject approximately the same size throughout. Try it and see if you suddenly feel as if you're in a Spielberg or Cronenberg film.

THE Z-DEPTH CHANNEL

Depth, usually known as Z-depth in 3D packages, can be saved out as a separate image channel that can be stored with some image formats when you render a scene. The Z-depth channel contains information regarding the distance of the objects in the scene from the camera. Some compositing software packages can use the Z-depth channel, which can allow you to add and adjust 3D effects such as depth of field after the scene has been rendered. Additionally, Maya 8 can now composite depth images directly in a camera view, which is great for placing objects in a scene that has a depth-mapped background plane.

Setting the Camera and Resolution

Maya allows you to create as many cameras as you want in order to render your scene. You can also set up multiple cameras to render a scene simultaneously from different angles. Finally, you can also render a scene from any of Maya's orthographic (top, front, and side) and perspective cameras.

By default, when you create a scene, the perspective camera is already set up to render. Choose **Window** → **Rendering Editors** → **Render Settings** to open the Render Settings window and look at the settings in the Common tab. You will find a Camera attribute. In the drop-down menu next to Camera, you'll see persp, which refers to the perspective camera. Expand this menu and you'll see a list of all the other cameras in the scene. By selecting one of these other cameras, you are changing the camera that will render the scene (see Figure 13.3). Choosing the last option in the list—**Add Renderable Camera**—creates a new section in the Render Settings window, where you can select an additional camera to render the scene. By selecting this option several times, you can add as many cameras as you wish to render out your scene.

Select the perspective camera from this menu, and then open the Attribute Editor for the perspective camera. In the tab for the perspective camera's shape node, you'll find an Output Settings folder. Open this folder, and you'll see a check box next to the Renderable attribute. This indicates that this camera will render the scene. Open the attributes for the orthographic cameras in the scene and you'll find that this attribute is automatically deselected for these cameras.

How do you make sure the correct camera is rendering the scene? Let's look at an example.

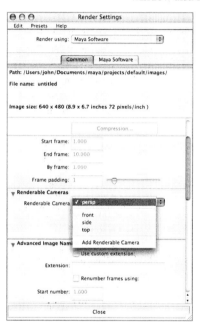

Figure 13.3

The drop-down menu in the Render Settings window allows you to choose which cameras will render the scene.

1. Create a new scene.

2. Create a cube at the origin.

3. Create a new camera, select it in the Outliner, and rename it renderCam.

4. Position the camera so that it is looking at the cube from an angle that is noticeably different from the perspective view.

5. Open the Render Settings window.

Once again, in the camera list you should see the persp camera listed, indicating that the perspective camera will render the seen. Click the menu arrow to display the camera list and you should see renderCam listed. However, since persp appeared as selected in the camera list, the scene will be rendered from the perspective camera. Want to switch to renderCam? Choose renderCam from the list. Close the render settings window, and then open this window again; renderCam should appear as the rendering camera. As noted earlier, to render from both the persp and renderCam cameras in one batch render, choose

Add Renderable Camera from the list, select persp as one of the cameras and renderCam as the other. When the scene renders, you will get two image folders, one for each camera. This can be a little dangerous because you might leave these settings on by mistake and end up rendering the scene from multiple cameras when you don't intend to do so. This can double (or triple or quadruple, depending on the number of cameras you've left "on") your render time.

RENDERING HOUSECLEANING

Don't assume that just because you've done all your test renders with a particular camera that camera necessarily will render the scene. Always double-check the render output settings of a camera before starting a batch render. Failure to check which camera is selected to render a scene has been the cause of many a wasted render hour. Also, avoid giving your cameras a long name such as tonyCharacter_left_big_toe_render_camera_version1. When you batch render, you'll end up with extremely long filenames, and you can miss that tonyCharacter_left_big_toe_render_camera_version1 has been set to Renderable because the name is too long to be completely visible in the Camera drop-down list in the Render Settings window. Always double-check each camera's output settings before starting a batch render.

Setting the Resolution

The resolution is the size of the two-dimensional image Maya creates when you render a scene. In Maya, the resolution controls are located in the Render Settings window, shown in Figure 13.4. The attributes in the Render Settings window will be discussed in more detail in the next section, but let's open the Render Settings window and focus on the resolution attributes.

Maya borrows a lot of terminology from the world of motion picture cameras. For instance, you'll see the terms *Film Back* and *Film Gate* in the attribute settings for your camera. Film Back refers to a plate in a physical camera upon which the negative sits. This relates to the actual size of the negative. A 35mm camera has a 35mm film back. Film Gate refers to the metal gate that holds the negative against the film back. The film gate in a real camera overlaps the negative so that only the region inside the gate is exposed to light. There can be more than one size film gate for a 35mm camera.

The resolution is set in the Image Size section of the Render Settings window. These settings determine the size of the images rendered in the Render View/IPR window as well as the size of the resolution gate displayed in the camera. And, of course, the Image Size settings determine the resolution for all batch renders. This is one reason you might want to visit the Render Settings window at the start of a project: all your test renders in the render view will be at the resolution you set in the Render Settings window. You can use one of the many presets in the Resolution drop-down menu, or you can create a custom

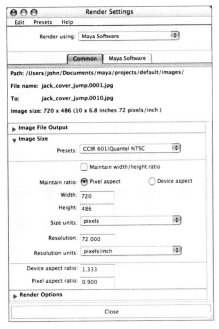

Figure 13.4

You specify the properties of your rendered images in the Render Settings window.

resolution by entering numbers in the Width and Height fields. As long as the Maintain Width/Height Ratio check box is enabled, the corresponding numbers in the Width and Height fields will automatically update when you enter a new number in either the Width or Height field. This is handy because you can then quickly change the settings to one-half or one-quarter size for test renders.

If you are rendering for video output, remember that video stretches the height of the pixel, which means that an image intended for video will look squished on a computer monitor. The pixel aspect ratio for video is rectangular rather than square, making the ratio 0.9. (You can see this when you choose CCIR 601/Quantel NTSC from the Resolution drop-down menu.) A pixel aspect ratio of 1.0 creates an image made up of square pixels, which is how a computer monitor displays an image.

Between the render settings and the camera attributes, you'll see resolution expressed in a number of ways. Many related ratios refer to the dimensions of the final image as well as the dimensions of the pixels that make up the image.

Image Aspect Ratio Simply the resolution of an image represented as a ratio, or X/Y. For example, typical video is 720/486 = 1.48.

Pixel Aspect Ratio The Y/X ratio of the actual pixels that make up the image. The square pixels a computer monitor uses have a pixel aspect ratio of 1.0. Video uses nonsquare pixels with a ratio of 0.9 (1.0/1.1).

Device Aspect Ratio The image aspect ratio multiplied by the pixel aspect ratio. For video that is 1.48 × 0.9 = 1.333.

Film Aspect Ratio The Camera Aperture attribute represented as a ratio X/Y. For video, that is 0.816/0.612 = 1.333.

If your final output is video but you want to view your animations on the computer unsquished, you can test-render using an image aspect ratio of 720 × 540 or 640 × 480. You can then set your resolution to a standard video resolution for final renders or use your compositing or editing software to convert the test renders to nonsquare pixels, or 720 × 486. Just be sure not to expect good results if you "upsample" a 640 × 480 image to 720 × 486 because the pixels of the original image are being blown up in this case, which can result in ugly artifacts.

Most of the time choosing one of Maya's preset resolutions will get the job done just fine.

When animating in Maya, you can choose to see a representation of the resolution in your camera window by choosing **View ▸ Camera Settings ▸ Resolution Gate** from the menu in your camera's viewport. You can also choose to see your safe action and title-safe regions from this menu. These controls are also available in the camera's Attribute Editor in the Display Options folder.

You can further adjust the display of these regions by fine-tuning the Overscan, Film Back, and Film Gate settings in the camera's Attribute Editor.

Let's take a look at how to work with Maya's display settings.

1. Return to the scene you created in the previous example or create a new scene, and open the editor for the perspective camera.

2. Switch your perspective view to the perspective camera by choosing Perspective from the camera pane's panel menu.

3. Turn on Resolution Gate, and just for fun, turn on the Safe Action and Title Safe regions.

4. Open the Attribute Editor for the perspective camera. As you increase the settings for the Overscan attribute in the display options, you'll see the visible area around the resolution gate increase. This region won't be visible in your final render, but it is often useful to see while animating.

Maya's camera settings emulate real-world cameras as much as possible. This makes sense when you consider how often an animator has to collaborate with filmmakers when making a composite of CG renders with live-action background plates. For this reason, Maya makes your life easier by giving you a menu of presets for the Film Gate settings. If you choose 35mm TV projection from the list, your resolution will automatically switch to a film aspect ratio of 1.333. The Film Back and Film Gate settings in the Attribute Editor only become important when you're working with live footage. If you are creating your entire scene in Maya, you don't necessarily have to adjust these settings and you can stick to setting resolution in the Render Settings window. If you are trying to match live footage, however, it is essential that your Film Back and Film Gate settings match the footage you will be working with. You should be able to use the presets or obtain the necessary settings information from the filmmaker.

When you set up your camera's resolution in Maya, your film gate and resolution should align. You can verify this by selecting the Display Film Gate and Display Resolution check boxes. If the solid green line (resolution) does not match the Film Gate (dashed green line), you need to change the Film Gate selection to match the aspect ratio in the Render Settings window.

Resolution is one of the most important factors determining how long it takes to render a frame. It's not a bad idea to do test renders at half the final resolution and then switch to a higher resolution when you're ready for a final render. A setting of half the final resolution will reduce your test-render times to approximately 25 percent of final render times.

Maya also allows you to change the size units, as well as the pixels per inch or pixels per centimeter, of your render, allowing for more control when the desired final output is print rather than to a monitor. Users of Adobe Photoshop will be familiar with these settings because they resemble Photoshop's image size controls. Most video and computer work can be done at the default 72 pixels per inch. Work for print is often done at 300 pixels per inch or more. Common print sizes are shown in the bottom section in the list of image size presets.

Image Planes and Environment Settings

An image plane is a simple 2D plane that is attached to and perpendicular to a camera. When you are creating a model from reference sketches, image planes can be a great help. You can also use them to match an animation to live footage by mapping an image or a sequence of images to the plane. And, new with Maya 8, you can even composite current objects with a depth-map-enabled background image.

You can create an image plane in the Environment section in the camera's Attribute Editor by clicking the Create button next to Image Plane. A dialog box will open in which you can choose the file you want to use as an image plane as well as how the image plane will be displayed in the camera and whether it will be visible in other cameras. You can choose to use an image sequence as well, in much the same way you use an image sequence for a texture. This is helpful for matching live video to an animation.

To use the in-camera depth compositing feature, first render out an image with depth information in it. This image must be in the IFF format, and it should be an integer multiple of the viewport (for example, 1280 × 960 if the viewport is 640 × 480). Set the rendered image as the background by selecting the camera, and in the Attribute Editor, under the Environment section, create an image plane and attach the rendered image to it. Next, twirl down the Depth section for the image plane and check the Use Depth Map box to enable depth compositing. At this point, objects in the scene will be properly sorted according to depth with the background image, as shown in Figure 13.5 where the torus is composited with the background image, which contains prerendered geometric primitives.

> Be sure that your render settings match those of your imported video. If the imported video image has a pixel aspect ratio of 0.9 and you render your geometry as square pixels, things may look distorted when you composite your video and animation.

The camera's Environment section also has a simple setting that you can use to change the color of the background when you render with that camera.

Figure 13.5

Compositing geometry (the torus) with a pre-rendered background

Adding Depth of Field

Depth of field is a simulation of a photographic trait in which objects within a certain range of the camera are in focus and objects outside that range are blurred. While computer-generated images are by nature completely in focus, controlled depth of field can be dramatic and can often help in the storytelling of an animation because it can guide the viewer's eye toward objects of interest in the scene, so Maya provides depth of field as a rendering option. Both Maya Software and mental ray rendering engines can create depth of field; however, the quality of mental ray's depth of field is often superior to Maya's software render.

Maya's software render creates depth of field as a postprocess effect. This will add to your render time, so keep that in mind. Try this quick exercise to create a depth-of-field effect in Maya.

1. Open DOF.mb from the CD.

2. Select renderCam from the Outliner, and open its Attribute Editor.

3. Render an image from renderCam (in the render view, make sure you choose **Render → Render → renderCam**), and store it in the render view (choose **File → Keep Image In Render View**).

4. In the Attribute Editor for renderCam, turn on the Depth Of Field setting. Make sure Focus Distance is set to 7 and F Stop is set to 5.6.

5. Render the image again and note the difference. The hydrants in the foreground are clear, whereas the objects in the middle and background are increasingly blurry.

6. Set Focus Distance to 15 and render again. Now the objects in the foreground and background are blurry and the objects in the middle are clear.

You can control the amount of blurriness by adjusting F Stop. Just as in a real camera, a lower F Stop value will create more blur (though since this is a postprocess for Maya, it will result in a longer render time). F Stop and Focus Distance are keyable attributes. Try setting some keyframes on them to increase the drama of a scene by creating a film technique called the "rack focus," where the area in focus shifts between two objects.

The Focus Region Scale attribute refers to the area of focus set by the Focus Distance attribute. Think of it as a box with the focus distance at the center. A larger focus distance will mean that a larger area of the scene around the focus distance will be in focus.

Focus Distance and Focus Region Scale are measured in scene units. Often it can be tricky to determine the correct focus distance from the camera when you want a specific part of the scene in focus. Fortunately, you can employ a few tricks to create a more interactive depth of field control. Try this setup.

1. In the DOF scene, create a distance tool by choosing **Create → Measure Tools → Distance Tool**.

2. Click in two different locations in the scene to create the two distance locators.

3. Point-constrain locator1 of the Distance tool to the camera by selecting the renderCam and the locator1 in the Outliner. Then from the Animation menu set, choose **Constrain → Point** (be sure that Maintain Offset is unchecked when you create the constraint so that the locator will snap to the camera's position).

4. Choose locator2 from the Outliner, and move it to a position you want in focus for the scene. You can see the distance expressed in units above the Measure tool.

5. Choose **Window → General Editors → Connection Editor** to open the Connection Editor.

6. Load the distance dimension's shape node into the left side of the Connection Editor.

7. Load renderCam's shape node in the right side of the Connection Editor.

8. Scroll to the bottom of the list for the distanceDimension's Shape Node attribute in the Connection Editor and select the Distance attribute.

9. In the middle of the list for renderCam's shape attributes, select the Focus Distance attribute (see Figure 13.6).

Now when you move locator2, the focus distance of the camera will update automatically. This makes animating the focus distance as easy as setting keyframes on locator2. To examine this camera rig, open DOF2.mb from the CD.

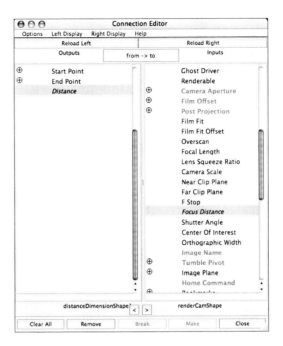

Figure 13.6

You can link the Distance attribute of the distance-DimensionShape1 to the render-CamShape in the Connection Editor.

Sometimes it is more economical to render from Maya as separate passes and then add the depth-of-field effect in your compositing software. This is especially true when you need to make changes after the fact. To do this effectively, you'll need to render with a Z-depth channel.

Adding Motion Blur

In the real world, when an object moves quickly in front of a camera, the object is blurred in the direction of the motion because the camera's iris is open for a finite period of time, allowing the object to move across the view plane while the shutter is open. Like depth of field, motion blur in CG is a post-render effect added by Maya to make images look more like those captured on real film. Adding motion blur to your animation can make an object's movement smoother and more realistic, whereas not using motion blur can make the images stutter, as if they are being filmed using a stop-motion technique. (Traditional stop-motion animation does not have motion blur because the images are captured one frame at a time no matter how fast they are moving. If you want to simulate this "Ray Harryhausen" style of animation, you can try rendering fast-moving skeletons or dinosaurs without motion blur.) To achieve the motion blur effect, you have to turn on Motion Blur in the Render Settings window.

The Maya Software renderer lacks the ability to add motion blur to an object's reflection or refraction on another surface. However, the mental ray renderer is able to achieve this—keep this is mind when you are deciding how to best render a scene with motion blur and reflections or refractions. Creating motion blur with mental ray is covered in the next chapter. Rendering motion blur with Maya Software has a few other limitations—for instance, shadows do not blur accurately.

Motion blur comes in two flavors: 2D and 3D. Two-dimensional motion blur is faster than 3D and is calculated after the frame is rendered. It essentially adds a 2D blur filter to the objects moving in the frame based on their motion in the frame. It is not as accurate as 3D motion blur, but it works well in most cases and is far faster to calculate than 3D motion blur. Two-dimensional motion blur is fine for surfaces that are far from the camera or when you don't need a lot of detail in the blur.

When you render using 3D motion blur, Maya's rendering engine calculates the motion blur based on the position of the moving object and camera in the frames before and after the frame that is currently being rendered. Three-dimensional motion blur is your best choice when an object changes direction or when you are concerned about the level of detail in a shot. As you can imagine, this more accurate blurring effect will add significantly to render times. You can turn motion blur on and off on a per-object basis by opening each object's Attribute Editor and turning off Motion Blur in the Render Stats section. Usually you need motion blur only for objects moving quickly or those that are moving close to the rendering camera.

To control motion blur for the overall scene, use the Render Settings window. In the Motion Blur section in the Maya Software tab in the Render Settings window, the Blur By Frame setting allows you to control the amount of blur. Entering a higher number results in a greater amount of blur. When using the 2D type of motion blur, the Blur Length setting will adjust the streakiness of the blur. Adjusting Shutter Angle in the camera's Attribute Editor under the Special Effects section also affects the amount of blur. Once again, higher numbers mean more blur.

When rendering a scene that has a lot of objects, figure out which objects need to be blurred and which don't. If you leave Motion Blur on for all the objects in the scene, your renders can be significantly longer, even if distant or nonmoving objects are not blurred. Adjusting motion blur settings through the Outliner can quickly lead to insanity if your scene contains many objects. Selecting all the objects in the scene and then opening the Attribute Spread Sheet is often a better way to go about this. The Attribute Spread Sheet is found under **Window → General Editors → Attribute Spread Sheet**. The Attribute Spread Sheet is an interface that allows you to edit attributes for multiple selected objects all in the same window.

Figure 13.7
The amazing driver-less convertible is blurred as it races down the street.

Open the scene `motionBlur1.mb` from the CD. Turn on Motion Blur in the Maya Software tab of the Render Settings window, and try various numbers for the Blur By Frame value under the 3D motion blur settings in the motion blur folder. Try setting render-Cam's shutter speed (in the renderCam's Attribute Editor under the Special Effects section) to 360. Keep the images in the render view for comparison. Try experimenting with 2D motion blur as well. See Figure 13.7 for an example.

Using the Render Settings Window

The Render Settings window is arguably the most important window you'll work with when creating an animation. This is where you turn your geometry, shaders, lighting, rigs, dynamics, and scripts into something for the world to see. If you were baking a cake, this window would be the controls on the oven. It is important to understand the settings in this window and even more important to go through them carefully each time you prepare to render, especially if you are setting up a batch render. Few experiences are more painful than realizing that you've just rendered 7000 blank frames moments before you have a meeting with a client (or before you proudly show your freshly rendered sequence to a significant other who's heard enough of your talk about this animation thing already).

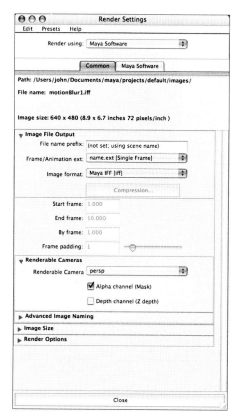

Figure 13.8

Figure 13.8

A look at the settings in the Common tab in the Render Settings window

Before you render, you should understand and determine what you plan to do with the images after you have rendered them. A visit to the Render Settings window before you start modeling, texturing, and animating, as well as when you are ready to start your final render, is an essential practice.

The Render Settings window consists of two tabs and a choice of rendering engines. The Common tab and its settings remain consistent regardless of the renderer you decide to use. The drop-down menu at the top of the Render Settings window is where you choose your renderer; it's usually set to Maya Software by default. Let's leave it that way for now. The second tab's settings depend on the Render Using option selected in this drop-down menu and therefore change accordingly. We will cover Maya's rendering engine here. The settings for mental ray are discussed in detail in the next chapter.

Let's start with the attributes in the Common tab (see Figure 13.8). Think of this as your "what, where, when" tab.

In the Common tab you'll see the path to the currently selected image folder and the name of the image or image sequence. The path to your image folder depends on how you set up your project in your project settings. The name of the image file or sequence of files is derived from the scene name, but you can change this using the fields in the Image File Output section.

If you don't enter anything in the File Name Prefix field, the image file will take the name of your scene file. You can type whatever you want here, but if you're going to take the image file or sequence into a compositor, you might want to give the sequence a name that's short, recognizable, and without spaces or special characters. Leaving this field blank so that it takes on the name of the scene file is a perfectly acceptable practice and not a bad way to remember which scene created which image sequence when projects get big.

Frame/Animation Ext is a drop-down menu from which you can choose how the image or sequence will be labeled. This is an unassuming menu that's just asking to be overlooked when you start a batch render. If you are rendering a single frame, you can choose from the first two options, which essentially allow you to have your image labeled with or without a frame extension. Always label your images with an extension. Even if you work on a Mac, which normally doesn't require extensions, many compositing packages do require them and the images could end up on a Windows or Linux PC, both of which require extensions.

If you want to render a single image, it might be easier to work with the Render View window than to set up a batch render for just a still. The Render View window is discussed later in this chapter.

The next five options in the Frame/Animation Ext drop-down menu are specific to image sequences created in a batch render. This is where you decide how you want to position the frame extension and sequence numbering in the image sequence:

- Name.#.ext creates a sequence that looks like `myimage.1.tif....myimage.4000.tif`.

- Name.ext.# creates a sequence that looks like `myimage.tif. 1...myimage.tif.4000`.

- Name.# will look like `myimage.0001...myimage.4000`.

- Name#.ext will look like `myimage0001.tif...myimage4000.tif`.

- Finally, the new name_#.ext will produce files named like `myimage_0001.tif...` `myimage_4000.tif`. This last format has been added to ease compositing with packages that expect only one period before the file's extension.

Name[Multi Frame] and name.ext[Multi Frame] become active when you're rendering directly to a movie format such as AVI or MOV.

What's the difference between all these formats? That depends on what you're going to do with the image sequence and what your compositing software prefers when you import the sequence. If you choose a naming format your compositor does not recognize, you might have to use some kind of file renaming utility to convert the image sequence to a more acceptable naming format. This is an easy place to make a mistake if you're not paying attention. The safest bet is to choose the format name.#.ext or name_#.ext, but look into your compositing software's documentation just to make sure. Even better, if you are not sure what your compositing package prefers, render out a test sequence of, say, 10 frames and read the images into your package. If there is a problem with the format you've chosen, it's much better to discover it with a quick test render than it is to discover it after rendering hundreds of frames with the wrong naming convention.

Below the Frame/Animation Ext drop-down menu is the Image Format drop-down menu, from which you can select your desired image format. Once again, the format you choose depends on what you plan to do with the image and what your compositing or editing software prefers.

> You can choose to render directly to a movie format such as AVI or MOV, but this is not recommended, at least not for long or final renders. If you render an image sequence rather than a movie file and your machine crashes during render, you can always pick up rendering the sequence from where you left off. If you render straight to a movie format and your machine crashes, you will have to start the render over again from the beginning because the movie file will be corrupted. Rendering to a movie format can be efficient, however, if you are creating quick test renders to check animation and render settings.

The next four fields are grayed out unless you choose an image sequence format from the Frame/Animation Ext menu. Start Frame and End Frame allow you to choose which part of the animation you want to render. By Frame allows you to choose whether you want to render one frame at a time, or more, or less. You can render a scene backward by inputting a higher start frame value and a lower end frame value.

It is not uncommon to render by half frames by entering 0.5 in the By Frame field. Animators do this occasionally when working with scenes with heavy dynamics elements like particles or to get around having to render fields for video. If your project settings are at 30 frames per second and you render with 0.5 as your By Frame setting, you essentially end up with the animation at 60 frames per second or, to put it another way, twice as many frames. You can convert this back to 30 frames per second in your compositing software and achieve the same kind of smooth motion you get from rendering with fields but without the hassle of rendering with fields directly out of Maya. Field rendering can now be accomplished in your video compositing or editing software.

FIELDS AND TELEVISION SETS

Field is a term derived from an imperfection in the television. Older TVs (and many today) were manufactured inexpensively, and that meant that they could not render out their entire screen in one "pass." Thus a cheat, called interlacing, was developed whereby the even horizontal lines were rendered out on pass number one and the odds were rendered out on pass two. On pass three, the even lines were rendered again, and so forth. (Some TVs render out the odd frame first, so the process is reversed). While this slower scan rate allowed for inexpensive TVs, it creates all sorts of issues with fast-moving objects and potential brightness on a TV. Today's more expensive HD televisions often allow progressive scan, which means the entire screen is rendered in one pass (even and odd fields together). This is preferable to interlaced signal since there are no motion or brightness issues, and thus the image looks brighter and crisper on a progressive scan TV (assuming the signal from your TV station is in progressive mode as well). However, even today, a progressive-scan-capable TV will cost more than one that only provides an interlaced image at the same resolution. Next time you are at an electronics store, look at the fine print and find a TV that has 1080i resolution, and one that has 1080p and note the difference in price between the two (assuming they are the same size screen). The *i* stands for *interlaced*, the *p* for *progressive scan*, and the interlaced TV costs substantially less than the progressive scan one.

Of course, you need to consider two important items when oversampling the frame rate. First, if you alter the frame rate of the render, you will want to make sure that you change the frame numbering in the Renumber Frames section in the Render Settings window. Check the Renumber Frames Using check box, and then adjust the Start Frame number and By Frame number accordingly (1 and 1 in these boxes works fine). As you do this, you can look at the bold type at the top of the Render Settings window to see how your sequence will be renumbered. Second, if you render with a By Frame setting of 0.5, your render will take twice as long and will require twice as much disk space that it would if you were rendering with a By Frame setting of 1.

In some cases, you might choose to render every other frame or every third frame. This is a common practice when creating animations for the purpose of previsualization. Once again, make sure you adjust your frame numbering settings.

Frame Padding allows you to choose how many zeros you want in your frame sequence labeling. For instance, entering the number 4 here yields `myimage.0001.tif`. It's good to have some frame padding in your image sequence because many compositing packages will read in files out of sequence if padding is not used. Using frame padding will make life easier for you and the people you work with regardless of the software you're using, so it's good to always use padding.

In the Renderable Cameras section, you'll see options for rendering out alpha (mask), and depth (Z-depth) channels. Enabling the alpha channel creates a mask around the scene rendered, making it easier to composite the render in with other images. Z-depth is a special channel that stores depth information as an 8-bit gray image. Only a few image formats such as IFF can use this extra channel, and not all image formats allow for an alpha channel. TIFF, Targa, SGI, and IFF are safe bets for rendering with an alpha. As for depth channels, if an image format is selected that doesn't allow depth maps in it directly, Maya will create a separate set of images with only depth information in them.

> Maya calculates Z-depth based on the position of an object relative to the rendering camera's clipping planes. This updates for every frame. Checking Auto Render Clip Plane in the camera's Attribute Editor can cause errors in your Z-depth render because Maya automatically updates the clipping plane for each frame, so be sure to turn this feature off if you will be rendering depth information in your scene.

Under Advanced Image Naming there is a field that will allow you to use a custom extension for your images. In most cases, you won't need to use it. As discussed earlier, the Renumber Frames option is useful when you are rendering by a different frame increment. Also if you are rendering just a section of a scene, you can use the Renumber Frames option to renumber the frames so they will fit within a range you have previously rendered. For example, if you decide to render frames 241 through 360 but you'd like them to be numbered 1 through 120, you can use the Renumber Frames field. You can also use this field when you are rendering a scene that starts at a negative frame value or if you are rendering a scene backward.

The Image Size section was covered earlier in this chapter in the section on setting the camera and resolution.

In the Render Options section, you'll find the Enable Default Light check box and fields for specifying MEL scripts that perform pre- or post-render functions. The MEL fields are advanced options that are not normally used by individuals and are beyond the scope of this book.

The default light is there so that if you render a scene without first adding any of your own lights, you will still see your objects. This light can affect the lighting in your scene, however, especially if you are using global illumination in mental ray. It's usually a good idea to turn this light off after adding any of your own lights in the scene regardless of how you render. This just ensures that you're getting what you want when you render.

> If you don't add any lights and render your scene only to discover a black image, check to see if the default light has been turned off.

At this point we've covered the basics of the Common tab render settings. Let's take a look at the settings in the second tab, which depend on the rendering engine you've chosen for your scene.

Rendering with Maya Software

The second tab in your Render Settings window is your "how" tab. The settings here cover the quality of your image and change depending on which renderer you are using: Maya Software, Maya Hardware, Maya Vector, or mental ray. Many of these settings are tied to settings in the Attribute Editor for your cameras, textures, and geometry. To try Maya Software rendering, be sure Render Using is set to Maya Software and click the Maya Software tab (see Figure 13.9). In the Anti-Aliasing Quality section, the Quality drop-down menu contains presets that automatically enter settings for the rest of the attributes in the Maya Software tab. If you choose one of these presets and then alter the settings, this setting will automatically change to Custom.

As you move from the top presets on down the list, the quality improves and the render times increase. For most final renders, the Production Quality settings are a good place to start.

Anti-Aliasing and Image Quality

The anti-aliasing, or smoothness, of a render in Maya is calculated on both a geometry level and a shading sampling level independently. Geometric anti-aliasing is calculated first, and you control it in the Render Settings window by choosing settings from the Edge Anti-Aliasing drop-down menu. Adjusting the tessellation of an object in its Attribute Editor can also affect its smoothness.

Smaller objects can flicker when rendered, even when Edge Anti-Aliasing is set to the highest level. To fix this, turn on the geometry anti-aliasing override in the object's Attribute Editor and adjust the number of samples. This option is available only when Edge Anti-Aliasing is set to High Quality or Highest Quality.

The Shading field in the Number Of Samples section determines the anti-aliasing quality, or relative smoothness, of the objects, textures, and lighting in the scene. A setting of 1 causes the image to render fast, but the shading will look jaggy. Higher sampling values will produce smoother-looking results but cause the image to take longer to render. Notice that the shading samples change when you select different settings from the presets in the Quality drop-down menu. By choosing Highest Quality, you turn on adaptive sampling. Adaptive sampling is more efficient because it adjusts the level of shading samples on a per-pixel level as needed. You can use the sliders to set a maximum level of shading samples.

The Number Of Samples section has additional levels of control for 3D motion blur and software-rendered particles. As you might have guessed, increasing these settings will increase render times but will also help in producing superior image quality.

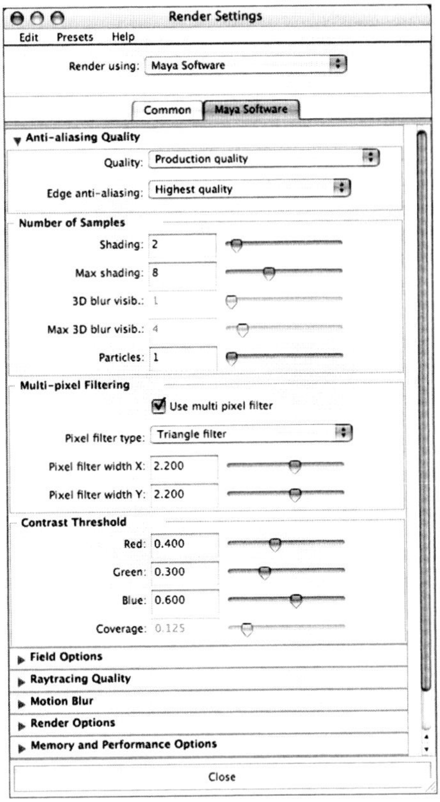

The Multi-Pixel Filtering section is available only when High Quality or Highest Quality is chosen in the Edge Anti-Aliasing drop-down menu. These settings allow for an additional level of softening to the render.

The settings in the Contrast Threshold section are related to adaptive sampling and are therefore available for adjustment only when Highest Quality is chosen from the Edge Anti-Aliasing drop-down menu. When Maya Software renders an image with adaptive sampling, each pixel is compared with its five rendered neighbors. When a certain threshold is met, based on the values in the red, green, and blue contrast threshold settings, additional sampling is applied to the pixel. Operation of this feature will be affected by the amount of contrast in the rendered image. The default settings are based on the contrast sensitivity of the human eye.

Figure 13.9

A look at the settings in the Maya Software tab

Field Rendering in Maya

Field rendering is used for rendering images that will be displayed by an interlaced video monitor. Video monitors display an image in alternating lines or fields (see the sidebar "Fields and Television Sets" earlier in this chapter). Each field can be thought of as a half image. The alternation of the fields is known as interlacing. The options in the Field Options section of the Render Settings window allow you to specify how you want the fields to be rendered:

- Rendering Frames is equivalent to rendering without fields.
- Both Fields, Interlaced combines the two images into one image. On a computer screen the image will look as though it has been broken into horizontal lines.
- Both Fields, Separate renders each half frame as a separate image file that you can combine in your editing or compositing software.
- Odd Fields and Even Fields render only the half of the image corresponding to the selected (odd or even) field.

Field rendering can be tricky and often requires some planning and testing. Some software packages use the terms *odd* and *even*, some (such as Adobe After Effects) use *upper* and *lower*. Field rendering will result in smooth movement of objects on a video screen; however, if you render incorrectly, the movement will look jerky or will flicker. Test some variations of a small segment of your animation in which there is a lot of movement. View it on a video monitor as soon as you can if you decide to render fields directly from Maya. The safest bet is to render frames and convert to fields in your compositing or editing software.

Raytracing in Maya Software

By default, Maya Software uses a rendering method known as scanline. Scanline rendering is fast, simple, and usually sufficient for basic scenes. It is a system in which the objects in a scene are sorted and rendered based on their distance from the camera.

Raytracing is a system in which rays are shot from the camera into a scene. If these rays encounter reflective or refractive objects/textures, they are reflected or bent off the surface. If these reflected or refracted rays encounter another object in the scene, that object then appears in the reflective or refractive surface of the initial object. Raytracing is generally thought of as a more realistic rendering method than scanline because of its ability to create reflections and refractions. Raytraced images take longer to render than scanline, so should be used only when needed.

Raytracing is enabled globally in the Render Settings window when you select it in the Raytracing Quality section. If you have set up your lights to create raytraced shadows or you have raytraced reflections and refractions on your shaders but they are not rendering correctly, chances are it is because you have not enabled raytracing in the Render Settings window. You use the sliders in the Raytracing Quality section to specify the number of samples used when you're creating a raytraced image. A finer level of control over raytracing is found in the Attribute Editor for the shaders and lights used in the scene. To achieve a truly spectacular level of realism in your images, you might want to consider using mental ray, which is discussed in the next chapter.

When working with reflections and refractions, you will need to bounce between the Render Settings window for Maya Software, the attributes of the objects being reflected and refracted, and the shaders attached to the objects being reflected and refracted. For raytraced shadows, you will need to work with the shadow-casting lights, the objects casting shadows, and the Render Settings window. For instance, if you have an object inside a glass that you would like to see refracted, you will need to ensure the following:

- That Visible In Refractions is selected in the Render Stats settings in the Attribute Editor for the object inside the glass
- That the shader attached to the glass has refractions enabled in its Raytrace Options menu
- That Raytracing is enabled in the Render Settings window
- That your primary light has Raytraced Shadows enabled to produce proper shadowing

Reflections follow a similar set of requirements with the exception that if you have raytracing on in the Render Settings window, reflective materials such as Blinn and Phong will have their reflectivity on by default. You can control reflection amount and overall color by using the Reflectivity slider in the Attribute Editor for these materials.

Raytraced reflections, refractions, and shadows are expensive to render. You can set limits on the rays being used to create these effects by using the sliders in the Raytracing Quality section in the Render Settings window and also by using the sliders in the Attribute Editors for the shaders attached to raytraced objects. The controls in the Render Settings window will affect all the raytraced shaders in the scene. If, in the Render Settings window, the limit on the numbers of rays being used is lower than the limit set on the raytraced shader, the global limit will be used, whereas if the global limit is higher than that of a particular object, the object's limit will be used.

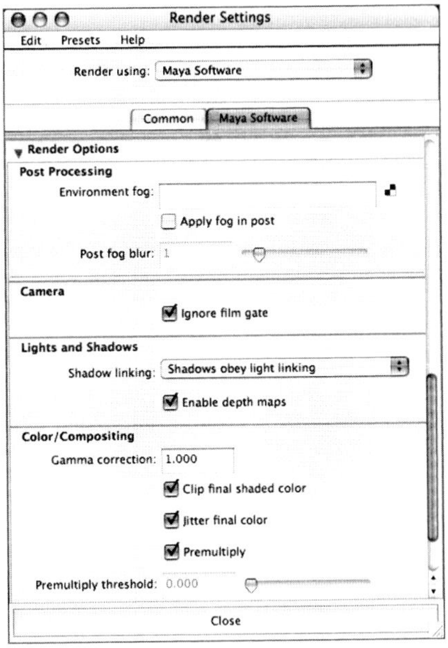

Figure 13.10

The Render Options section of the Render Settings window

Render Options

In the Render Options section in the Maya Software tab of the Render Settings window (see Figure 13.10), you'll find some additional controls that will affect how your rendered images look.

First, you can create environment fog. (You can also create this in the Hypershade window.) Environment fog allows you to simulate the effect of particles in the air that diffuse light. This can increase the sense of depth in a scene as objects will fade as they are farther from the camera.

Ignore Film Gate is on by default, which means that the Resolution Gate settings will be used to determine the size of the rendered image. If this option is unchecked, Maya will render the objects visible in the film gate and everything outside that will be rendered with the background color.

Shadows Obey Light Linking is also on by default. This means that shadows in the scene will be cast according to how the lights and objects have been linked in the Light Linking menu (choose **Window → Relationship Editors → Light Linking**). If this option is off, shadow-casting objects will cast shadows regardless of whether they are linked to lights. As you can imagine, turning this off can yield some strange results.

Maya 8.5 now includes shadow linking as well as light linking. Using this feature, you can link only certain objects to shadow calculations, potentially reducing render times by a great deal.

Enable Depth Maps is a global switch that, when on, allows depth-map shadows to be cast by lights that have them enabled.

The Color/Compositing section has some controls that affect how the rendered images will behave when you bring them into a compositing program such as Adobe After Effects. Gamma refers to the degree of brightness of an image. In some cases, the gamma of your rendered images may need to be corrected, depending on what you will do with them in compositing after rendering.

Clip Final Shaded Color ensures that the color values in the final image remain in a range from 0 to 1. This keeps the images from becoming overexposed.

Jitter Final Color reduces banding in areas where there should be a smooth gradation.

Premultiply ensures that objects rendered in Maya are not anti-aliased against the background color. If this is off, the Premultiply Threshold setting will be enabled.

Memory and Performance Options

The options in the Memory And Performance Options section allow you to control how Maya optimizes renders by using file caches, instances, tessellations, and the bounding box when calculating displacement maps (see Figure 13.11). These settings are meant to cut down on render times, and it's usually safe to leave them at their default On state. Consult the Maya documentation for more information on these settings.

The raytracing options allow for a global control of the level of detail for raytraced objects in a scene. Recursion Depth can be set to 1 for simple scenes or increased to 2 or 3 for more complex ones. Likewise, the Leaf Primitives and Subdivision Power settings can be increased for more complex scenes. The Subdivision Power setting is sensitive and should be increased only slightly if the scene is complex.

The Multi Processing option allows you to either use all available CPUs for rendering or set the number of CPUs via a slider. This setting is meant for multiprocessor machines or render farms.

Additional Options

The options in the IPR Options and Paint Effects Rendering Options sections control the shading, shadow, and motion blur for IPR renders and Paint Effects rendering. Turning off unneeded options in the IPR section will increase the speed of IPR renders and save disk space, though obviously at the cost of reduced fidelity to the final image.

In the Paint Effects options, if Enable Stroke Rendering is off, Maya will not render Paint Effects strokes. This is a global control you can use when you need to render a scene quickly without Paint Effects. Conversely, if you want to see only the Paint Effects strokes, you can select Only Render Strokes. Read This Depth File is necessary if you need the Z-depth information for the rendered strokes for compositing. The IFF format is the only type of image that can contain depth information. Consult the Maya documentation for the particulars of how to include depth information using the IFF format.

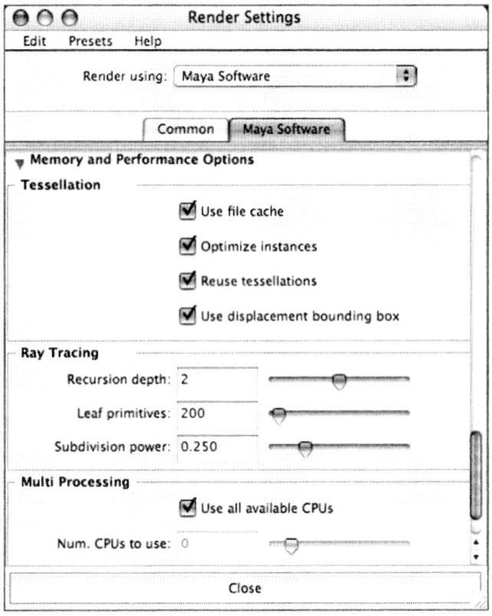

Turning on Oversample in the Paint Effects Rendering Options section can increase the quality of your Paint Effects strokes by rendering them at twice their resolution. Of course this will mean longer render times for the scene. The Oversample Post Filter option applies a filter to further increase the smoothness of the oversampled strokes. These options can be helpful when rendering Paint Effects hair or other fine elements.

Figure 13.11

The Memory And Performance Options section of the Render Settings window

Hardware Render and Hardware Render Buffer

Rendering with Maya hardware and with the hardware render buffer are two related but different processes, and the overlap can be a little confusing. The difference primarily concerns the quality, the process, and the abilities of the two renderers. Both types use your computer's graphics card (rather than the main CPU) to render images. Naturally this means that the type of graphics card you are using will affect how the images are rendered. A list of qualified graphics cards is available on the Alias website at `www.alias.com/glb/eng/support/maya/qualified_hardware/index.jsp`. If your card is not on the list, it can most likely still be used, but the results can't be guaranteed.

Most often, hardware rendering of either type is used to render certain types of particles and to produce faster, simpler renders. The hardware render buffer essentially renders each frame into a window on the screen. The rendered image is then captured by the hardware and saved to disk. The biggest problem with this system is that you must be careful to ensure that no windows are overlapping the buffer window. Leaving your screensaver on during a long render can also cause problems. To access the hardware render buffer, choose **Window → Rendering Editors → Hardware Render Buffer** (see Figure 13.12). To access the settings, choose Attributes from the Render menu at the top of the Hardware Render Buffer window.

Figure 13.12

The convertible as seen in the Hardware Render Buffer window

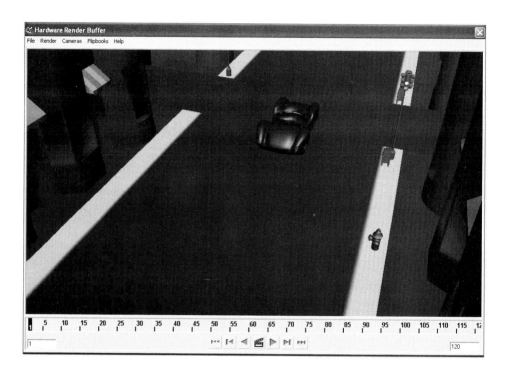

Macs are less susceptible to screen overlap and screensaver issues than Linux or Windows machines. When rendering a scene via the hardware render buffer, the render window can be hidden and the screensaver can run without causing problems on a Mac. This feature is useful since you can get other work done on the computer while hardware rendering is taking place.

You access the Maya Hardware renderer through the Render Settings window, and it has several advantages over the hardware render buffer. You can batch-render with Maya Hardware, and it supports features the buffer does not. In addition, the images tend to be a higher quality; particles also look better using this method. Some features that are supported by Maya Hardware rendering include per-pixel specular highlights, bump maps, motion blur that is superior to that produced with the hardware render buffer, shadows, reflections, displacement maps, normal maps, shader translucency, and ramp and Blinn shaders.

The options available on the Maya Hardware tab in the Render Settings window (see Figure 13.13) include the ability to choose between 8 bytes per channel and 16-bit float per channel, transparent shadow maps, color and bump resolution, and hardware geometry caching. Geometry caching allows your graphics card to cache geometry data when it is not being used for other tasks. This can sometimes improve performance.

Vector Rendering

As mentioned at the start of the chapter, Maya can render both bitmap and vector images. Vector images can be imported directly into other vector programs, such as Illustrator and Flash. This is useful because it is difficult to create 3D images inside a vector graphics program. Vector images have the advantage that they tend to be small and they can be scaled to any size without losing quality. The disadvantage of using vector images is that it can be difficult to create a photo-realistic image if that is your intent.

> Vector rendering should not be confused with Toon rendering. They are similar in look and are related in some ways, but they are not the same. Toon shading uses a combination of shaders and Paint Effects strokes to create the look of a cartoon object. Toon shaded objects are rendered with Maya Software or mental ray and not the Vector renderer, and they produce bitmap (or raster) images rather than vector ones. The new Toon Shading tools are discussed in detail in Chapter 15.

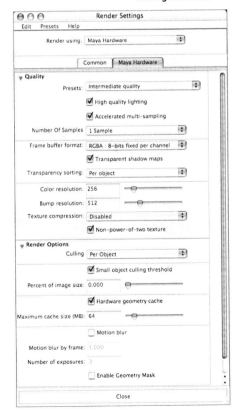

Figure 13.13

Maya Hardware settings are accessed through the Render Settings window.

The settings for a vector render will be affected by the file format you choose in the Common tab of the Render Settings window. You can render a vector image to a bitmap format such as Targa or TIFF; however, if you want to edit the vectors in another program, such as Adobe Illustrator or Macromedia Flash, choose a vector format. These include SWF, SWFT, EPS, AI, and SVG, which are conveniently grouped at the top of the list of file formats in the Common tab.

When you choose Maya Vector from the Render Using menu in the Render Settings window, you'll find controls for how the vector image will be drawn. The controls displayed depend on your chosen format (Figure 13.14 shows the Render Settings window with SWF as the chosen output mode). For instance, the Flash format allows you to choose a frame rate for the Flash animation as well as the version of Flash you want to render to.

The Curve Tolerance and Detail Level Preset settings affect your render time and image size. A lower tolerance will create many more lines per curve, which will look closer to the original model, but the file size will be larger than one rendered with a higher tolerance setting.

You can specify the detail level through a preset, or you can enter it manually. The detail level is fairly self-explanatory: more detail means a larger file size and longer render time but a more detailed image.

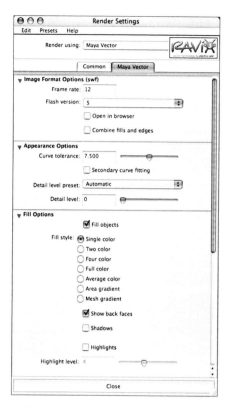

The Fill Options section allows you to control how the shaded image will look. Vector rendering supports anisotropic, Blinn, Lambert, Phong, and Phong E shaders. Figure 13.15 shows some examples of various fill options rendered with Maya Vector. Several variations of the settings have been used to create the images. The upper left has been rendered with a single fill color and no edges. The upper right has been rendered with a single color and with hidden edges selected in the edge options. The lower left has been rendered with a four-color fill and with edge detail selected in the edge options. The lower right has been rendered with mesh gradient selected for the fill options as well as edge detail chosen for the edge options.

The Edge Options settings allow for control over the outline curves drawn around the fill shapes. To create a wireframe version of the model, choose Hidden Edge.

Vector rendering supports only point lights. If the scene contains no point lights, one will be created at the position of the camera at render time. Shadows are available only for some render formats, such as SWF.

Figure 13.15

The convertible is shown rendered with Maya Vector.

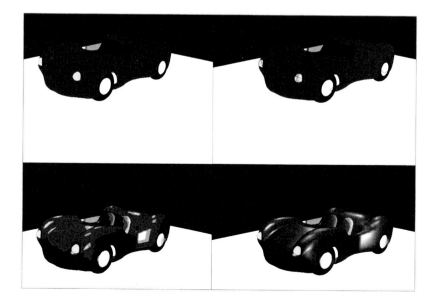

The SWF format can be imported into Adobe's Flash 8 and edited there. The image or sequence will appear in Flash as separate layers similar to render passes. There will be layers for color, specular, shadows, reflections, and transparency depending on your model, settings, and shaders.

Working in the Render View Window

The Render View window is a useful tool for fine-tuning the way your scene will render. When you initiate a render in the Render View window, you can see Maya creating the image in real time. The Render View window works for Maya Software, Hardware, and Vector as well as mental ray. You'll also use this window for IPR (Interactive Photorealistic Rendering). We'll cover that in the next section.

You can access the Render View window in several ways. If you have the Status line visible, you can click the clapper board icon to open the Render View window and immediately start rendering the active view. You can also choose **Window → Rendering Editors → Render View** and display the Render View window by choosing it from the panel window. This can be a great setup when you're using a split-screen layout. You can keep the Render View window handy while adjusting your scene and then render and rerender as necessary. Figure 13.16 shows the Render View window with a completed render of the convertible.

Figure 13.16

The Render View window allows you to tune your scene by rendering and storing stills.

New with Maya 8.5 is the ability to open the render view without instantiating a new render job. The Open Render View button (to the left of the Render View clapper board icon) opens the Render View window but doesn't begin a new render. This can be very useful if you've closed the Render View window after rendering an image and wish to open it again without waiting for Maya to rerender the scene.

At the top of the Render View window, you'll see a toolbar with File, View, Render, IPR, Options, Display, and Help menus. The File menu has options for loading and saving images. Often, if you need to save a single image, it is preferable to render using the Render View window and save from the File menu rather than creating a batch render for a single image.

The View options allow you to look at the red, green, blue, and alpha channels of an image as well as take a snapshot of an unrendered camera view.

The Render menu allows you to choose which camera you want to render from. Unless you change this setting, the Render View window will always render from the previously selected camera while the window is open.

Below the menu bar is a series of icons that control what you see in the Render View window. Clicking the first clapboard icon renders the image from the same camera as the most recent render. Clicking the clapboard with a red square renders a user-selected region of the image. This is a big timesaver if you just need to tune a section of the image and you don't want to wait while Maya redoes the entire image. To render a region, click and drag in the render view image; a red square should appear where you drag. Click the Render Region button to see the image update within the red square. If you change something in the scene and click the button again, you'll see the area in which the change was made update.

When working in the Render View window, you can zoom and pan around a rendered image by using the same hot key/mouse button combinations that allow you to navigate in a camera view window. This is useful for closely inspecting your rendered images. If you need to snap back to actual size, you can click the 1:1 button on the render view panel menu.

Often, when it looks as if your image has been rendered with jagged edges and artifacts, you have zoomed in slightly in the Render View window by accident. Remember to click the 1:1 button before you try to solve the problem by cranking up your anti-aliasing and render quality settings.

The Render View window's most useful feature, next to IPR, is the ability to quickly compare renders by storing images. Try this:

1. Create a simple scene with a NURBS sphere.

2. Create a spotlight and point it at the sphere.

3. Attach a Blinn shader to the sphere.

4. Set the intensity of the light to 1 in the light's Attribute Editor.

5. Render the image in the Render View window by clicking the clapboard in Maya's uppermost toolbar.

6. The Render View window should open automatically and an image of the sphere should be created quickly.

7. On the Render View window's toolbar, click the Keep Image icon, which looks like an arrow pointing into an open box, or choose **File → Keep Image In Render View**.

8. Change the intensity of the light to 0.4 and render the image again.

9. Once the image has been rendered, click the Keep Image icon again.

10. Using the scroll bar at the bottom of the Render View window, you can go back and forth comparing the two images. You can do this for as many images as you like as long as you store each image after rendering. If you want to remove an image from this buffer, you can scroll to it and click the remove image icon, which looks like an arrow pointing up out of a box.

The ability to save and review renders is handy for tuning an image and making comparisons. An even handier tool is Maya's IPR feature. When you render an image, some statistics will appear as an overlay at the bottom of the Render View window, including size, zoom level, rendering engine, frame, render time, camera, and render layer when applicable.

Using Interactive Photorealistic Rendering (IPR)

Maya's IPR feature is another useful tool for tuning a render. It works best when adjusting textures, lighting, glows, optical effects, depth-map shadows, motion blurs, depth of field, and many other aspects of a render. However, it doesn't work with raytracing and a few other rendering features, though it does work with mental ray. In fact, IPR for mental ray will allow for previewing raytraced reflections and refractions, which is an advantage over IPR with Maya's rendering engine.

When you use IPR, you create a render that uses a special image format containing information specific to your scene. This is not a format for a final render, such as IFF, TARGA, or TIFF, but rather a format used exclusively in the IPR window. Using IPR is similar to using the Render Region button mentioned earlier except that with IPR, the rendered region updates automatically when you make a setting change to certain elements in your scene and the rerender is usually much faster (close to real time if the scene is not too complex). Try this:

1. Open the IPR file from the CD.

2. Click the IPR button on Maya's toolbar, or, if the Render View window is open, click the IPR button on the toolbar. The scene will slowly start to render. It might look slightly different from the software render, but that is OK. This render is for tuning various settings. Maya is creating the initial IPR image from which we can tune our render. Rendering an IPR region will not work until we've created this initial IPR render.

3. Once the image has rendered, click and drag a square somewhere on the surface of the car's body. A green box should appear as you drag in the Render View window. This is the IPR render region.

4. Open the Attribute Editor for the area light in the scene, and slowly move the Intensity slider up and down. As you move the slider, you should see the lighting change in the IPR render region box.

5. Try changing the color of the shader applied to the car body. You'll see it update as you make changes.

IPR will not update if you change the model or the camera view. If you do this, you will need to create a new IPR render from which you can tune the image. You can save IPR images if you are working on a scene in which creating an IPR image takes a long time.

The IPR image will allow you to select objects and nodes related to them in your scene by right-clicking in the IPR window. Try clicking the car chassis in the render region of the IPR image generated in the previous example. The Blinn shader assigned to the car will become the selected item.

Layer Rendering, Compositing, and Editing

Rendering and compositing often go hand in hand. The concept is simple: you render your scene in several passes and then combine them as layers in a compositing program such as Adobe After Effects or Apple Shake. Often if a small change needs to be made, it is much faster and easier to do so in the compositing software than to rerender the entire scene in Maya. If you've ever worked with a picky client (and all good clients are picky), you know that the changes are numerous and frequent.

Render passes can be separated by specific objects and elements—such as background scenery and foreground characters—or they can be the diffuse light, specular highlights, shadows, reflections, ambient occlusion, and other elements that make up the texturing and lighting of a specific object. Or they can be both. Maya's render layers, which were completely overhauled in version 7, provide an extremely powerful set of tools with which to control and manage exactly what renders and how it does so.

Let's start with a simple exercise to get into the swing of using render layers.

1. Open the file convertible_textureLayers.mb from the CD

2. Switch your camera to renderCam and render a still. You should see a little red toy convertible in your Render View window.

3. Open the Render Layer Editor by choosing **Window → Rendering Editors → Render Layer Editor**, or simply click the Render radio button on the Layers palette (situated under the Channel Box by default). Clicking this button switches from display layers to render layers.

4. In the Outliner, select the convertible group.

5. From the Layers menu in the Layer Editor, choose **Create Layer From Selected** or click the create new Render Layer From Selected Objects icon (it is the one with the blue sphere and the yellow gear).

6. In the Layer Editor, you will notice two layers, masterLayer and layer1, as shown in Figure 13.17. MasterLayer is selected. Do another render from the renderCam. Everything should look the same.

7. In the Layer Editor, switch to layer1. In the camera view, you'll notice that only the car remains: the ground plane and the lights have disappeared. Do another render from renderCam.

This new render shows the red car but no ground; the lighting has also changed because the scene lights are not included in render layer1. The lights and ground need to be added to layer1 in order to be visible in the layer1 render.

1. From the Outliner, select areaLight1, directionalLight1, nurbsPlane1, and spotlight1. Right-click layer1 in the Layer Editor and choose Add Selected Objects.

2. Notice that the lights and ground now appear. Do another render from renderCam. Store the image. Notice that in the Render View window, *Layer: layer1* appears in the text at the bottom over the image. If you switch to masterLayer in the Layer Editor, the image will look the same as the one from layer1; however, *Layer: masterLayer* will now appear in the text in the overlay. If the words *Layer: composite* appear, go to the Options menu in the Layer Editor and uncheck the Render All Layers check box.

What we've just demonstrated is that objects and lights can be on more than one render layer. How is this useful? Let's continue with our example scene to find out.

1. Select layer1 from the Layer Editor, right-click, and choose layer1. In the pop-up menu, rename the layer redCar.

2. From the Layer menu, choose **Create Empty Layer** or click the Create New Empty Render Layer icon (the one with the yellow gear but without the blue sphere). Rename the layer greenCar. Notice that when you switch to this layer, everything disappears. If you were to render, you'd see a black screen. Hey, at least it would render fast.

Figure 13.17

The Render Layer Editor with new layers

3. Select the geometry and lights from the Outliner, and right-click the new greenCar layer in the Layer Editor. Choose Add Selected Objects. Everything appears in the camera view. Switching from one layer to the next shows no difference.

4. Select the body of the red car and open the Hypershade. From the Materials tab, find greenPaint shader. Right-click the Shader icon and choose Assign Material To Selection.

5. The car turns green. Do a render from renderCam with the greenCar layer selected in the Layer Editor. Now we have a nice green car.

6. In the Layer Editor, switch back to the redCar layer. The car turns red. Render and you have your red car back.

7. If this is not working as described, check to make sure that Auto Overrides is selected in the Options menu of the Render Layers window.

As the example above shows, you can have the same object on many layers, textured completely differently on each layer, which has very powerful repercussions for rendering work flow. Rendering variations of our car object is simple. Furthermore, each render layer can have a different lighting setup. But hold on—we've just begun. There is a whole lot more to this. Thus far we have created layers with alternate texturing on a per-object basis. Now let's create layers with alternating texturing on a per-component basis.

A new feature of Maya 8 is the ability to duplicate render layers. If, say, you have several layers that you wish to be nearly identical, you can duplicate a "master" layer, and modify each version much more quickly than having to create each layer from scratch.

1. Using the convertible_textureLayers.mb file, open the Hypershade window and find the shader hubCap1 material swatch. Right-click and choose Select Objects With Material. You'll notice that the polygons on the wheels that form the hubcaps are now selected. The wheels are a single polygon object with a separate shader applied to those polygons that make up the hubcap.

2. Switch to the greenCar layer in the Layer Editor. In the Hypershade, find the hub-Cap2 layer. Right-click and choose Assign Material To Selection.

3. Render out images from redCar layer and greenCar layer. Store the images in the Render View window, and compare the renders from each layer. You'll notice that the hubcaps on the green car have a lower diffuse value so they appear darker. You have successfully created layers with alternate texturing on a per-component basis.

If you open convertible_textureLayers2.mb, you'll find the scene set up as described.

In addition to altering textures or showing different objects on different layers, you can separate a render into its constituent parts using layers. Let's try creating separate passes for the specular and diffuse shading of the convertible.

1. Open the scene convertible_renderPresets.mb from the CD.

2. Select all the objects and lights from the Outliner.

3. In the Render Layer Editor, choose **Layers → Create Layer From Selected**.

4. In the Render Layer Editor, select the new layer, which is called layer1. Right-click the layer and choose **Presets → Specular**. You will notice that the clapper board icon to the left of the *layer1* text turns red to indicate that render passes have been enabled for this layer.

5. Render an image from renderCam with layer1 selected in the Layer Editor. What appears in the render view is the car model with just the specular highlights, as shown in Figure 13.18.

6. Repeat the process, but this time choose **Presets → Diffuse**.

7. Render the scene again with layer2 selected. You'll see the image appear with just the diffuse values of the shaders.

Figure 13.18

Rendering out just the specular pass

The render presets include Luminance Depth, Occlusion, Normal Map, Geometry Matte, Diffuse, Specular, and Shadow. A description of each render element follows.

Luminance Depth Renders a grayscale image based on the distance from the camera. This is similar to rendering with Z-depth and can be used to determine the positions of 3D geometry in a 2D compositing package. The settings of the camera's clipping planes can affect how this image is rendered.

Occlusion Requires mental ray for rendering. In fact, choosing this preset automatically sets the layer to mental ray for rendering. It also assigns a surface shader with an ambient occlusion node to the geometry in the layer. This is often used for dirt passes or as an alternative for final gather.

Normal Map Renders out normal map information, which allows normal information from high-resolution models to be applied to lower-resolution models. Normal mapping is found in many current high-end video games, allowing lower polygon models to appear to have much more detail.

Geometry Matte Renders the geometry in the layer as a mask for compositing.

Diffuse Renders the geometry with only the diffuse values. No shadows or specular highlights are included.

Specular Renders only the specular highlights on the geometry. No alpha channels are rendered for this preset, as the expectation is that this layer will be multiplied in with the color and/or diffuse layers. Reflections will also show up in a specular pass if they are enabled for the shader. This makes sense since, technically, specular highlights are a diffuse type of reflection.

Shadow Renders shadows only. The shadows are visible in the alpha channel of the rendered image.

You can assign an object to a number of layers, each layer can have one of these presets, and the resulting image can be composited in image-editing or compositing software (the duplicate layers feature comes in handy when creating all of these render pass layers). Furthermore, you can assign a different render setting for each of these preset layers. The layer settings function as a Render Settings window override. In other words, you can have mental ray render the occlusion pass and use Maya Software for the diffuse pass and so on. If you prefer fewer layers (and less control), you can tell Maya to render a given layer with multiple passes: right-click on the layer, and choose Attributes. In the Attribute Editor window that pops up, open the Render Pass Options section and choose any elements you wish to have rendered out for this layer: Beauty (a composite of all elements), Color (the color information), Diffuse (diffuse, or nonspecular, lighting and color), Specular (for specular lighting information), and Shadow (to capture shadows on a separate pass).

Let's take another look at the previous example.

1. Choose layer1 from the previous example (the one set to the Specular preset). (Or open `convertible_renderPresets2.mb` from the CD and choose layer1.)

2. Notice that the Render Settings window icon next to the render layer label changes when you add a preset. A red mark appears. Click this icon for layer1. The Render Settings window opens. The words *Render Using* appear in orange next to the list of renderers. Choose mental ray.

3. From the mental ray tab in the Render Settings window, choose Preview from the Quality Presets section (mental ray will be discussed further in the next chapter).

4. Click the Render Settings window icon for render layer2. The Render Settings window will pop open or change if it is still open. Choose Maya Software from the list of renderers. Choose Intermediate Quality from the Quality Presets menu at the top of the Maya Software tab in the Render Settings window.

5. With the Render Settings window open, click back and forth between layer1 and layer2 in the Layer Editor. You can see the Render Settings window update with the appropriate settings for each layer. This means you can use more than one type of render setting for a single scene.

6. Click the master render layer to open the Render Settings window, which is updated with tabs for all four types of renderers. This includes the rendering engines not necessarily applied to your render layers.

> The settings for your Render Settings window override will stay consistent across multiple layers. In other words, you can't have two versions of settings for mental ray or Maya Software settings for two different render layers.

The advantage of using render layers is almost unlimited flexibility. You can create an unlimited number of layers for the objects in your scene and their compositing passes.

Additionally, you'll notice that the shading in the openGL Shading windows updates to give you a preview of what will be rendered in the render pass. If you would like to assign a separate renderer such as mental ray or Maya Hardware to a layer without relying on the use of a preset, click the Render Settings icon for that render layer to open up its Render Settings window and right-click over the Render Using label. From the options in the pop-up menu, choose Create Layer Override and then choose your renderer from the Render Using menu. The words *Render Using* will change to orange indicating that you have set an override for that layer.

> Be aware that display layers affect the objects on render layers. If you have an object assigned to a display layer as well as a render layer and the visibility of that display layer has been switched off, that object will not be visible when you switch to the Render Layers menu, nor will it render as long as the display layer is switched off. This means you should double-check your display layers before starting a render or if an object that should be in a render layer is not showing up in the viewport.

Now that you have a taste for what the new render layers can do, let's look at how they work in more detail. You may have noticed that the first time you create a new render layer, two layers actually appear in the Layer Editor: the new layer and the master layer. The master layer is always on regardless of whether you are using render layers. It is hidden when other layers are not present, and appears in the Layer Editor when you create a new render layer. Notice that the box next to the Master Layer label is empty. An *R* appears in the box next to the label for new layers in the Layer Editor. The *R* indicates that the layer is renderable. When you start a render, a subfolder in your images folder is automatically created and named after each render layer (and each pass, if multiple passes are created for a given layer). The images from each render layer are put into its corresponding subfolder. The master layer is not renderable by default once other render layers have been created, but you can make it renderable by selecting the empty box next to the label.

The master layer contains all the objects in a scene. It is a reference point from which Maya calculates the differences on other layers. If you have numerous lighting setups and variations of an object all assigned to different render layers, rendering the master layer could get ugly. This is why it is off by default. Notice that the master layer in the Layer Editor has no option icons. Right-clicking the master layer does not provide an option menu either.

A great time-saving feature introduced with Maya 8 is the ability to "recycle" render layers. To understand this feature, assume you have created 5 render layers, each with 3 render passes (say one each for diffuse, specular, and shadow). When you choose to render your scene, Maya must render out 15 (5 × 3) images and save them out each time you wish to rerender the scene; obviously this can get time consuming, especially if you wish to change only an element or two on a given layer. By recycling selected render layers, you instruct Maya to pass over these layers when you rerender the scene, saving render time in the process. In our example, recycling 4 of the 5 layers would mean only 3 images would have to be rerendered for the new iteration of the scene. To enable recycling on a given render layer, check the recycle symbol (two curved arrows, as seen in Figure 13.17). If the symbol is green, the layer will be recycled; if red, it will be rerendered.

The real power of render layers is demonstrated by your ability to customize how the individual layers render; you do so through overrides. We have already demonstrated how to apply Render Settings window overrides. Now let's look at material overrides and attribute overrides.

1. Open the file `convertible_materialOverrides.mb` from the CD.

2. From the Outliner, select the convertible group and all the lights.

3. From the Layer Editor under the render layer settings, choose **Layers → Create Layer From Selected**. Do this twice (or choose **Layers → Copy Layer** to duplicate the first layer) so that you have two new render layers as well as the master layer.

4. Click the sphere icon next to the layer2 label in the Layer Editor to open the Hypershade. Keep layer2 selected in the Layer Editor.

5. Find the reflectionShader shader.

6. Right-click the swatch for the reflection shader in the Hypershade and choose Assign Material Override For layer2, as shown in Figure 13.19. By doing this you are assigning the same shader to all the objects in that render layer. Here we use this feature to create a reflection pass for all the objects in this layer. Notice that the sphere icon in the Layer Editor has turned blue. Now when you click it, the Attribute Editor opens for the shader applied to this layer.

Figure 13.19

Selecting Assign Material Override For layer2 in the Hypershade

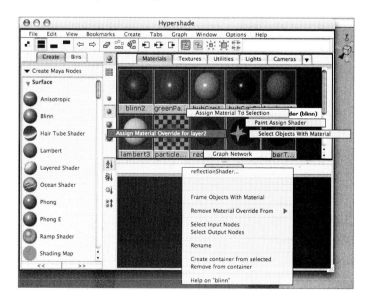

You can combine overrides so that a layer can have a Specular preset render override with a particular renderer chosen as well as a material override with its own reflection settings. This works better in some cases than in others. By its nature, a Diffuse preset will not render reflections regardless of the material override applied to the layer.

7. Select the headlights on the car.

8. In the Layer Editor, choose **Layers → Create Layer From Selected**.

9. Layer3 should appear in the Layer Editor. Double-click the layer3 label and in the pop-up type **glow**.

10. Right-click the glow layer label and choose Create New Material Override. This is another way to create an override, using preset material overrides. From the list, choose Surface Shader.

11. In the Layer Editor, click the blue sphere. The attributes for the new surface shader should appear. Change the Out Color to yellow. Move the slider on the Out Glow Color to a dark gray color.

12. Render the scene from renderCam. You now have a separate layer for the glowing headlights.

You can also create overrides for attributes on a per-layer basis. This is handy for separately rendering motion blurs, shadow casting, visibility in reflections, and so on. To see how this works, let's try another example.

1. Open the file `convertible_attributeOverrides.mb` from the CD.

2. Select the geometry and lights from the Outliner, and from the Layer Editor, choose **Create Layer From Selected**.

3. Do a quick render and verify that the car is casting shadows on the ground.

4. Click the flag icon next to the label for the new layer to open the Attribute Editor for the layer. You'll see a list of overrides.

5. In the Attribute Editor, click Override for Casts Shadows. The Casts Shadows box will contain a check mark. Click this check mark to clear the box.

6. Do another render with layer 1 selected in the Layer Editor. Notice that the car is no longer casting shadows.

Experiment with the other settings in the layer1 attribute overrides. Between the various levels of overrides available through the presets, material overrides, and attribute overrides, you should be able to fine-tune your renders for optimum compositing. It may take some practice before you can create a work flow that makes sense to you or your group. The guiding principle should be neatness—because all the subfolders and image sequences can quickly create a big mess on your hard drive—and efficiency—creating enough passes that you can avoid rerendering as much as possible, instead doing tweaks in your in the compositing package.

After a little bit of toying around, you'll notice that the presets are really just a combination of material and attribute overrides. You can create your own presets as well. Try combining a material override and some custom attribute overrides to the objects in a layer. Then right-click the layer label and choose **Presets → Save Preset**. Name and save your preset. Create a new layer with some objects, and open the Preset menu again. You'll see your custom preset there, ready to apply.

Rendering for Photoshop

Users of Adobe Photoshop may find that render layers resemble Photoshop layers. This is not by accident. In fact, the render layers are equipped with some of the familiar compositing modes found in packages such as Adobe Photoshop and After Effects. These include Normal, Lighten, Darken, Multiply, Screen, and Overlay. These modes determine how the pixels in a rendered layer interact with the pixels in the layers beneath them. The following exercise will familiarize you with rendering directly to Photoshop layers.

1. Open the layerModes.mb file from the CD.

2. Open the Layer Editor and switch to render layers. You'll see five layers and the masterLayer.

3. Click each layer. You'll see that a different hemisphere has been assigned to each layer. The background has its own layer as well.

4. When you expand the menu just above the layers in the Layer Editor, you'll see a list of compositing modes. Each layer has been assigned a different mode. The layers have been named after these modes for the sake of clarity.

5. In the Options menu for the Layer Editor, choose **Render All Layers**. A window will open with three choices: Composite Layers, Composite And Keep Layers, and Keep Layers. Choose Composite And Keep Layers.

6. Click Apply And Close. Make sure there is a check next to Render All Layers in the option box.

7. Open the Render View window, check the Render All Layers option under the Render menu, and render the current frame. You'll see each layer rendered separately and then a final composite with all the layers together.

Each layer has a different mode, meaning the pixels that make up each layer have been combined using an operation, such as multiply, or screen, with the layer below. By choosing Composite And Keep Layers from the option box in the Layer Editor, you'll see that each layer has been stored separately in the render view and that they are all together in the last image. You can save the composited image or the layers as a Photoshop file from the render view; however, the composite will not be divided into layers in the Photoshop file. To ensure that you get each layer separately, you need to create a batch render with PSD Layered (psd) as your selected image format.

> You can change the order of the layers in the Layer Editor. Select a layer and MM click and drag it up or down. The object in the scene will not move, but the order in which the layers are composited will.

Batch Rendering

Batch rendering is the process in which Maya takes your scene and renders each frame sequentially, creating either an image sequence or a movie file. As mentioned previously, you almost always want to render an image sequence rather than render directly to a movie file.

You set up the batch render parameters in the Common tab of the Render Settings window, as discussed earlier. Once again, pay close attention to how your images will be named and the names padded, the position of the image numbering, and the extension before starting a batch render. Also pay attention to where the images will be written on your disk. Batch renders can take a long time and can create a large number of files. You want to ensure that you have sufficient disc space and that you know what your final files are named and where they will be stored so you can retrieve them later.

To start a batch render, switch to the Rendering menu set and choose **Render → Batch Render**. The options for batch rendering are simple. You have a choice of how many processors you want to use if your machine has more than one. You can also simply select Use All Available Processors and let Maya use the available resources automatically.

Once a batch render starts, you can monitor its progress in the Script Editor or Feedback line. You can see about how long each frame takes to render, as well as other statistics, in the Script Editor's History pane. In addition, if the render fails, you can sometimes find out why in the Script Editor. You can view the most recently rendered frame in a batch render by choosing **Show Batch Render** from the Render menu. The render view will appear, displaying the current frame in progress. It's a good idea to check here after a few frames have been written to disc just to make sure you are rendering what you expect.

Once a batch render has finished, you can view the sequence by launching FCheck or a third-party image viewer from Maya by choosing **File → View Sequence**.

If you are rendering to a layered Photoshop format, the Photoshop file should appear in your images folder. The file should contain each render layer as a separate Photoshop layer. The settings for the blending modes will be retained from your choices in Maya.

The Ultimate Rendering Checklist

Here is an example of a checklist you might want to create for yourself when preparing to batch-render a scene. Put it on a sticky note and paste it to your monitor or have a colleague or coworker go through it with you before you send off a batch render.

1. Check rendering engine—Maya Software? Hardware? mental ray? Vector?

2. Is the animation set up to render a sequence rather than a single frame?

3. Are the correct frames entered in the frame range settings?

4. Will the files be named correctly? Frame padding?

5. Is the correct file format selected?

6. Will an alpha channel be rendered with the files? Will a depth channel be rendered?

7. Is the correct camera or cameras set to be renderable? Are others set not to be renderable?

8. Are the files going to the correct folder or folders?

9. Will render layers be used? If so, are they set up correctly with the correct objects assigned?

10. Is the resolution correct?

11. Do I have all the settings correct for the image quality I need (anti-aliasing, contrast threshold, raytracing, and so on)?

12. Does the frame sequence need to be renumbered?

13. Is the default light on?

14. Is motion blur set for the correct objects in the scene?

If you make a habit of going through this checklist every time you send off a batch render, you can save yourself the hours of aggravation that comes with discovering that your batch render job failed to render what you expected.

Summary

You should now be familiar with the concept of rendering and how to use Maya's native tools to create images and image sequences from your scenes. We've looked at how to create and animate cameras, set the resolution, and set the options in the Common tab of the Render Settings window. We've also looked at how to render using the Maya Software, Hardware, and Vector renderers, and we've looked at how to use render layers when compositing. Finally, we've looked at some of the effects you can create using motion blur and depth of field.

The next chapter covers rendering with mental ray, which is yet another tool you can use when creating images in Maya. Many of the concepts discussed in this chapter will carry over to the next and help you in your understanding of mental ray.

CHAPTER 14

Advanced Rendering with mental ray

mental ray is a photo-realistic rendering application that accurately renders physically correct simulations of natural light, motion blur, fog, depth of field, caustic effects, and more.

mental ray is the leading rendering software for high-end commercials and is a major contributor to the film industry. It is a high-end rendering option that has been integrated into Maya's work flow to a high degree as of Maya 8.5. mental ray has been used to create some fantastic, ultrarealistic shots in films such as *The Matrix Trilogy*, *The Brothers Grimm*, *Poseidon*, *The Hulk*, and others. This chapter will cover the following topics.

- Introduction to mental ray

- Understanding render settings

- mental ray custom shaders

- Lights, shadows, and fog

- mental ray motion blur

- Indirect illumination

- Image-based lighting and HDRI

- Surface approximation and displacement maps

Introduction to mental ray

mental ray, a stand-alone software package, is integrated within Maya (as well as other 3D packages) and provides outstanding image quality and realistic image effects. mental ray renders scene files from a host program like Maya in its own mental ray (.mi) format, which means that when you invoke mental ray to render within Maya, your current Maya scene is translated into a mental ray scene; you can view the progress of this translation from the Script Editor or from the Command line Feedback line. Not all Maya features are supported by mental ray, and some features do not render in the same way they do with Maya's Software renderer. For example, shaders evaluate different results, object tessellation is different, and mental ray does not support Paint Effect strokes unless they are converted to 3D. Normal maps, hardware rendering, and the capability to render volumetric fur are features that are new to Maya 8 and 8.5. Figure 14.1 shows the render settings for mental ray.

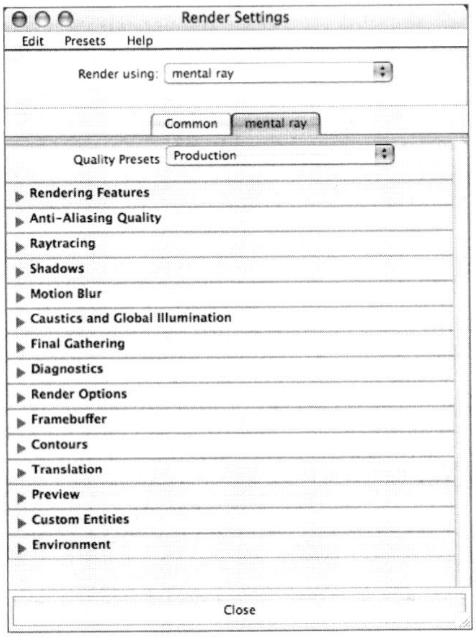

So, what is mental ray? Separate software you say, with limits and its own files? All this sounds confusing. It's actually not confusing at all because Maya handles all the conversion and translation under the hood. All you need to know is how to select mental ray within Maya and render. Although there may be some differences and limitations to using mental ray within Maya, the benefits by far outweigh any troubles.

mental ray for Maya usually is loaded by default. If it's not, choose **Window → Settings/Preferences → Plug-in Manager** to open the Plug-in Manager window, and load mental ray with the Mayatomr.mll option.

To select mental ray for rendering, open the Render Settings window by clicking the icon on the Status line or by choosing **Window → Rendering Editors → Render Settings**. From the Render Using drop-down list, select mental ray (see Figure 14.1) to enable the mental ray tab (to the right of the Common tab) which enables rendering with mental ray.

Another simple way to enable mental ray is to use the Render View toolbar drop-down list, which is shown in Figure 14.2.

You can easily set mental ray as your default renderer:

1. Choose **Window → Settings/Preferences** to open the Preferences window.

2. Select Rendering from the Categories list on the left, and then select mental ray from the Preferred Renderer drop-down list (see Figure 14.3).

Figure 14.1

The Render Settings window, the heart of mental ray. This is the main port to controlling all mental ray features.

Figure 14.2

The Render View toolbar. The Render drop-down list lets you alternate between Maya's renderers.

mental ray gives you a high degree of control over your renders. The Render Settings window lets you control render settings, and through a variety of other settings (windows and tabs) you can further customize unique attributes on objects, lights, shaders, and more. Throughout this chapter we will discuss most of these windows and attributes.

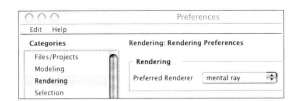

Figure 14.3

Make life easy and set mental ray as your default renderer.

Understanding Render Settings

The Render Settings window provides all the options for controlling mental ray renders. You use the Common tab to specify common attributes such as image format, resolution, and frame padding; the Common tab works the exact same way as any other built-in renderer you use.

The mental ray tab in the Render Settings window is the heart and soul of mental ray. It's where you control image quality, motion blur, indirect illumination, and much more. The following section provides detailed descriptions for key features as well as how they work.

> Get in the habit of turning off the default light in the Common tab of the Render Settings window when working with mental ray. You want full control over lighting, without any "default" light influencing the render.

Rendering Features

The new Rendering Features section of the mental ray tab in the Render Settings window, shown in Figure 14.4, provides a quick way to adjust the "big ticket" render settings for your render. Setting the primary renderer controls the general quality and speed of the render. Scanline is the "cheapest" rendering mode and should be used if there is little motion in the scene and no reflective or refractive surfaces. Rasterizer provides for scenes with rapid motion (but no reflections or refractions), while Raytracing allows for refractive and reflective surfaces, but at the cost of slower render times.

Figure 14.4

The Rendering Features section of the mental ray tab

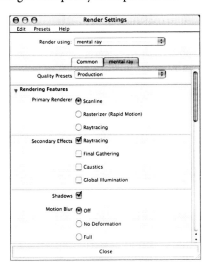

While the primary render engine is set via the top controls, the raytrace mode will enable itself for portions of the scene that need it if Raytracing is checked in the Secondary Effects section. Final Gathering, Caustics, and Global Illumination can be enabled here as well (we will discuss these render elements later in this chapter). You can also enable shadow casting through the bottom section. If shadows are enabled, motion blur can be controlled via the radio boxes below the Shadows check box: Off disables motion blur, No Deformation attempts to keep rendered geometry close to the geometry's shape, while Full allows for full motion blur, at the expense of distorted (fast-moving) geometry and potentially longer render times.

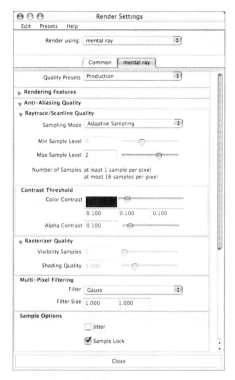

Anti-Aliasing Quality Section

The Anti-Aliasing Quality section in the mental ray tab of the Render Settings window controls the quality of an image by specifying the color values for each pixel during the render phase (see Figure 14.5). Anti-aliasing is accomplished by sampling colors within a certain region, comparing them with a contrast threshold value, and filtering the result to provide smooth transitions from one color area to another.

When an area in a scene needs to be placed within the space of a single pixel, you can use only one color value, although the scene can contain a variety of colors that represent that pixel space. Sampling and Contrast Threshold, which can be found within the Anti-Aliasing Quality section, provide a way to compare colors on a subpixel level before determining the color value for each pixel, producing highly accurate anti-aliased renders.

Figure 14.5

The Anti-Aliasing Quality section provides most of the controls for adjusting shader aliasing in the render.

Some of mental ray's features, such as realistic depth of field, require extremely high sampling values, thus quickly becoming memory- and time-intensive renders.

Raytrace/Scanline Quality

In this section are options to control the precision mental ray will use to determine pixel colors. If you have Adaptive Sampling chosen (the default), mental ray adjusts its sampling based on the requirements of the scene, using the Max Sample Level slider setting as an exponent to adjust the required samples; with the slider set at 2, 1 sample is the minimum, 16 the maximum. With fixed sampling, the Max Sample Level slider sets the exact number of samples per pixel. With Custom Sampling chosen, you use the Min Sample Level and Max Sample Level sliders to specify the min and max sample levels independently of each other. When using adaptive sampling, mental ray uses the Min Sample Level to compare the region with the contrast threshold. It then determines whether or not to sample at a higher level, the highest being the Max Sample Level value.

The sampling level increases the number of blocks that are sampled at an exponential rate. Negative values take fewer samples than there are pixels, which is known as infrasampling. A value of zero samples once per pixel, and values greater than zero exponentially increase the samples taken within each pixel, known as oversampling, which provides for higher-quality renders but at the expense of render time. For example, 1 sample (2 to the power of 2) equals 4 sampling blocks, 2 samples (power of 4) equals 16, 3 samples (power of 6) equals 64, and so forth, the number of blocks always being equal to a value of 2 raised to the power of *nx2* samples.

> Because sampling is adaptive, increasing the minimum level greatly increases render time and forces mental ray to oversample regions that otherwise require fewer samples. It is best to set Min Sample Level to a low value.

Contrast Threshold

The settings in the Contrast Threshold section control which sampling level, between the Min Sample Level and Max Sample Level, is used to calculate the value of a given pixel. These settings act as a metering device to compare contrast between two sampled colors (neighboring sampled blocks within a sample region). As long as the contrast between sampled colors exceeds the values in the Contrast Threshold section—in other words, more contrast than permitted—mental ray continues to increase the sampling level for the sample region until the Max Sample Level is reached or until the sampled values are within the Contrast Threshold limit.

> You can increase quality by using lower values in the settings in the Contrast Threshold section. The lower the value, the longer the render time.

Multi-Pixel Filtering

The settings in the Multi-Pixel Filtering section provide options for better blending, or smoothing, between pixels by determining how to filter a cluster of pixels. Different filter types use different means to blend pixel color values; higher filter values use a larger cluster of pixels and cause more blurring. They should thus be used with caution because they can overblur your image as well as slow down the render.

Sample Options

The Sample Lock and Jitter settings are both ways to control the sample locations with an intention of resolving artifacts such as banding, noise, or flickering in image sequences.

Checking Sample Lock forces mental ray to sample the same locations, reducing noise or flickering. Checking Jitter forces mental ray to offset the sample location during an image render, which is useful for reducing banding artifacts such as visible gradient values.

In practice, for test renders use a Min Sample Level of –2 and a Max Sample Level of 0. Set all Contrast Threshold sliders to 0.1 or higher, and choose Box filtering under the Filter drop-down list in the Multi-Pixel Filtering section. In production, typically the Min Sample Level and Max Sample Level values are between 0 and 2 and Contrast Threshold between 0.1 and 0.05. Use Gauss or Mitchell Multi-pixel Filtering. If there is no need for the alpha channel, leave Alpha Contrast set to 1, preventing it from slowing down the render.

Using the Quality Presets drop-down menu at the top of the Render Settings window is an excellent way to see what Maya considers appropriate values for various settings for anything from draft- to production-quality renders.

Figure 14.6

The Raytracing section enables better optimization for raytracing during the render. A good handle on these settings helps in reducing render times.

Raytracing Section

The Raytracing section of the Render Settings mental ray tab (see Figure 14.6) provides controls for enabling and limiting raytracing. By default, mental ray initiates each render as a scanline render.

With scanline rendering, the scene is sorted in a 2D viewing plane from the camera's perspective, which is then used to examine color values for each visible point in this projected viewing plane.

Scanline rendering is used to reduce the overhead of calculating raytrace rays, which initiate from the camera and travel (bouncing around) through the scene's reflecting or refracting surfaces. Thus, initially the color for each point is examined using the scanline algorithm, and if, when the color is being processed, a ray must change its direction, as with a reflection or refraction, raytracing is initiated. When the trace has completed to the depth you specify (as discussed next), mental ray resumes the scanline process for examining the color value for the next point.

Raytracing Limiting Attributes

Raytracing could theoretically extend to an infinite number of bounces if we didn't set limits. The Reflections and Refractions attributes dictate the maximum number of times a single ray can change its direction; these attributes limit the number of rays that may be used, reducing rendering overhead. If the Reflections value is met, no further reflections are calculated for a given ray. If an environment shader exists when the reflection limit is reached, that color is returned for the reflection. The Refractions attribute limits a ray from penetrating and redirecting through surfaces when the index of refraction (IOR) value is other than 1. An IOR of 1 is evaluated as regular transparency and is rendered using scanline rendering because the ray does not change its direction, instead passing straight through the object.

The Max Trace Depth attribute acts as an overall raytrace limiting value for the total of both Reflections and Refractions. This value limits the number of times a single ray can reflect and refract. For example, if Max Trace Depth is 3, any combination between reflection and refraction rays is limited to no more than three rays (for example, one reflection, two refractions). The Shadows attribute limits the amount of times a ray can be redirected to create a shadow, much like the Reflections and Refractions limiting attributes. With a Shadows value of 0, shadows will not appear; at 1, shadows appear; and a value of 2 or greater will cause shadows to appear in reflections as well. These settings are global to the scene, but you must also specify them locally. For a source light casting raytraced shadows, you must increase the Ray Depth Limit attribute under the Raytrace Shadow Attributes rollout in the light's Attribute Editor.

The Reflection and Refraction Blur Limit settings determine how blurry reflections and refractions are. The higher the number, the blurrier reflected or refracted objects appear when rendered.

The settings in other sections of the Render Settings window will be discussed throughout the chapter as they are used.

mental ray Custom Shaders

You can adjust shaders for mental ray in two ways. One way is to use mental ray attributes, found in the mental ray section of the Attribute Editor's tab for most Maya shaders (see Figure 14.7). These attributes provide control over how Maya shaders render with mental ray.

The other way to adjust shaders for mental ray is to use the mental ray shader library, which comes with its own collection of shaders, textures, utilities, and more—all found under the Create mental ray Nodes (or Create All Nodes) drop-down option in the Hypershade window or through the Create Render Node window. (If you don't see the Create mental ray Nodes Tab, click the Create Maya Nodes Create bar and choose Create mental ray Nodes.) Some of these additional shaders provide an entire set of tools for rendering effects, such as subsurface scattering and contour rendering (which provides a cartoonish look).

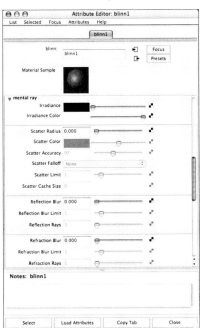

Figure 14.7

mental ray attributes for Maya shaders are portholes to powerful mental ray features such as blurry reflections and refractions.

Applying a Custom Texture

You can use mental ray shaders combined with Maya shaders, providing the unique power of the best of both worlds. For example, a common practice for rendering texture-based occlusion is to connect the mental ray Occlusion texture to the Ambient Color channel of a Lambert shader or, even better, to the Out Color attribute on a surface shader. This practice will become clear with the following exercises. Occlusion refers to the blocking of light (occluding) that occurs based on the distance between geometry, such as objects in near proximity, and folds or cracks on a surface. As surfaces become closer, they block light from passing through, creating a "soft lighting" effect. To aid in creating occlusion maps, Maya has an Occlusion texture as an option for a pass in the Preset Passes setting in the Render Layer Manager (see Chapter 13). Passes are extremely powerful for compositing. When you apply Occlusion as a pass for a render layer, Maya automatically creates a surface shader and maps an Occlusion texture into its Out Color attribute, creating a custom shader for you. You will see this shader pop up in the Hyper-shade window when you choose to create an Occlusion pass from the presets. In the following tutorial, we will look at establishing some of these connections.

1. Open the scene occlusion01.mb from the CD. In the Hypershade window, create a mental ray Occlusion texture by selecting the Create mental ray Nodes tab on the left-hand pane and choosing **Textures → mib_amb_occlusion**.

2. MM drag and drop the Occlusion texture over the Lambert1 shader (the default shader), and select ambientColor from the pop-up list. Set the Lambert1 Color value to white.

3. Render the scene (using the mental ray render engine); notice that no lights are being used, so what you see is entirely the shader at work. This shader darkens objects in near proximity based on light occluding values provided by the Occlusion texture. To improve the quality (reduce the splotchiness of the image), increase the number of samples of the mib_amb_occlusion1 texture. Try 64, then render. Figure 14.8 shows the result. This grayscale render can be composited atop a "normal" render (using multiply, soft light, or other compositing modes) to create a soft, global illumination type image.

4. Delete the Occlusion texture and apply a new Lambert shader to all objects. In the Render Layers Editor, create a new render layer and assign all objects. (See Chapter 13 for more details on the Render Layer Editor.) RM click the new layer (not master-Layer), and choose **Presets → Occlusion**. A new shading network should appear in the Hypershade window, driving the occlusion texture to the Out Color of a surface shader. Examine this network to see how you can manually adjust this texture as we did in the previous steps.

The mental ray documentation provides detailed information for most of the mental ray shaders.

As you can see, connections with mental ray textures are handled in the same way as with Maya textures and are thus easy to use. The one exception is in the way mental ray shaders are applied to an object. Figure 14.9 shows two shading engines connected to Maya and mental ray shaders. The shading engine is the node that drives the connections between objects and materials. Maya and mental ray shaders have separate connections on the shading engine, thus allowing for both Maya shaders and mental ray shaders to be connected simultaneously; however, while rendering, mental ray–specific shaders over-write the Maya shaders.

Figure 14.8

Ambient Occlusion makes any render appear more esthetic and interesting.

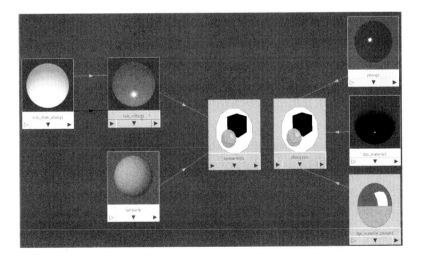

Figure 14.9

Custom mental ray shaders connecting into Maya's shading engine. These connections are different from Maya's connections.

Applying a Custom Shader

If you haven't already switched over to the Create mental ray Nodes bar, in the Hypershade window, click the Create bar and choose Create mental ray Nodes from the pop-up menu. Create any number of mental ray shaders as you would Maya shaders and examine their properties. You'll notice that they are different from Maya shaders. They have controls only for diffuse color, ambience, and a few additional attributes, depending on the shader.

mental ray shaders are much different from Maya shaders and do not provide control for all the attributes that define a surface at render time, such as Transparency, Reflection, and Refraction. These attributes need to be connected in a certain way to allow their use. The Shading Engine node on the left in Figure 14.9 shows a typical connection scheme for a mental ray Phong shader to a mental ray Reflective node (a mental ray Sample Compositing node), which is connected to the shading engine. Shading engines are created by default for every new shader and are labeled SG (Shading Group) with the additional prefix name matching the shader type, such as, for example, lambert2SG. To examine these connections in the Hypershade window, open the shader.mb file from the CD. This scene has a few connections using mental ray shaders, textures, and other nodes.

Figure 14.10

mental ray light attributes for an Area light

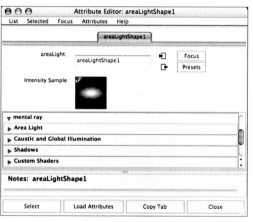

Under the mental ray tab for Maya shaders are Reflection Blur and Refraction Blur attributes that allow for rendering distance-based blurring. This enables mental ray to support realistic reflection and refraction blurring. For example, when you place your finger on a non-planar reflective surface, the reflection of your arm rapidly loses "focus" as your wrist, forearm, and upper arm get farther from the point of contact on the surface. The down side of these attributes is that as the values increase, so do the render times. The time is worth it, however, as these attributes add great realism to renders.

mental ray Lights, Shadows, and Fog

Maya lights work well with mental ray, particularly Point, Spot, and Directional lights. You can find additional mental ray attributes for these lights in their mental ray tab in the Attribute Editor (see Figure 14.10); thus, you should prefer using them with mental ray renders. Not all the settings exist for each light type; hence, these attributes are based on settings that mental ray supports for each light type. New with Maya 8, you can directly use Area lights with mental ray (rather than having to define an area attribute for a Point or Spot light).

The mental ray additional light attributes include Caustic And Global Illumination, Shadow Maps, Area Light (area lights), Custom Shaders, and Light Profile (only for Point lights). The Light Profile setting is a very useful tool, enabling use of light descriptions from light manufacturers that describe realistic light characteristics for a specific light, a great advantage for architectural or theatrical previsualization rendering.

Area Lights

Area lights are now created simply by choosing **Create → Lights → Area Light** from the main menu set. Area lights are extremely powerful, mimicking the way natural light spreads out from a real-life light source.

Technically, mental ray places several emitting Point lights within the Area light's light-emitting region. This light region is defined by the size of the geometric shape that appears around the source light once the Area Light attribute is enabled (see the following tutorial, "Creating Area Lights"). The fact that Area lights scatter light from a region rather an infinitesimal point in space is significant because it enables scattering light as if it is from an actual physical size source light. This allows for soft shadow and light-wrapping effects to appear. A powerful mental ray feature not found in Maya's rendering engine is that this characteristic also provides real specular highlights based on the source light's actual size (region).

Creating Area Lights

Open the `arealight_01.mb` scene from the chapter folder on the CD. The scene consists of some simple geometry, a curved reflecting back plane, and a Point light. Notice that the perspective camera is keyed in place for render tests. Anti-Aliasing Quality is set low for reducing render times, as area lights can quickly become an expensive render. Save snapshots in the render view for comparing images.

1. Verify that the default light is disabled and render a frame. If you do not see the object and Point light reflecting in the back plane, make sure raytracing is enabled.

2. Create an Area light (notice that it defaults to a rectangular shape) and move it into the same position as the Point light; then delete the Point light. Rotate the Point light so the aim vector is pointing down and to the left a bit from the persp camera's point of view. Render an image. The light quality changes, and light does not emit behind the rectangular light shape (opposite the direction arrow that shows the direction light is being emitted). The light will likely be a bit dimmer now, but we can adjust that later.

3. Check the Use Light Shape box to enable light shapes, then enable the Visible check box from the bottom of the Area Light tab and render. This makes the Area's light shape visible in the render. For example, this can be used to make a halogen or fluorescent source light visible. Note that you can see the light in the reflection but not in

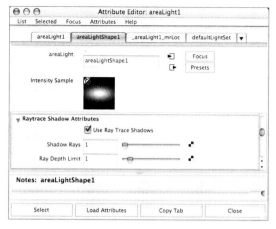

Figure 14.11

Enabling raytracing shadows for mental ray Area lights. Only the Ray Depth Limit attribute is relevant.

the scene itself: this is due to the fact that the light is emitting light away from the persp camera. If you move the camera or rotate the light so that it is emitting toward the camera, you will see the light in the scene.

4. In the Shadows section (not the mental ray shadows tab), under Raytrace Shadow Attributes, enable Use Ray Trace Shadows (see Figure 14.11) and render. This enables raytrace shadows with mental ray. Only the Ray Depth Limit attribute should be used with area lights. This attribute controls how many times a shadow can be reflected; in other words, how many times the shadow can bounce from one reflection to the next.

5. Notice that there are no shadow reflections on the wall. To remedy this, increase the value of Ray Depth Limit to 2, and rerender.

6. Notice how the shadow accurately spreads out from the object. This effect is known as a soft shadow, but here its quality is low. Increasing the sampling under the Area Light tab will improve the quality. Set the High Sample Limit value to 16 and render. Notice that both the shadow and reflected shadow quality greatly increase, as well as the render time. Setting High Sample to 32 improves quality even more, at the expense of higher render times. Also note that the penumbra around the Area light's reflection in the back wall gets less grainy with higher sampling rates.

7. Area lights provide for five shapes to be used as light emitters from the Area Light section (enabled by checking the Use Light Shape box); each scatters light based on its geometric shape. Experiment with them and notice that the light and shadow behavior depends on the shape you use. Note that cylinder and sphere both are visible in the scene as well as the reflection: they emit light in a full 360 degree range rather than being one-sided.

8. Reselect a rectangular shape for the **Area** light, then scale the Area light's rectangle that appears around the source light nonuniformly on the X axis in the viewport. Render with different scales to see how the shape scale controls the light spread (light wrapping around an object) and soft shadow.

9. The Shape Intensity field controls how bright the Area light appears in the scene. You can reduce the value to less than 1 to reduce the apparent brightness of the light. Note, however, that the light remains as bright as before in the reflection.

Controlling the Sampling Quality

mental ray Area lights, as explained earlier, are basically a cluster of Point lights randomly placed within the Area light shape. Thus, a rectangular Area light can have 4 × 4 Point lights arranged into a grid on the surface that act as light sources that cast light into the scene spread within a rectangular shape. The light direction is bound by whether you are using a rectangular or disc shape, which both spread light in 180°, or the sphere and cylinder shapes, which spread light in all 360°.

Consider both Sampling and Anti-Aliasing settings when adjusting Area light quality.

SAMPLING

The Sampling attributes under the Area Light section control how many source lights are placed within the light region. Use them with care because high values greatly increase the render time. Use Sampling to try to reduce graininess in soft shadows by increasing the number of samples, effectively providing more rays for calculating soft shadows.

The High Samples setting sets how many Point light emitters are set in the X and Y dimensions of the Area light. Obviously, the more emitters, the less grainy the rendered image, but at the cost of higher render times. The High Sample Limit setting controls how many bounces a light ray will go through before mental ray reverts to the Low Samples setting. Typically, after only a few bounces (reflections and refractions) there is no need to use a high number of light samples to get good results, so this setting can be left fairly low. The Low Samples setting controls how many point light emitters exist once the High Sample Limit number of bounces occurs. Leaving this at the default of 1 should normally be fine.

Shadows

mental ray shadows can be either raytraced or scanlined. Shadow maps are non-raytraced shadows created with the scanline rendering algorithm. Raytracing provides precise shadows, color transparent shadows, and Area light soft shadows as well as support shadowing through volumetric effects, such as casting shadows from dust or clouds. Both raytrace and detail shadow maps support motion-blurred shadows.

Scanline shadow maps have the advantage of being faster to calculate as well as providing a means for storing and reusing shadow information (hence the description as *maps*), provided the shadow remains the same. The shadow maps method also provides the ability to use OpenGL acceleration. The mental ray implementation of shadow maps also includes the ability to render transparent shadow maps with fine shadow detail—a major advantage over the Maya Software rendering engine.

Scanline shadow maps also render soft shadows; however, this is not as precise a calculation as you can get with raytrace shadows. The scanline soft shadow is merely a blurring effect of the shadow outer rim based on specified values within the light attributes. Normally, however, this effect is more than adequate for a shadow.

Raytrace Soft Shadows

Open the raytrace _01.mb scene from the CD. This scene consists of a Spot light aimed at a transparent object as well as a reflective wall. The camera has two keyframes for different render perspectives.

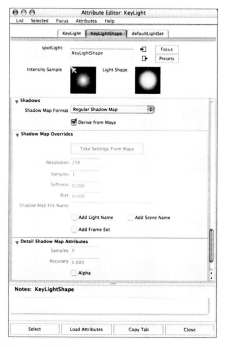

Figure 14.12

Shadows and detail shadow map attributes for mental ray lights. Detail maps support color transparency and motion blur shadow maps, reducing the need to raytrace and improving render times.

1. Select the spotlight (which is renamed KeyLight) and display the Raytrace Shadow Attributes in the Attribute Editor under the Shadows section. Enable Use Ray Trace Shadows, set Ray Depth Limit to 2, and render. You can see that raytrace shadows provide for color transparency in shadows.

2. Set the Light Radius attribute to 2 and render. Notice that the soft shadow appears, but with poor quality. Increase the Shadow Rays attribute's value to improve the quality. Try using a value of 20.

The raytraced soft shadow falloff is based on the distance from the object, a realistic shadow effect. Also, the shadow accurately represents transparency and color. The shadow softness is also visible in reflections. This type of soft shadow is adjusted in a different manner than the Area light soft shadow, which is tuned from the mental ray Area Light tab.

Shadow Map Attributes

Shadow map attributes are available in the mental ray section of Maya Lights, as shown in Figure 14.12. The shadow map is mental ray's equivalent algorithm for Maya's depth map shadow maps.

By default, the shadow map settings are derived from Maya's shadow maps, easing their creation. However, unchecking the Derive From Maya check box gives you access to a number of Shadow Map Overrides controls, where you can set map attributes directly for the mental ray engine. The Take Settings From Maya option transfers the current depth map values from the Default Shadows section into the mental ray Shadow Map section, thus allowing you to easily transfer settings from Dmap shadows to mental ray shadow maps. Resolution defines the size of the shadow map image, just as with depth map shadows.

Softness blurs the outer rim of the shadow (the terminator line), providing for fake soft shadows. Samples controls the soft shadow quality; an increase in value increases quality. These soft shadows are in no way realistic; their softness is solely based on the values and are not distance-based shadow falloffs. You use the Shadow Map File Name text box to enter a name for storing and reusing the shadow map.

If you select Detail Shadow Map from the pop-up menu at the top of the Shadows section, you have access to the Detail Shadow Map Attributes section to fine-tune the quality of shadow maps when using the detail scanline shadow algorithm. See the "mental ray Motion Blur" section later in this chapter.

> Don't forget to disable Shadow Casting and Receiving for objects that do not require these settings because they can decrease the shadow quality by using much of the image map resolution real estate. You can disable these attributes for every shape in the Render Stats tab in the Attribute Editor.

THE SHADOW METHOD

Under the Shadows area of the Render Settings mental ray tab, Shadow Method controls how mental ray calculates shadows. Unchecking Shadows disables both scanline and raytrace shadows. The Simple, Sorted, and Segments options all relate to raytrace shadows only. Shadow Linking can be set to Obeys Light Linking (the default and most commonly used setting), be On for all objects, or be Off. See Figure 14.13.

Figure 14.13

The Shadows area of the Render Settings mental ray tab

The Simple shadow method looks for shadow-casting objects between the light source and an illuminated point on a surface. Once a fully opaque object is found, the shadow is evaluated, and at that point mental ray stops calculating shadows for a given ray. This prevents calculating unnecessary shadows for objects that may still be in the ray's path.

Sorted works in a similar way with the exception of first listing all the occluding objects and then examining their shadows based on which object is closest to the light. When the light is fully blocked, the shadow calculations terminate. This mode is more expensive to render and is used with custom mental ray shaders that require information on objects in the light's path.

Segments is the most expensive to render and is an advanced method for calculating shadows through volumetric effects such as clouds.

> Unless Sorted or Segments is required, use Simple to reduce render times.

SHADOW MAP SETTINGS

You can calculate shadow maps in three ways:

- Regular is the default shadow map algorithm that mental ray uses.
- With Regular shadows selected, checking the openGL Acceleration box accelerates calculating shadows based on hardware performance.
- Detail is an advanced algorithm for calculating shadow maps, enabling shadow map transparency as well as finer detailed motion blur.

Detail makes each mental ray shadow map a detail shadow map. Alternatively, you can choose whether to enable this as a global setting for the scene or on a per-light basis from the light's attributes by enabling the Detail Shadow Map attribute in the Shadow Map Format drop-down menu.

Rebuild Mode, in the Shadow Maps section, specifies how to rebuild or reuse shadow maps. Rebuild All And Merge enables mental ray to reuse the current shadow maps as well as append new information to the map. Reuse Existing Maps disables new calculation of shadow maps when old versions exist instead using ones previously created. Rebuild All And Overwrite forces all new shadow calculations and is the same as the older "off" setting in previous versions of mental ray. Checking the Motion Blur Shadow Maps check box enables calculating scanline motion blur shadow maps.

To experiment with shadow map settings, open the shadowmap_01.mb scene from the chapter folder on the CD. This is the same scene we used for the raytrace soft shadow tutorial.

1. Examine the light and open the Attribute Editor. Do a quick render of the scene. You will see the raytrace soft shadow from the previous tutorial.

2. Select KeyLight, enable Depth Map Shadows from the Shadows section for the key light, and render the scene. Notice that the shadow renders quickly and looks bad.

3. Set the shadow map resolution to 1024 and rerender. The low quality of the shadow is still apparent, and the transparency is not visible in the shadow.

4. Uncheck the Derive From Maya check box in the mental ray tab, set the resolution to 1024 once again, adjust Samples to 10, and rerender. Notice that the render slowed down but the quality did not improve. This is because the samples only increase the quality of a soft shadow. Set Softness to 0.030 and render again.

5. The soft shadow appears, although the quality is poor. Increase Samples to a value of 40 and render; you should see an improvement in soft shadow quality. The Softness values are sensitive; thus large numeric increases greatly influence the shadow spread.

6. Set Softness to 0.09, set Samples to 80, and rerender. Figure 14.14 shows the results of these settings.

These steps should clarify how Samples and Softness are coordinated. Notice that although the map resolution at 1024 looked jagged, we overcame the need to increase map resolution when soft shadows were applied. The resolution is also greatly influenced by the size of shadow-casting objects in the scene; hence, the need to remove Casts Shadows under the Render Stats section for objects that should not influence this calculation. When Cast Shadows is disabled, the depth map will be focused on a smaller region containing only shadow-casting objects, maximizing the use of the map resolution.

Let's look at the Detail Shadow Map option with the current scene:

1. In the Shadow Map Attributes section in the Attribute Editor, reduce Softness to 0.015, reduce Samples to 25, and render.

2. In the Render Settings window under Shadow Maps, select Detail from the Format menu and render.

Using Detail adds transparency to the shadow, although this is not as accurate as the raytrace color transparent shadow. In the motion blur tutorial, you will see more advantages for using detail shadow maps.

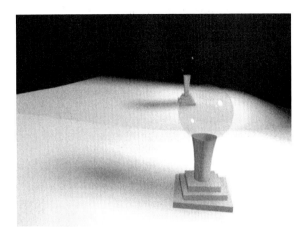

Figure 14.14

Cranking up the samples and softness values of mental ray shadow maps

Fog

mental ray provides two completely different ways to render volume light/fog.

- Using mental ray custom shaders to render mental ray participating media effects. Participating media is an effect that realistically simulates particles that exist in air and "participate" in the lighting solution, absorbing and reflecting light.

- Using the Maya volume fog shader in the Light Effects tab on the Maya lights window; however, with mental ray the work flow for controlling the fog quality is a bit different. The Maya fog shader is by far faster and easier to handle, but if you can afford to use mental ray participating media effects, the results are truly impressive. The downside is that participating media effects take longer to render and are harder to master.

The quality of volume light is based on a balancing act between settings. Let's experiment with fog.

1. Open the fog01.mb scene from the CD. A spotlight(spotLight1) casts fog through blinds onto a sphere. The blindsCNTRL node has a CNTRL attribute that opens and closes the blinds. PointLight1 is there for lighting the front side of the wall and should not be adjusted. A Fog shader has been applied to spotLight1 in the Light Effects tab with Fog Spread and Fog Intensity values of 2. In the Depth Map Shadow attributes, the Fog Shadow Intensity and Samples settings control volume light quality with Maya Software renders; these values are set to 3 and 80. The scene is set up for rendering with Maya Software renders.

2. The perspective camera has keyframes to help view the scene. While on frame 1, render using the Maya software renderer. Notice how volume light spreads through the blinds with clear lines and creates a clear break around the sphere.

3. Now switch to mental ray and render. The image quality is poor primarily because the Fog Shadow Intensity and Samples settings do not influence mental ray; thus we need to set volume samples in some other way.

4. Navigate to the fog coneShape1 tab from the top part of the Attribute Editor and expand the Render Stats section. In this section is a Volume Samples Override attribute (see Figure 14.15) that controls volumetric samples with mental ray. Enable this attribute and render at frame 2.

5. Notice that the fog has completely disappeared. This is because the override is set to 0. Start increasing the Volume Samples value.

   Set a value of 2 and render frame 1. As you increase the samples, the quality will improve; however, this may overblur the fog. Set a value of 30. Render, save a snapshot, set a value of 15, and then rerender. When you compare the snapshots, the relative difference should be clear: 15 samples, while acceptable, has more identifiable grain, whereas 30 samples produces a less grainy but slightly more blurry image.

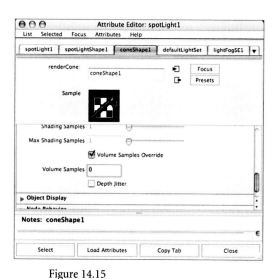

Figure 14.15

The Volume Samples Override check box is the secret to mastering fog with mental ray.

6. The other contributors to mental ray fog are the spotLight1 spread and intensity values. Expand the Light Effects section, set Fog Spread to 1, and then render. The fog seems to have toned down but looks better. Increase the Fog Intensity value to 6, render, and save a snapshot.

7. Now set Fog Intensity to 12, and set Fog Spread to 1.1. In the fog coneShape1 tab, set Volume Samples to 30, render, and save a snapshot. Compare this snapshot with the snapshot from step 6. Notice that the fog has much finer lines but requires more intensity to be visible. The Fog Spread value can increase the intensity and make the fog look thicker/richer as well as spread out more from light rays. Set Spread to 2, set Intensity to 1, and render. Notice that a much smaller intensity value was required to make the fog visible.

One last issue to address is the fog falloff rate, which can be controlled by setting a higher falloff rate for spotLight1. Hide the blinds layer, set Fog Intensity to 2, set Fog Spread to 1, set light Decay Rate to Quadratic, increase light Intensity to a whopping 350,000, and render.

mental ray Motion Blur

Motion blur is caused by movement of objects that are captured on film during the time the camera shutter is open. The amount of motion blur is based on how long the film is exposed to the scene.

Maya benefits greatly from mental ray's ability to render realistic motion blur effects. mental ray realistically blurs lights, texture colors, shadows, caustic light, global illumination, and anything else that would be affected by motion blur in real life. For example, in the case of a camera moving through the scene, everything in its line of sight is affected by motion blur (increasing render time, of course).

mental ray motion blur is supported by both raytracing and scanline rendering. The Render Settings window for mental ray provides one primary area that is used for controlling motion blur settings (see Figure 14.16). In addition, the Raytracing and Shadows sections also have contributing attributes that primarily control scanline motion blur and shadows.

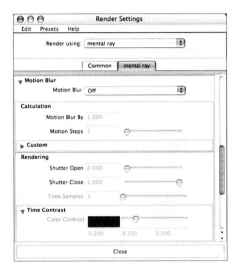

Figure 14.16

The Motion Blur settings provide control for simulating more realistically how the shutter exposure time influences film.

Motion blur calculates the blur factor based on sampling an object's transformation and deformation over a given time interval, which is set with the Motion Blur By attribute in the Motion Blur section. Think of this time interval as an overall scale that ranges from 0 to 1 and represents the range of time that is used to sample motion. The Motion Steps setting controls the accuracy of motion blur by sub-sampling a single frame based on this number. In other words, if Motion Steps is set to 2, mental ray divides the current frame in half and examines the motion blur across each half frame to better determine the exact motion blur. The Shutter Open and Shutter Close attributes determine when within that time range the shutter should open and close. For example, you can specify to open the shutter from one half the time range until the end; this enables offsetting the motion blur factor as well as reduces the number of samples that are taken throughout the time interval. The upcoming tutorials will help you understand these settings.

To increase the motion blur effect, increase the difference between Shutter Open and Shutter Close or increase the Motion Blur By factor.

The new Time Samples setting controls how many time samples are taken at different points in the image plane as a frame is rendered. In a way this is like anti-aliasing "jitter" done to offset the effects of sampling too regularly when creating motion blur. Increasing the Time Samples setting improves the quality of motion blur at the expense of longer render times.

Scanline motion blur provides accelerated ways to calculate motion blur using the Rapid scanline rendering algorithm found by choosing Raytracing from the Primary Renderer drop-down menu.

If raytracing features are required, use the default Scanline because Rasterizer (Rapid Motion) does not support raytrace features. If you require motion blur in reflections, use either the Scanline or Raytracing option. Under the Quality Preset options at the top of the Render Settings window are several preset Rapid options to choose from.

Controlling Motion Blur

To see mental ray motion blur in action, open the mb_01.mb scene from the CD. The scene consists of a single propeller with some animation, as well as a keyframed view on the perspective camera. The propeller colors are there to enhance your ability to follow their motion. The key light is casting a soft shadow map, and Shadow Maps is set to Detail. Renders for this tutorial should be at frame 15.

1. The Motion Blur attribute in the Motion Blur section enables selecting the method that will be used to calculate motion blur. Set this attribute to No Deformations. No Deformations will blur only object transformation, rotation, and scale and will not blur object deformation such as blend shapes. It approximates the motion blur based on the objects' start and end positions during the time interval and then blurs between.

2. Render the scene. The motion blur appears to be linear, meaning there is no interpolation for the propeller between the shutter open and close time. To remedy this, increase the Motion Steps attribute to a value of 6. Each time you increase Motion Steps, mental ray interpolates another step within the motion blur sampling time interval. Render again and note that the end of the propeller now shows a curved motion blur rather than a linear one, as shown in Figure 14.17. Increasing the new Time Samples setting improves the quality of motion blur by reducing graininess, making the blur look smoother. Try setting Time Samples to 6 and note the subtle difference this brings to the blurred propeller.

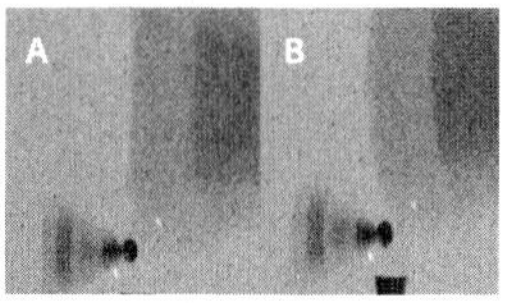

Figure 14.17

Increasing Motion Steps. (a) The linear nature of motion blur with one step. (b) An arcing motion blur using six steps.

The Full motion blur method is a realistic calculation of motion blur that takes longer to render but provides more accurate results. This motion blur blurs deformations as well as translations; thus, it blurs effects such as soft bodies and blend shapes. The Full method examines motion on a per-vertex level.

Controlling the Shutter

The Shutter Open and Close settings together determine when the shutter is open during a frame. You can delay the start time by increasing Shutter Open above 0 and decrease the end time by lowering Shutter Close below 1. Adjusting these settings allows you to offset the motion blur within a frame as well as decrease or increase the blur effect—having the shutter open a small amount of time decreases the blur effect, as if the camera has a very fast shutter speed (like a video camera); a large opening time increases the blur effect, softening up the render.

1. Set the Shutter Open and Close values to 0.5 and render. Obviously, there is no motion blur since the shutter never opened. Shutter affects motion blur, so we still see the object rendered.

2. Now set Shutter Close back to 1 and render. Compare this snapshot with the previous render that used a Shutter Open value of 0. Notice that the motion blur arc is much smaller and is offset, taking place only on the lower half of the previous blur. Now set Shutter Open to 0 and Shutter Close to 0.5. Hopefully you can anticipate that it will render only motion blur for the first half of the time interval. Notice that the quality is better when we render shorter shutter times because less sampling is needed.

Tuning Quality

You can improve the quality of motion blur renders by adjusting the Time Contrast values in the Motion Blur section. These values work in a similar way to the anti-aliasing contrast threshold values, but here they apply only to motion blur effects and determine how many motion samples are taken within the time the shutter is open. Lower values improve quality and slow the render time. The Time Contrast values let you fine-tune the sampling quality in red, green or blue independently from the rest of the scene without a need to increase anti-aliasing contrast threshold quality.

1. Reset the scene with a Shutter Open value of 0, a Shutter Close value of 1, and a Motion Steps value of 6.

2. Change the time contrast for the color channels (RGB) to a value of 0.08 and render.

Clearly there is an increase in quality (reduction of graininess) as well as an increase in render time. The propeller colors are easier to follow because mental ray supports motion-blurred textures as well as reflections, shadows, and anything else that would need to be motion blurred.

Motion Blur Shadows and Raytracing

The main difference between scanline and raytracing motion blur is in the quality of the shadow. Raytracing provides for better motion-blurred shadows, which also respect color and transparency values. By contrast, shadow maps don't work well with motion blur. However, detail shadow maps solve this problem, enabling better-quality motion-blurred shadow maps. This eliminates a need for raytrace shadows. Object motion blurring should yield the same result using either scanline or raytrace motion blur.

When using shadow maps for shadows, use the Detail Shadow Maps format in the Shadow Maps section of the mental ray tab in the Render Settings window, which calculates motion-blurred shadow maps that better resemble a ray-traced motion-blurred shadow. The only consideration is that detailed shadow maps require an increase in detail samples to appear smoother and more accurate. The downside is that the shadow blur does not inherit color by default. Although Detail Shadow Maps provides for transparency levels in shadow maps as well as motion blur edges, the color is based on the Transparency color specified under the shader.

Choosing the Detail Shadow Map selection in the Shadow Map Format drop-down menu in the mental ray section for a light source can improve the shadow quality by enabling you to increase the Samples and Accuracy attributes in the Detail Shadow Map Attributes below. The Samples attribute determines how many samples are taken on a subpixel level. When this is set to 0, default values are used. Increasing Samples to 1 reduces the quality, and a setting of 6 greatly improves quality.

Experiment with these attributes using a simple animated semitransparent sphere translating through the scene under a shadow-casting light. Also experiment with motion cameras, lights, and caustic light effects. Motion blur with mental ray is a feature that yields truly realistic results, much more powerful than Maya software's motion blur.

> When you're trying to render both motion blur and depth of field, the render times increase exponentially. If you do need both effects, try adding the depth of field with a non-motion-blurred Z-depth pass in a compositing package.

Indirect Illumination

mental ray enhances Maya with an ability to render realistic light simulations by introducing global illumination, caustic light, and final gathering capabilities, which calculate indirect light influence between objects. Without indirect light capabilities, such as when using the default software renderer, Maya can use only direct lighting (or first order lighting) to calculate light influence in a scene, requiring unusual light placement and generally resulting in less-realistic results.

Unlike direct lighting, indirect lighting tries to mimic the natural behavior of light. For example, in the case of direct lighting, if you place one light directly above a desk, that light source affects only the tabletop. With indirect lighting, as in real life, the entire room is influenced by light, including areas directly beneath the table.

Global Illumination and Caustic Light

Global illumination and caustic light relate to the diffusive, specular, and glossy reflection and transmission of light from one object to another. Global illumination calculates the reflected diffuse light contribution, and caustics calculate the specular and glossy reflection and refraction of light—for example, a magnifying glass that focuses light through the lens, creating a hot spot on a diffusive surface. Caustic light and global illumination are separate in mental ray; thus, each can be fine-tuned independently.

Both are calculated with the help of photons, which can be thought of as light particles emitting from a light source. The light emits photons with a given color value and light energy value. The light then travels throughout the scene, bouncing from one object to another, until finally the energy is lost or there are no more surfaces to hit. Each photon leaves its mark at every point of contact as well as inherits some color influence from the surface. Thus, photons transfer color influence between surfaces, which is known as color bleeding.

Irradiance

Irradiance is a term that describes the total incoming light intensity at a given point from the scene. You can also think of irradiance as the overall contribution of light from object shaders or photons in the scene cast upon a specific point. To further clarify, this relates to measuring light influence for every point in the environment from its surroundings.

> Each shader in Maya has an Irradiance and Irradiance Color attribute in its mental ray tab. This attribute is used with indirect illumination for fine-tuning the influence irradiance has on that object.

Final Gather

Final Gather determines the light and color effects that objects have on each other. You can use Final Gather as a means for lighting a scene and/or as an additional way to improve the lighting. The main advantage of Final Gather is that it examines irradiance in the scene based on surface color values and does not use lights for illuminating objects. Final Gather is the process of casting individual rays from a hemispherical region around points on a surface, known as Final Gather points and Final Gather rays, which are used to sample light and color influences from other surfaces. Each Final Gather ray can bounce twice in the scene before returning values that influence that Final Gather point. Final Gather is not a photon-tracing process.

> Final Gather rendering is commonly used with image-based lighting and HDR Images, which provide lighting information via a texture map on an object rather than via lights. We will examine HDR lighting in the section "Image-Based Lighting, Physical Lighting and HDRI" later in this chapter.

Global Illumination Rendering

Let's explore global illumination (GI) rendering with a tutorial.

1. Open the `room_01.mb` scene from the CD. The light object areaLight1 is an Area light that we will use to emit photons through the blinds into the room. This scene is set with a low-quality setting to reduce rendering times. Render through camera1, frame 1 to see the direct light influence.

2. Enabling global illumination is divided into two parts. The first is to define areaLight1 as a photon-casting light. In the Attribute Editor for the light, in the mental ray settings, expand the Caustic And Global Illumination section (see Figure 14.18), which controls the photon physical properties such as energy, initial color, photon decay rate, and number of photons to cast. Enable Emit Photons and leave the rest of the options at their default values.

3. The second part of enabling global illumination is found in the Caustics And Global Illumination section in the Render Settings window (see Figure 14.19). This section

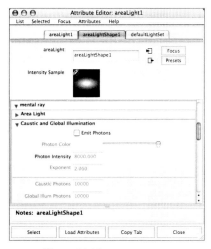

controls how photons are rendered, as well as limiting photon tracing (bouncing), just as with raytracing. This section also provides an option for storing photon map files that can be reused to prevent recalculating photon emission. Enable both Global Illumination and Rebuild Photon Map, and enter a name in the Photon Map File text box, as shown in Figure 14.19; then render through camera1 at frame 1. While rendering, notice that the Help line reads "mental ray Photon Emission," which describes the photon-casting process.

Comparing this render with the previous render, you can see a small, insignificant change in the room. However, it is obvious that the blinds, which are closest to the light, are influenced by the GI. What has happened is that the photon light energy is low and is overpowered by the direct light.

Figure 14.18

Emitting light photons from a Maya light, a method used for calculating realistic light bounce and color bleeding within the scene

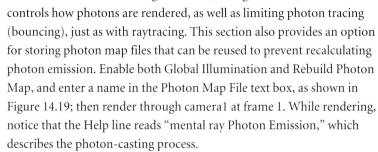

When rendering with global illumination, try matching the light and photon intensity and decay rates.

4. Set the arealight Decay Rate attribute to Linear and render. You now clearly see the area affected by global illumination. To affect the entire room, we must increase the photon energy. You can do so in two ways; both are found in the areaLightShape1 mental ray tab.

5. The first way to increase photon energy is to use the Exponent attribute, which controls the photon decay rate. The default value of 2 represents an inverse square falloff.

Change this to 1 and render. The falloff rate is now linear and ultimately carries more light and color into the scene. You can see a variety of colorful spots that represent the photons in the room.

6. The other way to increase the photon energy is to increase the Photon Intensity value, which represents the initial energy for each photon. Set Exponent to 2, increase Photon Intensity to 80,000, and render. The photons now have a more realistic light falloff using the inverse square falloff.

Controlling Global Illumination

Improving the quality and reducing the spottiness of a GI render require adjusting the attributes in the Caustics And Global Illumination section in the Render Settings window. To speed up this process, we created a photon map. Disable Rebuild Photon Map in the Render Settings window for the next few steps, and notice that when you render, there is no photon emission phase.

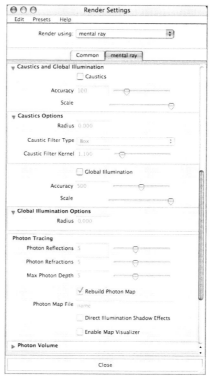

Figure 14.19

The heart and soul of indirect illumination, the Caustics And Global Illumination settings provide controls for simulating how indirect light travels and affects objects in the scene.

Use a photon map while adjusting settings in the Render Settings window. However, if you are adjusting light attribute settings, rebuild the photon map.

1. Set Global Illumination Options Radius to 1 and render. The colorful circles you see (see Figure 14.20) are photons displaying color, intensity, and their position in the scene. Radius defines the size for each photon. The most visible color bleeding effect is from the spheres that transfer different colors into the room. Increasing the Radius value causes more photons to overlap and blend. Set Radius to 5 and render. This increases color blending; however, the room is still full of spotty color stains. Global illumination depends on the number of photons used; their color, intensity, and radius; and how they blend together.

Reducing the stains is a balancing act between the Radius and Accuracy attributes in the Caustics and Global Illumination section of the Render Settings window (just below the Global Illumination check box). Increasing the Accuracy value determines how many photons should be considered while blending overlapping regions.

Figure 14.20

Light photon spread within the scene. Making these circles overlap and blend colors is the main concern for tweaking global illumination.

2. Set **Accuracy** to 1 and render. Notice that there is no blending. With Radius set to 5, increase the accuracy to 250 and render. Notice how the photon colors begin to blend.

3. Increase Radius to 10 and rerender. The scene has better photon blending.

4. Set Accuracy to 650 and render, constantly comparing the results. The large radius carries too much light intensity from the window frames onto the walls. We should probably use smaller photons and more of them for a better result.

When we increase Radius under Global Illumination Options, the scene colors will be more blurred and provide for an overall similar-toned global illumination solution. On the other hand, a smaller radius requires more photons and provides more detail and a nicer solution.

> For both Accuracy and Radius, there will be a point at which an increase in value will have no effect. Therefore, increase the radius and then adjust the accuracy. If the accuracy no longer affects the scene, increase the radius again and then increase the accuracy again. If the solution is not satisfying, add photons.

Improving Quality and Adjusting the Mood

There are not enough photons in the scene for blending well with small radius values. Let's fix that.

1. In the Render Settings window, set Radius back to 1, set Accuracy to 64, and then, under the attributes for areaLightShape1, increase Global Illum Photons to 100,000. Verify that Rebuild Photon Map is enabled, and then render. Notice how the photons are overlapping. Hence, a smaller increase in radius is required.

2. Try using the previous settings, Radius of 10 and Accuracy of 650, and compare the results. Color blending is better because of the increase in photons, but dark corners typically have darker photons and with a small radius will not inherit light from brighter photons. To clarify what's going on here, render with a radius of 4 and look at the top corner between the walls. Since the anti-aliasing settings contribute to the low quality, increase sampling when you need a higher-quality render.

To adjust the initial light color, change the Photon Color value in the Attribute Editor, which is a way of forcing warm/cold light schemes. This value should be in sync with the pointlight color value.

3. Change Photon Color to blue and enable Rebuild Photon Map in the Render Settings window. Set Accuracy to 64, set Radius to 1, and render. The effect should be clear because the room has completely inherited the blue color.

4. Now try using a bright color that will have less influence and provide for a nice mood, and render again.

Using the Map Visualizer and Adjusting Irradiance

You can visualize photon emission within the viewport rather than just in the render view. Let's experiment with the Map Visualizer, which is used to create 3D representations of maps of photons in the viewport.

1. In the Render Settings window in the Caustics And Global Illumination section, check the Enable Map Visualizer box (under Photon Tracing) and render. The Map Visualizer creates in the viewport a spread of red dots that represent the location of photons in the scene.

2. Choose **Window → Rendering Editors → mental ray → Map Visualizer** to open the Map Visualizer window. This window contains options for controlling the display of the red dots. Experiment with the values to better understand them. To remove the dots from the scene, choose the mapViz1 node in the Outliner window, which can be deleted at any time without affecting the render.

All object shaders have their own irradiance attributes. To control how they are affected by incoming light, adjust the Irradiance Color value found in the mental ray section of the shader's settings.

3. Select the blinds, adjust their shader (blinds_blinn) Irradiance Color value to 0.1 (V of HSV), and then render at frame 2. The blind's shader color starts to reappear rather than being completely white from the intense photon energy in that area.

4. Select the wall, increase its Irradiance Color value (V) to 0.9, and render. Notice that the wall is less affected by the light. You can experiment with adjusting these values for the spheres in that view.

Figure 14.21

**Using the Map Visu-
alizer to determine
where photons fall
in the scene**

Using a grayscale color for Irradiance Color will affect how much irradiance influences the shader to which it's applied. However, changing the color value will overwrite the scene irradiance color with the new color unless you use a very desaturated bright color.

Fine-Tuning the Direct Lighting

After adjusting the irradiance, we can improve the lighting by increasing the direct lighting influence. We are using an Area light to get a nice spill of light into the room—notice that the light is not casting soft shadows and has a low intensity. Now make sure that Global Illumination is enabled in the Render Settings window as well as Emit Photons for the light. You can disable Global Illumination to adjust the direct lighting, and then when you're satisfied with the direct lighting, enable Global Illumination and examine the direct light's effect combined with global illumination.

1. Set the intensity of the light to 100 with linear decay, and match the arealight's Color with Photon Color. Enable Use Raytrace Shadows under the Shadows tab, disable Rebuild Photon Map in the Render Settings window in the Caustics And Global Illumination section, and render a frame. A strong direct light with a nice light spill enters the room because we are combining Area light characteristics for direct lighting as well as global illumination for indirect lighting.

Figure 14.22

Combining global illumination and direct lighting provides softer, more natural lighting with color bleeding. However, the room is still dark and can use more lighting and caustic light.

2. Increase the Anti-Aliasing Min Sample Levels and Max Sample Levels values to 0 and 2 respectively, and then render. The room should look much better (see Figure 14.22), but it's still dark in certain Areas that should have influence from indirect light. There's also still some spottiness that will be resolved with the addition of Final Gather.

   To improve the lighting simulation, we will introduce final gather as an additional indirect light. We'll do so later in the Final Gather Rendering, combining GI with FG in that section of this chapter. In the next section, we will use caustic light to render indirect light influence for the glass objects on the table.

Caustic Light Effects

Most of this section builds on the terminology, technique, and tools used in the previous GI tutorial. In this section, we will examine how caustic light can affect the refractive objects on the table. As mentioned earlier, caustics calculate the specular and glossy reflection and refraction of light. Open `room_02.mb` from the CD. This is the same scene we've been using, but a Spot light (labeled causticsLight) is above the table and will be used to cast caustic photons into the room.

The objects on the table are refractive, semitransparent surfaces that would display caustic light in real life by focusing light onto the table. Global illumination and direct lighting have been disabled for the areaLight01 (from the previous tutorial) to speed up the process.

1. Render the scene with direct lighting to see the influence of the spotlight. Since this light will cast caustic photons, we could select to emit only specular light. However, in this case let's keep the direct light influence as well.

2. In the Caustics And Global Illumination section in the Render Settings window, enable Caustics with an Accuracy value of 64. This attribute works exactly the same as with global illumination. In the Attribute Editor for CausticsLight, enable Emit Photons in the Caustics And Global Illumination section. Notice that when Caustics is enabled, you can adjust only the Caustic Photons amount under the light. The same is true with global illumination.

3. Move to frame 3 (camera1) and render the scene with the current settings. The caustic light is barely visible because the energy is too low or the decay rate too high. You can increase caustic photon energy in the same way as with GI: set the Photon Intensity value to 80,000 and rerender.

Notice the detailed caustic light focusing through the refractive surfaces, as with glass, water, and other refractive surfaces (see Figure 14.23).

Figure 14.23

Caustic light simulating the effect of light transmitting through glass provides for interesting patterns on surfaces.

Adjusting Caustics and Combining with Global Illumination

Now let's fine-tune our scene by combining the global illumination solution with caustic light.

1. Save a snapshot in the render viewport and adjust the Render Settings. You can disable Rebuild Photon Map, as with global illumination, and now use the current map while adjusting the Accuracy setting under Caustics. Set Accuracy to 350 and render. Notice that the caustics are much more blurred than before.

> Caustic effects usually look better when sharpened, so using low caustics radius and accuracy values may yield a better effect.

2. Try finding a setting for Accuracy that you like, which normally should be balanced between an overly sharp and overly smoothed render. Use a value of around 120. Also increase Caustic Photons to 20,000 in the light's Attribute Editor, and don't forget to rebuild the photon map in the Render Settings window.

3. You can reduce the overall intensity of the caustic effect by changing the value for the Caustic Scale color under the Caustics section. Open the color and select a 0.5 V value (HSV).

4. Now let's combine GI and caustics. Select areaLight1 and enable Illuminates By Default. In the mental ray section of the Attribute Editor, enable Emit Photons, and in the Area Light section, enable Visibility. In the Render Settings window, enable Global Illumination.

5. Select CausticsLight, and set Global Illumination Photons to 0. For areaLight1, set Caustic Photons to 0. In both cases, leave Emit Photons on, which ensures that each light will emit the correct type of photons with respect to the role it plays in illuminating the scene.

6. Enable Rebuild Photon Map in the Render Settings window and render at frame 1. When the render is complete, you should see the effect of using both GI and caustics for indirect light, each contributing a different type of indirect illumination, one for diffuse light and the other for specular light. However, there are some unwanted color stains on the wall.

CAUSTIC SHADOWS

When using caustics, there is a problem with shadow casting: shadows will be opaque for transparent objects. You can render the scene in separate passes and then composite with a compositing package such as After Effects or Shake. This method requires that you render a separate shadow pass without caustics and then multiply it by the caustics color pass.

GI, Caustics, and Final Gather Object Overrides

The dots on the wall are from caustic photons. These appear because we are using a small number of caustic photons that will not suffice for coverage on that wall. There are two options for resolving: increasing the number of caustic photons and tweaking their values or, better yet, removing them completely from influencing the wall.

Figure 14.24

mental ray settings can be overridden on the object level.

mental ray provides a way to override caustics, global illumination, and final gather on a per-object basis. To do so, you select the object shape and adjust the settings shown in the mental ray section (see Figure 14.24).

1. To remove the caustics, simply enable Caustics Override for the wall and specify a Caustics Accuracy setting of 0. This forces mental ray to consider zero caustic photons on the wall.

2. Disable Rebuild Photon Map in the Render Settings window, and rerender a region on the wall to verify that the dots have been removed.

Final Gathering Rendering

Final Gathering (FG) is a means for rendering indirect light based on irradiance. As discussed earlier, this simply means that when an object is bright, it casts more light into the scene, and if objects get close to each other, they occlude light from their surfaces. For example, when you clap your hands, the palms of your hands get darker as they get closer. Final Gathering is commonly used to render an occlusion pass, which provides information on how objects occlude light from each other and how they self-shadow. An occlusion pass is typically rendered as a grayscale image that is then used to scale color values from the color pass during the compositing stage. Another technique is to retrieve the environmental influence cast on objects using an environment dome. This process renders an environment pass that describes the color influence from an image typically mapped onto an IBL node. You will see both of these in the following sections.

First, let's get acquainted with FG basics.

1. Open the FG_01.mb scene from the CD and familiarize yourself with it. It contains some Paint Effects objects that have been converted into a 3D mesh. The camera is keyed for two similar views on both frames 1 and 2. Follow the tutorial while rendering these views.

2. With the default light off, select the camera (perspShape) and display the Environment tab in the Attribute Editor. Change the background color to white, and render a frame. Obviously, the tree is black (no lighting) and the background is white.

3. In the mental ray tab of the Render Settings window, enable Final Gathering in the Final Gathering section (see Figure 14.25) and render. This is what a grayscale occlusion pass should look like.

4. Final Gathering will see the background color as an environment color that contributes to the irradiance in the scene. Experiment with the background color using different color values to see the effect it has on the tree. Note that Final Gathering only works if Raytracing is also enabled in the Raytracing tab.

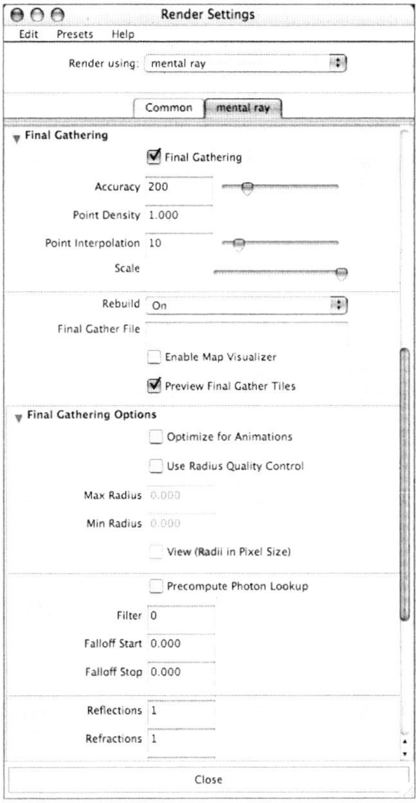

Controlling Final Gathering Settings

The Accuracy attribute in the Final Gathering section defines the number of rays that are emitted from each Final Gathering point. As this number increases, so does the render time and the quality; hence, the more rays used the better the interpolation of the irradiance influence.

It is very render expensive to emit Final Gather rays for each point on a surface on a microscopic level. When the Use Radius Quality Control check box (under Final Gathering Options) is checked, the Min and Max Radius attributes limit that area by defining a radius around a Final Gather point; within that radius no other points will cast rays. These attributes also define how the region should be illuminated using information from sampling the scene with Final Gather rays as well as averaging values from nearby Final Gather points.

Figure 14.25
Final Gathering render settings. This powerful addition to indirect illumination is probably the most-used method in production.

> For testing, use values around 100. In production, you might go above 1000 rays, especially to reducing flickering in motion sequences. Try keeping the value as low as you can since it directly influences render times.

> If you require fine detail such as when rendering self-shadowing within tight creases, you will want smaller Min and Max Radius values. However, if you just need to have some darkening without fine detail, use larger values, which will provide for faster renders.

The new Point Density setting controls the number of Final Gather points to be computed. Setting this number higher than 1 will increase both quality and render times. The Point Interpolation setting controls the number of other Final Gather points a given point will consider while rendering; the resultant points are interpolated over, smoothing out the grainy appearance that often accompanies Final Gathering renders. The more points considered, the smoother the final output, and increasing this value does *not* significantly increase render times. Note that when Use Radius Quality Control is enabled, Point Interpolation is disabled since the radius settings already determine how far each Final Gather point looks to do its interpolation. Finally, the Optimize For Animations check box enables a temporal interpolation where mental ray looks forward and backward across frames and smooths the results between frames, reducing the interframe flicker that is often associated with Final Gathering renders.

Now let's explore some FG settings.

1. Continue with the previous scene, with a white background color and looking at the view keyed at frame 1. Set Final Gathering Accuracy to 100 and render. Set Point Interpolation to 30 and render; save a snapshot.

2. Change Point Interpolation to 1 and render. Figure 14.26 shows the result. Compare this render with the previous render. We used exaggerated high values to emphasize the disparity you get when you use different values. When beginning to set up a scene, normally you should use the 10 percent rule of thumb: set Point Interpolation to 10 percent of the scene size. After examining your scene, change the values based on visual cues. Notice the finer shading on the leaves and under the roots using low values as opposed to high values.

3. Select the tree and display the Irradiance and Irradiance Color attributes on the LambertTree shader. Set Irradiance Color to any color and render. Notice that this overrides the irradiance color from the scene and uses the color you set.

Figure 14.26

Final Gather used to add natural light occlusion to the tree based on the irradiance levels applied from the scene's background color

Other important attributes are Max Trace Depth, Reflections, and Refractions in the Final Gathering Options section of the Render Settings window. They are exactly like the corresponding attributes under the Raytracing tab, as well as the Caustics And Global Illumination sections (see the Raytracing section earlier in this chapter). The default Max Trace Depth of 2 allows two Final Gather bounces, which is adequate for many scenes. However, the Reflections and Refractions defaults of 1 each is usually inadequate. mental ray uses the lowest of the settings for Max Trace Depth and Reflections/Refractions to determine how many bounces a light will take, so be sure to adjust both settings when you make changes to your scene. Although Final Gather uses single or multibounce diffuse rays, these rays can be reflected or refracted several times when hitting a reflective object, such as a mirror. Normally these rays don't need to refract or reflect more than twice.

Final Gathering can write to disk a final gather file that can be reused rather than having mental ray recalculate the final gather rays, provided the conditions in the scene don't change, much like with shadow maps or GI maps. The Rebuild pull-down menu under the Final Gathering section defaults to On, which forces Final Gather to recalculate each time you render. Off forces using the Final Gather map (whose name is specified in the Final Gather File field). Freeze allows appending detail to the map, which is useful for different applications: Final Gather calculates the map based on the rendered camera perspective; thus if the camera moves it can add detail to the map and reuse that information.

Combining GI with FG

In this final stage, we add Final Gathering for more indirect illumination in the room we dealt with in the sections on global illumination and caustics earlier in this chapter. The room's GI and caustics have been disabled. In the previous tutorial, the room still had many dark areas and lacked the occlusion effect between surfaces in near proximity, such as the table legs on the floor. Let's fix that.

1. Open the room_03.mb scene from the CD, select the white plane behind the window, and look at its shader (surfaceShader1). This shader will be used to drive illumination into the room from the window.

2. Enable Final Gathering in the Render Settings window and render a frame using the default values. (The lights have been disabled.) The white surfaceShader1 is not doing a good job illuminating the scene because its light value is fairly low. To increase the value, select the Out Color value in the surfaceShader1's attributes: with the Color Chooser, set the V (value) to 10, and then render.

3. Try setting a value of 40 and render again. Notice that the increase in value has a direct influence on the irradiance in the scene. This type of behavior directly relates to the advantage of using HDR images, which is covered in detail in the following section.

4. Select the camera, and in the Environment tab, set a bright color for the background. This color can set a warm or cold mood. Render and notice how some of the darker areas are now brighter. That's because we are providing bright "light" influence from two directions, one from outside the room and the other from inside the room (in front of the camera).

5. Save a snapshot, enable Secondary Diffuse Bounces from the Final Gathering Options tab in the Render Settings window, and then render again. Enabling secondary bounces means that each ray can bounces twice before returning light and color values; thus, areas that are dark receive more light and color values. Notice that the far wall in the room is better illuminated now.

6. Enable Global Illumination and Caustics in the Render Settings window, and for both lights (areaLight1 and causticsLight), enable Emit Photons and Illuminates By Default. Next enable Visibility for areaLight1 in the mental ray attributes section. Render a frame using all indirect illumination features. Notice how Final Gather brings out some of the extra details required to create a more realistic render. Figure 14.27 shows the result of the rendered room, which is now a highly photo-real looking render. Compare it with images from the previous global illumination and caustic light renders.

Figure 14.27

Here's the combined indirect illumination render using global illumination, caustics, Final Gather, and direct lighting.

As mentioned in the section on caustic light effects, you can control specific Final Gather settings on a per-object basis. In the case of Final Gather, notice that you can adjust the min and max radius for each object. This approach can resolve some problems when rendering objects that have completely different scales, such as a highly detailed object in a large environment. For example, when a record player is placed inside a room; the record player's detail and scale is very different than that of the room.

Figure 14.28

The Environment section of the mental ray tab of the Render Settings window

The following sections will examine how both direct and indirect illumination can be used with image-based lighting.

Image-Based Lighting, Physical Lighting, and HDRI

Image-based lighting (IBL) is the process of using an image or sequence of images to define the lighting in the scene. The color values present in the image are sampled and used in one of the following ways: as directional lights, as irradiance values for final gather, or as photon emitters (global illumination). All these methods have one common denominator; that is, they all define lighting in a scene based on an image.

mental ray's Image Based Lighting button (see Figure 14.28) in the Environment section of the mental ray tab of the Render Settings window provides a way to create a spherical container that is used as a hemispherical bounding environment. This is known as an IBL node. The IBL node can be mapped with an image that is then used for casting light and color values into the scene (representing an environment) or just for transferring reflection values from an environment.

When an IBL node is created, a spherical object appears in the scene representing that node. This object can be translated, scaled, and rotated in the viewport. Figure 14.29 shows the Attribute Editor window for the IBL node. Notice the Infinite attribute, which is enabled by default. The IBL node is considered a light shader and can be found in the Lights tab in the Hypershade window, as show in Figure 14.30.

In Infinite mode, the IBL node acts solely as an infinite environment that mental ray uses for environmental influences such as reflections and light sampling and thus is not affected by the position or scale of the node. In this mode, the IBL node will always encompass the entire scene. However, the rotation is active and is used for orienting the image in the scene. In Finite mode (with Infinite disabled), all transformations have effect; thus, you can scale and position the IBL node in the scene. This provides an ability to light objects with an IBL node in a closed environment such as a room.

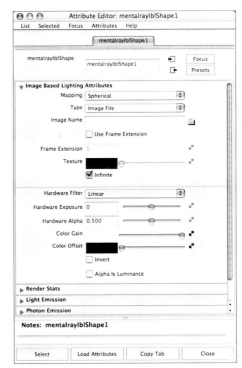

Figure 14.29

The IBL node attributes enable you to control how an image, typically an HDR image, can be used as a source of light, defining the environmental light influence and providing more realistic integration between 3D elements and live action shots.

Figure 14.30

The IBL node resides in the Lights tab of the Hypershade

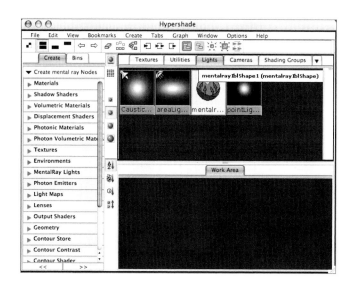

Finite mode image-based lighting uses Point lights rather the than Directional lights in Infinite mode. This greatly increases the render time because Point lights are more expensive to compute than Directional lights.

Physical Sun and Sky Simulation

New with Maya 8.5 is the ability to create a physical simulation of sun and sky (the button to create this effect is just below that to create an IBL node, as shown in Figure 14.28). Creating a Physical Sun and Sky node does essentially the same thing as creating an IBL, except that Physical Sun and Sky uses a procedural simulation to create a sun and sky surrounding the scene rather than relying on an image that you must provide. Thus, if you wish simply to render a scene using a sun and sky instead of a specific location that you must go out and shoot and then import into Maya, this new node will likely provide you with more than enough options to get the look you're after.

The mia_exposure_simple node is a new node mental ray uses to "squash" HDR images into the normal range of exposure your monitor can display. See the next section for more on HDRI and its uses.

Upon clicking the Create Physical Sun And Sky button, Maya turns on the Final Gathering option in the Render Settings window and creates two shading networks (mia_physicalSun1 and mia_physicalSky1), as well as an exposure node, and places them in the

Utilities tab of the Hypershade. In addition, a sunDirectionShape node is placed in the Hypershade's Lights tab. Adjusting the attributes of this node network by selecting the physicalSky1 node in the Attribute Editor (the physicalSun1 node is driven by the sky node) lets you adjust the lighting and sky conditions to get the look you want. A simple scene (`simpleSky.mb` on the CD) rendered with physical sun and sky simulations is shown in Figure 14.31. Note that only the sun simulation (in conjunction with Final Gathering) is lighting the scene.

Figure 14.31

The Physical Sun And Sky simulator showing an early evening lighting condition

High Dynamic Range Images (HDRI)

High Dynamic Range Images (HDRI) can better represent the light value present in real life by recording the light intensity value for different exposure levels and thus provide for a high dynamic range of light stored in an image. Real-life light values are not limited by any range, such as the typical 0 to 1 range in a computer. For example, when we look into the sun, we must immediately look away because the light intensity is so great, while at a cave mouth, light will fall away into complete darkness. The ability to retrieve the contribution of light based on its intensity in real life and use it with CG opens the door for more realistically simulating real-world light. For example, HDR images are used to sample light from outdoor environments that are then applied as lighting values onto 3D vehicles, providing an almost hyper-real quality to the cars. This has become common practice for car commercials and a feature of many special-effects-intensive films.

Let's explore the IBL node and Final Gathering.

1. Open the `IBL_Light01` scene from the CD and familiarize yourself with it. The objects represent different types of materials, from fully reflective to simple Lambert shaders. We will examine how HDRI with IBL can be used to light the scene.

2. Make sure that the default light is off, and create an IBL node by clicking the Create button in the Image Based Lighting tab in the Render Settings window. A wireframe sphere representing the IBL node appears in the viewport. If you do not see the sphere, you can scale it down; the scale is irrelevant because we are using Infinite mode.

3. Select the IBL node and open the Attribute Editor. In the Type attribute drop-down list, select Texture and then change the Texture attribute from black (default) to white. Then render, which sets the environment to white.

4. Notice that the white background reflects on reflective objects. Let's add lighting with final gathering. Enable Final Gathering with Point Interpolation of 20. (See the section "Final Gathering" earlier in this chapter for details.) Render a frame.

5. Notice that with final gather, all the colors come out and there is also a nice degree of shading, as seen in Figure 14.32. To increase the light intensity (irradiance), in the Image Based Lighting Attributes tab (for the mentalrayIblShape1 node) click the Color Gain color, increase the V (HSV) value to 2, and then render. This increases the light intensity and with HDR images acts as a means for controlling the exposure level.

Now let's look at how IBL, Final Gathering, and HDRI work together.

6. From the Type attribute drop-down list, select Image File, which enables mapping an image file to the IBL node. Using the Image Name drop-down list, load the image `lat_long_ldr.tiff` from the CD. If you zoom out in the viewport, you can see the image displayed (in shaded mode) on the IBL node; you can control this display with the Hardware Filter and Alpha attributes. Reset the Color Gain value to 1 and render. As Figure 14.33 shows, the chrome ball in particular now shows the image surrounding it.

The Mapping attribute (set to Spherical) provides two methods for mapping images onto the IBL node. The difference is in how images are wrapped around the IBL node. Both angular and spherical images can contain a 360° panoramic view, representing an environment. We used a latitude-longitude image (as with a globe), which is used with spherical mapping. An angular map looks like a reflective chrome ball and is mapped using the angular method. Both image formats are displayed in Figure 14.34.

Figure 14.32

Image Based Lighting on three spheres

Figure 14.33

Results of using a texture map for the Image Based Lighting environment

7. The image is visible in reflections and provides some lighting for the scene. Save a snapshot. We will now replace this image with its HDR version.

8. Load lat_long.hdr into the texture file and rerender. The dynamic range is visible on diffusive surfaces and reflective surfaces. Notice the differences in the sky and clouds on the reflective sphere. The image is dark, so increase the Color Gain value to 2 and render. Figure 14.35 shows the resulting image.

9. Replace the HDR image with ANGULAR.hdr and change Mapping to Angular. Render and see how the scene reacts to the new environment. Tumble around in the scene and notice how the angular image wraps around the IBL node. Compare this with the spherical mapping method in the viewports.

Figure 14.34

Latitude-longitude vs. angular HDR images. Both types can be used with the IBL node and wrap around the scene, providing environmental light influence.

Figure 14.35

IBL with a High Dynamic Range image as texture

Controlling Exposure

You can render an HDR image at different exposure levels. Although you can view only one exposure level at a time, the entire dynamic range is present, from low to high exposures. The IBL's Color Gain attribute value increases the range being used but does not do an overall washy increase with HDR images as with a standard image. This might be a bit difficult to comprehend; a few experiments as well as reading more about HDR imaging should suffice to master this technique. The best way to further your knowledge is by looking up Dr. Paul Debevec's website at www.debevec.org or www.hdrshop.com. As a convenience to the user, mental ray now includes a resampler node, mia_exposure_simple, that allows you to remap a HDR image back to low resolution for display on your monitor. See the Maya documentation for more on how to use the exposure node.

Now let's look at IBL, HDRI, and Light Emission:

1. Continue with the previous scene and disable Final Gathering.

2. In the IBL Attribute Editor, in the Light Emission section, which is shown in Figure 14.36, enable Emit Light and render.

3. Notice that the shadow is clear and based on the sun direction. This demonstrates how HDR images can provide information for lighting based on light intensity in the HDR image. Change the IBL image to the Spherical, lat_long.hdr and render to see the difference.

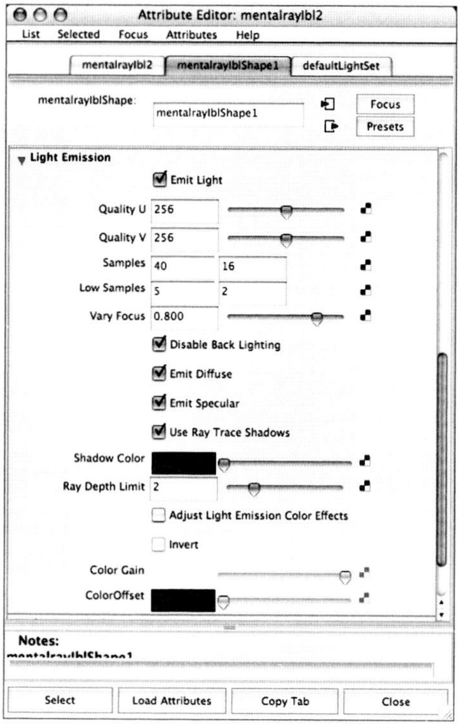

Figure 14.36

You use the Light Emission options to simulate Directional lights influenced by color and intensity captured from the image used with an IBL node.

Quality U and V determine the resolution for the image that is mapped to the sphere. The actual image is reduced in resolution to match the U and V values. IBL uses every pixel in the down-sampled image as a Directional light. Thus, increasing the Quality U and V settings increase the number of lights available to light the scene; decreasing these values speeds up render times.

The Samples setting determines which of those available Directional lights should actually be used. This is another filtering process for optimizing the render times, as it takes a long time to render 256 × 256 Directional lights. Sampling takes two numeric values that correspond to primary and secondary lights, also referred to as key and fill lights. The primary number (first numeric field) tells mental ray how many of those pixels that have a higher range should be used; the secondary numeric field uses values that are more average (midrange) in the image. With HDR this is particularly important, since an image can have an extremely high range of light values; thus, sampling more key lights or more average lights can greatly affect your render.

When Light Emission is used, the intensity of the HDR image is controlled by the Color Gain value in the Light Emission section. To control this value, enable Adjust Light Emission Color Effects.

The Low Samples setting refers to how many light samples should be used when Final Gathering is enabled. This value should be much lower than the Samples value since Final Gathering adds a lot of lighting into the scene.

The rest of the attributes are fairly straightforward and are used in the same way on other nodes, particularly lights. They include Emit Diffuse and Specular as well as Use Ray Trace Shadows and Shadow Color, all of which should be familiar to you.

You can adjust the quality of the image by setting higher values for the Quality U and V and Samples and within the Anti-Aliasing Quality section. However, use low values while testing scenes.

Scattering

New to mental ray on Maya 8 is a scattering property that simulates, in straightforward fashion, subsurface scattering. Subsurface scattering is the effect wherein light penetrates a surface (rather than bouncing straight off of it) and then is scattered below that surface, dissipating from a point to a larger, fuzzier area and picking up color from what is below the surface before returning to the surface and exiting, when the light rays are seen by our eyes. Though this effect might sound obscure, we see it every day: everything from blood, car paint, and milk to marble and porcelain produces subsurface scattering, and of course our very own skin does so as well, its color being partially determined by the blood vessels and fatty tissue that lies just beneath it (obviously this effect is more visible on those with fairer skin).

Subsurface scattering has several subtle visual cues. First, light picks up complex color attributes because of the path a given ray travels beneath the surface of an object. Second, light looks softer bounced off of a subsurface scattering object because the light is diffused from its original point. Third, light can "bloom" around the edges of objects because it can travel for a distance under the surface before bouncing out to be seen. For this last effect, consider a marble bust or a person's face when it blocks a light source. While you cannot see the light source itself, you can see light spilling around the edges of the bust or face, producing an often striking rim light effect; if you're still having trouble imagining this effect, just get a friend to stand in front of a light bulb in an otherwise dark room and you'll see the effect right away.

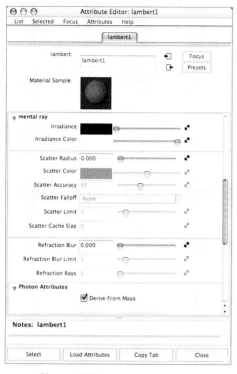

Figure 14.37

The mental ray Scattering controls for a shader

Without an effect like subsurface scattering, objects tend to look very hard and "plasticky," so for realistic images, subsurface scattering is a sought-after effect. Unfortunately, subsurface scattering is a very computationally expensive and complex effect to achieve, which is where mental ray's new Scattering setting comes into play: with a few simple adjustments, you can create an effective approximation of subsurface scattering in just a few minutes, whereas before the effect would have taken a great deal of effort. The Scattering attribute is available for the anisotropic, Blinn, Lambert, OceanShader, and Phong (including Phong E) shaders.

To see scattering in action, let's turn our favorite model, Machismo, into a marble statue. Open the `Mac_for_scattering.ma` file on the CD. You will see Machismo there, smoothed one time (so that his face in particular is more rounded), and a basic three light setup with key, fill, and back spotlights lighting him. A camera (camera1) has been added to the scene and keyframed into a couple of positions that will show off different features of subsurface scattering. Machismo's shader, a default Lambert (lambert1), has had a slightly tweaked 3D marble shader added to it to give the feeling that he's carved out of a block of marble. Render the scene and note that the "bust" looks reasonably like marble but it is lacking in subtle light interaction. This is where subsurface scattering comes in to play. Keep a copy of this render for comparison with your later renders.

> Though marble normally includes specular components and thus would be better suited to a Blinn type shader, we wanted to keep specular highlights out of the scene so you can see the scattering effects better.

To create a scattering effect, open the Attribute Editor for the lambert1 shader, and in the mental ray section (shown in Figure 14.37), change Scatter Radius from 0 to some larger number; for now, change the number to 1. Comparing this render to the default one, you will immediately see that the general lighting is much brighter than before, thanks to light scattering across and under the surface of the model. In addition, the shadow areas (under the armpits and the left side of his cheek, for example) are much less dark, also because of the scattering. Figure 14.38 shows the difference between these renders. Raise the radius to 10 and rerender; here the difference is very subtle but shows even more light scatter in the shadow areas, reducing the overall contrast of the render. Change the radius back to 1 before proceeding.

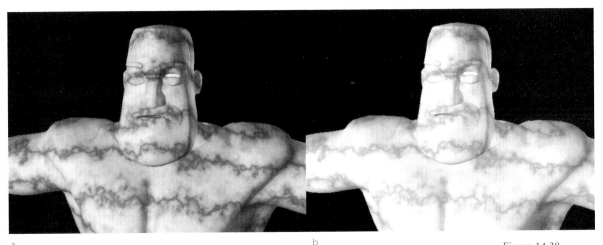

a   b

Figure 14.38

Rendering without subsurface scattering (a) and with scattering, radius 1 (b)

The effect is fairly subtle with a full-coverage lighting scheme. To see it better, let's turn off the key and fill lights (spotlight1 and 2) by turning their intensities down to 0. Try rerendering with a scatter radius of 0 and 1 and you will see a now more obvious difference between a render with and without subsurface scattering (see Figure 14.39). In particular, note how light bleeds around to the front of the figure here, lighting the right side of Machismo's face, chest, and arms, which do not receive any direct light. With a large radius value, like 10, scattering actually washes out detail on the model; the effect of raising the radius value is to make the model appear smaller and smaller so that the material is less thick and more light bleeds through and around it. If you move to frame 2, where the model directly blocks the light as seen from the camera, you can see the effect of changing the radius value even more.

Figure 14.39

Using only a backlight and rendering without subsurface scattering (a) and with scattering, radius 1 (b).

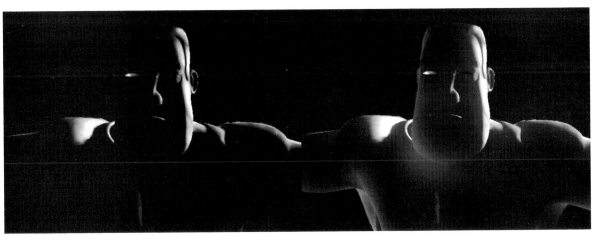

a   b

The other attributes in the mental ray Scattering controls adjust how the scattering effect works. Scatter Color adjusts what color light that scatters within the model should pick up. By making this color very different from the model color, you can make the model look like it has a complex color structure beneath its surface (this effect is more subtle but more interesting with front and back lighting on it). Scatter Accuracy adjusts how many points are taken into account for scattering; the higher the number, the greater the realism of the scatter effect, but more memory and time is required to render it. Scatter Falloff is just like light falloff, determining how quickly light dissipates as it scatters within the model. For a more realistic effect, try Linear or Quadratic for the falloff calculation. Scatter Limit limits the total number of times a ray can bend and bounce to determine pixel color. A value of 5 or 10 for this is adequate for most purposes; turning Scatter Limit down to 0 turns off the scatter effect. Scatter Cache Size determines how many scatter points are stored in a scatter cache. The more points used, the better the render efficiency but the more memory is used. Unless you have a low memory situation, leave this setting at 0, which tells mental ray to cache all scatter points.

Via some relatively simple controls you can create a very convincing (and complex) effect, one that was outside the pale of normal rendering artists just a few years ago.

Surface Approximation and Displacement Maps

The Approximation Editor (see Figure 14.40) provides a way for overriding Maya's tessellation with mental ray tessellation, which is achieved by attaching mental ray–specific tessellation instructions to objects. mental ray provides better tessellation methods and more control over fine detail, such as around trimmed surfaces without uniformly increasing the tessellation for the entire surface.

Applying an approximation description is fairly straightforward. Create a NURBS sphere, and then open the Approximation Editor by choosing **Window → Rendering Editors → mental ray → Approximation Editor**. The Approximation Editor displays the current selection's approximation methods. Notice that they all read DeriveFromMaya, which

Figure 14.40

The Approximation Editor is mental ray's port for applying mental ray–specific tessellation instructions to objects.

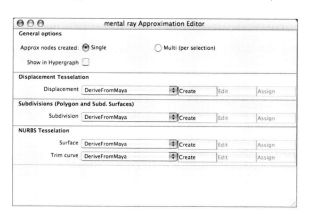

means that currently no custom approximations are attached to the sphere. Thus, mental ray will take the tessellation settings from Maya.

If you select a multipatch model and then enable Single, one approximation is created for all the surfaces/patches. If you enable Multi, a new approximation is created for each surface. Selecting the Show In Hypergraph option opens the Hypergraph window and displays the new approximation connections.

Open the Attribute Editor, verify that the sphere is selected, and then click the Create button for Surface in the NURBS Tessellation section of the window (Mac) or click the Create button for Surface Approx. (NURBS) (Windows/Linux). Notice that a new window pops up in the Attribute Editor, displaying the mental ray surface approximation options. In the Approximation Editor next to Surface Approx NURBS), you'll see mentalraySurfaceApprox1, which is the new approximation you just attached.

Once an approximation is created, it is kept in the scene. Thus, the active approximation can be replaced by another approximation from the list under any of the approximation tabs in the Approximation Editor. Click Create again for the SurfaceApprox (NURBS). For the Create button to become available again, you need to first switch to DeriveFromMaya. A new approximation is created and attached to the surface. You can now select the previous mentalraySurfaceApprox1 from the list and click Assign to swap the new approximation with the old one.

Presets and the Approximation Method and Styles

The Approximation window in the Attribute Editor provides several tessellation options. The following is a brief summary of this extensive and technical topic. Detailed explanations for all the tessellation methods can be found in the mental ray documentation.

The Surface Approximation Preset

The Presets list provides a selection of settings that drive the Approx Method and Approx Style attributes (note that the Approx Style attribute is only available for certain Presets or Methods). The low to high quality for each preset drives the settings below the Approx Style. For example, the Regular Grid Low Quality preset provides fewer Subdivision U and V values than the High Quality option, and both are based on the same method and style.

The Surface Approximation Method

The Approx Method options provide control over setting the "rules" for how to approach the surface tessellation. For example, should it be adaptive tessellation based on the size in pixels, meaning surfaces closer to the camera receive more tessellation as with the Length/Distance/Angle method? Or should it be based on the surface patches as with Parametric and Regular Parametric? Both methods control NURBS surface tessellation. Parametric is also used for polygon surfaces and acts as a subdivision control during the render.

The Surface Approximation Style

The Approx Style option dictates how the surface is tessellated based on the method you choose. Thus, the method you choose dictates where adaptive subdivision should take place, for what part of the surface, and how it will be achieved.

Approx Style provides different algorithms for controlling how the surface is subdivided into triangles; the difference is in the way mental ray handles adaptive subdivision. The four options are Grid, Tree, Delaunay (only for NURBS), and Fine. Fine is known to be an expensive, high-quality subdivision style that creates uniformly sized triangles and is dense. Tree is known for localizing subdivision in a treelike progressive manner, thus reducing the overall tessellation for the surfaces. Grid will use a uniform grid across the surface, providing for a denser grid in more detailed areas; this results in excessive tessellation that might not be required. Delaunay will try to optimize the tessellation by triangulating toward areas with more angles; this method can cause very unpredictable results.

Now let's experiment with approximation control.

1. Open the approx_01.ma scene from the CD and select the NURBS sphere with the trimmed hole (nurbsSphere1). In the Approximation Editor, Edit becomes active when you choose mentalraySurfaceApprox1 for the Surface Approx (NURBS). Select Edit to view the approximation settings, and then render at frame 1.

2. Notice the jagged edges on the outer rim. To improve this you can simply increase the U and V subdivisions from 1 to 2 in the Attribute Editor (mentalraySurfaceApprox1). Notice that the method is set to Parametric, and then render.

3. There is an enormous increase in quality because every increase of the subdivision value using the Parametric method exponentially subdivides each patch (surface between isoparms), thus greatly increasing the triangle count for every patch on the surface. This is not exactly an exponential increase. The arithmetic that is being used is more complex.

4. Change the Approx Method to Regular Parametric, which subdivides surfaces as a whole, and render. Notice that it looks horrible since it is applying only two subdivision levels for the entire surface. However, the trimmed area looks fine because it uses a separate surface approximation. Increase U and V Subdivision to 40 and 40, and then render. Notice that the subdivision level acts differently when used with Parametric or Regular Parametric.

5. Create a new Trim Curve (Mac) or Trim Curve Approx. (Windows/Linux) under NURBS Tessellation in the Approximation Editor for the sphere and render frame 2. Save a snapshot in the render view, and then in the Attribute Editor increase N Subdivisions to 4 and render again. You will notice the increase in the trim surfaces quality. The Trim approximation affects only areas that are cut out and has no effect on border curves.

6. Select the polygon sphere and move to frame 3. In the Approximation Editor, create a Subdivision (Mac) or Subdivision Approx.
(Windows/Linux) under the Polygon and Subd Surfaces section,
make sure it is assigned to the object, and then render a frame.
Select Edit for this poly approximation, and in the Attribute Editor, fix the hole by specifying the type of conversion that should be
used—select Quads To Triangles from the Conversion attribute at
the bottom—and render. Increasing subdivisions will, as expected,
increase the quality and reduce the render time. Render with a
subdivision of 6 and notice the increase in quality. Under Parametric, the subdivision increases uniformly across the surface.

Figure 14.41

The Displacement Approximation section

7. Change Approx Method to Length/Distance/Angle, which allows
control over how the object subdivides based on the camera and
pixel space. Render a frame and note the low quality. The Min and
Max Subdivision attributes control how many times a triangle can
subdivide, and the Length, Distance, and Angle attributes control
the rules that determine when more subdivision is needed; thus,
this is an adaptive subdivision process. Length specifies the maximum length for each edge, Angle specifies the maximum angle allowed between two
neighboring faces based on the normals, and Distance tries to subdivide until the
faces are no more then *n* units away from the surface. The values for these three
attributes are set in scene units or, by enabling View Dependent, set in pixel size units.
Any Satisfied specifies that once the criterion for one of the three controls is met, the
subdivision process will stop. Change Length to 1, enable View Dependent, and then
render. Each edge length will not exceed a value of 1 pixel.

Displacement Mapping with mental ray

mental ray provides the ability to render extremely detailed displacement maps without
artifacts. This is known as fine displacement and uses the Fine Approximation style for
tessellating, providing extremely high-quality adaptive tessellating. mental ray displacement works with both direct and indirect illumination.

Let's experiment with fine displacement.

1. Open the `dissp_01.ma` scene from the CD, and select the Poly plane. Notice a shader
connected to the displacement of the poly plane. Render and you see that the result
isn't particularly impressive using Maya feature displacement. Select the plane, and in
the Approximation Editor create a Displace from the Displacement Tessellation section (Mac) or Displace from the Displace Approx. section (Windows/Linux). In the
Attribute Editor (see Figure 14.41), select the Fine View Low Quality preset, and
notice that Approx Style changed to Fine. Render an image and compare with the
previous render.

2. Select the Grid texture (used for the displacement), and under the Color Balance section in the Attribute Editor, increase the Alpha Gain value from 1 to 3 and render, which increases the displacement value. Create a Maya Fractal 2D texture, apply it to the Grid Color Gain value, and then render. There is no effect because the Alpha Gain instead of the color value controls displacement. The alpha for the Grid texture is taken from the Filler and Line Color values. Connect the Fractal1 texture to the Filler Color and render. You can control the height from the Grid Alpha Gain as well as from the Fractal1 Color Balance attributes; experiment to see their effect.

We recommend you render this scene with Final Gathering and an IBL node to see their effects with displacements. Figure 14.42 shows displacement with HDRI and Final Gathering.

> When using an advanced procedural texture network, consider piping the color values through a luminance node into the displacement. This enables you to control the displacement amount through the color values rather than through the alpha gain.

Figure 14.42

Displacement rendering with mental ray provides detailed tessellation and amazing results.

Summary

In this chapter we examined the fundamentals needed to control mental ray renders in detail. Particularly with mental ray, the settings can make or break a render because some renders can get processor intensive. Knowing how to optimize is critical for success.

We looked at mental ray settings; custom shaders; lights, shadows, and fog; motion blur; indirect illumination; IBL and HDRI lighting; the new Scattering effect; and surface approximation and displacement maps. The most important feature we discussed is the increasingly common use of HDRI with final gathering in today's industry for simulating real-life lighting. We recommend that you further research HDR imaging and spherical harmonics, particularly if you're interested in advanced imaging and photography.

If you are solely interested in being a modeler or an animator, a basic occlusion render can demonstrate your model or animation with a nice aesthetic render, which might help you avoid some extra work with texturing and rendering.

CHAPTER 15

Toon Shading

Maya's Toon Shading provides a set of tools that let you create the look of hand-drawn, cartoon-style animation from the 3D objects in your scene. Toon Shading in Maya is actually quite simple to use but powerful, producing high-quality cartoon-style renders. Using the Toon Shading tools, you can create cartoon characters that exist in 3D space or add stylistic touches to your photo-realistic scenes.

We will use a hands-on approach to explore the Toon Shading tools by taking a simple 3D scene and applying the Toon Shading lines and fills to create a cartoon look. We'll also take a look at how to use the tools in a science-fiction environment. It is recommended that you review the chapters on shading and rendering (Chapters 12 and 13) before going through the exercises in this chapter. This chapter will cover the following topics.

- **Understanding Toon Shading**
- **Applying fills**
- **Generating toon lines**
- **Toon line techniques**
- **Using Paint Effects strokes with toon outlines**
- **Toon line modifiers**

Understanding Toon Shading

The Toon menu under the Rendering menu set (shown in Figure 15.1 and also available as a shelf) lets you access the tools you need to create the toon effect. Toon Shading is similar to vector rendering or the output of a vector program like Adobe Illustrator in that the rendered image resembles lines that define shapes filled in with colors, as in traditional cartoons ranging from *Snow White* to *Scooby Doo*. However, the Toon Shading tools and techniques are different from vector rendering and produce different, more specialized results, and thus the two should not be confused. The Toon Shading toolset uses a combination of ramp shaders to fill the shapes and Paint Effects strokes, or offset meshes, to create the drawn outlines. You can render toon-shaded objects using Maya Software, mental ray, and Maya Hardware; however, mental ray and Maya Hardware require a few additional steps in order to get the objects to render correctly. Toon Shading works with NURBS, polygons, and subdivision surfaces, and you can apply Paint Effects brush strokes to the outlines to create a variety of styles.

Applying Fills

Let's walk through the process of applying toon shaders to a scene and do a little exploring along the way. Open the toon1.mb scene from the CD and switch to the Rendering menu set.

The scene shows three goofy-looking mushrooms on a hill, as shown in Figure 15.2. There is a directional light in the scene, and no shaders have been applied to the surfaces. The geometry is composed of NURBS, but as mentioned, you also can use polygons or subdivision surfaces with Toon Shading.

1. In the perspective view, switch to the shotCam.

Figure 15.1

The Toon menu

Figure 15.2

Three gray mushrooms

2. From the Toon menu in the Rendering menu set, choose **Set Camera Background Color → shotCam** to open the Color Chooser. Select a nice sky blue. This menu option is essentially a shortcut that lets you to change the background color in the camera's Environment tab without having to open the camera's Attribute Editor.

3. Select the hill shape, and choose **Toon → Assign Fill Shader → Solid Color** to apply a surface shader to the hill shape, then open the Attribute Editor to the surface shader. Change the color of the surface shader to a nice grassy green.

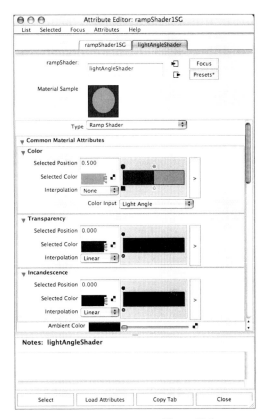

The Assign Fill Shader options are essentially shortcuts to several presets you can use for your toon-shaded objects. These presets are surface shaders and ramp shaders identical to surface and ramp shaders you create in the Hypershade. The only difference between using these toon presets and creating and assigning a ramp shader from the Hypershade is that the presets have already been set up with some toonlike attributes—in the case of the solid color, the preset creates a surface shader and assigns your chosen color to it. You don't have to use these specific shaders, but they are a nice place from which to start.

Figure 15.3

The Attribute Editor for the Light Angle Two Tone fill. It's actually a ramp shader preset to look like a toon fill.

4. Select the mushroom1 shape, and choose **Toon → Assign Fill Shader → Light Angle Two Tone** to assign a ramp shader to the mushroom. The colors on the ramp are indexed based on the light angle. The diffuse and specular values have been set to 0, and the translucency has been set to 1. Change the colors from gray and white to dark purple and light purple (see Figure 15.3).

5. Select the mushroom2 shape and choose **Toon → Assign Fill Shader → Shaded Brightness Two Tone**. The colors on this ramp are indexed based on the diffuse shaded brightness. The diffuse value has been set to 1, and the specularity is at 0. Change the gray and white colors to dark orange and yellow.

6. Select the mushroom3 shape, and choose **Toon → Assign Fill Shader → Shaded Brightness Three Tone**. This is the same as the previous example with the exception that the ramp has three colors instead of two. Set the three colors on the ramp so that they go from dark green to light green.

7. Render the scene from the shotCam and compare the differences in how each mushroom looks (see Figure 15.4).

By now you should have a good idea of how the fill presets in the Toon menu work. Try applying the other presets to the mushrooms. Change the colors and the interpolation on the ramps to achieve different looks. Here's a brief description of the other presets, all of them shown in Figure 15.5:

Dark Profile A ramp shader with the ramp colors indexed based on the surface brightness. The diffuse value is at 0.5, and the translucency has been set to 0.25. The incandescence ramp has a dark gray set for the first color on the ramp, causing a dark area to appear around the edges.

Rim Light A ramp shader much like the Dark profile preset except that the indexed colors are dark and medium gray and the incandescence ramp has white as the first color with a linear interpolation to black. This creates the effect of a white highlight on the edges of the surface.

Circle Highlight A ramp shader similar to the previous two shaders with the exception that it has a specular value of 1 and a ramp mapped to the specular color. The specular ramp goes from black to white with no interpolation, causing a white highlight to appear as the specular reflection. This shader is great for shiny surfaces such as plastic or metal, and works well for classic Anime-styled robots.

8. If you're happy with how your mushrooms look, apply fill shaders to the eyeballs and eyelids of each character and the teeth on mushroom3. Or you can open `toon2.mb` from the CD. Render a frame and take a look. So far, fills are quite easy. The fun begins when we start applying the outlines to the geometry.

9. Select mushroom1, and choose **Toon → Assign Outline → Add New Toon Outline**.

10. A thick black line appears around the outline and across some of the edges of the mushroom. In the Outliner, you'll see a new node labeled pfXToon1. Select this node and open the Attribute Editor.

11. Set the Line Width attribute to 0.033.

12. In the camera view, tumble around the mushroom and observe how the outline updates according to the camera angle.

13. Render a still to see how the outline will look (see Figure 15.6)

Figure 15.5

The three remaining toon shader fill presets. From left to right they are Dark Profile, Rim Light, and Circle Highlight.

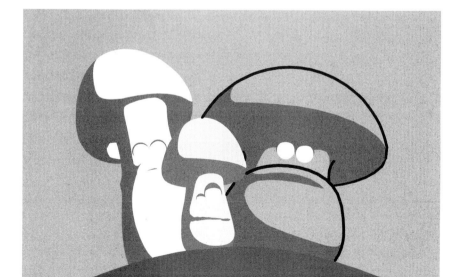

Figure 15.6

Mushroom1 with a toon outline applied

The outline is a special type of Paint Effects stroke that updates according to the angle of the camera. The pfxToon node has a transform and a shape node just like most other objects in Maya. You can actually select the transform node and move it away from the mushroom shape; it will still update according to the view.

Generating Toon Lines

You can create four types of toon lines for your objects: profile, border, intersection, and crease lines. Profile lines are the objects that define the outside shape of the object. They are drawn along the silhouette of an object at the point where the outermost edge turns away from the camera. If you draw a smiley face on a piece of paper, the profile line is the circle that defines the edge of the face. If you use Paint Effects strokes for your lines, Maya continually regenerates them, depending on the view of the camera. If the scene becomes heavy with toon lines, performance can slow, which might cause you to consider using the Offset Mesh option instead.

You can generate profile lines in two ways. They can be composed of Paint Effects strokes or an Offset mesh. In the Attribute Editor for the pfxToon1 node is a Profile Lines menu that you can use to choose how you want to build your profile lines. Profile lines are Paint Effects strokes by default. If you switch to the Offset Mesh option, a new node will be created that you can see in the Outliner. The new node is a group called pfxToon1ProfileMeshes, and in the group is a geometry node called polySurface1. This is a polygon object, offset slightly from the original object with its normals reversed. If you look in the Render Stats of the polySurface1's Attribute Editor, you'll notice that shadow casting and receiving is off and that Double Sided is switched off. The object takes on the color that you have set for the toon line. This is a totally different way to create the effect of toon outlines than using the Paint Effects option. Some advantages of using an offset mesh are that they update faster than Paint Effects strokes in the viewports, they render in mental ray and Maya Hardware, they are stable when animated, and they show up in reflections and refractions (see Figure 15.7).

Using Paint Effects strokes for your profile lines also has its advantages and disadvantages, which we will explore in depth in the next section.

Border lines are drawn around the open edge of geometry or at the border between two shaders. In the Attribute Editor for the pfxToonShape node is a menu for choosing whether you want border lines at the open edges of your objects, at the boundary of a shader on your object, or both. We'll use border lines to add detail to some of the facial features of our mushroom characters.

1. Select the two eyelid objects in the mushroom1 group, and choose **Toon → Assign Outline → Add New Toon Outline**. Note that you can apply one toon line to multiple objects.

2. Set the width of the line to 0.033.

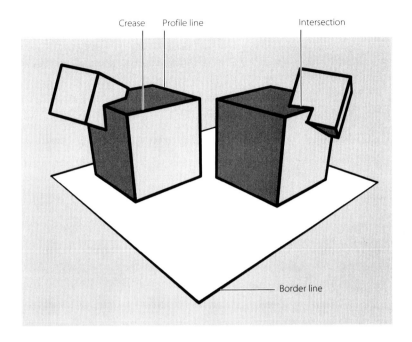

Crease Profile line Intersection

Border line

Figure 15.7

A render showing the different types of toon lines. The cubes on the left use Paint Effects strokes for the lines, and the cubes on the right use an offset mesh.

The eyelid shapes are hemispherical cups above the eyeballs. Since they have an open end, a border line is created on the edge of the lids.

Crease lines occur at hard edges on polygon objects. If you create a polygon cube and create a toon line for it, crease lines are drawn on the edges of the cube as well as the profile if the Crease option is on. Crease lines are not view dependent. In the Attribute Editor for the pfxToon node is an option for Crease Angle Min and Max, which controls which edges will have crease lines by the settings in the fields. You can use crease lines to draw lines around each polygon in your object if you want to achieve a wireframe look. To do this, apply a toon line to a polygon object, set Crease Angle Min to 0, and turn off Hard Creases Only (See Figure 15.8). New to Maya 8 is the ability to turn off backfacing creases so that Maya doesn't generate crease lines for portions of the object facing away from the camera, which creates fewer lines, making the scene lighter to interact with. To access this control, select the pfxToon1 node, open the Attribute Editor, and in the Crease Lines section, uncheck the Backfacing Creases box.

Intersection lines appear where two objects that have the same toon line node applied intersect. If you look at the purple mushroom with the toon line, you'll

Figure 15.8

Turn Hard Creases Only off and bring the Crease Angle Min down to achieve a wireframe look on a polygon object with toon lines applied.

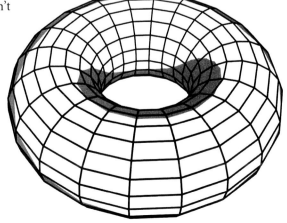

see that there is no line on the bottom edge of the mushroom. This is because the mushroom and the ground geometry intersect. To place a line there, we need a single toon line applied to both the ground and the mushroom geometry. A single object can have multiple toon lines applied. These lines can overlap as well. Let's try this:

3. Select the mushroom1 geometry and Shift+select the hill geometry.

4. Choose **Toon → Assign Outline → Add New Toon Outline**.

5. Open the Attribute Editor for the new toon line (pfxToon2).

6. Set Profile Lines to Off.

7. Set Border Lines to Off.

8. Uncheck Crease Lines.

9. Check the Intersection Lines box to turn intersection lines on.

Now you have a line where the mushroom and the ground intersect. This line will update if you move the mushroom around or off the ground. It is a Paint Effects stroke and cannot be made an offset mesh.

Maya 8 now supports local occlusion, which allows for more accurate representation of toon outlines when objects have multiple faces that are close together. Without local occlusion, toon lines can run into other objects, hurting definition of the objects and muddying the sense of shape and intersection for them. Once a toon line has been created, you can access the Local Occlusion drop-down menu in the Common Toon Attributes section of the Attribute Editor for the pfxToonShape2 node. The choices are Off (default), Line Surface, and All Toon Surfaces. Line Surface generates local occlusion only by other surfaces generating lines, while All Toon Surfaces generates occlusion for any surface assigned to the same pfx node. Unless you have a specific reason to use Line Surface, the All Toon Surfaces option is preferable. Figure 15.9 shows how local occlusion works for a scene with overlapping geometric primitives.

Toon Line Techniques

A single object can have multiple toon lines applied, or a single toon line can be applied to multiple objects. It depends on what you want to do with your scene. If you want a consistent look for all the objects in your scene, it might be easiest to use one type of line for everything—that way the options can be accessed through a single node. If you look at the Attribute Editor for a pfxToon node, you'll notice that below the Common Toon Attributes are controls for each of the four types of lines, thus allowing you to control the way each type of toon line looks without having to apply a different toon line to the same object. In other words, if you apply a toon line to an object and you want the border lines to be a different thickness than the profile lines, you can use the controls in the Border Lines section of the toon line's Attribute Editor.

In some situations you might want the flexibility of having multiple toon line nodes in a scene or even on the same object. We'll look at some examples that should give you ideas about the philosophy behind the techniques. We'll also look at some options for varying the way the lines are drawn and how you can use Paint Effects brushes to modify your toon style.

1. Open the `toon3.mb` scene from the CD.

2. In this version of the mushroom scene, a single toon line has been applied to all the mushrooms, the mushroom eyes, the eyelids, and the ground. The only things that do not have a toon line applied are the NURBS curves that make up the pupils on the eyes. This is because toon lines can only be applied to meshes; they can't be applied to curves. However, Paint Effects strokes can be applied to curves. Let's fix this so that our mushrooms have proper eyes.

3. Choose **Window → General Editors → Visor**. On the left side of the Visor window, be sure the Paint Effects tab is selected, then scroll down and select the toon folder. Here you will find a number of Paint Effects strokes that resemble our toon lines, plus some fun variations.

4. Select the Smooth brush from the folder.

5. Choose **Edit → Select All By Type → NURBS Curves** to select the pupil curves.

6. With all the pupil curves selected, choose **Paint Effects → Curve Utilities → Attach Brush To Curves**. The pupils will become giant black balls.

7. In the Outliner, select the newly created strokes and choose **Paint Effects → Share One Brush**. This way you can change all the strokes applied to the pupils by changing the settings on just one of the brushes.

8. Open the Attribute Editor for one of the strokes and set the Global Scale value for the brush stroke to 0.165.

9. Render a frame.

Now let's do something interesting. Select the pfxToon1 node in the Outliner and open its Attribute Editor.

1. Try changing the width and color of the profile lines, border lines, and intersection lines to become familiar with how you can control these independently. The Maya documentation has good descriptions of each of the attributes in the Profile Lines, Crease Lines, Border Lines, and Intersection Lines rollouts. The following steps demonstrate how you can use some of these settings to alter the look of your toon-shaded objects.

Figure 15.9

Overlapping geometric primitives rendered with local occlusion off (top), using Line Surface occlusion (middle), and using All Toon Surfaces occlusion (bottom)

2. Make sure Smooth Profile is checked in the Profile Lines tab and increase Profile Width Modulation. This will vary the width of the profile lines depending on their curvature, causing the render to look more like a loose sketch and less like CG.

3. Scroll down to Curvature Based Width Scaling and try different settings in the graph for the curvature width. This will also vary the width of the lines based on curvature.

4. Under Common Toon Line Attributes, set Lighting Based Width to 1.0. This makes the lines thin where the surface is light and thicker where it is dark. It does not show up in the camera view but will display when you render (see Figure 15.10).

5. Return Lighting Based Width to 0, and bring Profile Width Modulation to 0. Next to the field for Line Width Map in the Common Toon Attributes section, click the Texture button and choose Noise Texture from the pop-up window. Render the scene and note how the line looks like a scribbled marker. Adjust the settings in the Alpha Gain section in the Color Balance tab of this texture to increase or decrease the thickness of the lines. Animating the texture will cause the line to have a nervous wiggly quality (see Figure 15.11).

6. Remove the noise texture by right-clicking in the field next to Line Width Map on the pfxToon node and choosing Break Connection.

As you can see, you quickly can create a unique look for your toon lines by adjusting the settings in the pfxToon node.

Figure 15.10

Applying Lighting Based Width to the toon outline causes the lines to be thicker where the surface is dark. Combine this with Profile Width Modulation, and the result is a looser, less "CG" line.

Figure 15.11

Mapping a noise texture to the Line Width Map setting is another way to create a nervous, wiggly line.

Using Paint Effects Strokes with Toon Outlines

Now let's see how you can use Paint Effects brushes to enhance your toon look. Any Paint Effects stroke can be applied to toon lines. You can also layer multiple Paint Effects strokes over your toon lines to create a variety of outline styles.

> If working with Paint Effects is confusing, feel free to jump ahead to Chapter 17, which covers Paint Effects in detail.

1. With your previous file open (or after opening the `toon3.mb` file off the CD), choose **Window → General Editors → Visor** to open the Visor window.
2. Open up the toon folder.
3. Select the brokenWiggle.mel line style.
4. Choose **Toon → Assign Paint Effects Brush To Toon Lines**.
5. Render the scene. You'll see that the toon lines now look thin and scribbly (see Figure 15.12). Try a few more of the line types in the toon folder.

Figure 15.12

Figure 15.12

Paint Effects strokes can be used to alter the toon outlines. In this case, the Broken Wiggle line has been applied.

6. Assign the doodle line to the toon lines. To edit the settings for the doodle line, you have to open the Attribute Editor and use the input/output arrows to move to the doodleLine1 node. You'll have to scroll past a number of nurbsTessellate nodes to get to the doodleLine1 attributes.

7 The doodleLine1 node is a Paint Effects brush with the same type of settings as all the Paint Effects brushes. You can also layer toon lines to create some really interesting looks.

8. Select the geometry for the three mushrooms and the hill, then choose **Toon → Assign Outline → Add New Toon Outline**. A new pfxToon2 node appears in the Outliner. A thick line is drawn around the mushrooms and the ground.

9. Select the pfxToon2 node in the Outliner.

10. In the Visor window, open the toon folder and select brokenGlopLine.

11. Choose **Toon → Assign Paint Effects Brush To Toon Lines**.

12. Open the Attribute Editor for pfxToon2, and scroll through the outputs until you find the Attribute Editor for brokenGlopLine1.

Figure 15.13

A smear brush has been layered on top of the doodle line stroke applied to the mushroom and ground geometry. This smears the colors around, creating a messy smudged effect.

13. From the **Brush Type** menu, choose **Smear**.

14. Render a still. Notice how the doodle line and the edges of the fill are still visible but have been smeared around by the broken glop line that is layered on top of doodle-Line1. The second toon line was applied only to the mushroom and ground geometry, so you'll notice that the eyes have not been affected (see Figure 15.13).

TOON SHADING EXAMPLES

Maya 7 comes with a number of example files you can use for study. To access them, choose **Toon → Get Toon Example**. The Visor window will open with a number of sophisticated toon-shaded objects that you can drag into your scene. Each example has a description of the effect included in the scene file. To further explore how you can use Toon Shading in your scene, take some time and explore these examples.

Toon Line Modifiers

The tools that you use to create the toon-shaded look are flexible enough that they can be used however you'd like in order to bring your own original ideas to life. They are actually not limited to cartoon settings; with the added flexibility of replacing toon outlines with Paint Effects strokes, you can use the toon outline tools to enhance stylistic or even photo-realistic scenes. In this example, we'll use the toon line tools in conjunction with Paint Effects and the toon line modifiers to enhance the look of a stylized science fiction setting.

1. Open the `station1.mb` scene from the CD and render a still from the perspective camera (see Figure 15.14).

    The scene is composed of a single polygon object with a Blinn shader applied. There are a couple of area lights and some spheres with a glowing surface shader applied to simulate lights. The beam object is a lofted NURBS surface with a transparent Lambert applied. This object has keyframes on its Y rotation and is grouped and positioned so that it looks as though the station is emitting some kind of beam.

2. Select the station object, and choose **Toon → Assign Outline → Add New Toon Outline**.

3. Select the pfxToon1 node from the Outliner.

4. Open the Visor window, and from the glows folder, select the neonYellow brush.

5. Choose **Toon → Assign Paint Effects Brush To Toon Lines**.

6. Open the Attribute Editor for the pfxToon1node, and move to the neonYellow1 brush. Set the Global Scale to 0.5.

Figure 15.14

The space station in its default state

7. Render a still.

8. In the Attribute Editor for the pfxToon1 node, scroll down to the Line Resampling options and turn on Resample Profile, Resample Crease, and Resample Border. You can also turn on Local Occlusion in the Common Toon Attributes tab. These adjustments should fix most of the errors in the details of the lines.

9. In the Attribute Editor for the neonYellow1 brush, scroll down to the Shading section and move the Incandescence1 slider down until it is at about the same place as the Color1 slider.

10. Render another still (see Figure 15.15).

11. This scene will be getting a little heavy with toon lines. To speed up performance, go to the Attribute Editor for the pfxToon1 node and turn off Display In Viewport. The toon lines will still appear when you render the scene but will no longer appear in your interactive view, which will speed up your interaction with the scene.

12. Select the beam object in the beamGroup.

13. Choose **Toon → Assign Outline → Add New Toon Outline**.

14. Select the pfxToon2 node from the Outliner.

15. Open the Visor window, and from the glows folder select the goldSparks brush.

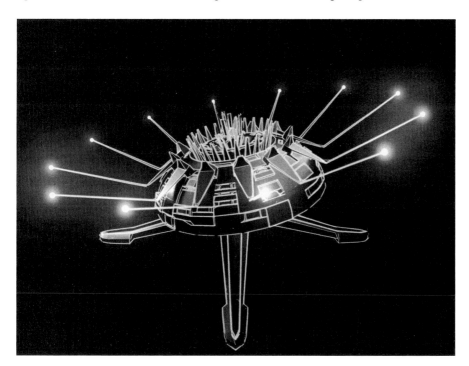

Figure 15.15

The station model with neon toon lines

16. Choose **Toon → Assign Paint Effects Brush To Toon Lines**.

17. Open the Attribute Editor for the pfxToon2 node and move to the goldSparks1 tab.

18. Set Global Scale for the goldSpaks brush to 2.0.

19. Render a still.

20. Select the pfxToon2 node from the Outliner.

21. Choose **Toon → Create Modifier**.

A wireframe sphere will appear. This is similar to the Soft Modification tool; however, instead of deforming geometry, it alters attributes on the toon lines as well as on the Paint Effects strokes applied to toon lines. You can use this to create some interesting effects. We're going to animate it so that the station emits a crackling ball of energy that travels up the light beam every 20 frames or so.

1. In the Outliner, select the lineModifier1 node.

2. Expand the beamGroup and Ctrl+select curve1 so that both lineModifier1 and curve1 are selected.

3. Switch to the Animation menu set and choose **Animate → Motion Paths → Attach To Motion Path ❏**.

4. In the Motion Path option box, choose Start/End. Set Start Time to 1 and End Time to 20.

5. Make sure that Follow is selected, set Front Axis to X, and set Up Axis to Y.

6. Click Apply.

7. Select the lineModifier1 node from the Outliner and open the Graph Editor.

8. Select lineModifier1, and press the F key so that the animation curve for the motion path is visible.

9. In the View menu, enable Infinity at the bottom of the menu so that you can see how the curve behaves after frame 20.

10. In the Curves menu, with the lineModifier1 curve selected, choose **Post Infinity → Cycle**. The curve for the motion path should now repeat every 20 frames.

11. Close the Graph Editor and play the animation in the perspective window. You should see the lineModifier1 tool move up the beam every 20 frames.

12. Move to a frame where you can see the lineModifier1 tool above the station. Frame 4 or 5 should be fine.

13. Select the lineModifier1 tool and scale it in X, Y, and Z to about two units each.

14. Open the Attribute Editor for lineModifierShape1.

15. Start adjusting some of the settings and see how they affect the brush strokes attached to the toon lines. Render a frame, and then use the Render Region tool in the render view to select the area around the lineModifier1 tool. This will save you time as you preview the adjustments you make to lineModifier1.

16. Try these settings:

> Width Scale = 1.983
>
> Width Offset = 0.2
>
> Surface Offset = 0.5

Under the Brush Tube Attributes, try these settings:

> Force = 0.3
>
> Directional Force = 0.3
>
> Displacement = 0.4
>
> Directional Displacement = 0.7
>
> Tube Scale = 3.5

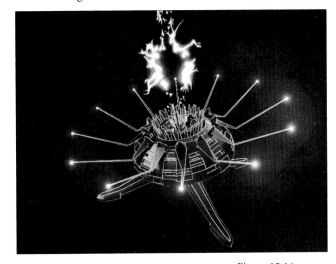

Figure 15.16

The pulsing energy ball, rising out of the space station

17. You can also try adjusting the Dropoff graph to see how the stroke reacts at the edges of the modifier tube.

18. You can also adjust the settings on the goldSparks stroke to redefine the look of the pulsing energy. Figure 15.16 shows the energy ball emanating from the station.

19. Open the `station2.mb` file from the CD to see the completed scene.

Since the brush strokes are attached to toon lines that update according to the camera angle, animating the camera will further enhance the crackling effect on the spark strokes.

20. In the lineModifierShape1 Attribute Editor is an option for modifying the color. Since the goldSparks stroke has replaced the original toon lines, this option will not have an effect on the sparks. However, if you use a modifier with a regular toon line, this can create some interesting effects.

To see a rendered version of the animation, open `station.mov` from the CD. To complete the animation, you can parent an orange Point light to the lineModifier1 shape, keyframe the intensity up and down as the energy pulse comes out of the station, and set the falloff to linear.

Modifiers can be used with the offset mesh toon line style; however, the controls in the brush tube attributes will not have an effect since they only work on Paint Effects strokes.

Summary

Using Maya Toon Shading tools is a great way to add some style to your animations. However, like many of Maya's tools, it becomes much more interesting when you find new and unexpected ways to use them beyond their obvious application. For example, you can combine the use of intersection toon lines and Paint Effects strokes to create interactive splashes where a boat hull meets water or sparks where bullets hit a wall.

After reading through this chapter, you should have a good idea of how Toon Shading works, and you should feel comfortable enough to do some exploring on your own. You should understand the toon fill shaders as well as how to apply and use both Paint Effects outlines and offset mesh outline. The Maya documentation has detailed descriptions of each node and attribute associated with Toon Shading. In addition, the examples that come with Maya are a great source of ideas.

In the next chapter, we will introduce Maya's built-in scripting language, MEL, showing how it is the basis of how Maya operates and how it can be used to simplify and automate many of the tasks you perform while using the program.

CHAPTER 16

Maya Embedded Language (MEL)

This chapter introduces Maya's embedded scripting language, MEL. You will learn how Maya uses MEL, you'll see how you can increase your productivity by automating repetitive tasks using MEL, and you'll learn some basic pointers on how to program with MEL, as well as where to look to continue learning about this deep, powerful part of Maya.

Although MEL does require a bit of programming savvy, you really don't need to know a great deal about computer programming to use it—at least not at the basic level. If you have never programmed before, MEL may seem a bit baffling at first, but don't worry: even if you never plan to do any real programming with MEL, you will find that this chapter contains information that will allow you to use MEL to control Maya in powerful, high-level ways, often without your having to do any programming yourself. If you do have some previous programming experience, MEL's syntax will seem straightforward. If you know C or C++, MEL will look very familiar. Maya 8.5 now also supports the Python programming language; experienced MEL scripters should read the sidebar describing how to integrate the languages.

- **Fundamentals of MEL and scripting**
- **The Script Editor**
- **Getting help with MEL**
- **MEL programming techniques**
- **Debugging MEL scripts**
- **Creating procedures and scripts**
- **Dissecting other programmers' work**

MEL Is Fundamental

Maya Embedded Language (MEL) is the underlying layer upon which your interactions with Maya are built. When you open Maya, the program first runs several MEL scripts that actually build all the windows you see—that's right: Maya itself has no interface whatsoever. You can even run Maya from your operating system command prompt by typing `Maya -prompt`! Behind nearly everything you see in Maya is a MEL script.

What does this mean to the average Maya user? Simple: whatever the original interface programmers did, you also can do. You can write windows that have sliders, tabs, text fields, and buttons in them; you can create attributes in the Channel Box; you can even add menu items to the main menu bar. The fact that Maya is built on MEL is one of the program's most powerful features.

> Because Maya's syntax is similar to that of the C, C++, and C# programming languages, a good primer on one of these languages is good preparation for learning MEL. We recommend *Beginning Programming* (Wrox, 2005), *C for Dummies, 2nd Edition* (Wiley, 2004), and *C# 2005 for Dummies* (Wiley).

What Is a Scripting Language?

MEL is a scripting language, not a complete programming language (such as Java or C++). A program written in a programming language is compiled and becomes an independent program (such as the core program, Maya, which just runs atop your computer's operating system). A scripting language, on the other hand, resides inside another program (in this case, Maya) and is interpreted at every line rather than compiled. Because scripting languages are interpreted by the "mother" program, they are a bit slower than compiled programs—however, they require much less programming overhead than compiled programs do.

If you are a real "propeller head" and like to get into the guts of a program, you can create plug-ins for Maya using the C or C++ programming language. Maya has its own application programming interface (API)—appropriately enough named Maya API. MEL does just fine for 95 percent of the things most people want to do, however, and it isn't too difficult to learn.

Although the API is outside the scope of this book, you can contact Autodesk about using the Maya SDK to develop plug-ins for Maya.

The Script Editor

One of the best ways to get to know MEL is to use the Script Editor. MEL is a huge language (with more than 600 commands and about 75 functions), but the Script Editor will clue you in on how commands are used and allow you to "cut and paste" whole scripts together without the need to program a thing yourself. You don't even need to use the

Command line to enter the MEL commands. Operations you perform in the Maya interface are recorded as MEL commands in the Script Editor. With no knowledge of programming, you can actually copy-paste together a fairly complex script.

The Command line, which we discussed in Chapter 1, is just one input line in the Script Editor. When you type a command in the Command line, it appears in the Script Editor's history window and also in the output line, which is to the right of the Command line and is, in fact, the last line of the Script Editor's history window.

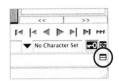

You can open the Script Editor in two ways: either choose **Window → General Editors → Script Editor** or click the Script Editor button in the lower-right corner of the screen. When opened, the Script Editor looks like Figure 16.1.

Notice that there are two panes in the editor. The top pane is called the history pane; the bottom, the input pane. To see the Script Editor in action, try the following. With the editor open, create a polygon cube (choose **Create → Polygon Primitives → Cube,** then double-click anywhere in the scene window). Now look at the history pane. The last lines of that pane should read something like this:

```
setToolTo CreatePolyCubeCtx;
polyCube -ch on -o on -cuv 4 ;
// Result:pCube1 polyCube1//
```

Figure 16.1
The Script Editor

What you see in the top pane is the command you told Maya to perform when you made your menu selection. The `setToolTo` command is a new feature in Maya 8 that implements the interactive primitive creation tool (this is on by default, but can be set to non-interactive creation in the primitives' option boxes). The `polyCube` command then creates a polygon cube where you double-click in the scene window; all the characters preceded by dashes (`-ch`, `-o`, `-cuv`, and so on) are "flags" that tell `polyCube` how to build the cube. For example, `-ch` stands for construction history, and when it's on, it enables construction history, and `-cuv` tells Maya how to create the UVs for this cube (in this case, the 4 means to create the UVs such that a texture will not be distorted when mapped to the cube). The semicolon at the end of the lines tells Maya the command is finished. (Nearly every line of MEL code needs a semicolon at the end.) There is also a result line, starting with the `//` characters, which provides feedback that the command was completed successfully (more on this later).

> Sometimes, more characters will fit into the input pane than we can squeeze into the printed page, so the semicolon is also your guide to where one command actually ends and the next begins. As you enter commands from this book into the Script Editor, you generally need to press the Enter key only after semicolons.

Change some of the attributes of the cube (scale, rotation, translation, and so on), and look at what appears in the history pane of the Script Editor. You can see that every command you perform in the interface is relayed to Maya's core program via MEL commands. For ease of reading, you can clear the top pane at any time. In the Script Editor menu bar, choose **Edit → Clear History** to clear the top pane of all commands.

Now try opening one of Maya's windows, for example, the Hypergraph window (choose **Window → Hypergraph: Hierarchy**). What do you see in the history pane? Probably nothing at all. To keep from cluttering the history pane, Maya's programmers created a filter that blocks from view in the history pane many of the MEL commands that users and programmers don't commonly need to see. Sometimes, however, it is useful to see everything that's really going on in Maya. Close the Hypergraph window, choose **History → Echo All Commands** in the Script Editor, and reopen the Hypergraph window. Now you should see something like this in the history pane:

```
editMenuUpdate MayaWindow|mainEditMenu;
HypergraphHierarchyWindow;
hyperGraphWindow "" "DAG";
addHyperGraphPanel hyperGraphPanel1;
HyperGraphEdMenu hyperGraphPanel1HyperGraphEd;
createModelPanelMenu modelPanel1;
createModelPanelMenu modelPanel2;
```

```
createModelPanelMenu modelPanel3;
createModelPanelMenu modelPanel4;
buildPanelPopupMenu scriptEditorPanel1;
buildPanelPopupMenu hyperGraphPanel1;
```

All these obscure looking lines of code represent the actual steps by which Maya builds the Hypergraph window for you. (Nearly all the words, such as `buildPanelPopupMenu`, are calls to other MEL scripts in the `~maya8.5/scripts/others` folder—the exact path will depend on your operating system. You can look through these other scripts to see how the window is actually constructed.) As you can see from this example, even the windows in Maya are created through MEL.

Now let's take a look at the input pane (the pane in the bottom half of the Script Editor window). First, empty your scene of all objects and clear the history pane; place your cursor in the bottom pane and type the following (you might want to turn off the Echo All Commands function first, to make reading the history pane easier):

```
polyCube -name myCube;
```

Press the Enter key on your numeric keypad (not the one on your main keyboard), or, alternatively, press Ctrl+Enter on your main keyboard. You should see the text disappear from the input pane and appear in the history pane. At the same time, you should see a cube appear at the origin of your scene, named myCube. Congratulations, you have just executed your first MEL command!

The line excerpted earlier that reads

```
// Result: myCube polyCube1 //
```

is called the *result line*. The two slashes at the beginning of the line are a comment marker that tells MEL to ignore the rest of that line. (You'll see these comment lines in all well-written MEL scripts, and we'll discuss annotating your code later.) MEL then displays the result of the operation (in this case, that it created the cube as you asked). If a problem occurs while making the cube, the result line contains an error message over a red background instead of a result message.

You have to use the numeric keypad's Enter key or press Ctrl+Enter because the alpha Enter key is reserved for inline returns. In other words, pressing the alpha Enter key just creates a new line in the editor window. To force the contents of the editor window to be evaluated (executed), you must use one of the two other options or highlight all the commands in the input pane and then press the alpha Enter key.

Now try this: delete the cube from your scene, and then triple-click the line in the history pane that you typed earlier (`polyCube -name myCube`). Once you have the entire line highlighted, copy that line into the input pane: MM drag into the input pane (or Option drag if you use a Mac). Now press Enter. You should see the exact same cube (called myCube) created at the origin of your scene, meaning that you have copied a command from the history pane and made a mini-script (called a macro) out of it. This is a simple example, but consider the power this little cut-and-paste trick gives you: you can "record" anything you like from the history pane and turn it into a MEL macro (or even a full-blown script). By storing this little script, you can return to it any time and, by cutting and pasting text or even clicking a button, run all the commands.

You can also easily create buttons for MEL commands on the shelf of your choice. Simply highlight the commands you want to put on the shelf and then MM drag the Com-

Figure 16.2

Several MEL script shelf buttons

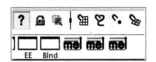

mand lines up to a shelf (Option drag on a Mac). Figure 16.2 shows a shelf with several MEL script buttons on it. We will create some shelf macros in the "Hands On" section later in this chapter.

What Is an Attribute?

As you likely understand from reading earlier chapters, an attribute (MEL uses the term Attr to refer to attributes) is any item that lives on a Maya node. (A Maya node is anything you can see in the Hypergraph or on the tabs at the top of the Attribute Editor.) This sounds a bit obscure, but it's really fairly straightforward: every item (except headers) in the Channel Box, such as rotateX, transformY, or scaleZ, is an attribute of an object that is termed a node, and this node is listed as a header in the Channel Box.

> For a basic NURBS sphere, the nodes are nurbsSphere1, nurbsSphereShape1, and makeNurbs-Sphere1. The attributes are all the other fields available (the ones with number or Boolean fields to their right). There are actually many more attributes on a node than are shown in the Channel Box by default. To see them all, select the object and open the Channel Control window (choose **Window → General Editors → Channel Control**).

LINE NUMBERS

For those accustomed to programming with MEL, there is a welcome (and much overdue) feature introduced in Maya 8: the input pane of the Script Editor window now shows line numbers along the left-hand side of the pane. Though it is still a relatively weak environment for programming large-scale scripts, the introduction of line numbers makes it much easier to program short scripts directly in the Script Editor window—and makes debugging much easier as well.

MAYA 8.5, MEL, AND PYTHON

New to Maya 8.5 is internal support for Python version 2.4.3, including the ability to run MEL commands within Python once your environment is properly set up. Python is a stand-alone scripting language (not dependent on the Maya environment) that is used extensively in the visual effects field. While the casual scripter can safely ignore Python, for those involved in larger companies with pipelines dependent on Python scripting, this new addition means that Maya can now be integrated fully into a production pipeline with great ease. In fact, given that all MEL commands (except those that duplicate Python commands, like math functions) are available inside Python, programmers can now use Python exclusively, calling MEL commands within scripts coded in Python.

The Script Editor now has two tabs in the input pane: MEL and Python. Selecting the MEL tab (chosen by default) tells the Script Editor to treat any input text as a MEL script and interpret it according to MEL syntax. Selecting the Python tab tells the Script Editor to interpret the input as a Python script. The Command line also has a toggle (at the far left), allowing you to input one line of MEL or Python script, depending on the toggled selection.

As Python's syntax is quite different from MEL's, calls must be rewritten to take account of proper syntax. For example, the MEL command `sphere -radius 5 -name ball` would be rewritten for Python as follows:

```
maya.cmds.sphere (radius =4, name ='ball')
```

The `maya.cmds` prefix notifies Python that a MEL command is going to be passed to it. The `radius` and `name` flags are then passed to the `sphere` command as arguments, rather than flags, as per Python's standard syntax.

In order to enable Python in the Script Editor, you must first enter the following line in the Python tab of the input pane:

```
import maya.cmds
```

This command loads the MEL command module into Python, allowing you to use MEL in any Python script. To reduce keystrokes when typing MEL commands in Python, you can choose to import into an alternate namespace. For example, the command `import maya.cmds as mc` allows you to type the following, which saves keystrokes:

```
mc.sphere (radius =4, name ='ball')
```

To automatically import MEL commands into Python upon Maya startup, you can create a user-Setup.py text file in the home scripting path (~home/Autodesk/maya/8.5/scripts) with the file containing the `import maya.cmds` command. Upon starting, Maya will "see" this file and automatically import the MEL commands into the Python scripting environment.

A proper introduction to Python scripting is outside the scope of this chapter. For more information on using Python in Maya, see the online help documentation. There are a number of books available for learning Python, including *Beginning Python* by Peter C. Norton et al. (Wrox, 2005).

When you build, alter, or animate an object, you're creating or changing one or more attributes on one or more nodes that make up the object—and, of course, all these changes are just MEL commands, so you can make Maya do the work for you. In this section, we'll take a quick look at how MEL works with attributes; later we'll get into more detail about how to build complex scripts using attributes.

You might have noticed when you adjusted certain attributes of myCube in the previous section that the Script Editor was filled with statements that started with setAttr. The setAttr statement tells MEL to set a certain attribute to a certain value. Likewise, the getAttr statement gets (reads) the value of an attribute on a certain object so you can use that value in another MEL statement. The addAttr statement tells MEL to add a custom attribute to a certain item. The listAttr command lists the node's attributes. Essentially, using the setAttr statement is the same as selecting an object, opening the Attribute Editor window, and changing a value in one of its fields. (Try changing a value in the Attribute Editor and you'll notice that the Script Editor history pane shows that a setAttr statement has been executed.)

The syntax (the rules of what goes where) for a setAttr statement is as follows:

```
setAttr [flags] objectName.attributeName value;
```

Flags, as you've seen, are any special requests for MEL to complete; the *object.attribute* name is the name of the item's attribute to set on a given node (such as myCube.translateX), and *value* is the attribute's value. The getAttr and addAttr commands have similar syntax. For example, we can move a cube called box to 10 on the X axis by typing the following in the Script Editor:

```
setAttr box.translateX 10;
```

Once you execute this command, your box moves from where it is to 10 on the X axis. (Of course, if you have no object node called box, you will get an error message.)

The way MEL (and Maya) references an attribute is similar to the way C++ and other object-oriented programs work. You reference the node, then type a period, and then add the attribute: Object.Attribute. If you don't specify the node on which the attribute is located, you'll get an error message. For example, typing setAttr translateX 10; generates an error message because Maya doesn't know what to translate.

Setting the translateX attribute is much like giving the move command: move 10 0 0. Unlike with the move command, however, setting the attribute of translateX does not affect the other two attributes (the Y and Z translate attributes). Also, the setAttr statement is far more flexible than the move command, which only can translate an object.

As a quick example of how `setAttr` works, let's make a box and manually set several of its attributes. Type the following in the Script Editor's input pane:

```
polyCube -n box;
setAttr polyCube1.sw 3;
setAttr polyCube1.w 5;
setAttr box.rotateY 45;
setAttr box.translateX -2.5;
setAttr box.translateY .25;
setAttr box.scaleY 0.5;
```

Can you figure out what each command does on your own? Try highlighting each line and pressing the numeric Enter key to execute it.

Highlighting one line at a time is a useful way to figure out what's happening in a script—and to see where things go wrong.

ENHANCING YOUR WORK FLOW WITH SHELVES

Although we briefly discussed shelves in Chapter 1 they might have appeared to be only somewhat useful. What makes shelves really useful is not just what appears on them by default, but the new buttons you can easily add to them. You can, for example, make any menu item a shelf button or place MEL scripts on the shelf, allowing you to perform complex tasks at the click of your mouse. Additionally, because you can create and use multiple shelves, you can make a shelf specific to a task. For example, you can devote one shelf to MEL scripts and another to common tasks for a specific project. To create a new shelf, choose **Window → Settings/Preferences → Shelf Editor**, select the Shelves tab, and click the New Shelf button. To switch to a new shelf (the Surfaces shelf, for example), simply select the shelf from the pop-up shelf menu, the gray "folder" button to the left of the shelf). (You can also customize shelf settings using the drop-down menu, the black triangle just below the shelf menu tab.) Maya includes a large number of preset shelves, making the shelf bar fairly useful "out of the box." To create a new shelf button from a menu item, hold down the Ctrl and Shift keys and choose the menu item from the menu bar (*not* the hotbox). A new button will appear on the active shelf, and clicking this button will be the same as selecting the menu item you chose.

To delete any shelf button, just MM drag it to the trashcan at the top right of the shelf bar. To move an item to a different place on the shelf, simply MM drag it to the place where you want it. Other shelf items adjust to the new placement.

You can create as many shelf buttons as you want (though you might have to scroll through the list if you create too many on one shelf) and/or delete any of the default buttons Maya provides for you, thus customizing your shelves to contain buttons that are the most useful to you. It's handy to place buttons for items such as the Hypergraph and Hypershade on the General shelf for easy access.

To change the way your cube is constructed, you reference the shape node (`polyCube1`), not the transform node, which you renamed `box` when the cube was created.

The first line builds a cube. The rest of the lines change some of the attributes, either on the shape node of the cube (the `polyCube1` node) or on the transform node (the `box` node).

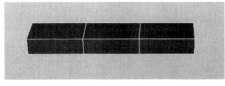

After the `polyCube` command, the next two `setAttr` statements change the subdivisions along the width and then change the width of the cube (now a rectangle) itself. The last four lines change the rotation, position, and scale of the cube's transform node (named `box`). The finished product should look like that in Figure 16.3.

Figure 16.3

The box, squashed

If, for some unknown reason, you need to create a flattened box over and over again in different scenes, you can simply MM drag (Option drag on a Mac) these commands to your shelf and make the object at the click of a button—quite a time-saver.

How to Get Help with MEL

Before we delve any further into the world of MEL, let's examine the powerful Maya help tools available to MEL scripters—and see how easy they are to use.

First, you have Maya's internal Help function. Because there are so many MEL commands and functions (about 700), the Help function is a quick and useful feature. (You can even type **help help** to get a look at how the `help` command works.)

Here's an example of the type of information available in Help. Open the Script Editor, and in the input pane type **help** followed by the name of the command you want help with (or just type it in the Command line below the main window). For example, to get help with the `setAttr` command, type this:

```
help setAttr;
```

Execute the command (press Enter on the numeric keypad, or press Ctrl+Enter on the keyboard), and in the Script Editor's history pane, you'll see the following result lines:

```
Synopsis: setAttr [flags] Name[...]
Flags:
   -e -edit
   -q -query
  -av -alteredValue
   -c -clamp
  -ca -caching        on|off
  -cb -channelBox     on|off
   -k -keyable        on|off
   -l -lock           on|off
   -s -size           UnsignedInt
 -typ -type           String
```

These result lines give you a quick look at the setAttr command: a synopsis of its syntax (or how to use it) and a list of flags that you can use with the command.

If you're an experienced programmer, this information might be all you need to use the command. If you're just starting out, however, you'll probably want more guidance. In that case, try typing the following in the input pane:

```
help -doc setAttr;
```

When you execute this command, Maya automatically opens your browser of choice and finds the correct HTML page in your help documents (on your hard drive) that contains the command you want help with. In the case of the setAttr statement, the following is displayed. (This is merely an excerpt—the actual page contains much more information.)

Synopsis
    SetAttr [flags] object.attribute value [value..]
ReturnValue
    None.
Description
    Sets the value of a dependency node attribute. No value for the
    attribute is needed when the -l/-k/-s flags are used. The -type flag
    is only required when setting a non-numeric attribute.
The following chart outlines the syntax of setAttr for non-numeric
    data types:
{TYPE} below means any number of values of type **TYPE**, separated by a space
[TYPE] means that the value of type **TYPE** is optional
A|B means that either of **A** or **B** may appear

Examples
sphere -n sphere;

        // Set a simple numeric value
        setAttr sphere.translateX 5;

        // Lock an attribute to prevent further modification
        setAttr -lock on sphere.translateX;

        // Make an attribute unkeyable
        setAttr -keyable off sphere.translateZ;

        // Set an entire list of multi-attribute values in one command
        setAttr -size 7 "sphereShape.weights[0:6]" 1 1 2 1 1 1 2

        // Set an attribute with a compound numeric type
        setAttr "sphere.rotate" -type "double3" 0 45 90;

```
// Clamp the value of the attribute to the min/max
// Useful floating point math leaves the value just
// a little out of range - here the min is .01
setAttr -clamp "anisotropic1.roughness" 0.0099978;

// Set a multi-attribute with a compound numeric type
setAttr "sphereShape.controlPoints[0:2]"
-type "double3" 0 0 0 1 1 1 2 2 2;
```

As you can see, a few examples can do a lot to clarify how a command is used.

You can also access an entire MEL manual online, for a more in-depth look at the structure of the scripting language itself. In Maya, choose **Help → MEL Command Reference** to open the main MEL reference page in your web browser, as shown in Figure 16.4. This web page contains information on all MEL commands, browsable by letter (at the top of the page), or you can browse by command category if you are looking for a command in a given area. Between the internal Help files and the online help on your hard drive, you can access excellent reference material rapidly.

Examining other users' scripts as guides for what you want to do is another great way to learn more about MEL—you can even copy and paste portions of scripts for your own use. (Just be sure that you have the author's permission.) For some example scripts you can study, see the sample MEL scripts on the accompanying CD, check out the "Maya Gems" section of the online help, or go to a website such as highend3d.com, which posts numerous user-created MEL scripts.

Figure 16.4

The MEL command reference document open in a web browser

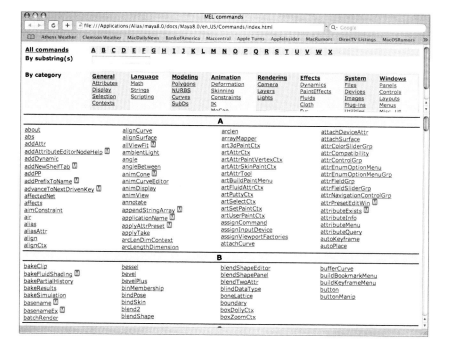

Hands On: Creating a Light Setup Using MEL

Now let's put our knowledge of MEL to use to create a small but useful script that creates a standard light setup you can place in any scene with a simple click of your mouse. The technique described here is "cut-and-paste scripting," which requires no programming knowledge. In this example, we will create a standard three-light setup (key, fill, and back), but you can alter this method to create any light setup you wish—or create multiple setups and put them all in the shelf to choose from for a given scene!

1. Open a new scene in Maya and clear the Script Editor history pane (choose **Edit** → **Clear History**). You can add a ground plane and objects, as we did, to see the effects of your lights if you wish; if you do this, be sure to clear the history again when finished.

2. Create a Spot light with Cone Angle of 40, Intensity 1, Penumbra of 10, and Cast Shadows on, and move it into the "key" light position: above and to the right of the scene (from the camera's perspective). You can also rename the spotlight something meaningful, such as keyLight. After you move the spotlight, copy all the lines of code generated from the history pane into the input pane. The code will look something like the following.

```
defaultSpotLight(1, 1,1,1, 0, 40, 0, 10, 1, 0,0,0, 1, 0);
rename "spotLight1" "keyLight";
move -r 0 0 9.028994 ;
move -r 11.075382 0 0 ;
move -r 0 3.945165 0 ;
```

For more elegant code, you might want to combine all the move -r statements into one line. To do so, just add up the numbers in each column and use one single move command.

3. Now create a second spotlight, turn off shadow casting, set Intensity to 0.5, rename it fillLight, and move it to the lower-left side of the scene (as seen from the camera). You can also adjust this light to a slight bluish color. When finished, add this code the input pane.

4. As a last step, create another light called backLight, with no shadows, a cone angle of 60, and an intensity of 1. Move the light to the back of the scene (pointing toward the camera), slightly to camera left and looking slightly down at the scene objects.

When finished (and after cleaning up the move and rotate commands a bit), you should have something that looks like the following code in the input pane. Figure 16.5 shows the results of the lights shining on a sample scene.

```
defaultSpotLight(1, 1,1,1, 0, 40, 0, 10, 1, 0,0,0, 1, 0);
rename "spotLight1" "keyLight";
move -r 19.764 22.101 20.838 ;
```

```
rotate -r -os -42.6 39.2 0 ;
defaultSpotLight(0.5, 1,1,1, 0, 40, 0, 10, 0, 0,0,0, 1, 0);
rename "spotLight1" "fillLight";
move -r -18.034 2.571 8.113;
rotate -r -os -3 -66.2 0 ;
setAttr "fillLightShape.color" -type double3 0.58425 0.63904 0.779 ;
defaultSpotLight(1, 1,1,1, 0, 60, 0, 10, 0, 0,0,0, 1, 0);
rename "spotLight1" "backLight";
move -r -7.937 8.956 -11.675;
rotate -r -os -29.4 -144.8 0;
```

5. MM drag the code (Option drag on a Mac) from the input pane into a shelf. Now when you click this button, the three lights will be created and moved into position for any scene you wish!

6. You might notice that the MEL button on the shelf is not the most descriptive icon in the world. To specify which MEL script this is, you can add some text (or even another icon) to the button. To add text to the icon, click the black triangle at the left of the shelf, and in the drop-down menu, choose Shelf Editor. In the Shelf Contents tab, scroll to the bottom of the list, where your new button should be, and change the Labels & Tooltips field to 3 light setup from its current value. Then, set the Icon Name field to 3Lts. The icon name will show up under the MEL icon in the shelf, and the labels text will appear if you pause the mouse over the icon. Figure 16.6 shows the finished button, ready to use!

Feel free to create more light setups, or other simple scripts you might find useful, and place them in a shelf for later use.

Figure 16.5

A three-light setup shining on sample geometry

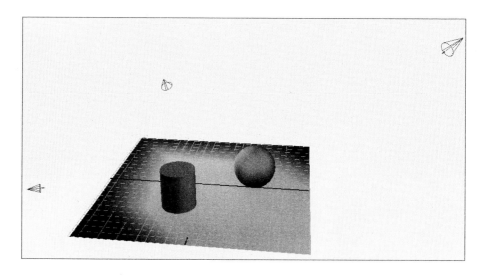

Figure 16.6

A customized shelf button for the three-light setup

Variables, Loops, and Branching

Now that we have looked at the basics of how to use MEL, let's take a closer look at how to create more sophisticated scripts using the language. If you've done any programming at all, you've probably been waiting for this point: the main reasons to program are (1) to create flexibility and (2) to take care of repetitive tasks. Flexibility comes through variables and branching; repetition is made possible through looping.

Variables

It's actually much easier to see what a variable is than to talk about it. Type the following in the Script Editor:

```
string $myVariable;
$myVariable = "hi there";
print $myVariable;
```

When you execute these commands, you'll see that `"hi there"` is displayed in the last line of the history pane, indicating that when you told Maya to print *$myVariable*, it displayed `"hi there"`. The first line of this script is called a *declaration* of the variable: `string` is the variable's type (a string is just text contained in quotes), and *$myVariable* is its name. The second line of the script assigns the string `"hi there"` to the variable *$myVariable*, and the third line tells the `print` command to output the contents of the variable *$myVariable*, which is `"hi there"`.

TYPES OF MEL VARIABLES

You use the following types of variables in MEL:

int An integer number—used to represent a whole number, such as 3 or –45.

float A decimal number—used to represent a real number, such as –3.71 or 472.86.

string A set of characters surrounded by quotes—used to store text, such as "hello world".

vector Three decimal numbers that make a vector number—used to represent a point on a three-dimensional grid, such as (26, 31.67, 6.724). A vector number is useful for three-dimensional information such as position (X, Y, Z coordinates) or colors (red, green, blue).

array A list of numbers—used to store lists of integers, floats, strings, or vectors. Arrays are useful for storing data about many similar items, such as the color of each particle in a group of particles.

matrix A two-dimensional array of floats or an array of float arrays. If this sounds confusing, you can think of it as a graph of rows and columns of floating-point data.

We'll examine various types of variables more closely as they are needed in this chapter.

Every MEL variable must start with the dollar sign ($) symbol so that MEL knows it's a variable. (This is easy to forget, and it causes strange errors—so remember your $ symbol!)

In the previous example, we could have typed the following after the `print` statement

```
$myVariable = "goodbye";
print $myVariable;
```

This would change the data in the variable *$myVariable* to the string `"goodbye"` and display it on the screen just after `"hi there"`. Thus, as you see, variables can be useful because they can store different data at different times as a program runs.

MEL has a convenience feature built into it for variables: you can declare and assign a variable in the same line. In other words, you can write the previous script as follows:

```
string $myVariable = "hi there";
print $myVariable;
```

There is no real difference between the two methods of declaring and initializing variables, except for less typing and better readability—you can use whichever method appeals to you (though most seasoned programmers opt to save keystrokes). You can also save keystrokes when declaring and assigning values to variables in other ways. Here are some examples of ways to declare variables:

- Integer

```
int $months = 11;  //standard declaration & assignment
int $days = 11, $year = 1977;  //2 assignments, comma separation
int $dollars = $pounds = $pesos = -14;  //multiple assignments
```

- of the same valueFloat

```
float $distance = -7.1;        //standard
float $height, $weight = 87.8;  //declare 2, assign 2nd
    $length = 3.4;             // implicit float declaration
```

- String

```
string $greeting = "Hello World!";  //standard
string $empty = "",                  //comma separator
    $hello = "HI!";                  //2nd line ends declaration
```

- Array

```
int $bits[5] = {0, 1, 0, 1, 0};  //standard
float $lengths[10];               //10 element float array with no
values
    $lengths[0] = 4.6;            //assignment of 1st element
string $class[5] = {"Jim", "Davy", "Dave", "Deborah",
"Wil"}; //string array assignment
```

It is always easier to read code that has appropriately named variables. Like well-written comments, well-named variables make life much easier when you revisit old code or deal with complicated scripts. For example, a variable named `$whisker_length` is much more meaningful than `$wl`.

IMPLICIT DECLARATIONS

You can implicitly declare variables in Maya by simply assigning them a value such as $var="hello". This assignment implicitly declares *$var* as a string variable because the quotation marks tell the interpreter that the value "hello" has the string data type. However, because it is more difficult to read implicitly declared variables, and more important, because it is easy to make mistakes when using implicit declaration, we recommend that you always take the time to explicitly declare each variable type.

Looping

Next, let's examine looping. Say you want to create five cubes in your scene using MEL commands. You can either type **polyCube -n box** five times or have MEL do it for you using the for loop. To build our five cubes, type the following:

```
int $i;
for ($i = 1; $i <= 5; $i++){
    polyCube -n box1;
}
```

Voilà, five cubes named box1 through box5. (You will need to move them away from each other to see them as separate objects. We'll automate this action in a moment.)

Notice that there is no semicolon after the for statement: MEL expects one or more commands (contained within the { } brackets) after the for statement, so a semicolon is unnecessary. Additionally, the closing bracket (}) functions as a semicolon, so a semicolon is also unnecessary on the last line. The syntax for the for loop is as follows:

```
for (initial_value; test_value; increment)
```

The *initial_value* is what the counting variable is set to at the beginning. The *test_value* is a Boolean statement (yes or no, 1 or 0, off or on, true or false) that determines whether to continue with another iteration of the loop. (See Maya's documentation on Boolean operators.) The *increment* is how quickly the counter increases in value (*$i++* is a shorthand way of saying "increase the value of *$i* by 1 each loop"). The for loop in the previous example can be read as follows: for i starting at 1, while i is less than or equal to 5, increment i by 1 every time the statements inside the brackets are executed.

To make this loop do a bit more for us, let's have it move the cubes on top of one another on the Y axis as it creates them:

```
for ($i = 1; $i<= 5; $i++){
    polyCube -n box;
    move -r 0 (2* $i) 0;
}
```

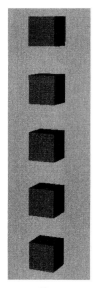

Now as the cubes are created, each one is moved up by twice the value of i, placing them atop one another, as shown in Figure 16.7.

There are several other types of loops in MEL. Following are the syntax and an example of each.

for – in

Syntax:

```
for (element in array){
    statements;
}
```

Example:

```
string $student;
string $class[3] = {"Brian", "Nathan", "Josh"};
for ($student in $class){
    print ($student + "\n");  // \n = go to the next line
}
```

Result:

```
Brian
Nathan
Josh
```

while

Syntax:

```
while (test condition){
    statements;
}
```

Example:

```
int $i = 0;
while ($i < 5){
   print $i;
   $i++;   //increment i by 1
}
```

Result:

```
01234
```

do – while

Syntax:

```
do {
    statements;
} while (test condition);
```

Figure 16.7

Cubes created and moved by a MEL script

Example:

```
int $i = 5;
do {
    print $i;
    $i-;    //decrement i by 1
} while($i > 0);
```

Result:

```
54321
```

Branching

Branching provides a way to ask a question and decide whether to take some further action based on the answer. (The for statement actually contains a branch in its *test_value* statement.) Let's modify our box building script, this time placing a conditional statement inside it:

```
for ($i = 1; $i <= 5; $i++){
    polyCube -n box;
    if ($i<=3){
        move -r 0 (2 * $i) 0;
    }
    else{
        move -r (2 * $i) 0 0;
    }
}
```

What happens when you execute these commands? The first three cubes are stacked up on the Y axis (when $i is less than or equal to 3), and the last two are stacked along the X axis (when $i is 4 and 5, and therefore greater than 3). The results of this script are shown in Figure 16.8.

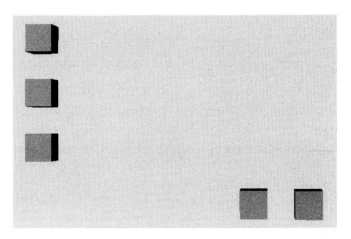

Figure 16.8

Creating and moving cubes using the for and if commands

In the abstract, the syntax for the `if` statement is as follows:

```
if (test){
    commands;
    }
else if (test){
    commands;
    }
else{
    commands;
    }
```

The `else if` and `else` statements do *not* have to exist for the `if` statement to work. The `else if` statement allows you to make as many tests as you like (your conditional statement can have as many `else if` statements as you want), allowing you to test for multiple possibilities within one large conditional statement. The `else` statement must always be last in such examples, and it is the "default" answer if no other conditions are met. All the commands for an `if`, `else if`, or `else` statement must be enclosed in brackets (`{ }`). If we want, we can increase the complexity of our create-and-move-box code with an `else if` statement:

```
for ($i = 1; $i <=10; $i++){
    polyCube -n box;
    if ($i <=3){
        move -r 0 (2 * $i) 0;
    }
    else if ($i > 3 && $i <= 6){
        move -r 0 0 (2 * $i);
    }
    else{
        move -r (2 * $i ) 0 0;
    }
```

Here, the cubes will stack along the Y axis if $i is less than or equal to 3, along the Z axis if $i is between 4 and 6, and along the X axis if $i is greater than 6.

> If there is only one line of commands after the `if` statement, you do not need the brackets. Always be consistent with the placement and alignment of your brackets; it becomes easy to forget a bracket with multiple `if` `else` statements, which can lead to unnecessary debugging.

Another way of branching is to use the `switch` statement. A `switch` statement branches based on a control. The control can be of type `int`, `float`, `string`, or `vector`. If the value of the control is equal to the value of one of the specified case values (which must be of the same data type as the control), the statements following that case value execute. Following is the basic syntax of the `switch` statement:

```
switch (control)
{
    case value1:
        statement1;
        break;
    case value2:
        statement2;
        break;
    case value3:
        statement3;
        break;
    ...
    default:
        statement4;
        break;
}
```

The `break` statement is used to exit the `switch` statement and prevent execution of subsequent case statements. The default statement executes if none of the other `case` statements are a match for the control. You can omit the `default` statement. You can also omit the break statement if you want the program to "flow down" to the next case statement. (This is fairly unusual, however, so use the `break` statement unless you're *sure* you understand what you're doing.)

Here is an example of the `switch` statement used with our build-a-box script:

```
for ($i = 0; $i < 3; $i++){
    polyCube -n box;
    switch($i){
        case 0:
            move -r (2 * $i) 0 0;
            break;
        case 1:
            move -r 0 (2 * $i) 0;
            break;
        case 2:
            move -r 0 0 (2 * $i);
            break;
        default:
            break;
    }
}
```

Here we create three cubes and move them each along a different axis. When i is equal to 0, we move it along the X axis, 1 along the Y axis, and 2 along the Z axis. When i is 3, we arrive at the default condition, which does nothing, so the new box is not moved.

Debugging MEL Scripts

If you have been careful typing thus far, you might have gotten away with creating scripts without seeing a MEL error message; in the work ahead, however (and certainly as you begin building MEL scripts of your own), you will encounter error messages, the most common of which is the syntax error. Every command has a particular structure or form that must be followed to execute successfully. Otherwise, the script interpreter won't know what to do with your command and will most often return a syntax error.

Although debugging a script is a bit of an art form, you can help yourself in a couple of ways. First, check the history pane when you execute a script: if the last line of your script is the last line in the history pane, the commands executed without an error. If, however, you get a comment line such as the following, you know that there has been at least one error in parsing the script:

```
setAttr box 5;
//Error: line 1:  No attribute was specified. //
```

Parsing is the programming term for the search that the script interpreter makes through the script to ensure that all the commands are correct.

The Feedback line (at the bottom-right of the screen and shown in Figure 16.9) turns orange-red to indicate that the MEL interpreter has discovered an error in your code. One way to identify quickly where these errors might lie is to turn on the Line Numbers In Errors option in the Script Editor (choose **History → Line Numbers In Errors** in the Script Editor menu), which causes Maya to print the line number where each error occurs. Generally, it's a good idea to keep this option on at all times. It does not slow Maya down in any significant way, and it provides useful information about where errors are occurring. Now that Maya displays line numbers in the input pane, it is fairly easy to scroll down to the proper line where an error has occurred.

As you begin scripting, one error that will probably creep in is forgetting the final semicolon at the end of a line. This can be difficult to spot if you're not aware of the problem. If you are getting errors in your script that don't make sense, try looking at lines above where the error occurred to be sure they all end with a semicolon.

Figure 16.9
An error reported in the Feedback line

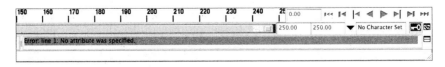

Finally, since MEL is an interpreted scripting language, you can execute a script one line (or one chunk of lines) at a time rather than as a whole. This can be a useful way to figure out where a problem is occurring in your program. A brief exercise will illustrate:

1. Type the following, but don't execute it yet:

```
print "hello, world!";
print hello, world;
```

2. Highlight the first line and execute it (by pressing the Enter key on your numeric keypad or Ctrl+Enter on your keyboard). You should see `hello, world!` displayed in the history pane.

3. Now highlight and execute the second line. You should see something like the following:

```
// Error: print hello, world; //
// Error: Line 1.12: Syntax error //
```

The first line executed properly, but the second had an error in it—the `print` command needs a string to work with, and you need to include quotation marks to identify the string. In a two-line script, spotting the error is simple; in a longer script, this method of going through the script one line at a time can be a great way to uncover problem spots.

A Comment on Commenting

Comments are a way for you, as a programmer, to document your code. Comments can be useful when you revisit old code, when you're writing code that may be confusing, or when others are reading your code.

Comments are identified by two forward slashes (//). When the script executes, the interpreter ignores anything that follows the two slashes on that line. Here are some examples of legal comments:

```
//Script written by: John Doe
polyCube -n myCube;     //create a cube named myCube
```

As you can see, a comment can be on a line by itself or at the end of a line of code.

For multiple lines of comments, as at the beginning of a script, you can also use /* to identify the beginning of a longer comment. Everything after these characters will be ignored by the MEL parser until it sees the paired characters */, which define the end of a long comment.

Always include comments at the top of a script describing what the script does, which arguments (inputs) it needs (you'll learn about arguments later in the section on procedures), who wrote and modified it, and when it was last modified. It's also not a bad idea to put in a "use at your own risk" line to indicate that some unforeseen problem could arise while using the script and that the author is not responsible for any mishaps because of the script's usage (ah, the joys of a litigious society).

You might think that these comments are of use only to others and not to yourself and you'd rather not bother with them if you don't plan to distribute the script. But remember that two months after you create the script, you might need to modify it, and if you can't figure out what you did or why, you'll waste a great deal of time hunting through the script instead of getting right to your modifications.

Always comment your scripts well (even the simplest ones). It's a habit (and for once, a good one), so get into it! Commenting well doesn't necessarily mean commenting everything though. In the CD files provided for this chapter, the scripts are a little overcommented for instructional purposes, but in most cases, if you have more comments than code, you have overdone it. Good code is self-documenting with comments included where you or someone else might need a little extra information about what is happening. Here is an example of poor, or overdone, commenting technique:

```
// z equals x plus y
$z = $x + $y;
```

Creating a GUI

Although typing commands into the Command line or input pane of the Script Editor is useful for simple tasks, it is often much more elegant (not to mention user friendly) to create a graphical user interface (GUI) window in your script to give users access to all the script's commands in a comfortable point-and-click environment. Although creating these windows can be somewhat challenging, nearly all high-quality scripts use them, so it is good to learn at least the basics of GUI creation using MEL.

Windows in Maya can be complex (just look at the Attribute Editor window for an example), but the basic way to create a window is fairly simple. At a minimum, you need three commands to make a window:

```
window -title "title" -wh X Y myWindow;
some kind of layout;
showWindow;
```

Executing the `window` command creates a window with a name that appears at its top (the `-title` flag), optionally a predefined width and height (the `-widthHeight` or `-wh` flag), and an optional name (the last item in the `window` command). The title of a window and its name are not the same: Maya refers to the `myWindow` name, while a user sees the window's `title`.

The `showWindow` command displays the window on the screen. (The window will never appear if you forget this line.) This command belongs at the end of a "make window" series of commands.

The layout commands specify the layout of the window. Some common types are columnLayout, scrollLayout, rowColumnLayout, and formLayout. The column layout creates a column, the scroll layout makes the window a scrollable window, the row-and-column layout makes a grid of rows and columns (like a table), and the form layout creates a flexible space that can be laid out in many ways. These layouts can also contain other layouts nested within them, creating the ability to make complex windows relatively easily. (The form layout is often the parent layout, with many other layouts inside it.)

Let's create a simple window that contains one button and one slider. Type the following in the Script Editor:

```
window -t "The Big Window!" -wh 400 200 myWindow;
columnLayout -cw 200;
button -l "Click this button" myButton;
text " ";
attrFieldSliderGrp -l "Slide this around" -min 0 -max 10 theSliderGroup;
showWindow myWindow;
```

These commands create a window (which Maya knows as myWindow but, as you see in Figure 16.10, is titled The Big Window!) with a width of 400 pixels and a height of 200

pixels. A column layout is then set with a width of 200 pixels. Next, a button (labeled Click This Button and known to Maya as myButton) is created; then a field-and-slider group is created (labeled Slide This Around and known as theSliderGroup) with a minimum value of 0 and a maximum value of 10. The text command just puts a space between the button and the slider group. Finally, we display the window via the showWindow command. Obviously it's not too difficult to create windows with buttons, sliders, or other objects in them.

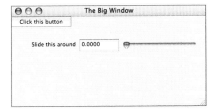

Figure 16.10
The Big Window!

If you make some errors typing the MEL script and then go back and try to run the script again, when you try to re-create the window, you might run into the following error message: Error: Object's name is not unique: myWindow. If you get this message, you need to delete the window myWindow. Even though it doesn't appear on the screen, MEL has created a UI object named myWindow. (The showWindow command is last, so an object can be created but not shown.) Thus, while myWindow doesn't appear, it can exist in your scene and it needs to be deleted. To do this, type **deleteUI myWindow** in the Command line or Script Editor and execute it. This command is useful as you create and troubleshoot GUI windows, so commit it to memory.

Now let's make our buttons do something. Clear all objects in your scene and create a sphere called "ball." Edit your script to include the -command and -attribute flags, as follows:

```
window -t "The Big Window!" -wh 400 200 myWindow;
columnLayout -cw 200;
button -l "Click this button" -c "setAttr ball.ty  5" myButton;
text " ";
attrFieldSliderGrp -l "Slide this around" -min 0 -max 10
                   -at ("ball.tx") theSliderGroup;
showWindow myWindow
```

The -c flag for button tells Maya to perform the quoted instruction each time the button is clicked. Thus, when this button is clicked, Maya sets the ball's Y position to 5 units. The -at flag in the slider group tells Maya to connect the slider and text field to the quoted attribute (in this case, the X translation of the ball). When you move the slider (or enter numbers in the text field), the ball moves back and forth between 0 and 10 on the X axis.

On the attrFieldSliderGrp, you can set the slider and text field to different minimum and maximum values. The -fmn and -fmx flags give the field's min and max values. The -smn and -smx flags give the slider's min and max values. Setting slider and text fields to different minimum and maximum numbers allows the user to enter numbers outside the slider's bounds, which can be useful if the user wants to override your default settings.

You can also create radio buttons and check boxes that perform functions when selected. (See the MEL documentation for more information on these.)

> As an exercise, which command could you place on the button to move the ball up 5 units every time the button is clicked? Hint: it's relative motion instead of absolute.

Now that you've seen how quickly you can create a basic window as an interface to your scripts, let's make a script that automatically creates an interface for controlling the lights in a scene. Make a new scene, and then create several lights and aim them at an object in the scene—or just use your light creation script from earlier in the chapter. Now enter the following in your Script Editor window:

```
string $sel[] = `ls -lights`;
string $current;
string $winName = "lightWindow";
if (`window -exists $winName`) {
    deleteUI $winName;
}
window -title "Lights" -wh 600 300 $winName;
scrollLayout;
```

```
rowColumnLayout -nc 2 -cw 1 160 -cw 2 400;
for ($current in $sel) {
    text -l $current;
    attrFieldSliderGrp -min (-1) -max 10 -at ($current + ".intensity");
}
showWindow $winName;
```

When you execute this script, Maya automatically creates a "light board" for you, allowing you to control the intensity of all lights in the scene from one floating window.

The most interesting portion of this script is the first line:

```
string $sel[] = `ls -lights`;
```

This line assigns to the variable string array *$sel[]* the name of every light in the scene. The `ls` command tells Maya to list the items that come after (in this case, `-lights` means "list all lights in the scene"); then the reverse apostrophes tell Maya to evaluate this command (which returns the name of each light) and read the results into the array *$sel[]* (the [] brackets indicate an array of strings).

Next, other variables are declared to store the "current item" *($current)* and the window name *($winName)*, and the script checks to see whether the window already exists—if it does, the script kills the old window (using the `deleteUI` command) so it can write a new one. This little piece of code is good to include in all your GUI scripts to ensure that you don't accidentally generate any errors if a window whose name is the same as the current window already exists. Then a window is created with a scroll layout (so the window can scroll if it's too small) and a row/column layout (a table). Next the script performs a variation of the `for` loop, called the `for...in` loop. The `for...in` loop looks through an array (in this case, *$sel[]*) and does one loop for each item it finds, placing the value of `$sel[number]` in the variable *$current*. The data type of *$current* must therefore match the type of *$sel[]* (in this case, they're both strings).

As you can see in Figure 16.11, the loop then displays the name of the light (in column 1) and makes a field slider group that's attached to the light's intensity setting (in column 2).

> If you want only the lights you have previously selected in the scene to be in the window, you can add the flag `-selected` to the `ls` command on the first line.

This little script should indicate how powerful a work-flow enhancer MEL can be: in just a few lines of script, you created a way to control potentially dozens of lights in a complex scene in a completely simple, intuitive manner. If you needed to create just the right light levels on 20 lights in a scene, it could take hours navigating to each light and adjusting it individually. This script could make the job a 10-minute effort instead.

Figure 16.11

**A GUI window show-
ing light controls**

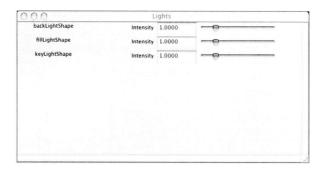

Figure 16.11

**A GUI window show-
ing light controls**

As an exercise, try creating sliders that let you adjust the light's colors as well as its intensity. (Hint: Three attributes, `colorR`, `colorG`, and `colorB`, control the red, green, and blue intensities.) If you really want to get crazy, try placing each group of controls for each light in its own subwindow (so `intensity`, `colorR`, `colorG`, and `colorB` are all inside a window). You'll need to know about the `setParent` command, as well as how to make a frame layout with the flag `-cll` (collapsible) set to true (to make each window close by clicking its triangle). You could also add check boxes to turn off each light's visibility so that you can see the effects of each light separately. You can find help for these commands in Maya's online reference documents, and if you get stuck, check out `lightBoard.mel`, one of the MEL scripts included on the CD.

Using Procedures and Scripts

In the past few sections, we've touched on most of the basic elements of MEL. However, all the pieces we've created so far won't work well if we try to give them to someone else or save them to our scripts folder. We haven't done anything to save the commands we've written in a format that Maya can read as a whole. Now we need to turn these bits of code into full-fledged (stand-alone) scripts that you can port from one place to another and trade with others.

In the following sections, we'll look at procedures and scripts. A procedure is the basic building block of a MEL script. At its fundamental level, it's simply another declaration line that tells Maya that all the contained lines form one named function. A script is just a collection of one or more procedures.

Procedures

In the abstract, a procedure looks like this:

```
proc myProcedure ()
{
commands
}
```

Maya executes all the commands in the curly braces every time you type **myProcedure** in the Command line or the Script Editor's input pane. myProcedure is the name of the procedure, and the parentheses can contain any number of declared variables that can either be called from another procedure or entered by the user when executing the procedure. As a simple example, let's write a procedure that creates a user-defined number of spheres:

```
global proc makeBall (int $num){
    int $num;
    for ($i = 1; $i <= $num; $i++){
        sphere -r 1 -name ("ball" + $i);
    }
}
```

LEARNING FROM THE MASTERS

No matter how much you learn in this chapter, space and time simply aren't sufficient here for you to learn everything MEL has to offer. One of the best ways to continue learning MEL is, quite simply, to look at (and copy from) other people's scripts. If you can go through each line of a script and figure out what it does, you will learn a great deal. Better yet, if you can grab some code someone else wrote and modify it to do what you want it to, you can really start to put together some neat and useful scripts to solve your everyday work bottlenecks— just be sure you have permission to use and/or modify the code first.

Enter this text in the Script Editor, and then execute it. You will notice that nothing happens in Maya. This is because the script as a whole has been "sourced" into Maya's memory: a procedure is stored in Maya's memory rather than executed immediately. Because the script now resides in memory, whenever you type **makeBall** followed by an integer number in the Command line or input pane, you'll get as many spheres as the number you typed (called ball1, ball2, and so on) in your scene. Typing **makeBall 5**, for example, makes five spheres named ball1 through ball5 in your scene. We've made this procedure "global" so that when it is saved as a text file, Maya can reference the procedure from within the following folder (more on this in a moment):

- Windows

```
\local disk (C:)\Documents and Settings\<user name>
    \My Documents\maya\8.5\scripts
```

- Macintosh

```
~home/Library/Preferences/Alias/maya/8.5/scripts
```

You know that a procedure is just a bunch of MEL commands contained in braces and given a name, so how would you turn our series of light board commands into a procedure? Like this:

```
///////////////////////////////////
global proc lightBoard (){
    string $sel[] = `ls -lights`;
    string $current;
    string $winName = "lightWindow";
    if (`window -exists $winName`){
        deleteUI $winName;
    }
    window -title "Lights" -wh 400 300 $winName;
    scrollLayout;
    rowColumnLayout -nc 2 -cw 1 160 -cw 2 400;
    for ($current in $sel){
        text -l $current;
        attrFieldSliderGrp -min (-1) -max 10 -at ($current + ".intensity");
    }
    showWindow $winName;
}
///////////////////////////////////
```

Once you source (enter) this procedure, each time you type **lightBoard** in the Command line, the procedure runs and you get a light board for all your lights.

It is a good idea to comment the beginning and end of every procedure (so it's easy to see where they start and stop). Two slashes (//) define the start of a comment.

Scripts

What is the difference between a procedure and a script? A script is just a collection of one or more procedures. Thus, the lightBoard procedure we just wrote is actually a script as well. A true script is also saved as an external text file and given a name, which must end in .mel, and the name of the script should be the same as the name of the last (global) procedure in the script (plus the .mel extension). For our light board example, we save the script as lightBoard.mel and store it in the scripts folder (see the preceding section for the full path). (When you choose Save Selected in the Script Editor, this is the default folder; so just save it there.)

Now let's make a simple script that contains two procedures to see how that is done:

```
// Source this script, and then type "makeBall <number>" in
// the Command line or Script Editor.  The procedure will make
// the number of spheres you specify and call them "ball1,"
// "ball2," etc.
// Created by:  John Kundert-Gibbs
// Last Modified:  April 16, 2005
// Use at your own risk.

/////////////////////////////////////////////
// makeIt creates the spheres and gives them names.
// This procedure is passed the number of balls you specify
// from the main procedure.
proc makeIt (int $theNum) {
    // $theNum must be redeclared internal to the procedure
    int $theNum;
    for ($i = 1; $i <= $theNum; $i++) {
        sphere -r 1 -name ("ball" + $i);
    }
} //end, makeIt
/////////////////////////////////////////////

/////////////////////////////////////////////
// makeBall is the main procedure you call.
// It just calls the procedure makeIt and passes it the
// number of spheres you specify.
global proc makeBall (int $num) {
    int $num;
    makeIt ($num);
} //end, makeBall
/////////////////////////////////////////////
```

All we've done with this script is to create a subprocedure that actually creates the spheres. The main (or global) procedure merely calls the subprocedure. (This is often the case with complex scripts—just look at the end of a script and you'll often find a small procedure that simply calls all the other procedures in the script.) The last procedure is the one that you call by typing **makeBall 5** in the Command line. This is (and should be) the only global procedure in the script—the makeIt procedure being a local procedure (and therefore not visible to Maya outside the script). Note that it is the *last* procedure that is your main procedure: as MEL is interpreted, the main procedure needs to come last because it references all the procedures above it.

"PROCEDURE NOT FOUND"

At times, Maya, for some reason, does not see a local procedure even when it is correctly placed within a script. When you get a "Procedure Not Found" error message, try redefining your local procedures to global and see if that removes the error. Additionally, if the script is stored in the default scripts folder for Maya 8.5, it generally finds these other procedures. To find out what your default scripts folder is, just choose **File → Source Script** in the Script Editor window, and look at what path is listed.

To begin your journey of discovery, take a look at the sample scripts on the CD that comes with this book. So that you get used to reading commented scripts, all comments about the scripts are inside the scripts rather than in a separate text file.

Summary

In this chapter, you learned both the basics and some more advanced aspects of Maya's MEL scripting language, and you gained some hands-on experience building tools and scripts to make Maya more useful and automated. You worked with variables, loops, and conditional branching and learned how to create custom GUIs to make the user interface experience more intuitive. For more useful and fun example scripts, be sure to check out the included scripts on the CD. They range from simple to complex and are a great resource for studying other people's code.

In the following chapter we will discuss Maya's Paint Effects tool and how it can be used to create visually interesting natural effects.

CHAPTER 17

Paint Effects

One of the primary challenges that both 3D software and computer developers face is re-creating natural phenomena such as trees, plants, rain, and gushing lava. These tasks require re-creating the seemingly chaotic patterns of organic forms with realistic motion rather than "sterile" 3D graphics such as those seen when 3D was first introduced in films such as *Tron*.

In the past, natural phenomena could only be created with dynamic simulations (rain, snow, water) or with procedural modeling, thus creating clusters of different models, such as grass blades or flowers and then tiling them repeatedly, which made for an enormous poly count. Paint Effects, which is a built-in paint program that ships with Maya Complete, drastically changes this approach by providing a unique ability to paint 2D and 3D natural phenomena intuitively within the viewport. No longer do you have to spend an enormous amount of time creating clusters of grass blades or modeling a tree or 10 from scratch. This might sound a bit unrealistic, since we know that 3D usually begins with a modeling process; however, with Paint Effects, traditional work flows are replaced with a natural and intuitive means for painting nature's phenomena in 3D, using an extensive brush library as you would within a 2D paint program.

- ▪ **Understanding Paint Effects**
- ▪ **Painting with Paint Effects**
- ▪ **2D canvas painting**
- ▪ **3D Paint Effects**
- ▪ **Paint Effects and animation**
- ▪ **Understanding tubes: a rose tree tutorial**

Understanding Paint Effects

Paint Effects lets you naturally paint using either a mouse or a pressure-sensitive tablet. The available selection of brushes lets you paint 3D Paint Effects objects that resemble a variety of natural phenomena and much more. When you paint an "effect" into a scene, you create a stroke that can resemble a stroke made through traditional means, such as with an air brush, crayons, or pastels. Paint Effects brushes can also produce special effects from the painted stroke, such as rain or trees, all with different looks and behaviors. You can animate these Paint Effects objects to mimic natural motion using custom attributes as well as the Paint Effects built-in dynamic features. Both provide methods for simulating gushing water, creating plants that react to wind, creating snow storms, and animating plant growth over time, to mention but a few. Paint Effects objects are represented by curves in the scene that are responsible for the placement of a particular effect in our 3D environment so that the paint effect is integrated within the scene when rendered.

Paint Effects objects are not real geometry—they are post-process render effects that are superimposed onto the Maya software render; thus they are actually composited into the scene. Maya has an outstanding integration process for Paint Effects that supports depth, transparency, and color influences from the scene in a way that makes it hard to believe that you are seeing only a post-process effect. Therein lies the tremendous advantage of Paint Effects over other software. For example, you might use another program to create your natural elements, but integrating it within a 3D scene consists of one of two options. The first is using a compositing package, which requires a skilled compositor to properly integrate depth, transparency, and light, assuming you are using the same camera perspective. The other option is importing the natural elements into Maya, which can become poly intensive and cumbersome. Paint Effects is completely integrated into Maya, so you don't really feel that it is only a post-process effect.

You can view Paint Effects within Maya at three display levels. Figure 17.1 shows one Paint Effects brush using these display modes, which are curve, mesh, and rendered. The rendered display can only be seen in the Paint Effects panel, which renders on-the-fly using OpenGL, allowing for good quality previews of the Paint Effects.

Figure 17.1

Paint Effects provides three display modes, which are from left to right, curve and mesh, both available in all views, and OpenGL rendered, which is available only within the Paint Effects panel.

Because Paint Effects is not actual geometry and provides different display modes, it reduces the overhead caused by either managing intensive poly scenes or intensive Paint Effects scenes. Using curve display can greatly improve interaction with intensive Paint Effects scenes. In addition, Paint Effects's limited dynamics do not rely on Maya's dynamics solver, which eliminates some of the inconveniences of using dynamics and allows you to easily view dynamic-style simulations while scrubbing the Timeline. That's a huge advantage when compared to conventional dynamics. This is possible because Paint Effects dynamics are driven by expressions that define natural behavior and evaluate without a need to cache simulations.

Although you can't modify a Paint Effects object by shifting vertices, Paint Effects objects can be converted into 3D objects that can then be modified at a vertex level. Paint Effects animation is conserved after converting into a 3D object, accepting any changes made to the stroke or brush nodes. Since Paint Effects is only supported by the Maya Software renderer, converting to 3D enables rendering Paint Effects using any other renderer, such as mental ray. Paint Effects can also be integrated with the Toon Shading system as well as Maya Hair. Also, Paint Effects brushes used with Hair can render with mental ray. For more information on Toon Shading, see Chapter 13.

Understanding Strokes and Brushes

Most nature effects rely on a variety of advanced techniques that address particular problems in CG. These techniques include creating dynamic simulations such as rain or fire and creating natural elements such as trees or flowers. The latter are commonly referred to as L-systems, which describe random growth or branching—for example, how a tree trunk randomly expands into branches, twigs, and leaves. Paint Effects can reproduce such dynamic and L-system simulations using tubes that emit from strokes as well as a variety of visual effects such as glows, lightning, and neon lights; all these and more are defined by the brush and its attributes.

At its heart, Paint Effects is all about painting. As you can with 2D paint programs, you can start by selecting a brush and then painting a stroke in the viewport using that brush. Conveniently, Paint Effects appropriately names these features strokes and brushes. Figure 17.2 shows a variety of brushes rendered in the Paint Effects panel window.

Every Paint Effects element is constructed by three primary elements—a curve, a stroke, and a brush. Figure 17.3 demonstrates the relationship between these elements. The curve 4 and stroke1 items are the transform nodes, which are attached to Maya shape nodes. The stroke shows two receiving inputs, one from the curve node, representing the stroke "path," and another from the brush node, representing the render qualities of the stroke. Notice that the brush node is connected to a Time1 node, providing the ability to animate brush attributes over time.

Figure 17.2

Paint Effects can create anything from a simple brush stroke to rain falling from cumulus clouds over a small town.

Figure 17.3

Paint Effects connections in the Hypergraph window demonstrate the relationship between transform, stroke, and brush nodes.

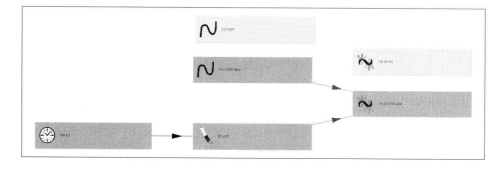

Strokes

Strokes represent the actual painted line similar to an artist's stroke; the strokes can be defined either as a color such as a crayon line or as a base to emit or grow effects such as rain or grass. These effects are referred to as tubes and are basically curves that extend out from the stroke and have brush attributes that define their rendered look.

All Paint Effects objects are based on tubes that "map" the Paint Effects form in the scene. These tubes define paint effects placement and size along the initial tube, which is the stroke. Tubes can be thought of as placeholders for the paint effects; hence, you can tumble around these Paint Effects (tubes) in perspective. Although paint effects are a post-process effect, they react to camera angles and have a real physical presence in 3D; thus, using nongeometric objects (tubes) for representing high-quality paint effects provides a significant boost in performance.

> Paint effects are not images mapped onto placeholder cards with an alpha and texture. Rather, they are full-fledged objects that can be viewed from any and every angle.

The stroke directly relates to the curve, which acts as a 3D placement guide for the initial stroke "tube." Hence, the curve's path within the scene defines the stroke shape and length. Basically, a stroke can be thought of as a curve (paint stroke) with unique attributes, such as thickness, display quality, and visibility.

Brushes

The brush defines physical properties for the stroke, or you might say the stroke's "look." This look can be any effect from more than 400 preset brushes that ship with Maya. In the Rendering menu set (press F6) choose **Paint Effects → Get Brush** to open the Visor window, displaying the Paint Effects tab (see Figure 17.4). You can see the Paint Effects folders and their root folder. Selecting any of these folders displays small preview images of the available brushes on the right side. To see the brushes more clearly, you can zoom and track within this window just as you can with any other 2D panel.

We refer to brushes as presets simply because they can be blended to form different brushes, much like mixing colors on a color palette, opening the door for creating an unlimited number of new looks that can be saved for later use. The difference between using a traditional brush such as crayon over an effects brush such as grass is in the way the stroke is displayed and rendered. A traditional brush colors the stroke along its path (dictated by the curve), whereas an effects brush emits tubes along the stroke; thus, the stroke does not render any color. Each brush has an extensive set of tabs and attributes, providing an enormous number of different effects and animation.

Autodesk provides good resources for sharing and downloading several brushes. Find them at the Autodesk community website (`www.autodesk.com`). You can also find more brushes in the Maya Paint Effects section at `www.Highend3D.com`. You can add all new brushes to the Paint Effects root folder, displayed in the Visor.

> Besides having special dynamic and flow animation settings, almost all attributes both on brushes and strokes can be animated.

Figure 17.4

The Visor window lets you see and select any of Maya's 400 preset brushes.

In addition to being able to choose from a multitude of brushes, you can render each brush as one of six available brush types in the Brush Settings window, as shown in Figure 17.5. The brush types are Paint, Smear, Blur, Erase, ThinLine, and Mesh. We will experiment with these brush types later in this chapter. The default is Paint, which renders Paint Effects by stamping images along tubes and is commonly used for clouds, smoke, fire, and glows.

Smear, Blur, and Erase allow for—surprise!—smearing, blurring, and erasing anything in the scene. For example, if you paint a stroke in front of a character and then use it as a Smear brush type, at render time it will smear the character based on the brush setting. An example worth experimenting with is to draw several strokes surrounding objects using different brushes (airbrush, plants, water) and different brush types (Smear, Blur, and

Figure 17.5

The six brush types available for Paint Effects

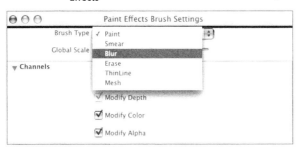

Erase) and examine their effects while rendering. This demands further experimentation once you complete this chapter. Paint Effects is powerful tool, especially when integrated with animation. In the Academy Award–winning short film *Ryan* (`www.nfb.ca/ryan/`), a must-see for all 3D artists, these brush types were used extensively to create what director Chris Landreth refers to as "psycho-realism" effects.

Thin Line and Mesh brush types are discussed in detail later in this chapter. For now, we will just mention that Thin Line renders tubes directly without stamping along the tube length and Mesh renders geometric forms (also without stamping). Thin Line brushes are typically used for hair, and Mesh brush types are used with more geometric effects such as trees and plants. A common practice in Maya 8.5 is to use the Thin Line brush type with Maya Hair or Toon shading. With respect to Toon Outlines, different brush types are supported; therefore you may use the default Paint brush type. Using Thin Line may benefit effects that are meant to appear as thin paint strokes, similar to hair or pencil strokes. However, for strokes that may appear more like a cloud brush or a pastel brush, using the default Paint type is more suitable.

Painting with Paint Effects

You can use Paint Effects to paint on a 2D canvas or directly into the scene. When painting in the scene, you can further choose whether to paint on the scene grid (default), paint a texture on a model, or paint 3D Paint Effects onto the model surface, which are then constrained to the surface. This is a particularly nice feature, which results with brushes that inherit the transformation and deformation from an object. For example, a Paint Effects stroke used for hair (not Maya Hair) is bound to the head's motion.

Paint Effects can be painted either directly into the scene or within a special Paint Effects panel that provides two work environments—a 2D canvas and a 3D scene. When you are working in the 3D environment, the current perspective camera view is displayed. Although you are able to tumble and track, as with the perspective view, painting in 3D within the Paint Effects panel is different because it enables viewing Paint Effects in a rendered preview quality, based on OpenGL. This permits painting more intuitively while viewing the actual rendered result. Another significant difference between the two work environments is that the Paint Effects panel is meant to be used for painting. Thus, when it's loaded, the Paint Effects tool (the brush) is active—meaning that by default you cannot accomplish normal tasks such as selecting objects.

> You paint using the Paint Effects tool, which loads by default into the Tool Box when the Paint Effects panel is active. When you switch to perspective view, the Paint Effects tool remains active.

Working within the Paint Effects panel might be a bit difficult to fully comprehend, so let's clarify it. Create a primitive cube to help identify the scene orientation, and then open a floating Paint Effects panel by choosing **Window → Paint Effects**. Make sure that Paint Scene mode is set in the Paint menu within the Paint Effects panel (shown in Figure 17.6). Notice that if you tumble the perspective viewport, the Paint Effects panel updates, matching changes in the perspective.

Figure 17.6

The Paint Effects toolbar

If you hold down the left mouse button and drag across the Paint Effects panel, you draw a stroke into the view using the default brush. To momentarily switch from the painting mode into the normal perspective mode (for selecting objects), hold down the Ctrl key and select the cube rather than paint a stroke. Normally you would work without a floating panel by replacing the perspective view with the Paint Effects panel. To do so, from within any view choose **Panels → Panel → Paint Effects**. Ultimately, the best work flow is achieved by pressing the 8 key, which toggles the panel on and off.

The Paint Effects panel provides different ways for controlling its settings; one is by using global settings. From the Maya Rendering menu set (press F6), choose **Paint Effects → Paint Effects Globals** to open the Paint Effects Globals window in which you can tweak global settings for both paint environments (Canvas and Scene). Most of these settings are self-explanatory. All these attributes can be found elsewhere within the Paint Effects toolbar or the brush attributes. We will review some of them later in this chapter.

The Toolbar and Painting Basics

Press the 8 key to open the Paint Effects panel. Figure 17.6 shows the Paint Effects toolbar that is displayed in the top portion of this panel. This toolbar consists of a menu bar and an iconic toolbar that provide some shortcuts to commonly used options. Hover the mouse pointer over these icons to display a tooltip. While you are working with Paint Effects, these icons update based on the work environment (Scene vs. Canvas) as well as the selected brush; hence, some brushes reveal additional icons. The Paint menu in the panel enables switching between the Scene and Canvas work environments. Canvas is used for painting textures, and Scene enables painting directly into the scene. Switch between the two to see the difference. The following steps will provide a basic introduction for painting effects within the Paint Effects panel:

1. With the panel set to Scene, choose **Brush → Get Brush** to open the Visor window and select the airTranspRed.mel brush from the airbrush folder.

2. Paint a stroke in the Paint Effects panel. The most common way to change the stroke thickness is by simultaneously holding down the B key and the LM while dragging in the viewport. This scales the brush size, just as it does with the Artisan tool. Notice a spherical wire display growing in scale, which represents the brush tip. Another way to adjust brush scale is by opening the Template Brush window from the toolbar icon or by choosing **Brush → Edit Template Brush**. Then change the Global Scale attribute shown (partially) in Figure 17.5.

The Template Brush Settings window provides all the necessary controls for tweaking the brush settings. This window allows you to adjust pre-paint settings, in the same manner as you would adjust post-paint settings for existing brushes (3D strokes).

3. After you set the brush to a "thick" stroke, paint another stroke and then adjust the stroke display by choosing **Stroke Refresh → Rendered** from the Paint Effects toolbar. You should see a transparent red stroke in the view. Tumble in the panel and notice how the view switches on-the-fly to an interactive display mode that provides fast scene interaction.

4. From within the Paint Effects panel, choose **Stroke Refresh → Wireframe**, which switches the display to the wireframe mode. Also known as the interactive display mode, this is used to display Paint Effects in other views outside the Paint Effects panel. If the Paint Effects panel display has not updated the display mode to wireframe, it is because OpenGL views require some sort of view change, such as tumbling the view, to force an update. The panel also provides a separate menu for controlling the scene geometry shading from within the Object Shading menu; thus, you can display 3D models in wireframe while looking at rendered strokes.

Controlling Strokes

When you paint a stroke in the view, it is painted into the scene depth on the perspective grid based on the brush position. As you move the brush higher up, you are actually painting farther in depth (usually along the Z axis). You can see this by the Paint Effects tool, which scales in size based on its position in depth (top to bottom in the view). Tumble the view to see the stroke positioned along the scene grid. Open the Paint Effects tool attributes in the Stroke Settings rollout (see Figure 17.7) by choosing **Brush → Tool Settings**. When the Paint At Depth attribute is disabled (by default), you paint on the grid as you have been doing so far. Thus, when painting a stroke from top to bottom, you are actually painting from farther away from the camera toward the screen. If you enable Paint At Depth, you will notice that the paint brush tip changes from a spherical representation to a circle that also scales based on the pointer's location in the view. In this mode, your first click within the view initiates a stroke depth, meaning a depth "slice" is selected for painting. The pointer selects a location in depth, which enables painting at that depth "slice" on an imaginary grid. For example, if the scene orientation is Z forward and Y up, the pointer will select a depth slice along the Z axis and paint onto the XY plane rather than the grid when you paint a stroke.

Figure 17.7

The Stroke Settings rollout, where you set your brush settings for painting

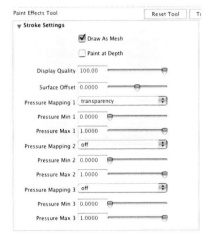

The pressure mapping attributes provide a way to control the stroke when using a tablet. Thus, you can map the tablet to influence almost any brush attributes as well as set a min and max range of influence.

The Draw As Mesh attribute controls the interactive display for the stroke, providing a choice for whether the stroke is displayed as a curve or as a mesh. The mesh display provides a better representation of what Paint Effects look like in the perspective view. Create a new scene and select the dahliaRed.mel brush (under flowers). Enable Draw As Mesh and disable Paint At Depth; then paint a stroke in the Paint Effects panel. Disable Draw As Mesh and paint another stroke to see the difference. To display the interactive mode in the Paint Effects panel, set Stroke Refresh to Wireframe. Press the 8 key to toggle to perspective. Both strokes appear in the same interactive mode and thus maintain their display settings; one is displayed as a mesh and the other as curve (see Figure 17.8).

If your plants seem dark, you might want to disable Force Real Lights. Choose **Paint Effects → Paint Effects Globals → Scene**.

Figure 17.8

Curve and mesh display modes seen in the perspective view. Mesh display provides reasonable reference for the Paint Effects render appearance, at the cost of slower scene interaction.

In the perspective view, select the mesh stroke and display the strokeShape section in the Attribute Editor (see Figure 17.9). This window, as opposed to the Stroke Settings window, provides control over existing strokes using the same attributes. Thus, once a stroke has been drawn, you can still tweak the stroke "drawing" settings. Setting Display Quality is straightforward; move the slider to see the effect. Toggle Draw As Mesh on or off, providing control over each stroke's display. This sort of display characteristic (Draw As Mesh) can be applied with any brush whether it's a traditional or effects brush. Other useful features are the Min Clip and Max Clip settings in the End Bounds rollout. This enables clipping the amount of tubes that emit along the stroke. Your stroke should have a few sprouting flowers. Reduce the Max Clip value to see how it clips flowers from the stroke as well as shortens the curve display.

> Min and max clipping is useful when working with a large number of tubes that emit from a stroke (for example, several trees). You can tweak values while displaying an individual tree and when satisfied display the remaining trees.

By now you should know how to create 3D Paint Effects strokes in your perspective view or in the Paint Effects panel. When you paint in 3D, for each stroke in the Attribute Editor, there are the four nodes (transform, stroke, brush, and time), which we examined earlier in the section "Understanding Strokes and Brushes." The Template Brush Settings window provides the same settings available within the brush node for an existing stroke, as in the case of the flower. The flower's brush settings in the Attribute Editor window should read dahliaRed1, with all the brush attributes displayed below it. Now let's examine some brush basics with painting on a 2D canvas in the Paint Effects panel.

Figure 17.9

The Stroke attribute settings for an existing selected stroke can be used to toggle mesh display on and off, as well as to set several other stroke appearance settings.

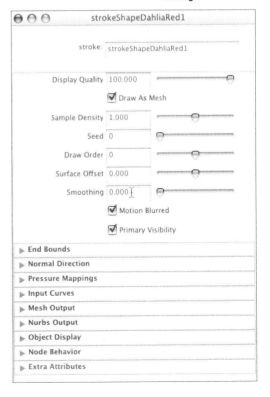

2D Canvas Painting

Like all 2D paint programs, Maya's Paint Effects has pros and cons. Some of the pros are its ability to easily paint textures while displaying the result in 3D, to create tileable textures, and to use a variety of unconventional paint brushes that also respect depth values in 2D. The cons are that the standard paint programs support more features, such as layering, blending modes, masking, color corrections, and filters. From an artistic perspective, working with Paint Effects is much like working with a real canvas, enabling you to smear, blur, and erase paint strokes as well as blend colors and brushes. At that level, it is a powerful and responsive tool that is well integrated into Maya. Another great advantage is the ability to paint textures in real time on objects in the scene, alleviating the typical strictly polygon limitation found with most third-party 3D paint programs.

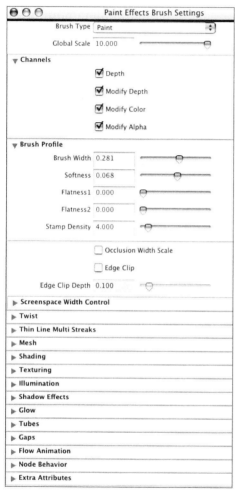

When you choose **Paint → Paint Canvas** from the Paint Effects panel toolbar, a few options that are typically used when painting on the canvas appear in the toolbar. The toolbar Canvas menu provides standard controls that include setting image size and color, as well as controlling wrapping effects used for creating seamless textures. Choosing **Canvas → Canvas Undo** is good for only one undo level and is the only way you can undo 2D canvas strokes. Zooming and tracking in the canvas is the same as with other orthographic views. Choose **Canvas → New Image** to open the Paint Effects New Texture window, select a resolution and background color, and apply the settings.

Select a brush by clicking the Get Brush icon, and then paint a few strokes on the canvas. To clear the canvas, click the Clear Canvas icon, which is the first icon on the left of the toolbar. You can save a canvas as an image file by choosing **Canvas → Save As**, and you can export the alpha channel within the image. You can also save the depth channel as an image file (RGB not Z depth) by choosing **Paint → Save Depth As Grayscale**. These Paint Effects images are normally saved in the sourceimages folder in the project folder.

Using Brushes in 2D

As with all brush settings, you can choose whether to adjust values for the template brush, or you can adjust settings for an existing brush in the Attribute Editor. With respect to painting in 2D, these settings always need to be applied on the template brush since strokes on canvas don't create brush nodes that can later be adjusted.

Figure 17.10

You use the Brush Settings section to adjust the brush characteristics before applying a stroke.

Let's examine some of the brush features while painting onto the canvas; note that they work the same way while painting in 3D. Open the Paint Effects Brush Settings window (choose **Paint Effects → Template Brush Settings** or press Ctrl+B) and keep it handy. Figure 17.10 shows the brush settings.

Brush Types

Open the Visor window, select a brush, and then paint a few strokes onto the canvas, making sure you adjust the scale by holding down the B key. If you have a pressure sensitive tablet, you will see that it reacts appropriately. After you paint a few strokes, select a traditional brush (crayon, airbrush, or pastel) and change the brush type to Smear in the

Template Brush Settings window. When you paint over the previous strokes, you will see how this provides a way to smear paint. The Thin Line and Mesh types are meant to be used only when painting in 3D and will be examined later in this chapter.

The Channels Section

You use the options in the Channels section (brush settings) to specify which channels will be painted onto the canvas or rendered when painting in the scene. Disable Modify Alpha and paint another stroke on the canvas. Then display the alpha channel by clicking the Display Alpha Channel icon on the Paint Effects panel toolbar. You will see that the stroke has no alpha, unlike previous strokes, which all have alphas.

When you are painting on the canvas, each brush also paints into the depth channel, which enables better brush integration. Normally, if you paint two strokes, the second is on top of the first. When Depth is enabled (the default), the stroke is painted with a depth channel. Modify Depth enables interaction with existing depth values from other strokes. Figure 17.11 shows different color noodles painted with two strokes, using both Depth and Modify Depth. Notice how the different noodle strokes interact based on their depth values. Figure17.12 shows the depth channels for this image, which was exported with the Paint menu. You can see how depth is retained while drawing on a 2D canvas.

Figure 17.11

Painting strokes with depth on the canvas. Notice how the strokes interact, retaining their depth value—a truly unique characteristic among paint programs.

Figure 17.12

The depth channel that was created while painting Figure 17.11. In this image, the difference between "noodles" closer to the camera (in white) and those farther away (gradually darkening) is clear.

The Brush Profile Section

The Brush Profile section is where you set the size and general painting behaviors of the brush. Clear the canvas, and from the Visor window choose **Brush → Get Brush → Grasses**. Select the astroturf.mel brush, paint a stroke on the canvas, increase the Brush Width value, and paint another stroke. This scales the region of effect for each brush, in contrast with Global Scale, which scales the entire effect. To clarify, when you are painting grass, Global Scale increases the scale of each grass blade; Brush Width provides more coverage in the scene using the same scale. Clear the canvas and select the default paint brush from the airbrush folder. Paint a line on the canvas, and adjust the Softness attribute that feathers the borders. Theoretically you can feather the borders of trees, plants, and any other brush. Reset the brush settings by choosing **Brush → Reset Template Brush**.

Earlier we mentioned that using Paint (brush type) stamps images along the stroke, as opposed to other brush types. Select the cumulus.mel brush from the clouds folder and paint a stroke. Now change Stamp Density to 0.1 and draw another stroke; notice that only one stamp appears. Change Stamp Density to 1 and draw yet another stroke. Notice that the images are stamped based on this value; the higher it goes, the more dense the stamping. If you change to the Thin Line brush type, Stamp Density is disabled since it is irrelevant for this type of brush, which doesn't utilize stamping.

Tubes

Paint Effects strokes can basically be categorized according to whether a stroke emits tubes. To enable emitting tubes, you can click the Make Tubes icon on the toolbar or choose **Paint Effects → Template Brush Settings → Tubes** and enable the Tubes section (see Figure 17.13). This enables emitting tubes for both 2D and 3D strokes. The other main attribute found under the Tubes section is Tube Completion, which determines whether a tube will stop "sprouting" when you stop painting and is demonstrated with a small exercise later, because it is best seen in 3D. The sections within the Tubes section, such as the Creation section, provide further control over specific tube characteristics, meaning fine-tuning how tubes are drawn on the canvas or in the scene.

Select any simple airbrush from the Visor window and enable Tubes. Notice that the moment tubes are enabled, additional icons appear in the Paint Effects panel toolbar. These icons include the Tubes Per Step (TS) setting, which can also be found in the Creation section, within the Tubes section of the Template Brush Settings window. Tubes Per Step defines the number of tubes that emit from the stroke. Note that Tubes Per Step is not the total number of tubes along a stroke but rather a multiplier that controls the amount of tubes for a given distance, based internally (the calculation is hidden from the user) on points along the stroke. Needless to say, increasing TS will greatly increase the number of tubes that emit along the stroke. With Tubes enabled, paint a stroke and notice that you no longer define paint along the stroke but rather emit

Figure 17.13

The Tubes section, the heart of Paint Effects, enables you to sprout or emit effects from the stroke.

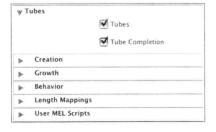

paint (tubes) in random directions from the stroke's "path." Increase the TS value using the slider to the right of TS within the toolbar and draw additional strokes and more tubes appear to sprout along the stroke.

To see how the Tube Completion attribute works, from the toolbar, choose **Paint → Paint Scene** (if prompted, there is no need to save), choose **Brush → Get Brush → Trees → treeBareBrown.mel**, and start painting a stroke in the view. When you see the third tree begin to sprout, release the mouse button (or lift the tablet pen). Notice that the paint effect automatically completes. Thus, while painting with Tube Completion turned on (the default), Paint Effects automatically finishes sprouting each effect to its full potential.

Disable Tube Completion from the Template Brush Settings window and then start painting another stroke just as before. This time when you stop painting, Paint Effects also will stop sprouting tubes. Basically all effects that "sprout" from the stroke appear with some time delay, especially when you're painting in 3D. When Tube Completion is disabled, the Paint Effects taper down toward the end of the stroke instead of automatically complete "growing." Press 8 to toggle to perspective and select the stroke. In the brush's Attribute Editor, display the Tubes section and toggle Tube Completion on and off to see the attribute's effect.

Additional 2D Brush Settings

By now you have gained a good fundamental understanding for creating 2D and 3D paint effects. The following sections examine additional settings for controlling brush appearances. These include color controls as well as controls for blending brushes, as you would with traditional painting. In addition, we look at creating a tileable texture for a 3D surface as well as directly painting textures on surfaces. The ability to paint directly on surfaces is extremely powerful, especially for creating texture hold-out masks for procedural shaders. To clarify, using Paint Effects we can directly paint white to black masks on a surface and export them as images to be used as hold-out masks within a shading network, to control transparency along the surface, for example. This is just one powerful advantage gained with the ability to paint textures directly on surfaces within Maya instead of a third-party application.

Color, Transparency, and Incandescence

In the Canvas view, for each stroke that you paint, you can set color, transparency, and incandescence values in the Template Brush Settings window Shading section or from the toolbar in the Paint Effects panel. With 3D, you can further refine these values using the Shading section for an existing stroke. You use the toolbar C and T sliders to define the stroke's color and transparency. When using tubes, C and T define the tube's base values, and C2 and T2 define the tip color and transparency. To find these additional settings, which are available only when tubes are enabled, choose **Shading → Tube Shading**. Some of these attributes involve randomizing the hue, saturation, or value as well as setting incandescence for tubes. To see these settings in action, create a new scene and experiment with them using the noodles brush.

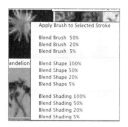

Figure 17.14

Blending brushes provides almost unlimited creative opportunities and acts much like an artist's paint palette.

Blending Brushes

Blending brushes is much like mixing colors, with the added benefit of mixing unique Paint Effects brushes.

1. Select the vineLeafyThick.mel brush from the plants folder and draw a stroke.

2. From the flowersMesh folder, right-click tigerBud.mel and notice that a few blending options appear (see Figure 17.14).

3. Select Blend Brush 50% and draw a stroke (see Figure 17.15). You just created vine leaves with tiger buds—now that's cool, especially when you realize this also applies in 3D.

Blend Brush blends both shading and shape. If you choose Blend Shading, the shading will transfer. If you select Blend Shape, the original shape changes and the shading is preserved. For example, selecting the daffodil.mel brush and Blend Shading 100% with the roseRed.mel brush creates red daffodils. An additional window makes blending brushes more intuitive. Choose **Paint Effects → Preset Blending** to open the Preset Blending window. Any brush you select will mix based on the current settings within the preset. Experiment with these settings and mix more than two brushes at a time to discover yet another powerful Paint Effects feature.

Figure 17.15

A figment of imagination, vine leaves with tiger buds, easily made possible by blending brushes

You can select a new brush in the Preset Blending window by setting both Shading and Shape to 100%.

After you create a brush, saving it is fairly straightforward. Choose **Paint Effects → Save Brush Preset** to open the Save Brush Preset window (see Figure 17.16), which displays the current brush settings. Enter a name and overlay label (overlay text displayed over the shelf icon) and then define an icon. With the Paint Effects panel open, select Grab Icon and drag a selection marquee over a portion of the painted stroke, which grabs that area as an icon for the brush. Choose whether to save it into the Visor Paint Effects folders, which then requires you to select the appropriate folder, or the shelf, which then adds the brush and icon to the Paint Effects shelf.

Figure 17.16

Saving your own brush preset as well as defining a custom icon directly from the Paint Effects panel

Creating Tileable Textures

When you are painting in 2D, the canvas can wrap around both U and V (horizontally and vertically), thus providing a way to easily create tileable textures. To set this up, click the two arrow icons from the toolbar, Wrap U and V, or choose **Canvas → Wrap** and select one of the two options. Figure 17.17 shows an image that has been painted using the wrap features and tiled several times in a paint program. To shift an image so that you can see how it tiles, choose **Canvas → Roll → 50% Horizontal**. This shifts the horizontal image corner halfway into the canvas so that you can inspect the seam.

Figure 17.17

Tileable textures using the Wrap feature. Notice that the upper-left corner is tiled repeatedly.

Painting Textures in Real Time

You can paint or edit an object's texture in two ways: you can adjust the texture in the canvas or paint directly onto the object. Split the view layout into two panels side by side, one for perspective and the other for the Paint Effects panel canvas mode, and then follow these steps:

1. Create a NURBS sphere, and from the Rendering menu set (press F6) choose **Texturing → 3D Paint Tool** □. In the File Textures section, select Color under Attribute To Paint, and then click Assign/Edit Textures to open a window in which you can define the file texture resolution, format, and similar attributes. Click Assign/Edit Textures again. Now a texture file is assigned to the color channel for the sphere. If you already have a texture assigned, you only need to specify which channel to use. Once a channel is selected, paint strokes are then applied to that channel, meaning that color is added to that channel's texture file. Channels include the different color channels available from under the assigned shader, such as color, transparency, ambient color, specular color, and any other color channel that may be mapped with a texture file.

2. You can start painting a texture in the perspective view using Paint Effects brushes by enabling Paint Effects in the Brush section. To do so, click the Last Brush icon on the left or click the Get Brush icon farthest to the right. Notice that the two icons on the right enable editing the Paint Effects brush settings as well as selecting a brush directly from the Visor window, much like tools available in the Paint Effects panel (same icons). Select Get Brush, select a plant brush, and start painting on the sphere. In the File Textures section, select Save Textures, which will write a texture file to the 3DPaintTextures folder in the project folder. (Save the scene beforehand.)

3. Now let's use the canvas to edit the texture we created. In the Paint Effects panel (Canvas mode), choose **Canvas → Open Image**, browse to the 3DPaintTextures folder, and load the image we just saved. (This could be any image, regardless of the 3D texturing tool.) Apply some color to it in the canvas.

4. Finally, to display the changes, choose **Canvas → Auto Save** from the panel menu, which automatically saves the image after every stroke and updates the texture displayed on the sphere in the perspective view when Hardware Texturing is enabled (by pressing the 6 key).

Figure 17.18

The main Paint Effects menu available from the Rendering menu set

3D Paint Effects

We have already discussed much of what there is to know about the similarities of painting in 3D and painting on a 2D canvas, but with 3D there are even more Paint Effects options. In the following sections, we primarily focus on brush settings found in the Attribute Editor or on options available from the Paint Effects main menu (see Figure 17.18).

Work in the Paint Effects panel only when you need to see the rendered effect; otherwise, for better performance, use the perspective view. Press the 8 key regularly to toggle between views. Don't forget that you can also switch the Paint Effects display from mesh to curve under the Stroke settings.

Painting onto Geometry

Paint Effects enables painting 3D effects directly onto geometry surfaces. To see this for yourself, in a new scene create a NURBS sphere and scale it up a bit. In the Rendering menu set (press F6), choose **Paint Effects → Make Paintable** to enable painting directly onto the sphere surface. Open the Visor window, choose **Feathers → downRed.mel Brush**, and then draw several strokes onto the sphere surface. Notice how the strokes follow the sphere surface curvature. An excellent use for this is painting grass or plants over a terrain surface, immediately filling the scene with natural elements and providing for a less sterile environment.

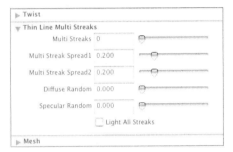

When objects that have strokes painted on their surface deform or move, the stroke "sticks" to the surface. Apply a Lattice deformer from the Create Deformers menu in the Animation menu set, and deform the sphere. Notice how the strokes are appropriately affected. If you display the Paint Effects Tool settings and enable Paint At Depth, the first point you select on the surface selects the depth slice. From that point on, that depth is maintained as you paint.

Paint Effects can produce great hair simulations. For example, you might use Paint Effects for sideburns, which stick to the face as they deform with blend shapes. (And unlike the Hair module, Paint Effects ships with Maya Complete.)

Figure 17.19

Thin Line brush settings in the Attribute Editor for a selected stroke. These settings are used to control how additional tubes sprout along each "initial" tube. Thin Line is great for creating Paint Effects hair, Maya Hair, and toon outlines.

The Thin Line Brush Type

Thin Line is an alternative brush type for rendering effects that require a large number of tubes in a typically dense form without any significant volume (per tube), such as hair. The Thin Line method renders tubes directly without stamping images along its path. You can use this method with additional multistreak attributes (see Figure 17.19) that provide a way to greatly increase the number of "hairs" surrounding a single tube and renders up to 100 times faster than the default Paint brush type. Keep in mind that Thin Line brushes excel at rendering high-quality lines and should not be used with objects that require volume, such as trees. This is a great brush for rendering Paint Effects strokes with Maya Hair or Toon Shading. Using Thin Line as a brush type for toon outlines can form some really complex and cool-looking effects.

Let's look at how we can create a single stroke of hair. In the following section we'll look at how to share the brush we'll use with several other strokes to cover the head with hair.

1. Open the `Hair01.mb` scene from the CD. Select the head model, and choose **Paint Effects → Make Paintable**. Toggle to the Paint Effects panel, and from the Visor window, select a hair brush from the hair folder. Draw a stroke along the head's surface.

2. Thin Line provides better tools to make this single stroke appear denser. Press Ctrl to momentarily disable the paint mode, select the stroke, and then display the Brush tab in the Attribute Editor. Under Brush Type, select ThinLine, which enables the attributes in the Thin Line Multi Streaks section.

3. Increase the Multi Streak attribute to about 5. You should see that the render in the Paint Effects panel displays more tubes around that stroke.

You control the multistreak offset from the stroke center line with the Multi Streak Spread 1 and Multi Streak Spread 2 attributes. Multi Streak Spread 1 controls the offset of the tubes at the base of the stroke, and Multi Streak Spread 2 controls the offset at the tips. Thus, you can make the hair appear to spread out more at the top (see Figure 17.20). Diffuse and Specular Random provide a way to randomize both the diffuse and specular brightness to make it appear more natural, and Light All Streaks forces the render to apply lighting to each tube.

FORWARD TWIST

The Twist section in the Paint Effects Brush Settings window provides some additional features for controlling the Paint Effects display that can optimize performance. These attributes work well when you choose **Brush Profile → Flatness 1 and 2**, which flattens the tube's tip and base. Open the `twist.mb` scene from the CD, and select the tree. Set Flatness 1 And 2 to a value of 1. Notice how the tree loses volume and converts to flat geometry. From a performance point of view, there are fewer polygons to calculate, which is an improvement. Thus when the tree would be viewed from a side angle, it would appear flat, just like a 2D card surface (such as a geometrical plane surface). A common trick when using 2D cards for planting images such as tress or people into a 3D scene is to ensure that they always face the camera. This means their flat side is never made visible during the render. In Paint Effects, this technique can be applied by choosing **Twist → Forward Twist,** which will constantly orient the tree so that it faces the camera. Enable the Forward Twist attribute and notice how the poly faces are always facing forward regardless of the camera's position. Forward twist and flatness don't work well with Paint Effects that have been converted to 3D, although you can use flatness for artistic reasons.

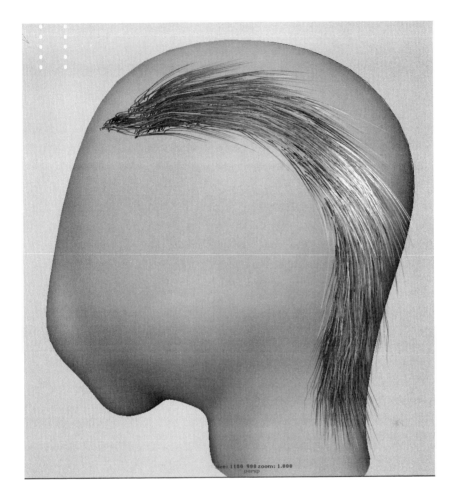

Figure 17.20

An example of one Thin Line stroke using multistreaks to increase the number of strokes (tubes) visible along the initial stroke

Sharing and Transferring Brushes

You must have noticed that every time you paint a stroke, a new brush is attached to it. If you want to paint several strokes that share the same brush, you can use the Share One Brush option; here's a quick demonstration.

1. Open the Hair02.mb scene from the CD. This scene has an initial stroke of hair on the head. The hair has been tweaked with the Path Follow Brush and Path Attract attributes appropriately. You'll see more on this in the "Hands On" section later in this chapter.

2. Using several brushes, draw strokes over the head surface to fully cover the hair region. Even when using the same brush settings, you will need to tweak each stroke separately under its brush settings.

Figure 17.21

After you enable Brush Sharing for several strokes, all brushes conform to the last selected brush, which makes controlling several brushes an easy task.

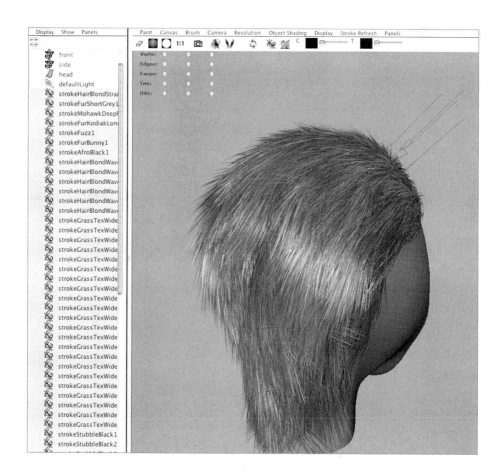

3. In the Outliner, select all the strokes you created. The last stroke should be the primary stroke, in this case strokeShapeHairBlondStraight1. This is the brush we want to apply to the rest of the strokes. Choose **Paint Effects → Share One Brush**, which then applies the brush settings to the selected strokes, as shown in Figure 17.21. Any settings you change on this brush will apply to all the strokes. If at some point you want to detach the brush, select Remove Brush Sharing. Each stroke is then adjusted from its own brush settings. You can examine the scene Hair03.mb on the CD.

Using Control Curves

Control curves are merely curves you might have created using the CV tool and are used as attractor paths for tubes, for example, to stylize hair. Let's quickly examine a scene to get a better handle on this.

1. Open the ControlCurve.mb scene from the CD. You will find three curves on top of the sphere and a stroke of hair that has been painted on the sphere surface.

2. Select strokeHairThatGirl1 and Curve1, and then choose **Paint Effects ⇸ Curve Utilities ⇸ Set Stroke Control Curves**. Immediately you see the hair wrap around the curve.

3. Select strokeHairThatGirl1 and Curves 2 and 3, and then reapply Set Stroke Control Curves to add influence from the remaining curves. Notice that the top curve has no more influence. When you add new curves, the previous curves are disabled. To remedy this, select the stroke and all three curves and then reapply them as control curves.

4. In the Stroke Attribute Editor, choose **Input Curves ⇸ Control Curve** to display the curves that currently influence your stroke. To control the effect of these curves, navigate under the brush (hairThatGirl1) attributes and choose **Tubes ⇸ Behavior ⇸ Forces**. The Curve Follow, Curve Attract, and Curve Max Dist attributes control how tubes react to control curves. Figure 17.22 shows the sphere using control curves.

5. Set Curve Follow and Curve Attract to 0. Curve Follow makes tubes try to flow in the same direction as the curves. Gradually increase this value to see this effect. Curve Attract attracts the tubes toward the curve path. Gradually increase this value to see how, when Curve Attract is combined with Curve Follow, the hair wraps around the curves. Curve Max Dist controls the distance in world units that the curves will apply influence. If this attribute is set to 0, there is no distance limit.

Figure 17.22

Control Curves lets you stylize tubes by attracting them to curves. In this case, three spiral curves influence different strokes on a sphere.

The Mesh Brush Type and Displacement Mapping

You use the Mesh brush type to render Paint Effects brushes based on triangulation rather than on the default stamping method. This method is better for rendering geometric Paint Effects such as plants, trees, buildings, and some other miscellaneous brushes. The Visor window provides some default Mesh brushes, which are better with this brush type; however, that doesn't prevent you from converting any other brush to this type using the Brush Type attribute. Mesh brushes provide an ability to better render flat and hard-edge surfaces, and they extend Paint Effects's ability to render displacement mapping, environment reflections, and more precise texture mapping coordinates based on an actual 3D mesh. The Mesh brush type enables attributes found in the Mesh section (see Figure 17.23). These attributes control some of these characteristics, which are disabled with other brush types.

Open the MeshBrush01.mb scene from the CD. This scene includes a Mesh brush that has been converted to 3D. (See the section "Converting Paint Effects to 3D Geometry" later in the chapter.) The reason for this conversion has nothing to do with the Mesh brush abilities; it is simply easier to view some of its characteristics on actual geometry. All the attributes we examine work exactly the same with the corresponding Paint Effects stroke. You will also see that even after you convert a brush to 3D, it maintains a direct connection with the attributes under the brush settings.

Mesh brush tessellation has three primary elements: length and width divisions and subdivision levels. Divisions along the tube length remain a function of the Segments attribute, which is true for all brush types and specifies how flexible the tube is when deformed or, in other words, how smooth the tube curvature is when it deforms. Segments can be found in the Attribute Editor for a selected stroke under the **Tubes ▸ Creation** section. Select the brush in perspective and increase Segments to 20 (under roseRed1). Notice that the divisions along the tube length increase.

Figure 17.23

The Mesh section under the brush settings in the Attribute Editor for a selected stroke controls the mesh quality for Mesh brush types. You primarily use the Sub Segments slider for better displacement mapping.

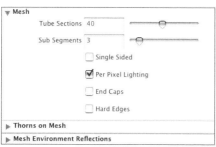

In the Brush Attribute Editor, expand the Mesh section (see Figure 17.23). Tube Sections controls the divisions along the width of the mesh. Increase this value to 13 and notice that this transforms this four-corner tube into a round tube. Sub Segments further subdivides each polygon, increasing tessellation exponentially. However, when used with mesh brushes (not converted geometry), Sub Segments influences only displacement calculation. Thus, if there is no displacement, its value is irrelevant. Increase this value to 3 and notice that the mesh gets denser. Sub Segments is the reason for converting the stroke to a 3D polygon mesh. This attribute is not visible with Paint Effects brushes that have not been converted, and hence we are using a converted stroke to visually see its effect for the purpose of this tutorial.

Sub Segments is used to improve the quality of displacement mapping, which is only supported with Mesh brush types. Furthermore, Mesh brushes only support displacement mapping using the displacement option under the brush settings for a selected stroke. You can find this feature under Map Displacement section (within the Texturing section), which can be enabled when using a Mesh brush. Needless to say, you can use a converted stroke with any type of displacement mapping because it is geometry in the scene rather than a Paint Effects brush. Enable the Map Displacement attribute from the Texturing section. You should see how the surface bumps out based on the texture (checker map); however, the quality is poor. Increase Tube Sections to 60, Sub Segments to 6, and Segments to 30. You now should have an object similar to Figure 17.24. Notice how these attributes control tube tessellation. If you had used the nonconverted version of this tube, you would see this exact same effect only within the Paint Effects panel render mode.

Under Map Displacement for a selected stroke, there are additional attributes that control surface displacement. Displacement Scale controls the displacement intensity, and Displacement Offset displaces regardless of tube width. Adjust these values to see their effect. Bump Intensity and Bump Blur relate to the bump factor just as with regular Maya shaders, meaning that they are independent from the displacement mapping. The Bump Intensity attribute works if you enable Per Pixel Lighting in the Mesh section.

To display other options for Mesh brush types, go to the Mesh Environment Reflections section (found within the Mesh section). These options enable faking environmental reflections. These are mapped reflections that can be tweaked with the various attributes found in this tab; however, they will not reflect actual geometry in the scene. If you want Paint Effects brushes to reflect real geometry in the scene, your only option is to convert to 3D and use a standard reflection shader. To display one last Mesh-related option, Thorns On Mesh, which enables growing thorns from the geometric faces and can be tweaked using the settings below, which are fairly straightforward. Thorns On Mesh doesn't convert to 3D, thus it only works with Paint Effects Mesh brush strokes.

> Choose **Paint Effects → Mesh Quality Attributes** to display a collection of Mesh-related attributes, normally found under various brush tabs. These attributes let you conveniently tweak Mesh quality settings for either strokes or 3D converted strokes.

Brush Illumination and Texturing

Paint Effects controls illumination and texturing from its internal shading engine, which allows access to several control settings through the Brush Attribute Editor. Some of these settings include options for influencing Paint Effects with scene lights, faking shadows, making tubes glow, and using your own file textures for mapping.

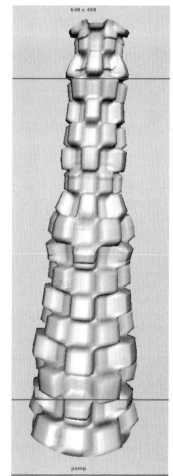

Figure 17.24

Mesh displacement mapping controlled in the Mesh and Texturing sections. This Paint Effects brush had to be converted to a polygon mesh to enable previewing displacement mapping in perspective; otherwise, this effect would only be displayed within the Paint Effects panel in stroke-rendered mode.

Texturing

We reviewed the basic color attributes for Paint Effects in the section "Using Brushes in 2D" earlier in this chapter. You were introduced to controlling stroke color as well as applying shading qualities for tubes along their length. Paint Effects lets you use textures rather than just color values. There are different texturing methods, and each has specific behaviors. Texturing is controlled in the Texturing section (see Figure 17.25) and is combined with the shading values when enabled.

In the Texturing section, you can choose whether to map color, opacity, and displacement (displacement only for Mesh brushes) using the options in the Texture Type drop-down list. You can choose to map an image file, a checker map, a U or V ramp, or a fractal map. All provide control over the brush texturing. Furthermore, each type can use different mapping algorithms available from the Map Method attribute. If you choose to use an image file, you can load an external file by browsing to an image under the Image Name attribute, which is at the lower portion of this section. A good understanding of Maya texturing (see Chapter 12) makes this section self-explanatory.

The quality of displacement mapping is based primarily on available geometry for displacing the surface; see "The Mesh Brush Type and Displacement Mapping" in this chapter for more details. When enabled, opacity mapping is controlled by the Tex Alpha 1 and Tex Alpha 2 attributes, which define transparency for the Tex Color1 and Tex Color2. Let's look at an example.

1. Open the `texturing.mb` scene from the CD and select the stroke. Enter the Paint Effects panel, Paint Scene mode, and choose **Stroke Refresh → Rendered**. You should see the textured tube in your Paint Effects panel. Display the Texturing section in the Attribute Editor for the selected brush (roseRed1).

2. In the Texture Type drop-down list, select Checker; notice how the texture on the selected tube updates in the Paint Effects panel's OpenGL rendered preview. Change Repeat U and V to 15 and 5.

3. Enable Map Opacity; notice how the textured tube becomes partially transparent. To make the white checkers transparent, set Tex Alpha 1 and 2 to 0 and 1.

4. Disable transparency by disabling Map Opacity and enable Map Displacement. Notice that the tube bulges (a bit) based on the checker map. Increase Displacement Scale to 2; the surface doesn't appear to change much.

5. Choose **Paint Effects → Mesh Quality Attributes** and increase Tube Sections to 20, Sub Segments to 6, and Segments to 40. Now reduce the displacement scale; it should appear similar to the exercise from the section " The Mesh Brush Type and Displacement Mapping." This clarifies how the mesh quality controls the displacement for both Paint Effects strokes and converted geometry.

To better understand these settings, create several brush strokes and investigate their texture settings.

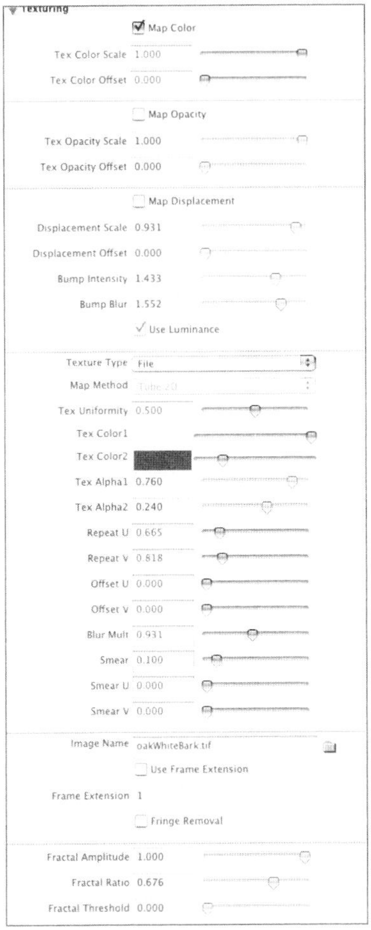

Figure 17.25

The Texturing section is the heart of Paint Effects shading, ultimately acting much like a surface shader in the Hypershade. Within this section you have control over color, opacity, displacement mapping, and loading external image files.

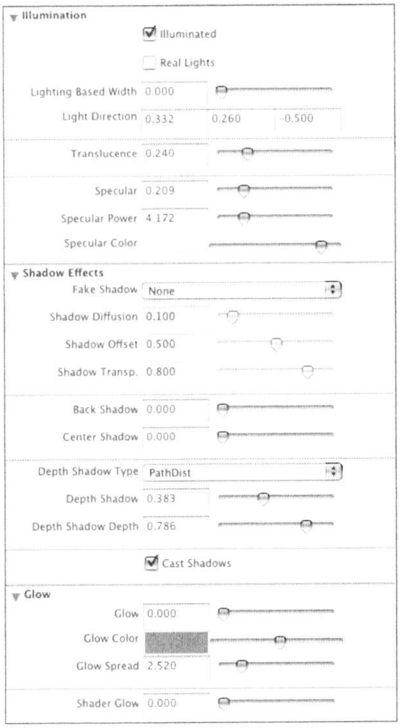

Figure 17.26

Illumination, Shadow Effects, and Glow sections under a brush node in the Attribute Editor

Illumination and Glow

Illumination and glow are controlled from their own sections, which are shown in Figure 17.26. Paint Effects can use either fake illumination or scene lights to illuminate strokes. If Illuminated is disabled, Paint Effects will not render light qualities such as specular light or react to light intensity; only the shading attributes will be used, much like using ambient light. Once Illuminated is enabled, the Paint Effects brush reacts to either the scene lights or the Paint Effects directional light settings. To clarify, if you enable the

Real Lights option, the light qualities are taken from the scene light; otherwise, you can set the light directionality and specular qualities using the settings in the Illumination tab.

You can easily set Paint Effects glow in the Glow section by setting the Glow (amount), Color, and Spread attributes, all self-explanatory. Furthermore, you can select whether to use the Paint Effects glow or Maya's Shader Glow, which work exactly the same as the Shader Glow settings. Increasing the Shader Glow attribute enables using the ShaderGlow1 material from within the Hypershade window, yielding more control over the glow effect.

Shadows

You can control shadows in Paint Effects by using real depth map shadows based on scene lights or by faking shadows based on settings in the Shadow Effects section, which is shown in Figure 17.26. To use real shadows, simply enable Cast Shadows at the bottom of the section; this option supports using depth map shadows only.

For fake shadows, Paint Effects provide some fairly decent ways to control the shadows. This includes simulating the shadow darkness within denser areas of a stroke. For example, when you're using some sort of dense Paint Effects brush, the areas near the bottom or center of the stroke should appear darker than areas near the tip, as with grass blades.

The Shadow Offset option for fake shadows works like a Photoshop Drop Shadow effect. For example, this option can be good for a Paint Effects image that is up against a wall, like the plant shown in Figure 17.27. When this type of effect is used, the Shadow Offset attribute determines the distance for offsetting the shadow on an imaginary plane behind the brush. The following attributes apply to both 2D and 3D Cast shadows. Shadow Transp provides control over shadow transparency, and Shadow Diffusion provides a means for blurring (diffusing) the shadow, thus faking a soft shadow effect, which normally would require intense shadow computation.

Figure 17.27

The effect of using 2D offset fake shadows, similar to a paint program's "drop shadow" effect. The shadow is cast behind the stroke with an offset.

Figure 17.28
Center Shadow is used to darken tubes along the stroke "curve" path, simulating light occlusion caused by tubes on the exterior portion of the stroke.

The 3D Cast option in the Fake Shadow drop-down list provides better control over fake shadows and includes some really useful features. This method is based on casting a shadow onto an imaginary plane beneath the Paint Effects stroke. The settings below Shadow Transp provide ways to fine-tune the fake shadow effects on the actual Paint Effects tubes, which define how tubes will be darkened as well as how the darkening spreads along the tube length. These settings work with both fake and real shadows, since they only influence tubes. The Back Shadow attribute is used for darkening tubes facing away from the light. The Center Shadow attribute is for darkening tubes near the center of the stroke (see Figure 17.28) and simulates some sort of light occlusion that tubes would cast on their neighboring tubes, such as the way grass blades do within a clump of grass; however, this darkens the tube uniformly along its length.

The Depth Shadow Type drop-down list provides more choices for simulating light occlusion, typically in dense clusters of tubes; this should not be used with Center Shadow. Depth Shadow adds to the Center Shadow attribute an ability to fine-tune the shadow effect along the length of the tube. If you select PathDist from the Depth Shadow Type drop-down list, the tubes near the stroke center line will be most affected by darkening; thus the interior tubes seem to be receiving less light than exterior tubes. SurfaceDepth affects areas at the lower portion of all tubes (the roots) regardless of the distance from the stroke; thus areas close to the tubes' surface appear darker. Both these options take effect only if the Depth Shadow value is greater than 0. Depth Shadow and Depth Shadow Depth control the amount of shadow effect and the extent of the shadow effect along each tube.

Figure 17.29

Shadow on the
plane created using
3D Cast Fake Shad-
ows along with Path
Distance (left) and
Surface Depth
(right) for simulating
fake light occlusion
along the tubes
themselves

Figure 17.29 compares the effects of the Path Distance and Surface Depth options. Notice that the shadows cast on the surface remain the same regardless of the method, although tube-shading qualities have changed. Open the shadow.mb scene and experiment with these attributes to learn how to control fake shadowing; for photorealism, the Shadows section is probably one of the most important found under the brush settings. First, render with 3D Cast alone, and then add Surface Depth and adjust its setting. Once you clearly see that the lower portion of the grass has darkened, switch to the Path Distance option and compare the results.

Stroke Pressure

The Stroke section in the Attribute Editor has a Pressure Mappings section that provides options for defining the pressure along the stroke for scaling any brush attribute. If you have a tablet, you can map the pressure from the tool settings. However, if you want to fine-tune pressure-mapped values, you can do so from this tab. To try this, open the glow01.mb scene from the CD. In the Pressure Mapping tab for the stroke, you will see Pressure Map 1, 2, and 3. Notice that 1 and 2 have been mapped to scale and transparency. You can adjust the range value to define the min and max values for those attributes. Change some of these values and see how the stroke immediately updates in the Paint Effects panel, rendered mode. When you go to the Pressure Scale section of Pressure Mappings, the graph depicts a decreasing curve in value, which defines the pressure values from start to end. The curve is then clamped to the range provided by the mapping Min and Max values. This method is great for making strokes appear more natural.

Gaps

You use the options in the Gaps section in the brush Attribute Editor to create intervals along the stroke path, much like a dotted line (see Figure 17.30). Open the scene used in the previous section, glow01.mb, and display the Gaps section in the Attribute Editor. View

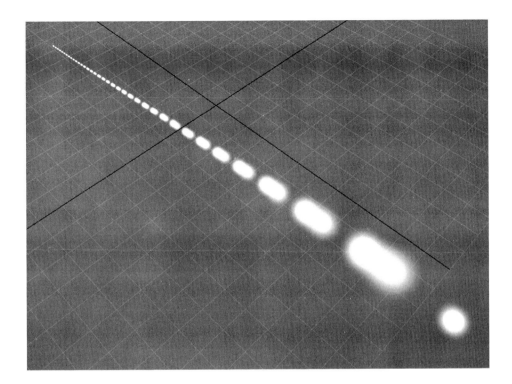

Figure 17.30

Gaps and pressure mapping make strokes look more realistic.

the scene in the Paint Effects panel, rendered mode; this allows you to see the values influenced in real time if you drag sliders slowly up and down. Adjust Gap Size and notice that this value defines the gap distance between the visible portions proportionally to the Gap Spacing attribute. At a value of 1, the stroke disappears. Gap Spacing defines the proportions between the gap size and the tube size. Gap Rand provides some sort of random offset between these values.

Paint Effects and Animation

Paint Effects provides several settings and ways to achieve brush animation. We will look at ways to mimic natural motion using the Behavior section in the tutorial at the end of this chapter. Another great place to achieve brush-based animation is in the Flow Animation section, which provides a way to animate brush growth over time (for example a flower sprouting from the ground or lightning coming down from the sky). Other ways to animate or deform Paint Effects include using springs, pressure-mapped curves, or soft body curves to control the stroke. We will experiment with flow animation and springs. A nice technique for integrating Paint Effects with Maya's dynamic engine is to paint strokes over a soft body mesh, which then deforms the curves based on the soft body motion. The motion inherited from the soft body relates to the fact that curves on surfaces will inherit surface deformations.

Flow Animation

The Flow Animation section contains options for creating unique animation with Paint Effects. These include animating texture flow (including displacement mapping) along tubes and animating tubes growing and diminishing over time. All these attributes are measured in seconds. The `FlowAnimation.mb` scene on the CD has three strokes, each on a separate layer, demonstrating different aspects of flow animation. You will also find four video clips that demonstrate the rendered results using different flow animation techniques. Two of those clips show the same brush rendered with and without Stroke Time enabled.

Flow Speed determines how fast the flow progresses, such as gaps and textures moving along the tubes, as well as the flow direction. The direction is defined by positive vs. negative numbers; positive values flow from start to end, and negative numbers flow in the opposite direction. Texture Flow determines whether the texture or gaps appear to progress along the tubes.

Time Clip enables using the remaining attributes (Stroke Time, Start Time, and End Time) to animate growth-type animations. Typically this should not be used with Texture Flow. Start Time defines when the tubes first appear, and End Time defines when tubes disappear. Thus, the difference between the two values defines a lifespan for the visible portions of the stroke.

When Stroke Time is disabled, the tubes grow from the stroke outward, thus initially appearing along the full stroke span and then gradually growing. When Stroke Time is enabled, the tubes grow from the starting point of the stroke toward the end (based on Flow Speed values of course). Finally, using the Momentum attribute (choose **Tubes → Behavior → Forces**), you can slow down the appearance of growth over time. These are best understood with some simple experimentation, which you can explore on your own using the `FlowAnimation.mb` scene.

Spring Animation

Spring animation is yet another wonderful Paint Effects feature. It lets you mimic spring-like motion for Paint Effects, such as hair reacting to motion. Let's examine this with a quick tutorial.

1. Open the `spring01.mb` scene from the CD. This scene includes a sphere with some feather strokes painted on its surface. The sphere has some animation. Scrub the Timeline to confirm that the strokes are attached to the sphere. For springs to work properly, you must have keyed animation.

2. Select all four strokes, and choose **Paint Effects → Brush Animation → Make Brush Spring** ❑. Notice that you have some settings for controlling the spring behavior. Spring Stiffness controls the spring flexibility. Higher values increase the spring effect, and a value of 0 disables spring motion. Leave these at the default, click Apply, and then scrub the Timeline; you should see the feathers reacting more naturally to motion.

Springs are added as an expression. Thus, the only way to conveniently adjust these settings is to change the settings in the Make Brush Spring option box and reapply the effect. Spring Damp controls how fast the spring reacts to the motion; lower values provide a faster reaction time.

Understanding Tubes: A Rose Tree Tutorial

So far we have discussed most of the sections and settings in the brush Attribute Editor, leaving the detailed tube-related explanations for this section. To quickly recap: Once a stroke has been drawn, you can enable tubes. If you choose not to emit tubes, all brush settings control how an effect is applied along the stroke rather than defining an effect emitting from the stroke. Let's explore some of the key features and open the door for further experimentation.

The following sections include a running tutorial and recommended exercises for visualizing tube abilities. The final tutorial scene is available on the CD (RoseTree.mb). We will create a flower tree by blending an oak tree brush with the rose flower brush. Complete all the steps in the perspective view. To see the rendered stroke, toggle to the Paint Effects panel momentarily. Note that the brush stroke should be set to Draw As Mesh. If your computer performance slows down, you can decrease Display Quality under the stroke or use the curve display for most of the time.

> Throughout this exercise, feel free to use settings of your liking. This is an artistic process, not a technical one.

Creating the Initial Rose Tree

To create the initial tree, follow these steps:

1. Open the Visor window, find oakWhiteMedium.mel in the TreesMesh folder, right-click on the oakWhiteMedium icon, and choose Apply Brush To Selected Stroke. This will set 100% of the brush stroke's influence to the white oak preset. Next, go to the flowersMesh folder and find roseRed.mel, and then right click-select Blend Brush 20%. Doing this makes the stroke influenced by 80 % oakWhiteMedium.mel and 20% roseRed.mel. Draw a stroke in the perspective view; you should have something similar to Figure 17.31.

2. With the curve selected, disable Real Lights in the Illumination section of the brush's Attribute Editor. Notice that we have a tree with thorns and small pale roses. Disable Branch Thorns by choosing Thorns On Mesh in the Mesh section. You can always add them back later. Notice that Brush Type is set to Mesh.

Figure 17.31

Blending the oak and rose brushes results in a tree with pale roses and lots of thorns. This scene will need some custom tweaking to look better.

All about Tubes

In the Tubes section of the brush's Attribute Editor (see Figure 17.13 earlier in this chapter) are three main sections—Creation, Growth, and Behavior—that are responsible for different tube characteristics. Used together, they provide several unique settings that can greatly "offset" the Paint Effects look. The options on the Creation section set the initial tube size, width orientation, and more. Growth controls how tubes branch out, and Behavior controls deformation and simulating forces such as blowing wind or turbulence.

3. To disable leaves, go to the Growth section within the Tubes section and disable Leaves. Notice that the roses look pale and disfigured; this is because we blended only 20%, maintaining more of the tree appearance. (We will address the rose appearance in the section "The Growth Section" later in this chapter.) Disable Flowers and Twigs so that you are left with about four tree trunks. If you don't see the trunks, make sure Draw As Mesh is enabled in the strokeShape tab.

4. In the Texturing section, increase Tex Alpha 1 and 2 to a value of 1. You might have noticed that the tree inherited some transparency from the flower.

The Creation Section: All about Appearances

The Creation section has a variety of settings that control the initial emission of tubes, and we have already touched on some of these attributes. Tubes Per Step defines even tube distribution between stroke steps. Tube Rand provides a means for randomizing this distribution along the stroke.

5. Set Tube Rand to zero, and increase Tubes Per Step to 0.18. You should have a fairly even distribution of trees along the stroke. Start Tubes defines how many tubes will be created on the first point of the stroke, regardless of Tubes Per Step. Increasing this value creates a cluster of tubes around that first point; experiment and see. Set Start Tubes to 0, and set Tubes Per Step to 0.1. Three or four tree trunks should be visible.

As you have already seen, Segments defines subdivisions along the tube's length. The number of segments available defines the deformation ability of the tube. Since we are using a Mesh brush type, set Tube Sections appropriately. See the section "The Mesh Brush Type and Displacement Mapping" for details.

> Once deformations are applied in the Behavior section, a change in segments can greatly change the tree's appearance. Increasing this value can "ruin" the look you've created. It is best to anticipate this and set enough segments in advance.

Segments are also used to calculate steps along a tube for animation purposes. Each distance between two segments is considered a step, regardless of the actual distance. Thus, offsetting the segment spacing acts as a means for controlling the animation progress, for example, when animating growth. You can offset the spacing with the Segment Length and Width Bias attributes. Length Min and Length Max provide a way to increase the tube height. Using the Length Max value, however, is more applicable for defining some random height between tubes. Experiment with these values.

6. Tube Width 1 and 2 define the base and tip width. Width Rand and Width Bias work together to randomize this width. Set Width Rand to 0.3, and then slide the Width Bias to see its effect.

Other settings include Width Scale, which provides a ramp for changing the tube width along its length. Each point along the ramp has a value that, when selected, can be set numerically within the Selected Value attribute or placed roughly on the ramp. Interpolation controls how the change in width is evaluated per point. Experiment with the ramp to see how you can add points and change the appearance of the tubes. Tube Direction controls whether the tubes emit outward from the stroke or along the stroke's path; toggle this value to see the change.

Figure 17.32

The Creation section settings used for this tutorial displayed in the Channel Box. Once you are familiar with the brush settings, you can easily access them from the Channel Box.

Elevation Min and Elevation Max attributes control the "Leaning Tower of Pisa" effect within the given min and max values. This makes the tubes lean toward the stroke and also forces the tube to deform. Azimuth Min and Azimuth Max act as a rotational plane for the elevation. Thus, when the tube leans down, you can force it to aim in another direction by adjusting the azimuth. Experiment with Elevation and Azimuth to see how they are related. We will continue to work using one tree by setting Start Tubes to 1 and Tubes Per Step to 0. When you're done, you can reintroduce more trees. Figure 17.32 shows the settings we used for the Creation section.

The Growth Section: Controlling Tube Branching

The Growth section (see Figure 17.33) simulates the branching of tubes from its available sections, which include Branches. The Twigs, Leaves, Flowers, and Buds options each contain several attributes that provide ways to tweak that particular characteristic. Fortunately, most (not all) of their settings are similar. Thus, once you master one, you've actually mastered them all.

Normally, Branches splits the root tube (tree trunk) into more tubes (branches). Each branch can be further divided into twigs and, of course, into leaves, flowers, and buds. With the oak tree brush that we are using, twigs branch out first from the tree trunk; then branches will split, and then twigs split and further branch out. This might seem opposite to the norm, but it is a powerful feature that you can enable in the Twigs tab. Although Branches is enabled under Tubes, no branches are visible. Go to the Twigs section to fill the tree with twigs and branches. Disable Branches and you should see just the twigs along the tree trunk.

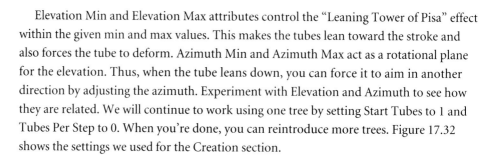

Figure 17.33

The Growth section enables additional sprouting of elements from the source stroke (tube) and is similar to L-systems.

In this case, Twigs settings control the split along the tree trunk. Normally this is controlled in the Branches section.

TWIGS

Twigs split in a radial cluster around a given point on the tube, forming an appearance similar to a palm tree when applied to a tree trunk without branches. You can control how many clusters sprout along the tube as well as several other settings to create randomness between individual twigs. This might explain why they are referred to as twigs. The difference between twigs and branches is that branches can further split into more branches, and twigs split only once along the tube. Thus twigs can be thought of as sticks distributed along a branch.

7. Go to the Twigs section in the Growth section to display the Branch After Twigs attribute, which enables you to select which comes first. With this attribute enabled, the twigs precede the branches. Go to the Branches section, disable Middle Branch, and notice the tree's appearance has greatly changed. Go to the Twigs section and you

should see branches splitting the tree trunk. Reset these values so that the twigs are visible and Branch After Twigs is enabled.

8. Twigs In Cluster and Num Twig Clusters define how many twigs exist in each cluster as well as how many clusters are created along the tube length. Set Twigs In Cluster to 2 and Num Twig Clusters to 1. You should see one cluster with two twigs. Increase Num Twig Clusters to 2, and notice how another cluster appears with two twigs. Slowly slide Twigs In Cluster up to see how it sprouts more twigs in each cluster. Leave this at 6 and 2 while you examine other attributes in this tab.

The following list provides explanations and steps to follow while adjusting the twig settings; experiment with them and eventually use values of your choice. Most of these attributes are meant to help randomize the twig appearance to make it more natural. Many of these attributes are found in other Growth sections and have a similar effect; thus, if you know one, you know them all.

Because we want to randomize the location of twigs along the tube, we'll use several clusters, each with one twig. Figure 17.34 shows the settings we used for the Twigs section.

Twigs In Cluster	1
Twig Dropout	0.177
Twig Angle1	36.179
Twig Angle2	3.393
Twig Twist	−0.315
Twig Length	0.691
Twig Start	0.523
Num Twig Clusters	14.68
Twig Base Width	0.641
Twig Tip Width	0.165
Twig Stiffness	0.342
Branch After Twigs	on

Figure 17.34

The Twigs section settings in the Channel Box

TWIGS TAB ATTRIBUTES	WHAT IT DOES
Twig Dropout	A method for randomly pruning twigs, reducing their count and providing a more natural (chaotic) feel. Increase this value to see how twigs are omitted from the clusters and thus produce a more natural appearance.
Twig Base and Tip Width	These settings are used to control the base and tip radial width for twigs: both are self-explanatory, and can easily be understood with little experimentation.
Twig Start	An initial point along the tube where twigs will start to appear. The value is a percentage of the total tube length. Slide the value between 0 and 1 to see the effect.
Twig Angle 1 and 2	These attributes define the angle between sprouting twigs and the main tube, for example the angle between branches and the tree trunk. Angle 1 relates to twigs from the surface up, and angle 2 refers to twigs at the top portion of the tree. Decrease angle 1 first, and then experiment with angle 2.
Twig Twist	This attribute is used to offset the placement of the twig clusters around the tube. It does not deform twigs so they appear twisted but rather rotates the cluster around the tube axis, offsetting its location, and always above the first twig cluster. Increase Num Twig Cluster and experiment.
Twig Stiffness	This attribute provides additional fine-tuning control over twig sensitivity to deformations applied from the Behavior tab. This value determines twig resilience to these deformations. At a value of 1, the forces have no effect.
Twig Length and Length Scale	Twig Length defines the length of each tube, and the Twig Length Scale graph provides a way to scale the length based on the cluster's position along the tube. Note that this scale factor acts uniformly on all twigs at a particular position, thus two twigs at the same "height" position along the tube's length will share the same scale. Change some of these values to see their effect.

Split Max Depth	1.802
Split Rand	0.164
Split Angle	24.873
Split Size Decay	0.7
Split Bias	0.144
Split Twist	0.453
Start Branches	0.24
Num Branches	2
Branch Dropout	0.101
Middle Branch	off
Min Size	0

Figure 17.35

The Branches sections settings in the Channel Box

BRANCHES

Now let's work on the branches.

9. Go to the Branches section to split the twigs into branches. Because we are using branches on twigs, these settings define the branch characteristics for each twig. These settings also apply the same characteristics to branches on the root tube. The main characteristic of Branches is that it enables branching out several times. Once a tube branches out, the following branch can branch out further and so forth. Let's examine this with a few simple steps. Figure 17.35 shows the final settings we used for this section.

10. Set Start Branches, Split Max Depth, and Split Rand to 0; only twigs are visible. Num Branches defines the number of branches that should be created at each split; set this to 2. Split Max Depth specifies the number of times a tube will branch out. If you increase this gradually, you will see twigs splitting along their length. Notice that the number of times each split divides is based on the Num Branches value. Start Branches defines how many branches form at the splitting point, in this case at the first split on each twig. Increase this value gradually to see its effect. For now leave it at zero.

11. To control the length of branches, go to the Twig Length section. Experiment to see the effect.

The remaining settings are similar to twig settings; prune branches with Branch Dropout. Split Angle spreads out the branches. Split Size Decay provides a way to taper the branch width along its length based on the twig scale it has branched out from. At a value of 1, they are equal in scale. Lower values make them thinner toward the end, and values greater than 1 make them appear thicker toward the end—an interesting effect. Apply settings of your liking or use the ones in Figure 17.35.

LEAVES AND FLOWERS

By now you should have no problem tweaking Leaves and Flowers. Both provide a multitude of options for controlling their appearances. Let's quickly run through the important points relevant to this tutorial.

12. Go to the Leaves section within the Growth section, which fills the tree with leaves, including on the tree trunk, again an influence from the rose brush. Go to the Leaf Location section and set On Secondary Branches Only to On. This omits leaves from the tree trunk. You can also tweak Leaf Dropout to prune some leaves as well as decrease their scale with Leaf Length.

An important option available for leaves is Leaf Forward Twist. When this option is enabled, the leaf always faces the camera so that flat edges don't appear in the render.

Recall that we created the rose bush with a Blend setting of 20%, which was enough to get the initial flowers on the brush tips. It would have been better, however, to blend at

100% so that the flowers transfer with all their color and shape instead of appearing dull. We'll fix that next.

13. Create another stroke using just the rose brush, and then copy the settings and color values under Flowers from the roses to the tree. Notice that the image file for the flowers has already been transferred but that color settings are dull and need to be corrected. This demonstrates a workaround for getting full-bodied roses on the tree branches. Figure 17.36 shows the settings we used for the flowers.

We are now ready to start deforming the tree to make it look more interesting, as well as add some natural forces to simulate a wind breeze. At this point, your tree should look similar to Figure 17.37.

When you render the tree, it may seem rigid. Since this is a Mesh brush, Map Displacement is probably applied to the tree. You can either decrease Sub Segments to 1, which leaves little displacement, or greatly increase this value.

THE BEHAVIOR SECTION: DEFORMATION AND NATURAL MOTION SIMULATIONS

The Behavior section of the Attribute Editor provides additional choices for deforming and animating Paint Effects. As always, the best way to understand settings is by experimenting with them. For now, in the Growth section, disable all options except Twigs. Now only the initial tube and twigs are visible.

THE DISPLACEMENT SECTION

The Displacement section provides several ways to deform tubes as well as control the amount of deformation along the tubes' length. These include Noise, Wiggle, and Curl, which all affect the tubes in different ways. The Frequency value for each deformer controls the amount of deformation along the tube; thus, high-frequency values provide a lot of "curls" or lots of "noise" along the tube. The Offset values provide a way to offset each effect that, when animated, can yield a flowing appearance—for example, noise flowing across the tube. Move this slider for each of these deformers to get an idea of how this might look animated.

Finally, Displacement Delay, which is the first attribute in the Displacement section, provides a way to taper the influence from all other forces under this section. This "delays" the effect from kicking along the tube's length. Thus, when you diminish these deformations toward the tube base—for example, when used with Curl—the curls can seem to taper toward the tip, based on how much curl effect is applied. Experiment with these values. See if you can create a spiral tube that tapers toward the base or tip, and make sure that no other forces are applied while you experiment. Figure 17.38 shows the settings used for both the Displacement and Forces sections.

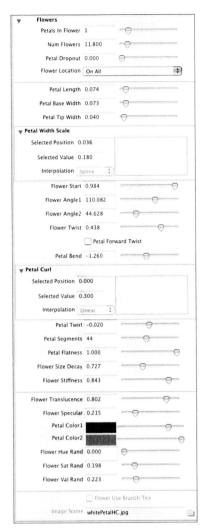

Figure 17.36

The transferred settings from a rose brush to a tree brush, displayed in the tree Attribute Editor

Figure 17.37
The rose tree with red roses at the tips

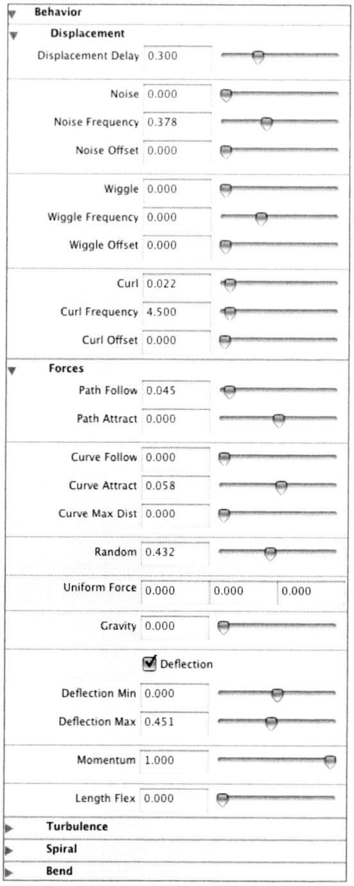

Figure 17.38
Displacement and Forces attribute values in the Attribute Editor for the rose tree

FORCES

This section provides some interesting options for creating different appearances. Figure 17.39 shows the same tree with different settings. The Path Follow attribute provides a way to influence whether tubes follow along the stroke path or the normal direction, similar to going to the Tube Direction section within the Creation section. Path Attract makes the tree tip appear to lean down toward the stroke path. Experiment using positive and negative numbers with both these attributes. Curve Follow, Attract, and Max Dist. are discussed in the section "Using Control Curves" earlier in this chapter. All three attributes apply only when you have set control curves to influence the stroke.

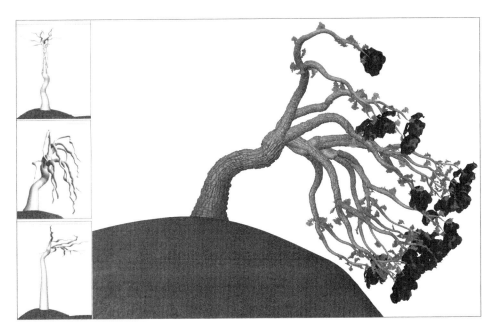

Figure 17.39

Displacement and Forces attributes utilizing different values for displaying a few of the different effects those values may produce

Random, probably one of the most useful attributes in this section, provides a way to apply forces in random directions and random intensities. This is similar to applying turbulence to a soft body. Higher values increase the tree's deformation by increasing the force's influence. Deflection, which enables Deflection Min and Max, provides a way to prevent the forces from influencing beyond a certain height above the ground. Increase Gravity so that the twigs appear to fall below the tree surface, enable Deflection, and then increase the Deflection Min level. As you increase the Deflection Min level, notice how the lower parts of the twigs seem to flatten out on an imaginary plane that lifts them up. We used these settings to make the tree appear to spread out. Momentum is used to control flow animation over time. See the section on flow animation earlier in this chapter for more details on the Momentum attribute. Keep in mind that Momentum should be set to 1 because values lower than 1 will deform the tube. Finally, Length Flex provides a way to limit the tube's flexibility with respect to forces. This limits the amount of stretching that can occur along the length of the tube due to forces. At a value of 0, there will be no stretching.

SPIRAL AND BEND

These sections contain simple, straightforward settings for deforming brushes and are powerful when combined with animation. Spiral can make the tree appear to sway from side to side, and Bend can make the branches appear to fold in or spread out like a fist.

TURBULENCE

This sections adds magic to your Paint Effects by letting you define effects such as a strong wind or merely a light breeze.

1. Turbulence Type provides a few types of settings that define how the turbulence will affect the tubes. You can read about each of these settings in the Maya documentation. Select Tree Wind, which applies turbulence in a way that affects the outer branches more then the inner branches and thus simulates treelike characteristics. Scrub the Timeline to see how the tree reacts to the turbulence. This is a huge shortcut for many complicated tasks, enabling us to work intuitively and adjust settings without worrying about scripting complex expressions.

2. Interpolation controls how smooth the motion will appear. Play a few frames to get a feel for Linear, and then switch to Smooth Over Time And Space and replay the sequence. The branches appear to ease in and out rather than suddenly change in direction as with Linear interpolation.

The remaining settings control the wind behavior, or more precisely, the turbulence characteristics. Turbulence defines the wind intensity. Increasing this value makes the wind appear stronger. Turbulence Speed defines the rate of change for the turbulence over time. Increasing this value intensifies the wind shear.

> Experiment with these values while playing the Timeline. You will see how intuitive this process can be, allowing you to immediately see changes in motion. This speaks for itself, showing off one of the greatest features in Paint Effects.

Before you're done with the scene, try setting fake 3D cast shadows and add some grass or plants on the surface near the tree and maybe even a few clouds in the sky.

> If the refresh is too slow, you can disable Draw As Mesh under the stroke and adjust the animation using the curve display.

Converting Paint Effects to 3D Geometry

Now that you have animation applied to the tree, you might want to render using a different renderer, such as mental ray (see Chapter 14). Another great advantage to Paint Effects is its ability to convert brushes into polygon or NURBS objects. This key feature is significant to Paint Effects.

1. Open the most recent scene with the tree animation, and select the tree in the perspective view. From the Maya menu, choose **Modify → Convert → Paint Effects To Polygons ❑**. The most important attribute is Poly Limit, which specifies the number of polygons that can exist in the converted mesh. Click Apply to convert to 3D. With

this tree you should probably set a high poly limit. Don't be afraid to enter 1,000,000, which will give Paint Effects a "free hand" while converting. This doesn't necessarily mean it will use the specified amount; however, it won't subtract from the tessellation you set using the Paint Effects Mesh Quality window.

2. With the tree selected (the stroke and not the polygon you just converted to), open the stroke Attribute Editor. Under Mesh Output, you can change some of the conversion settings. Thus, even after converting to 3D, you can still choose whether you want to output quads instead of triangles as well as change the Poly Limit. All these changes take immediate effect on your converted stroke. The Color Per Vertex option provides game artists some extra options for how the texturing is converted.

You can convert to NURBS patch modeling, which seems to work efficiently and create a "clean" model. If this interests you, experiment with objects that don't have several leaves or flowers to get a feel for it. Using polygons with Paint Effects is a better choice in most cases.

HISTORY AND PAINT EFFECTS

Even after converting Paint Effects to geometry, the brush settings still apply if the history is maintained. Not only is animation maintained, but you can also apply changes to most brush settings and have them affect the converted geometry. This is really outstanding; it also provides you with an ability to combine rigid dynamics such as collisions with Paint Effects objects, since they are no longer merely a postprocess effect. (See the section "The Mesh Brush Type and Displacement Mapping" earlier in this chapter for information about the mesh-related tessellation features.)

Choose **Paint Effects → Mesh Quality Attributes** while fine-tuning mesh resolution.

KEEP EXPERIMENTING

The key for learning the vast number of Paint Effects attributes and settings is to play around with them. Search for new and creative ways to apply effects. For example, try painting particles into specific locations in the scene using the Particle tool and then distribute Paint Effects trees on each particle using the Particle Instancer tool. Another great benefit with Paint Effects is rendering different tree animations and then applying them to 2D placement cards in your scene. You also can use a rendered motion sequence as a mask for a light source. This means that by rendering a simple tree with a breeze, you can then use that sequence as a gobo for the light. Essentially this method will enhance your renders with realistic natural motion, casting shadows and adding more mood.

Because Paint Effects is purely an Autodesk invention, the software engineers at Autodesk take great pride in its ability, and every single attribute is covered in detail in the Maya help files. See these help files for specific descriptions of any Paint Effects attribute. Most important, take time to adjust to Paint Effects, as it takes some time to master. Start by gradually introducing simple natural elements to your scenes, such as grass or plants that simulate natural motion. You will gradually find more interesting ways to apply Paint Effects to your creations.

Summary

After completing this chapter, you should feel comfortable with Paint Effects and its abilities. Paint Effects is particularly powerful for 3D artists who want to avoid using dynamics for simulating natural phenomena or modeling natural elements, taking advantage of the ability to paint an effect naturally within the scene using only their most powerful tool, their imagination.

In this chapter, first we looked at how Paint Effects integrates into a 3D scene. We then explored brushes and strokes and looked at painting in 2D, followed by painting real-time textures. We then examined 3D painting with the Thin Line and Mesh brushes as well as transferring, sharing, texturing, and animating 3D Paint Effects. This was followed by the rose tree tutorial, in which you created a tree using different brushes, animated it, and finally converted it to a poly tree ready to be rendered in your renderer of choice.

CHAPTER 18

Rigid Body Animation

The next several chapters explore a different way of animating in Maya: using physical simulation rather than keyframed animation. This chapter introduces the concepts of simulation using rigid body dynamics, a system that solves animation for large, "rigid" objects (such as a baseball bat or a flower pot) under physical forces (such as wind and gravity). Often, using rigid body simulation can produce physical animation in a much more efficient and believable manner than can traditional keyframing.

- Describing rigid body dynamics

- Creating a simple rigid body

- Working with fields and impulses

- Animating active versus passive modes

- Adding constraints to a rigid body

- Using the Rigid Body Solver

- "Baking" rigid body animations into keyframes

Rigid Body Dynamics Basics

Rigid body dynamics is part of a physics simulator in Maya that mimics the motion of real-world solid objects as they move under the influence of physical forces (such as gravity or wind) and collide. The equations describing the motion of rigid bodies were developed in the late nineteenth and early twentieth centuries and is considered one of the crowning achievements of "classical physics" (along with, among other things, the description of moving fluids). Rigid body dynamics is different from the traditional Maya animation in that you do not set keyframes on the objects to move them; Maya governs their motion through its dynamics engine instead. If you've ever tried to keyframe even the simple motion of a ball bouncing on the ground, you know how difficult it is to make the ball look as if it is bouncing for real. If you try something more difficult, such as bouncing a cube off a wall, you can quickly become frustrated trying to make the collisions look realistic.

Rigid body dynamics takes the tedium out of animating complex physical motion and automates much of the process. Using rigid bodies is straightforward: you convert one or more existing geometries into rigid bodies; create any fields you want to influence them; give the rigid bodies initial motion for their position, velocity, and impulse; and play back the animation to run the simulation. Maya's dynamics engine does the calculations to make the body or bodies behave realistically based on your initial information; you don't need a degree in physics to animate rigid bodies effectively, just a bit of practice with the settings.

> Maya also uses its dynamics engine to create many other effects, including particles, fluids, hair, and cloth, each of which will be covered in the following chapters.

The two types of rigid bodies are passive and active. Passive rigid bodies are *not* affected by fields and cannot be moved by collisions, though they can take part in collisions. Passive rigid bodies can also be keyframed to move or rotate. Active rigid bodies, on the other hand, *are* affected by fields and will be moved by collisions; however, they cannot be keyframed. The dynamics engine controls the translation and rotation attributes of active rigid bodies, so you can't move them around on your own.

Generally, a passive rigid body is a stationary collision surface such as a floor, a wall, or some other object that is fixed to the world. An active rigid body is any kind of falling, moving, or colliding object (a basketball or a coin, for example). Although it would seem a great disadvantage that active rigid bodies cannot be keyframed, you can convert rigid bodies from passive to active at any time in an animation, allowing a rigid body to be passive for a time and then to become active; thus you can keyframe an object for part of an animation (to move it into position or keep it with another object for a time) and then invoke the rigid body engine to create a physically accurate simulation. A good example of this interchange between passive and active rigid bodies is a character throwing a ball: as the character winds up to throw, you keyframe the arm and ball into position, but as soon as they release the ball, you use rigid body dynamics to control the ball's flight.

The next section will walk you through a simple example to show how rigid bodies work.

Creating a Simple Rigid Body

One of the simplest (or at least most intuitive) and familiar physical motions is that of a ball dropping onto a level floor. Since this is such a familiar action, and since it's so easy to reproduce at home (a tennis ball and kitchen floor do nicely!), dropping a ball on a floor is a good way to understand the basics of rigid body simulation. To set up the simulation, follow these steps:

1. Create a new scene in Maya. Create a NURBS or polygon plane and scale it out to about the size of the Maya grid. Now make a NURBS or polygon sphere with a radius of 1 and move it above the plane. Your scene should look like Figure 18.1.

2. Select the plane, and from the Dynamics menu set, choose **Soft/Rigid Bodies → Create Passive Rigid Body**. The plane is now a passive rigid body and will act as the floor.

Figure 18.1

A sphere placed above a plane

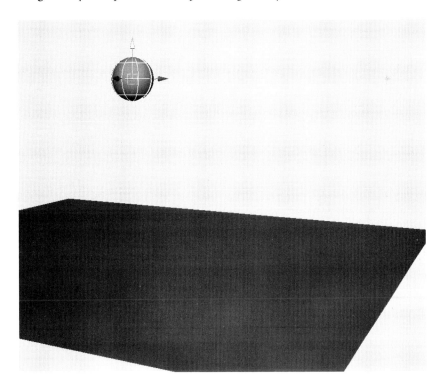

3. Select the sphere, and from the Dynamics menu set, choose **Soft/Rigid Bodies →
   Create Active Rigid Body**. The sphere is now an active rigid body.

4. To allow dynamics simulations to play back properly, the playback rate has to be set
   to Play Every Frame so that the physics engine can calculate what it needs before
   going on to the next frame. Either choose **Window → Settings/Preferences → Preferences** and choose Settings/Timeline or click the Animation Preferences button at the
   lower right of the screen to display the Animation Preferences window.

5. In the Playback section, choose Play Every Frame from the Playback Speed drop-
   down list.

6. Close the Animation Preferences window, rewind the animation, and play it back.

> Rigid bodies can be created from NURBS or polygonal geometry, but not subdivision sur-
> faces. If you want to create a rigid body from a subdivision model, first convert it to polygons.
> You can "fake" physics on a subdivision model by duplicating the object, converting it to
> polygons, and parent-constraining the subdivision version to the polygon version. Then run
> the simulation on the polygon version and turn the polygon version's visibility off.

OVERSAMPLING

Oversampling lets you determine the number (it must be an integer) of substeps per frame
for dynamic simulations. To edit the rate, choose **Solvers → Edit Oversampling Or Cache Settings**. By default, the Over Samples value is 1, meaning that the dynamics will be evaluated
every frame. If you raise the Over Samples value to 10, for instance, then Maya will evaluate
the dynamic simulation 10 times for every frame. Increasing the Over Samples value can help
fix excessive dynamics behavior by providing a more accurate simulation, but it can slow
down playback. New to Maya 8 , you can specify an oversample rate for dynamics playback
without changing the frame rate.

Apparently something's still missing, since nothing at all happened! Even though we
have two rigid bodies in our scene, we're still missing an important ingredient: we need to
provide either force fields or some initial motion. Although we can go into the rigid body
channel and adjust the initial velocity attributes of the ball, let's instead create some gravity to produce a more realistic scenario.

1. From the Dynamics menu, choose **Fields → Gravity**.

2. Choose **Window → Relationship Editors → Dynamic Relationships** to open the
   Dynamic Relationships window, shown in Figure 18.2.

3. Choose nurbSphere1 in the Outliner on the left side of the window, and make sure gravityField1 is highlighted in the selection window on the right. If it's not, click gravity-Field1 to highlight it.

> A shortcut to creating a rigid body and attaching it to a field is simply to select a geometric object (before you make it a rigid body) and then create a field. When you do so, Maya automatically makes the selected geometry an active rigid body and connects it to the newly created field. You can even select multiple geometries and make them all rigid bodies by creating a field.

If you select the sphere and then click to create the gravity field, the two will automatically be connected. (If there are other active rigid bodies that you haven't selected, they will be unaffected by this force.) Selecting objects to be affected by a field before creating the field saves time when working with rigid body simulations.

Rewind and play back the animation to see the ball fall to the plane, bounce a few times, and come to rest. If the animation is cut off in the middle, increase the animation Range Slider to about 200 frames.

> It is important to rewind your animations and to have the animation preferences set to Play Every Frame when working with simulations. Because each frame depends on the ones that came before it, Maya must play through each frame to calculate the position of each object at each frame. If, on working with a rigid body animation, you discover strange behavior in the simulation, be sure your preferences are set to Play Every Frame and that you are rewinding the timeline before you play the animation.

Now let's see how changing settings for our rigid body scene affects the animation. In the Channel Box, you'll see rigidBody*n* listed under the shape node for the object you select. For now, select the plane, and then click the rigidBody1 text to expand the Channel Box attributes for the rigid body.

The Channel Box shows numerous rigid body channels, giving you detailed control over the rigid body. The primary attributes to deal with for now are Mass, Bounciness, Damping, Static Friction, and Dynamic Friction. Change Bounciness to 0.9 and replay the animation. (Remember to rewind first!) On the first bounce, the ball should bounce nearly as

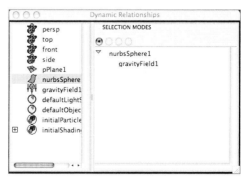

Figure 18.2
The Dynamic Relationships window

high as the height from which it was dropped, and it should take longer to settle to rest as the animation plays. Now try setting Bounciness to 2. What happens? The ball bounces farther up each time, soon disappearing from view—talk about a superball! In our virtual world, not only do we get to simulate reality, we get to break the rules if we want.

The Mass, Bounciness, Damping, Static Friction, and Dynamic Friction settings all contribute to how the ball reacts when it collides with the ground plane. Try playing with some of these settings, such as Static Friction, Dynamic Friction, and Damping—for both the ball and the plane—to see how the bouncing motion changes. However, keep in mind that Mass is a relative attribute—relative to other objects in the simulation. Since a passive rigid body essentially has an infinite mass, the Mass setting won't matter for the plane or the ball colliding with it. Also, changing the mass of the ball won't make much difference because gravity is a universal force and it affects all active objects in the same way. Mass really only comes in handy when two or more active rigid bodies collide. Their different masses will govern how much momentum is transferred from one object to the other and how their trajectories are altered. Later, you'll see where Mass can be used effectively in a simulation.

> Trying different values for all the attributes is a good way to explore how rigid bodies work. Set up a scene and try different settings for each of the channels of each rigid body. Take notes and scribble down settings—with time you'll be able to predict which values cause which behaviors.

You can also experiment with the initial velocity and impulse attributes of the active rigid body ball. Although initial velocity starts the ball out moving in one or another direction, impulse is like a tiny (or big) rocket engine connected to the ball, causing it to accelerate more and more the longer the impulse is applied.

Using the Rigid Body Solver

If a dynamics simulation is not running properly or you are experiencing poor playback, you can adjust how Maya calculates its rigid body simulations. Adjusting settings is most useful for scenes in which you need precise collision detection and interaction in the simulation. You can open the rigidSolver attributes window—the Rigid Body Solver—by choosing **Solvers → Rigid Body Solver Attributes** from the Dynamics menu set or by selecting a rigid body, opening the Attribute Editor (press Ctrl+A), and selecting the rigidSolver tab. The controls in this window allow you to adjust how Maya calculates the simulation in order to fine-tune it for speed or accuracy. Let's look at the solver in action. Create an empty scene, add a plane and a sphere (at some height above the plane), and make the plane a passive rigid body.

Before making the sphere a rigid body, let's make the shape a bit more complex. First, increase the sections and spans to 16 or more each (on the makeNurbSphere1 node). Then mold the sphere into some bizarre, angular shape (the more angular, the better), something like Figure 18.3. You can create this shape quite easily using Maya's Artisan utility (choose **Edit NURBS → Sculpt Geometry Tool ❐**). Or you can just pull individual CVs out of the sphere. Select the sphere, and choose **Fields → Gravity** to automatically create an active rigid body out of the sphere and attach it to the gravity.

When you play back the animation this time, Maya will probably go just a bit slower—this time, it has to keep track of a lot more surfaces! If you play back the frames one at a time (and look under the plane), you'll probably also be able to see a few points where some of the sphere's surfaces poke through the plane, as shown in Figure 18.4.

At full-speed playback, you probably won't notice these errors, but at times you might want to correct problems like this—or perhaps speed up playback for a particularly complex simulation. In these situations, you can use the Rigid Body Solver menu to adjust how Maya calculates its rigid body simulations. Essentially, the Rigid Body Solver gives you some control over the way Maya's dynamics engine handles the mathematics involved in the movement and interaction of rigid bodies. As you've just seen, complex shapes interact in complex ways, and adjusting calculation options via the solver is useful when the result of using Maya's default settings isn't accurate or fast enough to look realistic.

Either way you open the Rigid Body Solver, you'll see the window shown in Figure 18.5, which allows you to adjust the solver to meet your needs.

Figure 18.3

A modified sphere above a ground plane

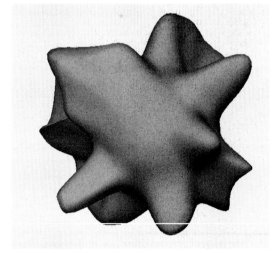

Figure 18.4

The modified sphere poking through the ground plane

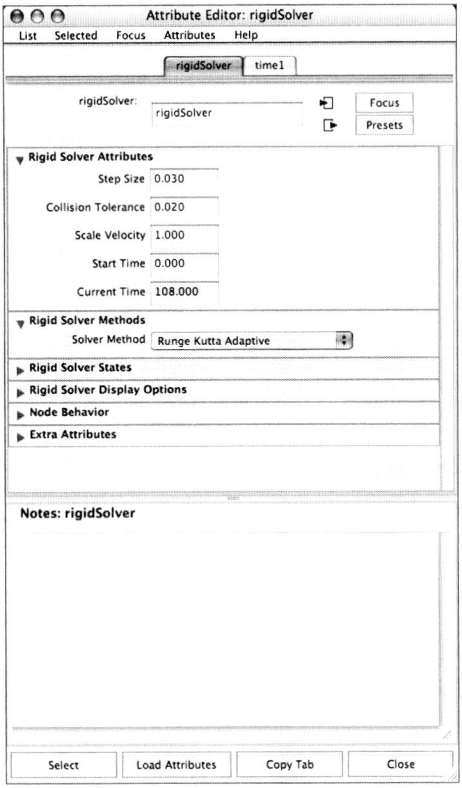

Attribute Editor: rigidSolver

List   Selected   Focus   Attributes   Help

rigidSolver | time1

rigidSolver:
rigidSolver
Focus
Presets

▼ Rigid Solver Attributes
Step Size   0.030
Collision Tolerance   0.020
Scale Velocity   1.000
Start Time   0.000
Current Time   108.000

▼ Rigid Solver Methods
Solver Method   Runge Kutta Adaptive

▶ Rigid Solver States
▶ Rigid Solver Display Options
▶ Node Behavior
▶ Extra Attributes

Notes: rigidSolver

Select | Load Attributes | Copy Tab | Close

Figure 18.5

**The Rigid Body
Solver window**

Notice the Rigid Solver States and the Rigid Solver Display Options sections of the window. Here you can turn most major functions on and off. As an example, try the following:

- Click the Display Velocity check box, and play back the animation. You will see an arrow that points in the direction of the sphere's velocity; its length represents the speed of the sphere.

- Clear the State check box. The animation now does nothing because clearing this check box turns off the solver. (This is a good way quickly to eliminate dynamics so that you can concentrate on other elements of an animation.)

- Clear the Contact Motion check box. Now the sphere strikes the plane, but it no longer bounces because dynamic motion from the contact is no longer calculated.

Try clearing each of the check boxes in the Rigid Solver States section in turn and see what effect this has on playback. When you're finished, reset the check boxes to their default state to ensure that your simulations work as expected in the future.

The Rigid Solver Methods section of the window offers three choices, though normally you will use the default method, Runge Kutta Adaptive. If you have a complex simulation, however, and either want to view it more quickly in interactive playback or don't care about the accuracy of the simulation for your final rendering, you can (temporarily) set the method to either Runge Kutta or Midpoint. Midpoint is the least accurate but fastest. Runge Kutta is a compromise between the two extremes. For a dented ball, you probably won't see much difference between the three methods.

RUNGE *WHAT?*

The Runge Kutta and Runge Kutta Adaptive options are named for the Runge Kutta solution, a mathematical method for solving an interlocking system of differential equations using first-order derivatives. In Maya, time is broken into discrete steps (referenced through the Step Size field in the Rigid Solver Attributes section), and the integral of the equations is approximated at each step. Although the technique is mathematically complex, it is fast and accurate enough for most applications.

The top—and most useful—section of the Rigid Body Solver window is labeled Rigid Solver Attributes. Using the Start Time, Scale Velocity, Step Size, and Collision Tolerance fields, you can alter the speed and/or accuracy of your rigid body simulation. Let's look at each option:

Start Time   Specifies when the Rigid Body Solver begins to function. For example, if you set Start Time to 50, the Rigid Body Solver will not start working until frame 50. The Current Time field is for reference only (you cannot modify it) and contains the current frame of the animation.

Scale Velocity   Used only if you have checked the Display Velocity check box in the Rigid Solver Display Options section—the Scale Velocity value lets you scale the arrow that sticks out from the rigid body, making it fit within your scene view. This option does not affect the way an animation simulates—it merely gives the artist better information about the scene.

Step Size   Defines the "chunk" of time (measured in fractions of a second) into which the solver divides the Timeline. A smaller Step Size setting means more calculations per second of animation, but it can also mean a more accurate simulation. If you have trouble with rigid body interpenetration errors (meaning that two bodies have "pierced" each other, as in our example), reducing the Step Size setting is a good place to start.

Collision Tolerance   Tells Maya how carefully to evaluate frames where collisions take place. A large collision tolerance will speed up playback, but collisions can become inaccurate.

Try setting Collision Tolerance to 0.8 and play back your animation. You will notice that the sphere doesn't bounce correctly on the plane. Now set Collision Tolerance to 0.001 (the smallest possible value). If there were instances when the sphere stuck through the plane before, they should no longer appear (or at worst they should poke through only a little bit).

Experiment with different Step Size and Collision Tolerance settings and see how the changes affect the simulation. Often you can get away with making either Step Size or Collision Tolerance large, as long as you keep the other element small. Finding a compromise between speed and accuracy for a complex simulation is often the key to using rigid body dynamics effectively.

Speeding Up Calculations with Additional Solvers

Each additional object a rigid solver has to keep track of can multiply the calculation time. To compensate for this, you can speed up calculations by isolating parts of a simulation and assigning additional solvers to each part. By making some changes in the deformed sphere scene you created in the previous example, you can see how this works. (If you no longer have that scene, just create a ball and a plane, make the ball an active rigid body and the plane a passive rigid body, and then create gravity. Play back the animation to be sure the ball bounces off the plane.)

Now create a second Rigid Body Solver and assign the ball to it.

1. Choose **Solvers → Create Rigid Body Solver** to create a new solver, which will be called rigidSolver1 (or 2 or 3, depending on how many others you have created).

2. To set the new solver as the default (so that all new objects converted to rigid bodies will be assigned to it), choose **Solvers → Current Rigid Solver → rigidSolverX**. (rigid-SolverX is the solver you want to establish as the default.)

Since we have already created both rigid bodies using the same solver, we need to assign one of the two bodies (the ball) to the new solver—rigidSolver1. Unfortunately, there is no button to do this, but you can do it with a quick bit of MEL scripting.

3. In the scene window, select the sphere, and then, in the Command line, type the following:

```
rigidBody -edit -solver rigidSolver1;
```

This command tells Maya to edit the Rigid Body Solverfor whatever objects are selected in the scene.

Now play back the animation again. This time, the ball should pass right through the plane. Although the plane and the ball are both still affected by gravity, they no longer interact because they "live" in different solver states.

If you want to edit the settings of your new rigid solver, be sure it is selected (choose **Solvers → Current Rigid Solver**), and then choose **Solvers → Rigid Body Solver Attributes**. This opens the Attribute Editor with the rigidSolver1 selected.

Finally, with rigidSolver1 selected, you can create a new plane (or other object), make it a passive rigid body, and play back the animation. Because both the ball and the new plane share the same solver, they will collide properly.

Speeding Up Calculations by Controlling Collisions

Keeping separate rigid body objects on different solvers can be an important work-flow efficiency. Particularly in scenes with multiple dynamic rigid bodies that need to behave differently from one another, multiple solvers afford you better interactivity.

Furthermore, you can manage the collisions on rigid bodies on an individual object basis as well, for an even finer degree of control. By toggling the Collision attribute (found toward the bottom of the Channel Box for the rigidBody node of the object) on or off for a rigid body, you can control whether that object collides with all other rigid body objects in the scene. This attribute controls only *all* the collisions of that object, not collisions on a per-object basis.

For more detailed control, you can toggle the collisions between only two or more objects as opposed to turning all objects' collisions on or off.

To control collisions, follow these steps:

1. In a new scene, create a ball and ground plane, make the ball an active rigid body and the plane a passive rigid body, and then create gravity to attach to the ball to make it bounce off the plane. (You should be an expert at creating this scene by now!) Check the playback to make sure the ball bounces off the plane properly.

2. Add a NURBS cone to the scene, and place it above the ground plane and one or two units directly under the ball.

3. To make this cone an active rigid body and attach it to the existing gravity, choose **Window → Relationship Editors → Dynamic Relationships** to open the Dynamic Relationships window, and connect the cone to the existing gravity. Maya automatically creates an active rigid body out of the cone and attaches it to the gravity. Your scene should look similar to Figure 18.6.

Play back the simulation and you'll see both the ball and the cone fall to the plane. The ball will hit the cone, bounce off its tip, and push it to the side on its way back down (or it may interpenetrate the cone—if so, try adjusting the rigidSolver settings). Now let's try to get rid of the collisions between the ball and the cone. If we turn off collisions on the cone through its Collisions attribute, the cone won't collide with the ball, but it also won't collide with the ground, which is a problem. If you tried turning off collisions on the cone through the Collisions attribute, turn them back on.

Instead, select both the cone and the ball and choose **Solvers → Set Rigid Body Interpenetration**. Play back the simulation and you'll see that the ball and cone will both bounce off the plane, but not off each other. To turn the collisions between the ball and cone back on, select them both and choose **Solvers → Set Rigid Body Collision**.

In addition to the collision controls under the Solver menu, each rigid body object has an attribute called Collision Layer. This attribute separates object collisions in a scene so that not all objects in the scene have to collide. You can assign different collision layers to different objects to speed up calculations, simplify animation, achieve particular effects, and so on.

Figure 18.6

A scene with cone and ball as active rigid bodies

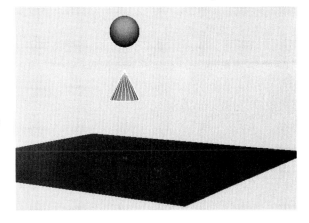

Let's create an example to show how collision layers work. We'll shoot a series of cubes at each other, first without collision layers and then with them.

1. Start a new scene, create a NURBS plane, and scale it out fairly large so that objects can bounce off it.

2. Create a polygonal cube (polygon cubes are easier to deal with than NURBS cubes because they aren't made up of multiple subshapes). Move the cube up above the plane and duplicate it three times, moving each cube a little away from the next.

3. Select all three cubes and duplicate them, moving the new group of cubes off to the other side of the plane (see Figure 18.7).

4. So you can tell which cube is which, use the Hypershade to assign red, green, and blue textures to each pair of cubes. (To create the textures, open the Hypershade, create three new Lambert textures, assign basic red, green, and blue colors to each shader, and MM drag the texture on top of the appropriate cubes.)

5. Select the ground plane and make it a passive rigid body. Then select all the cubes and create a gravity field (thus making the cubes active rigid bodies). Set the gravity field low, to 2.0 or so, so that the cubes will hit each other before dropping to the plane.

6. Now select the cubes on the right, and under the rigidBody*X* section of the Channel Box, set the initial velocity in X to –10. (You may need to adjust this number, depending on how far apart the cubes are.) Select the cubes on the left and set their initial X velocity to 10.

7. When you play back the animation, you should see the cubes collide and bounce around a bit on the ground plane, as shown in Figure 18.8. (If the cubes interpenetrate, try setting Step Size to a small number in the Rigid Body Solver window.)

Figure 18.7

Creating six colored cubes atop a ground plane

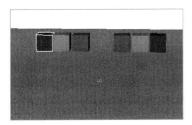

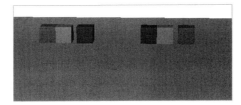

Figure 18.8

Cubes colliding (all on one collision layer)

Figure 18.9

Cubes colliding (in separate layers)

Now we will see how setting these cubes in different collision layers affect the simulation. Select both red cubes and set their Collision Layer channel (toward the bottom of the rigidBody channels) to 1. Set the green cubes to layer 2, and set the blue cubes to layer 3. On playback, you should see the red cubes bounce off each other and pass right through the green and blue cubes (the green and blue cubes will similarly only interact with each other), and then the whole lot of cubes will fall right through the ground plane! Obviously we have a problem here: the ground plane is set to Collision Layer 0, which doesn't interact with layers 1 through 3. Fortunately Maya has a "collide with everything" setting for the collision layer: –1. Select the ground plane and set its collision layer to –1 and you should get correct behavior, as shown in Figure 18.9.

When animating a scene heavy with dynamic objects, such as shattering glass, controlling collisions with layers is an invaluable part of your work flow.

Working with Fields and Impulses

Once you create an active rigid body, you can control its movement in a few ways. You can set values directly for its impulse, initial velocity, and spin attributes, as you'll see later this chapter. You can also control movement secondarily through collisions with other active or passive rigid bodies.

In addition, fields affect the movement of active rigid bodies by exerting a specific force on them. For example, if a shot calls for particles of dust to blow around in a scene, you can use an air force to create a dynamic simulation. Fields are useful because they closely resemble forces in nature that affect the movement of objects in real life. You've already seen how useful the gravity field is.

The same primary attributes control all fields: Magnitude, Attenuation, Use Max Distance, Max Distance, and Volume Shape. The Magnitude attribute governs the strength of force applied from the field to the object(s), and Attenuation is a factor that determines the amount the strength of the field diminishes as the distance between the field and object increases.

Magnitude and Attenuation essentially govern how much the field directly affects the dynamic object. The Use Max Distance, Max Distance, and Volume Shape attributes, however, in effect define the field's maximum area of influence. These three attributes allow dynamic changes in specific regions of 3D space.

With Use Max Distance turned on, the Max Distance attribute dictates how close the object needs to be to the field for the field to have any influence. Objects beyond the Max Distance value from the field's location are not affected.

An easier way to govern the region of influence on a field is to use the Volume Shape attribute to define a specific volume for the field. Dynamic objects in that volume are affected by the field's force. Volume Shape gives you a visual representation of the region of influence and can be transformed. Actually seeing the volume of influence of a field is much more interactive than using just the Max Distance setting to define its extents. With Volume Shape, you can see your dynamic objects and their proximity to the field and the extent of its influence, and you can animate the physical shape of the volume to create your desired effect.

This exercise will show you how fields work.

1. In a new scene, create a passive rigid ground plane that is scaled to fit the grid, and then create eight spheres.

2. Place the spheres in two rows of four facing each other as in Figure 18.10, with one row closer to the origin than the other row.

3. Select the spheres and create a gravity field.

4. Select the spheres again and create a radial field. Change its Magnitude to –1, and change its Volume Shape to Sphere. Set a keyframe for its scale to be 1, 1,1 at the first frame.

5. Go to frame 80, and scale the field's sphere volume up until it's about the size of the ground plane.

Figure 18.10

Eight spheres lined up to face each other

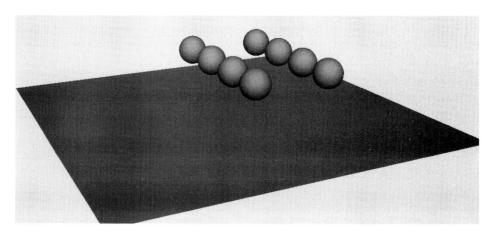

When you play back the simulation, you should see the radial field affect the spheres in the middle of the row closer to the origin first. As the volume of the field increases, it affects the other spheres as well. Try changing the volume shape to a cylinder or a cube and replaying the simulation. Also try changing the magnitude of the radial field to try to get some of the spheres to escape the field's volume once they bounce around inside a bit.

Let's now see how to use rigid bodies to create a realistic simulation of a bullet being fired from a really big "gun" at a planet. We'll use a small cylinder for the "bullet" and a big sphere for the planet, but you can model just about anything you want and substitute those objects in their places

1. Create a sphere with a radius of 500 units, translate it down −500 in Y, and name it planet. Scale your view out so you can see the top of the planet.

   Because of the large size of this sphere, you may find that your camera "clips" the sphere so you cannot see it completely. To deal with this issue, select your viewing camera (choose **View → Select Camera**), open the Attribute Editor (press Ctrl+A), and in the Camera Attributes section, set Far Clip Plane to a larger number, such as 10,000.

2. Create a cylinder (named bullet), and scale it so that it looks about the size of the cylinder in Figure 18.11. You might want to color the bullet differently from the color of the planet for clarity. (Also feel free to model a "gun" to shoot the bullet out.)

It really doesn't matter how big the bullet is, as long as it looks good to you. (We rotated it sideways and stretched it out a bit.) Just be sure to place the bullet a little above the surface of the planet or you'll get rigid body interpenetration errors, which will be problematic for your simulation.

3. Make the sphere a passive rigid body (choose **Soft/Rigid Bodies → Create Passive Rigid Body**), and make the cylinder an active rigid body (choose **Soft/Rigid Bodies → Create Active Rigid Body**).

Figure 18.11

Create a curved planet surface and bullet.

You could add a simple gravity field to these objects, but gravity pulls everything in the same direction. What you need here is a field that's centered on the planet; we'll use the Newton field (named after Sir Isaac). The Newton field creates a gravitational "well" in the planet that will attract all active rigid bodies to it, its force depending on the distance between the planet and the object. This slightly more complex version of gravity will produce a ballistic arc for the bullet as it travels around the surface of the planet.

4. Choose **Fields → Newton**; then Shift+select the sphere and choose **Fields → Use Selected As Source Of Field**. In the Outliner or Hypergraph, you will now see a Newton field parented to the planet.

5. Select the cylinder, and then choose **Window → Relationship Editors → Dynamic Relationships** to open the Dynamic Relationships window.

6. Click the Newton field to highlight it—this connects the cone to the Newton field.

7. Set the frame length to 1000 or more, and play back the animation.

> When you attach a field to an object by selecting the field, Shift+selecting the object, and then choosing **Fields → Use Selected As Source Of Field**, you are using the object as a source of the field's force. The field will travel with its parent object and can be used to create a wake or turbulence as the parent object passes rigid bodies or particles.

The bullet should fall and land on the surface of the planet, bounce a bit, and stay there or perhaps roll around a bit on the surface of the sphere. If not, try setting the magnitude of the Newton field to 6 or 7 and see if that helps.

Now we're simulating planetary gravity; what we're missing is the thrust (or impulse) that a gun uses to expel a bullet from its chamber. With the bullet selected, look under the rigidBody2 section in the Channel Box and set the bullet's impulseX to about 5. (Depending on the direction you rotated your bullet, this might be impulseZ instead.) The bullet will now accelerate quickly away from the "gun," obviously not a realistic scenario. To accurately portray a gun, we need to create a quick impulse to simulate the explosion of gun powder in the firing chamber. To do this, we need to keyframe the impulse off a frame or two after the simulation starts.

1. Select the X (or Z) impulse, move the Time Slider to the first frame, set a value of 20 for Impulse, and RM choose Key Selected.

2. Go out to frame 3, and set the value of impulseX to 0. (The impulse will fall off from 20 to 0 over the two intervening frames.)

IMPULSE OR INITIAL VELOCITY ATTRIBUTES?

Instead of keyframing the Impulse channel to give the rocket a short thrust, you can also set its Initial Velocity attributes. The Initial attributes (Initial Velocity in XYZ as well as Initial Spin in XYZ) give the rigid body only a starting thrust of motion but do not continue to provide thrust as Impulse does. Therefore, Initial Velocity is better suited for rigid bodies that should have a burst of motion only at the beginning of the simulation, and the Impulse attributes are better for acceleration at any time during the simulation.

When you play back the animation, the bullet should fire, arc over the planet for a time—and fall *through* the surface! Not exactly the results we were looking for. The problem is as follows: the tessellation of the sphere (how Maya's simulation engine chops it up into bits) is too low for the size of the sphere. You can solve this problem in four ways. The first is to use the Rigid Body Solver attributes as discussed in the previous section. For our purposes here, the most useful controls in this window are Step Size and Collision Tolerance. Step Size controls how frequently the solver runs its equations (in fractions of a second). The Collision Tolerance setting controls how accurately the collisions are calculated. For both controls, the smaller the number, the more accurate the results, but conversely the more time it will take to run the simulation. Thus, you will want to set the values as large as you can get away with for a given scenario.

The second way to fix the collision detection problem is to increase the U and V spans of the sphere to force the tessellation; however, this method will require you to delete and re-create the rigid body on the sphere to work. The third way is to increase the tessellation factor of the rigid body itself. With the planet selected, open the Attribute Editor, select the rigidBody1 tab, and twirl down the Performance Attributes rollout. The tessellation factor is set to 200 by default, but you can increase this to a significantly higher number until the bullet no longer falls through the planet. Be aware, however, that the higher the tessellation, the longer it will take the simulation to solve.

The fourth way is to use a stand-in proxy object for the planet. Under the Performance Attributes rollout is a Stand In menu from which you can select Cube or Sphere; because the planet is a spherical object, choose Sphere. (A stand-in is mathematically calculated, rather than tessellated, so it is far more robust for collision detection.) This method, though only useful if your objects are nearly spherical or cubic, is fast to solve and thus the method we use here.

Once you have a good basic simulation, you can tweak settings to get different effects. Setting the initial impulse higher will, of course, make the bullet travel faster (and farther).

With enough impulse, you should get the bullet to orbit the planet rather than crashing back into it (a value of 45 worked well for us). Giving it too much impulse will cause the bullet to fire off into space. You can also add a drag field to the bullet to slow it down as if air were present in the simulation (be sure Attenuation is set to 0, and play with the Magnitude setting); if you do this, you will note that you need to increase the impulse by a great deal to get the bullet to travel the same distances.

Play around with various aspects of this simulation until you feel you really understand how everything works together. This "playing" is a crucial step in learning how Maya's simulation engine works, so take the time to do it. Once you have an interesting simulation, save your file for use later in this chapter.

Animating between Active and Passive Modes

We will create a simple pool table break to explore animating with rigid bodies that switch from active to passive modes. In production work, dynamics is typically used as a helping hand as opposed to an all-encompassing solution. Getting real-life motion from dynamics is a terrific boost to a scene, but rarely is dynamics alone enough to get a shot. Thus it is important to understand how to switch between keyframe and simulated motions in order to "set up" dynamics simulations properly.

We will create a basic pool table out of cubes, a set of 10 pool balls, and a cue ball. We will then keyframe the cue ball to strike the other balls and let the dynamics engine take care of the rest.

Creating the Objects

We don't need a realistic pool table for our simulation—a few well-placed boxes will do the trick nicely. In fact, even when you have complex geometry in a scene, it's usually best to run your simulation using simple geometry to speed up your calculations.

First we'll create the objects for the pool table and balls.

1. Create a polygon cube and scale it twice as long as wide (the thickness can be fairly small). Figure 18.12 shows the pool table when it's completed.

2. Create several more polygon cubes and place them around the table as "bumpers" for the balls to hit. Don't forget to leave spaces where the pockets of the table would be, and, above all, *don't let the bumpers touch the table or each other*. It is extremely important to avoid letting rigid bodies intersect each other when a simulation begins. Rigid body interpenetration can lead to certain objects being ignored during simulation. Should an interpenetration event happen, an error will display in the Script Editor.

3. Create a cue ball from a NURBS sphere and place it on one side of the table, slightly above the table surface.

4. Create the number balls (or duplicate the cue ball), and place them into a triangle on the other side of the table, being sure not to let them touch each other or the table surface. See Figure 18.12.

5. Select all the balls, then choose **Modify → Freeze Transformations** to zero all the attributes of the pool balls.

"Zeroing" the transforms of an object resets all the values of that object's transformation attributes (Move, Rotate, and Scale) without moving the object. This will effectively reset the object to seem as if it were created at its current position as opposed to the origin (or other) point. Some Maya functions, particularly when dealing with history, respond much better when the object to be affected is first "zeroed."

Freezing the transformations is generally a good idea when dealing with dynamics because it makes them "cleaner" for Maya to deal with. In addition, deleting any construction history attached to a dynamic object can help to avoid any significant slowdowns or strange results. Unless you need the history to remain on the object, it's always a good idea to delete it before making the object a rigid body.

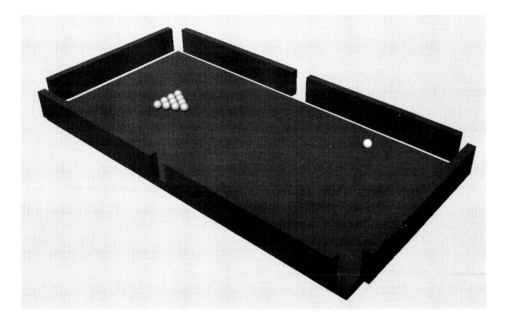

Figure 18.12
A simple pool table

Defining the Simulation

Now we'll begin defining the dynamics of the scene.

1. Select the elements that make up the pool table, and in the Dynamics menu set, choose **Soft/Rigid Bodies → Create Passive Rigid Body**. If need be, open the Options window and make sure the settings are all reset to their defaults first. (In the Options window, choose **Edit → Reset Settings**.)

2. Select all the pool balls in the scene and convert them to active rigid bodies by choosing **Soft/Rigid Bodies → Create Active Rigid Body** (with default settings). It actually does not matter if you create the cue ball as an active or passive body because we will be animating it first as a passive body so that we can set keyframes on it.

3. Now you need to create and attach a gravity field to make things stick to the table. Select the balls and choose **Fields → Gravity**. Again, make sure the settings are at their defaults before applying the gravity.

The dynamics are now set up in the scene and awaiting animation. If you play back the animation now, you should see the balls move around a bit on the table surface. Gravity is pulling them down whatever little distance they were placed above the surface, and they are bouncing off each other a bit as well. Although we can adjust settings such as friction and bounciness to get rid of this motion, it is actually easier to make all the balls passive until just before they are struck.

4. Select all the balls in the scene, go into the Channel Box, and set the active channel of the rigid body to Off. Now you should see no motion at all when you play the scene forward.

Animating the Scene

We will animate the scene by animating the cue ball toward the number balls using keyframes and then setting the active channel to On and allowing the dynamics engine to calculate where all the balls go.

1. Select the cue ball and set a passive key for it by choosing **Soft/Rigid Bodies → Set Passive Key** at the first frame of the animation. This will set the translation and rotation keys for the ball as well as key off the active status of the rigid body.

2. Go to frame 5, move the cue ball so that it is just about to strike the apex of the triangle, and set another passive key (see Figure 18.13).

3. Go to frame 6 and turn the cue ball into an active rigid body by choosing **Soft/Rigid Bodies → Set Active Key**. The ball becomes an active rigid body, and Maya's dynamic simulator takes over and calculates its motion from here. The ball inherits the momentum we set on it with the keyframe animation.

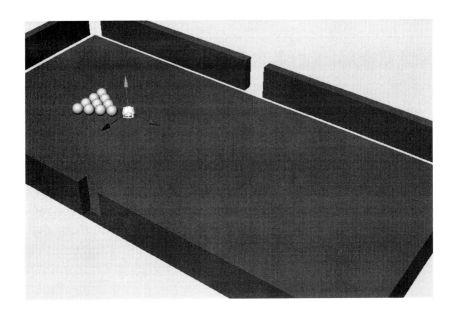

Figure 18.13

Keying the cue ball to strike the number balls

4. On frame 5, set a passive key for all the number balls. Then, on frame 6, set an active key for them. As of frame 6, the animation will run automatically as Maya simulates the interaction of the balls and the table.

What you have done here is force the cue ball to become an active rigid body just as the balls are about to collide. This timing lets you take advantage of the sphere's "inheriting" speed and rotation from its keyframed movement so that it will smash into the balls with a good deal of force. To alter the trajectory of the cue ball, simply move it at frame 1 or 5 and reset a passive key on it.

ACTIVATING WITHOUT SETTING KEYFRAMES

You can manually turn the Active attribute on and off without setting keyframes on translation and rotation automatically. Select the rigid body object, and in the Channel Box, toward the bottom of the rigidBody channels, is the active channel. Type **on** or the number **1** to turn the object from a passive rigid body to an active rigid body and keyframe it. To toggle it back to passive, type **off** or the number **0** in the active channel and set a keyframe. Although this method works for the most part, Autodesk advises users to use the Set Active Key and Set Passive Key commands instead.

When you play back the animation, you will likely notice that the balls come to rest quickly after the collision, and (depending on collisions) you might see one of the balls fly off the table entirely. To solve these problems, you can adjust the magnitude of gravity from its default of 9.8 to something larger, such as 50. You can also reduce the static and dynamic friction values for the table and balls from 0.2 to a small value such as 0.01 and increase the bounciness of the balls to a number such as 0.9 since the balls are highly elastic in their collisions and thus most of the momentum of the balls is conserved in the collision. Reducing friction allows the balls to slide and roll more easily, while a high Bounciness value lets the momentum of the cue ball transfer efficiently to the other balls. Again, it is best to play with different settings until you get a simulation you like. Figure 18.14 shows an effective simulation running, and the CD contains a file, `poolTable.mb`, that has numbers set well if you want to see a completed example.

As you can see in this example, rigid body dynamics is a balancing act of setting various attribute values. This balancing act can become a convoluted process at times, but with patience and some careful note taking, the process becomes easier. Playing with the numbers over and over again is a great way to familiarize yourself with how dynamics works; you'll begin to see the forest through the trees.

Figure 18.14

A good pool-break simulation

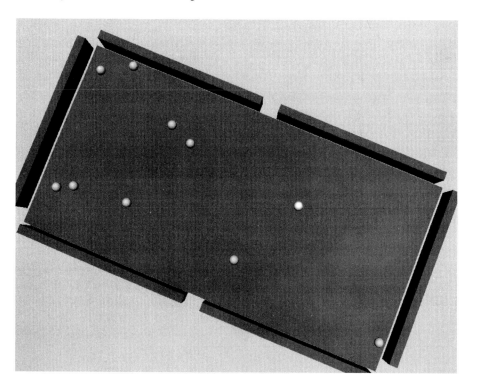

Adding Constraints to a Rigid Body

As a more complex example of using rigid bodies, along with constraints, let's create a toy called kinetic marbles. This is a popular desk toy in which a series of five chrome marbles are suspended from strings. You swing a ball to strike one end of the series, and the momentum travels through the series and swings up a ball on the other end, which then swings back down to knock the other end back up and so on. Along the way, you'll learn how to add constraints and how to adjust the Rigid Body Solver to speed up some complex calculations.

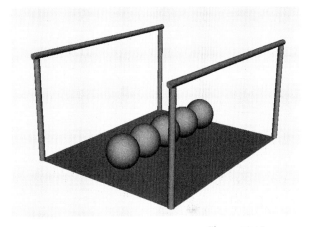

Figure 18.15

Chrome balls in a frame

First we'll create and set up the kinetic balls.

1. Create a new scene. Create a NURBS sphere and move it up to rest on the ground plane (set Translate Y to 1) as the center ball. Duplicate the sphere four times, and then line up the balls with a small gap between each pair of balls.

2. Build a frame around the balls to set up the desk toy, as shown in Figure 18.15. You're more than welcome to design your own fancy frame, but for now, cylinders and a plane will work. We'll use this frame just for placement and scale purposes, but you can also have the balls interact with the frame if desired.

   Be sure that each ball is slightly separated from the balls on either side (so that they don't touch each other). Otherwise, when you create the rigid bodies, you will get an interpenetration error and the simulation will break down. After you create your first duplicate and then move and rotate it, you can use the Smart Transform option in the Duplicate Options window to do the rest. Each duplicate will be moved into position automatically.

3. Select all the balls and convert them to active rigid bodies. With the balls selected, create a gravity field and set its Magnitude to 50.

> Alternatively, if you create the gravity without any of the spheres selected, you can connect them through the Dynamic Relationships window. With the unconnected sphere selected, choose **Window → Relationship Editors → Dynamic Relationships**, and highlight gravity-Field1 to connect it to the sphere. Select any other unconnected spheres and connect them to the gravity one by one in the Dynamic Relationships window.

In a real kinetic ball desk toy, a string attaches each ball to the side rails of the frame. The balls swing front to back on the strings that hold them. To make the balls swing from the horizontal bars, we will use dynamic constraints. Just like animation constraints, dynamic constraints create a relationship between dynamic objects to constrain them together.

4. Select the first ball in the series. Choose **Soft/Rigid Bodies → Create Nail Constraint** and a Nail constraint will appear at the center of the sphere already selected.

5. Move that node straight above the ball and place it inside one of the rails. Select the ball again and create another Nail constraint, placing it on the other rail. Create two Nail constraints for each ball, and place them on the rails as shown in Figure 18.16.

6. Move the outer two nail pairs in toward the center just a little bit to force the balls together when you run the simulation, as shown in Figure 18.17.

Figure 18.16

Place Nail constraints on either rail of the frame.

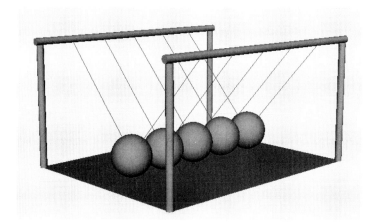

Figure 18.17

Adjusting the Nail constraint

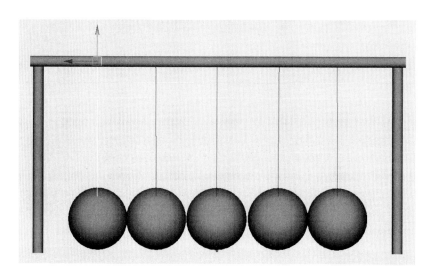

7. Run the simulation (play back the scene), and you'll notice that the balls won't fall straight down due to the gravity. They will instead settle in together because they are being held up by the Nail constraints. This constraint causes the balls to act as if they are hanging from a string that is nailed to a ceiling. Since you moved the constraints on the outer pair of balls, the whole set should "jiggle" just a bit when you run the animation.

8. To put the balls into the "knocking" motion these toys are known for, you'll need to set an initial motion on one of them on the end. Select the ball on the left end of the series and set its Initial Velocity Z attribute to –30. You will want the ball to swing up and away from the other balls; gravity will force it to swing back and strike the series of balls.

9. Set your frame range to a large number such as 5000, and rewind back to frame 1. Play back the scene. You'll see the end ball swing up and back to hit the others. They will all jerk to the right and bounce around a bit—not quite the correct behavior. We need to find the proper rigid body attributes to make the toy work correctly.

10. Select all the spheres, and in the Channel Box set Bounciness to 0.9. Change Static Friction to 0, and make sure Damping is set to 0. (If there is too much bouncing after the initial animation, you can set the Damping value to some small number, such as 0.05, to cause the balls to return to rest more quickly.)

When you rerun the simulation, you'll see that the toy works rather well. Figure 18.18 shows how the end balls bounce back and forth.

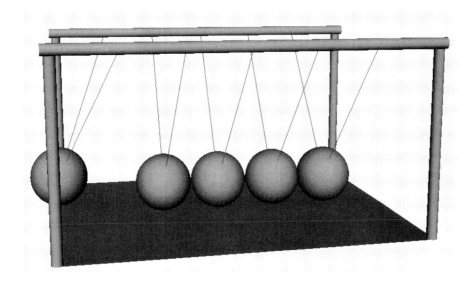

Figure 18.18

The kinetic ball toy in action

11. Now let's finesse the scene a little bit. Let's get rid of the first ball's swing up. Instead, it would be cleaner for the first ball to swing down from the top of its arc. Play the scene until the ball reaches the top of its arc and then click Stop, but don't rewind the animation. Choose **Solvers → Initial State → Set For All Dynamic**. This programs the current state of all dynamic objects into Maya as the initial state, meaning they will all start in this position.

12. Now select the first ball, and set its initial velocity in Z back to 0 so it doesn't rise up any farther. When you rewind the animation now, the ball on the end will swing down and the other balls will have settled down some already. Figure 18.19 shows the initial state of the kinetic marbles.

You can try different gravity and dynamic settings to see how the simulation is affected. As soon as you change one setting, you'll find you have to compensate by adjusting another setting or two to make sure everything animates properly. As an exercise, try to get the kinetic marbles to stay in motion as long as possible, or try lifting two balls into the air on the start frame.

Figure 18.19

Once initial states are set, the marbles will start in the correct position.

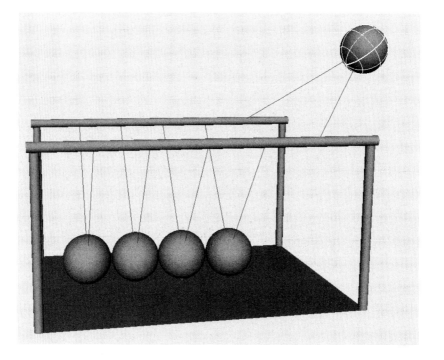

Converting (Baking) a Rigid Body Animation into Keyframes

As a final step in working with rigid body animations, it can be valuable to be able to tweak the animation that the simulation engine gives you. Although rigid body simulation cannot be keyframed (except for property values), you can "bake" a simulation into keyframes. *Baking* is the term Maya uses for creating a set of keyframes that mimic the dynamic motion of a rigid body simulation. These keys mimic the motion of the rigid object, but you can go into the Graph Editor (or other editors) and adjust individual frames or even tweak more global motion. Although this is a great help for minor tweaks, it can become complex to maintain the "feel" of the original simulation when adjusting these keyframes, so it is best to get the rigid body simulation as close to correct as possible before moving on to baking the animation. If you might eventually want to return to your rigid body simulation and save a *different* copy of your project before you bake the simulation. You can't go back once the simulation is baked!

> Baking rigid body simulations is also a necessity when you render using multiple machines. Whereas you need to render out simulations on one (and only one) CPU, keyframed animation can be split up and rendered on a CPU farm.

Select the cubes in the previous example (or just open any scene with rigid body animation in it), and choose **Edit → Keys → Bake Simulation ❑**. In the option box, be sure Hierarchy is set to Selected and Channels is set to From Channel Box. Then select the rotation and translation channels in the Channel Box and click the Bake button. You will see the animation proceed forward as Maya simulates the motion, adding keyframes as it goes.

Once the animation is complete, select any of the cubes and open the Graph Editor. You should see something like Figure 18.20. Note how the first collision, which changes the cube's direction of motion, shows up as a spike in the X translation portion of the graph.

On closer inspection, you will likely notice that the simulation generates a *lot* of keyframes—one for each frame, in fact! You can reduce the number of keyframes in a couple of ways. The simplest is just to delete them, which should work for the rotation channels of the cubes (as they had no initial rotation). You can also choose **Curves → Simplify Curve** from the Graph Editor window (alter settings for this control for different effects).

You can also, of course, move the curves around in time and space, allowing for the cube, say, to bounce when it is still above the ground plane or to have it off by itself but still "interacting" with the other objects. Try playing around with one or more of the curves to see how the keyframes relate to the motion you see in the scene window.

Figure 18.20

A simulation baked into keyframes

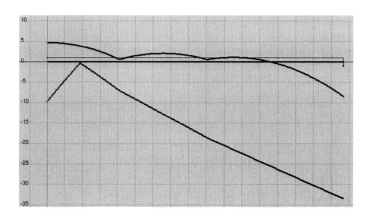

Summary

In this chapter, you saw how easy it is (relatively speaking) to get Maya to do the work for you when simulating real-world events such as objects falling and colliding. You also saw that you can convert rigid bodies from passive (keyframeable and not affected by fields) to active (not keyframeable but affected by fields) and that, when a passive rigid body becomes active, it inherits the motion it had before. This allows rigid bodies to work within a keyframed animation and with keyframed characters. Finally, you created more complex interactions and adjusted the rigid solver to give realistic, but faster, simulations and learned about baking simulated animations into keyframes for further tweaking.

In the next chapter, we will deal with a different type of simulation: particle simulation. Where rigid bodies take up a volume of space, and interact in complex ways, particles are essentially small points in space that do not interact with each other, only the forces applied to them. As opposed to rigid bodies, there can be tens of thousands of particles in a scene, so particles are excellent for simulating various natural and statistical phenomena such as fireworks, smoke, and sparks.

CHAPTER 19

Using Particles

One major reason for Maya's popularity among professionals and effects houses is the power of its dynamic particle simulation tools. Maya's particles are fast and flexible. Through the use of fields, expressions, and MEL scripts, you can create everything from fiery explosions and brilliant fireworks to a swarm of attacking bees.

The best way to learn is to do, so this chapter features a lot of exercises to familiarize you with the power of particles. Get ready to do some work over the next few pages. The chapter features the following topics:

- What are particles?
- Using particles for effects
- Manipulating particles with fields and goals
- Advanced particle expressions

What Are Particles?

A particle is essentially a point in 3D space. You animate this point indirectly using fields, forces, expressions, and occasionally some MEL scripting. Typically, particles are born from various types of emitters or emitted from surfaces or even textures. Once born, they live for a while in the world of a Maya scene where they are acted upon by fields, collision surfaces, goals, expressions, and sometimes some MEL scripting. And then they die (unless you specify that they live "forever"), leaving the scene and possibly freeing some memory for more particles. Using particles is quite different from your everyday keyframe style of animation, so it takes some getting used to.

Think of a particle as a snowflake and it all makes sense. You don't animate the snowflake itself; rather, you manipulate the particle/snowflake by animating the attributes of the forces that affect it—wind, gravity, and surfaces like a house or the ground being the most obvious. Particles can be rendered as points, multiple points, streaks, multiple streaks, blobby surfaces, clouds, tubes, instanced geometry, and sprites. Some are rendered in Maya Software, and some can only be rendered using Maya Hardware. In many cases, particle animations need to be composited into a scene.

A Maya particle object is a shape node with anywhere from one to several million particles. The individual particles do not have transform nodes, so you can't keyframe them. The particle shape itself, however, does have a transform node, and this does have translation and other channels available for keyframing.

Animating with particles in Maya is a vast topic. Some professionals specialize solely in particle animation. The best way to understand the particle animation work flow is to dive in and get your hands dirty with some exercises. As you follow along, the fundamental concepts will be explained. The goal of this chapter is to get you comfortable enough with particle animation that you can move on to explore more advanced techniques and even create some techniques of your own.

Autodesk is in the process of changing the entire simulation framework for Maya to the new "nucleus" solver methodology. In version 8.5 of Maya, only the new nCloth simulation package uses the nucleus solver to simulate cloth, but Autodesk notes that it plans to roll out the nucleus solver for particles and other entities over time. See Chapter 23 for more on the new nCloth and nucleus solver.

Using Particles for Effects

The first exercise will be creating a simple laser sword effect. We are going to use particles to create a beam of vibrating light that forms the blade of the sword. This exercise will introduce you to a typical work flow for using particles and emitters to create a visual effect.

1. Open the `laserSword1.mb` file from the CD.

2. Play the animation. You will see a NURBS curve grow from the handle of the sword. The sword then rises to the air and takes a couple of slashes.

We need to get some particles into the scene and attached to the blade of the sword. The two most common ways to get particles going are to draw them into the scene using the Particle tool and to use an emitter to shoot them into the scene. In this case, an emitter makes more sense since we want the blade to emit particles to achieve the vibrating laser effect. Drawing the particles with the Particle tool would give us a static cloud of particles. We want the particles to emit from the blade of the sword, so we are going to turn the NURBS curve into a particle emitter.

3. Rewind the animation to the beginning. In the Outliner, expand the sword group and the parented laserSwordHandle group. Select the curve labeled sword.

4. With the curve selected, choose **Particles → Emit From Object** ❒ from the Dynamics menu set.

5. Name the emitter laserBlade.

6. From the Emitter Type menu, choose Curve.

7. Set the rate to 1000.

8. Click Apply, and play the animation.

You'll see a cloud of dots grow out of the sword and spread all about the scene in a big mess. In addition, if you stop and move the Timeline back and forth, you'll get some strange results. When you create a particle animation, you are actually creating a simulation that is time dependent. The particles determine what they do next based on what they've just done. Therefore, you always need to play your particle simulations from the beginning so that they behave correctly—that is, until you create a particle disk cache, but we'll get to that in a moment.

It is also crucial to set your playback preferences to Play Every Frame rather than real time for the simulation to work properly. To do this, open the Preferences window (**Window → Settings/ Preferences → Preferences**), click the Timeline item on the left, and set Playback Speed to Play Every Frame.

Particle Lifespan

Now let's tame our particle laser blade. This is where the fun begins.

1. Rewind and play the animation a few more times.

Our main problem at this point is that the particles are flying off the blade and going on forever. To control this, we need to shorten the particle's lifespan. It sounds cruel, but what we are doing is shortening the amount of time each particle exists in the scene before it disappears. You'll see in a moment that many attributes are tied to a particle's lifespan.

2. Select the **particle1** attribute from the Outliner, and open its Attribute Editor. Select the particleShape1 tab. From this point, we will be adjusting the particle's shape node attributes as well as the emitter, which is attached to the curve. This process represents a typical work flow in which you first create a "default" particle setup and then begin to tune the simulation.

3. Scroll down the Attribute Editor for the particle1 shape node until you find the Lifespan Attributes section (see Figure 19.1).

4. You'll notice that the Lifespan Mode attribute is set to Live Forever. From the menu list, choose Constant, and set the Lifespan Mode attribute to 1.0. Play the animation from the beginning again and make sure the animation is looping.

5. You'll notice that now the particles don't last as long and the emission is a little less messy. You can now adjust the numeric Lifespan attribute. While the animation is playing, set this to 0.5. The simulation updates immediately, and the particles' lives are shorter. This attribute is measured in terms of seconds. The particles now last 12 frames (24 fps × 0.5). Set this attribute to 0.1 to keep the particles even closer to the curve.

6. Take a look at the other options in the Lifespan Mode menu. You'll also see Random Range and lifespanPP Only. Choose Random Range.

7. Stop the animation. You'll see that Lifespan Random is now available. This is a modifier for the Lifespan attribute. Putting a value in here will alter the lifespan randomly by plus or minus that value. Set Lifespan Mode back to 0.5, and set Lifespan Random to 0.25. The particles now last anywhere from one half to one and a half times as long as the setting in the Lifespan attribute.

8. LifespanPP Only allows you to set the lifespan range on a per-particle basis for a finer level of control. The other settings affect the particles on more of a group level. Sometimes that's all you need. However, setting a per-particle lifespan allows you to tie other per-particle attributes to the lifespan of each particle.

9. Set the Lifespan Mode attribute to lifespanPP Only, and scroll down in the Attribute Editor until you find the Per Particle (Array) Attributes section (see Figure 19.2). Things get a little more complicated at this point, but follow along closely and it will start to make sense.

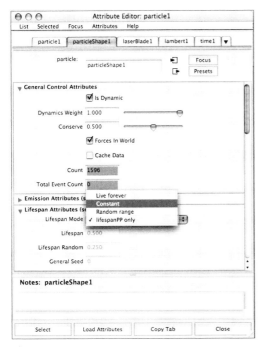

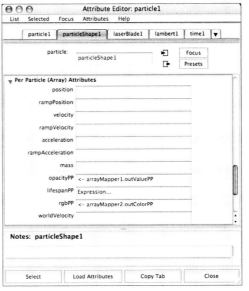

Figure 19.1

You use the Lifespan Attributes section to specify how Maya will determine the amount of time particles exist in the scene.

Figure 19.2

The Per Particle (Array) Attributes section of the particle shape's Attribute Editor. This is where you enter expressions and create ramps that will control how each individual particle behaves in the scene.

Per-Particle Array Attributes

Animating particles can lead to giving one a bit of a god complex, but that's okay. They're only pixels, so you can't cause too much damage. Up until now we've been looking at the attributes of our particles on sort of a group or ant-hill level. When we start adding per-particle attributes, it's as if we are moving to the level of controlling the lives of the individual ants. In other, less metaphorical terms, the two levels of control we have are at the particle shape node (or group) level and at the per-particle level. Sometimes the difference is subtle; sometimes it is substantial, depending on what you're trying to do.

Right-click the empty field next to lifespanPP in the per-particle attributes and choose Creation Expression to open the Expression Editor (see Figure 19.3). We are about to enter our first particle expression. This window will become very familiar as you work with particles.

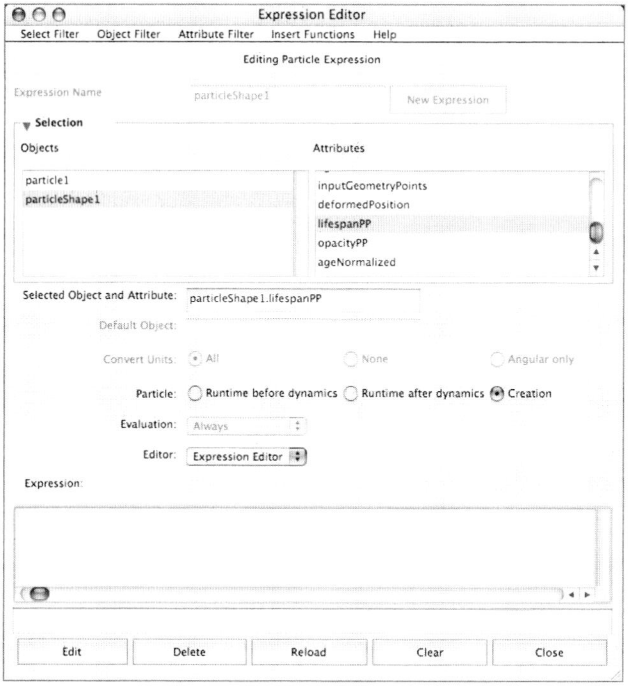

Figure 19.3

The Expression Editor opens when you choose to enter an expression in the per-particle array attributes.

Figure 19.3

The Expression Editor opens when you choose to enter an expression in the per-particle array attributes.

Creation and Runtime Particle Expressions

The two types of particle expressions are creation and runtime (the runtime type being further split between runtime before dynamic calculations and runtime after dynamic calculations). Creation expressions affect the attributes set at the time each particle is born; they can be thought of as the particle's DNA. Runtime expressions are attributes or changes to attributes that occur after a particle is born and can affect it up until the time it dies; this is the life story of a particle. The two types of expressions can interact and affect each other.

When you are born, your height is genetically encoded. Even though you're not 6 feet tall at birth, you can think of height = 6 feet as a creation expression for your height attribute. Sooner or later you're going to be 6 feet tall. Now, if at some point during your life your legs are replaced by bionic extendo-legs and you achieve a height of 10 feet, you could think of the corresponding expression as a runtime expression. Height = 10 feet is something that has happened after your birth, during your lifetime. The runtime expression can override the original creation expression height = 6 feet. Remember this analogy when you are trying to figure out whether an expression you want to write should be a creation or runtime expression

For the time being, we only need to concern ourselves with a creation expression for the lifespanPP attribute. Right-clicking the lifespanPP attribute and choosing Expression opens the Expression Editor with our particle attribute selected. You'll see that particle-Shape1 is highlighted in the Selections box and lifespanPP is selected in the Attributes box. In the Selected Object And Attribute field, we already have the syntax for the first part of the expression.

1. Make sure that Creation is selected in the particle options above the Expression box. Highlight the text in the Selected Object And Attribute section (`particleShape1. lifespanPP`). MM drag it down to the large expression editing area below. (On a Mac you have to copy it from the field and paste it into the box.)

   > If at some point while writing an expression you click another attribute or object, all the text in the expression editing area will disappear forever. This is why it is often a good idea to compose more lengthy expressions in a text editor such as Notepad or TextEdit and then paste the expression into the Expression Editor when you need to do a test.

2. In the expression editing area, change the text so that it reads `particleShape1. lifespanPP=0.5;`. Click the Create button at the bottom of the window and play back the animation. The animation should look exactly the same as when we had a constant lifespan mode of 0.5.

3. Right-click the lifespanPP field in the per-particle section of the Attribute Editor and choose Creation Expression. The Expression Editor will open again with your expression in the main field. With the animation still playing, change the expression to read as follows:

   ```
   particleShape1.lifespanPP=rand(0.1,0.3);
   ```

4. Click the Edit button at the bottom of the window. Your animation should update while it's playing.

We have now set the lifespan for each particle to be at a random range between 0.1 seconds and 0.3 seconds. This is similar to setting a random range in the Lifespan Mode attribute of the particle shape. However, each particle now has a unique lifespan attribute, which can be accessed by other attributes. This is a big advantage of the per-particle (array) attributes.

> Using expressions is a powerful way to control your particle simulations as well as many other aspects of Maya. How do you come up with expressions? How do you know when to use them? Mostly it comes from practice, experience, and borrowing ideas from other animators. This is why it's a good idea to get involved with the Maya community through websites such as Autodesk's the-area.com, cgsociety.com, and highend3d.com, as well as online forums, magazines, and user groups. Once you've studied the work of other animators and understand a few expressions, coming up with your own will become easier and easier.

The Conserve Attribute

Let's take a step back and look at our laser sword. It's a bit on the meek side. It needs to be thickened up, and a little color wouldn't hurt either. First, let's beef up the sword by increasing the emission rate of the particle. Before we continue, you might want to save your work if you haven't already.

1. Stop the animation and in the Outliner find the sword curve. Expand the sword in the Outliner and you'll find an emitter called laserBlade1 parented to the sword curve. In the perspective window, you'll see a small circle on the sword curve. That's the emitter icon.

2. Select the emitter and open its Attribute Editor. Set the Rate (Particle/Sec) attribute to 8000 and play the animation.

The sword looks a little better, but it's still leaving too much of a trail of particles (see Figure 19.4). We can fix this by lowering the Conserve value on the particle shape.

Conserve is short for conservation of energy. The default value is 1. At 1, a particle loses no energy as it is emitted into the world. Lowering this value has the effect of slowing the particle down after it leaves the emitter. It loses energy as it travels. Setting Conserve to zero will essentially freeze the particle in space. Generally you don't have to lower this amount much to see an effect.

Figure 19.4

The circle at the center of the sword curve represents the emitter.

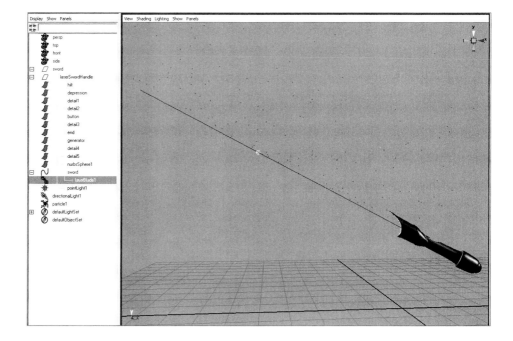

3. Set the Conserve attribute of particleShape1 to 0.5.

4. Scroll down to particleShape1's render attributes. From the Particle Render Type menu, choose MultiPoint. Click the button for Add Attributes For Current Render Type. A new list of attributes appears, as shown in Figure 19.5.

> In Maya you can display the particles in a scene in 10 basic ways. You must render some with Maya Hardware, and others you must render with Maya Software. Those that require software are indicated by the (s/w) next to their names in the list. We'll take a look at some of these throughout this chapter. Each particle type has extra attributes that are specific to it. These attributes are activated when you click the Add Attributes For Current Render Type button.

5. In the new list of attributes for MultiPoint, set Multi Count to 10, Multi Radius to 0.15, and the point size to 1. The MultiPoint particle replaces each single particle with a tiny cloud of particles. You control the size of the cloud and the number in each cloud with the newly added attributes.

6. Now we have something that looks more like a laser sword. Of course it is a bit on the gray side. Let's add some color. Scroll down to the Per Particle Attributes list and click the Opacity button that appears below the list. In the pop-up options box, choose Add Per Particle Attribute. This adds a new Opacity attribute to the list of per-particle attributes above.

> If no opacityPP option is added to the list, try closing the Attribute Editor and opening it again, or press the Load Attributes button at the bottom of the Attribute Editor to force the list to update. Sometimes the list doesn't refresh properly.

Figure 19.5

New attributes are added when you click the Add Attributes For Current Render Type button.

7. Right-click the box next to the opacityPP attribute in the list, and choose Create Ramp.

8. Right-click the opacityPP attribute and choose arrayMapper1 .outValuePP → Edit Ramp. A ramp texture will appear in the Attribute Editor.

The ramp determines the per-particle opacity value over the course of the life of each individual particle.

The value at the bottom of the ramp is 1, represented by white. The bottom of the ramp is the birth time of the particle. The value at the top is 0, or black. The top of the ramp is the death of the particle. So over the course of the particle's life, the opacity moves from white (1.0) to black (0). This ramp gives us a little more control over how the particles fade out. See Figure 19.6.

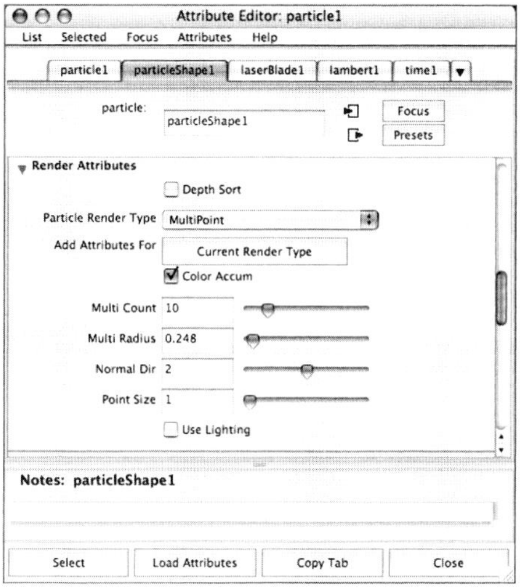

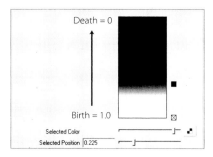

Figure 19.6

A ramp texture controls the opacity of each particle over its lifetime. The bottom of the ramp represents the particle at birth; the top represents the particle at death. Over the course of the life of the particle, the opacity value moves from 1 to 0 because of the way the colors on the ramp have been set up.

9. Delete the gray color in the middle by clicking on the box to the right of the gray area on the ramp and move the black slider down so that its position is at .360. Create a new color value on the ramp by clicking in the white value. Move it up the ramp so that the gray area between the white and black is smaller. By doing this we have further refined the shape of the blade as it moves around. See Figure 19.6 for reference.

10. We're going to use a similar process to add color to the blade. Click the Color button next to the Opacity button in the Add Dynamic Attributes section. Choose Add Per Particle Attribute again.

11. In the same way that we added a ramp to the opactityPP attribute in steps 7 and 8, add a ramp to the new rgbPP attribute in the list.

12. Right-click the rgbPP field again and choose arrayMapper2.outColorPP → Edit Ramp.

13. Use the ramp controls to create a ramp that moves from light blue at the bottom to a dark blue at the top. Don't make the light blue too light. This ramp works just like the opacity ramp. Each particle starts its life bright blue and then grows gradually darker until it fades out. Since the per-particle lifespan is set to a random range, the sword will look as though it is vibrating because each particle will have different opacity and color values on any given frame.

14. Play the animation. Now we have a nice blue laser sword. Looks a little dull, though. Open the Attribute Editor for particleShape1. Check the Color Accum box. Play the animation.

15. *Color Accum* refers to color accumulation. The colors of the particles now become additive. In denser areas of the particle, the color will glow bright white. In sparser areas, it will show more of the per-particle color—in this case it's blue. If the whole sword is too white, try adjusting the colors on the color ramp and darken the blues a bit.

The Hardware Render Buffer

The sword is looking good, so it's time to render a short sequence. The MultiPoint particle type requires Maya Hardware or the Hardware Render Buffer to render. Using Maya Hardware will often yield better results than the Hardware Render Buffer, but let's practice using the Hardware Render Buffer anyway.

1. Rewind the animation to the beginning, and open the Hardware Render Buffer by choosing **Window → Rendering Editors → Hardware Render Buffer**.

2. Make sure the camera in the Hardware Render Buffer window is set to the perspective view. You can move the view in the buffer window the same way you track, tumble, and dolly in the perspective view.

3. Open the attributes for the buffer by choosing **Render → Attributes** from the menu bar at the top of the buffer.

4. In the Attribute Editor, enter **laserSword** as the filename. Set the start frame to 1 and the end frame to 145.

5. From the Resolution menu, choose 640 × 480.

6. Under the Multi-Pass Render Options section, click Multi Pass Rendering to activate it, and choose 3 from Render Passes. Using Multi-Pass renders out 3 (or however many frames you've selected) for each rendered frame and then blends these frames together to create a smoother look for the final image.

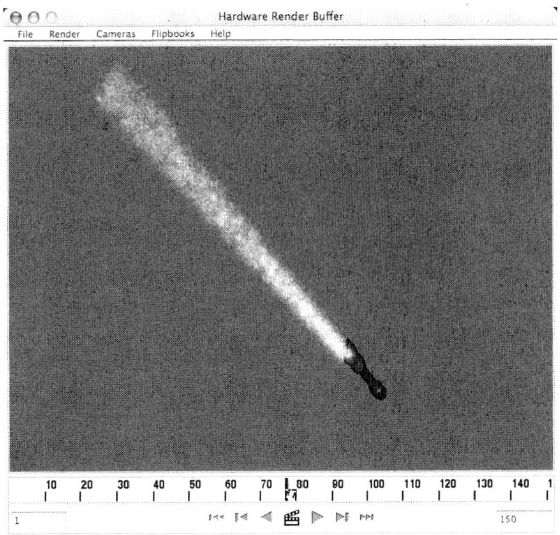

Figure 19.7

The laser sword as rendered in the Hardware Render Buffer. The particles make a nice-looking laser beam.

7. Leave the rest of the settings at their default values, and make sure the background color in the Display Options section is black or dark gray.

8. Play the animation to about frame 50. Click the clapboard icon at the bottom of the render to see a rendered still. It should take three passes to render the image. The particles shift position in each pass and are then blended to create a smoother, fuzzy appearance.

9. Rewind the animation and choose **Render → Render Sequence** from the menu bar at the top of the buffer.

The Hardware Render Buffer renders out each frame three times, takes a screen grab, and then stores the image to disk. It's important to turn your screensaver off and avoid having any interface windows overlapping the buffer while it's rendering. If you increase the number of passes in the Multi-Pass Render Options section, the image will look smoother but it will take longer to render because each frame will be rendered more times. You can also add motion blur to the render (see Figure 19.7).

> Macs are generally immune to the need to keep the Hardware Render Buffer Window front-most, so if you're using a Mac, you can go ahead and work on something else while the render progresses.

When the animation has completed rendering, you can view the sequence by choosing it from the Flipbooks menu.

Congratulations. You have successfully created your first particle animation. To see a completed version of the animation, open laserSword2.mb from the CD.

Now let's look at some ways to control the movements of particles.

Manipulating Particles with Fields and Goals

The two most common ways to move particles around are by using fields and goals. Fields are like forces—think gravity, air, and turbulence—that affect static particles or particles already in motion. When you need to move a particle, fields are generally your first resort. Furthermore, you can add multiple fields to your particles. The Maya documentation has a detailed description of how each field works. A goal can be any object in the scene, even other particles. Goals are like magnets that attract particles. More than one goal can affect the behavior of particles.

Open the file goalsAndFields.ma from the CD. Several display layers have been created, each with an identical particle grid. The particles have been set to render as spheres. You can easily create the grid using the settings in the option box for the Particle tool. Creating a particle grid by using the Particle tool is an example of creating a particle without the use of an emitter.

Each display layer has a different field applied to it, and the top layer is using a goal. Play the animation and compare the behaviors of the particles. Next we'll create a project that gets into actually creating and adjusting fields.

Using Multiple Fields with Particles

Open the file snowGnome1.mb from the CD. You'll find a pathetic little garden gnome whose life is about to get a little worse. The gnome is a single polygon object.

1. Create a volume emitter by switching to the Dynamics menu set and choosing **Particles → Create Emitter ☐**.

2. Name the emitter snowStorm, and set the emitter type to Volume. Set the rate to 100, and click the Create button.

3. At the origin you'll see a cube or a sphere. This is the volume emitter (see Figure 19.8). Move the emitter 7 units in X and 11 units in Y. Scale it so that it is 3 × 3 × 7. Make sure the Volume Shape in the Volume Emitter Attributes section is set to Cube.

> A volume emitter can be in the shape of a cube, a sphere, a cylinder, a cone, or a torus. You can set this in the Attribute Editor of the emitter in the Volume Emitter Attributes section. Naturally these settings apply only if your emitter is a volume.

4. Select the particle shape that was created with the emitter and open its Attribute Editor. In the Render Attributes section, switch to Blobby Surface (s/w), and click the Add Attributes For Current Render Type button.

5. Play the animation a few frames so that some particles appear on the screen. The blobby surface particles appear as gray circles. They're probably huge at this point. Set their radii to 0.2.

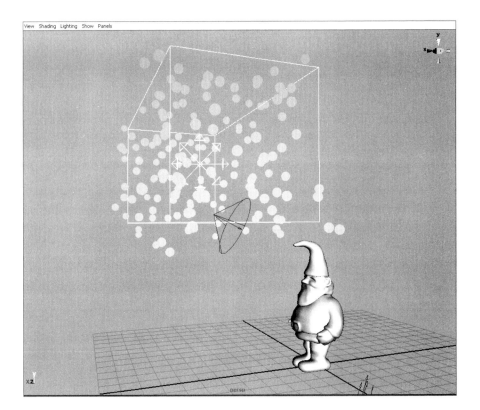

Figure 19.8

The volume emitter above the gnome

6. Rewind and play the animation. The particles are created randomly in the space defined by the cube emitter. From there they spread out as an omni directional emitter would.

7. Select particleShape1 and choose **Fields → Gravity**. Select the Gravity Field, and in its Channel Box set Magnitude to 5, set Attenuation to zero, and ensure that Use Max Distance is set to Off.

The Magnitude attribute refers to the overall strength of the field. Attenuation refers to the amount that the strength diminishes as the distance between the particle and the field increases.

8. When you play the animation, the particles fall. You can affect the speed of their falling by adjusting the magnitude of the Gravity field. Adjusting the dynamics weight or the conserve properties of the particle shape will also affect the rate at which the particles fall, but since this is an attribute of the particle shape, it will affect the way in which the particles interact with any other fields you add. That does come in handy sometimes.

You can add as many fields as you'd like to affect the way the particles behave. Here we'll add an air field to blow the snow toward the garden gnome figure.

1. With nothing selected, create an air field by choosing **Fields → Air**. If you play the animation, you'll notice nothing different happening. We must first attach the field to the particle by selecting the field and then selecting particleShape and choosing **Fields → Affect Selected Object(s)**. This is another way to attach a field to a particle as opposed to creating a field with the particle selected.

2. Choose **Window → Relationship Editors → Dynamic Relationships** to open the Dynamic Relationships window. This is a helpful tool for visualizing the various dynamic connections in a scene and for making and breaking those connections. The left side resembles the Outliner. Choose particle1 from the left side. In the Selection Modes pane, choose Fields. You'll see both the Gravity and the Air fields. If you select one of the fields, the highlight goes away, meaning the connection is broken. At this time, make sure both the Gravity and Air fields are connected to particleShape1.

3. Select airField1 in the Outliner, and move it 12 units in X and 8 in Y.

4. In the Channel Box for the Air field, set Magnitude to 5. Set Attenuation to 0, and turn off Use Max Distance by typing **0** in the Use Max Distance field. Scroll down and set the direction attributes to −1 for X, 0 for Y, and 0 for Z.

5. Play the animation. You should see the particles blowing toward the gnome. They should fly right through the poor guy.

6. You can control how the Air field affects the particles by adjusting its magnitude. You can control its direction by turning on Use Max Distance and repositioning the field.

7. With the Air field selected, click the Show Manipulators Tool button in the Tool Box. You now have interactive controls for the magnitude, max distance, and attenuation.

8. With the Show Manipulators tool still activated for the Air field, click the blue switch below the Field icon. You can cycle through additional interactive controls for the direction, speed, and spread of the Air field. Play with these controls and note the effect they have on the particles. When you get the hang of it, set the field back to a magnitude of 5 and turn off Use Max Distance. (A max distance of −1 is the same as turning off Use Max Distance.)

9. Now let's see if we can have some fun with our garden gnome. Select particleShape1 in the Outliner, and Ctrl+select the Gnome object. From the Particles menu, choose **Make Collide**. Play back the animation.

10. You will likely notice that playback is now a little slower, since Maya has to calculate all those collisions. However, now the particles are bouncing off the garden gnome—it looks as if he's being pelted with Ping-Pong balls. Let's make them stick a little. Select particleShape1 and open its Attribute Editor. Click the geoConnector1 tab. This tab has four attributes: Tessellation Factor, Resilience, Friction, and a new Offset attribute.

Tessellation Factor is like a collision resolution control. The higher you set this, the more accurate the collisions with the geometry; increasing Tessellation Factor will also slow down the playback of your animation. For the time being, leave this at 200. Resilience is how "bouncy" the collision is: higher resilience leads to larger bounces off a given surface. Friction controls how much a particle slides around a surface on an angled collision: high friction leads to particles that tend to stick to the surface. Finally, the new Offset attribute controls how far off a surface a particle will "collide" with it. This setting is important for particles that appear to have volume (such as blobby particles) because all particle collisions are calculated as if a particle is a mere point in space. By adjusting (or even keyframing) the offset value, you can force larger particle representations to not interpenetrate the collision surface.

1. Set Resilience to 0 and play the animation. You'll notice that now the particles don't bounce as much; some even stick and slide off the gnome.

2. Set Friction to 1. Now you'll notice that the particles stick to the gnome. Move Friction down to 0.5 and the particles stick and slowly move down the body of the gnome.

3. Set Offset to around 0.2 and notice that the particles now collide above their mid-point, which will create a more realistic look for the collisions.

The next problem is that the particles that don't hit the gnome but keep flying off into infinity. We need to create a ground plane for the snow to land on.

1. Create a NURBS plane and scale it up so that it covers the area around the gnome and where the particles are falling. Set the number of spans to 16 × 16.

2. Select particleShape1 and the NURBS plane and choose **Particles → Make Collide**. Find the node for geoConnector2 in the Attribute Editor and set Resilience to 0, Friction to 1, and Offset to about 0.1. Now when the animation plays, the particles stick to the ground as well as to the gnome.

3. The blobby surface particle type has some interesting properties, the first of which is that you can use a shader to color it. Select the particle and open up the Hypershade. Find the radioactiveGoo shader, right-click its swatch, and choose Assign Material To Selection. Play the animation until some particles are in view, and then render a frame using Maya Software.

4. Gnomey is being attacked by glowing green balls. To get them a little more gooey, raise the Radius and Threshold values in the render attributes in particleShape1's Attribute Editor. The threshold controls how much the blobby surfaces will attract each other and form into blobs. You have to render this to see how it looks; this property is not shown in the camera view. Try a value such as 0.6 for radius and 0.5 for threshold.

Figure 19.9

A garden gnome covered in radioactive goo

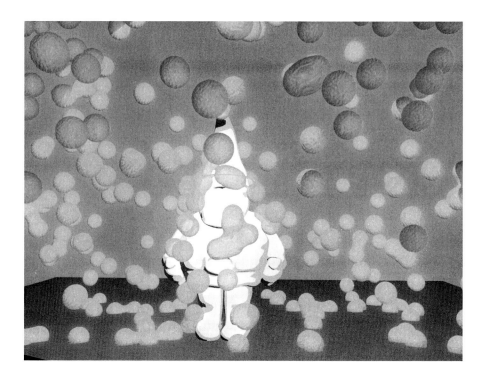

Finally we can render the poor gnome and watch in horror as he's covered in radioactive goo (see Figure 19.9). Before we render, however, we should create a cache for our particle simulation.

Particle Cache

A particle cache is a file sequence that is written to your disk and contains all the position data for the particle simulation. As you can imagine, this can take up a lot of disk space if you have a large number of particles in your scene. Double-check your available space before creating a particle disk cache. The reason to use a particle cache, however, is that it allows us to scrub through the scene in Maya so we no longer have to play the scene from the beginning each time. It also ensures that when we render the scene, the particles move the same way each time. This becomes especially important when we use random numbers in expressions, and especially if we intend to render out a sequence on several render machines. Otherwise, we could have unpredictable behavior in our final renders.

> Explicitly setting a seed number for the random lifespan—such as seed (particleID);— produces repeatable results, so try this method if you really need random but repeatable behavior.

To create a disk cache for our gnome scene, follow these steps:

1. In the Dynamics menu set, choose **Solvers → Create Particle Disk Cache ❐**.

2. In the option box, you'll see a field in which you can enter the path to a folder for your cache. By default, this is set to a subfolder of the current folder.

3. By default, the cache will be created based on the frame settings on the Timeline. You do have the option to use the start and end frame as they are in the render settings. Set the Timeline to go from 0 through 100 and leave this option unchecked.

4. Select the particle1 shape in the Outliner, and click the Apply button for the particle disk cache. You'll see the Current Frame Indicator go through the Timeline; however, nothing will update in the camera view until the end. That's okay. Maya is just writing files to your disk.

5. Once this is done, you should be able to scrub back and forth in the Timeline and see the animation. If you decide to change the simulation, you'll need to delete the particle disk cache; otherwise, nothing will change. To do this, choose **Solvers → Memory Caching → Delete**. You'll notice that you have options to enable and disable caching here as well.

6. If you're happy with the animation, set up a software render, take a break, and come back and check it out when it's done. See Chapter 13 for information on Maya software rendering.

Goals

Goals are one of the most useful tools for controlling particle simulations. Goals attract particles based on parameters you set. Any object can be a goal, including another particle shape. Goals are easy to animate, and are straightforward to incorporate into expressions. Let's play with some goals so you can get the hang of it.

1. Open the scene goals1.mb from the CD. You will see an emitter at the origin and a locator at the edge of the grid. The emitter is set to omni directional with a rate of 200 particles per second. Play the animation and observe the behavior of the particles.

2. The particles currently spread outward into the scene in all directions from the center of the emitter. Select particle1, and then select the locator. From the Particles menu, choose **Goal ❐**. Set Goal Weight to 0.5. Play the animation.

3. You'll see the particles shoot out toward the locator. At a goal weight of 0.5, they tend to overshoot the locator. Open the Attribute Editor for particle1 and find the Goal Weights And Objects section. Play the animation and try moving the locator1 slider up and down as it plays. This adjusts the weight of the goal, or the strength of the attraction. At a weight of 1, the particles are instantly placed at the position of the locator. At 0, the goal has no effect.

You can create as many goals for a particle system as you wish. Each goal will attract particles based on its goal weight attributes, causing the particles to "balance" between the different goals.

4. Adjusting the goal smoothness also affects how the particles make their journey toward the goal. Try adjusting this while the animation plays as well.

5. Set Goal Weight at 0.5, set Goal Smoothness to 3, and then adjust Conserve of the particlesdown to 0.7. The particles slow down as they reach the goal because they are losing energy as they travel. The overshoot is lost as well.

Goals and fields can also be combined to control the movements of particles. In this next section we'll add a Drag field to a particle that is already being influenced by a goal object.

1. Set Conserve back to 1.0, and add a Drag field to the particle by selecting particle1 and choosing **Fields → Drag**. Move the Drag field icon so that it's blocking the particles from reaching the locator shape, and then adjust its magnitude to 100. The particles slow down as they move through the Drag field. Fields and goals can work together in a particle simulation.

2. Delete the Drag field and create another locator. Move this locator 12 units in X.

3. Select particle1 and then locator2, and choose **Particles → Goal**. Make sure that Goal Weight is set to 0.5 as it is for locator1. Play the animation.

4. If you look from the top view, you'll see that the particles form a line equidistant from the two goals. Each goal is exhibiting the same amount of attraction on the particles, so they are stuck in between.

5. Open the Attribute Editor. Open the Goal Weights And Objects section. You'll see that a set of attributes and options identical to those for the locator1 goal have been added. While the animation is playing, try adjusting the sliders for locator1 and locator2. You'll see the particles moving closer to whichever goal has the higher value. You can add as many goals as you want to the particle shape and use them to guide your simulation.

6. Select the check box next to locator2's Goal Active attribute. We'll deactivate this so that we can work on the locator1 goal.

7. In the Attribute Editor, move up to Lifespan Attributes and choose LifespanPP Only. Just as in the previous exercise, we will add a Lifespan Per Particle attribute.

8. In the Attribute Editor, move down to the Per Particle (Array) Attributes section, right-click the lifespanPP field, and choose Creation Expression from the pop up options.

9. In the Expression Editor's main field, type the following:

```
particleShape1.lifespanPP=rand(2,3);
```

This will set the lifespan for each particle to a random range between 2 and 3 seconds.

10. In the Attribute Editor's PerParticle (Array) Attributes section, right-click the goalPP attribute above lifespanPP and choose Create Ramp. Once you see `<-arrayMapper1.outValuePP`, right-click again and choose Edit Ramp.

11. Adjust the ramp so that it is black from the bottom to about halfway up, make sure the top is white, and set Interpolation to Smooth. Play the animation.

12. The ramp is adjusting the goal weight of the particles over the lifespan of each particle. At birth, each particle has a goal weight of 0. As a particle ages, the value moves up the ramp. Toward the top, it starts moving toward a value of 1 and the particle starts to zoom toward the goal. You can have a lot of fun adjusting the values in the ramp and thus controlling how the particles approach the goal.

13. Stop the animation and go back to the Attribute Editor for the particle. Right-click the goalPP value again and choose Edit Array Mapper from the pop-up. Set Min Value to 0.01 and Max Value to 0.5. This changes the ranges in the ramp so that now black = 0.01 and white = 0.5. This is another handy way to fine-tune the simulation.

14. Right click the goalPP attribute, and choose Break Connection to get rid of the ramp that controls the goalPP.

15. Move back up to the Goal Weights And Objects portion of the Attribute Editor and click the Create goalWeight0PP button. This adds another attribute to the per-particle array attributes.

Per-Particle Goal Attributes

The per-particle goal attribute, which works for each goal that affects a particle, provides yet another level of control for your simulations. You can add ramps to each goal or access each goal in expressions or both.

> The attribute you create here is called goalWeight0PP. Maya numbers the goal weight PP attributes in the order in which the goals are added to the object, starting with 0. This may be a little confusing, but essentially our goal weight for locator1 is referenced in the per-particle array and in the Expression Editor as 0. If we added the second goal weight per-particle attribute, it would be goalWeight1PP.

We'll try out the goal attribute in this exercise.

1. In the Per Particle Array Attribute section, right-click goalWeight0PP and choose Creation Expression. Under the lifespanPP expression in the Expression field, type `particleShape1.goalWeight0PP=.5;`. Click the Edit button. This sets the goal weight for locator 1 to 0.5, much the same as we had before.

2. In the Expression Editor, switch to Runtime Before Dynamics and type the following:

```
particleShape1.goalWeight0PP=0.5+(0.5*sin(time));
```

What this expression is doing is calculating the time in seconds and taking the sine of that value. This new value is then assigned to the per-particle goal weight for locator1. Taking the sine of time will create a value that moves smoothly between −1 and 1 while the animation plays. It's a sine wave.

However, we don't want a goal weight of negative 1, so we are halving the value by multiplying it times 0.5, and then to that value we add 0.5. Thus, our sine wave has been cut in half vertically and bumped up so that now we get a value from 0 to 1. Play the animation, and you'll see how the attraction of the particles to the goal alternates between strong and weak. If you set the Conserve attribute to 0.7, it's a little more obvious.

Now we'll look at how two goals can interact with each other to alter particle behavior.

1. Make the second goal active by clicking on the check box under the locator2 value. Set the value to 0.5. From the top view, you'll see the particles move somewhat organically between the two goals.

2. Go back to the runtime expression for the goalWeight0PP attribute and edit it. Replace sin with noise, and play the animation. Now the particles move randomly between the two goals.

You can continue to develop this animation by adding a per-particle attribute for the locator2 goal. Try mixing ramps and expressions between the two goals. By combining all the techniques in the example we just discussed, you should be able to come up with a variety of ways to control article simulations. Of course, we're not done yet…

Soft Body Dynamics

There comes a time in every animator's life when they need a little jiggle. Soft body dynamics are a great way to get some jiggling motion in your animations, and they are fairly easy to set up. When you convert an object to a soft body, you are essentially turning all its vertices or CVs into particles. Fields, goals, and expressions can then act on these particles, and the object as a whole deforms as the particles move. Soft body dynamics can be used to create a jiggling secondary motion and simple cloth and fluid effects. Let's take a look at this in a couple of exercises.

1. Open the file `jellyCube1.mb` from the CD.

2. In this file you'll find a fairly dense polygonal cube and a bumpy plane. The cube and plane are both deformed with the same lattice. The cube has been animated sliding around the bumpy plane. If the lattice is visible, hide it by deselecting **Deformers** from the view panel's Show menu. This will make the animation of the cube easier to see.

3. Select the green pCube1 object, and from the Soft/Rigid Bodies menu in the Dynamics menu set, choose **Create Soft Body ❐**.

You can turn an object into a soft body in three ways:

Make Soft Turns the vertices into particles.

Duplicate, Make Copy Soft Allows you to make a duplicate copy in which all the vertices or CVs are soft but the original exists as well. This is useful because you can make the vertices on the original object goals for the particles on the soft object.

Duplicate, Make Original Soft Similar to Duplicate, Make Copy Soft but reversed so that the duplicate object can be made a goal object. This works well when you turn a lattice that is deforming an object into a soft body.

Let's see how this works by turning the animated cube into a soft body object.

1. Rewind the animation, and then choose Duplicate, Make Copy Soft.

2. From the other options, make sure that Hide Non-Soft Object and Make Non-Soft A Goal are checked. Deselect Duplicate Input Graph.

3. Set the weight at 0.5 and click Apply.

4. Play the animation.

Things are definitely looking goopy. In fact, the new gelatinized cube is leaping off the ground when it stops. Essentially each vertex of the non-soft, hidden object is a goal for each particle that composes the soft, visible object.

1. If you look in the Outliner, you'll see a new object called copyOf pCube1. Expand this object and you'll see the particle that comprises the vertices of this soft object.

2. In the Outliner, make sure Shapes is selected from the Display options. Find the shape node for the original pCube1 object. It should be written in blue, indicating that it is hidden. Select it, and from the Display menu on the toolbar, choose **Show Selection**. Rewind and play the animation.

3. Now you can see both the original object and the soft body copy. Notice how they interact. Select pCube1's shape node, and from the Display menu on the toolbar, choose **Hide → Hide Selection**.

The behavior of our soft body is not unlike the behavior of the particles in the goal exercise that we completed in the previous section, so we know we can control the movement of the soft body in a number of ways. We can turn down the conserve on the particle shape, we can adjust the goal weights, or we can add fields. We probably don't want to mess with the lifespan of the particles because making them die off could produce some strange results. Soft bodies also provide another alternative for controlling the goal weights per particle. We can interactively paint the goal weights on the cube using Maya's Artisan tools. For soft bodies, this is a good place to start.

Here's how to paint the goal weights on a soft body object:

1. Select the bumpy plane under the cube and turn off its visibility. Rewind the animation and zoom in on our cube o' jelly.

2. First let's set our goal weights to 1.0 for all the particles. Select the particle shape in the Outliner, and in its Channel Box or Attribute Editor, make sure the goal weight is 1.0. Now we have a starting place from which we can edit. If you play the animation, the jiggly motion should be gone.

3. Select the soft body cube geometry, and from the Soft/Rigid Bodies menu, choose **Paint Soft Body Weights Tool ❒**.

4. This is not unlike painting bone or deformer weights. We're going to use the brush to paint on all our weights. The cube should turn white, indicating that the goal weights are at 1. Set the radius of the brush to a comfortable size; fairly large is fine. We don't have to get too detailed.

5. Set Paint Operation to Replace and Value to 0.5. Start painting the upper part of the cube. We want to leave everything on the bottom of the cube at 1.0 so that it still follows the ground correctly (see Figure 19.10).

6. Once you have the top three-quarters of the cube painted gray, switch the Paint operation to Smooth and click the Flood button a few times. This will turn your blotchy paint job into a nice gradient.

7. Drop the Artisan tool and play the animation.

8. The bottom looks good, but the top is still a little crazy. Select the cube and choose the Paint Soft Body Weights tool again. In the Paint Operation section, choose Add and set Value at 0.25. Click the Flood button. This will raise the gray value to 0.75. Play the animation again.

You can continue to edit the weights of the soft body until you're happy. Try painting different values on different parts and then smoothing, and adding until you get close to the look you want. Sometimes three layers smoothed out looks good: 1.0 at the bottom, 0.75 in the middle, and 0.5 at the top.

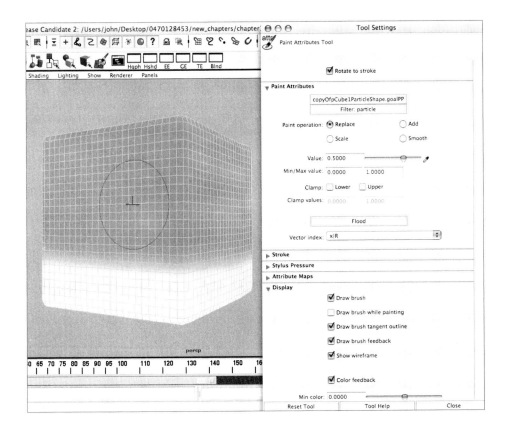

Figure 18:10

**Using Maya Artisan
to paint the soft
body goal weights**

What we have now looks goopy, but not like jelly. Jelly has a rippling effect that goes through the object when it's disturbed. To get this, we'll need to add springs to our soft body.

Soft-body springs are different from the rigid-body spring constraints. Soft-body springs can be added between each particle vertex on a soft body to help with the effect.

1. Select the cube and choose **Soft/Rigid Bodies → Create Springs** ❑.

2. In the options that appear, set Creation Method to Wireframe, set Wire Walk Length to 2, and turn off Use Per-Spring Stiffness, Use Per-Spring Damping, and Use Per-Spring RestLength. Set Stiffness to 100, and set Damping to 0. Leave Rest Length at 0, and leave End1 and End2 Weights at 1.

3. Click the Create button. Maya may take a few seconds to update.

4. When the springs are created, you'll see lines between each particle. The depiction of the springs in the camera view can slow down playback. To hide the springs you can deselect **Dynamics** from the view panel's Show menu or hide the spring object in the Outliner.

5. Play the animation and observe the results.

When you use springs on a soft body, your soft-body object might completely freak out and explode. Don't panic; you're computer hasn't turned on you (yet). This happens when the stiffness setting on the springs is at a high value. If this happens, you'll need to adjust your oversampling and your playback rate. To do this, go to your Timeline preferences and set Playback Speed to Play Every Frame and set Playback By Value to 0.5. Then in the Dynamics menu set, choose **Solvers → Edit Oversampling Or Cache Settings**. In this dialog box, set Oversamples to 2. Your animation will play back slower, but the exploding soft bodies should stop.

 Soft body dynamics can add subtle effects to character animations. Open the file soft-BodyCheeks.mb from the CD. Play the animation and observe the movement of the jowls (see Figure 19.11). It's a little exaggerated, but you can see how some secondary animation like this could be helpful. The setup is similar to the jelly cube animation. You can select the head in the scene and activate the Paint Soft Body Weights tool to see how the goal values have been applied.

Figure 19.11

A character's head has been turned into a soft-body object. The goal weights on the cheeks have been painted using Artisan.

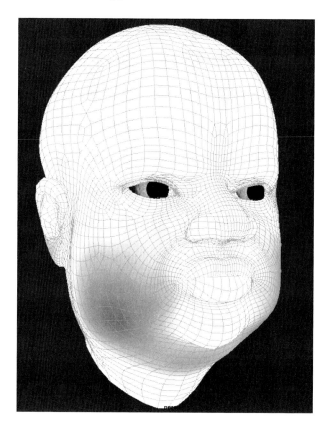

Sprites and Instances

Maya has some built-in particle effects that have their own expressions and scripts. You'll find them in the Effects menu in the Dynamics menu set.

One of the most useful is the curve flow. This effect allows you to create a stream of particles that follows a path. Let's test it out.

1. Open the curveFlow1.mb file from the CD.

2. You'll see a simple helical curve. Select this curve, and from the Dynamics menu set, choose **Effects → Create Curve Flow** ❐.

3. Set the name of the effect to stream, make sure the option to attach the emitter to the curve is enabled, set the number of control segments to 8, and set the subsegments to 4. Set Emission Rate to 100, Random Motion Speed to 0.5, Particle Lifespan to 5, and Goal Weight to 1. Click the Create button.

4. After a few seconds you'll see nine circles and locators appear along the curve. Click the Play button and a stream of particles will appear at the bottom of the curve and gradually make their way to the top, going through each circle along the way.

5. The circles along the curve are goals that guide the particles along the curve. If you open the Attribute Editor for the particle shape, you'll find that in the Per Particle (Array) Attributes section, a number of expressions have been created automatically. You can try editing these expressions if you are curious; certainly this is a good way to learn about expressions. However, if you just want to tune the way the particles move along the curve, you can select the stream group in the Outliner, and in its Channel Box you'll find a number of custom attributes you can edit. These include the goal weight of the particles, random motion, and the position of each goal along the curve.

Now let's make this a little more interesting by getting some sprites involved.

Sprites are a particle render type that consist of flat, square planes that are oriented to be perpendicular to the camera at all times. This allows you to map an image file or image file sequence to the planes so that your particles can look more complex, like smoke or fire. Sprites also have a consistent size so that if you zoom the camera in closely, they don't dissipate the way points or streaks do. Sprites must be hardware rendered however, which can be a drawback depending on what you want to achieve. Let's test a sprite on our curve flow simulation.

1. Select the particle in the curve flow scene, either through the Outliner or in the perspective view.

2. Open the Attribute Editor for the particle's shape node. In the Render Attributes section, choose Sprites. Click the Add Attributes For Current Render Type button to add attributes for this render type.

3. You might think that the image would be mapped to the sprites by adding a color attribute; however, the image is actually mapped using a shader. Select the particle shape and assign a Lambert shader. Lamberts work best since they have no specularity, which would be ignored by the particle anyway.

4. Make sure that Hardware Texturing is enabled in your perspective view, and open the attributes for the Lambert shader applied to the sprites.

5. In the color channel of the Lambert shader, click the checkerboard icon. We will map a file texture that is on the CD to the sprite. Choose File from the Create Render Node box, and make sure that it is mapped based on normal.

6. In the Image Name attribute under File Attributes in the File1 node, open the dialog box and browser to find the `spriteImage.tif` file located in the Chapter19 sourceimages folder on the CD.

7. When the image is mapped onto the sprite, you'll see a black flower pattern. The image preview in the File1 Attribute Editor's Texture Sample looks more like a fuzzy white dot. This is because the TIFF file itself consists of a white dot in the color channels and a flower shape in the alpha channel (see Figure 19.12). You'll also notice that the Lambert texture assigned to the sprite has a file texture mapped to both the color and transparency channels automatically. This happens when the imported file texture already has an alpha channel.

> You can create a sprite file texture in any image-editing software package, use photographs, or even create and render it out of Maya. However, you need to keep your image sizes small since each image is mapped to a particle. Try not to use anything larger than 128 × 128 unless you have a lot of RAM. Usually, 64 × 64 is just fine.

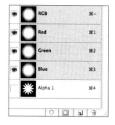

Figure 19.12

The channels for the sprite image as they appear in Photoshop's channel palette

8. Making the original sprite image white allows us some flexibility when changing the color of the sprite. Select the particle shape node, and in the Attribute Editor, click the Color And Opacity button in the Add Dynamic Attributes section. For both attributes, choose Add Per Object in the pop-up.

9. Scroll back up to the Render Attributes section and you'll now see numeric input fields for red, green, blue, and opacity. Enter 1.0 for red, 1.0 for green, and 0.5 for blue to make the sprites a nice pale yellow. Set the opacity at 0.8.

10. You can adjust the size of the sprites using Sprite Scale X and Y, and you can change the rotation by adjusting Sprite Twist. There are also per-particle sprite attributes you can add if you want to control these attributes with expressions. The Sprite Num attribute is available when you use a sequence of images for the sprites.

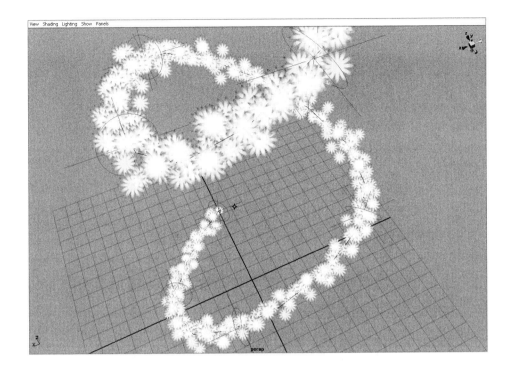

Figure 19.13

Particle sprites along the curve flow object

11. The Depth Sort attribute ensures that the sprites closest to the camera are in front. Make sure this is enabled.

12. You can render these particles using Maya Hardware or the Hardware Render Buffer (see Figure 19.13.). The file curveFlow2.ma on the CD contains the proper settings for this scene.

> The Sprite Wizard can make the task of assigning an image to your sprites a little easier. To use it, select your particle before assigning a particle render type, and choose **Particles →** **Sprite Wizard**. The wizard will walk you through setting up your sprites and will also make your life easier when you want to assign an animated image sequence to the sprite texture.

Particle Instancing

Particle instancing is similar to using particle sprites except that you are replacing each particle with a 3D object rather than with a 2D image. These objects can even be animated. This works well for creating swarms of bugs or other tiny, icky creatures, and it has the advantage of using software rendering as opposed to hardware, making compositing easier.

1. Select the particle shape object and switch the render type back to points.

2. Create a NURBS torus and scale it down to 0.25 in X, Y, and Z.

3. Select the torus and then the particle, and choose **Particles → Instancer (Replacement)**. The default options are fine.

4. When you play the animation, you'll see a delicious stream of donuts spiraling toward the heavens. The particles are related to the original geometry in the same way that an instanced object is related to the original. If you add a shader or rotate the original, the instances will update. However, since this is a particle, you can control some attributes using expressions as well (see Figure 19.14).

5. To control the orientation on a per-particle level, you will need to create a custom, vector, per-particle attribute and then set up some expressions to establish values for it. Creating expressions and custom attributes is covered in the next section. In the Attribute Editor for the particle, you will find an Instancer (Geometry Replacement) section where you can connect items such as position, orientation, and cycles to other attributes, including custom per-particle attributes. The file curveFlow3.mb on the CD contains the proper settings for this scene.

Figure 19.14

Particle instancing using a torus

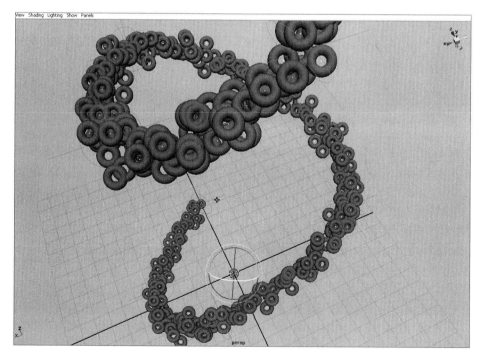

Advanced Particle Expressions

This final exercise is going to be a bit of a leap. If you have followed along so far and are comfortable with the type of animation workflow we've used in the previous exercises, you should be up for the challenge. If you're already familiar with animating particles, this section might teach you a few new tricks to try out on future projects.

This tutorial will take you step-by-step through the process of creating a particular effect: an eerie spectral cloud with elements of a time-lapse look. We want a turbulent cloud to appear in the air, grow, and then taper off. And we want some controls so that we can edit the effect after it has been set up. These controls are simple locators that could be animated or parented to the limbs of a wraithlike character. We're going to look a little closer at the goal weight per-particle and goal world position per-particle attributes as well as some ways to use ramps with expressions.

First, we want a turbulent stream of particles. We'll control their size and visibility by creating relationship between their per-particle position and the position of a locator.

1. Create an emitter, make it a volume emitter, and set its volume type to sphere. Name it cloudGen. Set the rate to 400.

2. The emitter should appear at the origin. If you play the animation, a semi-dense cloud of particles will spew out from within the sphere. Select the particle shape and choose **Fields → Uniform**.

3. The uniform force is just a force that pushes the particles in a particular direction. Really, the gravity field is a uniform force that pushes particles down in Y. Move the icon for the force a few negative units in X, just so that it's easier to see.

4. The force should start pushing the particles in the positive X direction. If nothing happens, double-check the connection between the particle and the field in the Dynamic Relationship Editor.

5. Let's calm down the motion a little. Set the conserve of the particle shape to 0.7.

6. Now let's randomize the motion. Select the particle shape and choose **Fields → Turbulence**. Set Magnitude to 30, and set Attenuation to 0. Make sure Use Max Distance is set to Off.

7. That looks cool, but the turbulence pattern itself is a little static. Let's get the noise pattern of the turbulence to animate a little. Select the turbulence field. In its Channel Box, right-click the PhaseZ attribute and choose Expressions.

8. In the Expression Editor, type the following in the Expression field:

    ```
    turbulenceField1.phaseZ=sin(time);
    ```

This expression moves the phase of the turbulence back and forth in Z over time in a sine wave pattern. Play the animation. Looks neat. You can also try `noise(time)`, which randomizes values from –1 to 1 in a connected manner that looks very natural.

9. It's not a bad habit to immediately assign a per-particle lifespan attribute to the particle shape. Even if you end up with something plain like a per-particle lifespan of 1 second, at least you have the attribute there, set up, and ready to use as an input value in any subsequent expressions or ramp. As we did in previous exercises, set Lifespan Mode to lifespanPP Only. Scroll down to the PerParticle (Array) Attributes section, right-click the Expression field, and choose Creation Expression.

10. For the creation expression type the following:

`particleShape1.lifespanPP=rand(5,7);`

11. Already this looks good enough for your demo reel. Okay, no it doesn't, but it does look rather cool. Switch the Particle Render Type setting to Cloud(s/w). For the time being, do not click the Add Attributes For Current Render Type button.

12. Create a locator and move it about 12 units in X. This will be our size control, which will help us create a sort of time lapse, condensing water vapor effect.

Figure 19.15

Attribute Editor buttons for each goal object allow you to add the new goal weight, position, normal, tangentU, and tangentV per-particle goal attributes.

We are going to set up a relationship between each particle's position and its proximity to the locator. From this, we will control the radius of the particle so that it appears and disappears as it passes the locator. For this, we'll use the goalWorldPostionPP attribute. You cannot directly animate this attribute; it just tells you the world position of a goal as it relates to each particle, but this is a useful input value to drive expressions. To get at this value, we need to make the locator a goal and also create a per-particle goal weight attribute.

1. Select the particle, Shift select the locator, and choose **Particles → Goal**.

2. If you play the animation, you'll see the particles shoot at the locator depending on the goal weight set when the goal command was activated. We'll eliminate this in a second with the Per-Particle Goal Weight attribute. Open the Attribute Editor for the particle. In the Goal Weights And Objects section, click the Create goalWeight0PP and the Create goalWorldPosition0PP buttons (see Figure 19.15).

3. Let's start by making a creation expression for goalWeight0PP. To do this, move down to the array attributes, right-click the goalWeight0PP field, and choose Creation Expression. In the Expression Editor under the lifespanPP expression, enter the following:

```
particleShape1.goalWeight0PP=0;
```

Click the Edit button.

4. If you play the animation, you'll see that it looks just as it did before we added the goal. However, now we have access to the location of the goal through the goalWorldPosition attribute. The locator goal is acting as a way to get additional information about the scene in the expression.

5. Go back up to the render type for the particle object and switch from Cloud(s/w) to numeric. Click Add Attributes For Current Render Type. You'll see each particle turn into a string of numbers. In the new attributes area, you'll see a field for attributeName. In this field, type **goalWorldPosition0PP**. The particles should look something like 12.000,0.000,0.000. By no strange coincidence is this the current location in X, Y, and Z of our locator goal object. If we move the locator and play the animation, these numbers will change accordingly (see Figure 19.16).

The numeric render type is a handy diagnostic tool. It doesn't render, but you can type the name of an attribute currently being used by the particle into the attribute name field and see the particle update accordingly. Try typing **birthTime** in this field, and you'll see the particles telling you when they were born in terms of seconds.

1. Switch back to Cloud(s/w) for the render type. Let's try working with the radius of our particle.

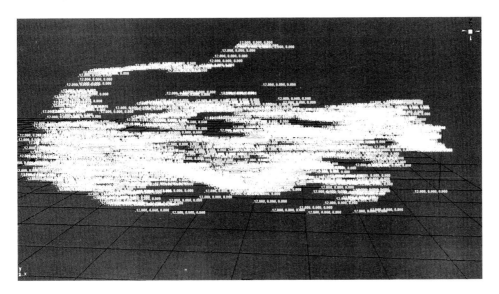

Figure 19.16

When the particles are set to the numeric render type, you can access per-particle information directly in the camera view.

Figure 19.17

**The Add Attribute
window allows you
to create new cus-
tom particle attrib-
utes or select from a
list of attributes.**

2. Click the General button in the area just below the
    array attributes section. From the pop-up menu,
    click the Particle tab and choose radiusPP from the
    list. You'll see a new radiusPP attribute added to
    the particle's array attribute list (see Figure 19.17).

3. Make a creation expression, as you did for the lifes-
    panPP and goalWeightPP attributes. The expres-
    sion should be `particleShape1.radiusPP=0.1`. If you
    play the animation, the particles are now smaller
    circles (see Figure 19.18).

4. We now have our creation expressions set up, and
    we've defined a starting point for our particles from
    which we can build some runtime expressions. With
    the Expression Editor open, select Runtime Before
    Dynamics Mode from the particle options.

First, we need to create some variables. These variables will hold values; we'll manipulate these values and then set the attributes equal to these new, manipulated values. Variables give us flexibility and allow us to gain greater control over the attributes.

Figure 19.18

**The turbulent cloud
of particles pushed
toward the locator**

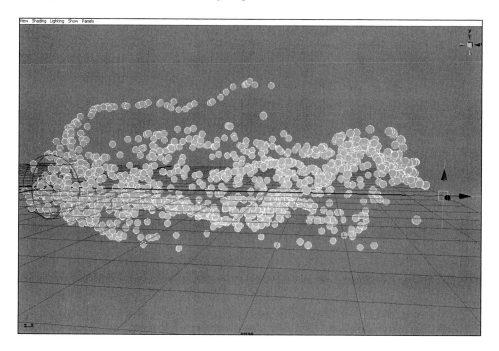

In each frame of a particle's life, the runtime expression will be executed, which is why expressions can be a little slow compared with other means of controlling attributes, such as Set Driven Keys, the Connection Editor, and utility nodes. However, they offer more direct, custom control. If expressions still can't get the job done, you can break out the MEL scripting (see Chapter 16). If that doesn't do it, you can use Maya 8.5's new Python script integration to create C++ style plug-ins for Maya. This new feature makes it a bit less scary to create powerful plug-ins that tie directly into Maya's API.

The first variable we'll create is one that will store the current per-particle radius value. We get this value each time the runtime expression is executed. Since the creation expression set this value at 0.1, for now we know this value will be 0.1. If the per-particle radius has changed by the end of the last frame, then at the start of the execution of this runtime expression, the variable will have that new value. Hopefully, this will become clearer in a moment. The syntax for creating a variable is as follows:

```
float $size=particleShape1.radiusPP;
```

In the first part of the variable syntax, we establish the type of number the variable will hold. In this case it is a float, which is a single positive or negative decimal number such as .1 or −3.14 or 0.33333333.

The second part of the variable syntax is the name of the variable. We chose $size since it is short and descriptive. Variable names must be preceded by a dollar sign ($).

We then set the variable equal to the value of the attribute we want the variable to contain. In this case, it is the radiusPP of our particle shape.

Finally, all statements must end with a semicolon in the Expression Editor. (If you forget, as everyone does now and then, Maya will let you know you've made a mistake by displaying an error message.)

Now let's create a variable to hold the location of the locator. We could make a variable just to hold the translate X, Y, and Z value of the locator, but instead we'll be using the new goalWorldPosition attribute we've set up. Why? There's a good reason that you'll learn in a little while. Type the following:

```
vector $goalPos0=particleShape1.goalWorldPosition0PP;
```

A vector is another variable type. A vector is a set of three numbers such as translate X, Y, and Z values or red, green, and blue values. Vectors can be added, subtracted, multiplied, or divided by other vectors directly. However, you can't perform mathematical operations between vectors and floats directly.

Now let's create a variable that will hold each particle's position. This will also be a vector. Type the following:

```
vector $pos=particleShape1.position;
```

Hold on a second. Up until now, whenever we've encountered a per-particle attribute, we've seen the giggle-inducing PP attached. However, position has no PP. You can verify this when you look at the list of attributes at the top of the Expression Editor. Why no PP?

Well, position is a per-particle attribute. It just is—and there's no PP attached. Just one of those things you learn and remember when you work with Maya. It's a quirk of the way Maya was programmed. More such gems are waiting to be discovered when you dive into the world of expressions.

One more variable to set up and we're on our way. We need a variable to store a threshold value for the distance between the goal shape (a.k.a. locator1) and the position of each particle. Since both of these attributes are vectors, our new measuring variable should be a vector as well. Type the following:

```
vector $dist=<<1,1,1>>;
```

Vector values are expressed as $<<x,y,z>>$.

Now we come to the meat of the expression. We're going to create a simple conditional statement that says, "If the distance between the particle position ($pos) and the goal position ($goalPos0) is less than our distance measure ($dist), make the particle's radius .3. If not, make it 0." Here is the syntax:

```
if  (abs($pos-$goalPos0<$dist)){
        $size=0.3;
        }
    else {
    $size=0;
        }
```

Of course this does nothing unless we now reset the radiusPP attribute equal to the new $size value. So the last line is

```
particleShape1.radiusPP=$size;
```

The syntax for finding the absolute value of a number is abs. If you remember from your high school math class, absolute value is the number itself without a negative sign. For example, the absolute value of −15.6 is 15.6, and the absolute value of 30 is 30. Since we work with a coordinate system that uses both positive and negative values, it's often necessary to get the absolute value of a position in order to measure distance in units properly.

Play back the animation. It should look kinda funky. The particles appear at the emitter, disappear, reappear near the locator, and then disappear again. Let's fix some of this.

1. In the Expression Editor, switch back to creation expression mode, and set the particleShape.radiusPP value to 0. This will ensure that the particle size at birth is also zero and that we won't see the particles popping up around the emitter.

2. That looks a little better. Let's expand the range of the visible particles. Go to the Runtime Before Dynamics mode and set our $dist variable to <<2,2,2>>.

3. Play the animation again.

Much better. But it would be nice if the particles grew in size as they approached the locator and then tapered off as they passed by. We could set up a complex loop within our expression to calculate this; certainly if the animation becomes more complex, we would need to do so. However, let's hack our way through this by using a ramp. Ramps are easy to control and give us a nice visual aid in tuning our particles. It's not the most elegant solution, but it will do in a pinch.

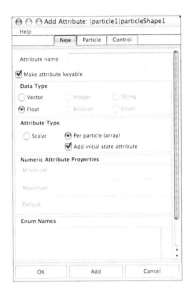

Figure 19.19

You can use the New tab in the Add Attribute window to create your own custom attribute.

1. To use a ramp, we need to create a per-particle attribute to hold it. We'll then set the radiusPP equal to the ramp based on the lifespan of the particle. Select the particleShape1 node, then choose Modify Add Attribute. We are going to create our own custom per-particle attribute (see Figure 19.19).

2. In the Attribute Name field, type **sizeScaleRampPP**. Set Data Type to Float, and set Attribute Type to Per Particle (Array). Leave everything else at the default. Click the Add button at the bottom of the panel and close the panel. You should see sizeScaleRampPP added to the list of array attributes.

3. Right-click sizeScaleRampPP and choose Create Ramp. By default, the ramp's input V value is set to the particle's age based on its lifespanPP value. That's fine.

4. Edit the ramp so that it has a line of white about three-quarters of the way from the top. The white should quickly transition to black at the top. See Figure 19.20 for some ideas.

5. Now we have to plug our ramp into the expression. Go back to the Runtime Before Dynamics section of the Expression Editor and replace

        $size=.3

   with

        $size=particleShape1.sizeScaleRampPP;

6. Play the animation. You should see a variation in size as well as a bit of ramping up and down in size as the particles approach and pass the locator.

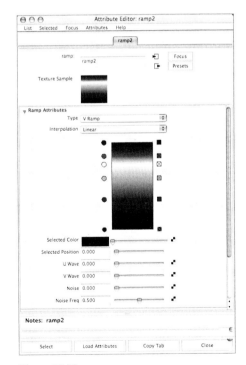

Figure 19.20

The ramp controlling particle size over lifetime

You can tune this part of the effect in three ways:

- You can edit the array mapper's max value and set it to a number other than 1. Try 0.3 or 0.5. This means that the upper limit—the white part of the ramp—is now 0.3 or 0.5 rather than 1, so the scale of the particles can't go beyond this value.

- You can adjust the position of the colors on the ramp, even add some gray or white bars so that the size fluctuates more over time.

- Since the ramp is tied to the particle's age, you can adjust the lifespanPP values in the creation expression. The random range for the lifespan adds a level of randomness to the size of the particles since the values of the ramp are tied to each particle's age.

The effect looks good. However, we have a lot of flexibility built in that we are not taking advantage of. Since we're using a per-particle goal position to determine where the particles appear, we can add another goal and hence another level of control. Plus, there's no reason why we can't animate the position of these goals.

First, let's add a goal.

1. Save your work and then create another locator.

2. Move this new locator (locator2) close to locator 1.

3. Select the particle shape, select locator 2, and choose **Particles → Goal**.

4. Open the Attribute Editor, and in the Goal Weights And Objects section, click the buttons under locator2 to add goalWeight1PP and goalWorldPosition1PP.

5. Add a creation expression in the field for goalWeight1PP.

> Remember, because of the order in which we added the goals, goalWeight0 and goalPosition0 refer to locator1 and goalWeight1 and goalPosition1 refer to locator2. A little confusing. We probably should have named our locators more clearly before adding them.

6. In the Creation Expression section of the Expression Editor, add a new line that reads as follows:

```
particleShape1.goalWeight1PP=0;
```

7. Switch to the Runtime Before Dynamics mode and add a variable for the new goalWorldPosition1 attribute. The line should look like this:

```
vector $goalPos1=particleShape1.goalWorldPosition1PP;
```

We have a new vector variable called *$goalPos1*.

Now we're going to change our expression, adding the new goal to the conditional statement. We will be saying, "If the absolute value of the distance between the per-particle position and the goal0 position is less than our distance variable *or* if the absolute value of the distance between the per-particle position and the goal1 position is less than our distance variable, use the ramp to control the size. Else, set the value to 0."

Here's the syntax:

```
If (abs($pos-$goalPos0<$dist)||abs($pos-$goalPos1<$dist))
     $size=particleShape1.sizeScaleRamp;
     else
     $size=0;
```

Play the animation. Try moving locator2 closer to the emitter to make sure it's working. Remember that the particle is a stream moving in the positive X direction. If you
move either locator too far out of the stream, you'll lose the effect.

Now things are looking rather neat (see Figure 19.21). For some additional fun, see if
you can create some randomness in the distance variable so that the region around each
locator grows and shrinks over time. This may require creating a float-variable, set to a
random or noise function, and then plugging this new variable into one or more of the
vector values of the $dist$ variable. Or you can use the sphrand function to generate random vector numbers and use that to alter the $dist$ value.

```
Float $noisy=(abs(noise(time))+2;
Vector $dist= <<noisy,noisy,noisy>>;
```

For one final touch, let's animate the position of the locators using an expression.
Select locator1, right-click its translate Z field in the Channel Box, and choose Expressions. For the expression, type this:

```
locator1.translateZ=sin(time);
```

Do the same for locator 2, but set its Z value to the following:

```
Locator2.translateZ=cos(time);
```

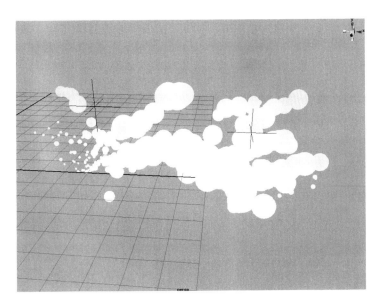

Figure 19.21

**The cloud scales as
it approaches the
locators.**

Here is the syntax for the creation and runtime before dynamics expressions:

Creation expressions:

```
particleShape1.lifespanPP=rand(5,6);
particleShape1.goalWeight0PP=0;
particleShape1.goalWeight1PP=0;
particleShape1.radiusPP=0;
```

Runtime expressions:

```
float $size=particleShape1.radiusPP;
vector $goalPos0=particleShape1.goalWorldPosition0PP;
vector $goalPos1=particleShape1.goalWorldPosition1PP;
vector $pos=particleShape1.position;
float $noisy=(abs(noise(time)))+2;
vector $dist=<<$noisy,$noisy,$noisy>>;

if (abs($pos-$goalPos0<$dist)||abs($pos-$goalPos1<$dist))
    $size=particleShape1.sizeScaleRampPP;
    else
    $size=0;

particleShape1.radiusPP=$size;
```

The cloud(s/w) render type has a shader applied to it automatically when you create it. It's called particleCloud1, and you can find it in the Hypershade. Feel free to experiment with the settings and try rendering a few frames of the particle cloud in the scene. When you are satisfied with the look, create a particle disk cache and render the animation. A completed version of this scene, called `cloud1.mb`, is located on the CD.

This effect would look cool wrapped around a ghostlike figure. The controlling locators can be parented to parts of the figure itself, allowing the fog to come into existence as it approaches the figure.

Summary

After reading this chapter, you should be familiar with how to create and work with particle systems. You should understand concepts such as particle lifespan and per-particle attributes and know how to create expressions for attributes and use ramps to control attributes. You should also understand how to use fields and goals with particle systems and particle collisions. This chapter also introduced working with soft body objects, particle sprites, the curve flow effect, and particle instancing. Finally, this chapter delved into the deeper world of advanced particle effects using expressions.

The next chapter introduces Maya Fluid Effects, which are similar in many respects to particles, but are better suited to creating effects like lava, fire, and pyroclastic smoke.

CHAPTER 20

Fluid Effects

The Fluid Effects simulation engine is one of Maya's most complex elements. Based on the Navier-Stokes equations that are a foundation of the science of fluid mechanics, Fluid Effects calculates the flow of viscous fluids over time, including piece-to-piece interaction of the fluid particles. (This interaction is a major difference between using Fluid Effects and using particles in Maya.) Although the underlying physics of the engine is highly complex, Maya wraps this in an elegant, easy-to-use package with a number of built-in presets available to help you create great effects quickly. Even with all the effort Autodesk has put into simplifying the Fluid Effects interface, however, the engine is so huge and powerful that there are in excess of 400 user-adjustable controls for how a fluid behaves and renders, a fact that becomes all too obvious when opening the Attribute Editor of a fluid. In this chapter, we will examine many of the most important Fluid Effects controls and how to use them to create the effects you want. Although we don't have space to go over every control, by the time you get done with this chapter you will have a solid idea of how to create and modify fluidlike effects to your liking for use in many situations.

This chapter covers the following topics.

- **What are fluids?**
- **Drag-and-drop fluids**
- **Creating and editing fluids from scratch**
- **Fluid attributes**
- **Ocean and pond effects**

What Is a Maya Fluid?

The Maya Fluid Effects package contains two separate, fundamentally different pieces, a true fluid simulator and a deformation/rendering engine called Ocean Effects. The 2D/3D simulation engine runs a nearly physically accurate simulation of fluids using the Navier-Stokes state equations to determine at any finite time interval where fluid particles are based on the behavior of neighboring fluid particles and generalized external forces such as temperature, density, and fluid velocity. As with Maya's particle system, each calculation depends on the state of the system on the previous frame (or fraction thereof); thus the simulation must play through every frame to produce valid results, which can become time consuming. Unlike Maya particles, however, fluids simulate connected flows, in which each fluid particle relates to others around it; for Maya's basic particles, there is no direct capability to do this. The Ocean/Pond Effects portion of the Fluid Effects package, on the other hand, does not use fluid dynamics directly. Instead, these effects use surface displacement, clever texture mapping, and some particle effects to produce convincing bodies of water that can simply be dragged and dropped into a scene that needs water effects. We will discuss Ocean/Pond Effects more fully in later sections.

Because of all the factors to be considered, running a fluid simulation carries a high computational cost. To minimize this overhead, Maya's simulations are contained within boxes called fluid containers (see Figure 20.1). Maya calculates fluid flow within these boxes but not outside of them. In contrast, Maya particles are calculated everywhere in the scene. A fluid container is further subdivided into small cubic areas called voxels, which define the smallest space in which a fluid is calculated. The more a fluid container is subdivided into smaller voxels, the more accurate the simulation but, conversely, the longer it will take Maya to simulate each frame. The primary difference between 2D and 3D fluid containers is the depth of the container. Although a 2D container is divided only in width and height, a 3D container can be arbitrarily subdivided in depth as well. A 2D container is much more efficient to simulate than a 3D one: if you double the number of voxels in width and height in a 2D container, the simulation time increases by a factor of 4 (2×2); if the number of voxels in a 3D container is doubled, the simulation time rises by a factor of 8 ($2 \times 2 \times 2$).

When creating a simulation, it is important to take into account the resolution of the simulation, as well as the intended output, and to balance the calculation times versus the quality of the final output. Fewer voxels means faster calculation times but lower resolution simulation; more voxels leads to higher resolution simulations but potentially much longer calculation times. Fortunately, Fluid Effects, especially for 2D fluids, is fast, allowing fairly complex systems to be simulated in near real time. When simulating fluid effects, especially 3D fluid effects, it is often best to get the general behavior of the system working using few voxels (low-resolution simulation) and increase the density of voxels only after the general behavior is acceptable. This speeds up calculation time, allowing you to view more iterations of the simulation in a given time, which can lead to more refined animations.

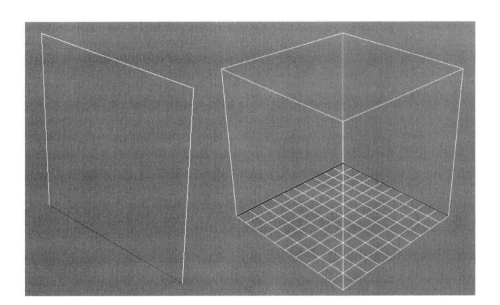

Figure 20.1

A 2D (left) and 3D (right) fluid container

Although you might assume that a 2D fluid would not be particularly useful for 3D rendering, for a more-or-less still camera, a 2D fluid can be quite convincing and can simulate and render much faster than a 3D fluid. A 2D fluid can actually have some depth, allowing for self-shadowing and other 3D effects. Although the illusion of depth breaks down if the camera rotates around the container, for many effects in which the camera is still, at a distance, or merely zooming straight in or out, a 2D fluid works well and is much faster to interact with and render than a 3D fluid.

NAVIER-STOKES EQUATIONS

The Navier-Stokes equations were developed in the 19th century by (you guessed it) Navier and Stokes. This set of three interconnected differential equations describes the motion of fluids as a series of small "particles" whose momentum, mass, and energy are conserved. (That is, these values do not change over time for the fluid as a whole.) In these equations, particles interact with one another, transferring momentum and energy (though not generally mass) to other particles. Computer fluid dynamics models evaluate the state of each particle for each time step Δt, where Δt is small, and use the results of the equations at this time step as the initial conditions for the reevaluation of the same equations for the next time step, $t+\Delta t$. The equations are complex to understand and have to account for boundary (the edge of a fluid, for example) and discontinuity conditions, which increases the complexity of these equations. Thus, evaluation of the equations is highly computationally intensive and can be slow, even on fast machines. For a thorough introduction to the Navier-Stokes equations, try a Web source such as www.navier-stokes.net.

So what can a 2D or 3D fluid simulate? Any single-fluid motion, such as clouds, explosions, smoke, fire, fog, lava, and mixing paint colors. With Maya's built-in presets, a generic version of most of these simulations is just a drag away, as discussed in the next section. Fluid Effects lets you view and render out the density gradient of a set of fluid particles over time as they interact with one another; react to velocity, temperature, density, and other fields; and collide off surfaces and/or the container itself. You can view and render the results either as cloudlike volumes, which can be texture mapped to taste, or as more substantial polygonal meshes that render as anything you want to texture them (water or lava, for example).

What Fluid Effects cannot simulate is two or more fluids interacting. A situation such as water pouring into a glass, for example, is a two-fluid simulations in which water from a pitcher (fluid 1) and water already in a glass (fluid 2) interact. Because Fluid Effects currently allows simulation of only one fluid, a simulation like this is not possible, though with some "cheating" of the density gradient, you can fake the effect using a steep drop-off from one density (the "water") to the other (the "air"), similar to the way a fire effect is created. Even with the single fluid restriction, Fluid Effects is useful for a range of effects and can save an effects animator a great deal of time creating complex naturalistic animation.

Fluids are different from Maya's particles. Although they both use some of the same kinds of simulation elements (for example, gravity, turbulence, and collisions), particles are calculated as completely stand-alone elements, no particle interacting with any other, nor will particles render as single objects (with the exception of the Blobby Surfaces and Clouds render types, which blend particles when they are close together). Although particles are quick to calculate, they are poorly suited for viscous fluid simulations because there is no global connection between particles; each particle behaves independently of all the others. Fluids in Fluid Effects, on the other hand, behave in more uniform large-scale ways because they are controlled by velocity (and other) gradients. Thus, Fluid Effects, while being slower to compute, is far better suited for situations in which the elements need to interact (such as fire, water, pyroclastic smoke, or lava).

> Particles can be influenced by fluids in a fluid container. Thus, particles can become part of a Fluid Effects simulation.

Here is a quick run-down of some of the most important fluid properties:

Density represents the material property of the fluid. Areas with high density will be visible in the simulation, and areas with low density will be transparent.

Velocity affects the behavior of dynamic fluids, moving Density, Temperature, Fuel, and Color values. Velocity is required for dynamic fluid simulations. It has both magnitude and direction. For dynamic simulations, Velocity values are based on the forces you apply to the simulation. You can also use Velocity as a fixed or static force to drive the simulation.

Temperature affects the behavior of a dynamic fluid via a gradient of temperatures in the container.

Fuel, combined with Density, allows a reaction to take place. Density values represent the material, and Fuel values determine the state of the reaction. Temperature can "ignite" the fuel to start a reaction (such as in an explosion). As the reaction unfolds, the Density and Fuel values dissipate until the reaction is over.

Color appears in a container only in which there is Density. You can apply color in two ways:

- Using the built-in ramp slider. A shader that is part of the fluid object makes it relatively simple to color your fluid object.
- Using a grid. A grid lets you control where color shows up in each voxel. Colors can behave dynamically so that they can mix.

We will cover all these fluid properties in more detail throughout this chapter.

Drag-and-Drop Fluids

The simplest way to create a fluid effect is to drop it into a scene from the Visor. By dragging a fluid example from the Visor, you get a premade simulation that runs well and looks good for any number of purposes without any work at all. We will cover how to create a fluid effect and an ocean effect via this method in this section.

To create a flame effect, take the following steps.

1. Open a new scene in Maya.

2. From the Dynamics menu set choose **Fluid Effects → Get Fluid Example**.

3. Click the Fluid Examples tab in the Visor (if it's not already highlighted), and click the Fire folder icon at the left (see Figure 20.2).

Figure 20.2

The Visor, showing various fire effects

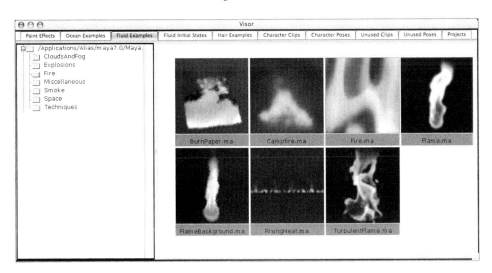

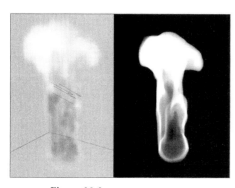

Figure 20.3

The flame simulation shown in the Maya scene window (left) and in a final render (right)

4. MM drag the Flame.ma icon onto your scene window, and play forward several frames into the animation. You should see something similar to the left image in Figure 20.3.

5. Render out a test image (as shown on the right in Figure 20.3) to see your instant flame. Just add a torch and a rocky wall and you're ready for some great dungeon effects!

Creating an ocean/pond effect via drag-and-drop is just as easy as creating a fluid effect. To create a stormy ocean, take the following steps.

1. Open a new scene in Maya.

2. From the Dynamics menu set choose **Fluid Effects → Get Ocean/Pond Example**.

3. Click the Ocean Examples tab (if it's not already highlighted) to display the various ocean and pond presets (shown in Figure 20.4).

4. MM drag the HighSeas.ma icon into your scene and play the animation in your scene window. You should see something that looks like the left side of Figure 20.5, with waves and a misty atmosphere.

5. Render out a test image from your animation to see the body of water in its final, rendered state, as shown on the right in Figure 20.5.

To create a sample pond, take the following steps.

1. Open a new scene in Maya.

2. Open the Visor (choose **Window → General Editors → Visor**), or alternatively, from the Dynamics menu set choose **Fluid Effects → Get Ocean/Pond Example**.

Figure 20.4

The Visor, showing various ocean shader examples

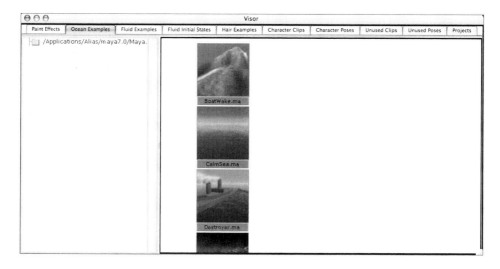

3. Click the Ocean Examples tab in the Visor (if it's not already highlighted) to display the various ocean presets.

4. MM drag the `WindingPondWake.ma` file into your scene and play the animation in your scene window. You should see something that looks like the left side of Figure 20.6, complete with a wake from an invisible "boat."

> Ocean Effects and 3D Fluid Effects simulations can take a long time to render due to the complex nature of their simulation, so be prepared to wait on renders, especially if you want to render at high quality or large size.

5. Render out a test image from your animation to see a pond simulation. Your rendered image should look similar to the right side of Figure 20.6.

As you should be able to tell from these three simple examples, it is extremely easy to create highly realistic fluid simulations. Try dragging other example files into Maya to see what they do. If you select the fluid container (for Fluid Effects and Ponds) or ocean surface (for Ocean Effects) and open the Attribute Editor, you can experiment with the parameters of these preset scenes. Real-world effects shots can benefit from slightly tweaked drag-and-drop Fluid Effects, as Figure 20.7 shows.

Figure 20.5

The High Seas ocean shader scene shown in the Maya scene window (left) and in a final render (right)

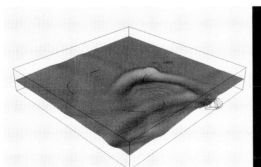
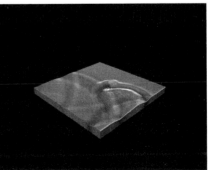

Figure 20.6

The pond simulation scene shown in the Maya scene window (left) and in a final render (right)

Figure 20.7

Drag-and-drop explosions (slightly modified) are used in a science fiction battle scene. *Copyright 2005, Clemson University Digital Production Arts.*

When you've finished playing around with these scenes, proceed to the following sections, in which we'll start from scratch instead of using a preset and show you how to create your own scenes. We'll also describe some of the more important attributes you can change to modify your scenes (or the included presets) to your specific needs.

Creating and Editing Fluids

Creating a 2D or 3D fluid from scratch isn't much more difficult than dragging a prebuilt scene in from the Visor. You have two basic options when creating a new container: creating an empty container or creating one with an emitter. If you want a fluid container with an emitter in it, it is obviously easier to create one with the emitter already inside, though adding an emitter is not at all difficult.

Creating a 2D Fluid

To create a 2D fluid, follow these steps:

1. In a new Maya scene, choose (from the Dynamics menu set) **Fluid Effects → Create 2D Container With Emitter**. This will create a new container (named fluid1 by default) with an emitter built in, as shown on the left in Figure 20.8.

2. Set your view to smooth shaded (press the 6 key on the keyboard), rewind the animation, and play it back to show a white gaslike substance being released by the emitter into the container, as shown on the right in Figure 20.8.

Be sure that you have your animation playback set to play every frame; if you do not, the simulation will break down. Choose **Window → Settings/Preferences → Preferences**, and then choose Settings: Timeline.

Figure 20.8

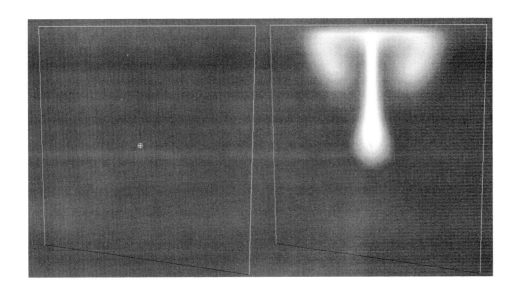

3. To add a second emitter to your fluid container, choose **Fluid Effects → Add/Edit Contents → Emitter**. Although a second emitter has been created, you will not see it in the scene because it is in the same location as the first emitter.

4. To see the new emitter, be sure it is still selected and move the emitter to a new location in X or Y. Be sure not to move your emitter on the Z axis. If the emitter leaves the fluid container, it will not emit a fluid any longer. (You can try this to see for yourself.) The need for the emitter to remain within the fluid container is one important difference between fluid and particle emitters.

5. Play back the animation again. You should see both emitters working and the fluids from both intermingling, as in Figure 20.9.

Fluid Interaction with Other Objects

To make a simulation a little more interesting, you can create any type of geometric primitive or particle and, placing it in the fluid container, let it interact with the fluid itself. To demonstrate this, use your basic 2D fluid from earlier (or create a new 2D fluid container with an emitter), and then create a NURBS torus (choose **Create → NURBS Primitives → Torus**). Stretch or deform the torus if you want, and then place it inside the fluid container. (Only a portion of the torus will fit within the container, of course, because it is 2D.) If you play back the animation now, the fluid will ignore the torus because the fluid and the torus have not yet been made to interact. To make the two scene elements interact, select the torus, Shift+select the fluid container, and choose **Fluid Effects → Make Collide**. Now play back the simulation and you should see the fluid wrap around the torus, as in Figure 20.10.

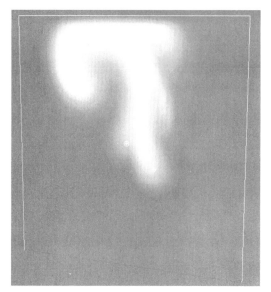

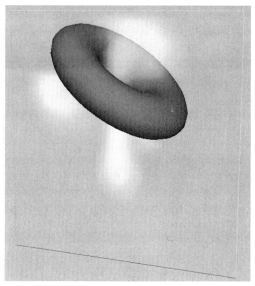

Figure 20.9

Two fluid emitters in the 2D container

Figure 20.10

A 2D fluid interacting with a torus primitive

Creating a 3D Fluid

Creating a basic 3D fluid is essentially the same as creating a 2D fluid, and the options in the Attribute Editor are much the same as well—which all makes sense since 2D fluids are just a special case of 3D fluids. On the other hand, 3D fluids are generally slower to manipulate because of the added computational challenges of a third dimension. Thus, although 3D fluids can be used in all cases when a fluid is needed, it is often wise to ask whether a 2D fluid can be used instead. For many purposes, a 2D fluid will work adequately and will simulate (and render) much faster. (See the "Hands On" section at the end of this chapter for an example of when a 2D container works fine for an effect.) In other cases, a 3D fluid is a must. In general, if the camera is fairly stationary relative to the fluid and the fluid does not need to create complex effects such as self-shadowing (which gives the impression of greater depth), a 2D fluid will work just fine. If the camera moves a great deal, or flies through the fluid, and/or if the fluid needs to create detailed shadows within itself, a 3D fluid is needed.

To create a 3D fluid with an included emitter, choose (from the Dynamics menu set) **Fluid Effects → Create 3D Container With Emitter**. You will get a cube with an included fluid emitter, which, if you play back the animation, will produce a 3D volume of gaslike fluid as shown in Figure 20.11.

Because 2D and 3D containers are essentially the same as far as attributes are concerned, we'll next examine fluid and container attributes using a default 2D fluid as a test case.

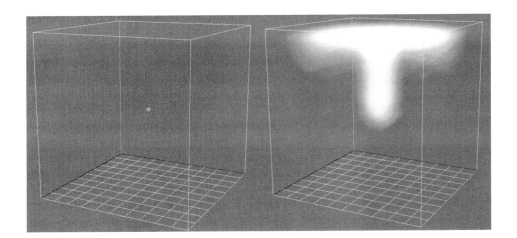

Figure 20.11

A 3D fluid container with emitter (left) and the emitter discharging fluids into the container (right)

Editing Fluid Attributes

Figure 20.12

The Attribute Editor for fluid1

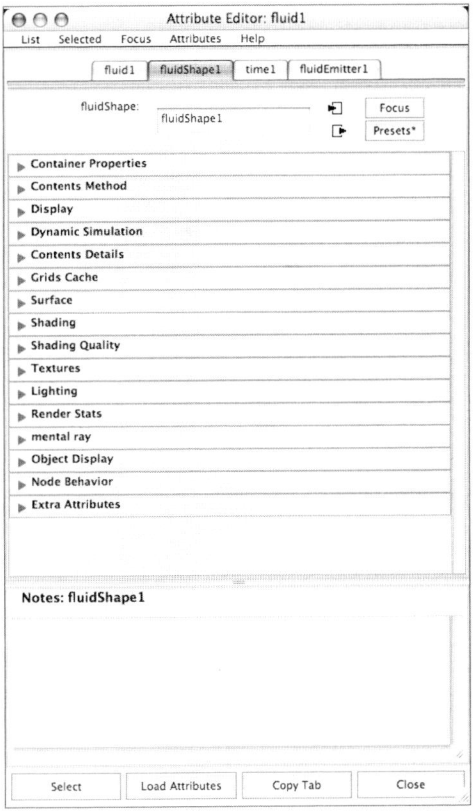

Now that you know how to create basic Fluid Effects, let's take a look at some of the attributes available to you to change the behavior of your fluid. First, create a default 2D fluid container with an emitter. Then select the container and open the Attribute Editor. You should see the fluidShape1 tab selected at the top, some sections (hidden behind twirl-down arrows) of attributes you can adjust, and a Notes section at the bottom of the window (see Figure 20.12). The Notes section at the bottom of the window is an area into which either you or anyone else can write notes about the current fluid. This is a great way for you to write down the specifics of a particular fluid you've built or for you to read about a fluid someone else has created. If, for example, you open one of the prebuilt fluids from the Visor and look at it in the Attribute Editor, you will see several sentences describing the particular effect and some suggested methods for modifying it.

The rest of the Attribute Editor contains a multitude of settings you can adjust to alter the behavior of either the fluid itself or the container in which it exists. Although we don't have the space to discuss every attribute, we will point out some of the most useful here. As with all dynamics simulations in Maya, a bit of experimentation is a great way to get to know all the attributes of a fluid, so feel free to play with settings.

The Container Properties Section

Starting with the top, let's first look at the Container Properties section of the Attribute Editor, which adjusts the resolution and behavior of the fluid container itself. The Resolution settings (set to 40 in X and Y by default) control how many voxels are in the container. A larger number (such as 100 in each direction) means a finer fluid simulation but one that runs slower due to the greater number of calculations that must be performed since there are more voxels over which to run the simulation. The Size attributes (set to 10 in X and Y and 0.25 in Z by default) control the size of the fluid container. (You can also use the Scale tool to interactively change the container's size.)

The Boundary X and Y attributes control how the container deals with fluids that reach container walls. By default, these are set to Both Sides, indicating that the fluid will react to all four walls (both sides in X and Y) and thus behave as if it's in a "room" from which it cannot escape. If, on the other hand, you want the fluid to interact with only one wall, to wrap (come up from the bottom of the container when it reaches the top), or simply not to interact with the walls at all, you can choose the appropriate condition from the pop-up menu. Figure 20.13 shows a higher resolution (100 × 100) fluid simulation running with Boundary X and Y set to None. The fluid passes through the boundary of the container (and thus disappears). This might be a more desirable behavior if, say, you wanted to create an outdoor campfire and didn't want the smoke from the fire to wrap back around to the ground once it reached the top of the container.

> When a fluid passes outside the boundaries of its container (which is possible when boundary conditions are set so that fluids can pass through them), it disappears completely from the scene. Thus, you will not generally want to show the boundary of a container that allows fluids to pass through it because it will reveal a harsh break between the simulated fluid and nothing.

The Contents Method Section

In the Contents Method section (below the Container Properties section) are several pop-up controls that determine how the fluid behaves within the container. For the default 2D fluid case, Density and Velocity are set to Dynamic Grid; Temperature, Fuel, and Falloff Method are set to Off; and Color Method is set to Use Shading Color. A dynamic grid updates its conditions over time, which allows the simulation to run. If you turn either Density or Velocity to Static Grid instead (causing the simulation not to update on each frame), the fluid will simply collect around the emitter instead of rising and filling the container.

Turning Velocity to Gradient mode instead and setting Velocity Gradient to an X Gradient causes all the emitted fluid to rise at a 45° angle away from the emitter, as in Figure 20.14. (Other Gradient options cause motion in different directions.) Changing the Temperature

Figure 20.13

A finer simulation (100 × 100 voxels) with boundary conditions set to None

Figure 20.14

Using an X Gradient velocity (rather than Dynamic Grid) on a fluid

and Temperature Gradient settings to Gradient and X Gradient causes a temperature gradient in the X direction to "heat" the fluid, increasing it more quickly and at an angle in the X direction. (This effect is more easily seen if you first reset the Velocity method back to Dynamic Grid.) Without fuel in the scene (see the next section for more on creating fuel), the Fuel setting has no effect on this simulation. Finally, Color Method controls how fluid color is calculated. The Use Shading Color option (selected by default) uses settings from the Shading section of the Attribute Editor to control color. Static and Dynamic Grid allow specific control over color (statically or dynamically as indicated), which you emit or paint into a container. (Use the Contents Details: Color section to control color in this case; see the section "Painting into Containers" later in this chapter for more on the subject.)

The Display Section

In the Display section of the Attribute Editor are controls for interactive shading of the fluid within Maya itself (as opposed to the Render controls, which control how it looks when rendered). You can display the rendered version of the fluid when in shaded mode (the default), you can set the display to Off, or you can set it to density, color, temperature, and the like. You can also turn on display of the internal grid within the container or set it to Outline (the default) or Bounding Box. You can turn on Numeric Display for fluid density, temperature, or fuel, displaying specific information about each voxel's attributes (though this is not normally useful to the animator). In addition, you can enable display of the velocity of all points in the container by choosing the Velocity Draw option; once this is enabled, you can adjust Velocity Draw Skip (reducing the number of arrows on the screen) and/or the length of each arrow. Figure 20.15 shows our basic simulation with velocity arrows drawn in.

The Dynamic Simulation Section

The Dynamic Simulation section of the Attribute Editor allows control over the physical simulation of fluids in a container. The basic control, Gravity, determines how a fluid is "pulled" in the scene. At the default (9.8), gravity pulls the fluid upward toward the top of the container at a sedate speed. If Gravity is made negative, it will pull the fluid downward instead. The magnitude determines how rapidly the fluid will rise or fall within the container. Viscosity determines how much each fluid particle "sticks" to its neighbors. A value of 0 means that they slide over each other freely; a value of 1 means that they all stick together (and thus don't move from the emitter). Friction determines how the fluid will react with the boundaries of the container (or objects with which it collides): a value of 0 means there is no friction, and a value of 1 means that all fluid cells that strike the container (or object) will stick to them completely. Damping controls how rapidly the motion of fluid particles is damped out. Figure 20.16 shows a fluid simulation with Gravity set to −10, Viscosity set to 0.3, Friction set to 0.5, and Damp set to 0.05.

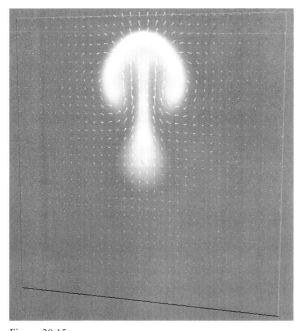

Figure 20.15

A fluid simulation with Velocity Draw indicating the speed and direction of fluid motion at each point in the container

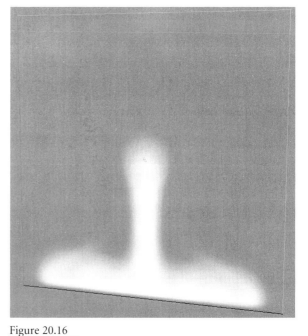

Figure 20.16

A fluid simulation with negative gravity and medium viscosity and friction settings

The Solver drop-down menu determines which simulation engine is used. (Navier-Stokes is best for most purposes.) High Detail Solve creates a more refined simulation (at the cost of calculation time), which can occur in all grids, in all except velocity, or in velocity only. (See the "Hands On" section later in this chapter for an example of using High Detail Solve.) Solver Quality is used with the High Detail Solve setting to determine just how refined the calculations will be. Grid Interpolator determines how finely a simulation is run: a Linear interpolation is coarser than a Hermite one but runs faster. Start Frame determines when the simulation begins running, the Simulation Rate Scale scales the timing of the simulation larger or smaller than default (setting this to a large value makes the simulation run very quickly and coarsely), and Disable Evaluation turns off the fluid calculations altogether. The Conserve Mass, Use Collisions, Emission, and Fields check boxes allow individual elements of the simulation to be turned on or off as work progresses on a scene.

The Contents Details Section

In the Contents Details section of the Attribute Editor (shown in Figure 20.17) are subsections dealing with Density, Velocity, Turbulence, Temperature, Fuel, and Color attributes, all of which are used to refine the behavior of the fluid itself. Some of the more interesting controls in this section are discussed here. Under Density are Buoyancy, which controls how positively or negatively buoyant the fluid is (negative buoyancy causes a fluid to drop instead of rise), Diffusion, and Dissipation. A Diffusion larger than 0 causes the fluid to scatter about the container rather than hanging together, and a nonzero Dissipation causes the fluid to disappear back into the normal (uncolored) state of the container.

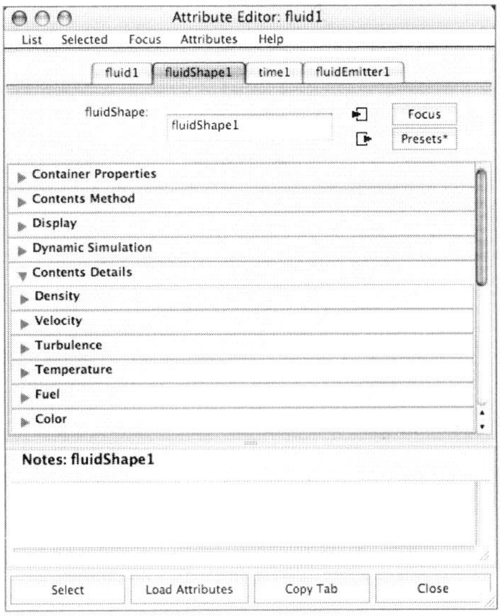

In the Velocity section, Swirl controls how many vortices are created in a fluid. Turbulence, Strength, Frequency, and Speed control how much a turbulence field will affect the fluid system. High values for all these settings produce something like Figure 20.18.

Under Fuel (which is disabled until you set Fuel Contents Method to Dynamic or Static Grid) are controls for Reaction Speed (how fast the fuel burns), Ignition Temperature (when the fuel is ignited), and Heat and Light Released from the fuel burn. If fuel and temperature are painted into the container (see the next section), the fluid simulation will look similar to Figure 20.19. In this image, the visible fluid has been pushed around by the temperature variation from the burning fuel, which was painted at the top right of the container, and (in its final rendered state) it will take on the color of the burning fuel as set in the Light Released settings.

Figure 20.17

The Contents Details section of the Attribute Editor

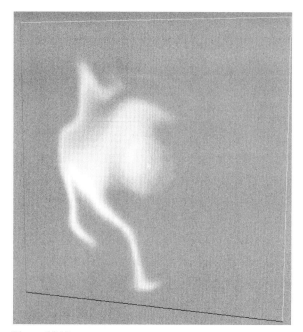

Figure 20.18

A fluid influenced by a strong Turbulence field

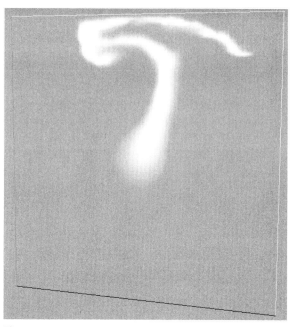

Figure 20.19

A fluid distorted by (invisible) burning fuel

The Grids Cache Section

The Grids Cache section of the Attribute Editor allows control over which portions of a fluid cache (used to speed up playback) will be read as a scene is played back.

The Surface Section

In the Surface section are controls for how the fluid itself is rendered. The two types are Volume Render (checked by default) and Surface Render (shown in Figure 20.20), which creates a more solid-looking fluid that can represent anything from water to lava. The Hard Surface option (available when the Surface Render option is selected) makes the fluid look more solid (and blocky), and the Soft Surface option makes the surface look more amorphous. Surface Threshold controls where the surface begins and ends: a low threshold includes most of the Fluid Effect (and density that is above ambient), and a high threshold includes only the densest sections of the fluid. The other attributes in this section control how the surface looks (and refracts) once it is rendered.

The Shading, Color, Incandescence, and Opacity Sections

In the Shading section (shown at the top of Figure 20.21) are controls for how the fluid is rendered. Most of these are similar to shading options you would come across in a shader

Figure 20.20

The fluid simulation from Figure 20.19 displayed as a surface rather than as a volume

network (see Chapter 12 for more on shading networks), but several options are unique tofluids. As an example, set the Dropoff Shape and Edge Dropoff options to Sphere and a small number (such as 0.05), respectively, and play the simulation back to see how the fluid reacts now. Dropoff Shape controls how the fluid's boundaries are computed. Cube creates an invisible cube around the object, causing the fluid to fade out when it comes in contact with the cube. A sphere, cone, or double cone shape (three other options) creates a spherical, conic, or bidirectional conic boundary. The Edge Dropoff setting controls how tightly the boundary shape is wrapped around the fluid object. The easiest way to see how these settings work is to run the simulation until you have fluid visible; then select Dropoff Shape and slide the Edge Dropoff slider back and forth to see how the boundary of the fluid changes.

The Color section allows control over the color of the fluid and which properties are mapped to color. You can choose a single value for color (the default condition) or, by clicking in the ramp slider at the right side of the Selected Color swatch, create a ramp of colors. (Click the Selected Color swatch to set individual colors on the ramp.) The Color Input controls which aspect of the fluid is being colored (and thus displayed and rendered), and the Input Bias moves all the ramp colors either up or down in case the default ramp settings are not set quite right. New with Maya 8 is an arrow to the right of the small ramps in this and other sections (shown in Figure 20.21); clicking this arrow causes the ramp to "blow up" to a larger size, allowing for easier editing of the ramp

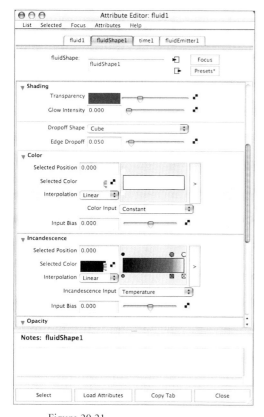

attributes. Figure 20.22 shows color settings adjusted in the blow-up ramp editor window and the results in the 2D container. The Incandescence settings work in just the same way as color, but they multiply their effects with the color settings, creating an incandescent effect when rendered.

Finally, the Opacity settings control which property of the fluid to map to opacity (Opacity Input) and how it is mapped (Opacity Ramp). The default linear ramp from 0 (transparent) at left to 1 (fully opaque) at right produces the effects we have come to expect when dealing with fluids thus far. If, on the other hand, you use Density as the Opacity Input setting and move the left ramp point up to 1, the entire scene becomes opaque (at the value set at the far left end of the Color ramp). This is because the entire fluid is *one* fluid; only the density changes are being displayed in this single fluid. Thus, if the entire fluid is made opaque, you can see that the container is filled with this fluid. By clicking within the Opacity ramp, you can add and change the curve, and by changing the Interpolation method (Linear by default), you can change how the ramp transitions from one opacity to another.

One other point worth mentioning here is that the color and incandescence ramp values can be mapped with a file or procedural texture simply by clicking the checkerboard button next to the Selected Color button when that point is selected in the ramp.

Matte Opacity adjusts how the alpha channel of the fluid renders. Using Opacity Gain with a Matte Opacity of 1 will create an alpha channel where the fluid renders. Other settings or values adjust this behavior.

The Shading Quality Section

The Shading Quality section controls how finely the fluid image will be rendered. The most important settings here are Quality (higher quality looks better but takes longer to render) and Sample Method, which can help get rid of bands using Jittered or Adaptive Jittered but at the cost of some noise in the final image. Using a higher-quality setting reduces the noise problem but with increased render times.

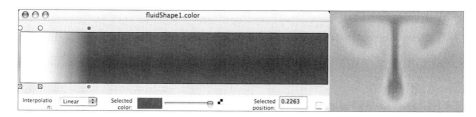

The Textures Section

In the Textures section of the Attribute Editor (shown in Figure 20.23) are controls allowing you to remap a given fluid in more refined ways than with simple coloring. What's more, these textures can be animated, giving the illusion of 3D motion to an otherwise static simulation. Thus, you can create, say, a 3D cloud simulation with a static grid (thus avoiding the computation involved in dynamically solving a large 3D grid) and just map the fluid with a moving texture, making it appear to be in motion. This is, in fact, how the stormyClouds preset is created. (If you check the attributes for this preset effect, all contents methods for this preset are turned off.)

Texture Opacity is the most obvious control. (Color and Incandescence are controlled in similar fashion.) After turning on Texture Opacity, selecting an option such as Billow from the Texture Type pop-up menu alters the basic look of the fluid into one that is more broken up, cloudlike, or billowy. At this point, altering Threshold, Amplitude, Ratio, and so on control the basic properties of the Billow (or other) texture type; playing around with Texture Type and these settings will create any number of different looks. Billow (and Volume Wave) also has a series of special controls at the bottom of the Textures section. By altering Billow Density, Spottyness, Size Rand, and Randomness, you can alter the basic look of the Billow texture to suit your taste.

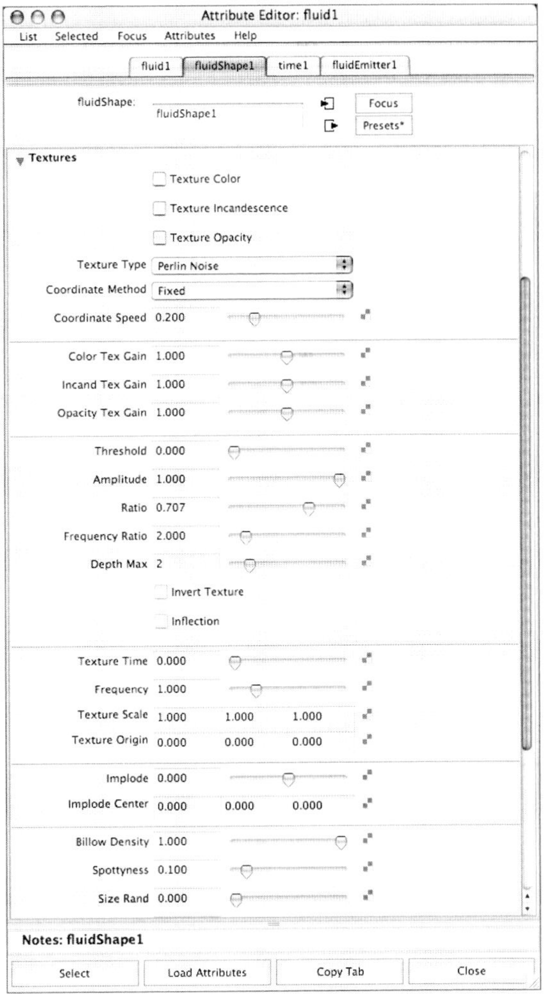

The Implode controls allow the texture to look as if it's imploding inward (with a controllable center of implosion). Finally, the Texture Time, Frequency, Scale, and Origin controls allow you to adjust elements such as the scale and frequency of the texture, and, using the Texture Time control, you can move through the texture (by moving the slider) to find the moment in texture time when the texture looks right to you.

Figure 20.24 shows our basic 2D fluid with a Billow texture and a higher than default frequency. As with most other attributes for Fluid Effects, most in the Textures section can be texture mapped by selecting the checkerboard icon at the right of the control.

If you play back your textured animation, you will likely notice that the texture stays in place while the fluid flows, which looks unnatural. By keyframing Texture Time (and many of the other attributes), however, you can animate the texture over time, giving the illusion that it is moving.

Figure 20.23

The Textures section of the Attribute Editor

Figure 20.24

The 2D fluid with a Billow texture on it

For example, if you play your animation back to a frame you like, choose **Fluid Effects → Set Initial State** (to set the current frame to the fluid's initial condition), set Velocity (under Contents Method) to Off (zero), and then keyframe the Texture Time attribute (RM choose Set Key with the mouse pointer over the words *Texture Time*) to different values over time, the fluid will appear to evolve over time even though it is now static—which you can observe if you play back the animation past your last keyframe. By combining dynamic simulations and moving textures (or just moving textures by themselves), you can create convincing effects that simulate quickly and render fast.

The Lighting Section

In the Lighting section of the Attribute Editor are a few controls that specify how the fluid itself is lit: self-shadowing and use of built-in or real lighting. Choosing the Self Shadow option allows the fluid to shadow itself, and clicking the Hardware Shadow check box allows you to see this shadowing in the Maya scene window. With self-shadowing on, volumetric fluids such as clouds will appear much more real than if they do not shadow themselves. If the Real Lights check box is off, Fluids uses a default directional light (whose position you can control via the Directional Light X, Y, and Z number fields); if you select Real Lights, the actual lights in the scene are used to calculate self-shadowing. Using real lights can be a better option, but it is much more computationally intensive than using the default light, so be prepared for slower renders.

Painting into Containers

Now that you have a good sense of how the various attributes of a fluid control its behavior and appearance, let's look at how to actually paint properties into a container. First, create a basic 2D fluid with *no* emitter attached. Next, choose **Fluid Effects → Add/Edit**

Contents → Paint Fluids Tool ❏. In the Paint Attributes section of the Options box, be sure the Paintable Attributes pop-up menu is set to Density, and then use your mouse to paint some fluid density into your scene. If you have a tablet, you can set the pressure of the stylus to change the amount of density (whiteness) of the fluid you're painting; otherwise, change the Value (Paint Attributes section) and Radius U and L values (Brush section) to alter the density and size of your strokes. After some strokes at different values and brush sizes, you should have something like Figure 20.25. If you then play back your animation, you will see the fluid move and swirl around under the influence of the default gravity and collisions with the container itself.

Figure 20.25

Various density strokes in a fluid container

Now that you know how to paint density, let's see what happens when you paint other properties into the container.

1. Set Gravity to 0 in the Dynamic Simulation section of the Attribute Editor. (You can check to see that your fluid now no longer moves from its initial position.)

2. In the Paint Fluids tool, erase the contents of your container by setting Value (in Paint Attributes) to 0 and clicking the Flood button.

3. Reset Value to 1 and paint a circle of density near the middle of the container. If you play back the animation, it should not move because gravity is no longer influencing it.

4. Set the Paintable Attributes pop-up to Temperature instead of Density. You should get a warning that you need to set the Temperature grid to Dynamic so the simulation will run properly. Click the Set To Dynamic button to allow this. You will notice that the container is now empty again: although the density you painted in the container is still present, you can no longer see it as you are now in temperature "mode."

5. Paint several strokes of high temperature (white) at the bottom-right corner of the container, as in Figure 20.26.

6. Switch back to Density on the Paintable Attributes pop-up and play back the animation. You should see the density of the fluid swirled around, responding to the high temperature of the bottom-right corner of the container (see Figure 20.27).

You can paint other properties into the container, including velocity fields (which will shove the density field around) and fuel, which, when burned by temperature fields above a threshold temperature (set in the Attribute Editor), will ignite, giving off heat and light and thus altering the look and position of the fluid density in the container. Try using the previous scene, but across the bottom of the container, paint in some fuel that touches the temperature area you painted on before. (When you are asked, be sure to set the fuel grid to dynamic.) If you leave the display set to Fuel, you can play back the animation and watch the fuel being consumed as it burns (as in the left image of Figure 20.28); if you set the display to Density, you will see the fluid density affected by the burning fuel (on the right in Figure 20.28).

Figure 20.26

Temperature strokes painted into the 2D container

Figure 20.27

Density of the fluid influenced by the (invisible) painted temperature

Figure 20.28

Fuel being consumed as it burns (left) and the fluid density affected by this burning fuel (right)

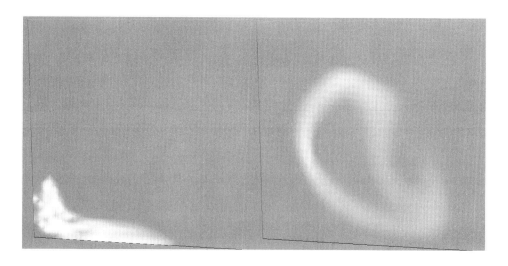

Creating an Ocean Effect

Creating an ocean effect from scratch is as straightforward as creating a 2D or 3D fluid container. From the Dynamics menu set, choose **Fluid Effects → Ocean → Create Ocean** to display a distorted, circular NURBS patch called oceanPlane1 in your scene (like the one in Figure 20.29) with a small "sample" patch showing the basic wave patterns you will see when the effect is rendered. If you render the scene out, you will see a basic set of waves against a blue background.

If you play back the animation in the scene window, only the sample patch at the origin will update. This is because Ocean Effects, not being true fluid simulations, create their ocean appearance and wave motion via texture mapping and displacement mapping, respectively. The new sample patch at the origin indicates what the general scene will look like when rendered, and at the same time, it updates quickly enough for interactive work. If you do a quick render of your scene at frame 1 and then rerender a section of your previous render at a new frame, you will see that the waves on the surface actually do move in the render, producing the appropriate illusion of a large body of water (see Figure 20.30).

> You will discover that rendering ocean surfaces is a long process, especially if you set anti-aliasing to a high quality. This occurs because the displacement and texturing process behind the effect is computationally expensive. One way to mitigate this trouble is to use a low-resolution and low-quality anti-aliasing on your test renders until you are happy with the general look of the ocean effect.

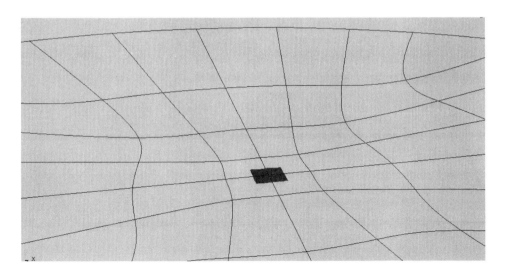

Figure 20.29

A long-distance view of the NURBS patch that contains the ocean shader

Figure 20.30

The basic ocean simulation rendered at frame 1 (on the left) and at frame 50 (on the right). The waves do not match up between frames, showing that the displacement map creating the wave effect is in motion.

Figure 20.31

The Attribute Editor, showing part of the Ocean Attributes section

Within the Attribute Editor, in similar fashion to Fluid Effects, are controls over the Ocean Effect itself, including wave height, turbulence, coloring, and so forth. None of these controls actually affect any kind of simulation; they simply control texturing and displacement.

To see how some of these controls work, select your ocean surface and open the Ocean Attributes section of the Attribute Editor (see Figure 20.31). First, notice that at the top, Type is set to Ocean Shader, which enables the controls below. In the Ocean Attributes section directly below the Type pop-up menu, some of the more important attributes are Time (which controls the animation of the effect and should be keyframed by default), Scale (which controls the scale of the simulation), Wind UV (which controls the wind speed, which in turn affects the wave height and motion), Wave Speed, and Observer Speed (which sets the observer in motion relative to the waves). Most of the other controls in the top two blocks of the Ocean Attributes section are fairly self-explanatory, and a bit of quick experimentation should get you familiar with how they affect the ocean.

The next three sections—Wave Height, Turbulence, and Peaking—use a ramp metaphor similar to several sections (like shading) in the Fluid Effects attributes. Wave Height, for example, uses the ramp to determine the size of the waves based on their wavelength. On the left side of the ramp are the smallest-wavelength waves, and on the right side are the longest; adding or moving points on the ramp, then, controls the height of the waves for each size wave. (A flat-line ramp makes all the waves the same size.) If, for example, you set the left side of the ramp to 1 and the right side to 0, the shortest, highest-frequency waves will be very large, and the longer waves will have no height at all, creating a ripple effect and causing the water to look more like a bathtub than an ocean. Doing the opposite (setting 0 and 1, respectively) makes for large, long-wavelength waves with no fine detail, producing a look that is too smooth for natural water. Experimenting with different values (usually above 0 across the board) produces much more satisfying results than either of these two extremes.

Figure 20.32

The basic ocean scene with the addition of white-capped foamy waves

Wave Turbulence, which is controlled in the same fashion as Wave Height, controls the turbulence (or random motion) of the waves. If Wave Turbulence is set to 0 across the frequency spectrum, all the waves line up perfectly, creating a smooth, unnatural look. Wave Peaking, which only functions if Wave Turbulence is greater than 0, creates a side-to-side (rather than up-down) motion to the waves so that they jitter back and forth over time. Again, setting this to a value greater than 0 creates a more random, dynamic-looking water surface, though at the expense of additional render time because Wave Peaking is computationally intensive.

> The wavelength of a wave, which is the inverse of its frequency, is the distance between two troughs (or peaks) of a wave. The two are related by the equation $\lambda = (\kappa / f)$, in which λ is wavelength, f is frequency, and κ is a constant representing the wave speed. Long-wavelength waves, then, have a long distance between each wave and thus look like large ocean swells—these would be the waves you would see crashing to the shore or the waves on which people surf. Short-wavelength waves, on the other hand, have a short distance between troughs, producing the detailed rippling of waves that exist on top of (or superimposed on) the larger waves. Thus, in general, you want your short-wavelength waves to have equal or smaller height than your long-wavelength waves.

At the bottom of the Ocean Attributes section are the Foam Emission, Threshold, and Offset values, which allow generation of foam at the tops of larger waves (the size of "large" waves being set by the Threshold value). You can create stormier ocean scenes by adding this foamy white-cap effect into the mix (see Figure 20.32).

Finally, in the Common Material Attributes section are controls for the color of the water. Here you can adjust water and foam color, incandescence, translucence, and the refractive index of the water, allowing you to create anything from highly photo-realistic water to the unearthly pink oceans of some alien planet.

One other important aspect of Ocean Effects is your ability to float any number of objects on the ocean surface itself. Because the surface is calculated through displacement mapping, you must use an expression that determines the displacement of any point on the surface to figure out how an object will float. Fortunately, Autodesk has made the process mostly transparent to the user: choose **Fluid Effects → Ocean → Float Selected Objects** to display options for floating objects on your ocean surface, including floating locators (to which you can later attach a camera or an object) and Buoy (a locator with a sphere attached), and the option to float any geometric object (Float Selected Objects) or create an unpowered or powered boat (Make Boat and Make Motor Boat, respectively).

These floating objects all work in similar ways (with varying options), so we'll just use Make Boat as an example. Into your basic ocean scene (or just create a new one), create some geometric primitive such as a NURBS cone, or add any model you want. With the object selected, choose **Fluid Effects → Ocean → Make Boats**. You should see your object now attached to a locator, which keeps track of floating the object. If you play back the animation, you will see the "boat" rocking up and down on the (invisible) ocean surface, as in Figure 20.33.

Creating a boat allows 3D motion of the object you create. If you use Float Object, the object will bounce up and down but won't rotate to stay tangential to the surface.

Figure 20.33

A cone "boat" floating on the ocean surface

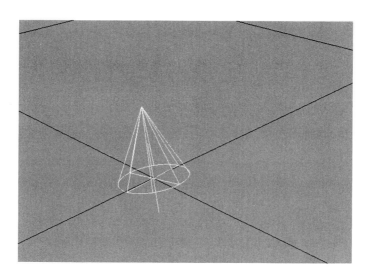

If you look in the Expression Editor (sort by expression name), you will see, under expression1, a long expression that actually does the dirty work of floating your object on top of the ocean. Fortunately you don't have to deal with this expression (unless you want to—in that case, have fun!). You can just open the Attribute Editor for locatorShape1 and twirl down the Extra Attributes section to display controls for the boat, all of which relate to variables in the expression you just viewed. After working through this chapter, you should find most of these settings easy to understand. As an example, you can choose to alter the buoyancy from its default 0.6. If you make the object less buoyant (like, say, 0.2), it will sink into the ocean, whereas if you increase buoyancy to a high number like 1.0, it will float like a beach ball just touching the waves. (You will likely have to increase Air Damping in this case, or the boat will jiggle around like crazy.) If you set the buoyancy to less than 0, the boat will sink like a stone. Thus, by keyframing buoyancy, you can cause the boat to rise up to the surface, bounce around on it, and then sink back down under the water again.

One unfortunate consequence of Ocean Effects being a displacement simulation is that the wake from a boat or other floating object is not calculated. Thus, while a boat floats on the surface of the water, it will not properly interact with the ocean, creating foam or waves as it floats or moves around the surface. You can solve this problem using the Create Wake feature. Simply select an ocean plane and choose **Fluid Effects → Ocean → Create Wake**. This creates a fluid emitter that creates ripples when it is still and a wake when it is moving.

Create Wake has three options: Wake Size, Wake Intensity, and Foam Creation. Wake Size sets the size, or scale, of the wake fluid container. Wake Intensity determines the height of waves created by the wake by filling in the fluid density attribute of the wake fluid. Positive intensities cause the ocean to bulge upward, and negative intensities make the ocean surface appear to bulge downward. Figure 20.34 shows a wake from an invisible

Figure 20.34

Creating a wake for the boat

moving "boat." (The wake emitter has been keyframed here to move over time, creating a more obvious wake behavior.) Unfortunately, the Options window for creating a wake does not accept negative values, so you will need to change the Fluid Density Emission attribute of the Ocean Wake Emitter after creating it in order to achieve them. The third attribute, **Foam Creation**, simulates the more turbulent aspects of a wake by adding something akin to heat to affected voxels over time, causing them to become turbulent and simulate foam. As with the rest of the Ocean Effects, these wakes operate through a series of shaders.

Creating a Pond Effect

Pond Effects are 2D fluid effects that are used to generate surfaces using a height map and a spring mesh solver. Thus, they fall somewhere between Ocean Effects, which are a displacement/rendering trick, and 2D/3D fluids, which are true fluid simulations. To create a pond, choose **Fluid Effects → Pond → Create Pond ▢**, select the size of the fluid container that you want to use, and click the Create Pond button.

Examining the Attribute Editor for a Pond Effect, you will notice that a pond is a 2D fluid, but some attributes are set differently from "normal" 2D fluids by default and the Pond Effect automatically has an initial state set. The most obvious differences are that the pond uses a height field and is calculated using a spring mesh solver instead of the normal Navier-Stokes solver. Unlike the Ocean Effect, a Pond Effect is stationary until some force is exerted upon it.

Ponds work well with wake effects, which you can add by choosing **Fluid Effects → Pond → Create Wake**. Since the wake fluid for a pond uses the same 2D fluid container used for the pond, there are only two options for creating a pond wake: Wake Intensity and Foam Creation. These options behave in a fashion similar to the options of the same names from the Ocean Effect's Create Wake feature. As opposed to the Ocean Effect (which relies on displacement mapping), it is possible to watch the deformation of a Pond Effect's surface in Maya, as you can see in Figure 20.35.

Figure 20.35

A Pond Effect with moving wake added

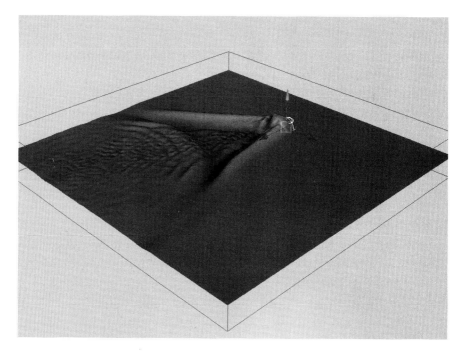

Hands On: Creating a Disappearing Cloud Effect for Machismo

Now that you understand the basics of creating Fluid Effects, let's have a little fun and create an effect that makes Machismo disappear into a poof of smoke. (This idea was inspired by the "bamf" effect created for Nightcrawler in *X-Men 2*, though we have gone a somewhat different direction with the final product to keep things simple and to show off some of the features of Fluid Effects, including the paintable falloff feature.) Follow these steps:

1. Open the BamfStart.mb file on the accompanying CD. There, as shown in Figure 20.36, is Machismo, posed and ready to disappear in a cloud of smoke. Note that Machismo's geometry becomes invisible at frame 10, which is where we'll start our "bamf" effect.

2. First we're going to create a new camera (choose **Create → Cameras → Camera**), move it into place so it shows Machismo from the side (see Figure 20.37), and lock the rotate and translate channels of the camera. (Select the rotate and translate channels and RM choose Lock Selected.) We do this because we will be creating a 2D fluid effect, which will depend on camera angle to work properly.

3. Now let's create a 2D fluid (without an emitter attached). Choose **Fluid Effects → Create 2D Container** ❑. Reset the settings and create the container. Rotate the container 90° in Y, and move and scale the box so that it resembles the box in Figure 20.37. In the Attribute Editor, set Resolution to 80 × 80 voxels in the Container Properties section.

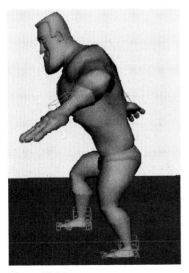

Figure 20.36

Machismo posed and ready to disappear

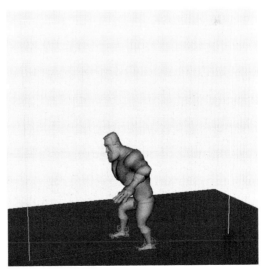

Figure 20.37

A 2D fluid container, rotated, moved, and scaled to surround Machismo

Figure 20.38

**Fluid Effects
Density painted
over Machismo's
silhouette**

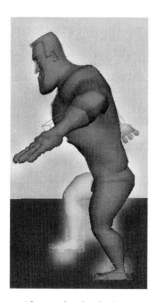

4. Now we will paint in some density in the basic form of Machismo. This will function as our initial smoke poof, so we want it to look like his silhouette (which is why we have locked our render camera). Select the 2D container, and choose **Fluid Effects → Add/Edit Contents → Paint Fluids Tool ❑**. In the Paint Attributes section, set Paintable Attributes to Density, choose Replace as the paint operation, and be sure Opacity (under Brush) is set to 1. Adjust the brush radius (hold down the B key and drag the mouse back and forth over the container to adjust the radius), and paint over the silhouette of Machismo. (Be sure to paint the inside of his body as well; you can turn off the geometry layer to be sure you have filled in the whole body.) When finished, your scene should look something like Figure 20.38.

If you play back the scene right now, you will see a few problems. First, the fluid starts to dissipate at frame 1 rather than frame 10. Second, the density is visible too early. (It should appear as Machismo disappears.) Third, the smoke dissipation is very smooth and leisurely—we want a more violent, turbulent effect. Let's solve these problems one at a time.

1. With the 2D container selected, open the Attribute Editor. In the Dynamic Simulation section, set Start Frame to 9 rather than 1. This disables the dynamics until frame 9. (We choose frame 9 rather than frame 10 because otherwise there's a slight hitch on the first frame before the dynamics really take effect.)

2. With the 2D container still selected, move the Timeline to frame 9 and set a key on the visibility of the container to Off. Move to frame 10 and set a key to turn the visibility On. Now the Fluid Effect appears at the same time that the geometry disappears.

3. Now we need to make a vacuum effect (as if the air is being drawn into where Machismo's body used to be) and add some turbulence and a few other tweaks to get the simulation to look right. To create the sucking effect, select the 2D container, and then choose **Fields → Newton ❑**. Set Magnitude to –500, set Attenuation to 0, and leave everything else at its default state. When you click OK to create this field, it is automatically attached to the 2D container. With the field still selected, go to the Channel Box and set the Apply Per Vertex channel to On to allow the field to operate over each voxel independently. When you play back the animation, the sucking effect is a bit too strong. We need to keyframe the effect off after a time. Set a keyframe at Magnitude –500 at about frame 17, and set another key with Magnitude at 0 at about frame 19 (with all suggested settings here, adjust to your satisfaction).

4. Now that we have a decent vacuum effect, let's add some turbulence so the smoke dissipates in a more violent manner. With the 2D container still selected, open the Contents Details section of the Attribute Editor, and then open the Turbulence subsection. Set Strength to 0.5, set Frequency to 30, and set Speed to 1. This will produce some high-frequency noise to disturb the dissipating smoke.

5. Now let's tweak a couple of other settings. Under the Dynamic Simulation section, set Damp to 0.05, and keyframe Viscosity to 0.2 and Gravity to 9.8 at about frame 16 (RM choose Set Key with the cursor over the text). At frame 26, set Viscosity to 0.005. At frame 50, set Gravity to 200. Adjusting viscosity lets the smoke react more like a thick liquid at the start of the simulation and like a thin smoke at the end of it. Adjusting gravity makes the smoke effect rise more quickly at the end of the simulation, so the effect doesn't hang around too long. There are, of course, dozens of other settings you can adjust to get just the effect you want, so feel free to experiment with anything that looks interesting in the Attribute Editor.

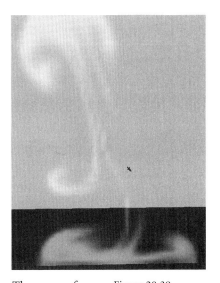

Figure 20.39

Creating a high-detail solution for the smoke effect

We can also create high-quality solves, which show much more detail in the smoke tendrils. Let's enable this mode to get a higher-quality result.

1. With the 2D container selected, open the Dynamic Simulation section of the Attribute Editor and set High Detail Solve to All Grids. This induces the high-quality solve mode, creating a more subtle effect, as shown in Figure 20.39.

2. This simulation is quite fast and visually interesting. We can leave the effect as is and render it out. (Be sure to set the render quality to the highest settings to get good results.) However, let's go one step further by painting in a falloff grid, similar to what we did earlier when painting the density grid. To paint this grid, select the 2D container. (You will want to rewind to frame 1 and temporarily turn the visibility of the container to On so you can paint the falloff into the grid.) First we need to adjust a few settings so that we can see and simulate the falloff grid. In the Attribute Editor, under the Contents Method section, set Falloff Method to Static Grid; in the Shading section, set Dropoff Shape to Use Falloff Grid; in the Display section, set Shaded Display to Falloff. Now you can see the falloff grid as you paint it.

3. Now reinvoke the Paint Fluids tool, and under the Paint Attributes section, set Paintable Attributes to Falloff rather than Density. As before, paint around Machismo's silhouette using the replace paint mode. This time, however, move well outside the body outline because we want the smoke to be visible beyond the body. You will also want to change to the smooth mode and paint over the edges of your "figure" to make the falloff boundaries as gentle as possible. When finished, your falloff grid should look similar to Figure 20.40.

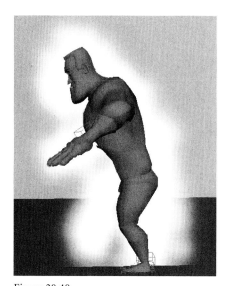

Figure 20.40

Painting the falloff grid

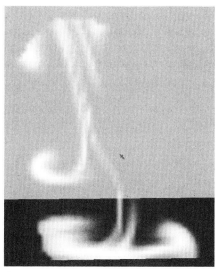

Figure 20.41

The smoke puff contained within the painted falloff region

To see your density grid again, select any tool other than the Paint Fluids tool (for example, choose the Select or Move tool). When you play back the simulation, the smoke is now "trapped" within this falloff region, as shown in Figure 20.41. You can open BamfComplete.mb on the CD to see the completed scene or view the bamf.mov file to see Machismo disappear in a puff of smoke!

Summary

Although fluids are complex, computationally expensive effects to achieve, this chapter has shown that, with Maya's Fluid Effects, it is fairly easy and fast to create all sorts of rich, naturalistic effects without having to delve into complex equations and algorithms. By adjusting various parameters of a prebuilt simulation, you can get any number of smoke, fire, cloud, water, and ocean effects—or, if you want to start from scratch, you can quickly build simple or complex effects of your own making, as exemplified by the hands-on example.

With this package in your arsenal, you should feel confident in your ability to create all sorts of natural (or supernatural) effects for your animations. With a bit of practice, you should be able to craft anything, such as a stormy ocean, a boiling volcano, or a steaming cup of coffee. What you can do is limited only by your imagination and ingenuity!

CHAPTER 21

Maya Hair

Hair is a powerful part of the Maya Unlimited package, allowing you to create complex hair motion, realistic hairstyles, and other dynamic effects. You will learn how to set up hair on a character's head, use constraints and forces to create a hairstyle, produce a realistic look using Paint Effects, and drive a skeletal system using dynamic hair curves.

- Fundamentals of hair systems

- Creating hair

- Controlling hair systems

- Styling hair

- Dynamics and collisions

- Rendering hair

- Creating cache

- Using dynamic curves to drive a skeletal system

Fundamentals of Hair Systems

Maya uses a special node called a hair system to control the dynamics of a group of follicles. Each follicle contains a hair curve and can influence how individual hair strands look and behave. When making hair systems, you can create hair as paint effects and/or NURBS curves. Paint effects can achieve realistic-looking strands of hair by using strokes that follow simulated hair curves. If you opt for creating NURBS surfaces, you can use lofting and other surface-building modeling operations.

Think of a hair system as a master level of control over a character's hair—that is, over a group of follicles. These follicles are influenced by gravity, turbulence, stiffness, collision, and many other attributes of the hair system. A scene can contain multiple hairSystem nodes, allowing you to easily create different types of hair dynamics for different parts of your character. As you will see, follicles can override certain settings of the hair system, allowing you break up uniformity and completely control your character's hair.

Active and Passive Follicles

When creating hair, you can make either active or passive follicles. A follicle represents a clump of a specified number of hairs. Hairs within each clump inherit exactly the same dynamics. Active follicles are dynamic and independent from other follicles in the hair system. Although more physically accurate, a head filled with too many active follicles can be extremely inefficient computationally. Passive follicles interpolate the dynamic behavior of neighboring active follicles and thus are less accurate, but using them is far more efficient than calculating every hair.

The number of passive follicles is determined by the passive fill value when the hair is created. Generally, if you want fairly uniform-moving hair, you can use a greater number of passive follicles. If you already have a hair system of active follicles, Maya makes it easy to add passive follicles by using the Paint Hair Follicles tool. You can also change a follicle back and forth from active to passive in the follicle's Attribute Editor. Figure 21.1 illustrates how a passive follicle's shape interpolates between neighboring active follicles.

Start, Current, and Rest Positions

A follicle has three positions: Start, Current and Rest. Throughout your work flow, you will constantly switch between viewing each of these states, accessed by choosing **Hair → Display**. The Start position displays the shape of the hair at the beginning of the simulation. This display mode allows you to easily select individual active follicles for adding constraints or altering per-follicle attributes. The Start position can be set to whatever the current state of the hair is by selecting the follicles and choosing **Hair → Set Start Position → From Current**. When you rewind to the start of the simulation, the hair will begin simulation from this Start position.

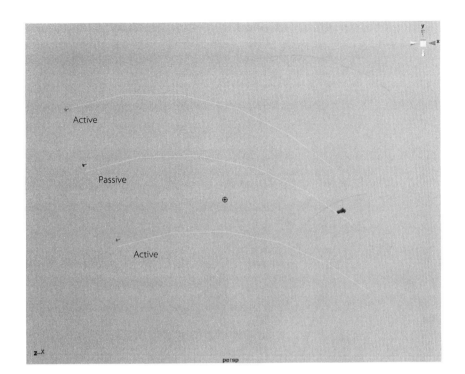

Figure 21.1

The passive follicle's shape is determined by the interpolation between the two active follicles.

The Current position is the pose of the hair at any given frame. Start and Rest positions are often set from the current position at a desired frame. If you play back your Timeline, but the hair does not simulate, you may not be viewing the hair system in the current position mode.

The Rest position refers to the goal shape of the hair follicles. When a Rest position is set (often from whatever the ultimate desired hairstyle is), the follicles try to retain the rest shape. You can see the Rest position from the start or current frame by choosing **Hair →** **Set Rest Position**.

How to Make Hair

Maya provides a variety of options for creating hair. Before you add hair to your scene, be sure you know the results you want. Do you want short or long hair? Do you want to style it or let it fall naturally? Do you want it to appear as individual strands or drive a mesh? Fortunately, you can apply the powerful dynamics of Maya Hair to all these options. You can either let Maya place hair for you or manually paint where you want it. You can even transplant hair between characters!

Create Hair

You can automatically generate hair on any NURBS surface or polygonal mesh. Maya allows you to specify the number of follicles to generate in the U and V directions on a surface. Since hair generation depends on the UV coordinates, be sure that you first lay out the UVs for any polygonal meshes. (Automatic mapping works fastest.) Occasionally, you might notice bald spots after creating hair. Most likely, this is the result of the UVs not being properly laid out.

When creating hair, you can specify the length of the hair, a randomization factor (so that the follicles are not all evenly spaced), the desired format for output, and other options. Points Per Hair controls how many control points are created along the hair curve. The more points per hair, the more detail a hair can inherit. Generally, longer hair should have more points per hair to ensure a smooth look.

Through each follicle's node (accessed via the Attribute Editor) you can specify whether the created hairs are Static, Passive, or Dynamic. Static hair is not affected by forces and can be manually keyframed. Passive hair curves interpolate neighboring active hair curves, making the simulation less expensive than a completely dynamic hair setup. Dynamic hair reacts to forces and the motion of the object to which it is attached. You can also specify whether you want to create hairs on the grid of the selected surface or on selected faces. Another great option is the ability to specify whether to create additional hair follicles in a new hair system or add them to an existing one.

When creating hair, you may notice many additional nodes and objects within your scene file. You will have hair systems, output curves, follicles, cache nodes, constraints, and other components. Since a hair system contains many components, Maya provides a way to select just what you want from the hair system. Select any element of the hair system and then convert the selection to what you want by choosing **Hair ⇢ Convert Selection**. Using this tool allows you to quickly select components without having to hunt through the Outliner.

Deleting such an intricate system of nodes can be a nightmare. Maya makes deleting all the components of a hair system easy: select any part of the hair and choose **Hair ⇢ Delete Entire Hair System**. All hair components related to your selection will be removed. If you want to assign a selection to a new or different hair system, simply choose **Hair ⇢ Assign Hair System**.

WHAT ABOUT SUBDIVISION SURFACES?

Maya does not support adding hair to subdivision surfaces. If you want hair to appear to be on a subdivision surface, first add hair to a polygonal or NURBS skullcap. You can then hide the skullcap geometry. Alternatively, you can attach the hair system to the polygonal base mesh of the subdivision surface.

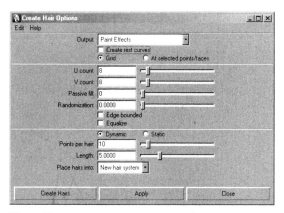

Figure 21.2

The Create Hair Options window presents one method for creating hair.

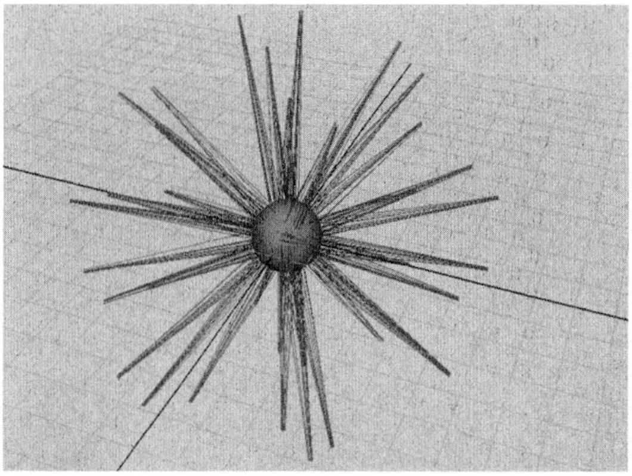

Figure 21.3

A simple hair simulation created on a sphere

In the following example, we will create hair on a simple NURBS sphere and play back the results.

1. In a new scene, create a NURBS sphere.

2. With the sphere selected, under the Dynamics menu set, choose **Hair → Create Hair □**.

3. In the Create Hair Options window (see Figure 21.2), choose **Edit → Reset Settings** and then click the Create Hairs button.

4. You'll see that Maya created a number of Paint Effects hairs sticking out from around the sphere (see Figure 21.3). Click the Play button on the Timeline to see the hair simulate.

> In order for this or any dynamic simulation to properly calculate, the playback speed should be set to Play Every Frame in the Timeline preferences.

Paint Hair Follicles

Suppose you want greater control over how hair is placed on your object. The Paint Hair Follicles tool not only allows you to paint active or passive follicles directly on your model, it also lets you trim or extend the hair length, delete follicles, and change all sorts of other attributes—all by using an interactive brush!

1. In a new scene, create a NURBS sphere.

2. Under the Dynamics menu set, choose **Hair → Paint Hair Follicles □** to display the Paint Hair Follicles Settings window, shown in Figure 21.4. Because we're working with a paint tool, the Artisan window also appears so that you can adjust various brush settings, if necessary. The default settings in the Artisan window should be fine for this exercise.

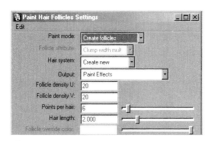

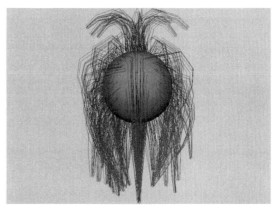

Figure 21.4

The Paint Hair Follicles Settings window gives you control over follicle attributes.

Figure 21.5

Paint Hair Follicles allows you to paint follicles with various properties.

3. In the Paint Hair Follicles Settings window, choose **Edit → Reset Settings**.

4. Change the Follicle Density U and Follicle Density V values to 8.

5. In the perspective view, use the brush to draw follicles on the sphere. Notice that if you want more detail in the gaps, you must increase the U and V follicle density in the settings.

6. You can also alter the length of the hair you just painted, allowing you to create custom haircuts and styles. Under Paint Mode, select Extend Hairs, and change Points Per Hair to 10. Freely paint on the sphere to extend existing follicles.

7. Click the Play button on the Timeline to see your custom hair simulate. Your results should resemble those found in Figure 21.5.

Presets and Transplanting Hair

Maya ships with a library of preset hair examples accessible through the Visor and allows you to transplant hair between surfaces. Each hair preset comes with great notes from Autodesk on how the hair system was created and tips for properly simulating and lighting the chosen style. Transplanting hair can be a useful feature if you have many characters in your scene that can have similar hair; you no longer need to start from scratch every time you want to place hair on a character. In the following example, we will use a hair preset and transplant it to a sphere.

1. In a new scene, choose **Hair → Get Hair Example**. In the Visor you will see 12 presets created by Autodesk.

2. Pan down, RMB click BunBack.ma, and choose Import Maya File BunBack.ma, or just MM drag the icon into your scene window. The hair file should then import into your scene. Close the Visor window.

3. In the Outliner, under hairAll, if you click either the hairSystem1 or pfxHair1 nodes and then open the Attribute Editor, you will see in the Notes section detailed steps and tips on creating, shaping, simulating, and lighting the hairstyle. These resources are useful for learning how to create your own unique styles and for properly using these presets.

4. Create a sphere. Scale and position it so that it closely matches the hair's shape. We will transplant the hair to this sphere.

5. Select the hairAll node, and then Shift+select the sphere. Choose **Hair → Transplant Hair** ❒. The Transplant Hair Options window opens (Figure 21.6).

If you want to move instead of copy the hair to the sphere, uncheck Copy Follicles. You can choose Match UV or Nearest Point for the transplant. Match UV is good when transplanting between similar objects. Nearest Point attempts to match the follicle layout on a completely new surface, but if your new surface is not closely matched in space to the current hair system, you will get unwanted results. Finally, you can place the new hair into the same hair system or into an existing hair system. If you choose Same Hair System and toggle Copy Follicles on, the hair system will be duplicated. If Copy Follicles is turned off, the follicles use the current hair system. If you have a hair system that already has a specific look and feel, you can place the hairs into this existing hair system by choosing it from the list.

6. With Copy Follicles unchecked, Nearest Point selected, and hairs placed into the same hair system, click the Transplant Hair button. The hair has now moved from the imported skullcap to your new sphere (see Figure 21.7).

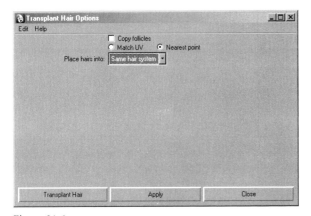

Figure 21.6

The Transplant Hair Options window allows you to apply an existing hair system to a new model.

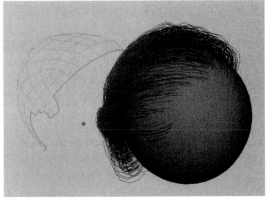

Figure 21.7

Hair preset transferred to a sphere

Hands On: Apply Hair to a Head

Much of this chapter explores Maya Hair on an applied model. The goal of this exercise is to create a typical example of dynamic hair with realistic looks and motion. You will be creating a relatively short female haircut, with a part down the middle. Since the hair style we are after has three distinct parts (the back and the left and right sides), we are going to use three hair systems to easily control each section. The hair will then be styled to the shape we want and set up for dynamic motion.

Creating Follicles on a Head

This portion of the exercise shows how to create hair follicles on sample head geometry. (Feel free to use a head you have modeled instead of the provided one if you want.) There is no one correct way to create hair; since we have a high-resolution head model, a skull-cap is used for faster computation and to prevent the hair being dependent on the final head model (thus hair modeling can begin before a finished head model has been created). The three parts of the hair are color-coded on the cap in order to make painting the follicles for each hair system easier.

1. Open the `HeadNoHair.mb` scene file from the CD. You should see a female head with a skull cap, as in Figure 21.8 (you may have to press the F key to focus on the model because it is not at the origin).

2. The hair style we are going for has three distinct parts; we will create the back of the hair first. Select the skullcap, and then choose **Hair → Paint Hair Follicles** ❑.

3. After resetting the tool to default settings, change the U and V follicle densities to 10, which will allow for at most 10 follicles to be created along the U and V directions on the skullcap. Since the hair is going to be medium-length, set the length to 10 and set Points Per Hair to 26, as shown in Figure 21.9.

Figure 21.8

Apply hair to a skull-cap rather than to the actual head model. Color-coding your skullcaps for different hair sections eases your work flow.

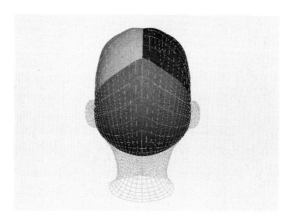

4. In the perspective view, use the brush to draw as many follicles on the back red portion of the head (see Figure 21.10) as Maya will let you (about 17 total). Don't worry if a follicle is slightly within another color section. Since Maya only dynamically simulates these follicles, they will act as "drivers" for the thousands of hairs that will eventually be added to the head.

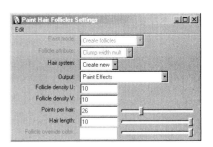

Figure 21.9

Setting follicle properties for the back of the head

5. With the Paint Hair Follicles Settings window still open, select Create New under the hair system list, and change the U and V follicle densities to 15. Paint follicles on the blue partition. Since the hair on the green and blue partitions ought to have more variety in length, we increased the UV follicle densities in order to produce more follicles. If any follicles appear not to stick straight out, change Paint Mode to Delete Follicles and paint to remove problem areas.

6. Once again, with the Paint Hair Follicles Settings window still open, select Create New under the hair system list to create a third hair system. Paint follicles in the green partition. You should now have a head full of active follicles (see Figure 21.11).

Adding Collision Constraints

The first step to successfully shaping hair is to create collisions between the hair and the skin. Objects can be set as colliders by choosing **Hair → Make Collide**. Collisions, especially with high-resolution models, can be computationally expensive. Because of this, Maya has preset sphere and box collision constraints that are much faster than dense mesh collision. Other constraints will be explained later.

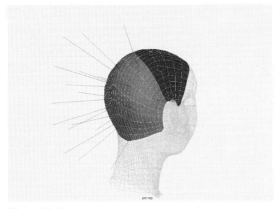

Figure 21.10

Active Follicles are added to the back section of the head. These follicles will eventually drive thousands of hairs.

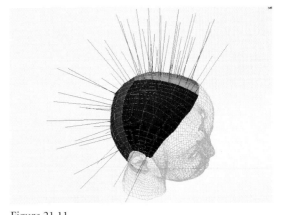

Figure 21.11

Multiple Hair Systems are used to better control the simulation of active follicles.

All hair constraints in Maya have a Curve Indices attribute that contains an array of follicles over which it has an effect. Unfortunately, this index cannot be appended easily to or significantly modified without using MEL scripting. When a collision constraint is added to a hair system, the outPin output of the constraint is connected into the inputHairPin input of the hair system shape node. Although you can connect other hair systems to the collision constraint by using the Hypergraph, the Curve Indices array in the constraint will not change. Therefore, the same number of curves that are affected on the first hair system will be affected on the subsequent hair systems. If the subsequent connected hair systems contain more follicles, the excess follicles would not collide. Consequently, attaching multiple hair systems to a single constraint is not recommended; each hair system should be attached to its own collision constraint.

The procedure then for making multiple hair systems interact with a seemingly similar constraint is to point-snap multiple colliders together, group them, and then manipulate the group so that they all translate, rotate, and scale together. Let's see how this works by adding colliders to our hair example.

1. Continuing from the previous example (or by opening `HeadActiveFollicles.mb`), change the display quality of each of the three hairSystemShape nodes to 1. (Select the hair system, open the Attribute Editor, click the hairSystemShape tab, and alter the Display Quality settings.) This allows for faster playback when simulating the hair.

2. Play your animation. You will see that the follicles fall directly downward inside the head (see Figure 21.12), with no collision. Rewind to frame 0.

3. Select hairSystem1Follicles, and choose **Hair → Create Constraint → Collide Sphere**. A collision sphere called hairConstraint1 is created.

4. Create two more collide spheres for hairSystem2Follicles and hairSystem3Follicles.

Figure 21.12

When simulating with no collision, follicles fall straight down, penetrating the head geometry.

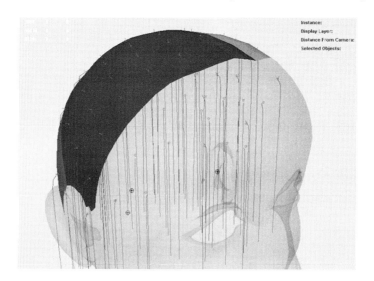

5. We will now transform all three colliders identically so that they collide similarly. Create a locator and move it into view. Point snap each of the three colliders to the locator so that they occupy the same 3D space. (Alternatively, move the colliders to the same World Space coordinates.)

6. Group the three colliders together and call the group CollidersGrp. Center the pivot on the group (choose **Modify → Center Pivot**). You can delete the locator created in the previous step now that our colliders move together.

7. Using the front, side, and perspective views, move and scale CollidersGrp so that it encapsulates the head. If it doesn't fit perfectly, that's okay.

8. Play the Timeline. You will see that the hair now collides with the collision spheres (see Figure 21.13). Rewind to frame 0.

The method just described is only one of many solutions for creating colliding hair. As there is no one correct way of setting up these collisions, experiment with your scene for results that match your needs.

If you prefer to create the multiple sections of hair under a single hair system, you can append new follicles to hair collisions by using the Assign Hair Constraint command, which is new to Maya 8. This command is discussed in the Constraints section of this chapter.

Styling Hair

After placing the active follicles in your scene, you are ready to style the hair. Styling is typically done by using a combination of fields and constraints. All of Maya's dynamic fields can be applied to influence the hair; so if you wanted to curl the hair tight, you could apply a Vortex field to the hair system. Uniform fields are great for simulating styling hair with a blow-dryer. Once the hair is in the general pose for the style you want, you can use constraints on select hairs to fine-tune the style.

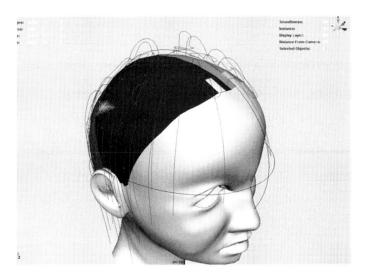

Figure 21.13

Follicles now collide with the collision constraint.

Forces and Hair

A powerful feature of Maya's dynamics is Interactive Playback, which allows you to run dynamics in real time. While Interactive Playback is enabled, you can move constraints and change forces interactively to shape the hair. We will now continue our example by using uniform fields and Rubber Band constraints to style the hair.

1. Continuing from the previous example (or by opening `HeadCollide.mb`), select hairSystem1 and add a uniform field by choosing **Fields → Uniform ❑**.

2. In the Uniform Options window, reset to defaults and change Magnitude to 5000.0. Also, change Direction X and Y to 0.0, and change Direction Z to −1.0. Click the Create button.

3. If you play back the simulation, you will see the hair on the back of the head flow backward. Stop the playback and go to frame 0. We will now add uniform fields to the other two sections.

4. As before, add uniform fields in the [−1.0, 1.0, 0.0] and [1.0, 1.0, 0.0] directions to hairSystem2 and hairSystem3, respectively. These fields will help generate a part down the middle of the hair.

5. Choose **Solvers → Interactive Playback** from the Dynamics menu set. You should now see the hair spread out in different directions (see Figure 21.14). Next, select each of the uniform fields and change Magnitude to 0.0. The hair should now fall gently into place. Stop the Timeline.

6. If you are happy with the results of how the hair falls around the head, select all follicles (you can select their groups) and choose **Hair → Set Start Position → From Current**. Now when you rewind to frame 0, the hairs will remain in the simulated pose rather than popping back to their default shapes (see Figure 21.15).

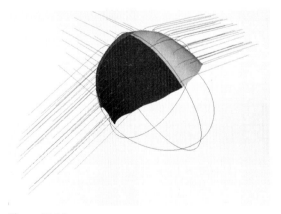

Figure 21.14

Uniform fields are used to simulate using a blow-dryer to style the hair.

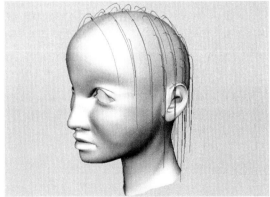

Figure 21.15

Hair rested and colliding with the head after using uniform fields to style

Constraints and Hair

Although forces are great for generally arranging the hair, specific tweaks can be achieved by using constraints:

Rubber Band	If the distance between the constraint and the hair exceeds the rubber band length, the hair will be pulled toward the constraint.
Stick	At any point in the simulation, if the distance between the hair and the constraint is less than the start distance, the hair is pushed away. If the distance between the hair and the constraint is more than the start distance, the hair is pulled toward the constraint. Rotating or scaling the constraint has no effect.
Transform	Similar to a stick constraint, only it can also be rotated and scaled. Useful for attaching hair to another object that manipulates it.
Hair-to-Hair	Binds hair together to make a clump.
Hair Bunch	Acts similarly to self-collision, yet more efficient. Repels hairs that intersect each other.

Rubber Band, Stick, and Transform constraints are all similar, yet each has its own advantages. Each of these constraints creates a connection between the constraint locator and each of the affected follicles. When using a Rubber Band constraint, imagine a rubber cord as the connection between the constraint and the affected follicles. The length of these connections is set at the start frame of the simulation. If the constraint is moved during simulation so that the length of the distance between the constraint and the follicle is more than the rubber band length, the affected follicles move with the constraint. There is no effect on the follicles if the constraint is moved so that the length of the connection is less than the rubber band length.

Imagine a Stick constraint as having rigid poles connecting affected follicles to the constraint locator. Stick constraints are similar to rubber bands in that the affected follicles move as the constraint moves away, but differ in that if the distance between the hairs and the constraint is less than the start distance, the hair is pushed away, forcing the distance from hair to constraint to remain constant.

A Transform constraint acts like a Stick constraint when translating. Transforms differ from Sticks in that rotating and scaling the constraint locator accordingly manipulates the affected follicles. Typically, Transform constraints are used when another object manipulates the hair. For example, if you use hair to create a leash, two Transform constraints can be attached to the dog's collar and the owner's hand.

Hair-to-Hair constraints bind hairs together so that they act as a clump. This type of constraint is useful for simulating a ribbon. Hair Bunch can be used to repel hairs from one another and is less expensive than self-collision.

Figures 21.16 and 21.17 show how each of these five constraints affects curves. In Figure 21.17, the Rubber Band affects the rightmost curve the most and affects the leftmost curve the least. The Stick affects each of the curves similarly because of its rigid

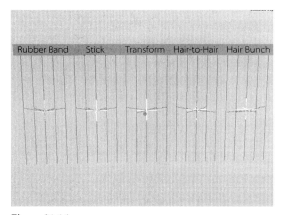

Figure 21.16

Examples of each constraint added to five curves, before they are translated

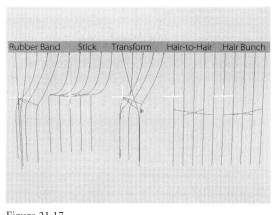

Figure 21.17

Examples of each constraint translated 2 units in –X and 1 unit in –Y

connections. Notice how the Transform keeps the rigid connections such as the Stick, yet the hairs are rotated in response to the movement. The Hair-to-Hair and Hair Bunch constraints do not affect the follicles if the constraint is moved. If, however, the rod holding the curves moves, the Hair-to-Hair curves will not collide with each other, but will have individual motion, while the Hair Bunch curves will move uniformly.

New to Maya 8, you can add follicles to existing hair constraints or reassign constraints to different follicles. This feature can really cut down on the number of colliders and constraints in your scene. To use this tool, select follicles you wish to add and then the constraint. Choose **Hair → Assign Hair Constraint** ❑. When Replace is checked, the selected hair constraint is reassigned to the selected hair follicles. When Append is on, the selected hair constraint adds the selected hair follicles to its influence.

> You can assign hair constraints only to follicles that are within the same hair system. Grouping or parenting constraints from various hair systems will achieve the effect of one constraint driving multiple hair systems.

If you would like to test these constraints for yourself, open the scene file `ConstraintsStart` `.mb` from the CD.

To add a constraint to a scene, for example, do the following:

1. View the Start position of the hair by choosing **Hair → Display → Start Position**. In this viewing mode, you can easily select individual follicle curves.

2. Select the curves you want to modify, and select the constraint you want by choosing **Hair → Create Constraint**.

3. Place the constraint in your scene. The location of the constraint relative to the affected follicles determines the start length of the connections between the hair and the constraint locator.

4. View the current position of the hair by choosing **Hair → Display→ Current Position**. Toggle the interactive playback and interactively move the constraint to set the hair into the position you want.

5. Assuming you want to keep the resulting shape and set it to be the default hairstyle, select the follicles and choose **Hair → Set Start Position → From Current**.

Using constraints on individual hair follicles is a great way to adjust the position of any "stray" hairs that did not set properly when creating the main hairstyle. Of course, the same constraints can pull out a few individual hairs so that the hairdo has some irregularity or messiness.

Altering Hair Lengths

Although simply deleting CVs from the hair in order to shorten it is permissible, Maya provides two ways to alter the length of hair: the Extend/Trim options in the Paint Hair Follicles Settings window and the Scale Hair tool. In addition, the Paint Hair Follicles tool can paint a variety of attributes, including Extend and Trim operations that alter the hair based on the number of points per hair selected. The advantage to using this tool is that the hair will remain the same shape; it will simply shrink or grow. To change hair length using the Paint Hair Follicles Settings window, select the hair system containing the follicle(s) from the Hair System drop-down list, change Paint Mode to Trim or Extend Hairs. Then enter an appropriate Points Per Hair value and paint over your existing follicles to change their lengths. Note that the Points Per Hair value, and not the Hair Length value, controls the length of an existing follicle. Since hair dynamics are sensitive to the number of control points along the hair curve, it would be undesirable to simply change the length without altering the points per hair. An existing hair follicle has a set of dynamics custom to that follicle which would break if the ratio between length and points per hair changed.

The Scale Hair tool lets you interactively scale hair. You can scale either single follicles or the scene's entire hair by dragging left to grow and right to shrink. Scaling the hair also exaggerates the style and curl in the hair, so added or muted volume is a side effect. To help get rid of unwanted volume, scale a bit up, simulate, set Current Position to Start, scale a bit more, and repeat.

> Be aware that the Undo feature in Maya records every change to a scaled follicle (even if you have not released your mouse button). Thus, it can take numerous Undos to return to a pre-scaled state.

Modify Curves

At times you will want to manually edit the hair curves. Under the **Hair ▸ Modify Curves** menu are several tools to shape your curves however you want. You can edit only Start and Rest curves (by selecting them); Current curves' shapes result from simulation and cannot be directly modified. The Modify Curves menu features the following:

- Lock Length
- Unlock Length
- Straighten
- Smooth
- Curl
- Bend
- Scale Curvature

Often when manipulating curves, you need to lock and unlock the lengths to retain the length of the hull for the selected curve or CVs. When a curve bends too much for your liking, you can use the Straighten tool to straighten it. The Smooth tool simply reduces the curliness. Curl allows you to modify the frequency and amount of curliness to the selected follicle. The following section describes how to obtain curls for the entire hair system. Occasionally, though, having this level of control over each follicle is important. Scale Curvature simply allows you to lessen or exaggerate the curvature of the follicle by a scaling factor.

Curly and Wavy Hair

Styling hair goes beyond just the general arrangement achieved by forces and constraints. Perhaps you want a braided ponytail or curly hair for your character, which would be rather difficult to create using only forces. Thankfully, Maya lets you easily achieve these effects through the hair system and follicle attributes.

Curliness is controlled in the Displacements section of the hair system's attributes. (Select the hairSystem*X* node and open the Attribute Editor to access this.) The Curl attribute is a control for the amount of waviness in the hair belonging to the selected hair system. Since curling hair requires smooth arcs, be sure the Sub Segments attribute in the Clump And Hair Shape section is turned up to at least 3 or 4. The Curl Frequency determines how many curls to create. Keep this value low for wavy hair; turn it high for kinky hair. It is always good to add a touch of curl, even to straight hair, just to give it a bit more depth and realism (or else your hair will be completely flat). Figure 21.18 shows the effects of adding curl.

Randomizations of the clumping of hair through noise provide yet more realistic-looking results. There are several attributes in the Displacement section of the hairSystem node to help create great looking curls and waves. There are three noise methods: Random,

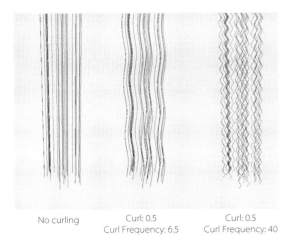

No curling   Curl: 0.5   Curl: 0.5
                 Curl Frequency: 6.5   Curl Frequency: 40

Figure 21.18

Different curling effects by affecting the Curl and Frequency attributes

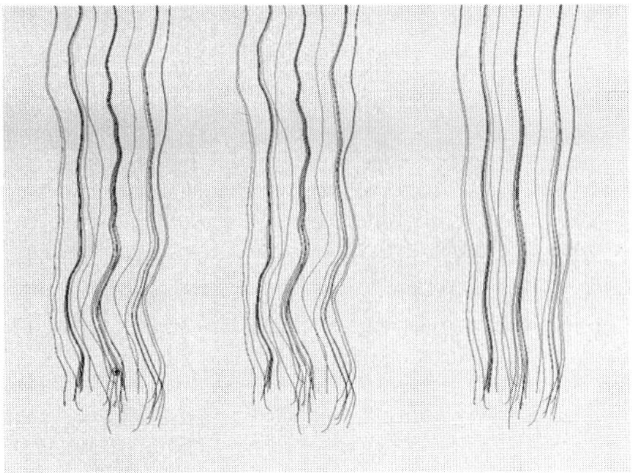

Clump noise   Surface UV noise   Random noise

Figure 20.19

Examples of the three noise methods. Noise allows for clumping for more realistic results.

Surface UV, and Clump UV. Random noise jitters the hair with no regard to neighboring-hairs and is good for frizzy hair. Surface UV creates noise in three dimensions (scaled in U and V directions across the surface, W down the length of the hairs) and is relative to the UV distribution of the hairs across the surface. Clump UV likewise has three-dimensional noise, but is not affected by the UV distribution across the surface. Surface and Clump UV noise are best used for natural-looking curls and waves. The frequency of noise can be scaled independently along the U, V, and W directions. Figure 21.19 illustrates the results of the three noise methods.

Sub Clumping refers to how individual hairs within each follicle clump cluster together. Adding sub clumping enhances a wet look to the hair, as if big chunks of hair were matted together. You can control the randomization noise and UV clumping attributes to achieve the sub-clumping effect you want. Figure 21.20 shows the effects of applying Sub Clumping to hair follicles.

Figure 21.20

Sub Clumping can be used for effects such as wet hair.

The Displacement scale allows you to change the amount of displacement applied along the length of the hair, controlling Curl, Noise, and Sub Clumping in the W direction. The left side of the graph represents the root of the hair; the right, the tip. Simply click in the graph to add or subtract displacement along the hair length, and drag in the pane to adjust the shape of the displacement curve.

No Sub Clumping   Sub Clumping

Figure 21.21

**Braids can easily be
created on follicles.**

Braids

Braiding virtual hair may seem like a daunting task, but it is straightforward using Maya's
per follicle Braid attribute. Simply select the follicle you want to braid and check the
Braid attribute. You must have enough sub segments in your hair (found in the hair system's attributes) for the curves to properly display. Also, adjusting Hairs Per Clump in
the hair system's attributes and the Density Mult value in the follicle's Render Overrides
will provide the volume needed for a successful braid. Modifying the hair system's clump
width will allow you to simulate the hair being tied together at the end of the braid (see
Figure 21.21).

SIMULATING HAIR GEL USING START CURVE ATTRACT

A great feature of Maya Hair is the Start Curve Attract attribute, found in the Forces subsection of the Dynamics section of a hair system node. This attribute controls how much attraction simulated hair has to the start position curves.

Through simulation and constraints, you can simulate the hair curves to a style you want,
set the start position (**Hair → Set Start Position → From Current**), and then adjust the Start Curve
Attract attribute to determine how stiff the hair conforms to the starting position.

By default, the value for Start Curve Attract is 0.0, meaning that the hair curves will not
adhere to the shape of the start curves. Increasing this value will attract the hair to the start
position, simulating hair spray or hair gel. A maximum value of 1.0 will hold the hair stiffly to
the start position shape.

When the Start Curve Attract attribute is higher than 0.0, you can alter the Attraction
Damp value, found directly underneath in the Attribute Editor. This value adds a damping
effect to the attraction force, resulting in quick springy hair for a low value or slow-moving,
flowing hair for a high value.

Adding Thickness to Hair Coverage

Often the active follicles alone look quite sparse in your scene. Once you decide on their general style, you will want to add thousands of hairs to fill in the gaps. You can do so in a few ways.

To increase computational efficiency, the shape and motion of hair is determined by a select few follicles designated as "active." Once these active follicles are shaped into the desired style, passive follicles can be added to give more thickness to hair coverage. These passive follicles interpolate their shape and motion from neighboring active follicles, so they don't significantly increase simulation time.

Two important attributes in the hair system's shape node to control thickness are Hairs Per Clump and Clump Width. Increasing these will add more hair to all the follicles in the associated hair system. On a per-follicle basis, the Density Mult attribute in Render Overrides can be adjusted to add fill in specific areas that need hairs.

Passive follicles are not required in every situation. Because of their efficiency over active follicles and to demonstrate how they work, we will add them to our ongoing example of placing hair on the girl's head.

1. Continuing our example, use your currently configured hair scene, or open `HeadAlteredLengths.mb` from the CD.

2. Choose **Hair → Display → Start Position** to view the follicles in their Start position (see Figure 21.22).

3. Select the skullcap and choose **Hair → Paint Hair Follicles** ❏. Choose Create Passive Follicles for the paint mode and hairSystemShape1 for the hair system. Since we are now trying to give more density to the hair, we will increase the U and V follicle density values each to 34. Since passive follicles derive their points per hair and length from neighboring active follicles, you don't need to alter the remaining options.

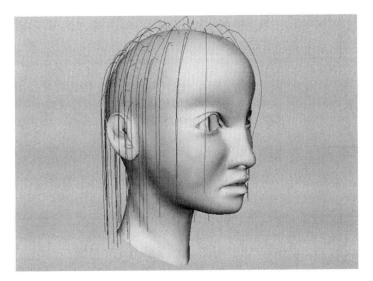

Figure 21.22

Depending on your desired hairstyle, you can alter follicle lengths after they have been created.

4. Paint onto the back side (red portion) of the skullcap. You will immediately see many follicles appear. Paint as many follicles as you can in this region. Test-render your scene to quickly spot any bald areas. If you can clearly see through any part of the hair you are trying to paint over, try increasing the U and V follicle density values in the Paint Hair Follicles Settings window.

5. Choose hairSystemShape2 for the hair system, and paint passive follicles in its respective region. Do the same for hairSystemShape3.

You will notice that once you've painted the hair using 34 as the general U and V follicle density, the top of the head is still quite bald. Every follicle in Maya has an associated clump of hair. By default, there are 10 hairs per follicle.

6. Since we are adding density to our hair, interactivity can quickly become limited. Place the Paint Effects and follicles of each hair system into their own display layer. We can now choose to view only the hair that we want to work with. Also, the Display Quality attribute of each hair system shape node allows us to control the amount of hair displayed in our preview.

7. Select hairSystem3 (the portion of hair attributed with the green partition of the skullcap) and open the Attribute Editor. In the Clump And Hair Shape settings, change Hairs Per Clump to 40 and Clump Width to 0.8.

8. To remove the chunkiness of the clumps, add a bit of thinning. (A value of 0.4 should suffice.)

> Creating a preset for the hair system in the Attribute Editor and then applying it to the other hair systems speeds up the work flow and assures that the hair has identical settings. Click the Presets button in the Attribute Editor to do this.

9. Repeat steps 8 and 9 on the other two hairSystem nodes, giving you a full head of hair. Feel free to paint in more passive follicles or adjust the clumping to tweak results (See Figure 21.23).

Figure 21.23

By adding follicle density to the hair systems, you can quickly add thousands of hairs that interpolate their shape based on active follicles.

Hair Dynamics and Collisions

Attributes for hair motion are controlled by the hair system. Follicle members of the associated hair system have a limited set of overrides in case you should ever want to control specific clumps. As seen previously, when styling the hair, forces inside Maya's dynamics can influence hair motion.

Attributes controlling a hair system's dynamics and collisions are found under the Dynamics, Collisions, and Turbulence sections of the associated hairSystemShape node's Attribute Editor. The following table briefly explains the function of each attribute:

DYNAMICS

Iterations	Controls the number of iterations per time step during solving. Hair appears stiffer when increased, but computation time is increased.
Length Flex	Controls how much a hair can stretch.
Stiffness	Controls the torsional flexibility of the hair.
Stiffness Scale	A graph that allows for adjusting the stiffness at points along the curve.
Drag	Simulates the friction of the air. A value of 0 will produce no drag, and a value of 1 will leave no follow-through.
Motion Drag	New to Maya 8, dampens the movement of hair curves relative to the movement of their follicles.
Damp	Dampens the dynamic effect. The lower the damping, the more energy and movement the hair has.
Friction	Controls the friction between the hair and a colliding surface.
Gravity	–Y force that is constantly applied to the hair.
Start Frame	Tells the simulation the frame on which to begin. If Current Time displays a frame before the start frame, the dynamics have no effect.

COLLISIONS

Collide	A toggle that turns on and off collisions.
Collide Over Sample	Controls the quality of collision sampling.
Collide Width Offset	Adjusts the offset of the collision in the event of penetration.
Self Collide	A toggle that turns on and off collisions between hairs.
Repulsion	The amount of repulsive force applied in the event of a collision.
Static Cling	Controls how much clinging occurs between hairs.
Num Collide Neighbors	Controls the number of neighbors the hair collides with. Increased number of neighbors negatively affects playback speed.
Collide Ground	A fast and efficient way to make hair collide with an infinite ground plane.
Ground Height	Determines the height of the collision ground.
Draw Collide Width	Displays the width of the collision around the hairs.
Width Draw Skip	Controls the quality of display of the Draw Collision Width.

TURBULENCE

Intensity	Controls the intensity of the turbulence.
Frequency	Controls how quickly turbulence changes over space.
Speed	Rate that the turbulence pattern changes over time.

new

General Work Flow Speedups

By the time you have modeled and styled the hair in your scene, interaction time will often come to a crawl. The following suggestions illustrate how to temporarily simplify the hair system to help with this excessive computation time.

Collisions

When animating hair in a complex scene, you can temporarily turn off collisions to get the correct general motion and dynamics of hair and to save computation time. Turn off collisions by unchecking Collide in the hair system's attributes. When a good basis of the dynamics is in place, enable collisions again to get accurate results.

When testing hair motion with collisions enabled, it is best to use a low Collide Over Sample value. If the hair noticeably penetrates the collision surface, increase Collide Over Sample and Collide Width Offset. If you have hair that needs to interact with a ground plane, such as a mop, use the Collide Ground attribute instead of creating a collider from a plane geometry because Collide Ground does not impact the efficiency of the solver.

Selected Visibility

Since hair tends to clump with itself, you do not need to preview the entire head of hair when simulating motion. Drawing 100 follicles instead of 10,000 really makes a difference in performance! Keeping Display Quality in the hair system's attributes to a minimal value will dramatically increase playback speed. Adding each set of hair to its own display layer lets you better organize your scene and show only the parts of the hair you are currently working on.

Selected Simulation

Just as we don't need to see every single hair we previsualize, we don't need to simulate every hair when working on body animation. In the hair system attributes, the default Simulation Method setting is All Follicles. Changing this to Off hides the hair system, and it will not simulate. This can be useful if you are simulating another part of your scene unrelated to the hair. Setting Simulation Method to Static keeps the hair system still, but the hair will move along with the underlying surface it "grows" from. Setting Simulation Method to Dynamic Follicles Only will only display and simulate active follicles. Since passive follicles often are used to fill in the gaps in hair renders, they don't need to be simulated until the active follicles are correct.

Cache

As with other dynamic systems in Maya, caches are used to save simulation data so that you can scrub through your animation, save time by not having to calculate the simulation over and over, present multiple versions of a simulation to your director, and send scenes to a distributed renderer.

To create a cache for your hair simulation, select a hair system and choose **Hair →
Create Cache** ❒; the option box is shown in Figure 21.24. You can specify whether to cache the frames set in the current render settings, the Time Slider range, or specific start and end frames. You can also choose to over- or undersample the calculation depending on the complexity of your scene. When you create the cache, Maya will play through the specified frames and "record" the data for each follicle into a * .mchp file located in the data folder of your current project. Warning: You must have a project set and your scene saved to see this cache file in the appropriate folder! This is one of the biggest traps Hair presents to users.

A cache node, called cache_yourHairSystemName, contains a link to the cache file that is attached to the hair system, as shown in Figure 21.25. Through this node you can load various caches if you want to view multiple versions.

Suppose you want to completely change the animation from which your cached hair is growing. You will need to delete the cache so that it can be resimulated with the newer animation by selecting the hair system and choosing **Hair → Delete Cache**.

At times you might want to delete only a portion of the cache. Go to the frame where you want to begin truncation and choose **Hair → Truncate Cache**. Frames before the current frame retain their cache, and frames afterward lose cache information. This command is useful if you have a minor animation tweak and don't want to recache the entire simulation. By choosing **Hair → Append To Cache**, you can add to an existing cache.

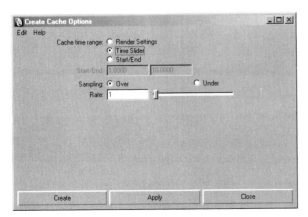

Figure 21.24

Cache allows you to save a simulation to disk, eliminating the need to calculate dynamics for each frame.

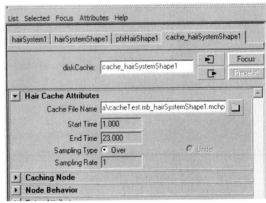

Figure 21.25

Saving multiple versions of your cache, each recording different simulation attributes, allows you to quickly view simulations without recalculation.

Rendering Hair

Although hair dynamics are quite complicated, equally intimidating is realistically rendering the intricate details of hair. Thankfully, issues such as ensuring hair thickness and controlling the variety of colors are easy to solve using the powerful shading options provided by Maya.

Depending on what you choose as your output format, you have a variety of options for rendering hair. Paint Effects are most often used to simulate realistic-looking strands of hair. If the output format is dynamic NURBS curves, surfaces can be created from these curves.

Paint Effects

If you are using Paint Effects as your hair output, you control the shading primarily though the associated hair system. Under the Shading section in the hair system, you can select the overall hair color. Maya gives you full control over the many slight colorations hair can exhibit. Often, hair seems to appear darker toward the base. Hair Color Scale allows you to multiply interpolated color values into the overall hair color. The leftmost color represents the root of the hair. One of the most influential color attributes of the hair system falls under the Color Randomization options. These sliders allow you to control the color of random streaks of color typical in realistic hair. Multi Streaks is the number of added sub hairs for each hair clump, allowing for many more Paint Effects tubes with little added computation time. Multi Streaks can be modified within its own section in the hair system attributes. Figure 21.26 shows some basic hair, and Figure 21.27 shows the same hair with Multi Streaks turned on.

Figure 21.26

Paint Effects with Multi Streaks turned off. Notice how thin the hair follicles appear.

Figure 20.27

Paint Effects with Multi Streaks turned on. This approach adds volume to follicles with little additional computation time.

If your scene uses NURBS curves as output, you may want to apply a Paint Effects brush to the dynamic curves. To do this, select the hair follicles and open the Visor (choose **Window → General Editors → Visor**). Click the Paint Effects tab and click the brush you want. (At this point, the follicles in the scene view and the brush in the visor should be highlighted.) Choose **Hair → Assign Paint Effects Brush To Hair**.

If you render at this time, you may notice that the paint effects don't really render the way you expect; they are thin and numerous and may have odd colors. Remember that under the Shading section of the hair system attributes, the Hair Color and Hair Color Scale are multiplied with the base Paint Effects colors. To make Maya ignore these features, make the hair color white and delete the nonwhite colors on the Selected Color graph. To change the thickness and number of strokes, change Hairs Per Clump and Hair Width, found in the Clump and Hair Shape section of the hair system's attributes.

See Chapter 17 to learn more about Paint Effects.

Geometry

Through using NURBS curves as the output or by making a curve dynamic, hair curves can be used to create surfaces that move like hair. Using curve extruding and lofting, surfaces can be constructed that retain the history of the dynamic follicles. This is useful if you want to make geometric "chunks" of hair rather than Paint Effects hair or if you want to make ropes, simple cloth, and other dynamic objects. The following example will create a dynamic plane, illustrating how simple it is to make an existing NURBS object dynamic.

1. In a new scene, create a NURBS plane, and set the U and V spans to 5 or so. You can scale it however you please.

2. Select the plane and switch to component mode. Select two opposite isoparms on the edges of the plane, as shown in Figure 21.28. Convert these two isoparms into curves by choosing **Edit Curves → Duplicate Surface Curves** (using the default settings) from the Surfaces menu set.

3. Delete history on the scene and delete the plane. You should be left with two curves. Although this is a roundabout way of obtaining two parallel curves, you can apply this method for more complicated objects.

4. Select both curves and choose **Hair → Make Selected Curves Dynamic** from the Dynamics menu set. This creates hairSystem1, hairSystem1Follicles group, and hairSystem1OutputCurves group.

5. Select the two curves in the hairSystem1OutputCurves group (it is easiest to access these curves via the Outliner) and loft them together. It is important not to delete history on this lofted surface. It should look identical to the plane from which the curves were made.

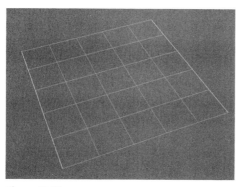

Figure 21.28

Edge isoparms of a NURBS plane can be used to create curves that will serve as boundaries of dynamic geometry.

Figure 21.29

Creating a surface out of lofted hairs will create dynamic geometry controlled by a hair system.

6. For each follicle in the hairSystem1Follicles group, change the PointLock attribute to Base in the Channel Box.

7. Play back the Timeline. You should see the surface fall like a piece of cloth, similar to Figure 21.29. Depending on the UV resolution of the plane you created in step 1, you may need to add CVs to get a more clothlike surface. To do this, select the curves in the hairSystem1OutputCurves group and the actual curves on each follicle. Rebuild these curves to a higher number, such as 20. Remember, the more CVs you have on a dynamic curve, the looser and silkier it is.

One other method for creating dynamic geometry is using curves to drive a skeletal system. This topic is discussed in its own section shortly.

Painting Hair Textures

Maya contains the Paint Hair Textures tool, allowing you to use the 3D Artisan brush to paint in baldness, hair color, and specular color. To use this handy tool, select a hair system and choose **Hair → Paint Hair Textures → Baldness** or **Hair Color** or **Specular Color**. The hair density and color are modified based on where you draw on the object. This is a great tool for visualizing various hair maps in 3D. You can also add your own 2D grayscale images for baldness, hair color, and specular color. The field for inserting a baldness map is found in the Clump And Hair Shape section of the hair system's attributes. Specular and Hair Color map filename paths can be found in the Shading section.

Lighting and Shadows

The final step in using software rendering for hair is properly casting self-shadows. Shadows really add to the realism of the Paint Effects hair. Typically, you want a key light with a high intensity (1.5–2.0) to create nice contrast between light and shadow. In the Shadows section of the light's attributes, turn on Use Depth Map Shadows, since Maya cannot raytrace Paint Effects shadows. For optimal visual results, turn off Use Mid Dist Dmap and alter the Dmap Filter Size to get smoother-looking shadows. You may need to adjust the Dmap Bias slightly to a greater value to allow more light to shine through the hair and to solve any shadow artifact problems.

mental ray for Maya

You can render hair using mental ray, eliminating the need to do a separate software render pass. The results and setup are a bit different than when using the software renderer. (See the Maya documentation for more on rendering hair with mental ray.) If you are using multi streaks in your Paint Effects hair, they will not show up in mental ray. To achieve the same effect, you can increase the number of hairs per clump.

Be sure that the Render Hair check box is enabled in the Features section of the mental ray tab of the Render Settings window. Hair rendered with mental ray tends to look a bit darker than when rendered in software mode. You can adjust the hair color and lighting to compensate if your hair appears too dark. The mental ray renderer allows you to use accurate depth-of-field composition; depth of field in the software renderer is not accurate. Hair can be affected by motion blur in mental ray and is fully integrated into the scene rather than being a Z-depth composite post process, which provides higher accuracy and realism than the basic Maya renderer. See Chapter 14 to learn more about using the mental ray renderer with Maya 8.5.

Using Hair to Drive a Skeletal System

The powerful dynamic system on which hair is built can be used to create many effects in your production. By making existing curves dynamic and then attaching these curves to skeletons, you can achieve great secondary animation on geometric objects. You can make a curve drive joints in several ways. Through MEL, you can develop expressions to update the location of joints based on locations of corresponding CVs on the dynamic curve. A more straightforward method is to use IK splines to connect the hair curve motion to deformable geometry.

To begin the process of transferring the dynamics of a hair curve to geometry, first create a skeleton. Since the number of CVs of the curve we will create equals the number of joints, be sure to provide enough joints for smooth deformation. After your skeleton is created, smooth bind it to your geometry. Then, with Point Snapping enabled, draw a 1-degree curve along the skeleton, a CV for each joint.

The rest of the process is described using an applied example of geometric hair on our previous head model. The scene provided has the hair already modeled, skeletons created for each strand, and a standard curve spanning each skeleton.

1. Open HeadGeoHair.mb from the CD. We are only concerned with making the front half of the hair dynamic since the rest of the hair is curled up into buns and thus won't move. Figure 21.30 shows the hair with skeletal bones created for the front hair

strands. There are two groups of hair strand objects: StaticHair and DynamicHair. Other scene components are organized in obvious group name structures. Also, for organization purposes, display layers have been created for the head, static hair, dynamic hair, skeletons, and hair curves.

2. Turn off the visibility of all layers except HairCurves. You should see curves that represent the front portion of the hair. Select all the curves and choose **Hair → Make Selected Curves Dynamic**. This will create follicles from the curves, a HairSystem1 node, and a new hairSystem1OutputCurves group.

3. Turn off the visibility of the HairCurves layer (which now by default contains the hair follicles). If you play the Timeline, the curves on screen should appear dynamic. Rewind to the first frame.

4. We will now use IK splines to make the hair skeletons follow these new dynamic curves. Turn on the visibility of the HairSkeletons layer. You should now see all the skeletons and the dynamic curves. In the Animation menu set, choose **Skeleton → IK Spline Handle Tool** ❐. In the Options box, reset the tool and uncheck Auto Parent Curve and Auto Create Curve, allowing us to specify the dynamic curves as our driver.

5. On one of the skeletons, with the IK Spline Handle tool, select the root joint, then the end joint, and finally the associated dynamic curve. You will see an IK handle appear at the end of the skeleton with a line connecting the root to the end. Repeat this method for each of the other eight skeletons. When you finish, your scene should look like Figure 21.31. If you see unwanted twisting in the IK spline, refer to the Advanced Twist Controls under the IK Solver Attributes portion of the IK Handle's attributes. For more information on IK splines, see Chapter 8.

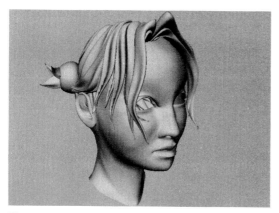

Figure 21.30

Even geometric hair can be driven by the power of Maya Hair.

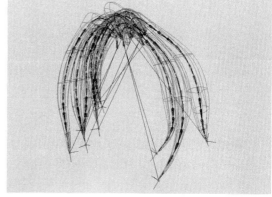

Figure 21.31

IK splines spanning the skeletons allow you to control skeletons by dynamic hair curves.

6. You should now have IK splines on each of the skeletons. Turn on the visibility of the DynamicHair layer and play the Timeline to see the hair geometry move with the curves. Rewind to the first frame.

7. Now we need to set up the dynamics and motion of the hair. In the Outliner, under the HairCurves group, select all the follicle nodes. Using the Channel Editor (so that we can change attributes for all selected objects), change pointLock from BothEnds to Base, making the hair attached only at its base instead of both ends.

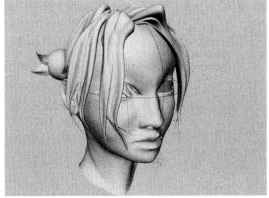

8. If you turn on the visibility of the Head layer and play back the simulation now, the hair droops down low and penetrates the head geometry. Rewind, select the follicles in the HairCurves group and choose **Hair → Create Constraint → Collide Sphere**. The sphere will appear at the origin, so translate and scale it to roughly surround the character's head. After placing the collide sphere, parent it to the head geometry. When you now play back the scene, you should see something similar to Figure 21.32.

Figure 21.32

Dynamic geometric hair colliding with a collide sphere

9. To make the hair stay in its proper rest position, select the hair curves and choose **Hair → Set Start Position → From Current**. With the curves still selected, choose **Hair → Set Rest Position → From Current**.

10. Since the dynamic hair curve positions are dictated by the associated follicles, parent the HairCurves group to the head geometry. Then, to make the hair simulate better, select the hair system and under the Dynamics section of the attributes, try some of the following values: Since a low iteration value can make the hair simulate too "silky," up the Iterations value to something like 30. To add to the stiffness of the hair, set Stiffness to a higher value, such as 0.8. Finally, to help the hair flow a bit better and "glide" to place smoothly, up the Damp to around 10 or so. If you wish, you can add simple animation to the head, rotating or moving to test the dynamics. Feel free to adjust any settings to cater to your animation.

11. The final step is to make the hair strands collide. An unfortunate side effect of using multiple curve-to-skeletal systems is that the geometric surfaces do not collide; only the hair curves do. Nevertheless, you can enable self-collisions by turning on the Self Collide attribute. (Select the hair system, and then, in the Channel Box, turn on selfCollide.) If strands are still penetrating, you can adjust the stiffness scale, adjust per follicle stiffness, or add Hair-to-Hair or Stick constraints. Figure 21.33 shows the geometric hair in various animated poses.

Figure 21.33

**When dynamic
hair curves and IK
splines are used,
even geometric
hair can dynami-
cally simulate.**

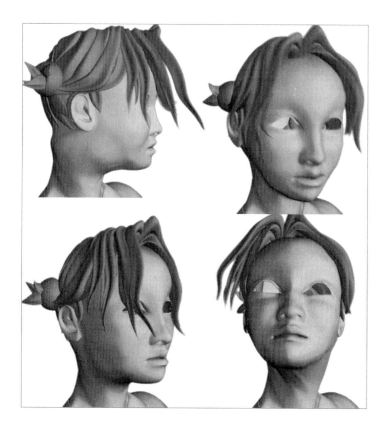

This is just one example of how curves can drive skeletons that in turn manipulate geometry. Any object that needs dynamic secondary animation can be set up quickly using IK splines and dynamic curves.

Summary

This chapter has explored the features of Maya Hair, and you should now be able to successfully create dynamic hair on your characters. Whether you want a realistic-looking scalp or a custom stylized look, Maya provides a wide assortment of options for your use. Furthermore, Maya Hair can be used to drive many special effects, whether by creating surfaces from dynamic curves or using hair to drive skeletal systems. Remember that the Visor contains some fantastic examples of hair, with great notes. You can learn a lot by playing with these presets and adjusting their attributes. The power inherent in Maya Hair, in addition to Cloth and Fur, makes the Maya Unlimited package worthwhile for your production needs.

The following chapter will discuss digital fur creation. Although hair and fur are similar in some respects, Maya treats them as completely different systems, each with unique settings and attributes.

CHAPTER 22

Maya Fur

Maya's Fur system lets you create fur for your character by using mapped attributes and setting values. The fur module has a number of uses for effects, such as creating moss on a rock a la time lapse photography. The fur in Maya has come a long way since its introduction and is made even more powerful with mental ray rendering. Furthermore, plug-in renderers such as Pixar's RenderMan for Maya will create even more astounding fur looks with minimal effort.

In this chapter, you will see the common use of Maya Fur—that is, for characters—in a hands-on example in which you create fur for a muskrat character. Keep in mind that Maya Fur is best used for short fur and short hair as opposed to long hair or shaggy fur because it is not capable of advanced reactive motion as typically seen with long hair. (For that, you'll need Maya Unlimited's Hair feature, discussed in the previous chapter.) However, Maya Fur is capable of movement, which you can control with keyframe animation or through dynamic fields.

- **Creating, editing, animating, and rendering fur**

- **Fur attribute maps and attractors**

- **Hands On: Adding fur to a character**

Creating Fur

Fur is mapped onto single or multiple NURBS or polygonal surfaces. A word of warning for polygonal surfaces, however: you must set nonoverlapping UVs on the surface that range between zero and one in texture space. (See Chapter 12 for more information on assigning UV values to polygons.) Fur relies on surface-mapped attributes that themselves rely on surface UVs for placement. For polygonal characters, more than likely, UVs have already been created, so this should not pose any issues. In other cases, you could even create a NURBS surface to match the polygonal areas of your current non-UVed model if you wish.

It's best to simply begin creating fur to see how easy this process can be. The work comes in making Maya Fur look and behave the way you want. To that end, it is prudent to know early on which renderer you plan to use. Maya's software renderer handles Maya Fur well, though you may find that mental ray does a more solid job, especially when the fur is self-shadowing. Using a plug-in renderer that supports Maya Fur, such as Render-Man for Maya, will change the work flow according to the renderer when you detail the look; however, the work flow when creating fur for Maya software rendering and mental ray rendering is exactly the same. Switching between the software and mental ray rendering for fur is quite easy, and we will cover both in this chapter.

Now, on to making some fur. We'll start by creating some simple fur on a NURBS primitive to get the hang of creating and editing fur. For this exercise, you'll map a Mohawk haircut onto a NURBS sphere to learn how to create and position fur as well as how to set various attributes to control its look.

Switch to the Rendering menu set and make sure the Fur module is loaded (if you do not see the Fur menu in the Rendering menu set). If not, choose **Window → Setting/ Preferences → Plug-in Manager**. In the Plug-in Manager, check the Fur.mll box in the list of plug-ins. You can also click Auto Load to On if you want Maya Fur to load whenever you run Maya.

Once you have Maya Fur loaded, create a NURBS sphere, and with the sphere selected, choose **Fur → Attach Fur Description → New**. Your sphere should now look like that in Figure 22.1. Usually white lines will pop out from the sphere. These are locators giving you visual feedback on the fur. They also give you color feedback by default, hence the white color in most default settings. You have now created a *fur description* for this fur effect. That's all there is to creating fur on a NURBS surface. Editing the fur description to be exactly what you need is the real trick.

The visual feedback for fur in your scene windows is revealed with locators. If you do not see anything after you attach a fur description or open a scene file with fur in it, check to make sure that locators are shown in your view panel (choose **Show → Locators**).

Figure 22.1

**The sphere with
fur attached**

Fur Feedback Settings

Open the Attribute Editor. It will be focused on the sphere if it's selected. To focus the Attribute Editor on the fur, select the locators. The Attribute Editor will now display the nurbsSphere1_FurFeedbackShape node, as seen in Figure 22.2.

This is where you can adjust the feedback properties to increase or decrease the level of feedback detail for your fur. You can enable or disable color feedback here. Disabling color feedback will turn the locators to the default Maya blue color when they're unselected. You can choose your tip and base color in the Fur Description attributes (covered in the following section). Figure 22.3 shows an example of color feedback enabled with a yellow base and red tip on each fur follicle. This is a simple setup, but when you are dealing with more intricate fur designs, you might want to increase the quality of the fur feedback.

The more locators you have giving you feedback, the better idea you'll have of how your fur is located on your surfaces. You can change the number of feedback locators by adjusting the U Samples and V Samples attribute values. Be careful not to set these values too high, though, as Maya will take an increasing performance hit the higher you go. Generally speaking, 32 for U and V is adequate for most tasks.

Figure 22.2

The FurFeedback-
Shape node,
accessed through
the Attribute Editor,
allows you to adjust
the real-time feed-
back properties of
your fur.

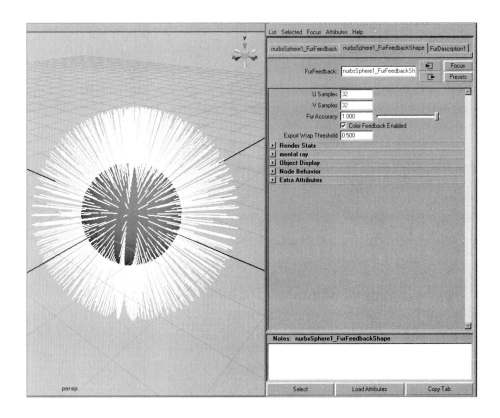

Figure 22.3

You can customize
the color feedback
to better organize
and preview your fur
descriptions.

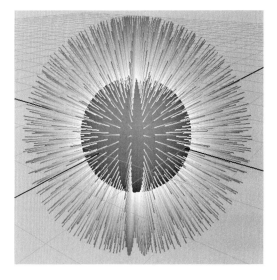

Furthermore, to adjust the feedback on *how* the fur itself looks, you can move the Fur Accuracy slider to adjust the detail level for each fur locator to give you feedback on the curl, bend, or shape of the fur. The thickness of the fur, however, will not be reflected in the feedback; you will have to render a test frame.

New to Maya 8.5, you can fine-tune gaps that may occur on combed fur along UV border edges by changing the Export Wrap Threshold value. Typically, you will not need to alter this value, but if the interpolation of fur along the UV border edges looks off, you can tweak this value to between 0 and 1.

Adjusting the Fur Description

This is where the real work begins. As you see, creating fur can be quick and easy; the work of getting your fur correct is all about creating the proper value maps. Switch to the Fur-Description1 tab from the FurFeedback tab in the Attribute Editor. (Your fur must be selected, of course.) Take a look at the fur attributes before we head back to the Mohawk haircut for our sphere.

> You can also access the Fur Description attributes by choosing **Fur → Edit Fur Description → FurDescription1** (or whatever the name of your fur) without having to select the locators representing that fur.

Table 22.1 lists and describes all the fur attributes. The first controls you'll see for a fur description—the first three in this table—set overall parameters of the fur. The rest of the attributes define how the fur will render. Skim this table, and then use it as a reference when you begin to create your own fur descriptions later in this chapter.

ATTRIBUTE	DESCRIPTION
Light Model	Changes the render of the fur according to how you want your scene lighting to affect the fur. A value of Ambient means that only base and tip ambient colors are calculated to create the final fur color. Ambient + Diffuse means that base and tip colors are added to the base and tip ambient colors. And finally, Ambient + Diffuse + Specular adds a specular highlight to the fur color.
Density	Governs the thickness of the overall fur on the surface. This is perhaps the most often changed attribute when creating fur because tweaking this value significantly changes the look of the fur. The higher the density, the longer the fur will take to calculate and render; so it's important to find the best setting for a proper look and a reasonable render time.
Global Scale	Uniformly adjusts the scale of Base Width, Tip Width, Length, and Offset values for your description.
Base Color and Tip Color	Sets the color of the fur to grade from the bottom to the top.
Base Ambient Color and Tip Ambient Color	Sets the ambient color to grade from bottom to top of each hair.
Specular Color	Sets the specular color of the hair when light strikes it.
Specular Sharpness	Sets the size of the overall specular across the whole fur description.

Table 22.1

Fur Attributes

continued

continues

ATTRIBUTE	DESCRIPTION
Length	Sets the length of each hair.
Baldness	Sets areas on the surface where there is little to no fur. This attribute is typically used with a map. A value of 1 indicates full fur; a value of 0 indicates no fur.
Inclination	Sets the angle at which each hair stands from the surface. A value of 0 is perpendicular, and a value of 1 lays the fur flat on the surface.
Roll	Rotates the fur at its root about the surface's V axis, with 0 at –90° and 1 at 90°
Polar	Rotates the fur at its root about the surface normal, with 0 at –180° and 1 at 180°.
Base Opacity and Tip Opacity	Sets the transparency of the fur at its base and tip respectively.
Base Width and Tip Width	Determines thickness of the hair at the base and tip respectively.
Base Curl and Tip Curl	Determines how much the hair curls at its base and tip. At 0.5, there is no curl. At less than 0.5, the hair curls in one direction, and at a value higher than 0.5, the hair curls to the other side.
Scraggle	Adds an element of randomness to the orientation of the fur by adding kinks to the individual hairs.
Scraggle Frequency	Governs how often the scraggle kinks occur.
Scraggle Correlation	Defines how each hair's scraggle corresponds to the scraggle of the other hairs. At a value of 1, all scraggle is in unison, and at a value of 0 every hair scraggle is different.
Clumping	Governs how parts of the fur clump together. The higher this value, the more hairs are pulled toward the center of a clump area.
Clumping Frequency	Sets how many clumps occur across the surface. This ranges from 0 to 100. The higher the value, the longer the render time, however.
Clump Shape	Determines whether a clump is concave or convex, that is, whether it bows in or bows out. The range is –10 (concave) to 10 (convex).
Segments	Defines how many segments a hair has: the more segments fur has, the smoother each hair will be. So, the longer the fur, and the more reactive to movement you need the hairs to be, the higher the segments should be set.
Attraction	Sets the amount of attraction the description will have to attractors, which are used for fur movement.
Offset	Sets the distance from the surface where the fur root starts.
Custom Equalizer	Deals with the use of customized equalizer maps for any fur description. Equalizer maps compensate for any uneven distribution of fur across a surface with uneven parameterization.

Figures 22.4, 22.5, 22.6, and 22.7 all correspond to Fur attributes. Figure 22.4 shows the effect of Inclination. Figure 22.5 shows how the Roll attribute affects fur. Figure 22.6 illustrates the role of Polar on fur, and Figure 22.7 demonstrates the effect of Fur Clumping, which is great for making fur look wet. In these figures, some of the fur has been curled to give you a visual clue as to the attributes' effects.

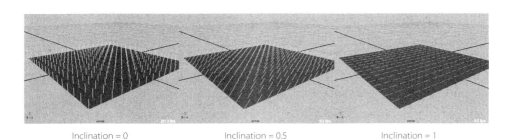

Figure 22.4
Effects of the *Inclination* attribute on fur

Inclination = 0   Inclination = 0.5   Inclination = 1

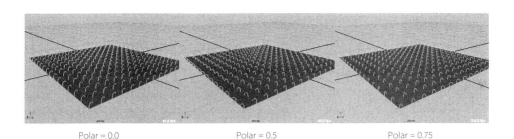

Figure 22.5
Effects of the *Roll* attribute on fur

Roll = 0.5   Roll = 0.0   Roll = 1.0

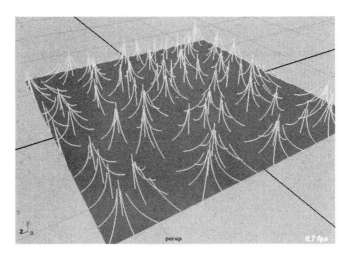

Figure 22.6
Effects of the *Polar* attribute on fur

Polar = 0.0   Polar = 0.5   Polar = 0.75

Figure 22.7
This example shows how fur clumps together with a Clumping value of 1, a Clumping Frequency of 25, and a Clump Shape of 0.

Back to the Mohawk

Let's jump back into the haircut and get our hands dirty again. First, change the name of the fur from FurDescription1 to mohawk_fur. Set Length to 0.15. Now we'll create baldness maps to place the Mohawk on the sphere. Creating this baldness map will give you the perfect idea of how to create and use maps for almost any other fur attribute.

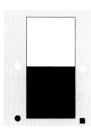

Figure 22.8

Set the ramp to a simple black-to-white gradient first.

1. RM click the Baldness attribute, and choose **Create New Texture** from the marking menu to open the Create Render Node window. Select a normal ramp (not projected) and name it baldness_ramp. You should notice that all the locators in the fur feedback disappear from the sphere. This is because the baldness of the fur is reading its values from the bottom of the ramp up. You will only see the feedback for whatever color is set to the bottom of the ramp, at first. This is merely in the feedback of the locators, so no worries just yet. Now change the ramp to a black-and-white gradient with Interpolation set to None (the result is shown in Figure 22.8).

2. To get visual feedback on how the ramp on the baldness will affect the fur's positioning, we're going to use an old trick: we'll set this baldness_ramp as the color of the sphere. This will give us immediate feedback as to where the ramp's colors are on the surface. Follow these steps:

    a. Open the Hypershade.

    b. Create a new Lambert and attach baldness_ramp to the Color attribute.

    c. Assign the Lambert to the sphere.

    This places the ramp on the sphere, and entering texture view mode (by selecting 6 in a view panel) will give you a view of how and where the baldness ramp will affect the sphere's fur. If you don't see anything on your sphere, make sure that Hardware Texturing is turned on in the Shading menu of your view panel.

3. Place the ramp's black and white shades as shown in Figure 22.9. Placing a white stripe down one side of the sphere inserts a strip of fur on that side of the sphere, which you can see as white on the sphere.

> Textures mapped onto Fur attributes must be baked before they have any effect on the fur description. Any subsequent changes made to these textures will need to be rebaked to affect the fur. Most fur attribute maps are effective at a 512 × 512 resolution. Higher map resolutions are called for in more intricate fur designs.

4. Notice that you still don't see any locators. For a map to have any effect on the fur, it must be "baked" into a fur attribute map. Maya Fur cannot read this texture node directly from the Baldness attribute. To bake the baldness, open the Attribute Editor for the fur description (choose **Fur → Edit Fur Description → mohawk_fur**) and

choose Baldness from the Bake Attribute drop-down menu. Set Map Width to 512 and Map Height to 512. These two values specify the size, in pixels, of the map file that Maya will write out to apply to the Baldness attribute of this fur description. Click the Bake button. Locators will now appear along the white stripe of the sphere. Disconnect the ramp from the Lambert's Color attribute to remove it, and make the sphere gray again.

5. Rotate the sphere to place the Mohawk on top of the head, as in Figure 22.10.

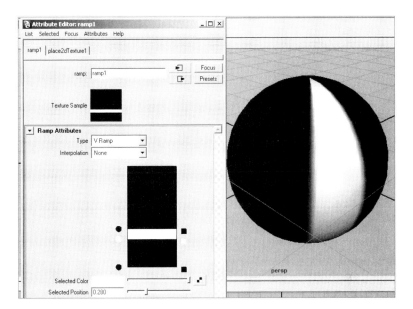

Figure 22.9

Place a white stripe down one side of the sphere.

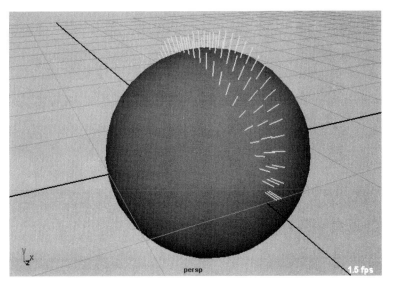

Figure 22.10

The first cut at making hair

You can refer to the scene file Haircut_v01.mb in the Haircut project in the Chapter 22 folder on the CD to check your work or to catch up to this point. In order to properly load in the fur's texture maps, make sure you set your Maya project to the Haircut directory in the Chapter 22 folder on the CD (do this by choosing **File → Project → Set**, navigate to the Haircut directory, and click OK.)

Painting Fur Attributes

We easily placed the Mohawk on the sphere, so now we can do some trimming and more detailed placement using the Paint Fur Attributes tool. Using the Maya Artisan toolset of brushes, you can paint attribute values to create your fur. This is one of the easiest ways to edit your fur settings, from creating length maps to combing the fur's direction.

Since we're done with the ramp texture, select it in the Hypershade and delete it. The baldness has already been baked to the fur description, so we will not lose the Mohawk by deleting the baldness_ramp node. For better control, you'll now paint the rest of the baldness of the Mohawk using the following steps:

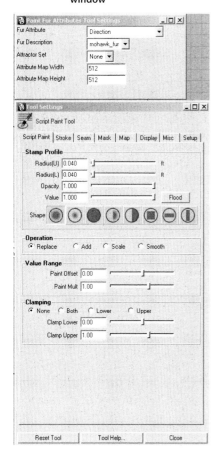

Figure 22.11

The Paint Fur Attributes Tool Settings window and the Tool Settings window

1. Select the sphere and choose **Fur → Paint Fur Attributes Tool ❐** to open the Paint Fur Attributes Tool Settings window and the Tool Settings window, as shown in Figure 22.11. The cursor will change to the Artisan paintbrush icon.

2. Set the attribute you want to paint onto the surface and the fur description that is affected in the Paint Fur Attributes Tool Settings window. Choose Baldness from the Fur Attribute drop-down menu. Make sure that Fur Description is set to mohawk_fur. Leave Attribute Map Width and Height at 512; that map size will be more than enough. You can of course increase it for more intricate maps and surfaces.

3. In the Tool Settings window, adjust the size of your brush. Click the Display rollout, and turn on the Color Feedback option so that you can see as you paint. Paint a baldness map, using a value of 0, to pull the fur back from the poles of the sphere, as shown in Figure 22.12. Exit the Paint Fur Attributes Tool Settings window by selecting any other tool (for example, by pressing W for the Translate tool).

4. Change Length to 0.5 from the original 0.15 we set to lengthen the hair. Now we will use the Paint Fur Attributes Tool Settings window again to paint a length map to make the edges of the Mohawk shorter than the middle. Before we do that, let's increase the fur feedback detail so that we see more of our Mohawk haircut. Select the locators, and open the Attribute Editor. Set both U Samples and V Samples to 64. You will notice twice the number of locators now.

5. To paint the length shorter on the outer edges of the haircut, select the sphere and choose **Fur → Paint Fur Attributes Tool** ❐. It's always a good idea to invoke this tool with the option box to gain access to the brush settings right away. Set Fur Attribute to Length in the Paint Fur Attributes Tool Settings window. In the Tool Settings window, set Operation to Scale and Value to 0.5. This scales the fur length from its current value of 0.5 by half wherever you paint on the sphere. Paint the outer edge of the Mohawk to create a shorter outer rim of fur, as shown in Figure 22.13.

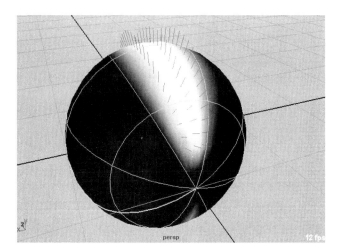

Figure 22.12

Paint a map that leaves the poles bald using a value of 0 for the bald areas.

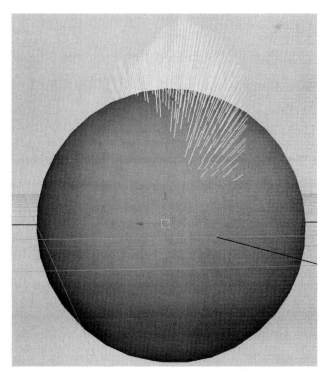

Figure 22.13

The Mohawk with shorter hair around the edge

6. Now's the time to test out the fur and see how it looks. Create a Spot light as a key light for your test scene, aim the light at the sphere from above and at an angle, and create a Directional light as a fill light aiming from the opposite direction. In the Render Settings dialog box, under the Common tab set Image Size Presets to 640 × 480, and under the Maya Software tab set Quality to Production Quality. Leaving all the other fur settings at their defaults, render a frame of the sphere with its new haircut. You should have something like Figure 22.14.

7. The fur looks more like little plastic spines right now. We'll adjust the color, density and the width of the fur to make it a proper punk rock hairstyle. Choose **Fur → Edit Fur Description → mohawk_fur** to open the Attribute Editor for the fur. Set Base Width to 0.008, and set Tip Width to 0.003. That is fairly thin; you will use widths of about 0.01 to 0.02 in most cases.

8. If you render now, the hairs will look better, but sparse. Change the Density setting from 1000 to 20,000. Run a render and you will see something more like a real haircut.

9. Now let's add color. Set Base Color to a dark red-brown. Set Tip Color to neon green. This is a punk hairstyle after all! Setting Base Color to brown will give you a sense of roots for the hair. Even if the fur is supposed to be an even color, you'll want the base color darker than the tip color to make the hair look more natural. (Since less light reaches the root of a hair, it will appear to be darker.) Run a test render and check it out.

10. To add more realism to the fur, add a little transparency to the tips. Set Tip Opacity to 0.635 and you'll notice in your next render that the hair will look more natural. Reducing Tip Opacity is a good trick and is frequently used.

11. Let's try shaping the hair a bit. Set Roll to 0.6 to slick the Mohawk back just a little bit. Add a little randomness to the haircut by setting Scraggle to 0.1. This will add just a little randomness to make the fur hairs slightly kinked, leading them to point in slightly different directions. Figure 22.15 shows the fur haircut.

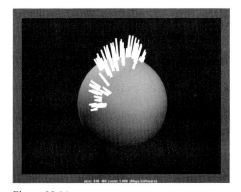

Figure 22.14

The sphere's haircut

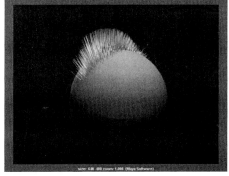

Figure 22.15

The Mohawk haircut after a little scraggle is added

Combing Fur Direction

Let's add some flare to the Mohawk on our sphere by first creating a bit of a part down the middle of the hair. For this, we will use the Paint Fur Attributes Tool Settings window to *comb* the hair into position.

First, make sure you have an Inclination value greater than 0 or a value other than 0.5 for Roll, Base Curl, or Tip Curl. Select the sphere, and choose **Fur → Paint Fur Attributes Tool ❑** to open the Paint Fur Attributes Tool Settings window.

> For the Comb function to work, you *must* have a value greater than 0 set for Inclination or a value other than 0.5 set for Roll, Base Curl, or Tip Curl. Combing the fur creates a fur attribute map for the Polar attribute. But to be able to see any changes to the fur when the Polar attribute changes, you will need some angle set on the fur to begin with.

Leave the Fur Attribute mode on Direction. Set Value to 0.03, and use a small radius brush. Use the brush to stroke the fur into the desired location, to split the Mohawk and to flare it out from the middle of the haircut. You will have to experiment with the direction of your brush strokes to point the fur in the right directions. Figure 22.16 shows the flared-out fur.

As you can see, the work of getting fur to look right lies in the editing. Creating and or painting maps to assign to the Fur attributes is the key to making proper fur. You will see this more in use when we add fur to a character at the end of this chapter. Using short

exercises such as the Mohawk on a sphere is important since actually using fur—becoming accustomed to how it works—is the best way to learn how to apply it effectively in your animations. Save this Mohawk haircut; we'll be using it later to add some movement to the hair. You can also load the file Haircut_v02.mb from the CD to check your work against it.

Figure 22.16

The Mohawk is flared out using the Comb function.

Fur Attribute Maps

Where do these maps get saved out? In your project folder structure you will notice a fur folder with its own set of subfolders called furAttrMap, furEqualMap, furFiles, furImages, and fur ShadowMap. These folders hold all the fur images and maps that Maya needs to describe and render your fur. The maps you bake or paint become IFF image files and are called fur attribute maps, or fur attrs for short. Whenever you save your scene file, Maya appends the filename to the fur attr file and places it in the fur/furAttrMap folder of your project. The files are named like this:

sceneName_furSurfaceName_furDescription_attribute.iff

Figure 22.17 shows a sample set of fur attr files in the fur/furAttrMap folder of this project. Notice the filenaming convention. This makes it easy to identify which map file controls which attribute of the fur. When working in an operating system that limits the number of characters you can have in a filename, it will be best to keep your naming conventions for files and objects short. For example, when you burn cross-platform CDs, some operating systems will not be able to handle filenames of more than 32 characters.

> When you change projects or create a new project and save the scene file into that new project, the fur attribute maps are resaved into the new fur/furAttrMap folder of that project by default.

Having separate files that are used to map your fur attributes is a handy way to control and edit your fur, but it can lead to an awful lot of files over the course of a long project. Once you are confident that you will not need to adjust your fur maps or move your project, you can set Maya to prevent new fur attr maps from being written. Choose **Fur → Fur Render Settings** to open the Fur Globals window, and set Copy Attr Maps to Never under the Fur Render Options rollout. This will reduce the number of fur attribute map files in your project, but it may cause confusion since the map filenames may no longer correspond with the scene filename.

However, unless you are really pressed for disk space (fur attrs take up little space), it's better to leave the setting at its default. This way you can be confident that each fur attr filename will match the appropriate scene filename. You might want, though, to keep a notebook log of the current files in use and use your notes to purge older fur attribute files as you go along.

Editing Fur Attribute Maps

Once a fur attribute map has been written, you can edit the maps in the fur description's Attribute Editor. Choose **Fur → Edit Fur Description → mohawk_fur** to open the Attribute

Editor. In the Details section (see Figure 22.18), you will find an entry for all the fur attributes.

Each entry gives you access to the fur attribute maps that have been painted or baked out into files. In the Mohawk scene, open the Length and the Maps sections. As shown here, you will find two sliders and two text boxes to adjust the map as well as the path and filename of the actual file mapped to the length of the Mohawk.

The Map Offset setting increases or decreases the overall value of the map applied. The Map Multiplier setting multiplies the values in the map file to increase or decrease the effect of the map on the fur. The Noise Amplitude setting creates random noise patterns in the map to create variations in the fur, and the Noise Frequency setting controls the rate at which the noise is created.

Experiment with a Noise Amplitude setting of the length map to create variation in the Mohawk. Set the value to about 0.15 for a nice effect. Try changing the Map Offset and Map Multiplier attributes to see how they affect the fur's length. Reset them to their original values when you're done experimenting.

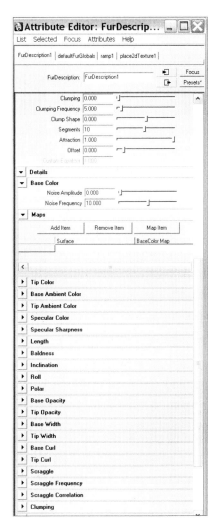

Figure 22.18

The details of the fur attributes shown here with the Base Color details expanded in the Attribute Editor

Detaching Fur Attribute Maps

To reset a fur attribute that has been baked or painted, you must detach its fur attribute map from the fur attribute through the Details section. For example, to reset the length of our Mohawk haircut, choose **Details → Length → Maps**. Click the map's filename, and then click the Remove Item button to disconnect the map from the attribute. This will not delete the file itself, however. And, if you change your mind immediately, you can undo the detach operation.

Detaching the texture from the attribute itself (instead of removing the map) will not affect the attribute since it has been baked. The map file needs to be removed to reset that particular fur attribute.

Creating Motion for Fur with Hair Systems

Well, that's all fine and dandy, but what does it mean? It's all jibber-jabber until you get to use it, right? Well, then, let's get our Mohawk hair to flutter in the wind. Load your last version of the Mohawk haircut, or use Haircut_v02.mb from the Haircut project folder on the CD. In order to properly load in the fur's texture maps, make sure you set your Maya project to the Haircut directory in the Chapter 22 folder on the CD (do this by choosing **File → Project → Set**, navigating to the Haircut directory, and clicking OK).

In older versions of Maya, fur movement was controlled with a couple of attractors that allow you to add simple movement to fur with keyframe or dynamic animation. You could have used IK handles, FK rotations, or soft-body-based deformations to animate the attractor chains. The fur then mimicked the movement of the attractors.

Although the theory of using attractors hasn't changed, the practice certainly has. Fur movement relies on hair curves attached to the fur description. This allows for a better dynamic reaction for the fur since the hair curves can be smooth curves of any length or shape while previous fur attractors could only respond to a three-joint chain for movement. Furthermore, you can even use the hair curves to style the fur as well as add motion.

> Fur attractors created in previous versions of Maya will still work properly in Maya 8.5, although any new attractors you need for your existing fur will have to be created with curves instead.

You can create hair curves to drive your fur motion by either creating a grid of hair curves that flood the surface with curves used to control the fur movement or by placing hair curves on specific points or faces on your model surface. See Chapter 21 for a discussion of hair curves.

Creating Attractors

We will add movement to the Mohawk haircut from the example in this chapter using hair curves.

1. With the `Haircut_v02.mb` file loaded, RM click the sphere and choose **Surface Point** from the marking menu. Select six points on the surface, as shown in Figure 22.19, along the line of the Mohawk. You cannot select CVs; you must select surface points to create hair curves at those locations on the surface.

> You needn't use dynamic curves as attractors. You can use static (nondynamic) curves in the Create Hair Options window and adjust the CVs of the curve(s) to style your fur or even to hand-animate the curves if you are the obsessive-compulsive type.

2. With those surface points selected, create the hair curves by choosing in the Dynamics menu set **Hair → Create Hair □**. In the option box, select NURBS Curves for Output and check the Radial button for At Selected Points/Faces. Check to make sure Dynamic is selected and that Length is set to 1 with 10 points per hair as shown in Figure 22.20. Click Create Hairs and you should have a result similar to Figure 22.21.

3. Select the newly created hairSystem node in the Outliner and then choose **Fur → Attach Hair System to Fur → Mohawk_fur**. This attaches the dynamic motion of the hair curves to the fur to create movement. That's it!

Select the sphere, and set some translation keyframes in your scene to move it around. When you play back your scene, you will notice the hair curves moving around quite a bit in reaction to the movement. But notice that the Mohawk fur is also moving in reaction to the fur. In Figure 22.22, the Mohawk fur is bent over, but only in the middle. Play back the scene and stop it while the sphere is in mid-movement to see the fur frozen in reaction to the movement of the sphere.

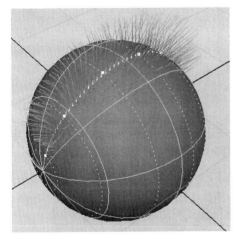

Figure 22.19

Select surface points to place your hair curves as fur attractors for the Mohawk.

Figure 22.20

The Create Hair Options window

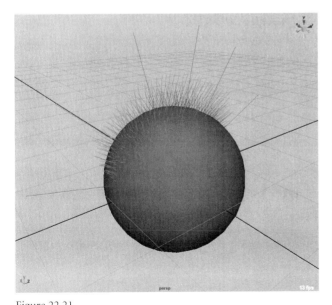

Figure 22.21

These hair curves will be used to control the Fur movement.

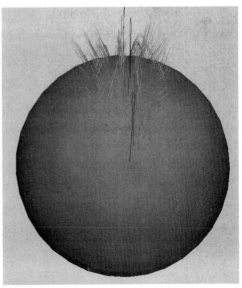

Figure 22.22

The curve attractors are affecting only the middle of the Mohawk fur.

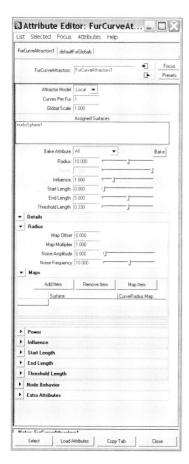

The hair curve attractors are affecting the fur only in the middle of the haircut. We will have to edit the newly created Curve Attractor Set node. Choose **Fur → Edit Curve Attractor Set → FurCurveAttractors1**. This node holds all the attributes needed for the attractor. Notice that the Attribute Editor is laid out similarly to the layout for a fur description node. (See Figure 22.23.)

The Radius setting controls the sphere of influence the attractor or attractors have over the hairs. With a low setting, demonstrated in Figure 22.22, the attractor controls only the hairs that are closer to it. Try increasing the Radius setting, but you will notice that the fur does not respond to affect all the Mohawk still. The Radius setting of 10 is more than enough, so this is not the culprit, but if you decrease the radius, note how the rest of the Mohawk stops responding to the curves. Our problem (as long as the radius is set to a high number such as 10) is actually due to the length of some of the fur.

For the attractor we created for the haircut to be effective on the entire length of hair, we need to adjust the Threshold Length attribute. This value sets the minimum length of the hair it takes for an attractor to act upon it. Since some of our hairs are less than the default 0.33 Threshold Length, change this value to 0.05. Notice how the whole Mohawk now dips in Figure 22.24.

Load the Haircut_v03.mb scene file from the Haircut project on the CD to check your work to this point. In order to properly load in the fur's texture maps, make sure you set your Maya project to the Haircut directory in the Chapter 22 folder on the CD (do this by choosing **File → Project → Set**, navigating to the Haircut directory, and clicking OK).

Other Curve Attractor Settings

The Influence setting controls how much the attractor affects the fur, with higher values creating greater influence and zero turning off all effect. The Power attribute controls how the influence of the attractor diminishes along the stem of the hair. With a value of 1, the influence begins to diminish immediately from the tip to the root. With a setting of 0, the entire hair (within the confines of Threshold Length, Start Length, and End Length) is influenced evenly, with no falloff.

The Start Length attribute sets the start position of an attractor's influence, and End Length sets the end position. These attributes limit the area along each hair where the attractors actually have an effect. You typically want Start Length at 0, and you want End Length set to the shortest of all your fur lengths; otherwise, you risk the tips of your fur not responding to attractor movement, which leads to a funky result. You can have a value slightly longer than your longest hair to be sure.

Now the fur mimics the shape and movement of the attractors. When you change the Attractor Model setting from Local to Global, however, the fur hairs grow toward the closest attractor instead.

Set Attractor Model to Global and you'll notice that all the hairs on the Mohawk point toward the locator, as shown in Figure 22.25. In this case, moving the top node of the attractor affects the motion of the fur. This is great for animating the fur pointing in specific directions. The fur does still react to dynamic forces if you are using dynamic curves as attractors in global mode.

Finally, the Curves Per Fur attribute specifies how many attractors affect an individual hair. When this attribute is set to 1, each hair is influenced by the closest attractor. When set to 2, each hair is influenced by the two closest attractors, and so on. This attribute is useful when you've created a number of attractors or when you have multiple attractors at specific surface points of the surface.

Figure 22.24

Now the whole Mohawk moves with the curve attractor.

Figure 22.25

The fur points toward the attractor when Attractor Model is set to Global.

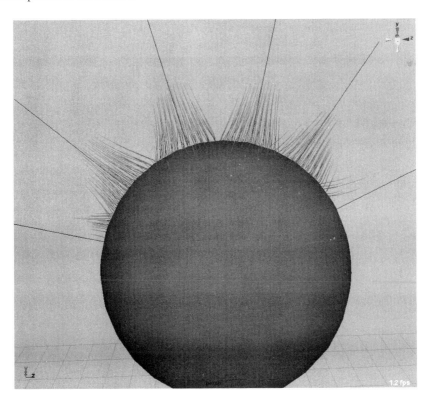

The trick for achieving good fur movement is to get in there and use fur and find how far it can go for your character or effect. There is really no better way to learn Fur, Maya, or anything for that matter. In the next section, we will jump in and put to good use the information in this chapter by adding fur to a character with multiple NURBS patches.

Adding Fur to a Character

Now that you have a grasp on how fur works, we add fur to a character, a muskrat superhero. The muskrat model is composed of several surfaces with varying UV directions and will pose an intriguing challenge to Fur. Adding fur to a multiple-surface character is a great exercise in how fur works in production. In this exercise, we'll deal with orienting fur to align properly across multiple surfaces, as well as with fur shadowing.

To begin furring the Mighty Muskrat character, you will load the model after it has been rigged, as shown in Figure 22.26. It is best to add fur after all the geometry is created and attached to the animation rig. It does not matter too much whether the model is textured, although it is helpful to have a clear idea of the texturing to be done on the model to help you set the proper colors and proper look for the fur itself. Figure 22.7 shows a rendering of the finished fur you'll create in this exercise.

Figure 22.26

The Mighty Muskrat ready for fur!

Figure 22.27

A finished rendering of the fur. Notice all the different surfaces of the character you'll need to cover.

We will use a rigged model of a muskrat character, but one that has no textures applied yet. To use this file, set your project to the MM_Fur project (from the Chapter 22 folder on the companion CD) and load the scene MM_Fur_v01.mb. This is the rigged character model with animation controls all set up for you to animate and test how the fur responds on a moving character. To complete it, you need add only the fur and the textures.

Adding Fur to the Head

Let's start with the more intricate task of adding fur to our muskrat's head.

1. Select the head geometry face. Choose **Fur → Attach Fur Description → New**. Figure 22.28 shows the head before fur is attached, and Figure 22.29 shows the fur locators after creation.

2. With that fur description now shown in the Attribute Editor, name the fur description MM_Face. Set a reasonable length for the fur description, say at about 0.08.

At this next stage, it is important to get the fur off our character's lips and out of his mouth. Also, there is no need for fur under the mask since it will not show; worse yet, if you don't remove it, it might poke up through the do-rag. It is best to start with a ramp on baldness as we did on the Mohawk haircut earlier in this chapter.

Figure 22.28

The character's head is selected

Figure 22.29

A fur description is attached to the head surface.

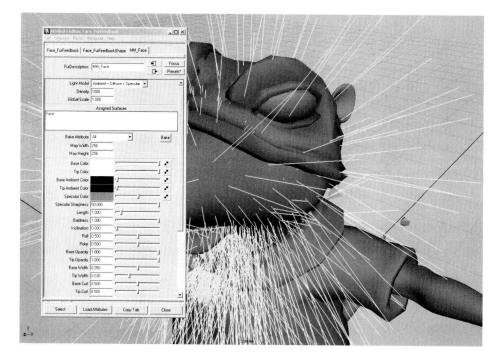

3. Create a ramp texture for the Baldness attribute of the MM_Face fur. Set the ramp to grade from black to white, and set Interpolation to None.

4. Once you assign the ramp to the Color attribute of the head shader as well as the Baldness attribute of the fur, toggle into texture mode (see Figure 22.30).

5. Select the mask and toggle it into template mode so that you can see the head and where the ramp position will line up. Switch the ramp to a U ramp so that the division of black and white is horizontal to the head, and adjust the color's positions so that the inside of the mouth is black and the rest of the head is white. This will get the fur out of our character's mouth. You will not be able to set the baldness for the rest of the head using the ramp due to the UVs of the geometry.

Figure 22.30

The Baldness ramp is seen on the face surface as a Color ramp to help position the fur interactively. The ramp is not placed correctly yet.

INTERACTIVITY AND THE RAMP SHADER

For an interactive work flow, you can set up the same ramp as the color on a Lambert shader. Then assign the shader to the head geometry to see the colors of the ramp as you position them, just as we did with the Mohawk exercise. This way you can see where the black and white of the ramp line up as you adjust it to place the black portions where you don't want fur. Make sure you remember which shader is attached to the head before you temporarily assign this new shader if you have assigned textures to your model already.

6. To commit this baldness pattern to the fur, bake the Baldness attribute. Set both Map Width and Map Height to 1024. In the Bake Attribute drop-down menu, select Baldness, and click the Bake button. This will create the fur baldness description file that maps to the surface to describe where the fur appears on the head. Notice in Figure 22.31 that the black areas of the mouth no longer have fur. Keep in mind that any changes you make to the Baldness ramp you will have to bake onto the fur before seeing any changes. The fur will not automatically update because its baldness is not attached to the ramp but to a map file being generated by the ramp each time you bake it.

7. To remove the fur from under the mask, we'll paint the attribute directly on the surface. Select the head geometry (called Face in this file), and choose **Fur → Paint Fur Attributes Tool** ❐ to open the Options window. The fur description should already be set to MM_Face. Set Fur Attribute to Baldness.

8. Choose an appropriate brush size, set its value to 0, and paint a bald patch under the mask and below the collar. Click the Display tab and turn on Color Feedback. This will show you the baldness value as you paint it. Paint the fur off the part of the head not visible under the mask, as shown in Figure 22.32. Use the Paint tool to finesse the edges around the lips, as shown in Figure 22.33.

9. When you're satisfied, save your work, put your feet up, and have a soda.

Figure 22.31

Getting the fur out of the muskrat's mouth using a ramp texture on the Baldness attribute

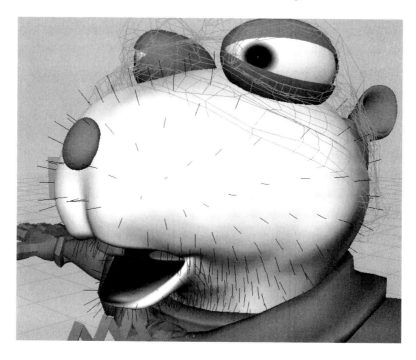

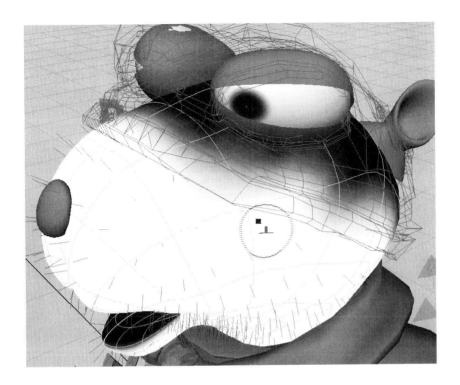

Figure 22.32
Paint out the areas where you don't want fur to appear.

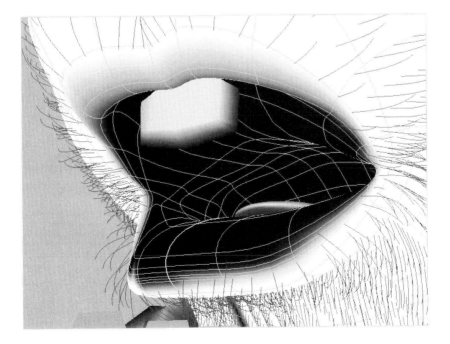

Figure 22.33
Paint carefully around the lips to keep them unfurred.

10. Reassign the head's previous shader, in this case a gray Lambert. Test-render a frame to see the fur on the character's head. It's not going to look good yet (see Figure 22.34). We still need to thin out, better position, change the density of, and properly light the fur.

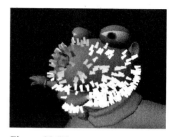

Figure 22.34

An early test render of the fur

11. Find a good thickness value for the fur. Choose **Fur → Edit Fur Description → MM_Face**. Set Base Width to 0.003, and set Tip Width to 0.002.

12. To position the fur, set Inclination to 0.7 to lay it down on the surface (not completely, though), and set the Polar value to 0.225 to rotate the fur to stroke along the face, as in Figure 22.35.

If you run a test render now, the muskrat will look as if he's at an acupuncture clinic as opposed to being a cute furry critter. The fur density is too low.

13. Change the Density value from 1000 to 200,000. Yes, yes, a big jump, but worth it! Change the color of the fur by setting the Base Color and Tip Color attributes to a golden brown.

14. At the top of the Attribute Editor for the fur, set Light Model to Ambient + Diffuse to avoid rendering out specular highlights. Sometimes fur looks better without the specular highlights. Untemplate the mask, and render a frame to check your work so far against Figure 22.36.

Figure 22.35

Laying the fur in the right direction along the face

Adding Fur Shadows

Don't panic yet; the fur is supposed to look that flat right now. We need to enable shadows for the fur to get it looking more real with a sense of depth. Shadows add a tremendous amount of realism and depth to any fur. But with Maya Fur, shadows are done a bit differently than with regular objects. To shadow fur, you must attach special Fur Shadow attributes to a light to allow the fur to self-shadow. The light does not need to cast shadows with depth maps or raytracing, however, for fur shadowing to work, as long as it is attached to the fur shadowing attributes.

To add shadows to a fur description, you select a scene light and use the Add To Selected Light command. To create shadows for the character's fur, follow these steps:

1. Create a Spot light to aim at the Mighty Muskrat's head from the front and at an angle. With the light selected, choose **Fur → Fur Shadowing Attributes → Add To Selected Light**. This will cause the fur to self-shadow based on the light from this Spot light. You will notice in the light's Attribute Editor that several new attributes are listed in the Fur Shading/Shadowing section, as shown in Figure 22.37.

2. Add a fill light with another Spot light to better light the scene. Add fur shadows to that light as well. When you run your render again, with the Spot light's fur shadowing enabled, you'll notice immediately a big change for the better in the fur's appearance. It now has a thickness to it, as shown in Figure 22.38.

3. Experiment with painting length maps to shorten some of the hairs around the mouth and around the cheeks so that they don't bunch up as much. Open the Details section in the Attribute Editor, and add about 0.1 to the length map's Noise Amplitude attribute to give the length a bit of randomness.

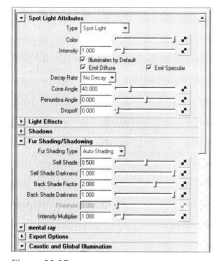

Figure 22.37

Fur Shading/Shadowing attributes

Figure 22.38

Fur shadowing gives a better sense of depth to the fur.

4. Add a small amount of scraggle and a tip curl of about 0.25. Last, open the Base Color subsection in the Details section and set Noise Amplitude to about 0.03. Open the Tip Color subsection, and set Noise Amplitude to about 0.02.

5. Render a test and judge for yourself how the fur looks on the Mighty Muskrat's face. You will go back and forth between renders to tweak the various fur attributes to get everything just right. The values used in this exercise should give you a terrific result for the face fur.

 Load the scene file `MM_Fur_v02.mb` in the MM_Fur project on the CD to check your work or to start the next section. In order to properly load in the fur's texture maps, make sure you set your Maya project to the Haircut directory in the Chapter 22 folder on the CD (do this by choosing **File → Project → Set**, navigating to the MM_Fur directory, and clicking OK).

Rendering Fur with mental ray

 Rendering fur with mental ray sometimes gives you cleaner results, particularly in the shadowed areas in animation. Not a lot of extra setup is needed. You can dive right in and render with mental ray as opposed to Maya Software at any time with your current fur setup on the muskrat. As a matter of fact, let's pick up right where we left off in the last section using `MM_Fur_v02.mb` in the MM_Fur project or your current scene file.

To render the muskrat with mental ray, follow these steps:

1. Open the Render Settings window, and change the renderer to mental ray. Set the Quality presets to Production.

Figure 22.39

Fur rendered by mental ray with depth map shadows and a hair primitive fur shader.

Figure 22.40

Fur rendered by mental ray with a volume fur shader

2. Render a frame of the muskrat's face with his existing fur setup. You should notice that the fur looks blown out and is now lacking shadows again on his face. This is because mental ray uses the regular shadow settings on the light and ignores the fur shadowing attributes we needed for the Maya Software renderer.

3. Select the spotlight directly facing him and turn on Use Depth Map Shadows in the Spot light's Attribute Editor window. You can leave the resolution set to 512 for now. Render a frame, and you should notice that the fur looks much healthier than before, as shown in Figure 22.39.

4. New to Maya 8, to help speed up renders you can specify the fur shader mental ray will use. The default fur shader, rendered in Figure 22.40, is Hair Primitive. To change the shader, choose **Fur → Fur Render Settings** and in the Attribute Editor of the defaultFurGlobals tab, twirl down the mental ray section. Notice that Fur Shader is set to Hair Primitive. Change this attribute to Volume and render another frame. While the quality is not as detailed as the Hair Primitive setting (see Figure 22.40), volume shading provides a faster algorithm for rendering mental ray fur.

That's it! If you do a side-by-side comparison of the fur rendered with mental ray and with Maya Software, you should see only a little bit of a difference in the shadow detail around the nose. mental ray renders the shadows a bit softer than does Maya's scanline renderer, but there is not much of an increase if at all in the render times. Overall, however, the two renders look much the same. Even so, we recommend that you have a good idea of what you want to render with before you get too far in your fur setup. For the most part, we like to rely on mental ray rendering for animated scenes with fur and shadows.

For the rest of the chapter, assume renders will be done in Maya Software, except where noted. If you choose to render with mental ray, your results will be much the same as ours in the chapter, with the exception of shadows. As mentioned in this section, you will need to enable shadows as normal for your shadow-casting lights to cast fur shadows in mental ray.

Adding Fur to the Ears

Since the ears are separate geometries from the head on our character model, they need their own fur descriptions. Because the only real differences between the ear fur and the face fur are density and direction, you can start with the same fur description created for the face and edit it to look good on the ears by duplicating the MM_Face fur description.

1. Choose **Fur → Fur Description (more) → Duplicate → MM_Face**.

2. Rename the duplicate fur description to MM_Ears, attach it to both ears by selecting the ears, and choose **Fur → Attach Fur Description → MM_Ears**. This will connect the existing fur description to the selection.

3. The maps set on the attributes of the fur description will not copy over to the duplicate fur description; however, that is not a problem because we need to re-create a baldness map anyway. Open the Paint Fur Attributes Settings window and use the Paint Fur Attributes tool to paint a baldness map to keep the fur out of the Mighty Muskrat's ear, placing it only on the back of each ear.

4. Set Length to 0.04, and add a noise amplitude on the length map of about 0.05. Set Polar to 0, and set Inclination to about 0.685.

Now, you've probably noticed that the fur on the left ear does not point in the same direction as the fur on the right ear. The fur should be pointing up on both ears, but it is currently pointing up only on the right ear (see Figure 22.41). You do not need to create a whole new fur description for the left ear with different Polar and Roll attributes to point the fur up.

5. Select the left ear and choose **Fur → Offset Fur Direction By → 270 Degrees** to set the fur in the same direction as the other ear. If you are using your own model, you may have to offset the direction of the other or both ears to get the fur to point up along the back of the ears.

6. Since the surface area of the fur is far less than that of the face, set the Density value to 15,000. Render a test frame. The fur on the ears should now match the face fur, as in Figure 22.42.

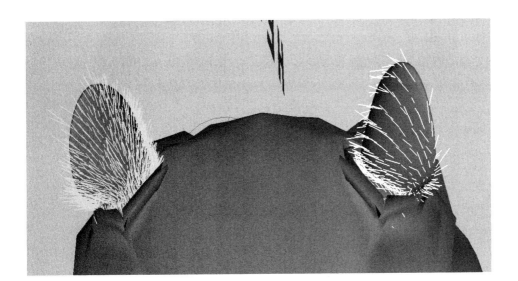

Figure 22.41

We need to perk up the fur on his left ear.

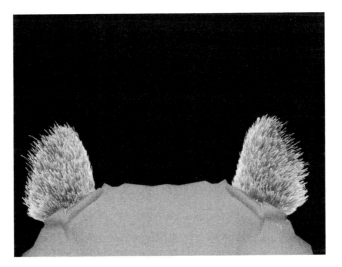

Figure 22.42

The fur direction on the ears is offset and the density is raised so that the ear fur matches the face fur.

Adding Fur to the Arms

Again, we have different surfaces for the arms of this character, so we will need to add fur to them on their own.

1. Duplicate the MM_Face fur description and rename it MM_Arms.

2. Select the arm geometry and attach the MM_Arms fur description to both arms.

Figure 22.43

Keep the fur point-
ing in the correct
direction.

3. You'll notice that the right arm's fur direction will be into the arm. We want the fur normals for this arm to be reversed so that the fur grows outward. Select the right arm surface and choose **Fur → Reverse Fur Normals** to flip the fur to grow back out. Also make sure the fur grows down the arm, as shown in Figure 22.43. Choose **Fur → Offset Fur Direction By** as needed.

4. Keep Length at 0.08, but set Noise Amplitude to about 0.15 in the Length details section in the Attribute Editor. Set Inclination to 0.6 to fluff it out away from the arm some.

5. Change Scraggle to about 0.14, and set Density to 10,000. Keep the other settings the same and render a test. Make sure the fur doesn't grow up through the gloves. Paint a baldness map if need be to keep the arm fur above the gloves.

Adding Fur to the Legs

To add fur to the legs, copy the MM_Arms fur description and rename it MM_Legs. You should notice that the fur on the legs is created in two incorrect directions, as shown in Figure 22.44.

Offset the fur direction on the left leg by 180 degrees and on the right leg by 270 degrees to get the fur to grow down (see Figure 22.45).

In the Length Details section, set Noise Amplitude to about 0.08. Run a test render, and make sure the Density setting copied over from the MM_Arms fur description (10,000) works for the legs as well.

If you are rendering with mental ray, remember to enable shadows for the lights in order to enable shadowing in the fur.

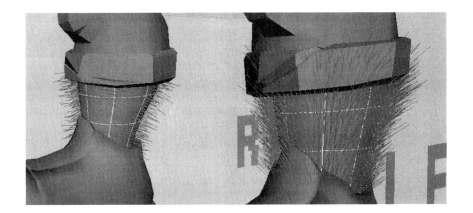

Figure 22.44

The fur direction is wrong for both legs.

Figure 22.45

Offset the fur direction to get the fur to grow in the proper direction.

Adding Fur to the Tail

Now we need to add fur to the muskrat's tail.

1. Duplicate the MM_Arms fur description and rename it MM_Tail.

2. Make sure the fur grows down the length of the tail, as in Figure 22.46.

3. Set Density to 35,000, and set Length to 0.12. Set Noise Amplitude to 0.2 to create a good amount of randomness to the tail fur.

4. Set Inclination to 0.75, and run a test render to make sure the density and length settings look good with the rest of the fur on the character.

To see a complete version of the character with fur, load the scene file MM_Fur_v03.mb from the MM_Fur project on the CD. In order to properly load in the fur's texture maps, make sure you set your Maya project to the Haircut directory in the Chapter 22 folder on the CD (do this by choosing **File → Project → Set**, navigating to the MM_Fur directory, and clicking OK).

Figure 22.46

Create the fur to grow down along the length of the tail.

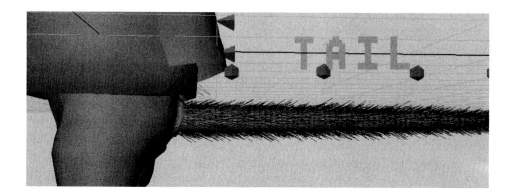

Summary

Using Maya Fur is a great quick way to add fur to a character or to create effects such as growing moss on a rock or tree face. It is a simple and effective fur solution that should cover a lot of needs. You will find that rendering with mental ray or even Pixar's Render-Man for Maya plug-in will provide some slightly different results that may give you better shadowing detail for animated characters without the possible render noise you can get from Maya's default scanline renderer.

To take our muskrat example even further, try adding attractors to the character's fur to add some movement to him. You can create a breeze movement to his fur as you animate him running or flying through the air. It is sometimes a great idea to create simple fur setups such as the Mohawk haircut on an ordinary sphere to test your ideas as well. The best way to gain experience with Maya Fur is to experiment and become aware of its abilities and limitations.

The most notable limitation is Fur's movement ability. Although there are numerous options to add movement to fur, they are effective only for slight movements. Additionally, Fur is best used for short fur or hair and is not recommended for long-hair effects. But it is possible to create a variety of effects with Maya Fur, including short hair fully covering a character, a pair of eyebrows, and a field of growing grass in a long shot.

CHAPTER 23

Cloth Simulation with nCloth

Maya's new nucleus cloth, or nCloth, simulation engine is a powerful new tool in the effects artist's toolbox. nCloth uses Maya's nucleus solver, a system of particles and "links" that can simulate almost any type of cloth in a stable, fast manner. Beyond traditional cloth uses, nCloth can also simulate such diverse objects as leaves, balloons, and even water effects. nCloth is available with Maya 8.5 Unlimited only; if you have an earlier version of Maya, or 8.5 Complete, you can read along in this chapter but won't be able to use the package yourself. (You'll find coverage of the previous Cloth implementation, now called Classic Cloth and supported by Autodesk for backward compatibility only, on the companion CD.)

This chapter covers the following topics.

- **What is nCloth?**

- **Creating an nCloth simulation**

- **nCloth properties**

- **nCloth constraints**

- **nCloth forces**

- **Using nCloth for a non-cloth simulation**

- **Creating a realistic simulation of a tattered shirt**

What Is nCloth?

Maya's nCloth, driven by Autodesk's new nucleus solver, is a system of particles connected by links that, via animation, forces, and collisions, drive geometric objects (a skirt, a flag, a pair of pants, a balloon, and so on) in a way that makes them appear to be made out of cloth or some other flexible material. If you have used Maya's soft bodies with springs before, the nCloth simulator should sound relatively familiar as it uses a similar method to create natural simulations. Unlike soft bodies, however, nCloth uses a solution optimized for nonstretching, nonshearing materials, making it ideal for use in solving cloth and clothlike materials.

> According to Maya documentation the nucleus solver might be used for other simulations (like soft bodies or water) in the future; at present, however, it is only being used in the nCloth engine.

nCloth can be created from any polygonal object (for NURBS or subdivision objects, you'll first have to convert them to polygons). Upon creating an nCloth object from a poly mesh, Maya places a single particle at each vertex, as shown in Figure 23.1. For quad-based faces, nCloth then places "links" going diagonally between the corner particles. These links help maintain stiffness and reduce shearing by maintaining the angle of the adjacent edges of the face. With triangular faces, nCloth will not place links between vertex particles, so it is best to work with quad polygon faces when creating models for later use as nCloth meshes.

When an nCloth object is created, the original polygon object is hidden, a new cloth object is created, and a new nucleus solver node is also created, assuming that one does not yet exist. If a nucleus solver already exists for some other object in the scene, you can choose to add the new simulation to the same solver or create a new solver for the new object. Figure 23.2 shows the elements of an nCloth solver displayed in the Hypergraph. Note that pPlaneShape1 (the original object's shape node) is hidden, the nClothShape1 and nucleus1 nodes are attached to a time1 node since they are implicitly animated for the simulation, and the outputCloth1 node (what is shown in the viewport) is driven directly by the nClothShape1 node. In the Outliner, the relationships are somewhat hidden: when you create an nCloth object, all that appears is a new nCloth1 node; however, as the Hypergraph view shows, a more complex set of relationships has been created for the simulation.

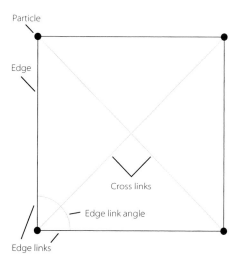

Figure 23.1

The components of a single "face" of an nCloth simulation

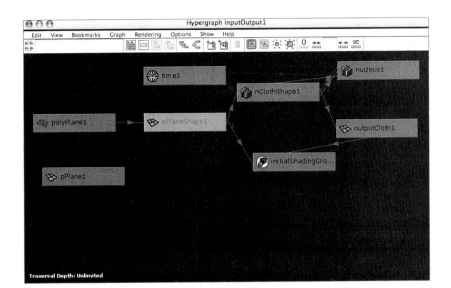

Figure 23.2

Connections for a
basic nCloth simula-
tion setup

Once an nCloth object has been created, the linked particles can be acted on by external forces, including gravity (which is included by default when creating a simulation), wind, turbulence, and so forth. In addition, objects, both "passive" objects in the scene and other cloth objects, can be set to collide with a cloth object during simulation. Collisions can be used, for example, to have a cloth skirt interact properly with an animated model, allowing the skirt to move as the character walks, jumps, or dances. Once again, for those familiar with particle or soft body simulations, forces and collisions will be familiar. Finally, constraints can be added to cloth objects, allowing certain portions of the cloth to remain attached to another object, or forcing "passive" geometry (like a button) to remain on the surface of a cloth, or even allowing the underlying geometry that originally created the cloth object to attract the cloth simulation back to its shape.

For a thorough introduction to particles, see Chapter 19.

Creating an nCloth Simulation

To demonstrate the basics of nCloth, let's create a simulation of a flag waving. While this simulation is a very straightforward use of cloth, it demonstrates changes to cloth settings quite clearly, so we will use it for the next several sections as our test bed for nCloth.

Open the flagstart.ma file from the CD. The file consists of a simple cylinder (the flag pole) and plane (the flag), as shown in Figure 23.3. The plane has been parented to the pole so that it follows the pole's motions, while the pole has a simple "waving" animation

Figure 23.3

Ready for the finish line: the basic flag pole/flag model

applied to it, starting at frame 50. Some basic textures have been applied to make it easier to see the simulation (press 6 to see the textures in your viewport). If you play back the animation, you will see the pole waving and the flag following along, but of course the flag at this point looks like a stiff polygon plane rather than a piece of cloth.

Creating a basic nCloth simulation is quite easy. Select the flag (plane), and then, from the nCloth menu set, choose **nCloth → Create nCloth** ❏. You will note that there are only two options in the Create nCloth option box: creating the cloth in Local or World Space Output environment (leave it set to Local for now), and choosing a solver. For now, your only choice is Create New Solver since you do not have another cloth simulation running in the scene. If you created another cloth object after creating your first one, you could choose to attach the new simulation to the same solver or to create a new solver for it. Click the Create Cloth button and you will see an nCloth1 node appear in the Outliner, and a small circle (or handle) at the middle of the flag, indicating that you have successfully created your simulation!

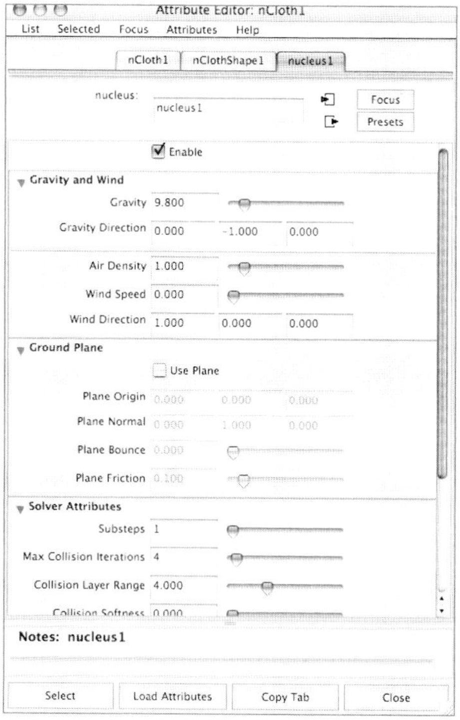

On playing back the simulation, a couple of problems are noticeable immediately. First, the flag just falls away from the pole because the simulation is not attached to it—note that even though the original poly plane was attached to the pole, the cloth version is only controlled by forces and constraints and thus is not. Second, the simulation appears very slow, with the flag plane drifting down at a low rate of speed. Let's take care of the second problem first. Select the nCloth1 node and open the Attribute Editor, then choose the nucleus1 tab at the top. As shown in Figure 23.4, the nucleus solver tab contains a number of options for adjusting how a simulation runs. For now, just change the Gravity setting at the top to a large number like 98. On playing back the simulation, you will notice that the flag falls much more quickly now. Gravity functions as a scaling factor for the animation: in general, the higher the gravity settings, the smaller the simulation will appear. Leaving gravity at its default 9.8 will make the flag appear to be very large, while a very high value like 1000 will make the flag appear to be a toy with very thin, silklike cloth. Setting it to 98 seems a good compromise to scale the simulation properly to a "normal" sized flag, but feel free to experiment with other gravity settings.

Figure 23.4

Properties of the nucleus solver at their default values

As always when playing back physical simulations, be sure you have your animation playback preferences set to Play Every Frame. If playback is set to Real Time, the simulation, which depends on the previous frame's state to calculate the next frame, will become bizarre and unusable. To set playback, open the Preferences window (**Window → Settings/Preferences → Preferences,** or click the small Animation icon at the bottom right of the Timeline—next to the "key" icon), and under the Timeline category, select Play Every Frame from the Playback Speed drop-down menu.

Now for the second issue: getting the flag to stick to the flag pole. For this, we need to create a Transform constraint, which locks certain vertices of the cloth to a positional and rotational constraint (which looks like a locator). We will then parent the constraint to the flag pole, locking those vertices to the pole itself.

Figure 23.5

A basic flag simulation using gravity and the Transform constraint. Now the flag mesh passes through the flag pole.

1. With the flag geometry selected, RM choose Vertex.

2. Toggle-select the top and bottom two vertices on the left-hand portion of the flag (the portion nearest the flag pole).

3. In the nCloth menu set, choose **nConstraint → Transform**. You will see a small cross (it looks like a locator) between the selected vertices, and in the Outliner a new node, dynamicConstraint1, has been created.

4. To lock this constraint (and thus the flag itself) to the pole, select dynamic-Constraint1, Shift+select the pole, and parent them together.

5. Play back the animation to see your flag falling (due to gravity) and waving while connected to the flag pole via the constraints, as shown in Figure 23.5.

We created our transform constraint for only a few vertices on the flag's mesh so that it will be easier to see how different cloth properties change the behavior of the cloth itself. This might or might not be an appropriate number of vertices for a "real-world" simulation: that depends on the needs of the given shot.

While our basic flag simulation looks pretty good now, there is an obvious problem with it: as Figure 23.5 clearly shows, the flag mesh passes right through the flag pole! While nCloth automatically creates self-collision behavior for the cloth, it does not create collisions with "passive" geometry in the scene. Obviously this issue needs to be dealt with before we can call even this basic simulation finished. Select the flag mesh, Shift+select the pole, and from the nCloth menu set, choose **nCloth → Create Passive □**. The Make Collide option box contains only one option: either to use the current nucleus1 solver for the collision or to create a new solver. Leave the choice set to nucleus1 and create the collision by clicking the Make Collide button. A new nRigid1 node will appear in the Outliner, and the

Figure 23.6

Adding "passive" geometry collision to the flag simulation

flag will now collide with the pole, as shown in Figure 23.6. Note that playback now is significantly slower than before, because of all the extra calculations that the solver has to perform to test for geometry collision. On the other hand, the simulation is now far more realistic since the cloth doesn't penetrate the flag pole! If you notice the flag getting stuck wrapped around the pole, don't worry about it too much; we'll deal with that issue later in the chapter.

We can also add additional forces, like wind or turbulence, to the flag simulation to create a blowing or billowing effect. Let's add some wind to see how this is done. Select the flag mesh, and then from the nCloth menu set, choose **Fields → Air ❑**. In the Air option box, click the Wind button, which presets a number of settings to get a good wind effect. Set Magnitude to 25, Attenuation to 0, Direction Y to 0, Direction Z to −1, and Speed to 10; then click the Create button to create the wind force. On playback you will now see that the flag is blown out toward the right of the screen (−1 in the Z direction) at a pretty good clip, as shown in Figure 23.7. The effect is most noticeable before the flag starts its waving animation and after it comes to rest at the end. For an even better look at your simulation, playblast the animation so that you can see the effects in real time. If the playblast looks too slow, or the wind is too strong, you can adjust settings as you wish to alter the simulation.

Now that we have created a basic simulation, it's time to look at how altering settings for the cloth, nucleus solver, constraint, and collision nodes affect the simulation itself. In order to keep the simulation as straightforward as possible for the next sections, delete the Air (wind) node before proceeding.

Nucleus Solver Properties

As you have probably already seen, there are a number of settings spread out across several nodes that affect the way a cloth simulation will proceed. Let's begin with the most fundamental controls for the simulation, contained in the nucleus solver node.

Either use your flag simulation from the last section (be sure to delete the Air node before proceeding) or open the `flagProperties.ma` file from the CD. We will use this file as the starting point for our exploration of nCloth's settings, so be sure to save a copy of the file in this state somewhere so you can go back to it easily.

Glance back at Figure 23.4 to see the default nucleus settings for an nCloth simulation. The first section at the top deals with gravity and wind settings, two forces that are deemed ubiquitous enough that they are built in as part of a cloth simulation. While gravity is on by default (set at 9.8 in the negative Y direction), wind is off by default. To enable wind, simply increase the Wind Speed value from 0. Adjusting Wind Direction and Air Density (how strongly the wind will affect the cloth) will then alter the simulation. The air and gravity settings in the nucleus solver node present a simple subset of the options available for Air and Gravity fields that you can add to a cloth simulation. See later in the chapter for more on adding fields to a cloth simulation.

> In the previous section we created wind by adding a force to the cloth mesh. Obviously we could have just used the wind settings on the nucleus solver node, but for the purpose of demonstrating forces, we chose to explicitly add the wind instead. Either method works fine, though combining both a wind force and the built-in nucleus wind can cause behavior that is difficult to control.

In the next section reside controls for using a default ground plane for collisions with the mesh. Checking the Use Plane box enables ground plane collisions, which are faster to calculate than a collision created with a physical object. Once the ground plane is enabled, you can control its origin , its **N**ormal attribute, and the bounce and friction of the interaction. By adjusting the Y element of the ground plane, you can make the virtual floor raise and lower (X and Z don't have much import unless you change the direction of gravity in the section above). The Normal attribute controls which way is pointing "up" for the ground plane; a Y value of 1 is usually what you want for this attribute. Bounce adjusts how bouncy collisions will be (with 1 being 100 percent resilience and 0 being no bounce whatsoever). Friction controls how much a cloth object will slide over a surface during tangential collisions. Figure 23.8 shows the flag colliding with a virtual ground plane with Origin set to 20 in Y.

The next section, Solver Attributes, controls the quality of the simulation, especially for collisions. The Substeps attribute determines how many sub-frame samples the solver takes to determine a simulation. A value of 1 (the default) is one sample per frame, which is fine for slow-moving objects. For cloth that is moving more quickly, 2, 4, or more sub-frame samples might be needed to accurately determine where and when collisions are taking place. If your cloth is getting kinked up or penetrating other objects, increasing the Substeps attribute could fix the problem, though the simulation will take longer to run due to the extra calculations involved. The Max Collision Iterations attribute controls how many recursive iterations the simulation is allowed to go through when analyzing collisions. Raising this number can help solve problems where cloth penetrates surfaces, sticks to (or gets buried in) surfaces, or simply looks incorrect—but again raising this number comes at the cost of longer simulation times. Collision Layer Range controls how many layers above or below the current solver layer nucleus will look for collisions. If you have six different solver layers enabled and the range is set to 3, then cloth on the solver1 layer will only collide with objects and cloth on its own layer and those up to three layers above it (see the next section on nCloth properties for more on collision layers). The Collision Softness attribute adjusts how far into an object the cloth can go before it "collides" with

Figure 23.7

Adding a wind force to the flag simulation

Figure 23.8

The flag colliding with a virtual ground plane 20 units above the origin

that surface and must move back out. A value of 0 (the default) means there is no inter-penetration, while a positive value means that the cloth can penetrate a surface a certain extent before moving back away from it.

In the Time Attributes section, the Start Frame value controls when a simulation will start. By increasing this value from one (to, say 40), you tell the solver to ignore the simulation until that frame. In the Scale Attributes section, Time Scale controls how fast the simulator effectively runs. A value of 2 here will make the simulator run twice as fast, making the cloth look heavier, for example. This attribute can be useful if you have a good simulation but need to adjust it to make the cloth work better within a larger animation framework. The Space Scale attribute essentially adjusts the units in which the simulator runs. As the simulator runs in meters by default, reducing the scale value to 0.01 alters the scale of the simulation to centimeters instead. Note that our changing gravity to 98 in the section above could be accomplished by altering the Space Scale value to 0.1 instead. The latter adjustment would have the added benefit of adjusting all other elements of the simulation to the same scale as gravity.

nCloth Properties

Now that you have a good idea about the nucleus solver, let's look at the properties of the nCloth node itself. In the Outliner, select the nCloth1 node and open the Attribute Editor. There are a number of sections here containing numerous controls over the properties of the cloth; we will go over the most important ones for each section. In a section by itself at the top of the window is a simple Enable check box. Unchecking this box turns off all cloth simulation, making it easy to disable the cloth solver if you are focusing on another aspect of the animation.

Surface Properties

The first section, Surface Properties (shown in Figure 23.9), is probably the most important for determining the way your cloth will behave and thus the type of cloth you are simulating.

First are two check boxes that turn Collision and Self Collision on and off. Self Collision is on by default, whereas Collision is enabled when you create a passive object with which the cloth collides. Turning either of these off disables it. Next is the Collision Layer setting, which prioritizes nCloth collisions. Two pieces of cloth (or cloth and a passive object) in the same layer collide normally. If one piece of cloth (or passive geometry) is on a higher level than another, the cloth on the lower level takes priority in collision calculations, driving collisions with higher level objects. This prioritization can be very useful in a situation where there are several objects colliding. For example, setting up a character's skin on layer 0, his shirt on layer 1, and a jacket he's wearing on layer 2 will allow the skin to drive collisions with the shirt and then the shirt to drive collisions with the jacket, as would happen in real-world interactions. Setting fractional layer values adjusts how much priority each layer has over the other: the closer the fractions to each other, the more equivalent the priority, and thus the interaction between objects. As noted in the previous section on the nucleus solver, you can set the collision layer range, which will limit which objects will interact with one another when colliding. In the shirt/jacket example, setting the layer range to 1 would mean that the skin would collide with the shirt and the shirt would collide with the jacket, but the character's skin would *not* collide with the jacket. This behavior might be preferable for a given simulation.

Next are Thickness and Self Collide Width Scale, which control how thick the cloth appears to itself and to passive collision objects in the scene. Thickness relates to all collisions (both self and with passive objects) and is how big each collision particle "sees" itself as being. A large thickness will make the particle appear big in collision calculations, making the cloth seem thicker, while a small value makes the cloth appear smaller, allowing the mesh to come very close to itself and other objects. The self-collide scale adjustment allows you to tweak the thickness value for self-collisions, so if you are satisfied with the general collision thickness attributes for the cloth colliding with passive objects but need the cloth to be a little thicker (or thinner) when colliding with itself, you can adjust this scaling value, which is multiplied by the Thickness setting.

The Solver Display and Color settings allow you to visualize the collision thickness values discussed in the preceding paragraph, as well as other values like links and weighting. Choosing Self Collision Thickness from the Solver Display drop-down menu, for example, shows the spherical range around each cloth particle where collisions take place (see Figure 23.10). These spheres are like Ping-Pong balls on the surface of the cloth, repelling other vertices that come within their radius. Once they are displayed, you can adjust the Thickness and Self Collide Width Scale and watch how the spheres' size adjusts to match the settings. The Color setting allows you to assign different colors to each type of displayed element.

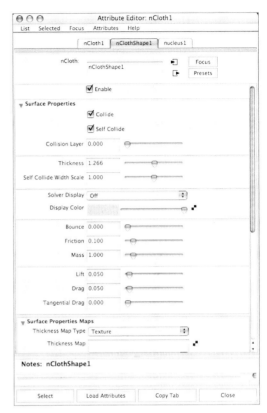

Figure 23.9

The Surface Properties section of the nCloth node

Figure 23.10

Displaying Self Collision Thickness for nCloth

Figure 23.11

Frame 40 of the flag simulation with a Mass setting of 0 (a) and 10 (b)

Next are the Bounce, Friction, and Mass properties of the cloth. Bounce and Friction relate to collisions and self-collisions, determining how much energy is transferred in collisions and how much particles "stick" when striking each other at non-perpendicular angles, respectively. Mass, on the other hand, determines how the cloth object reacts to all forces and collisions, effectively determining how heavy the cloth is in the simulation. A very small mass (like 0 or 0.01) will simulate a light material like silk; larger numbers like 1 or 10 will simulate material like cotton or heavy denim. Obviously the Mass setting is very important to the overall feel of your simulation. Figure 23.11 shows the difference the Mass setting makes to our flag simulation.

The Lift, Drag, and Tangential Drag settings control how cloth interacts aerodynamically with the air (and wind) in its environment. Lift is the same force that lets an airplane wing pull a plane off the ground, while Drag is the opposing force that drags the cloth to resist the force of the wind. Tangential Drag controls how much perpendicularity there is to the drag force: a value of 0 means that wind parallel to the surface will have no drag (and little lift), while a value of 1 means that the drag effect is equal for wind in any direction. Large settings for Lift, Drag, and Tangential Drag will cause our flag to billow in a wind, while a setting of 0 for all three will effectively make the flag impervious to a straight-line wind parallel to its surface.

Finally, you can create and add surface properties maps for Thickness, Bounce, Friction, Mass, and Wrinkle to your cloth object. These grayscale maps, which could be created in an image editor like Photoshop, provide for fine-tuning the entire surface's properties on a vertex-by-vertex level. Map colors that are black (0) create small values for their respective properties (like Thickness), while values of white (1) create large values for these properties. By adjusting the gray values throughout an image, you can adjust behavior down to a very fine level. See the section on painting nCloth properties for more on creating property maps interactively within Maya.

Dynamic Properties

Under the Surface Properties section is the Dynamic Properties section for the nCloth object (see Figure 23.12). The options here control how the cloth object will react to stresses as the simulation runs.

Stretch Resistance controls how resistive the cloth is to stretching as it is pulled or acted on by forces. A high value will maintain the cloth's dimensions, while a low value will allow the cloth to stretch, as if the material is a latex or spandex-type material. The Compression Resistance setting adjusts how resistive the cloth is to compression or crumpling. A low value allows the cloth to compress and crinkle, like paper or crinoline, while a high value makes the cloth resistant, acting more like denim or canvas. Bend Resistance and Bend Angle Dropoff control how the cloth object bends under stresses (like gravity or being pulled). High Bend Resistance values make the cloth behave like cheap new jeans, while a low value provides a more silky behavior. The Bend Angle Dropoff alters the Bend Resistance behavior based on the angle of the cloth: if the Bend Angle Resistance is greater than 0, at high angles (when the object is bent a great deal), cloth will have the full Bend Resistance value, but as the cloth flattens out, the cloth will progressively get less resistive to being bent. Shear Resistance controls how much the cloth object resists shearing—the sideways stretching of a flexible material. The greater the Shear Resistance setting, the more the cloth will resist shearing forces.

Restitution Angle and Tension specify how far the cloth object can be bent or stretched, respectively, before losing its ability to return to its rest state. The greater the number, the more the object can be deformed and still return to its rest state when forces are removed from it.

Rigidity specifies how flexible or rigid the cloth object is. If fully rigid (a value of 1), the cloth will not bend, acting instead as a rigid body object in the scene. If completely non-rigid (0), the cloth will act as a cloth object. Values in between create a hybrid situation. Deform Resistance controls how much the cloth wants to stay in its rest condition: a high value makes the cloth very difficult to deform, while a low value allows for easy deformation and also lets the cloth stay deformed after deformation. The Input Mesh Attract attribute controls how much the cloth object wants to return to its original shape (the shape of the original polygonal object from which it was created, or its set initial state shape). A high value forces the cloth object to return to its original shape if possible, given forces and collisions in the scene, while a low value decouples the cloth object from its original shape. The Input Attract Damp setting controls how much damping there is as a cloth object attempts to return to its initial shape. Obviously this setting has no effect when the Input Mesh Attract value is set to 0.

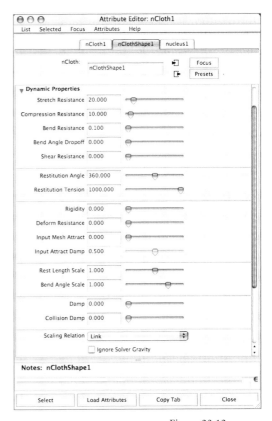

Figure 23.12

The Dynamic Properties section of an nCloth node

> You can set the initial state of a cloth object that is different from its original (creation) shape. To do so, go to a frame where the cloth object appears as you like (say, with the flag draped down over the pole), and choose Edit nCloth Initial State Set From Current to set the shape.

The Rest Length Scale and Bend Angle Scale settings scale how the length and bend settings are adjusted from frame 1 of the simulation. As these values are multiplied by the resting length and bend settings, a value of 1 maintains the current scales, while a larger value will stretch (or bend) the material out and a smaller value will shrink the material down. Figure 23.13 shows how a value of 2 for Rest Length Scale stretches out the flag material when the simulation plays back.

The Damp and Collision Damp attributes control how rapidly a motion or collision will be damped out when the forces stop acting on a cloth vertex. With no damping, there are often cases where one or two vertices will continue "jiggling" around after motion or collision activity, which is both unnatural and annoying (the flag simulation has this problem with the upper vertices near the flag pole at the end of the simulation). Increasing the damping values will damp out this effect. Be careful about setting the values too high, however, or your cloth will look like it's animating under water.

Figure 23.13

Increasing the Rest Length Scale value causes the flag to balloon outward on playback.

The Scaling Relation drop-down menu determines how the Rest Length and Bend Angle scaling values are applied to the cloth object. Link means the values are applied to all links between particles. Object Space determines the scaling values (including stiffness) based on the size of the object. World Space determines the scaling values based on object size, but stiffness is fixed in World Space size. When Disable Solver Gravity is selected, the solver will not use the gravity settings for the solution. This is the same as turning the Gravity setting (above in the window) to 0.

Finally, the Dynamic Properties Maps section (scroll down to see it) allows you to create texture maps defining a number of dynamic properties, including Stretch, Bend, Rigidity, Deform, Input Attract, Damp, and Collision Damp. See the preceding section, "Surface Properties," for more on creating dynamic properties maps.

Other Properties

The Pressure section of the nCloth node (see Figure 23.14) has settings that allow your cloth object to behave like a balloon or other object filled with gas. The Pressure Method drop-down menu determines how air pressure is determined: Manual Pressure Setting allows you to keyframe the pressure values as you wish, while Volume Tracking Method is more of a real-world simulation where the solver actually uses air influx and outflow values to calculate air pressure values within a cloth object.

The Seal Holes check box (at the bottom of the Pressure section) allows you to automatically fill the holes in a cloth object so that you don't have to worry about unintentional pressure leaks. If you wish to allow air to escape from your object, uncheck this box.

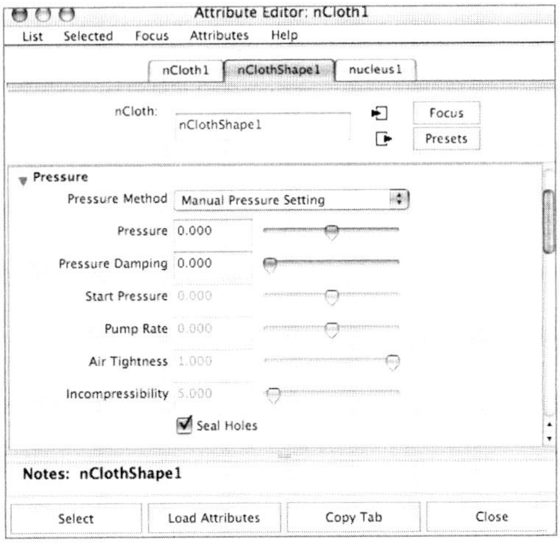

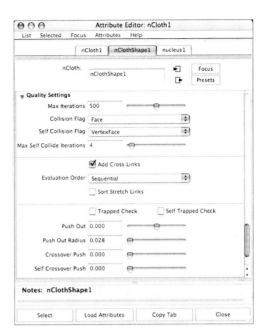

Figure 23.14

The Pressure section of the nCloth node

Figure 23.15

The Quality Settings attributes of the nCloth node

When Manual Pressure Setting is active, the Pressure setting controls how much pressure is in your cloth object. Pressure Damping damps the air pressure setting so that as you animate the pressure setting, the object won't jiggle around too much. When the volume tracking model is active, you still have access to the Pressure Damping attribute, but the other controls relate to creating a physical simulation of the air pressure within the volume of your cloth object. Start Pressure relates the relative pressure of the object with the surrounding air at the beginning of the simulation. A value of 0 specifies that the object is at the same pressure as its surroundings, meaning the object would be completely uninflated to start the simulation. Pump Rate lets the simulator know how quickly to inflate the cloth object, while Air Tightness specifies how permeable the cloth object is and thus how quickly air can escape from it. A low Air Tightness value will cause the object to deflate quickly when the pump rate is turned off. The Incompressibility setting controls how compressible is the air inside the cloth object—the more incompressible the air, the higher the relative pressure will seem to be, causing the object to be difficult to deform.

The Quality Settings section, shown in Figure 23.15, determines the accuracy of your cloth simulation. The Max Iterations setting clamps the maximum number of iterations the simulator can perform per frame (or sub-frame); the higher this setting, the better the overall quality of your simulation, but the longer will be the simulation times. The Collision

Flag and Self Collision Flag settings adjust how the nCloth object collides with other scene objects and itself, respectively. Adjusting these settings has a subtle but important effect on simulations because, for example, cloth vertices colliding with other vertices creates a different folding pattern than edges colliding with edges. Figure 23.16 shows the effect of the different settings for cloth-to-cloth simulation.

Self Collision Softness allows colliding objects to interpenetrate each other when the value is greater than 0. Self Collide Iterations clamps the number of iterations allowed when cloth-to-cloth collisions occur. The higher the number, the more accurate the simulation can be but at the cost of increased simulation times. The amusingly named Collision Insurance attribute scales out the collision size bounding box based on the relative velocity of the cloth. Raising this value from 0 can be a very effective way of taming a cloth simulation that is having difficulty with interpenetration when the cloth object is moving rapidly in the scene.

The Add Cross Links check box enables cross links on quad-based polygonal meshes. These links add stability and resist shearing forces for your simulation, so unless you have a specific reason to disable it (perhaps you wish to have your cloth shear a lot), you should leave this checked. The Evaluation Order drop-down menu has two choices, Sequential and Parallel. The Sequential setting evaluates link connections based on the order of polygons edges in the poly mesh from which the object was created. Parallel ignores this order, instead evaluating links from collision areas outward. While Sequential is a quicker calculation, Parallel will provide better results for simulations where significant collisions with passive objects are taking place. The Sort Stretch Links box enables sorting of links on the cloth object, which can help reduce stretching.

The Trapped Checked and Self Trapped Check check boxes are used to help resolve interpenetration errors with passive objects and with the cloth object itself, respectively. If your cloth (and passive) objects are in a "clean" (i.e., non-penetrating) state at the beginning of the simulation, checking these boxes will cause the solver to try to maintain a state without interpenetration, which can be very helpful in stabilizing a simulation where lots of interpenetration is happening. The other settings below the check boxes control how much and how strongly the interpenetration areas are pushed back to their "normal" state.

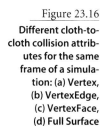

Figure 23.16

Different cloth-to-cloth collision attributes for the same frame of a simulation: (a) Vertex, (b) VertexEdge, (c) VertexFace, (d) Full Surface

a   b   c   d

Push Out sets how strongly a vertex will push away from another when trapped, while Push Out Radius sets the maximum distance over which the Push Out effect will take place. Crossover Push and Self Crossover Push use the contours of intersecting cloth and objects (or cloth with itself) to push cloth elements apart. These attributes are used for the start frame of the simulation, so making your cloth object "clean" (non-interpenetrating) at the start will obviate these controls.

The Time Attributes section contains information about the current time (frame) and when the simulation starts. Neither field can be adjusted in the nCloth node. To adjust the Start Frame attribute, go to the appropriate section of the nucleus tab (see the previous nucleus Solver section).

Painting nCloth Properties

While global settings for cloth can sometimes be all you need, there are many instances where it would be nice to control the value of a property, such as cloth thickness or bend resistance, over the cloth's surface on a vertex-by-vertex basis. There are two ways to accomplish this task: applying grayscale texture maps to the relevant attribute or painting the properties directly in Maya's viewport. While texture maps can potentially allow for more detailed control of these settings, painting them on is more intuitive and normally faster to accomplish, so we will discuss this method here.

The following cloth and dynamic attributes can be painted on an nCloth object: Thickness, Bounce, Friction, Mass, Stretch, Bend, Wrinkle, Rigidity, Deformability, and Input Attract (for information on each of these properties, see the previous section). You can paint these attributes on either as a texture map or as a vertex map. A texture map can have a higher resolution than the density of vertices on a cloth mesh, but the object must have a clean UV map for this method to function. A vertex map, on the other hand, will work on any cloth object, UV mapped or not.

For more on texturing and UV mapping, see Chapter 12.

As painting any property works in pretty much the same way, we will create two maps: a thickness map using the vertex method and a stretch map using the texture mapping method. From these examples you should be able to extrapolate how painting other attributes will work.

First, let's create the thickness map using the vertex map method. Use the flag simulation you have been using, or open the `flagProperties.ma` file from the CD. Select the cloth mesh and then, from the nCloth menu set, choose **Edit nCloth → Paint Vertex Properties → Thickness** ❑. This brings up the standard Tool Settings window for the Paint tool, and you will notice that the flag mesh turns black, indicating that the vertices all have a 0 thickness

Figure 23.17
(a) Painting a thick-
ness pattern on the
flag. (b) The result-
ing thickness values
displayed. (c) the
modified flag during
playback.

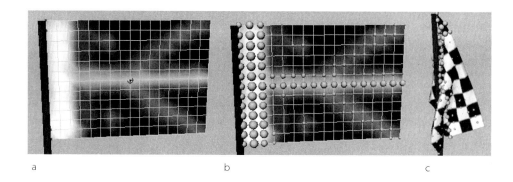

a   b   c

value, so they will collide as if the cloth is extremely thin. Adjust Opacity to something like 0.25, be sure Paint Operation is set to Replace and Value is set to 1, and paint on the cloth mesh. You can try for something reasonable, like a thicker material near the flag pole and thinner as it moves toward the tip of the cloth, but we opted for a more creative design, as shown in Figure 23.17a. As Figure 23.17b shows (by displaying the Self Collision Thickness values as spheres), the lighter the painted area, the thicker the cloth "appears" during self-collisions. Figure 23.17c shows the flag playing back during simulation.

Now let's paint on a stretch map as a texture map. First, go back to your saved file so that you don't have the thickness map painted on anymore (we do this to make it easier to see the effects of painting on the wrinkle map). Select the cloth object, then choose **Edit nCloth → Paint Texture Properties → Stretch □**. This time you will notice that the color begins as all white, indicating that the entire flag is highly resistive to stretching. Leave the color set to black (so that it subtracts from the current color), reduce the opacity to something small like 0.2, and paint on the surface of the object. Figure 23.18 shows the results of painting on a stretch attribute: the top (black) section of the flag stretches and droops more than the white section below it.

Figure 23.18
Painting a Stretch
pattern on the flag

Constraints

In addition to cloth properties and forces, constraints are useful for creating realistic simulations. While we have previously used the Transform constraint to lock some of the flag's vertices to the flag pole, there are other constraints that accomplish different tasks. Figure 23.19 shows the nConstraint menu in the nCloth menu set. Note that in addition to creating constraints, the menu contains options for painting on constraint properties and for converting texture maps into constraint property maps (see the previous section on Painting Cloth Properties for more on painting attributes on nCloth). Menu selections also allow you to edit set membership for the constraints (which vertices are affected by a constraint) and to delete an unwanted constraint. We will briefly present each constraint type.

The Transform constraint, which we have already used, locks selected vertices to a locator in space. Translating and rotating the locator forces the locked vertices to follow the constraint's motions, which then drives other parts of the cloth object as the simulation runs.

The Component To Component constraint is similar to the "button" constraint other cloth simulators use, but it's more flexible. Using this constraint, you can attach a passive object (such as a button) to a cloth object. This constraint also allows you to attach other cloth objects, such as a shirt pocket, to an nCloth object, which offers more functionality than the classic button constraint. Passive objects (like a button) will remain rigid while attached cloth objects will bend as expected.

The Point To Surface constraint attaches cloth to passive objects and is very useful for attaching elements of a mesh to an underlying object. For example, if a character's dress has "spaghetti straps" on the shoulders, you can use Point To Surface to force the straps to stick on the character's shoulders rather than sliding down and off of them.

The Slide On Surface constraint is a modification of the Point To Surface constraint, wherein the cloth object's vertices are "stuck" on a surface but can slide around to a limited extent. Using the spaghetti strap dress example, this constraint can keep the straps on the character's shoulders but allow them to slide around some as her shoulders move. This constraint (as with the Point On Surface constraint) can be used for cloth-on-cloth circumstances as well as cloth-on-passive-geometry situations.

The Weld Adjacent Borders constraint is somewhat similar to the Component To Component constraint but is specifically designed to allow the edges of two cloth objects to be constrained together and act as one object during simulation. For example, if you model a shirt sleeve and the body of a shirt as separate objects, you can use the Weld Adjacent Borders constraint to attach the shirt and sleeve together so that they will simulate as a single object.

The Force Field constraint applies a repelling force within a spherical area. The field can be applied to an object as a whole, but it's more useful when attached to individual vertices on a passive or cloth object. The field can then be used to repel areas of cloth that tend to penetrate other objects, locally correcting the simulation where needed. To attach a Force Field to vertices, select the vertices and then create the field.

The Attract To Matching Mesh constraint forces the mesh (or selected vertices) to conform to a passive scene object that has the same topology. In practice, you could duplicate the input mesh (from which you created your cloth object), deform that mesh into some different shape, and keyframe this constraint on to force the cloth object to "hit" the modeled shape on a given frame in the animation. While this moves away from a "true" cloth simulation, it allows you to direct the simulation so that cloth will achieve a certain look at a given time.

Figure 23.19

The nConstraint menu

The Tearable Surface constraint is a fun constraint that allows you to create tearable regions on a cloth object. Under stress (how much stress is determined by the Glue Strength attribute), the cloth will rip apart, creating a tear in the fabric. After creating the constraint, you can paint the Glue Strength attribute (determining which portions of the cloth will tear more easily) by choosing **nConstraint → Paint Properties by Vertex Map → Glue Strength**.

The Disable Collision and Exclude Collision Pairs constraints allow for individual cloth objects (or portions of each object) *not* to collide with other objects in the scene. The Disable Collision constraint disables collisions with all other objects (passive or cloth) in the scene, while Exclude Collision Pairs excludes only specific other cloth or passive objects from colliding. To create a Disable Collision constraint, simply select the cloth (or CVs on the cloth) for which you wish to disable collisions in the scene. For the Exclude Collision Pairs constraint, select all the objects (or CVs on the objects) for which you wish to disable collisions and then create the constraint.

Fields

While Gravity and Wind are built in as part of the initial nucleus solver, you can create a number of other fields to affect your cloth's simulation. These fields are the same as for particle simulation, so if you have used particles before, they should be familiar to you.

Fields can exist in three forms: stand-alone, volume, and object based. Stand-alone fields exist in the scene independently of cloth or geometric objects, affect all linked objects in a scene (unless Attenuation is on, in which case the field will decay as it moves away from the source), and can be transformed (rotated and scaled) to suit the needs of the scene. To create a stand-alone field, simply choose it from the **Fields** menu in the nCloth menu set (for example **Fields → Turbulence**).

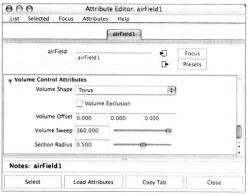

Figure 23.20

Creating a Volume Shape field in the Attribute Editor

Volume fields are also independent of other scene elements, but they produce their forces within a volumetric shape. Unlike the stand-alone fields, volume fields function only within a given volume described by the selected shape; outside this volume the force will have no influence over linked objects. You can choose the following volumes, which can be scaled to alter their shape, but not deformed: Cube, Sphere, Cylinder, Cone, and Torus. To create a volumetric field, first create a stand-alone field, and then, in the Attribute Editor's Volume Control Attributes section for the field, choose the desired volume shape from the drop-down menu (see Figure 23.20). Once a volume shape is selected, several options become available, depending on the type of shape selected. The Volume Exclusion check box inverts the effects of the field: when it's checked, only objects *outside* the volume will be affected by the force. The Volume

The effects of a volumetric turbulence field on the flag (gravity has been disabled to show the effect more clearly)

Offset (X, Y, and Z) fields allow you to offset the field from its creation point in the scene; while this control is potentially useful, it is much easier in most cases to just move the field volume around in the scene window. For objects like sphere and torus, you can alter the Volume Sweep attribute, which reduces the volume to only a portion of the full shape (a hemisphere rather than a sphere, for example). Finally, for the Torus shape, you can alter the Section Radius attribute, which changes the "fatness" of the torus shape. Figure 23.21 shows the effects of a toroidal turbulence field on the flag.

Finally, object-based fields are attached to nCloth objects themselves and produce forces based on the position and velocity of nCloth vertices as the simulation plays. The vertices of the nCloth object with a field attached act as sources for the field, which affects other objects in the scene. A wind/wake field, for example, can be attached to a cloth (or passive) object and will drag other cloth around depending on the motion of the force-generating cloth object. To create an object-based field, create the field itself, select the field, then Shift+select the nCloth object to which you wish to attach it. Choose **Fields Use Selected As Source Of Field** from the Fields menu to attach the force to the object (note that when connected, the field will become parented beneath the cloth object).

Following is a brief description of the fields that can be used with nCloth. The Air field simulates the effect of air on an object. Presets include Wind and Wake; Wind simulates wind blowing from a given direction, and Wake simulates the effect of air stirred up by a passing object (like leaves being blown about by a passing car). Drag simulates the effect of air friction on an object, dragging cloth back (resisting motion) as it is moved. Gravity is a uniform gravitational pull (normally in a negative Y direction) on an object. Newton, which is related to gravity, produces a "planetary" radial gravitational field that decreases as the square of the distance from an object. As this field simulates the effects of huge-scale objects (like planets) on one another, it might not be the most useful field for cloth. The Radial field is also a radial force, but it does not diminish in space, instead either sucking everything toward it or forcing it away in a spherical fashion. Turbulence disturbs a cloth object as if a swirling wind or other force were affecting it. Turbulence is very effective if you wish to create a more billowy cloth simulation. The Uniform field is similar to the Radial field, but Uniform forces everything in one direction, uniformly, whereas the Radial field acts in a spherical fashion. The Vortex field spirals objects toward it (or away from it) like water going down a drain. It can also be very effective in creating a tornado effect. The Volume Axis field moves cloth around a given axis within a volumetric shape and can be used to create effects where cloth is being moved around within a limited shape, such as, for example, clothing in a washer or dryer.

nCloth Caches

While nCloth creates excellent simulations, they can be slow to calculate, especially for cloth interacting with lots of forces, animation, and collisions, so it can be frustrating to have to resimulate the cloth each time you wish to play back the animation. nCloth caches come to the rescue here, as you can store the state of your simulation at each frame to disk. Using caches, you only need to simulate the cloth once. Then, in the future, Maya will read the cloth state from the disk, which makes playback go much more quickly, letting you access any point in the Timeline without simulating up to that frame and letting you focus on other elements of the scene (such as facial or lighting animation). Of course, if you change any cloth or solver properties, alter cloth-related animation, or add or change forces, collisions, or constraints, you will have to resimulate (and recache) the cloth to produce correct results.

In addition to simply saving cloth states out to disk, nCloth caching allows you to save out portions of your cloth simulation as geometry cache clips, which you can later combine and/or blend using the Trax Editor (see Chapter 10 for more on nonlinear editing and geometry caches). The hands-on section later in this chapter will deal with multiple caches in more detail.

Creating a cache is straightforward: select your cloth object(s), then choose **nCache → Create New Cache** ❑. The Create nCache option box, shown in Figure 23.22, contains a number of options that control how your cache is created and where it is stored. The cache directory is where the cache will be stored on your hard drive. By default, it resides in your project's data subdirectory, but you can specify anywhere (including an external hard disk if the cache will be large). As expected, the Cache Name field contains the name of the cache file you will be creating. The File Distribution choices alter how the file or files are stored for the cache. One File Per Frame creates a separate nCache file for each frame simulated, while One File creates one (often very large) file for the entire cache. If multiple cloth objects are chosen, you can check the One File Per Geometry option to create a separate file for each item selected (and for each frame simulated if that is chosen). In similar fashion to geometry caches, Maya creates a "master" XML file that stores information about all the other cache files it creates. When reusing a cache later on, you will normally access the cache via its XML master file rather than drilling down into the individual data files.

If you intend to manipulate the cache files in some way later on (for example, manually deleting some frames and replacing them with other files), you should choose to create one file per frame. Otherwise, using one file will work fine and create less mess on your hard drive. The Cache Time Range options allow you to cache simulation data only for the time interval you wish. Using Render Settings caches data for the frames set in the Render Settings window. Time Slider (the default) uses the current time slider to determine the range. Start/End lets you specify which frames to cache in the Start/End fields below. The Evaluate Every Frame field lets you control how often nCloth sub-samples the cloth when creating the cache. When you set this value lower than 1, nCloth will evaluate the cloth more than once per frame. The Save Every Evaluation field then determines how frequently the cache will save out your data. A setting of 1 (the default) should normally be used here because it saves out cached data for each frame (or sub-frame) that is simulated.

Once the options for Create nCache are set to your liking, click the Create button to run your simulation and cache the data to disk. Once the caching is completed, cloth will read its state from disk rather than resimulate it, allowing you to work with the scene much more quickly and freely than before. To check this, simply move the Timeline point to random places in the Timeline and watch the simulation update to its proper state.

After creating a cache for your cloth object, you have several choices for manipulating it, as shown in Figure 23.23. You can delete the cache, attach the cache to another file, disable the cache (which forces nCloth to resolve the simulation), or enable the cache. In addition, you can replace, merge, or append elements of the cache together or replace or delete one frame in the cache. You can also paint the weights of individual caches. If, say, you have one good cache for a shirt sleeve and another for the shirt body, you can paint the caches together, using that cache's good simulation for the sleeve but not for the shirt body and vice versa. Finally, you can create a polygonal "input mesh" for each frame of the animation from your cache using the Transfer Cloth To Input Mesh command. You can use these meshes as target shapes for the cloth during a later simulation or to extract a model of the cloth in its current state for a given frame or frames.

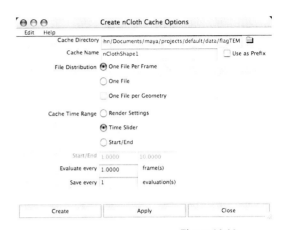

Figure 23.22

The Create nCloth option box

Figure 23.23

The nCache menu

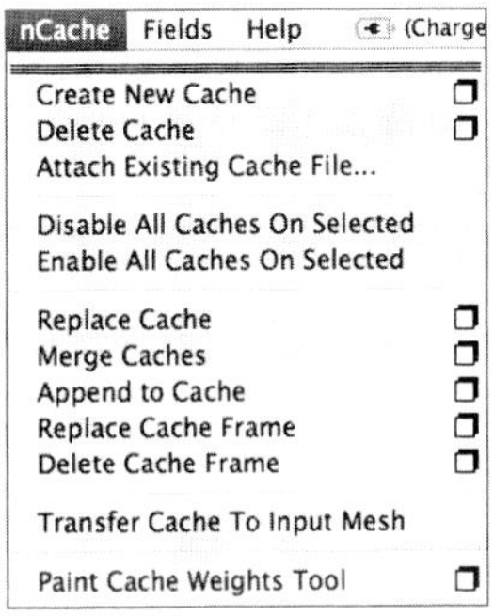

Hands-On: Creating a Tattered Shirt and Pants Simulation with nCloth

In this section we will use the skills learned in the previous sections to implement a basic cloth technical director (TD) work flow for a shot. Whether you are creating a small animated short, a blockbuster visual effects film, or an animated feature, there are a few principles and work flows that can help you when given the task to add dynamic cloth to a shot or scene.

For this example we will be using a character named Jack. Jack first appeared as an imaginative and lovesick hero in Clemson University's animated short, "First Impressions." Jack has a new look for this example. Let us imagine that Jack is now a marooned pirate exploring a tropical island. Jack's clothes are torn and worn out, which makes for a fun cloth simulation. Let's open up the Jack file and get started.

Open up the `jack_clothsetup.ma` file. It will also be useful to set up a Project space for your cloth scene. You will use this project space to hold your caches, scripts, and any other files. Choose **File → Project → New → ❑**. Name your project jack_clothsetup. Choose Use Defaults to fill in the Project Data Locations fields, then click the Accept button. This will create all the directories for your project in your `maya/projects/jack_clothsetup` directory. Figure 23.24 shows Jack, ready for cloth simulation.

If you play through the scene you will see that there is a character rig with keyframes. A simple range-of-motion test has been animated on the jack rig for use in cloth simulation testing. We will assume that for this character and the shots Jack will appear in, it is your job to build a cloth setup using Maya's nCloth and get the desired look for the cloth simulations.

Figure 23.24

Jack with tattered clothing ready to be simulated

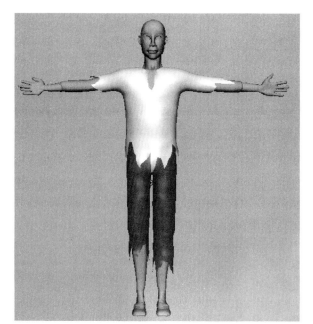

Here is a basic work flow for creating dynamic cloth for an animated character.

1. View the animation, checking for potential errors.

2. Cache out the animation.

3. Set up the cloth, constraints, and so on. Normally, in a production environment this process would be MEL scripted or you would be given a file that is already set up and you would import it in and attach the animation to it. Noting that this is a deforming/rigged character, we would make a geometry cache of the deforming character instead of bringing in the rig and deformers.

4. Iterate, trying different nCloth settings until you get the desired simulation, changing settings as needed.

5. Postsimulate cache blending and deformer cleanup.

6. Drive the "beauty" cloth with the simulated cloth through wrap deformers.

> There are two versions of the modeled shirt and pants. The difference is that one has a high number of polygons. We will call this version the "beauty" cloth, which is the geometry that will eventually be rendered out. The lower-resolution cloth will be used for our simulation. For this example, the simulation cloth has been provided, though normally the cloth TD would have to create it.

7. Hand off the beauty cloth to the lighter (maybe as a geometry cache so you don't have the nCloth solver and wrap deformer overhead).

We won't cover step 7 because we are focusing on the nCloth simulation (and not using this file in a production setting). We included the step to show how a real work flow would accommodate nCloth within it. In the following sections, we'll go through each step, describing how to get the best possible cloth setup and simulation for "pirate Jack."

Checking the Animation

When you first get your scene with your animated character, it is important to quickly examine the animation and the character's deformations. We will be looking for any areas that might cause us a problem during simulation. Many times a character's animation as seen through the shot camera can look great, but if you look more closely, there can be small issues that can get in the way of a cloth simulation. For example, cloth solvers don't do a good job handling limbs going through each other or through the body. The body will be used for cloth collisions, and if the cloth is forced through its collision object, the simulation can either fail or cause undesired simulation artifacts.

Some of the interpenetrations can be fixed by the animator very easily. However, some of them are part of the character rig's deformation. Some problem areas are where joints meet—behind the knees, the front of the hips, the elbows, and the arm pits. These issues can be resolved either through changing the rig or by adding your own deformers. There are various methods that can be used to fix the problem. Some include adding sculpt deformers or lattices in these areas to push the geometry apart. You can even set up these deformers to be turned on only when the knee or elbow bends. This can be done using Maya's Set Driven Key functionality by having the joint's rotation drive the envelope of the deformer.

For Jack's animation, the deformations seem to be pretty good. There is a small amount of self-penetration in the front hip areas when the legs are raised around frames 60 and 80. Also, if you look closely around frame 120, you can see that there is some overlap between the chest and stomach. This may or may not be a problem during simulation, but it is important to be aware of it if problems arise. If we do end up seeing problems, we can look at these frames more closely to see if action around them is the cause of simulation hang-ups.

Caching Out the Animation

When you first open up the file, the Jack character's geometry deformation is driven by the rig, including skinClusters and other deformers. The deforming geometry will be used for cloth collisions. We can speed up the performance of our simulations by baking out Jack's deformations using Maya's geometry caching system. This will make our working scene much lighter and our work flow faster. Although Jack's rig is fairly light and easy to move through the Timeline, many characters can have very complicated rigs with all sorts of deformation systems that drive the final look.

Usually a character's body will be made up of one surface. Jack, however, is made up of four separate pieces: his head, left forearm, right forearm, and torso/legs. To make sure we have everything we need, we will cache out each piece separately. We will use Maya's built-in geometry caching system to create these caches. Select **Animation → Geometry Cache → Create New Cache → ❑** and reset the options to their defaults. Using the default settings for each piece will create a cache in the /data directory of our project. Make geometry caches for the hands and body in the jak_bound_poly group and for the jak_basehead for a total of four caches.

Once the caches are created, we can duplicate the geometry and import the caches onto our duplicates. Select the jak_bound_ poly group, duplicate it, and rename the new group and the geometry by adding _cache to the end of the names. Next, duplicate jak_basehead and rename it jak_basehead_cache. Now group both jak_bound_poly_cache and jak_basehead_cache under a new group you will call jak_cache_data. We next need to delete the history on each of these new meshes and their parent groups. Do this by selecting the objects and choosing **Edit → Delete By Type → History**. This will ensure that there is no connection to the old rig.

Next we need to import our caches into each of these new meshes. Let's start with the head. Select jak_basehead. Then choose **Animation → Geometry Cache → Import Cache**. You can browse your /data directory and find the appropriate cache for the head geometry. Select the XML file associated with the head, jak_baseheadShape.xml, and click Import. Follow these same steps for the body and the hands.

It is also useful to have the joints from the rig so we can use them for attaching any deformers that may be used for creating our final look. This can be done easily by selecting all the joints in the jak_BOUND_JOINTS group and choosing **Edit → Keys → Bake Simulation**. With default settings, this will create a key at every frame for each joint.

Once the caches are imported and the joints baked out, we have all we need from the rig. You can delete the following objects from the scene in order to make it lighter: jack (the control rig), basehead, and jack_BASE_JOINTS. See Fig. 23.25 to make sure that your scene's Outliner matches the image. Your scene should now have only the cached character geometry, baked joints, and your garment and beauty cloth, which will make the animation run much faster.

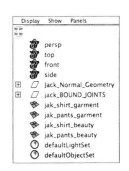

Figure 23.25

The Outliner showing the correct scene elements to start cloth simulation

Setting Up the Cloth Costume

We are now ready to set up Jack's costume using nCloth. Depending on the character and the requirements of the production, a character's modeled clothing can vary widely. It can be as simple as a skirt or as complicated as your imagination allows. Our character Jack has a clothing model that is fairly simple.

Part of our cloth setup will include creating wrap deformers between the "sim" and the "beauty" cloth so that the sim cloth drives the beauty cloth. You may ask why we don't just simulate the higher-resolution geometry. While it is true that for this example the beauty cloth is simple enough to simulate, in many cases the beauty geometry of a character can be double-sided to show thickness in the clothing and might have small details in shirt and pants that are modeled in, like buttons, seams, pockets, and cuffs. These details and the double-sided geometry would be very hard if not impossible to simulate efficiently, so simulating a low-res mesh and using that to drive the hi-res one is standard practice in the industry.

We will start by simulating the pants because the shirt will use the pants sim cloth as a collision object.

Turn off the display layers for the "beauty_cloth" and the "sim_shirt" so we can see the low res-pants clearly.

1. Select jak_pants_garment, and then Choose **nCloth → nCloth → Create nCoth** ❑.

2. In the options box, choose World Space Output, leave the solver set to nucleus1, and choose Create Cloth. This will create a new nucleus solver, nCloth node, and a new output mesh. jak_pants_garment will be hidden and used as the inputMesh for the nCoth node. The nucleus solver will most likely be named nucleus1 and will be connected to your nCloth object. Your nCoth object will most likely be called nCloth1 and its Shape node will contain all of the cloth properties for the pants.

3. Rename the nCloth node nClothPants and the shape node nClothPantsShape.

4. The output of your new nClothPants object is an outputMesh. This mesh will be named something generic like polySurface1. The outputMesh's Shape node will be named ouputCloth1. Rename these nClothPantsOutputCloth and nClothPantsOutputClothShape, respectively.

5. Rename the nucleus solver nucleusJackClothes so it is not as generic as nucleus1.

If we click the Play button now, the pants will fall through the character because we have not defined any collision objects, nor have we attached any portion of the pants to Jack's geometry. First we need to make the pants collide with the character's legs. The pants will only need to collide with the body portion of Jack. We will not need to make the hands and head into collision bodies. Of course, if the hands or head touched the pants, we would have to add them as collision objects.

We could use the bodyG_cache object for the collision, but in order to have more control over the collision object and for clarity, we will make a deforming copy of the body for collision purposes. Select bodyG_cache and type **polyDuplicateAndConnect** into the Script Editor. This command will create a duplicate of the bodyG_cache that will follow the motion exactly because the inMesh of the new object is connected to the outMesh of bodyG_cache. Rename the duplicate mesh jak_body_collsion. Because there are scale values on jak_body_collision's parent, we need to keep our new jak_body_collision object in the jak_bound_poly_cache group.

Also notice that we do not need all of the faces that are in the body geometry to collide with the pants. For example, the arms, feet, and most of the upper body are not needed for collision in this animation and will add unneeded faces to the collision calculations in our simulation, slowing things down for no good reason. One of the benefits of our duplicate geometry is that we can delete unneeded faces and the mesh will still deform as expected. Select the faces of jak_body_collision on the character's feet, as shown in Figure 23.26, and delete them. Now we have a clean, efficient piece of geometry to use as our collision object.

To create the collision object for the pants, we need to do the following steps.

1. Select jak_body_collision.

2. Choose **nCloth → nCloth → Create Passive □**.

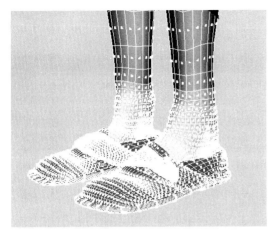

Figure 23.26

Selected feet faces

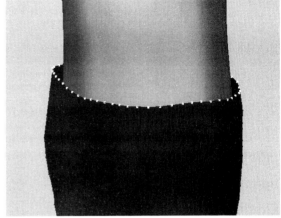

Figure 23.27

Selecting waist vertices to constrain to Jack's body

3. Select nucleusJackClothes as the solver.

4. Choose Make Collide.

This creates an nRigid node, which we will rename nRigidPantsBody to define it as the rigid node that will control the pants collision with the body. For now we will leave the settings at their default values.

If we play the scene now from the beginning, we will see that the pants collide with the body but they end up sliding off the character. This is because of a lack of constraints holding the pants up. In essence, Jack needs a belt to help keep his pants from falling off. We can add an nConstraint that will keep the waist of his pants connected to his body.

1. With the nCothPantsOutputCloth selected, RM choose Vertex.

2. Select the vertices at the top edge of the pants, as shown in Figure 23.27.

3. Shift+select jak_body_collision.

4. Choose **nCloth → nConstraint → Point To Surface**. This will create a dynamic-Constraint node.

5. Rename the dynamic constraint dynamicConstraintPantsWaist.

We now have pants that will collide with the body and stay constrained to his waist. Now that we have a basic setup for the pants, let's set up the shirt. Using jak_shirt_garment, create and rename your nClothShirt and nClothShirtOuputCloth. Use the same nucleus-JackClothes solver that you created for the pants. Also, use the same jak_body_collision geometry as a collision object for the shirt.

We will also need to make the simulated pants collide with the shirt correctly. As you know, the nCloth solves multiple layers of clothing in the same solver pass. However, to do this it needs to know what clothing layers are on top of one another. For this example, we will have three collision layers: the body will be assigned collision layer 0, the pants layer 1, and finally, the shirt will be assigned collision layer 2. This will allow the shirt to collide with both the pants and the body, and will help the pants stay inside the shirt where they overlap.

The shirt can use some nConstraints as well. The shirt collar and the slit in the neck of the collar will spread apart if we don't pin them closed. We will create a Point to Surface nConstraint to pin the collar of the shirt to Jack's body.

1. Select the vertices around the collar.
2. Choose **nCloth → nConstraint → Point On Surface**.
3. Rename the new dynamicConstraint dynamicConstraint_PTS_ShirtCollar.

We will also create Component to Component nConstraints in order to pin together the slit in the collar of Jack's shirt.

1. Select two vertices across from each other on the slit in jack's collar, as shown in Figure 23.28.

2. Choose **nCoth → nConstraint → Component To Component**.

3. Rename the new dynamicConstraint dynamicConstraint_CTC_ShirtCollar_01.

4. Create two more new Component to Component nConstraints on the other vertices on the edges of the slit using the same method you used in steps 1 through 3.

Now that we have created the basic simulation for Jack's shirt and pants, we need to tweak the settings to get the best simulation we can for them both.

Figure 23.28

Selected collar slit vertices

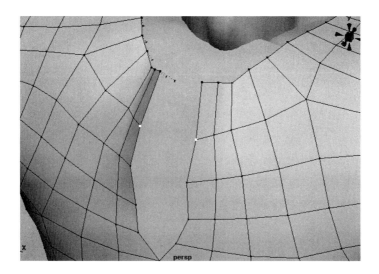

Changing Cloth and Solver Settings

When we run our simulation, we find several issues with the results that need to be resolved before the simulation will look good. This is where we get into more of an experimental portion of cloth simulation. Only with time and experience with a solver can you get the best possible results. nCloth and the nucleus solver are brand-new tools, so most Maya users are at an disadvantage in terms of experience. However, most cloth solvers are based on real-world dynamic forces, so using some intuition and a good dose of creativity, we can find a solution that will give us great results. One thing that is important to point out for this section is that any suggestions that are made about the manipulation of cloth attributes are exactly that: suggestions. You should take the opportunity presented here to explore nCloth and its abilities to be manipulated in interesting and fun ways. Sometimes the most unlikely choices can give you the best results.

For our example, we will leave the nucleus solver at its default settings. Let's start with the pants. With the default settings on the nClothPantsShape, the pants ride up on Jack's legs as he raises each leg and bends his knees. The pants have some nice motion, but they seem to be a little bouncy. In addition, the pants stretch and rebound much too much.

It appears that the springs or links that connect the vertices of the cloth mesh are too loose and are allowing the cloth to stretch and compress far too much. Let's try increasing the stretch and compression resistance. In the nCloth node, increase Stretch Resistance to 125 and Compression Resistance to 75. This helps with the stretching, but it adds some unwanted noise in the simulation. To try to compensate for this, we will increase Damp to 10, Collision Damp to 5, and Max Iterations to 2000. Other changes that help include changing Thickness to 0.2, Friction to 0.1, Point Mass to 0.5, and Trapped Check to On. The pants are also affected by the body collision object. Increasing the Friction value of nRigidPants to 0.5 lowers the amount of cloth that slides over the collision surface.

The shirt simulation has its own set of problems. Using the default settings, the springs, or links, are too loose and the shirt slides up toward Jack's head too much when he raises his arms and bends over. Also, there are numerous self-penetrations in the shirt when this happens. To solve this problem, we open the Attribute Editor for the shirt's nCloth node and increase the Stretch and Compression Resistance values to 125 and 75, respectively. Other changes include changing Thickness to 0.2, Friction to 1, Damp to 5, Collision Damp to 1, Max Self Collision Iterations to 40, Max Iterations to 2000, Point Mass to 0.2, Collision Layer to 2, Trapped Check to On, Self Crossover Push to 0.1, and Self Trapped Check to On. When we're finished making adjustments, we have a much improved, more stable simulation, as shown in Figure 23.29.

Figure 23.29
Jack with tweaked cloth simulation

Caching the Simulations

As noted earlier, cloth caching can be very useful both for speeding up scene interaction when cloth simulation is involved and for allowing later edits to the base cloth simulations. We can use the caching system to cache both the shirt and the pants at the same time.

1. Select nClothShirtOutputCloth and nClothPantsOuputCloth.

2. Choose **nCloth → Create New Cache** ❐.

3. In the option box, choose either One File Per Frame or One File and check the One File Per Geometry check box. For our purpose, the difference between caching modes is inconsequential.

4. Choose Create and the simulation will begin.

After a time, playback will complete and you will have the entire cloth simulation stored on disk. If you need to rerun the simulation, you will need to delete the cache and create a new one.

Sometimes we are able to get the desired motion with the simulation, or maybe we want to use part of one simulation and part of another to blend them together. We can use the Trax Editor to blend our caches together as explained earlier in this chapter. When blending caches together, it is sometimes useful to create a "bound" version of the cloth that is clean. This can be done by creating duplicates of the cloth garments and wrap-deforming them to the simulated cloth. These wrap-deformed cloth garments can then be cached out and used to blend to other caches that have been simulated. Another method for creating this "bound" cloth is to create a version of the costume with a Point to Surface constraint on the entire garment. By keeping the Strength value high, you will get a behavior to your cloth simulation that can be cached and blended.

Deformers such as lattices and clusters can be useful for manipulating a cached cloth simulation. This can be useful when a particular silhouette is wanted in your character or if you have some interpenetrations that you cannot quite resolve through simulation. It is important to understand that you will need to recache these deformed versions of our cloth in order to blend those caches in the Trax Editor.

Driving the Beauty Cloth

After all simulation, blending, and deforming of the cloth has been completed and you are happy with the results, it is time to use the low-resolution sim cloth to drive the motion of the beauty cloth. This last step can be done through the use of Maya's wrap deformers.

Go to the start frame and turn on the beauty cloth display layer to make the beauty cloth visible.

1. Select jak_shirt_beauty and Shift+select nClothShirtOuput.

2. Choose **Animation → Create Deformers → Wrap Deformer**.

This will allow the beauty shirt to be driven by the motion of the nClothShirtOuput cloth. Repeat steps 1 and 2 with the high- and low-resolution pants selected to drive the beauty pants via cloth simulation.

Now we have a beauty cloth that is ready to be passed to the next step in the production pipeline (usually lighting and rendering). One further step we could make would be to create a geometry cache for the beauty cloth. This way, when you are using this scene in the next stage of production, your scene doesn't have all the extra nCloth objects that are no longer necessary and make the scene heavy. For a look at Jack in action, see JackClothSim.mov on the CD, which shows the high-res mesh being driven by the simulation. Figure 23.30 shows a rendered frame from the movie.

As you can see from this example, nCloth can produce some great results with a bit of tweaking and experimentation. By using the concepts shown here, you will be able to get your own characters up and running with dynamic clothing driven by nCloth.

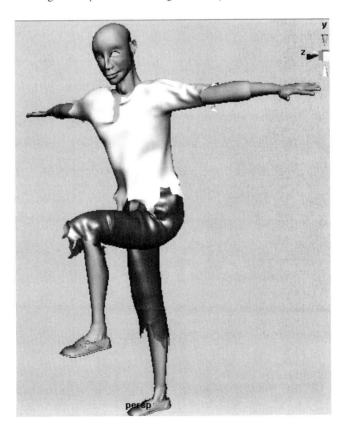

Figure 23.30

Jack with high-resolution shirt and pants driven by the low-resolution cloth

Summary

As you have seen, Maya's new nCloth cloth solver, which uses the nucleus engine to simulate cloth, is a robust, quick, and relatively simple way to create cloth from any polygon object. Creating cloth is straightforward, but there are numerous controls for it, allowing for precise simulation of the effect you wish to create. The ability to adjust solver and cloth properties, add forces and collisions, paint on attributes, and cache results make Maya's new nCloth one of the most powerful cloth solvers on the market and provides an excellent set of tools for technical animators looking to create realistic cloth effects for their characters.

Index

B

M

V

W